Race and Criminal Justice History

RHETORIC, POLITICS, AND POLICY

Revised First Edition

Arthur H. Garrison

Kutztown University

cognella | ACADEMIC PUBLISHING

Bassim Hamadeh, CEO and Publisher
John Remington, Executive Editor
Carrie Baarns, Manager, Revisions and Author Care
Kaela Martin, Project Editor
Abbey Hastings, Production Editor
Jess Estrella, Senior Graphic Designer
Alexa Lucido, Licensing Manager
Natalie Piccotti, Director of Marketing
Kassie Graves, Senior Vice President, Editorial
Jamie Giganti, Director of Academic Publishing

Printed in the United States of America.

cognella® | ACADEMIC PUBLISHING
320 South Cedros Ave., Ste. 400, Solana Beach, CA 92075

To Fay Garrison-Mitchell and Arthur E. Garrison, my
parents who have passed, Gale, my wife, and Dr. Maceo Ellison,
the patriarch of the family that has embraced me as their own.

"Soon after the great struggle began, we looked behind the army of white rebels, and saw … black people … and that they were all our friends. We have seen the white men betray the flag and fight to kill the Union but … we never saw a traitor in a black skin. Our comrades escaping from the starvation of prison … never feared to enter the black man's cabin … In all that period … no Union soldier was ever betrayed by a black man or woman. And now that we have made them free … we will stand by these black allies. We will stand by them until the sun of liberty … shall shine with equal ray upon every man, black or white, throughout the Union."

Boys in Blue speech (August 6, 1880)
James A. Garfield, Campaign Rally

"We will stand by them until the sun of liberty … shall shine with equal ray upon every man, black or white, throughout the Union." ***The road America did not take.***

****

"The Republican party offers to our brethren of the South the olive branch of Peace, and invites them to renewed brotherhood, on this supreme condition: That it shall be admitted, forever, that in the War for the Union we were right and they were wrong."

Nomination of John Sherman Speech (June 5, 1880)
James A. Garfield, Republican National Convention

"That it shall be admitted, forever, that in the War for the Union we were right and they were wrong." ***The road conservatives now dispute and abandon.***

****

"My countrymen, we do not now differ in our judgment concerning the controversies of past generations, and fifty years hence our children will not be divided in their opinions concerning our controversies. They will surely bless their fathers and their fathers' God that the Union was preserved, that slavery was overthrown, and that both races were made equal before the law."

Inaugural Address (March 4, 1881)
James A. Garfield, 20th President of the United States of America

"our children ... will surely bless their fathers ... that both races were made equal before the law." ***America chose Jim Crow and slavery by another name instead.***

Brief Contents

Detailed Contents

Student Learning Objectives Contents

5. Students will be able to explain the limits of Fourth Amendment protection and remedies for police use of force.
6. Students will be able to explain how a municipality can be held liable for policies and decisions that are made by its agents.
7. Students will be able to explain what limitations the Fourth Amendment places on police and municipal civil liability and criminal culpability.

1. Students will be able to explain and define the different types or racism and how social psychology has explained how each type operates within social dynamics.
2. Students will be able to define how social media in terms of television, movies, and crime reporting defines and supports negative images of Blacks, specifically defining Black males as criminals.
3. Students will be able to explain how negative perceptions of Blacks affects police perceptions of Black behavior and how these perceptions provides an explanation for disproportionate contact between police and Blacks.
4. Students will be able to apply social psychology theory to the issue of police use of force and race and explain how negative perceptions of Blacks affects police decisions to use force.
5. Students will be able to apply social psychology literature to social discourse and narratives regarding Blacks and crime and be able to differentiate different types of racism within political discourse and narratives.

1. Students will be able to put criminal justice policy and political perspectives in the larger context of American political history and the rhetoric regarding race.
2. Students will be able to link the development of the criminal justice system with the politics and policies of pre- and post-civil war America and why these social political contexts matter in understanding the formation of the contemporary criminal justice system.
3. Students will know who John Calhoun, Alexander Stephens, Jefferson Davis, Abraham Lincoln, James Garfield, Harry Truman, Orval Faubus, Strom Thurmond, George Wallace, Dwight D. Eisenhower, Barry Goldwater, John F. Kennedy, and Lyndon Johnson are and will be able to place these political figures in context with American political history and criminal justice history and explain their significance to both.
4. Students will be able to explain the link between rhetorical defenses of slavery and the inferiority of Blacks with rhetorical defenses of Jim Crow and how both were defended by the political argument of states' rights.

5. Students will be able to explain the link between the politics of civil rights, states' rights and the criminal justice policies of the 1960s.
6. Students will be able to explain the political rhetoric of the Republican and Democratic parties in social, political, and historical context.

1. Students will be able to explain how White Christians, both in Europe and in America, who were involved in the African slave trade and who owned slaves, justified their actions with the Bible as well as explain how abolitionists to slavery used the Bible to assert that slavery was evil. Students will be exposed to both arguments and will be able to explain why the former was due to manipulation and false interpretation of the Bible and the principles of Christianity.
2. Students will be able to explain why it matters that Christianity was used to place Blacks in an inferior position to Whites and how that belief survived slavery to form the foundation for Jim Crow laws and the adoption of second-class status for Blacks under the law enforced by the Supreme Court.
3. Students will be able to put the Civil War and the rise of Jim Crow in context with the idea of Black inferiority and the need for social control of Blacks.
4. Students will be able to explain Supreme Court jurisprudence supporting both the rise and fall of Jim Crow laws.

1. Students will be able to explain what the New York City Police Department (NYPD) Stop and Frisk program was and why the U.S. District Court held that it violated the Fourth Amendment and the Equal Protection Clause of the Fourteenth Amendment.
2. Students will be able to differentiate between an investigatory tool and a crime suppression tool in policing. Students will be able to discuss and apply Terry v. Ohio to the distinction between the two tools of policing.
3. Students will be able to differentiate between the police officer's ability to stop as compared to frisk a person under the Reasonable Articulable Suspicion (RAS) burden of proof and explain how the Fourth Amendment jurisprudence allows a stop and frisk on a lower level of proof than probable cause.
4. Students will be able to explain and differentiate between general population benchmarks vs. suspect race descriptive benchmarks to establish a disproportionate police activity based on race resulting in violation of the Fourth and Fourteenth Amendment.
5. Students will be able to explain how the NYPD stop-and-frisk program was defended both on the level of constitutional construction and political rhetoric by officials of the NYPD and the Office of the Mayor of New York. Students will be able to explain how

criminal justice policy is subject to political dynamics and debates and how elections can change those dynamics and debates and thus change the political policy.

Chapter Seven: *Black Incarceration and Social Control: American Political Choices and Criminal Justice Policy* 363

1. Students will be able to explain the history of American criminal justice in the post-bellum period and place that history in context with the criminal justice politics of the 1960s.
2. Students will be able to define peonage, convict leasing, criminal surety, and other forms of legal involuntary servitude laws that criminalized Blacks.
3. Students will be able to explain how the politics of the World War II and the Cold War added to the social and political background that supported the civil rights movement of the 1960s.
4. Students will be able to explain and describe the link between the fall of Jim Crow and the rise of conservative political ideology and the crime-control policies of the 1970s-1980s.

Chapter Eight: *The Modern Incarceration of Blacks within the Criminal Justice System* 407

1. Students will be able to explain the politics and policy dynamics of the 1980s and 1990s to explain modern criminal justice policy and its relation to Black disproportionate incarceration.
2. Students will be able to explain how the crack epidemic started and how federal laws under Ronald Reagan and Bill Clinton together formed the modern American criminal justice system. Students will be able discuss and describe how the political rhetoric of both democrats and republicans merged to negatively impact Blacks in urban neighborhoods and in public housing by both supporting a crime control model of criminal justice.
3. Students will be able to define the due process and crime control models and how each was adopted by various presidents in the second half of the twentieth century into the first decade of the twenty-first.
4. Students will be able to discuss how the modern narratives of crime and criminality have been used to shape and create criminal justice policy post-1960s, as well as differentiate the policies and politics of the 1970s, 1980s, 1990 and 2000s.
5. Students will be able to compare and contrast the criminal justice policies of presidents Reagan, Bush 41, Clinton, Bush 43, Obama, and Trump and the policy determinations each president made and the impact of those policies.

Chapter Nine: *Epilogue* 519

1. Students will be able to summarize the historical, social, political and societal factors that influence and define disproportionate involvement of Blacks in the criminal justice system.
2. Students will be able to explain and discuss the views of Frederick Douglass regarding the proposition that the U.S. Constitution is a pro-slave document and how Douglass rejected that proposition.
3. Students will be able to define social conservative political theory and understand its relationship to police use of force and the politics of police use of force as well as be able to distinguish the politics of police use of force from the law that governs police use of force.
4. Students will be able to explain and discuss recent research on police use of force and will be familiar with data from the Washington Post database on police use of force.

Charts, Tables, and Graphs Contents

Preface

THE HISTORY OF Blacks in America is a long history predating the Constitution by more than a century and a half. European colonization of North America has involved various nationalities, but Blacks have a unique history. The history of slavery in the Americas is a history of economics and trade. Two commodities, sugar and tobacco, would meet the demands of Europe for profitable goods. To satisfy demand for these products large single produce plantations were established with great demands for labor. That labor need was met by the international slave trade. First the Portuguese then the Dutch and then the British imported ten million western African slaves to the Americas. For sugar they are brought to Brazil and the Caribbean. For tobacco they are brought to Virginia, for rice they are brought to South Carolina, and by the nineteenth century for cotton they are brought to the mainland North America southern colonies.

Because of the institution of slavery and the principles it was based on, outside of economics, Blacks have a history all to their own compared to others who came to North American after the first colonies were settled in Jamestown, Virginia in May, 1607, and in Plymouth, Massachusetts in November, 1620. The Dutch brought the first Blacks to Jamestown, Virginia as slaves on August 20, 1619, to support the planting and harvesting of the first successful agricultural crop of the new colony, tobacco, and Blacks remained slaves in the colonies and then under the U.S. Constitution until April 9, 1865. The history of Blacks in America is a rich history of contributions to the poetry, arts, music, politics, law, and governance of America. But unlike other immigrant groups who also made contributions, Blacks in America begin their history chained to the bottom of ships while other people arrived by their own choosing. The point is that Blacks were brought to America for the sole purpose to serve and make other people's lives better. They did not come to America to make better lives for themselves. Blacks were a commodity to be used not a people to embraced.

This distinction begins to explain how Blacks have been perceived throughout American history. During the colonial and antebellum periods of American history, the population of Blacks (both slave and free) outgrew the population of White colonists and due to the ill-treatment by White colonists and slave owners, Blacks were perceived as a threat to societal safety. After the Civil War, Blacks were perceived as a social threat because it was believed by abolitionists and former slave owners alike that Blacks would not work without slavery and they would commit rape of White women if not socially controlled. In the 1970s through to today, Blacks are perceived as criminogenic. Criminal justice aside, Blacks in America have also been perceived a means to an end—either economic or political. By means to an end, I mean that they have been a catalyst or a means to address other political or economic ends. Blacks were the demarcation line in the economic and social distinction and disputes between the industrial north and the agricultural south. They were the political demarcation line between free and slave labor. They were the demarcation line between the colonies' drafting of the Declaration of Independence and the Constitution. They were the demarcation line of American politics for more than a decade before the Civil War and the demarcation line that broke over slavery in 1860. Jim Crow treatment of Blacks was the glue at the demarcation line of the North and South that healed the nation after the Civil War. Blacks were the demarcation line of the politics of the two parties in the 1940s through the 1960s that formed the modern political policy alignments of the Democratic and Republican Parties. Blacks are the demarcation line between those who assert the modern criminal justice system is just or unjust. At all of these demarcation lines, how Blacks were perceived and treated were the means of the solutions to the disputes by the competing parties. Blacks were a means to an end.

This book began as a discussion paper on the topic of disproportionate incarceration of Blacks presented at the 2015 American Society of Criminology (ASC) conference. Race and crime has been a subject within American political rhetoric and criminal justice research for centuries. The paper approached the topic of race and crime by putting the disproportionate incarceration of Blacks into a political, social, legal, and economic context. The goal of the paper was to assert that disproportionate incarceration was not simply the result of Blacks being criminogenic. The responses to the paper included developing the paper from a law review article into a book. This book is the result of that advice.

This book is written with specific premises. *First,* criminal justice policy in general and the relationship between criminal justice and race specifically cannot be understood outside of the study of American history in general and the legal, constitutional, and political history of America specifically.

Secondly, this book approaches the question of race and criminal justice with an interdisciplinary approach putting together American history, constitutional history, legal history, and political history in a chronological format along with research from social psychology, sociology, and constitutional law together to provide a perspective on why Blacks have always been disproportionately incarcerated within the American criminal justice system. Although the subject matter of this book is hardly untouched by scholarship, this book seeks to address the issue differently. Collateral issues such as poverty, healthcare, economic, and social injustice are not discussed in significant detail, but rather are used as background for the main topic of the book. The reader's focus is maintained on American political and social history and the political rhetoric and policies that explain how and why Blacks are disproportionately incarcerated and how and why they are disproportionately exposed to police use of force.

Lastly, one of the issues in addressing the issue of disproportionate incarceration of Blacks is the willful ignorance of many to consider how American history and the history of the criminal justice system as a tool of social control has negatively affected Blacks. American criminal justice is an institution that is the result of American history and policies. This book proposes that the political history of the modern Republican and Democratic parties, the criminal justice policies both parties have pursued over the past fifty years, the disproportionate incarceration and police use of force upon young Black males, and the distrust Blacks have for the criminal justice system are all built upon a social, political, legal, and psychological history that is more than two hundred years old.

It is proposed in this book that the incarceration of Blacks has been a social constant in America from slavery through Jim Crow through the late twentieth century through to the present day. This book examines both conservative and liberal political rhetoric by both Republican and Democratic leaders and explains how that rhetoric led to policies that supported Black incarceration as well as justified that incarceration.

I wrote this book with multiple purposes. On one level, I wanted a book that was not based on a specific ideological or political perspective, but rather a book that introduced the reader to the history, politics, and law that created the result of Black incarceration. I expose various perspectives ranging from incarceration of Blacks is reflective of Black criminality to critical race theory that advocates that Black incarceration is reflective of White social dominance and/or economic control. This book expands on these perspectives by examining other theories and scholarship including social psychology, political party history, American history, and Supreme Court judicial case history on race. The goal of this book was not to complete an exhaustive review of research, but to put various types of research together that is not found in other works addressing the dynamics of race, police, and criminal justice.

On a secondary level, I approached writing this book with the desire to expose the reader to the speeches and writings of key political leaders that have formed the modern political dynamics of America's two major political parties and the political ideas regarding race and criminal justice policy; as well as some of the significant Supreme Court and judicial decisions that established America's modern legal landscape. Thus, I expose the reader to extended reproduction of speeches and writings rather than brief quotes with commentary. My pedagogical approach is to allow the reader to read extended quotations of major leaders in American policy and let the reader to put them in context with various historical narratives provided throughout the book.

Lastly, many books on race and crime discuss the political changes of the 1960s and early 1970s and the "get tough on crime" policies of the 1980s and 1990s without providing a background to explain how these policies developed both rhetorically and politically. This book dedicates significant attention to the development of the political rhetoric that supported the criminal justice policies of the 1960s to the current policies of the Trump Administration. The reader will be exposed to the key political leaders of southern democratic and later republican politics that shaped the political landscape that created the modern American criminal justice system that disproportionately incarcerates Blacks and specifically young Black males.

I also wrote this book with the hope of fostering discussion and debate within classroom instruction. Students will be exposed to multiple perspectives on race and criminal justice and provides historical context for those perspectives. Regardless of a student's or an instructor's political perspective, this book allows for a more nuanced and informed discussion on the various issues on race and crime. This book is different from other books on race and criminal justice in that it provides the reader with historical, social, legal, and political facts from which opinions and perspectives can be formed without advocating a particular perspective to the exclusion of all others.

Although my perspective will be clear to the reader, the reader will not be presented with only my perspective as if that is the only one that can explain Black incarceration and police relations in America. The goal of the book is not to prove any particular ideological perspective, but rather to expose the reader to facts that can inform a particular ideological perspective.

This book is also written from an advocacy perspective in that perspectives and arguments regarding Black incarceration are confronted in a discussion approach. I present various views and directly argue with those perspectives allowing the reader to make their own determinations. Because I use first person extensive quotations to build or refute arguments and perspectives, the book does require active reading. I freely admit that passive reading will be insufficient. The chapters are longer than typical books and the reader will be expected to follow the development of facts and arguments and history. My hope is that the extra work that is required by the reader will be paid off with more robust discussion in class and a more sophisticated understanding of the various issues that have formed the current dynamics of Black involvement in the criminal justice system. I have written the book to be useful to those who do not have an extensive knowledge of history or social psychology or law. I provide the reader with backgrounds and explanations of American history to allow the reader to make their own judgements of assertions made throughout the book.

To facilitate student learning, each chapter begins with a list of student learning objectives and ends with a list of terms or key issue/people and a list of discussion questions based on the material in each chapter. These, I hope, will facilitate additional learning and discussion.

This book is comprised of both original research and revised sections of previously published work. *Chapter One* is an expanded version of the paper that was presented at the ASC conference and is also comprised of portions of a law review article I published in the *Rutgers Race and Law Review* in 2014. An expanded version of *Chapter Two* is published in the *George Mason University Civil Rights Law Journal* (2018). *Chapter Six* is a reprinting of material from the *Rutgers Race and Law Review* article. *Chapters Nine* and *Ten* are comprised of original research and the integration of various op-ed articles I have published in various local newspapers.

Two final points on how this book is designed for classroom use. *First*, I have written this book with the use of extensive reprinting of speeches by various political leaders, including those of the antebellum period and the civil rights movement and of past presidents. The reason is twofold. First, many students have never read or been exposed to the full context of famous quotes. My goal, put simply, is to expose students to the full context and meaning of sometimes famous quotes used in both academic and public discourse. *Secondly,* students exposed to the full quotation of some famous quotes will inoculate them from some of the political manipulation that has accompanied these quotes. Exposing the reader to full citations rather than small quotes minimizes uninformed use of ideas and the reduction of their meaning.

Lastly, although readings can be assigned in order of the table of contents, readings of chapters can be assigned out of order, or they can be assigned by focusing on specific subsections of various chapters in combinations that best suit the class instructor and the course. Although some of the chapters are extensive in length, they are divided into subject areas that can be read and used independent of other parts of the same chapter. Thus, the book does not require slavish following of chapter order or total chapter utilization. Different parts of a chapter can be assigned with parts of other chapters based on the focus of the course utilizing the book. As required for students, an instructor will need to think through the material in the book to fully maximize the material. I hope faculty will find the benefit of the material worth the extra effort.

Introduction

STUDENT LEARNING OBJECTIVES

1. Understand the connection between criminal justice and the history of race in America
2. Read perspectives on America regarding race and police brutality by President Barack Obama

****

America has a complicated history with race. America entertained slavery and legal racial discrimination on its shores for three and a half centuries. It also moved from explicit racial discrimination and government policies that made Blacks second class citizens to a country that elected a Black man president of the United States and extracted all systematic laws of discrimination from its books. Although one cannot dispute this progress, Blacks are still disproportionately arrested, convicted, and confined within the criminal justice system. The purpose of this book is to explore the social, political, historical, and psychological explanations for the chronic involvement of Blacks in the criminal justice system. This book will propose that the reason is much more complicated than simple explicit racism, though the explanation for the disproportionate incarceration begins with explicit racism. The disproportionate incarceration begins with how Whites have historically perceived Blacks. Both the social and structural impact of Jim Crow and its significance in the perception of Blacks as criminals to be controlled will be discussed throughout this book.

As discussed in Chapters One and Four, the modern conflation of race and crime occurred in the middle and late 1960s. After the summer of 1968 race riots, Dr. Martin Luther King, Jr. gave his famous *The Other America* speech to explain the social and racial animus that answered why the riots occurred. In part of his speech, Dr. King reflected on a conversation he had with a White man on an airplane who complained that Blacks don't do enough for themselves and that other racial groups have come to America and pulled themselves up, so why can't Blacks? His conversation is instructive in beginning to understand race and criminal justice in America.

> I remember the other day I was on a plane and a man started talking with me and he said ... you people don't do enough for yourself ... I know of other ethnic groups ... and they had problems just as negroes and yet they did the job for themselves, they lifted themselves by their own bootstraps. Why is it that negroes can't do that?
>
> And I looked at him and ... said *that he failed to recognize that no other ethnic group has been enslaved on American soil.*
>
> *Then I had to go on to say to him that you failed to realize that America made the black man's color a stigma.* Something that he couldn't change. Not only was the color a stigma ... his color was thought of as something very evil.
>
> ... *I had to say to my friend on the plane another thing that is often forgotten in this country. That nobody, no ethnic group has completely lifted itself by its own bootstraps.* I can never forget that the black man was free from the bondage of physical slavery in 1863. He wasn't given any land to make that freedom meaningful after being held in slavery 244 years. And it was like keeping a man in prison for many many years and then coming to see that he is not guilty of the crime for which he was convicted.[1]

As Dr. King explained to the man on the plane, it had only been fourteen years—after more than three centuries of slavery and Jim Crow—that the Supreme Court ruled in *Brown v. Board of Education* that segregation in America was based on the theory of inferiority of Blacks to Whites, and this theory had no place in American schools.[2] It had only been four years since Congress passed the Civil Rights Act of 1964, breaking the backbone of American apartheid dating back to 1865. In 2018 it has only been fifty years since the passage of the Civil Rights Act of 1968. To put the fifty years in perspective, for the first one hundred and seventy-nine years under the ratified U.S. Constitution Blacks did not, as a matter of law, enjoy freedom or equality in America. The protection of law is still relatively new when it comes to its application to Blacks. As Justice John Marshall Harlan in his famous dissent in *Plessy v. Ferguson* observed in 1896,

> We boast of the freedom enjoyed by our people above all other peoples. But it is difficult to reconcile that boast with a state of the law which, practically, puts the brand of servitude and degradation upon a large class of our fellow citizens, our equals before the law. The thin disguise of "equal" accommodations for passengers in railroad coaches will not mislead anyone, nor atone for the wrong this day done.[3]

---

1 Martin Luther King Jr., "The Other America," Speech at Grosse Pointe High School (March 14, 1968).

2 *Brown v. Board of Education of Topeka*, 347 U.S. 483 (1954).

3 *Plessy v. Ferguson*, 163 U.S. 537, 562 (1896).

It took America more than six decades for that atonement to begin with direct advocacy from the voice of a president. To put American apartheid in proper perspective, 2018 marks only fifty-five years since President Kennedy asserted that the time for civil rights had come, and freedom could not be said to reign in America when Blacks were discriminated against under the requirement of the law itself.[4] American race history involves two hundred and forty-six years (1619–1865) of slavery in the colonies and then under the U.S. Constitution. Slavery was followed by one hundred years (1865–1965) of Jim Crow Apartheid. To America's credit this history, one hundred years of legal Jim Crow, the legacy of two hundred and forty-six years of slavery, was stripped from the law in only fourteen years (1954–1968). To paraphrase Dr. King, it is true that the ark of American moral and political history is long, but it eventually bends toward justice.

In a speech on the fiftieth Anniversary of Bloody Sunday, President Barack Obama reflected on the rapid changes that America made when it came to terms with racial discrimination in the 1960s. The president said, "that's where we have to feel hopeful, rather than just say that nothing's changed—we have to say, 'Wow, we've actually made significant progress over the last fifty years.'"[5] The nation that was racially segregated in 1968 and needed laws to allow a Black man to move into a White neighborhood put a Black man into the White House in only forty years. The fact that racism is still an ongoing problem does not negate the truth that America is a far better place than it was only fifty years ago.

In 2015, President Obama used various occasions to reflect on the nature of race and criminal justice in America. On June 22nd, President Obama, while being interviewed on a local radio show, commented on the issue of race in America and said

> What is also true is that the legacy of slavery, Jim Crow, discrimination in almost every institution of our lives—you know, that casts a long shadow. And that's still part of our DNA that's passed on. We're not cured of [racism]. And it's not just a matter of it not being polite to say 'nigger' in public. That's not the measure of whether racism still exists or not. It's not just a matter of overt discrimination. Societies don't overnight completely erase everything that happened two to three hundred years prior.[6]

The proceeding chapters will provide historical support for President Obama's observation that discrimination is "still part of our DNA." But this history, the President asserted, must be viewed within the context of what has occurred over the past fifty years. He said that, "What I

---

4 President John F. Kennedy Address to the Nation on Civil Rights (June 11, 1963) at http://www.americanrhetoric.com/speeches/jfkcivilrights.htm. The impact of presidential rhetoric on race and policy is discussed in Chapter Four.

5 President Obama interview with Marc Maron (June 22, 2015) at http://qz.com/433923/obama-used-the-n-word-in-a-podcast-interview-to-nail-a-complicated-truth-about-racism

6 President Obama interview with Marc Maron (June 22, 2015) at http://qz.com/433923/obama-used-the-n-word-in-a-podcast-interview-to-nail-a-complicated-truth-about-racism

always tell young people in particular: Do not say that nothing's changed when it comes to race in America ... It is incontrovertible that race relations have improved significantly during my lifetime and yours, and that opportunities have opened up, and that attitudes have changed. That is a fact."[7] His point was that it is more than shortsighted and unjust to constantly assert America has not changed.

At the fiftieth anniversary of the Selma March, President Obama stated that, "To deny this progress, this hard-won progress—our progress—would be to rob us of our own agency, our own capacity, our responsibility to do what we can to make America better."[8] At the

---

7 President Obama interview with Marc Maron (June 22, 2015) at http://qz.com/433923/obama-used-the-n-word-in-a-podcast-interview-to-nail-a-complicated-truth-about-racism

8 Remarks by the President at the 50th Anniversary of the Selma to Montgomery Marches Edmund Pettus Bridge, Selma, Alabama, March 7, 2015, at https://www.whitehouse.gov/the-press-office/2015/03/07/remarks-president-50th-anniversary-selma-montgomery-marches

> During his speech, the President discussed the significance of the African American civil rights movement to the rest of the world and in world history.
>
> ... Young people behind the Iron Curtain would see Selma and eventually tear down that wall. Young people in Soweto would hear Bobby Kennedy talk about ripples of hope and eventually banish the scourge of apartheid. Young people in Burma went to prison rather than submit to military rule. They saw what John Lewis had done. From the streets of Tunis to the Maidan in Ukraine, this generation of young people can draw strength from this place, where the powerless could change the world's greatest power and push their leaders to expand the boundaries of freedom.
>
> They saw that idea made real right here in Selma, Alabama. They saw that idea manifest itself here in America.
>
> Because of campaigns like this, a Voting Rights Act was passed. Political and economic and social barriers came down. And the change these men and women wrought is visible here today in the presence of African Americans who run boardrooms, who sit on the bench, who serve in elected office from small towns to big cities; from the Congressional Black Caucus all the way to the Oval Office. (Applause.)
>
> Because of what they did, the doors of opportunity swung open not just for Black folks, but for every American. Women marched through those doors. Latinos marched through those doors. Asian Americans, gay Americans, Americans with disabilities—they all came through those doors. (Applause.) Their endeavors gave the entire South the chance to rise again, not by reasserting the past, but by transcending the past.
>
> This agency and significance is diminished when it is argued nothing has changed.
>
> We do a disservice to the cause of justice by intimating that bias and discrimination are immutable, that racial division is inherent to America. If you think nothing's changed in the past 50 years, ask somebody who lived through the Selma or Chicago or Los Angeles of the 1950s. Ask the female CEO who once

famous bridge, he said, "What happened in Ferguson may not be unique, but it's no longer endemic. It's no longer sanctioned by law or by custom. And before the Civil Rights Movement, it most surely was."[9]

Ten years after the Montgomery Bus Boycott (Dec 5, 1955—Dec 21, 1956—381 days), on March 7, 1965, Alabama State and local police stormed the Edmund Pettus Bridge in full riot gear and attacked Black marchers who were demanding the right to vote and were protesting the killing of Blackman named Jimmie Lee Jackson who had been shot, beaten, and killed by an Alabama state trooper. In response to the killing the march led by Congressman John Lewis, then chairman of the Student Nonviolent Coordinating Committee (SNCC), was scheduled to include walking from Selma to Montgomery Alabama. George Wallace, governor of Alabama, stated that there would be no march and he sent the Alabama State Troopers to prevent the march. The marchers were confronted by the state and local police at the Edmund Pettus Bridge which crosses the Alabama River. Eight days after the police riot, President Johnson in a joint session of Congress asked for the passage of the Voting Rights Act of 1965 and concluded his request saying, "[we] must overcome the crippling legacy of bigotry and injustice. We shall overcome."

In remembering Bloody Sunday President Obama commented on the contemporary issue of the post–civil rights movement era, disproportionate Black incarceration and treatment within criminal justice.

> Just this week, I was asked whether I thought the Department of Justice's Ferguson report shows that, with respect to race, little has changed in this country. And I understood the question; the report's narrative was sadly familiar. It evoked the kind of abuse and disregard for citizens that spawned the Civil Rights Movement. But I rejected the notion that nothing's changed. What happened in Ferguson may not be unique, but it's no longer endemic. It's no longer sanctioned by law or by custom. And before the Civil Rights Movement, it most surely was. …
>
> Of course, a more common mistake is to suggest that Ferguson is an isolated incident; that racism is banished; that the work that drew men and women to Selma is now complete, and that whatever racial tensions remain are a consequence of those seeking to play the "race card" for their own purposes. We don't need the Ferguson report to know that's not true. We just need to open our eyes, and our ears, and our hearts to know that this nation's racial history still casts its long shadow upon us.

---

might have been assigned to the secretarial pool if nothing's changed. Ask your gay friend if it's easier to be out and proud in America now than it was thirty years ago. To deny this progress, this hard-won progress—our progress—would be to rob us of our own agency, our own capacity, our responsibility to do what we can to make America better.

9 Remarks by the President at the 50th Anniversary of the Selma to Montgomery Marches Edmund Pettus Bridge, Selma, Alabama, March 7, 2015

> We know the march is not yet over. We know the race is not yet won. We know that reaching that blessed destination where we are judged, all of us, by the content of our character requires admitting as much, facing up to the truth ... we can make sure our criminal justice system serves all and not just some. Together, we can raise the level of mutual trust that policing is built on—the idea that police officers are members of the community they risk their lives to protect, and citizens in Ferguson and New York and Cleveland, they just want the same thing young people here marched for 50 years ago—the protection of the law. (Applause.) Together, we can address unfair sentencing and overcrowded prisons, and the stunted circumstances that rob too many boys of the chance to become men, and rob the nation of too many men who could be good dads, and good workers, and good neighbors.[10]

On the issue of race and criminal justice, President Obama, while asserting that America in 2015 is not the America of the 1960s or 1860s, concluded that the issue of racism within criminal justice has not been eradicated.

While the social, political, and economic progress regarding race is true and should not be superficially acknowledged, it is also true that there are two institutions within American society that reflect deep-seated racial divides, discrimination, and unequal outcomes. These institutions are the criminal justice system, in general, and American law enforcement treatment of Blacks, specifically.

In 1963, at the foot of the Lincoln memorial, Dr. King brought attention to police brutality and the need to recognize the value of Black people both socially and legally. Before he said he had a dream of equality and judgment by the content of character alone, he spoke of the need for Blacks to be equal as human beings under the promises of the great documents of America.

Social conservatives tend to hold up Dr. King as the hope of America, and they consistently invoke his dream uttered at the foot of Lincoln. As they invoke the goal—to be judged by the content of their character not the color of their skin—they ignore what Dr. King said before that famous prayer for America. Too many invoke the last few paragraphs of the speech as if that was the whole speech. The speech was about the social and economic injustice that Blacks suffered. *His speech asserted that under the great documents of America's founding*—the Declaration of Independence and the Constitution, the supreme law of the land,—*the social and economic injustices Blacks suffered should not have occurred in the first place.* It is this part of the speech that too many people are unaware of and it is this part of the speech that social conservatives intentionally ignore.

Dr. King made the case that the rights Blacks were due simply by being citizens of the United States and those rights had not been granted, certainly not before and not completely granted after Lincoln's famous emancipation. It was at this point, after discussing the

10 Remarks by the President at the 50th Anniversary of the Selma to Montgomery Marches Edmund Pettus Bridge, Selma, Alabama, March 7, 2015

historical social, political, economic injustice and cruelty, and abuse by the police and that this history was not worthy of a great nation under a Constitution and Declaration of Independence that were based on individual freedom, that he began to conclude with his famous dream for America.

What is more interesting about this last section of his speech is that it was not in the original draft. As Dr. King was speaking, Mahalia Jackson was sitting behind him and when he was close to the end of his speech she said to him "tell them about the dream Martin, tell them about the dream." It was at her urging that he ended his speech with the famous I Have a Dream that in America, Black children will be judged not by the color of their skin but by the content of their character and in so doing, in America, "All of God's children, black men and white men, Jews and Gentiles, Protestants and Catholics, will be able to join hands and sing in the words of the old Negro spiritual: 'Free at last! Free at last! Thank God Almighty, we are free at last!'"[11]

Although his dream has been the foundation upon which American aspirations on race have been housed for decades, there is more to the speech than the end.

The significance of this last section of his speech is what he said would constitute the foundation upon which the dream could rest. The point, of course, is that the foundation must be built and laid before the dream can be realized. The first thing he discussed in forming that foundation was the treatment of Blacks by the police, when he said, "There are those who are asking the devotees of civil rights, 'When will you be satisfied?' *We can never be satisfied as long as the Negro is the victim of the unspeakable horrors of police brutality.*" He said in the same famous speech, "I am not unmindful that some of you have come here out of great trials and tribulations. Some of you have come fresh from narrow jail cells. And some of you have come from areas where your quest for freedom left you battered by the storms of persecution and staggered by the winds of police brutality." The foundation under Dr. King's dream was the treatment of Blacks as human beings with equality and this equality under the law starts with how Blacks are treated by the police and the criminal justice system.

******

From the days of slavery, police brutality has been a key social and historical issue in America. In 2012, a Black seventeen-year-old was shot by a White Hispanic neighborhood watch captain in Sanford, Florida, because he looked like a criminal. When the boy, Trayvon Martin, confronted George Zimmerman, who followed him for blocks at night, a fight ensued during which Zimmerman shot Martin. In the subsequent trial, Zimmerman was found not guilty of murder. The reason why a civilian White Hispanic male could assume a Black teen wearing a sweat jacket with the hood on walking in a White middleclass neighborhood at night was worthy of suspicion of criminality and physical surveillance is part of the purpose of

11 Remarks by Dr. Martin Luther King at the March on Washington, Washington, D.C. August 28, 1963

this book. Why was Trayvon assumed to be criminal? He was coming home from a store in a neighborhood his father lived in. The divergent opinions of Whites and Blacks in America over the Trayvon Martin case and the acquittal of Zimmerman fostered the founding of the Black Lives Matter movement.

Fifty-one years after Dr. King said at the feet of Lincoln's memorial, "there will be neither rest nor tranquility in America until the Negro is granted his citizenship rights. The whirlwinds of revolt will continue to shake the foundations of our nation until the bright day of justice emerges," riots occurred in August 2014 when a Black man, Michael Brown, was killed by a police officer in Ferguson, Missouri, and in April 2015 when a Black man, Freddie Gray, died due to a broken neck while in custody inside a police transport van in Baltimore, Maryland.

There is no doubt, as President Obama asserted without hesitation, that many of the injustices that Dr. King listed have been removed from the law and society. "For Whites Only" hotels banning Blacks as patrons have been placed in the dustbin of history. But, battles over voting rights and the topic of this book criminal justice policy and its intersection with Blacks as a people to be controlled still remain.

The purpose of this book is to put the treatment of Blacks in the criminal justice system into a broader historical, social, political, legal, and psychological context. The historical and social context is that although it is clearly true that Blacks have progressed economically, socially, politically, and legally in America, that does not mean that racism and its systemic results are not in operation in the criminal justice system we have today. Although America has abandoned the Jim Crow policies of the 1870s through the 1960s and the political defense of segregation as a right of the states, the modern political discourse of America asserts that Blacks are supposed to be disproportionately incarcerated because they are disproportionately criminal compared to Whites. As discussed in this book, Blacks have historically been over represented in the criminal justice system well before the rise of the Great Society programs, which social conservatives blame for the breakdown of the Black family, which they claim is the sole reason for disproportionate incarceration of Blacks. The criminal justice system has acted as an explicit policy tool for the social control of Blacks from the end of the Civil War through the 1960s and the 1990s.

Chapter One provides an overall review of the socio-political historical development of the perception of Blacks as criminals resulting in the need to keep them under social control. The chapter begins with a review of the social conservative explanation of Black crime and poverty and Republican Party politics of denying the detrimental results of more than a century of discrimination. The chapter argues that Black disproportionate involvement in the criminal justice system predates the rise of the Great Society; the incarceration of Blacks within the criminal justice system originates with the fall of slavery and the need to control the now freed slaves. It asserts that the modern Republican Party was created between 1948 and 1968, and the catalyst for that birth was the political blowback resulting from the rise of the civil rights movement and its adoption by the Democratic Party. The criminal justice policies of incarceration and retribution from the late 1960s through the 1990s are a reflection of the history of both political parties in the 1960s.

Chapter Two introduces the reader to the Fourth Amendment with a focus on the limitations on the use of the amendment to protect Blacks from police use force. The chapter explores the law regarding the use of force and the availability of federal civil rights law, both civil and criminal, to seek redress of unreasonable use of force by the police. The chapter concludes that the principles of the Fourth Amendment, as great as they are, do not provide significant protection from abusive police use of force, but rather, it provides the police with a practical benefit of the doubt when they use force.

Chapter Three introduces how social psychology explains how the cultural perception of Blacks as dangerous influences how society and the police perceive the observed behavior of Blacks. The chapter will review how implicit and unconscious biases that Blacks are criminal *per se* influence how and why police interact with young Black males. Social psychology provides a broader context to the discussion of police and Black male interactions by explaining that these interactions have a psychological context, and racial bias influences the police decision to approach and begin interactions with Blacks. The chapter makes clear that racial bias, stereotypes, prejudice, and racism are not synonymous concepts. The nuanced differences between these concepts are discussed in detail as well as the distinctions between systemic and systematic racism. These concepts and distinctions are discussed within the context of police behavior and explain why a discriminatory result can occur without any explicit racial intent to discriminate.

Chapter Four returns to the political history of race in America, introduced in Chapter One, with a focus on the rhetoric of race and how presidents and national leaders spoke in opposition and in support of Blacks and their rights to constitutional civil rights and how that support and opposition manifested into specific criminal justice policies in the late 1960s through the 1990s. This chapter traces the speeches and policies of national leaders both antebellum and postbellum and during the civil rights movement of the 1950s–1960s. The rise of Strom Thurmond, George Wallace, Barry Goldwater, and the modern Republican Party is compared and contrasted with the policies of Harry Truman, John F. Kennedy, and Lyndon Johnson and the rise of the modern Democratic Party. The chapter also reviews the politics of conservatism, the Great Society, fear of crime and the backlash of White Northerners, as well as Southern Democrats to give context and explanation for the social politics that supported Republican and social conservatism regarding the criminality of Blacks in the modern day.

Chapter Five introduces how the Supreme Court and its jurisprudence from the middle 1800s through the early twentieth century provided constitutional support for Blacks being made second class citizens as a matter of law. This legal history also provides additional context for the Blacks' suspicion of the theory of states' rights and conservative opposition to federal intervention in race discrimination.

Chapter Six returns to police treatment of Blacks and their perception of Blacks as criminals with a case study of the New York City Police Department (NYPD) use of stop and frisk as a crime suppression tool, rather than an investigatory tool, and how crime statistics were utilized to justify disproportionate searching of Blacks. The chapter reviews how the NYPD argued in court that not only was the disproportionate stopping of Blacks constitutional, it was normal due to the fact that they were statistically disproportionately criminal. The chapter will focus on how the NYPD in a federal lawsuit utilized crime statistics to justify disproportionate police contact with Blacks. The legal arguments by the NYPD are supplemented by the political defense of the disproportionate application of stop and frisk by then New York City Mayor Michael Bloomberg and later disavowed by the change in policy by the current Mayor Bill de Blasio.

Chapters Seven and Eight return to the politics of race and crime introduced in Chapters One and Four with a focus on the modern racial arguments over Black-on-Black crime and the political rhetoric and resulting acceptance within the body politic that Blacks are supposed to be disproportionately arrested and incarcerated, because they are disproportionately criminal. The contemporary politics of interpretation of crime statistics and Black crime will be put in context by the historical criminalization of Black behavior and the incarceration of Blacks as a way to maintain social control after the fall of slavery in 1865.

Chapter Seven begins with a review of the Black codes, which were replaced by Jim Crow, and the system of involuntary servitude, which utilized the criminal justice system as a means to place Blacks in a state of slavery in full compliance with the Thirteenth Amendment, which allows for slavery as a means of punishment after conviction of crime. This involuntary servitude was established through a system of statutes comprised of criminal peonage, convict-leasing, criminal surety, mandatory employment (apprenticeship laws), vagrancy, and loitering laws. These laws carried mandatory prison sentences and fines which resulted in forced labor for private companies in coal mines, Southern swamps, and agricultural plantations. This system, together with Jim Crow segregation, made Black second-class social status a social historical constant. *Chapter Seven* concludes with a review of why this system of legally created criminal and second-class status began in 1865 and ended in the 1940s.

Chapter Eight focuses on the replacement of the Jim Crow system with conservative Republican politics and the rise of the crime control model of criminal justice in the 1980s. These policies were built upon the political blowback to the gains of the civil rights movement and the linking of the movement with social disorder and crime. These crime control policies began in the middle and late 1960s and gave rise to the abandonment of rehabilitation as an operating principle of the American criminal justice system and the adoption of retribution criminal justice policies. These policies included criminalization of drug use, the nationalization of drug law enforcement, three strikes, truth in sentencing, the crack cocaine 100 to 1 sentencing disparity, and the rise of mandatory and determinate sentences. These modern policies had the same net effect on Blacks as those of the late nineteenth century—the disproportionate incarceration of Blacks. This chapter reviews the rhetoric and policies of the last two decades of the twentieth century and the first decade of the following century that normalized Black incarceration. The chapter concludes with a comparison of the policies of Presidents Obama, and the resulting decrease in the general prison population and the disproportionate incarceration of Blacks, and policies of President Trump. The chapter reviews the policies of the Trump Administration under Attorney General Jefferson Sessions that are geared towards reverting back to the law and order, three strikes, and minimum mandatory sentencing strategies of President Clinton during the golden age of crime control theory politics.

Chapter Nine provides a summary of American political and criminal justice history and how both provide an explanation for disproportionate incarceration of Blacks and how this history provides a context for contemporary incidents of police shootings in 2015–2017. The chapter begins with a review of the rhetoric of Frederick Douglas, Attorney General Loretta Lynch, and President Barack Obama on the fears and hopes of Blacks and the promise of America despite Jim Crow. The chapter then proceeds to provide a summary of criminal justice history, in the context of American history, concluding with the issues raised by police shootings of Blacks and the resulting criminal justice reaction to those shootings.

Chapter Ten is a postscript on American rhetoric and politics which resulted in the election of Donald Trump as the 45th President of the United States. The chapter concludes with a review of the Charlottesville, Virginia incident and the racial dynamics of the debate over confederate memorials and the rise of the modern incantation of the "Lost Cause" as a result of the election of Donald Trump.

PEOPLE, KEY WORDS, AND CONCEPTS

Justice John Marshall Harlan
Dr. Martin Luther King
Trayvon Martin
Barack Obama
George Zimmerman
American Apartheid
Bloody Sunday
Brown v. Board of Education (1954)
Civil Rights Act 1964
Dr. Martin Luther King Speeches:

- *I Have a Dream* (1963)
- *The Other America* (1968)

Plessy v. Ferguson (1896)
Racism

DISCUSSION QUESTIONS

1. How did Dr. King explain racism to the man on the plane with him in the "Other America" speech? Why is it important to understand the effects of slavery and discrimination when discussing American history and the history of race in America?
2. In 1968, a federal law allowed Blacks to live in any home they could afford and that they could not be preventing from moving into a White community because they were Black. In 2008, a Black man moved into the White House as president. What is the significance of the change in American politics and society between 1968 and 2008?
3. What is the relationship between race and criminal justice?

CHAPTER ONE

Disproportionate Incarceration of African Americans

EXAMINING THE SOCIO-POLITICAL BACKGROUND OF A HISTORICAL CONSTANT

> I just feel that you people don't do enough for yourself ... other ethnic groups ... lifted themselves by their own bootstraps. Why is it that negroes can't do that? ... Then I had to go on to say to him that you failed to realize that America made the black man's color a stigma. Something that he couldn't change.[1]

STUDENT LEARNING OBJECTIVES

1. Students will be able to describe how political conservatives explain crime as it relates to race.
2. Students will be able to explain how the Democratic and Republican Parties developed their distinct political policies regarding criminal justice and how those policies were related to the politics of supporting or opposing the civil rights movement objective of dismantling Jim Crow.
3. Students will be able to explain the relationship between racism, crime, and the disproportionate incarceration of Blacks.
4. Students will be able to explain how history, sociology, political policy, and American political history provide explanations for the disproportionate incarceration of Blacks.

---

1 Martin Luther King Jr., *The Other America*, (speech, Grosse Pointe High School, Grosse Pointe, MI, March 14, 1968).

Parts of this chapter have been adapted from Arthur H. Garrison, "NYPD Stop and Frisk, Perceptions of Criminals, Race and the Meaning of *Terry v Ohio*: A Content Analysis of *Floyd, et al. v City of New York*," *Rutgers Race & the Law Review*, vol. 15. Rutgers Race & the Law Review, 2014.

5. Students will be able to define and debate issues of racism, criminal behavior, and perceptions of systemic vs. systematic racism.

****

While the reasons and explanations for why the criminal justice system and Blacks are disproportionately involved has been a source of academic and political debate for more than fifty years, the disproportionate involvement has been a historical constant since the end of the Civil War. This chapter begins the review of the political, social, historical, and psychological explanations of that constant by placing the disproportionality of Black involvement in the system within a larger context than the conservative orthodoxy that Blacks commit more crime and the liberal orthodoxy that the system is and has been corrupt and racist. This chapter will begin with an introduction of the orthodoxy of modern political conservatives, Chapters Four and Seven will provide a full discussion, followed by a rebuttal to that orthodoxy by reviewing historical incarceration data and the political history of the Republican and Democratic Parties post–World War II in regards to race and civil rights. This background will be used to propose that from the 1960s through the 1990s, Black incarceration through the criminal justice system served as a continuation of the social policy of controlling Blacks that began with slavery, which was followed by the Black Codes and, later, by the social/legal system of Jim Crow. Further, as the policy of Jim Crow was abandoned in the 1960s, it was replaced by the politics of White fear of Black crime. As this fear began to subside during the first decade of the twenty-first century, the rate of incarceration of Blacks began to decrease. Although the fear of Black criminality has decreased with crime rate, the politics of Blacks being criminogenic has remained a consistent theory within the Republican Party/social conservative social policy narrative.

The backbone to the use of the criminal justice system as an institution of social control of Blacks is the perception that Blacks are a criminal threat. Blacks are a social threat and are disproportionately represented in prison because of their disproportionate criminality. The Heritage Foundation, the chief think tank for conservativism and the Republican Party, best explains this theory of Black personal dysfunction and criminality.

> Policymakers at last are coming to recognize the connection between the breakdown of American families and various social problems.
>
> ...
>
> While this link between illegitimacy and chronic welfare dependency now is better understood, policymakers also need to appreciate another strong and disturbing pattern evident in scholarly studies: the link between illegitimacy and violent crime and between the lack of parental attachment and violent crime. Without an understanding of the root causes of criminal behavior—how criminals are formed—Members of Congress and state legislators cannot understand why whole sectors of society, particularly in urban areas, are being torn apart by crime. And without that knowledge, sound policymaking is impossible.
>
> ...

> The scholarly evidence, in short, suggests that at the heart of the explosion of crime in America is the loss of the capacity of fathers and mothers to be responsible in caring for the children they bring into the world. This loss of love and guidance at the intimate levels of marriage and family has broad social consequences for children and for the wider community. The empirical evidence shows that too many young men and women from broken families tend to have a much weaker sense of connection with their neighborhood and are prone to exploit its members to satisfy their unmet needs or desires. This contributes to a loss of a sense of community and to the disintegration of neighborhoods into social chaos and violent crime.[2]

Thus, if Blacks, conservatives argue, would get their families together and stop having children out of wedlock, the crime problem would be significantly reduced as would criminal justice control of them. The Heritage Foundation concluded that there "is a widespread belief that race is a major explanatory cause of crime. This belief is anchored in the large disparity in crime rates between whites and blacks."[3]

Internal family dysfunction as the explanation for Black crime and other social problems has been Republican Party and social conservative orthodoxy since the publication of the *Moynihan report* in 1965.[4] The House Budget Committee under the chairmanship of Paul Ryan, when he was the point man for conservatives and Republicans on poverty policy before he was elevated to the position of Speaker of the House, in an attempt to modernize the orthodoxy concluded that,

---

2 Patrick F. Fagan, *The Real Root Causes of Violent Crime: The Breakdown of Marriage, Family, and Community,* 1026 The Heritage Foundation Backgrounder 1, 1–2 (March. 17, 1995), *available at* http://www.heritage.org/research/reports/1995/03/bg1026nbsp-the-real-root-causes-of-violent-crime.

3 *Id.* at 4. To soften the assertion, Fagan also asserts that, "However, a closer look at the data shows that the real variable is not race but family structure and all that it implies in commitment and love between adults." *Id.*

4 See Daniel Moynihan, *The Negro Family: The Case for National Action* (1965).

See also a report by the Republican Majority on the House of Representatives Budget Committee on past presidential pronouncements on poverty. House Budget Committee Majority Staff, *The War on Poverty: 50 Years Later A House Budget Committee Report* (March 3, 2014) at 4 ("the single most important determinant of poverty is family structure. It has been the subject of fierce academic debate since the Moynihan Report—named after its author, then assistant secretary of labor Daniel Patrick Moynihan—was released in 1965. The Moynihan Report identified the breakdown of the family as a key cause of poverty within the black community."). See also Infra note 7.

In 1964 at his State of the Union Address President Lyndon Johnson said, "This administration today, here and now, declares unconditional war on poverty in America" and in 1988 at his State of the Union Address President Ronald Reagan said, "My friends, some years ago, the Federal Government declared war on poverty, and poverty won."

> No family can get ahead without a strong economy. But there are many factors that affect upward mobility. On the personal level, growing up in a two-earner household, completing formal education, and developing a habit and a store of savings are all significantly associated with higher rates of upward mobility. In addition, the Brookings Institution has shown that a combination of family conditions and patterns of behavior and achievement is the key to joining to the middle class.
>
> And at the neighborhood level, recent research has shown that areas with more two-parent households, a higher level of civic engagement, and fewer high-school dropouts enjoy higher average rates of upward mobility. Conversely, people who live in more geographically isolated areas, which often suffer from high levels of concentrated poverty and crime, are more likely to experience lower rates of upward mobility—even those who are not poor or do not engage in such activities themselves may be at increased risk of downward mobility.
>
> Poverty is a very complex problem [and poverty is both situational and generational].[5]

Because the report asserted that the causes and policy prescriptions for poverty are multivariate and did not reflect the orthodoxy of Republican and social conservatives that Black crime and poverty are the exclusive or predominant result of individual moral and cultural depravity, the report's explanation of Black family dysfunction did not garner support within conservative circles. But the report's conclusion that there was dysfunction has been a staple of Republican and social conservative social narrative for decades. The mainstream orthodoxy of Republican and social conservative thought on crime and poverty is more reflected in the commentaries of Bill O'Reilly.

> The reason there is so much violence and chaos in the black precincts is the disintegration of the African-American family. Right now, about 73 percent of all black babies are born out of wedlock. That drives poverty. And the lack of involved fathers leads to young boys growing up resentful and unsupervised. ...
>
> White people don't force black people to have babies out of wedlock. That's a personal decision; a decision that has devastated millions of children and led to disaster both socially and economically. So raised without much structure, young black men often reject education and gravitate towards the street culture, drugs, hustling, gangs. Nobody forces them to do that; again, it is a personal decision.
>
> ...
>
> The solution to the epidemic of violent crime in poor black neighborhoods is to actively discourage pregnancies out of marriage, to impose strict discipline in the public schools, including mandatory student uniforms, and to create a zero-tolerance policy for gun and drug crimes imposing harsh mandatory prison time on the offenders.

5 House Budget Committee, *Expanding Opportunity in America: A Discussion Draft From the House Budget Committee* (July 2014) at 5–6, 8, 21–23. See also Infra note 4.

> [The entertainment industry must stop glorifying youth who can't "speak proper English" and curse as a matter of normal course of language.] That child will never, never be able to compete in the marketplace of America ... never. And it has nothing to do with slavery. It has everything to do with you Hollywood people and you derelict parents. You're the ones hurting these vulnerable children. …
>
> It is now time for the African-American leadership, including President Obama to stop the nonsense. Walk away from the world of victimization and grievance and lead the way out of this mess. And that's the memo.[6]

As another social conservative commentator observed:

> Between 1890 and 1950, blacks had *higher* marriage rates than whites. Until 1970, black women were more likely to get married than white women—and that was despite the high mortality rates among black men, leaving fewer available for marriage. In three of four decennial years between 1890 and 1920, black men out-married white men. Whatever else may cause illegitimacy and its associated problems, it isn't poverty, discrimination, lack of education, unemployment or slavery. Black Americans had all those handicaps—and yet they still had strong families and low crime rates from 1890 until the 1960s. But in the '60s, liberals decided it would be a great idea to start subsidizing illegitimacy.
>
> …
>
> But we know poverty does not cause illegitimacy. The black experience from 1890 to 1960 proves it. It's the reverse, just as Bill O'Reilly said. If African-Americans started marrying again at their pre-Great Society rates, it would wipe out the entire black "culture of poverty."[7]

Even Speaker of the U.S. House of Representatives Paul Ryan, when he was the Chair of the House Budget Committee, could not resist advocating the orthodoxy that the Black family is the unitary and exclusive cause of Black poverty, dysfunction, and crime. When asked, "a boy has to see a man working doesn't he," Ryan answered,

---

6 Bill O'Reilly, "President Obama and the race problem," *The O'Reilly Factor Talking Points* (July 22, 2013, Fox News), Television. http://www.billoreilly.com/b/Bill-OReilly:-President-Obama-and-the-race-problem/945823226264545887.html; *see also*, Bill O'Reilly, "Are you your brother's keeper?" *The O'Reilly Factor Talking Points* (February 26, 2014, Fox News), Television. http://www.billoreilly.com/b/Bill-OReilly:-Are-you-your-brothers-keeper/-857498054410309943.html and Bill O'Reilly, "Why I went to the White House today" *The O'Reilly Factor Talking Points* (February 27, 2014, Fox News), Television http://www.billoreilly.com/b/Bill-OReilly:-Why-I-went-to-the-White-House-today/3176085340168095.html.

7 Ann Coulter, "Bill O'Reilly is smarter than Lawrence O'Donnell," anncoulter.com, August 7, 2013, http://www.anncoulter.com/columns/2013-08-07.html.

> Absolutely, and so, that's the tailspin or spiral that we're looking at in our communities. Your buddy Charles Murray or Bob Putman over at Harvard Business, those guys have written books on this. Which is, we have got this tailspin of culture, *in our inner cities in particular* [emphasis added], of men not working and just generations of men not even thinking about working or learning the value and the culture of work, and so there is a real culture problem here that has to be dealt with. Everybody's got to get involved. So this is what we talk about when we talk about civil society. If you're driving from the suburb you know to the sports arena downtown by these blighted neighborhoods, you can't just say, "I'm paying my taxes, government's got to fix that." You need to get involved. You need to get involved yourself, whether through a good mentor program, or some religious charity, whatever it is to make a difference. And that's how we help resuscitate our culture.[8]

Although research has shown that it is true that it is better for financial, emotional, educational, and structural reasons to be in a married two-parent household with a mother and a father caring for their children, it is highly simplistic and disingenuous to assert that all of the factors contributing to crime or poverty in a neighborhood can be explained and solved with the single solution of marriage with a father present in the home. I make no arguments that the presence of a *father* is of little significance in the life of a child, but there are multiple factors that result in criminality regardless of the presence of a father.

When Paul Ryan complained that "our communities" and "in our inner cities in particular" were in a tailspin because of Black "men not working, and just generations of men not even thinking about working or learning the value and the culture of work," he engaged the dog whistle of racial politics by conflating intergenerational poverty with simple intergenerational laziness and conflated both with race ("inner cities" is code for Blacks). But aside from the dog whistle, this kind of one dimensional thinking completely ignores the lack of working class living wage jobs in the urban and rural areas of America.

Poverty is a complex mix of societal ecological ***structural factors***, as well as interpersonal and individual ***psychological factors*** and ***social factors***. In other words poverty in America is a combination of how one thinks and where one lives. Returning to then Congressman Ryan's "inner city" statement, considering that unemployment rates in rural areas, Appalachia and Native American communities, are higher if not comparable to rates in urban America, he instinctively chose to say "in our inner cities in particular," which are predominately Black. The implication is that Whites who are underemployed, unemployed, poverty-stricken, and undereducated who live in high-alcohol and drug-infested rural communities nevertheless live in crime-free communities with stable married families, while Blacks in the same communities are simply criminogenic.

As any freshman-level introduction to criminology course, much less advanced study, makes clear, the explanations for why people commit crime are complicated and highly

---

8 Bill Bennett, *Morning in America*, (Salem Communications, March 12, 2014), Radio.

diverse. Crime results from individual, social, structural, and life course variables; crime is explained by the complicated interactions between people, among people, and between people and society. Neighborhood violence results from rational choice, the effects of ***social learning of aggression***, ***crime pattern*** and ***crime triangle*** (routine activities) theory, ***chronic intergenerational poverty***, ***intergenerational*** intra-neighborhood ***gang violence*** (and vendettas), the allure of violence and drug money, the inability of the police to prevent street-level violence or open-air drug (heroin, cocaine, and crack) selling in the 1980s, and chronic organized drug and weapons trafficking in rural neighborhoods and urban inner cities. These factors are compounded by the fact that the ***informal institutions of social control*** (family, church, employment, and schools), and the ***formal institutions of social control*** (police, courts, and corrections) have failed to provide safety for residents or to limit the power of gangs to intimidate and recruit. One of the reasons for the failure to limit the power of gangs is due to the proliferation of independent, small, and violent street gangs that replaced the larger organized street gangs dismantled by law enforcement in the 1980s–1990s. The result of the failure to control these smaller, more violent gangs is the creation of an environment that fosters violence, and sometimes purposeless violence, as a positive norm. ***Structural and chronic poverty*** creates a heightened need for survival and this need for survival creates the need for power and safety, which manifests in heightened violence.

All neighborhoods have a personality and sociology. Communities that are safe and secure produce behavior in accordance with that safety. In stable and safe communities aggression and violence are not the primary answers to interpersonal disputes nor are they the means to establish respect and order. Neighborhoods that are not safe and secure produce behavior in accordance with that lack of safety. Aggression and violence become the primary answers to interpersonal disputes and means to establish respect and order, which translate into to personal safety. Put another way, heightened need for vigilance for safety and security creates heightened levels of emotional and physical stress which results in emotional trauma which manifests itself in negative behavior (i.e., violence or hopelessness).

The constant need to maintain personal safety in an environment that does not provide a feeling of personal safety and one that provides risks to personal safety as a norm will also produce mental health trauma because of the culture of violence that the lack of personal safety produces. The trauma comes from either experiencing violence and sometimes mindless purposeless violence or the trauma from doing the violence. This trauma can manifest itself in depression, post-traumatic stress disorder (PTSD), drug dependency, mindless aggression, hopelessness, or any combination of these. The lack of security and stability can cause brain chemistry changes due to stress and the chronic stress can cause permanent psychological and behavioral adaptations, such as hypervigilance, automatic aggression response to environmental stimuli, and self-destruction behaviors.

These mental health reactions to structurally aggressive communities are experienced by all members of the community and all age groups. Very young children can develop these mental health issues without the cognitive memory of why they feel a certain way or react under stress a certain way. More significantly, intense trauma resulting in the development of post–traumatic stress disorder (PTSD) which can be caused by intense exposure to violence (i.e., murder, aggravated assault, etc.) or sudden violent death of a loved one can cause maladaptive behavior—including criminal and self-destructive behavior. As Dr. Brad Stolbach, a trauma psychologist at the University of Chicago, observed,

> PTSD is ... the responses to trauma [that] looks the same across populations, across ages, across genders. So what we see in soldiers and what we see in young people who've experienced life threat is very similar. As a matter of fact when you do give an opportunity to talk about the things that they are feeling they'll use almost exactly the same language to describe what they're experiencing.
>
> Much of the violence is really driven by untreated trauma rather than being driven by some criminal activity that people are benefiting from. So when you have people that are walking around traumatized, two of the ways that people often deal with that are to use substances to manage their emotions and to carry weapons in order to feel safe. Both of those things are going to increase the risk for them being harmed again, or for them doing harm to somebody else.[9]

The trauma of the violent act, murder for example, has a negative impact on the normal emotional processing of the loss of the loved one. It's this failure to grieve normally that creates emotional maladaptation to loss which can lead to other negative behavior.[10] The problem of maladaptation to the grief and trauma is amplified by each additional act of violence without emotional or cognitive relief which result in the violence being normalized in the minds and culture of the community. Death and violence becomes the norm not the exception and then people adapt their behavior to that reality in kind.

When looking at crime and violence in urban neighborhoods it's important to remember that urban cities don't suffer crime uniformly. Crime and violence is concentrated in certain neighborhoods that have been abandoned politically, socially and economically with little mental health services to deal with the traumas of life. In other parts of the city, mental health services and the medications that follow are made available for middle class residents who suffer from all types of mental health issues and the maladaptive behaviors that go with them. These services are minimally offered, if at all, in the marginalized sections of society.

Isolated communities that suffer from physical and emotional trauma due to violence as a norm also suffer from concurrent problems of chronic unemployment and the insecurity that it brings which manifests into a mentality of securing financial security at all costs—i.e., drugs, gangs and crime, violence. These dynamics result in focused and intense law enforcement and

---

9 Trymaine Lee, "Chicago Trauma: Counting Broken Bodies, But Not Broken Spirits," nbcnews.com, April 2, 2017 at https://www.nbcnews.com/news/us-news/chicago-trauma-counting-broken-bodies-not-broken-spirits-n740516.

10 Lee. See also, "MSNBC Special: All In America: Chicago," (December 29, 2017, MSNBC), Video. https://www.allinamericachicago.com/

the social disruptions to families that occur with family members chronically involved with the criminal justice system. These dynamics create an environment that is more prone to support behaviors that dehumanize and decivilize a people rather that humanize and civilize. I don't mean that inner city communities are uncivilized, but that the positive middle-class values that are fostered in middle class communities are not supported or fostered in inner city communities and the negativity that results decivilizes the environment regardless of the desires of the environment for the contrary.

Urban violence is the result of trauma, lack of mental health services, chronic unemployment, omnipresence of deviant employment, heightened aggression as a norm, heightened hypervigilance for safety, violent and sometimes purposeless violent behavior, chronic intensive law enforcement, intergenerational family involvement with the criminal justice system, emotional and psychological disorders (i.e., depression, PTSD, antisocial personality disorders, childhood personality disorders), family dysfunction (absence of fathers), and hopelessness. All of these factors support and amplify each other in creating an environment that is conducive to the worse of human behavior. The point is this, crime in inner cities is much more complicated than the simplistic and racist assertion by O'Reilly and others that crime is the exclusive result of the immorality of Black culture, lack of fathers in the home, and failure to enforce discipline in the schools.

Social conservative assertions, from both Black and White commentators, that Blacks are simply criminogenic, is an example of willful ignorance at best or racism at worst. The assertion that urban violence results from disproportionate criminality in Blacks is held by both Blacks and Whites, which raises a little admitted truth. As discussed in more detail in Chapter Three, Blacks can hold racist views of Blacks, just as Whites can. *Racism and negative perceptions of Blacks is not skin based*! Social conservatives, both Black and White, assert in the face of the complicated and contradictory history of racism in America that the implementation of the criminal justice system does not suffer from racism today. For example, David Clarke, a Black Sheriff from Wisconsin, testified before a congressional hearing that there is no racial bias in the criminal justice system, citing nothing more than an unnamed op-ed article on the *Justice Department Report on the Ferguson Police Department* and data from a PowerPoint slide.

> The same is true in arrest and incarceration data for African-American males. Participation rates in violent crime explain the disparity of why so many Black males are locked up in prison. Black makes are disproportionately involved in violent crime, and this violence is predominantly perpetrated against other Black people. It is not the result of a discriminatory criminal justice system.
>
> ...
>
> The police use of force data also tells a different story than the false narrative propagated by cop-bashers and the liberal mainstream media. A recent study that looked into police use of force between 2009 and 2012 showed this breakdown: 61 percent, or 915 of the 1,491 people who died from police use of force were White males, while 32 percent, 481, were Black males.

> It is a myth that police kill Black males in greater numbers than anyone else.
>
> Black-on-Black crime is the elephant in the room that few want to talk about. We could talk about the police use of force, but it does not start with transforming the police profession. It starts by asking why we need so much assertive policing in the American ghetto.
>
> Are police officers perfect? Not by any stretch of the imagination. Are police agencies perfect? Not even close. But we are the best that our communities have to offer.
>
> Instead, the conversation should be about transforming Black underclass subculture behavior. The discussion must start with addressing the behavior of people who have no respect for authority, who fight with and try to disarm the police, who flee the police, and who engage in other flawed lifestyle choices.
>
> ...
>
> What we are experiencing recently, it is not poor generally or Black people generally. It is the underclass behaviors.
>
> Kids growing up without fathers. School failure. Failure to stay in the workforce consistently. Failure to raise your kids. Father-absent homes. Those have nothing to do with the police.
>
> You can try to transform the police all you want, but as long as those behaviors, those lifestyle choices, are going to continue to grow in these urban centers, where the most assertive policing is needed, you are still going to have these confrontations.
>
> And when you try fight the police and disarm the police, so on and so forth, things are not going to end up well for you. I do not care how much more we pour into training. It approaches it as if it is linear. The world we live in is very asymmetrical.[11]

Sheriff Clarke testified before a congressional hearing on police use of deadly force disproportionately on Blacks, which he himself admits (32% of people shot by police are Blacks when they make up 13% of the total U.S. Population), and he offers that the real issue Congress should look at is "why we need so much assertive policing in the American ghetto [and] the conversation should be about transforming Black underclass subculture behavior. The discussion must start with addressing the behavior of people who have no respect for authority, who fight with and try to disarm the police, who flee the police, and who engage in other flawed lifestyle choices." As discussed in detail in Chapters Three, Six, Seven, and Eight the narrative asserted by Sheriff Clarke culminates in the conclusion that *Blacks are supposed be incarcerated,* and

---

11 U.S. Congress, House of Representatives, Judiciary Committee, *Policing Strategies for the 21st Century: Hearing before the Committee on the Judiciary,* 114th Cong., First sess., Serial Number 114–29, May 19, 2015 at 6, 88.

The power point presentation by Professor Richard Johnson, *Examining the Prevalence of Deaths from Police Use of Force* at slide 14 can be found at www.forcescience.org/forcepresentation.ppt and the op-ed "Holder Frames Ferguson PD For Racism Using Bogus 'Disparate Impact' Stats," which was published in *Investor's Business Daily* March 5, 2015, can be found at http://www.investors.com/politics/editorials/holder-frames-ferguson-pd-with-bogus-stats/.

they are supposed to suffer aggressive policing, because they are inherently criminal. As discussed in Chapter Three, this psychology, in turn, leads to fear of Blacks *per se*, and the assumption of Black criminality *per se* supports police aggressive use of force on Blacks, which is initiated by their color regardless of their behavior.

The logical conclusions of conceptions advocated by people like Sheriff Clarke also provide the context for political and policy determinations that have detrimental effects on Blacks. An example of this is the debate on racial profiling and whether Blacks are criminogenic. Sheriff Clarke echoed John Derbyshire, editor of the leading social/political conservative magazine, *National Review*, who wrote a famous article in which he asserted that opposition to racial profiling of Blacks simply places political sensitivities above the unfortunate truth that Blacks are criminogenic. These sensitivities, he argues, is based on irrational sensitivity to Black feelings and White guilt. Blacks, like the young in general and young males specifically when compared to the elderly and females, are more criminal, and police policy that focuses on Blacks because they are Black is as logical as focusing on the young more than the elderly and males over females. To do otherwise, Derbyshire and social conservatives argue, is to engage in political correctness at the expense of public safety. Innocent Blacks must suffer the effects of being members of a criminogenic race. As John Derbyshire wrote,

> By far the largest number of Americans angry about racial profiling are law-abiding black people who feel that they are stopped and questioned because the police regard all black people with undue suspicion. They feel that they are the victims of a negative stereotype.
>
> They are. Unfortunately, a negative stereotype can be correct, and even useful. …
>
> A policeman who concentrates a disproportionate amount of his limited time and resources on young black men is going to uncover far more crimes—and therefore be far more successful in his career—than one who biases his attention toward, say, middle-aged Asian women. …
>
> [T]he principle of equality before the law does not, and up to now has never been thought to, guarantee equal outcomes for any law enforcement process, only that a citizen who has come under reasonable suspicion will be treated fairly.
>
> It is on this special status accorded to race that … the Anglo-Saxon world has taken leave of its senses. The campaign to ban racial profiling [by] our over-educated, over-lawyered society … root[ed] in a fanatical egalitarianism [determined] not to face up to the realities of group differences … nursed and petted [by] guilt towards the behavior of our ancestors.
>
> [We must] shed the idea that deference to the sensitivities of racial minorities … trumps every other consideration, including even the maintenance of social order. To shed that idea, we must confront our national hysteria about race … [12]

12 John Derbyshire, "In Defense of Racial Profiling," 53 *National Review* 38, 39–40 (February 19, 2001) and Infra note 18.

The social politics of racial profiling is that since Blacks are simply more criminogenic and, as a result, pose a threat, the police should be unleashed on them. As discussed in Chapter Three, the significance to the proposition that Blacks are criminogenic is that it can lead to Blacks getting killed by police who also believe in these stereotypes.

As a side note, Derbyshire's racism was acceptable to the *National Review* in 2001, but his racism got out of hand when he published a blatant racist rant on his Web post in 2012,[13] in which he stated that Whites should stay out of Black neighborhoods; Whites should avoid groups of Blacks; Blacks, per se, are antisocial and violent towards Whites; and Whites should avoid beaches that have large numbers of Blacks, because that is the closest way a White person will come to being shot. It was this post that caused the *National Review* to fire Derbyshire for publishing views it did not support. I leave to the reader to discern any real difference between his 2012 post and his famous 2001 article.

In any event, the *National Review* and social conservatives consistently assert that Blacks are criminogenic. Criminogenic meaning Blacks are, by nature, criminals and more criminal than other racial groups. Post-9/11 American conservative think tanks, academics, and politicians have abandoned fears of being charged as being racists in making such claims. As one report noted in 2005,

> This report takes no position on causes of group differences in crime rates, except to point out that the ones that are most commonly proposed—poverty, unemployment, lack of education—are not satisfactory. As for the reality of those differences, the evidence is overwhelming: Blacks are considerably more likely than any other group to commit crimes of virtually all kinds, while Asians are least likely. Whites and Hispanics have intermediate crime rates.
>
> These differences are far greater than some that have given rise to significant public initiatives. Blacks are more than twice as likely as whites to be unemployed, and white household income is 60 percent higher than black household income. Blacks are twice as likely as whites to drop out of high school. Race differences of this kind have led to everything from affirmative action preferences to No Child Left Behind legislation.
>
> Americans are right to be concerned about these differences, but they are, relatively speaking, small. To repeat some of the more substantial differences in crime rates: Blacks are about eight times more likely than whites to commit murder, and *25 times* more likely than Asians to do so. Blacks are 15 times more likely than whites to go to prison for robbery, and *50 times* more likely than Asians.[14]

---

13 John Derbyshire, *Racial Politics: The Talk: Nonblack Version*, April 5, 2012, at http://takimag.com/article/the_talk_nonblack_version_john_derbyshire/page_2#axzz1rPInwjt2

14 "The Color of Crime," The New Century Foundation 1(2005): 19–20. http://colorofcrime.com/colorofcrime2005.html.

The report goes on to assert that because Blacks, being criminogenic, are convinced that racism exists in America, they are more likely to commit violent crime, and Whites need to know this in order to protect themselves.

> Assumptions about police bias are especially common among minority groups that have the most to gain from good relations with the police. Blacks, in particular, are convinced of police "racism." *In extreme cases, this belief leads to murderous rampages* like that of Brian Nichols with which this report begins. *It is not an exaggeration to say that his victims might be alive today if the facts in this report were widely known.* In countless less severe cases, a belief in police bias leads to suspicion, resentment, and lack of cooperation, all of which make it harder for the police to do their jobs, and more likely that minorities will suffer from crimes that could have been solved or prevented. How often do *assumptions about police—and societal—racism so anger blacks that they go beyond lack of cooperation to crime itself?* It is profoundly destructive for minorities to have exaggerated resentments toward the society in which they live. Uncritical repetition by whites of assertions about police bias only deepens these resentments. [Emphasis added][15]

Brian Nichols was a Black man who, while on retrial for rape, escaped from police custody in the Fulton County, Georgia, Courthouse and assaulted the sheriff deputy guarding him in the court house; killed his trial judge, the court reporter, and a federal law enforcement officer; and kidnapped and held a White female, Ashley Smith, in her home on March 11, 2005. Nichols surrendered himself the next day after Smith read him parts of *The Purpose Driven Life* by Rick Warren. I will leave it to the reader to consider the New Century Foundation conclusion that, "*It is not an exaggeration to say that his victims might be alive today if the facts in this report were widely known*" when the criminal acts of Nichols were blitz and rage attacks. He shot his judge and wanted to shoot his prosecutors (he shot the judge in his courtroom). Race had nothing to do with it. But, in fact, he was Black, and according to the New Century Foundation, that was enough warning.

Although the report lacks integrity (the authors lacked the courage to assign their names to it), the report is honest in the logical social and policy conclusions that Blacks are criminogenic by nature. The report concludes:

> Americans do not know the exact statistics, but they know that whites (and Asians) are less likely than blacks to rob them ... It is common to oppose publication of crime statistics for fear of creating "negative stereotypes," but statistical differences are the basis for important policy decisions.[16]

15 THE NEW CENTURY FOUNDATION. at 20 (emphasis added).

16 THE NEW CENTURY FOUNDATION, 20.

What are these "important policy decisions?" The report answers

> If one airline were three times more likely than other airlines to be involved in fatal accidents, would it be reasonable to avoid it? … People make choices, and risk affects their choices. If there are different risks associated with different groups of people it is legitimate to investigate and weigh those risks.[17]

The logical result of the belief that Blacks are criminogenic is that they should be avoided and surveilled more closely than peaceful Whites; and racial profiling is really criminal behavior profiling and its only political correctness that asserts otherwise.
In an article defending racial profiling, Taylor and Whitney echoed the same logic and conclusions as the New Century Foundation report.

> [People] have an intuitive understanding that men are more violent and dangerous than women. If someone in unfamiliar circumstances is approached by a group of strange men she feels more uneasy than if she is approached by an otherwise similar group of strange women. No one would suggest that this differential uneasiness is "prejudice". It is common sense, born out by the objective reality that men are more dangerous than women.
>
> In fact, it is just as reasonable to feel more uneasy when approached by blacks than by otherwise similar whites; the difference in danger as reflected by arrest rates is virtually the same. It is rational to fear blacks more than whites, just as it is rational to fear men more than women. Whatever additional precautions a person would take are justified because a potential assailant was male rather than female are, from a statistical point of view, equally justified if a potential assailant is black rather than white.
>
> …
>
> Everyone knows that young people are more dangerous than old people, and that men are more dangerous than women. We adjust our behavior accordingly and do not apologize for doing so. *Why then must we pretend that blacks are no more dangerous than whites or Asians?* But of course it is no more than pretense. *Everyone knows that blacks are dangerous, and everyone—black and white—takes greater precautions in black neighborhoods or even avoids such neighborhoods entirely*.[18]

---

17 THE NEW CENTURY FOUNDATION, 20.

18 Jared Taylor and Glayde Whitney, "Racial profiling: Is there an Empirical Basis?" *Mankind Quarterly* 42, no. 3 (2002): 285, 304, 308–310. (emphasis added); *see also* Derbyshire *supra* note 12 at 39 ("A policeman who concentrates a disproportionate amount of his limited time and resources on young black men is going to uncover far more crimes—and therefore be far more successful in his career—than one who biases his attention to, say, middle-aged Asian women."). But see, Bernard E. Harcourt, "Rethinking Racial Profiling: A Critique of the Economics, Civil Liberties, and Constitutional Literature, and of Criminal Profiling More Generally," *University of Chicago Law Review*, 71, no. 4 (2004): 1275, on why racial profiling, under rational economics—which it is based on—in fact does not provide police with a tool to reduce crime.

Sherriff Clarke, a Black conservative, agrees with the assertions of John Derbyshire and the New Century Foundation that the data shows Blacks are criminogenic and those who deny this fact are either uniformed, misinformed, or seeking political gain. He made his views clear when he testified before a House of Representatives hearing on police use of force on Blacks that

> Police use of force should be scrutinized—locally, that is. It should be examined in terms of factual data and circumstances that led to the police action and not from the emotional foundation of false narratives or catchy slogans like, "hands up, do not shoot," "no justice, no peace," or "Black lives matter." Let us leave that conduct for the public to engage in, not the mainstream media or those elected officials who cannot resist the opportunity to exploit the emotions of an uninformed or misinformed public simply for political gain.
>
> We will no doubt hear a lot of statistics thrown about today, some distorted to achieve a predetermined agenda. Others are legitimate.
>
> In 2013, the U.S. Department of Justice under Attorney General Eric Holder did a study in conjunction with the National Institute of Justice on traffic stop data. They found that when you use control factors that statistics and research require for legitimate findings, any racial disparities are attributed to differences in offending.
>
> The studies show that Black drivers violated speeding and other traffic laws at much greater rates than Whites. That conclusion of the study under an Eric Holder-led DOJ might be ugly to some, but is what the data and research have found.
>
> That same study showed that three out every four Black drivers said the police had a legitimate reason for stopping them.
>
> The same is true in arrest and incarceration data for African American males. Participation rates in violent crime explain the disparity of why so many Black males are locked up in prison. Black males are disproportionately involved in violent crime, and this violence is predominantly perpetrated against other Black people. It is not the result of a discriminatory criminal justice system.
>
> ...
>
> I do not control all law enforcement officers, but I am not going to let people indict them with this broad brush like we have the tendency to do sometimes.[19]

Clarke also stated that the real victims of the focus on police use of force and shootings of Blacks are the police and society due to the "Ferguson Effect."

> [W]e are at a tipping point ... about the psyche of the American police officer ... the constant bashing and maligning of the profession is starting to take its toll ... I talked to law enforcement officers from across this country, and the one common theme I heard

19 Supra note 11 at 5–6, 99. See Lynn Langton and Matthew Durose, "Police Behavior During Traffic and Street Stops, 2011," National Institute of Justice, Washington, D.C., NCJ 242937 September 2013.

> from them, first of all, their mindset is they are beleaguered right now. But the common theme that I heard is, you know, Sheriff, I do not know if I want to continue to take that extra step anymore, because I do not want to be the next Darren Wilson. …
>
> [T]hey look and they see that suspicious vehicle or they see that suspicious individual and say, maybe not today, I do not want this thing to go haywire on me and, next thing you know, I am one of those officers who becomes a household name in America.[20]

The adoption of White conservative critiques of Blacks by Black conservatives is not new and is reflected in Black literary culture. One example of Black conservatives adopting White conservative critiques of Black behavior and the conclusion that Black behavior, and not social and structural systems, is the direct cause of Black failure is shown in the movie *A Soldier's Story.*

In the movie, Sergeant Waters, the Black sergeant in charge of a Black platoon, complained about how the actions of "ignorant" Blacks can destroy the work of other Blacks. Waters asserted that after watching Blacks, White people conclude the "ignorant" behavior is normal, and the results of the behavior are to be expected, after all, these "coloured folks ain't supposed to have but so much sense." In the movie, while berating the members of the platoon, his answer to their complaint about his abuse and that they have to take similar abuse from the White soldiers, was, "yes you do. And if it wasn't for you southern niggers white folks wouldn't think we was all fools."[21] After all, if crime and poverty is simply solved by lazy Black men getting out of bed and going to work, as White social conservatives like Bill O'Reilly, Ann Coulter, Paul Ryan, and Black social conservatives like Larry Elder and David Clarke assert, one can easily look at inner city poverty and crime and conclude as Sergeant Waters did, what did you expect, "coloured folks ain't supposed to have but so much sense."

But not all Black conservatives have adopted White conservative narratives of Blacks or a myopic definition of poverty and the nature of poverty. For example, Bob Woodson, a Black conservative and president of the Center for Neighborhood Enterprise provides a more nuanced discussion of poverty and the moral issues attached to behavior found in poverty.

> But in addressing poverty … we tend to make the mistake of generalizing about poor people. Not everybody is poor for the same reason. I identify four categories of poor people. The first category of people are just broke. (Laughter.) … [B]ut the person's character is in place. And for them, they use welfare and assistance the way it was intended—as an ambulance service, not as a transportation system.
>
> And then, you've got category two, a person that confronts perverse incentives for maintaining—staying on—welfare. For instance, the single mom in Milwaukee … who saved $5,000 on welfare to send her daughter to college only to be charged with a felony …

20 Supra note 11 at 73–74.

21 *A Soldier's Story* (Columbia Pictures 1984).

> Category three would be someone who's physical or mentally disabled. But category four ... are those who are poor because of the poor choices that they make, the character flaws that they have. ... Just giving money ... injures with the helping hand.
>
> People on the left tend to look at the poor as if they're all category one. And people on the right tend to look at the poor as if they're all category four.
>
> [Y]ou need a strategy to address poverty to address the needs of each of these groups ...
>
> ...
>
> Final point is that also, I think, we have to destroy this false dichotomy that somehow if we spend more, we care more. If we spend less, we care less.[22]

Some Black conservatives understand that poverty, like crime, is complicated and not simply the result of inherent Black deviant behavior. But such understandings are not welcomed within the mainstream of White social conservative/Republican rhetoric, politics, or policy. The views of O'Reilly and Clarke are.

Returning to White social conservative explanations for crime, it is highly *intentionally dishonest* to assert that governmental policy and American sociopolitical and economic history has had no role in explaining the incarceration of Blacks. Leaving the social and political impact of slavery aside, consider the impact of a century of Jim Crow, segregation, and the imposition of economic and legal impediments on the ability of Black families to gain and maintain wealth intergenerationally in a capitalist system. In a capitalistic system, especially in the United States, wealth and economic success is intergenerationally created and transferred. By wealth, I mean wealth in all its various forms: financial, social, educational, professional, academic, moral, political, and societal. The exclusion of Blacks from a century of development and advancement created social, societal, and structural dysfunction and isolation that remains after its cause, Jim Crow, has been abated. Even Sherriff Clarke, the darling of White social conservatives, who asserts that racism has no explanatory power on the issue of Black disproportionate involvement or abuse by police, admits that American social policy provides the context for crime in urban communities.

> One of the things that is not addressed that we keep glossing over, and I said "we." We keep glossing over conditions that have led to the rise of the underclass of the American ghetto, where people can't find meaningful work. They have to send their kids to poor schools. Kids don't have a chance to reach their God-given potential to break out of that cycle of poverty, entrenched poverty.

22 American Enterprise Institute, "Expanding Opportunity in America: A Conversation with House Budget Committee Chairman Paul Ryan," (Panel discussion July 24, 2014).Transcript. http://www.aei.org/files/2014/07/25/-paul-ryan-event_175426104263.pdf.

> We have to look at some of the urban policies that have been enacted at the State and the Federal level that continue to feed into this growth of the underclass.[23]

Consider the historical impact of ***racial neighborhood exclusions***[24] (early 1900s), followed by ***legal restrictive covenants***[25] (1920–1948), followed by ***racial restrictive covenants in fact*** (1948–1968), and the ***red lining***[26] (1934-1968) of Black neighborhoods through the Fair Housing Administration (FHA) policies of insuring private housing and neighborhood development loans in White-only locations in major urban cities, which resulted in the physical, as well as social, political, and economic, isolation of Black neighborhoods.[27] These policies were compounded by government support of the ***rise of segregated White suburbs*** and the concentration of Black populations in the cities, the ***exclusion of Blacks from the benefits of the G.I. Bill*** and housing support granted to White servicemen after World War Two, in addition to the housing practices of ***blockbusting*** (real estate companies and banks forcing Whites out of city neighborhoods under the threat of housing devaluation due to Blacks moving in), ***real estate value manipulation*** (getting Whites to sell their homes at a loss, which were, in turn, overpriced and resold to Blacks), and ***racial steering*** (manipulating who moves into neighborhoods based on race and class). These policies resulted in the creation of concentrated poverty (political, physical, social, and economic) in selected sections (neighborhoods) of society. Add to this the use of ***racial profiling***[28] as a crime suppression strategy, as discussed in Chapter Six. Racial profiling serves as the politically correct[29] version of the belief that Blacks are criminogenic.[30]

---

23 U.S. House of Representative, Judiciary Committee, "Policing Strategies for the 21st Century," Supra note 11 at 88.

24 Racial residency laws were technically outlawed by the Supreme Court in *Buchanan v. Warley*, 245 U.S. 60 (1917)

25 Racial covenants were technically outlawed by the Supreme Court in *Shelley v. Kraemer* 334 U.S. 1 (1948). Michael Jones-Correa, "The Origins and Diffusion of Racial Restrictive Covenants," *Political Science Quarterly* 115, no. 4 (Winter, 2000–2001): 541.

26 Redlining was outlawed by the 1968 Fair Housing Act. See also, *Jones v. Alfred H. Mayer Co.*, 392 U.S. 409 (1968).

27 For a discussion on the history of Blacks in American urban cities see Douglas S. Massey, "Residential Segregation and Neighborhood Conditions in U.S. Metropolitan Areas," (391–434) in *America Becoming: Racial Trends and Their Consequences.* Volume I. Neil J. Smelser, William Julius Wilson, and Faith Mitchell (Editors) 2001.

28 *Floyd et al v. City of N.Y.*, 959 F. Supp. 2d 540 (S.D.N.Y. 2013); *see also* Bernard E. Harcourt, "Rethinking Racial Profiling: A Critique of the Economics, Civil Liberties, and Constitutional Literature, and of Criminal Profiling More Generally," *University of Chicago Law Review* 71 (2004): 1275.

29 For an example of defending racial profiling and the assertion that Black concerns over it are political sensitivities over the unfortunate truth that Blacks are criminogenic, see John Derbyshire, Supra note 12.

30 Supra notes 12–19 and accompanying text.

Although the racism and the legal structures of these policies have been negated, the physical structural (ecological) results of these policies are still in effect. The physical design and operation of the major urban cities in the United States all originated in the late 1800s through the 1950s, which means they all originated during the apex of American apartheid and predate the 1960s and the end of Jim Crow. The concentration of poverty in sections of urban neighborhoods is no accident; this historically results from policy. Consider that legal segregation in America only ended in 1968, one hundred and ninety-two years after the Declaration of Independence and one hundred and three years after the Civil War. As a matter of statutory law, the full political, economic, and social opportunities of America being made available to Blacks is only fifty years old.

When addressing the issue of crime and poverty in general, and disproportionate minority confinement specifically, two general policy approaches arise: conservative behaviorism and liberal structuralism. ***Conservative behaviorism*** asserts that the source of poverty and disproportionate criminal activity is Black negative pathology and behavior. Blacks engage in behavior, conservative behaviorists assert, that rejects the values of family and hard work, and poverty logically results. The policies of the Great Society further supplement this aversive behavior that results in crime. Racism, and the history of racism, has nothing to do with the result. ***Liberal structuralism*** asserts crime in general is caused by the social and/or economic inequities and/or political policies that isolate people and limit their options for success. These limits result in crime being an acceptable and/or the only available option for success.

Modern liberal structuralism, left-realism ***theory***, adapts classical liberal structuralism by retaining the assertion that social policy influences human behavior, but it adopts the proposition that individual behavior and choices also explain crime. The nuance of modern liberal structuralism is that it rejects the conservative proposition that the Great Society programs of the 1960s caused the breakdown of the Black family, and that breakdown is the exclusive source of Black crime and disproportionate incarceration; but accepts conservative theory that personal responsibility is a key issue in crime and that crime suppression is required to maintain society.

Returning to conservative theory, if social conservatives are correct that historical racism and the resulting social policy supporting racism from 1619 through 1968 have no role in explaining Black disproportionate incarceration, then the incarceration of Blacks should only correlate with the middle 1960s,[31] the rise of the Great Society programs, and the public policy of direct welfare payments to single mothers.[32] The Great Society programs, conservatives assert, are the cause of the fall of the Black family and *the* explanation of disproportionate

---

31 *Infra* notes 33,37–38, 58 and accompanying text.

32 "Since 1965, welfare spending has increased 800 percent in real terms, while the number of major felonies per capita today is roughly three times the rate before 1960. As Senator Phil Gramm (R-TX) says, 'If social spending stopped crime we would be the safest country in the world.'" Patrick F. Fagan, "The Real Root Causes of Violent

Black crime—which results in disproportionate Black incarceration. As the following data clearly shows, Black disproportionate incarceration *predates* the 1960s, the Great Society, unmarried mothers, the 1980s, and the rise of crack cocaine, and enhanced sentences, and it even predates World War I.[33]

As shown in Chart One,[34] official data from the Department of Justice shows that, as early as 1926, Blacks have experienced disproportionate incarceration. This disproportionate incarceration occurred before the Great Depression, despite the need for manpower during World War II and the Korean War, and well before the 1960s and conservatives' complaints and allegations of Black fathers failing to provide for their children. The data shows there was a significant increase in the incarceration of Blacks after World War II and during the rise of the civil rights movement. It is not an accident of history that Blacks have been disproportionately incarcerated, nor is it a recent historical occurrence. As discussed in the proceeding chapters, history provides a social, rhetorical, political, and policy context for an explanation of why the criminal justice system focused on incarceration of Blacks.

As discussed in detail in Chapters Four and Seven, during the subsequent twenty-five years after World War II American sociopolitical history brought turbulent change. This period involved the rise of the civil rights movement and the resulting social revolution of Black equality under the law and in society and the fall of the social Jim Crow system of White supremacy and Black inferiority under the law. This revolution was followed by the political revolution of the Great Society in 1964, in which the federal government took a direct role in reducing poverty and all types of economic inequality in the United States. These social and political changes were followed by the successful political blowback of social conservatives, urban White working class Northerners, and Southern Democrats beginning with the elections of 1966. This political blowback was supported by the merging in the American mind of social disorder, crime, and civil rights—all of which merged crime and Blacks (especially young Black men) as synonymous in the American political consciousness. This merging

---

Crime: The Breakdown of Marriage, Family, and Community," *The Heritage Foundation Backgrounder* 1, no. 3 (Mar. 17, 1995): 1026, http://thf_media.s3.amazonaws.com/1995/pdf/bg1026.pdf.

33 Michael W. Flamm, *Law and Order: Street Crime, Civil Unrest, and the Crisis of Liberalism in the 1960s* (2005), Douglas A. Blackmon, *Slavery by Another Name: The Re-Enslavement of Black Americans from the Civil War to World War Two* (2008), Arthur H. Garrison, "Disproportionate Minority Arrests, the Police and Juveniles: A Note on What Has Been Said and How It Fits Together," *The New England Journal on Criminal and Civil Confinement* 23, no. 1 (1997): 29–61, Arthur H. Garrison, "Disproportionate Incarceration of African Americans: What History and the First Decade of Twenty-First Century Has Brought," *Journal of Institute of Justice and International Studies* 11 (2011):87-116, *Infra* notes 37–38, 58.

34 Arthur H. Garrison, "Disproportionate Incarceration of African Americans: What History and the First Decade of Twenty-First Century Has Brought," *Journal of Institute of Justice and International Studies* 11 (2011): 87–116. (Charts presented here are revised and updated from those in my previous 2011 article).

began with the ascendency of the states' rights, limited government, and the crime control politics of Goldwater (1964) in Republican Party politics; the conservatisation of American national politics by 1968; the rise of Nixon's silent majority; the utilization of the Southern strategy, which resulted in the presidencies of Nixon (1968) and Reagan (1980); the disarray of the Democratic Party in 1968; and the expulsion of Social Conservative Democrats from the Democratic Party in the 1972 election. These sociopolitical events formed the foundation for the modern political discourse of American politics in which the Republican Party caters to White males (both suburban and urban high school–educated working class), states' rights, limited government, social conservatives, and the Democratic Party is dominated by various progressive, racial, gender, ethnic, urban, suburban, middle class, and working-class interests. Crime and race is one of the demarcation lines between the two parties; the Democratic party reflects the politics of civil rights and liberal attacks on the treatment of Blacks within the criminal justice system, and the Republican Party reflects the social blowback against the policies and goals of the civil rights movement and conservative defense of the incarceration of Blacks within the criminal justice system as being normal, because of the criminogenic nature of Black behavior.

The disproportionate incarceration of Blacks, which pre-dates World War I, has continued under subsequent presidents, and the political ascendency of American suburban White middle-class fear of crime in general, and specifically urban crime in 1964, was further reinforced by the advent of crack cocaine–motivated, violent urban crime in the 1980s. The crack cocaine epidemic in the urban cities resulted in the "get tough on crime" policies adopted by the federal government and all fifty states in the middle to late 1980s through the end of the 1990s. These "get tough on crime" policies included three strikes laws, increased building of maximum and super-maximum security federal and state prisons, mandatory sentencing laws, and truth in sentencing initiatives. The ***Comprehensive Crime Control Act of 1984*** signed by President Reagan increased federal penalties for marijuana, ended parole in the federal system, and created the mandatory sentencing guideline system with the creation of the Federal Sentencing Commission, in addition to reinstituting the death penalty.

As Chart Two shows,[35] by the time of President H.W. Bush, Blacks, who accounted for 13% of the total U.S. population, accounted for 50% of the total number of people incarcerated in the United States, a trend that would last from 1991 through 1995.

As shown in Charts Two and Three,[36] the disproportionate rate of incarceration steadily decreased from a high of 51% in 1993 to a low of 33% in 2016, a limited improvement considering Blacks in 2015 accounted for 13% of the total U.S. population. Review of Charts One, Two, and Three together shows that the incarceration of Blacks is a historical constant that spans decades before the rise of the Great Society and the 1960s. At the risk of

---

35 Garrison.

36 Garrison

being repetitive, conservative and the Republican Party orthodoxy asserts two propositions regarding Blacks and crime. First, the fall of the traditional family and American social values began its collapse with the policies of the Great Society. Secondly, Black disproportionate incarceration is the result of school failure, juvenile delinquency, crime, and violence, which is the direct consequence of the collapse of the Black family, which was caused by the welfare system programs of the Great Society, which encouraged unwed mothers to have children and to raise them without a father in the home. Blacks are disproportionately in prison because of their individual behavior, not because of racism in American social history or in criminal justice policies.

But, as the data shows, the incarceration of Blacks, in general, and Black men, specifically, is a historical constant. Blacks were disproportionately incarcerated long before Lyndon Johnson entered politics and policy making. When Johnson entered politics as a freshman member of House of Representatives from the State of Texas in 1937 under President Roosevelt, Blacks accounted for 25% of the total prison population, which was increasing from 22% in 1930, while Blacks were only 9.7% of the total U.S. population. The disproportionality of Blacks in the criminal justice system not only well predates the arrival and the ascendency of President Johnson in 1964 and the policies of the Great Society; it has been an American historical constant for various social, political, and legal reasons.

This historical constant of incarceration of Blacks is the result of social and political policies over time. As discussed in detail in Chapter Seven, from 1619 to 1865, these social and political policies included slavery and laws to control the movements of free Blacks. Consider the ***Fugitive Slave Acts*** (1793 and 1850), the ***Negro Seaman's Acts*** (1820s), and the advent of ***Southern slave patrols*** (the origin of policing in the South), for which the single purpose was to enforce slavery by controlling the behavior and movement of Blacks.[37] From 1865 to 1965, this historical constant included the social and political control the freed slaves through the policies of the ***Black Codes*** and ***Jim Crow*** in general, and specifically, between 1877 (the fall of Reconstruction) and the 1940s.

In the antebellum era, the South instituted slave patrols that would enforce order on rural slave plantations and patrol the Southern roads to prevent slave escapes. In the postbellum era, Southern police would enforce ***vagrancy laws*** to force Blacks into working relationships on plantations and the courts would enforce the ***criminal anti-enticement laws***, ***contract enforcement laws***, ***anti-emigrant agent laws*** and ***false-pretense laws*** that would make sure that as a functional matter Blacks did not leave the plantations. These laws together created a system of involuntarily servitude. ***Criminal anti-enticement laws*** made it a crime to hire Blacks that were in the employ of others—it established the proprietary claims over Black bodies. ***Anti-emigrant agent laws*** placed criminal fines on employment

37 Andrew E. Taslitz, *Reconstructing the Fourth Amendment: A History of Search and Seizure, 1789–1868* (2006); see also Sally E. Hadden, *Slave Patrols: Law and Violence in Virginia and the Carolinas* (2001), C. Vann Woodward, *The Strange Career of Jim Crow* (1955), *Supra* note 33, and *infra* notes 38, 58.

agents who were tasked with seeking workers from other states. ***False-pretense statutes*** criminalized Blacks leaving employment for other opportunities based on the theory that the Blacks had committed fraud when they took the first position by not intending to comply with the terms of the employment to the detriment of the employer. ***Contract-enforcement laws*** imposed a criminal fine for failure to satisfy the terms of a contract—a fine Blacks could not pay; ***vagrancy statutes*** facilitated the arrest and fining of Blacks for not being in employment (***apprentice laws***). The inability to pay these fines facilitated the system of ***peonage*** and ***criminal surety*** and ***convict-leasing*** occurred when fines could not facilitate Black labor. Both the contract-enforcement laws and vagrancy laws created a situation in which Blacks could pay the fine by "voluntarily" signing his labor over to a plantation owner to work off the debt of the fine or the bond imposed by the court. If no plantation owner would pay the fine in exchange for the Black labor, convict-leasing would be utilized.[38] The convict-leasing system provided forced labor in coal mines, swamps, and other areas in which White labor could not be found. This system of laws and practices as a whole were designed to keep Blacks in a status of near slavery by another name but in compliance with the Thirteenth Amendment.

This system also socially and psychologically conditioned American society to define Blacks as criminals and to expect to find them under criminal justice control. As discussed in more detail in Chapter Four, the political party loyalty realignments of the middle 1960s through the election of 1980, along with the economic changes that occurred in the 1970s and 1980s fostered various policies that affected Blacks and supported their disproportionate incarceration and isolation. In the 1970s, cities suffered deindustrialization because of manufacturing moving into the suburbs; the resulting loss of working class jobs and the victories of the civil rights movement allowed the Black middle class to leave the cities ("Black flight") in the middle to late 1970s, the result being the loss of middle class social, political, economic, and tax base support in many urban areas—leaving many urban Black neighborhoods in structural and social poverty.

---

38 See Chapter Seven for detailed discussion. See also, William Cohen, "Negro Involuntary Servitude in the South, 1865–1940: A Preliminary Analysis," *The Journal of Southern History* 42, no. 1 (Feb. 1976): 31–60, 34. Douglas A. Blackmon, *Slavery by Another Name: The Re-Enslavement of Black Americans from the Civil War to World War II* (2008). See also, Christopher R Adamson, "Punishment after Slavery: Southern State Penal Systems, 1865–1890," *Social Problems* 30, no. 5 (June 1983): 555, Earl Smith and Angela J. Hattery, "African American Men and the Prison Industrial Complex," *Washington Journal of Black Studies* 34, no.4 (2010): 387, Eric Schlosser, "The Prison Industrial Complex," *Atlantic Monthly*, Dec. 1998, at 52, Philip L. Reichel, "Southern Slave Patrols as a Transitional Police," *American Journal of Police* 7(1988): 51, Bruce P. Smith, "The Fourth Amendment, 1789–1868: A Strange History," *Ohio State Journal of Criminal Law* 5(2008): 663, Michelle Alexander, *The New Jim Crow: Mass Incarceration in the Age of Colorblindness* (2010) and Carol A Archbold, *Policing: A Text Reader* (2013). *Supra* notes 33 and 37 and *infra* note 58.

During the early 1950s and through the 1960s, the modern radicalization of American politics was fostered by various political/social events. *First*, White flight, which was the response to the Second Great Migration (1940–1970) resulted in the development of White only suburbs, like Levittown, which began the modern development of racially segregated neighborhoods. *Second*, political blowback occurred against the Democratic Party that occurred in the mid-term elections of 1966[39] by Northern suburban and working middle class Whites along with White Southern Democrats who resented the growth of the Great Society and the civil rights policies of President Johnson.[40] *Third*, starting in 1964 a political realignment occurred in which Black voters shifted from the party of Lincoln, the Republican Party, to the Democratic Party.[41] *Fourth*, the realignment of Blacks to the Democratic Party was matched by the transference of Southern White Democrats to the Republican Party, which began with President Truman in 1946.

When Truman signed executive order 9808 creating a committee on civil rights, he threw down the gauntlet to states' rights and Southern Democrats in his short and direct signing statement.

> Freedom from Fear is more fully realized in our country than in any other on the face of the earth. Yet all parts of our population are not equally free from fear. And from time to time, and in some places, this freedom has been gravely threatened. It was so after the last war, when organized groups fanned hatred and intolerance, until, at times, mob action struck fear into the hearts of men and women because of their racial origin or religious beliefs.
>
> Today, Freedom from Fear, and the Democratic institutions which sustain it, are again under attack. In some places, from time to time, the local enforcement of law and order has broken down, and individuals—sometimes ex-servicemen, even women—have been killed, maimed, or intimidated.
>
> The preservation of civil liberties is a duty of every Government-state, Federal and local. Wherever the law enforcement measures and the authority of Federal, state, and local governments are inadequate to discharge this primary function of government, these measures and this authority should be strengthened and improved.

---

39 See discussion in Chapter Four.

40 *Infra* note 46–52. President Johnson, after signing the Civil Rights Act of 1964 is said to have remarked to his press aide, Bill Moyers, "we just delivered the South to the Republican Party for a long time to come." Michael Oreskes, "Civil Rights Act Leaves Deep Mark on the Landscape of American Politics" New York Times (July 2, 1989) at https://www.nytimes.com/1989/07/02/us/civil-rights-act-leaves-deep-mark-on-the-american-political-landscape.html. See also, John Nichols, "When the Republicans Really Were the Party of Lincoln" (July 2, 2014) at https://billmoyers.com/2014/07/02/when-the-republicans-really-were-the-party-of-lincoln/.

41 For Example, See Leah M. Wright, "Conscience of a Black Conservative: The 1964 Election and the Rise of the National Negro Republican Assembly" *Federal History 2009* (2009): 32.

> The Constitutional guarantees of individual liberties and of equal protection under the laws clearly place on the Federal Government the duty to act when state or local authorities abridge or fail to protect these Constitutional rights.
>
> Yet in its discharge of the obligations placed on it by the Constitution, the Federal Government is hampered by inadequate civil rights statutes. The protection of our democratic institutions and the enjoyment by the people of their rights under the Constitution require that these weak and inadequate statutes should be expanded and improved. We must provide the Department of Justice with the tools to do the job.
>
> I have, therefore, issued today an Executive Order creating the President's Committee on Civil Rights and I am asking this Committee to prepare for me a written report. The substance of this report will be recommendations with respect to the adoption or establishment by legislation or otherwise of more adequate and effective means and procedures for the protection of the civil rights of the people of the United States.[42]

Chapter Four will discuss in detail the White Southern Democrat reaction to President Truman and his apostasy that the federal government had a role and responsibility to protect individual rights in the face of local and state intransience. The significance of his 1946 executive order was the forming the President's Committee on Civil Rights in 1946, which resulted in the desegregation of both the federal work force and the armed forces by executive order (9980 and 9981, respectively) in 1948 and the formation of the U.S. Commission on Civil Rights and the Civil Rights Division in the Justice Department through the passage of the Civil Rights Act of 1957.

The realignment of Blacks to the Democratic Party and the transference of Southern White Democrats to the Republican Party, which began with Truman, became irreversible with the Democrats passing the 1964 Civil Right Act[43] with support from Northern liberal Republicans. As discussed in Chapter Four, the liberal Republican wing of the party that supported the 1964 Civil Rights Act would be completely purged out of the party by 1980.

Fifth, the political ideological realignments of both parties began with the 1948, 1964, and 1966 elections in response to the Republican Party adopting the rhetoric and policies of

42 Harry S. Truman, "Freedom from Fear," signing statement on Executive Order 9808 creating the President's Committee on Civil Rights December 5, 1946 in *To Secure These Rights: The Report of the President's Committee on Civil Rights* (1947) at VII.

43 For example, See Stefano Luconi, "The Southern Strategy and the Post-New Deal Dynamics of the U.S. Party System," *Quarterly Journal of Ideology* 27, nos.3 & 4 (2004): 1.

Southern Democrat assertions[44] of states' rights[45] as advocated by Sen. Strom Thurmond[46] (D. South Carolina), Gov. George Wallace[47] (D. Alabama), Gov. Orval Faubus[48] (D. Kansas), Gov.

---

44 See *Supra* notes 40–41, 43 and Gary Miller and Norman Schofield, "The Transformation of the Republican and Democratic Party Coalitions in the U.S.," *Perspectives on Politics* 6, no. 3 (2008): 433.

45 As discussed in chapter four, the concept of States' Rights, it should be remembered, was birthed by the arguments of John Calhoun and other slave owning Southern leaders who opposed the power of the Union to place any limits on the expansion of slavery and asserted that slavery was both ordained by God and placed Blacks in the natural state God intended. The fall of slavery did not eliminate the idea that the states have a right to resist the national government when it sought to enforce federal Civil Rights laws on the segregated South. During the 1950s, the South asserted interposition the modern version of the antebellum theory of nullification.

Both concepts have been disavowed by history and even serious conservative leaders like Bill Bennett have bowed to the judgment of history. On his radio show a caller asserted that conservatives should be more media savvy and support conservative movements. Specifically, the caller asserted that conservatives should support a group of "black preachers" who had an online petition to "impeach" Attorney General Holder for his support of gay marriage on "states' rights grounds" to which Bennett said that was the wrong argument because "states' rights" was the "justification of slavery" and the "states' rights" argument has been "discredited" and could not be used as an argument for the defense of marriage. He asserted that the defense of traditional marriage is moral, philosophical, and religious. He said "states' rights was not the way to go, you have to use first principles." *Bill Bennett, Morning In America Radio Show* (March 4, 2014), *available at,* http://www.billbennett.com/show-archive/.

46 Thurmond led an insurrection within the Democratic Party in 1948, after President Truman ended segregation in the military and formed a commission to study civil rights, by running for president under the States' Rights Democratic Party, the Dixiecrats. The Dixiecrats took control of the Democratic Party in the South and Thurmond won 39 electoral votes. He left the Democratic Party and joined the Republican Party when Johnson signed the 1964 Civil Rights Act. He was a major leader in bringing the Deep South Democrats into the Republican Party during the late 1960s–early 1970s.

47 Wallace opposed integration and famously said at his inauguration as governor in 1963, "In the name of the greatest people that have ever trod this earth, I draw the line in the dust and toss the gauntlet before the feet of tyranny, and I say segregation now, segregation tomorrow, segregation forever." He is famous for standing in the doorway of the University of Alabama to prevent the admittance of two Black men to the University, forcing the Kennedy Administration to send the deputy attorney general, backed up by the nationalized Alabama National Guard, to move Wallace out of the way to allow the admittance and integration of the college.

48 Faubus opposed integration and ordered the Arkansas National Guard to prevent the integration of Little Rock Central High School in 1957 forcing President Eisenhower to nationalize the Guard and order the 101st Airborne Division to enforce the federal court order integrating the school. Faubus retaliated by closing the Little Rock high schools for the 1958–1959 school year.

Ross Barnett[49] (D. Mississippi), Sen. Barry Goldwater[50] (R. Arizona), Sen. Richard Nixon[51] (R. California), and Gov. Ronald Reagan[52] (R. California). This realignment was further supported by the Republican Party adoption of the states' rights theory of interposition, the modern version of the pre-Civil War Southern concept of nullification, in response to the civil rights movement of the 1950s and 1960s, and White opposition to forced integration and bussing[53] in the 1970s. *Sixth*, the Republican Party adoption of the Southern Strategy[54] achieved the twin goals of winning national presidential elections by cultivating both the Northern and Southern White male vote and the political restricting and segregation of the Black vote to urban areas. *Seventh*, in the 1972 election, after a heated and divisive political primary and convention, the Democrats selected George McGovern, and like the Republicans in the selection of Goldwater in 1964, the selection of McGovern changed the operating political orientation of the Democratic Party by expelling the foreign policy conservative wing of the party (what would come to be the neo-conservatives ("neo-cons") within the Republican Party) leaving social liberals and progressives in a dominant position within the party.

In 1968, the Democratic Party continued to suffer the abandonment of the South that began in the 1964 and 1966 elections when George Wallace, after losing the nomination of

---

49 Barnett opposed integration and had freedom riders arrested and imprisoned, and in 1962 opposed the integration of University of Mississippi when James Meredith was admitted. Barnett allowed a riot to occur on campus in which Meredith and a small detachment of U.S. Marshals were surrounded and attacked by an armed mob. It required the Kennedy Administration to send the U.S. Army military police from the 503rd and 716th Military Police Battalions to reinforce the marshals and later Kennedy had to nationalize the Mississippi National Guard to protect Meredith throughout his enrollment of the University.

50 Goldwater opposed the Civil Rights Act of 1964 and established the dominance of conservative, states' rights, opposition to the Great Society politics within the Republican Party in the 1964 Republican primary election as well as helped the facilitation of the transference of Southern Democrats to the Republican Party.

51 Nixon created and implemented the Southern strategy which solidified the transference of conservative, states' rights, opposition to the Great Society voters to the Republican Party.

52 Reagan became the embodiment of conservative states' rights and opposition to the Great Society politics, and he solidified the winning coalition of Southern White working-class democrats with Northern Republican voters. He opposed disinvestment in South Africa to end the Apartheid System, opposed the Martin Luther King Jr. holiday, opposed Affirmative Action programs, felicitated and provided support for the "get tough on crime" politics of the 1980s, and attacked social welfare programs by (1) supporting the assertion that they were immoral, (2) supporting the idea that the recipients of welfare support were urban, lazy, Black women, and (3) supported the policy assertion that they were not effective in reducing poverty.

53 David O. Sears; Carl P. Hensler; Leslie K. Speer, "Whites' Opposition to 'Busing': Self-Interest or Symbolic Politics?" *The American Political Science Review* 73, no. 2 (1979): 369.

54 *Supra* note 43.

the Democratic Party, formed the American Independent Party and won[55] 46 electoral votes and, in the popular vote, won almost ten million votes. More significantly, Wallace won five Southern states (Louisiana, Arkansas, Mississippi, Alabama, and Georgia), coming in second to Nixon in South Carolina, North Carolina, and Tennessee.[56] In 1968, the entire Confederate South voted Republican. The Democrat's loss of the South to the Republicans was complete and permanent. In the 1968 and 1972 elections, Nixon pioneered the strategy of using White fear of crime, implying, while allowing others to outright assert that the source of crime and disorder in America was the inner cities (i.e., Blacks) and the policies of the Great Society. The 1972 election rhetoric of running a campaign to restore "Law and Order" and being the party of the "Silent Majority" in order to win White male votes became the standard operating strategy for decades within the Republican Party. In no election since 1972 has a Republican run for president and in some way not raised the issue of law and order. The Republican Party would have one more realignment election, in 1980 with Ronald Reagan, which would solidify, unify, and organize the control of the Republican Party on a new and broad coalition of constituencies. The coalition that elected Ronald Reagan would also finalize the marginalization of Northern establishment liberal Republicans in the party. This winning coalition consisted of the Southern Democrats of Strom Thurmond (1948), Barry Goldwater (1964), and George Wallace (1968), supplemented by the Northern urban and rural working class moral majority White male presidential electorate of Richard Nixon (1968, 1972), supported by Reagan voters, which were comprised of social conservative, White Evangelical Protestant Christian, deregulation supply-side economics, small government, crime control pro-urban (city) law enforcement (as supposed to federal law enforcement),[57] reduced federal government (states' rights), and foreign policy neo-con voters.

This history of the political parties provides a background for the development of the criminal justice policy initiatives of the conservatives and the Republicans and the explanation for the modern continuation of using the criminal justice system as a tool for the social control of Blacks and the resulting disproportionate incarceration of Blacks. From 1964 through the 1990s, the responsibility for supporting the suppression of urban street crime, if not direct responsibility for suppressing it, shifted to the national government. This policy change occurred in no small part due to the urban race riots in Harlem (1964), Philadelphia (1964), Watts (1965), Atlanta (1966); the "long hot summer" riots of 1967, which included the riots in Newark (1967) and Detroit (1967); and the riots of 1968, including riots in Washington, D.C., Chicago, and Baltimore. These riots helped solidify the linkage between crime and Blacks in the American mind and linked civil rights and Great Society initiatives with crime and race.

---

55 David Leip's Atlas of U.S. Presidential Elections: 1968 Presidential General Election Results (2012) at http://uselectionatlas.org/RESULTS/national.php?year=1968.

56 Leip.

57 See discussion in Chapter Four.

Add to the political blowback from the civil rights movement and the urban riots the linkage of crime and Blacks that occurred as the result of the structural and criminological centralization of drug use and drug gang violence in urban cities in the 1960s and the rise of crack cocaine and the violence that followed in urban cities in the 1990s. The urban riots of 1964–1968 helped establish the rise of conservative politics in 1964 and its ascendency by 1972. Fear caused by the race riots provided a platform for conservatives (Republicans) to take control of the national political landscape, which culminated in the nationalization of federal funding of state and local urban crime suppression with the passage of the ***Omnibus Crime Control and Safe Streets Act of 1968***. From 1968 to present, this policy shift resulted in various criminal justice policies, like the war on drugs (1970s to 2008), the rise of the nationalization of drug control with the creation of the Drug Enforcement Administration, the passage of the ***Comprehensive Drug Abuse Prevention and Control Act of 1970***, and the "get tough on crime" policies of the 1980s and 1990s.[58]

These socio-political events were compounded by Black dissatisfaction with the Great Society's inability to produce actual reduction of poverty in urban cities. The failure of the Great Society's programs to make actual and significant change in the levels of poverty in the inner cities coupled with incidents of continued police brutality resulted in the urban riots (1964–1968), which resulted, as discussed above, in White suburban middle and working class voters' abandonment of the Great Society and the Democratic Party in the 1966 and 1968 elections. White abandonment of the Great Society and its growing resentment of the riots after the passage of major civil rights legislation that ended a century of Jim Crow social policy coupled with White middle class fear of Black radicalism (Black Panthers), which replaced the peaceful civil disobedience strategy of Martin Luther King Jr., further intensified the social-psychological link of civil rights demonstrations with riots and riots with crime, disorder, and Blacks in the American political consciousness.

An additional factor explaining the connection of race and crime is the assertion that crime resulted from deviant family structures in the Black community. This lack of traditional family structure with a father as the head of the home providing financial and disciplinary support and control of young Black males served as the defining explanation for crime for generations to come of social conservatives. This theory was adopted from a policy paper written in the Johnson Administration soon after the passage of Civil Rights Act of 1964.

58 *Supra* notes 32, 37–38. See also, Robert J. Sampson, and Janet L. Lauritsen, "Racial and ethnic disparities in crime and criminal justice in the United States," *Crime and Justice* 21 (1997): 311, Lincoln Quillian and Devah Pager, "Black Neighbors, Higher Crime? The Role of Racial Stereotypes in Evaluations of Neighborhood Crime," *American Journal of Sociology* 107, no. 3 (2001):717, Robert J Sampson and William Julius Wilson, "Toward a Theory of Race, Crime and Urban Inequality," in *Race, Crime, and Justice: A Reader* (Shaun L. Gabbidon & Helen Taylor Greene eds., 2005): 177, and Walker Newell, "The Legacy of Nixon, Reagan, and Horton: How The Tough on Crime Movement Enabled A New Regime of Race-Influenced Employment Discrimination," *Berkeley Journal of African American Law and Policy* 15, no. 1 (2013): 3.

In March 1965, *The Negro Family: The Case for National Action,* otherwise known as the ***Moynihan Report***, was leaked to the press, and it ignited a controversy regarding the status of the Black family and the impact of that status on American society as a whole. In 1965, Patrick Moynihan, Assistant Secretary of Labor in the Johnson Administration, wrote an internal government policy report to provide support for the unveiling of the declaration of the War on Poverty. Ten years after the beginning of the modern civil rights movement, with the Supreme Court decision of *Brown v. Board of Education* in 1954 and culminating in the landmark passage of the Civil Rights Acts of 1964 and 1965, policy attention shifted from ending racial Jim Crow and segregation to a focus on economic disparities and the failure of Black families to attain the American Dream.

In his famous "Freedom is not enough" speech at Howard University in June 1965, President Johnson said, "The voting rights bill will [establish the freedom to vote]. ... But freedom is not enough. You do not wipe away the scars of centuries by saying: 'Now you are free.' ... You do not take a person who, for years, has been hobbled by chains and liberate him ... and then say, 'You are free to compete with all the others,' and still justly believe that you have been completely fair. ... To this end, equal opportunity is essential, but not enough, not enough." This speech, along with Johnson's War on Poverty speech before Congress in January 1964, began four years of social programs, which resulted in Medicare, Medicaid, federal school loans, food stamps, and a host of others between 1964 and 1968. Patrick Moynihan authored Johnson's 1965 speech. Being at the cusp of leadership of major policy implementation, Moynihan was sidelined when his report leaked to the press.

The report made two conclusions regarding the state of the Black family. First, the Black family was dysfunctional and was getting worse as far as its stability. Second, the damage to the Black family could be addressed through direct social programs, the top being employment for the Black male and allowing the Black male to be the patriarch of his family with support from the Black female, just as it was in White families. Two factors caused the damage to the Black family, according to Moynihan. The first factor was centuries of slavery and Jim Crow and its impact on the structure of the Black family. As Moynihan explained, "[t]hree centuries of injustice have brought about deep-seated structural distortions in the life of the Negro American" and that the "Negro situation ... commonly perceived by whites in terms of the visible manifestation of discrimination and poverty," needed to evolve in order to consider "the effect that three centuries of exploitation have had on the fabric of Negro society itself." Moynihan asserted that the negative functioning of the Black family—low employment, high single mother birthrates, and low income—should be understood as the result of Jim Crow, not the endemic inferiority or criminality of Blacks.

The second factor was the matriarchal nature of the Black family in which the Black male was neither the bread winner nor the male role model of manhood for young Black males. This lack of Black male presence in the home leads to failure in school and the delinquent behavior of young Black male children. Moynihan asserted that because the "negro community has been forced into a maternal structure ... out of line with the rest of the American society," it has a weak family structure suffering from "a tangle of pathology." At the center of the tangle of pathology is Black male unemployment and the failure to hold a responsible position in the home, which resulted in "25% of Black families not [being] intact[,] 24% of Black children born illegitimate[, and] 25% of Black families were single female headed households."

Conservatives of the 1960s, as they do today, ignored the first factor and adopted the second factor as political orthodoxy. The report was only intended for internal government review as an empirical justification for the policies of the War on Poverty. The report aimed to justify the need for national action. Moynihan received national condemnation for his effort. Blacks—liberal ones anyway—cursed him and his report as blaming the victim and justifying racist ideals. Feminists, both Black and White, cursed the report for blaming women for the problem of the family and supporting a patriarchal view of America that was under direct challenge by the women's movement of the middle and late 1960s.

Due to the backlash, the report was abandoned by the Johnson Administration, and Moynihan left the Administration. By the 1980s, the report had reemerged as being prescient and evidence that the policies of the 1960s were a failure. As President Reagan asserted in January 1988, "the Federal Government declared war on poverty, and poverty won." Conservatives in the 1960s argued that social programs do not help the poor, and the problems of Blacks are of their own making to be fixed by them alone. Social conservatives, both Black and White, assert that with the end of legal Jim Crow, the responsibility and fault of their family structure belongs to them. The pathology within the Black family, it was asserted, was reinforced by social programs that removed the value of work and personal responsibility from Blacks specifically and the poor generally. Conservatives today, as they did in the 1960s, ignore the slavery/Jim Crow historical context Moynihan used to assert that poverty was attached to Black family structure. In doing so, conservatives distort the report by asserting that Moynihan was right—the issue of poverty lay with the Black family.

One cannot understand the *Moynihan Report* and its receipt in a vacuum. It was leaked one year after the rise of Goldwater and the conservative takeover of the Republican Party. It followed the summer riots of 1964 and preceded the urban riots of 1965–1968. By 1965 the civil rights movement was beginning to shift away from the philosophy of Dr. King to a more militant approach. Lastly, by 1965–1966 White fear of Black crime and its linkage to the civil rights movement began to form a political backlash against the War on Poverty that led to President Nixon and, later, the war on drugs and crime. The politics of the middle 1960s distorted the receipt of the report. The politics of the post-1960s have continued that distortion.

This post–World War Two 1950–1970 socio-political history created the modern and contemporary context for the social expectation that Blacks are supposed to be under social control. As shown in Charts One and Two, the results of these criminal justice policies resulted in the consistent yearly increase of the percentage of Blacks in prison from 35% (1975) during the Presidency of Gerald Ford to 41% at the beginning of the Presidency of Ronald Reagan (1981) to 51% at the end of the Presidency George H.W. Bush (1993). By the end of the eight-year presidency of Bill Clinton, the percentage decreased from 51% to 46%, and it continued to decrease from 46% to 41% by the end of the eight-year Presidency of George W. Bush. Under President Obama, the percentage continued to decrease from 41% to 33%. As

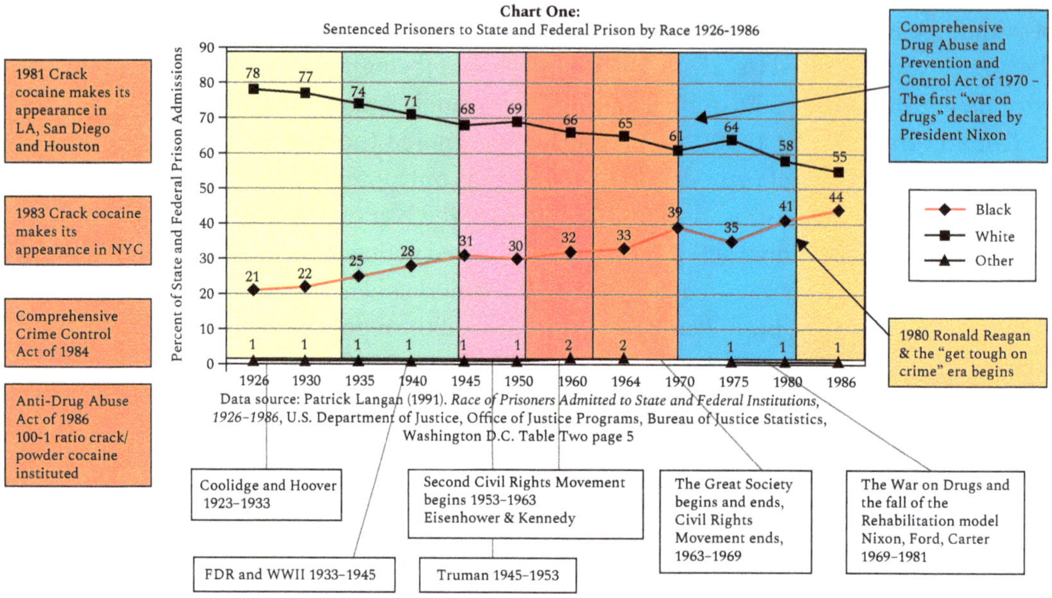

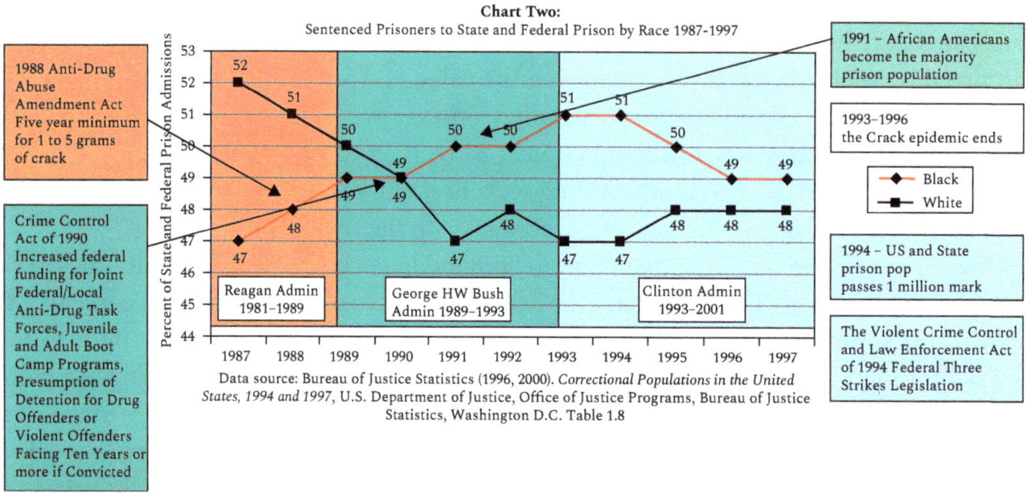

shown in Charts Three and Four, the reduction of the percentage of Black incarceration that occurred under President Clinton did so only when the politics of "get tough" on crime began to subside in 1998 and after the end the crack epidemic in 1994. For the first five years of the Clinton presidency, Black incarceration was between 51% and 49%, only to remain flat at 46% for the remainder of his term in office. The percentage of Black incarceration under President Obama decreased to its lowest point since 1964 (33%) from 41% in 2009 to 33% in 2016, five years after the passage of the ***Fair Sentencing Act of 2010***, which reduced the sentencing laws

Chart Three:
Sentenced Prisoners to State and Federal Prison by Race 1998-2016

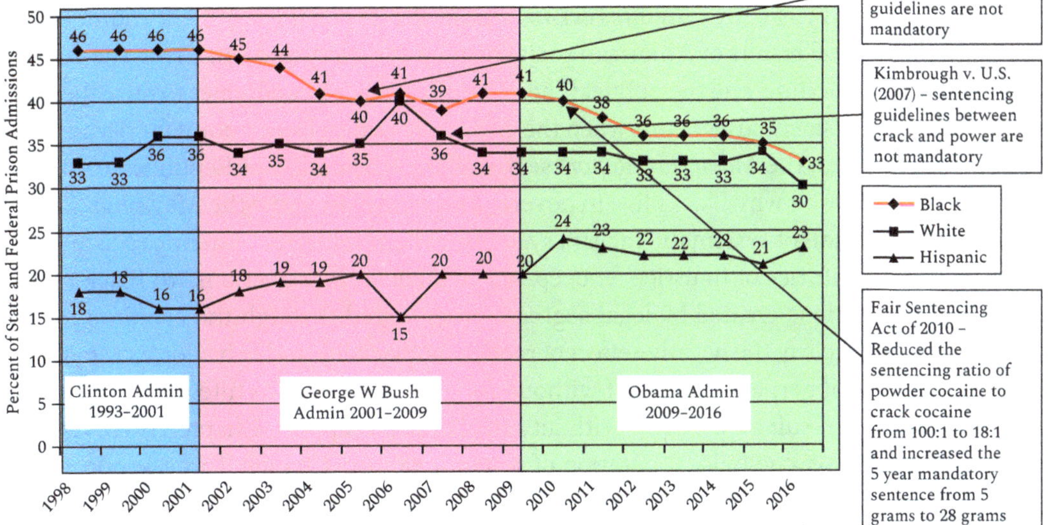

Source: Bureau of Justice Statistics (1999-2007). *BJS Prisoners in 1999-2016* U.S. Department of Justice, Office of Justice Programs, Bureau of Justice Statistics, Washington D.C.

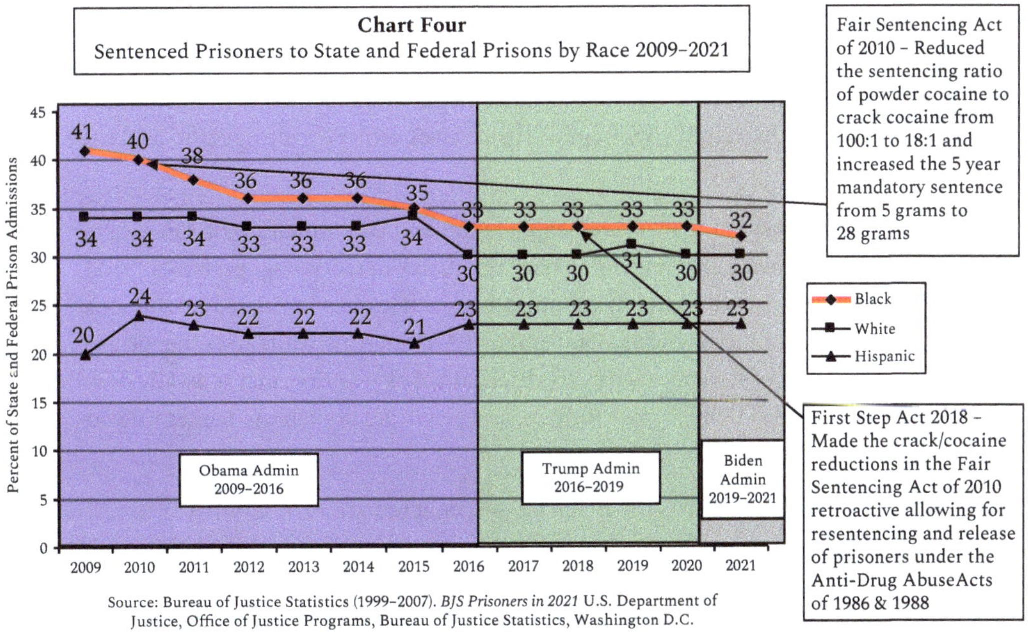

Source: Bureau of Justice Statistics (1999-2007). *BJS Prisoners in 2021* U.S. Department of Justice, Office of Justice Programs, Bureau of Justice Statistics, Washington D.C.

for possession of crack cocaine and seven years after the Supreme Court ruled that the federal sentencing guidelines were not mandatory.[59]

59 *U.S. v. Booker*, 543 U.S. 220 (2005) and *Kimbrough v. U.S.*, 552 U.S. 85 (2007)

With the fall of systematic legal racism (Jim Crow and legal segregation) in 1968, what remains is systemic racism. By ***systemic racism***, I mean White racial resentment and/or fear of Blacks, the structural results of American social history of slavery and Jim Crow, the current racial politics about crime, and the political "need" for Republican candidates to raise the issue of crime during presidential elections when the crime rate is at its lowest point for decades. As previously discussed, the *Moynihan Report* serves as the foundation of Republican and conservative orthodoxy on why Blacks live in poverty and crime. To quote the *Moynihan Report*, in the wake of the fall of systematic racism, systemic racism remains. Systemic racism is the result of "three centuries of injustice ... deep-seated structural distortions" to Black family social life—distortions created by legal segregation enforced through the criminal justice system. Systemic racism, the negative effect of racism on Black life and behavior, as Moynihan wrote, "is capable of perpetuating itself without assistance from the White world." Systemic racism is the social result of Jim Crow without active or legal support. Chapter Three reviews, in detail, the socio-psychological operation of systemic racism. Chapter Three, supported by Chapters Four, Five, and Seven, will provide a detailed review of the social, political, historical, and legal foundations of systemic racism in the face of the end of systematic racism as a result of civil rights movement.

The key in understanding systemic racism is that it does not require, and it assumes the lack of, affirmative and direct (blatant) racial prejudice and bias. Systemic racism is defined and operationalized by subtle but negative perceptions, portrayals, and treatment of specific types of Blacks as a group and then applying those negative perceptions to individual Blacks. Critical race theory, as discussed in Chapter Three, uses a more race specific and race accusatory definition.

> Systemic racism involves the racialized exploitation and subordination of Americans of color by white Americans. It encompasses the racial stereotyping, prejudices, and emotions of whites, as well as the discriminatory practices and racialized institutions engineered to produce the long-term domination of African Americans and other people of color. At the heart of systemic racism are discriminatory practices that generally deny Americans of color the dignity, opportunities, and privileges available to whites individually and collectively.[60]

As the Supreme Court held, "Just as the Black Codes, enacted after the Civil War to restrict the free exercise of those rights, were substitutes for the slave system, so the exclusion of Negroes from White communities became a substitute for the Black Codes. And when racial discrimination herds men into ghettos and makes their ability to buy property turn on the color of

60 Joe R. Feagin and Bernice McNair Barnett (2004). "Success and Failure: How Systemic Racism Trumped the Brown v. Board of Education Decision," *University of Illinois Law Review* 2004, no. 5 (2005): 1099, 1102–1103. See Chapter Three on aversive racism and racism without racists and how they explain systemic racism.

their skin, then it too is a relic of slavery."[61] The American context about race today is created by the American history of race. This history results in the perception of Blacks as criminal and a population to control, which creates a social perspective that they are supposed to be disproportionately arrested and incarcerated, because they are disproportionately criminal. If not controlled, at the very least, they are to be watched.

This narrative of crime having a Black face is reflected in how crime is discussed. As discussed earlier in this chapter Derbyshire, Clarke, O'Reilly, and social conservatives in general assert that the reason crime has a Black face is because Blacks commit most of the crime in America. The narrative that Blacks commit most of the crime in America is derived from the fact that Blacks are disproportionately arrested. The fallacy is that the latter does not establish the former. But that point aside, FBI arrest data proves that Blacks don't commit most of the crime. The data shows most of the crime committed in America is committed by Whites.

The differential criminality of various ethnic groups that Derbyshire says proves that Blacks should be feared on sight cuts the other way, and its Whites that should be the group to be feared. According to the most recent data, *FBI 2019 Crime in the United States* report, Whites commit the majority of rape, robbery, aggravated assault, and violent crime in America. Whites account for 69% of crime arrests while Blacks account for 26%. Whites accounted for 59% of all violent crime arrests while Blacks accounted for 36%. When using arrest data as a proxy for actual crime commission, a practice that has its own problems, ***crime is statistically White not Black***.

More importantly, arrest crime data as an explanation of crime has limits. Arrest data reflects police investigatory outcomes and it does not reflect actual guilt. In other words, crime arrest data represents a determination by the beginning of the criminal justice system not the definitive part of the system (the jury determination of guilt). The focusing on Black disproportionately in arrest data and arguing about why that statistic exists and what it means fosters and supports two political outcomes. First, it makes the face of crime Black. Second, it disconnects crime and Whites. It makes crime race specific and Black. That has policy consequences. Additionally, as discussed in Chapter Six, the New York Police Department's use of suspect race data as a benchmark and justification for disproportionate stopping and searching of Blacks resulted in civil liability for violation of the constitution in *Floyd et al. v. City of New York*.

Consider this point: most of crime in America is intraracial. But the narrative of crime is never White-on-White crime as a problem to fix. The narrative and politics is exclusively about Black-on-Black crime and then Black-on-White crime. Again, the choice of narrative has policy consequences. As discussed in Chapter Three, this narrative of Blacks and crime being synonymous creates a stereotype utilized by Blacks and Whites that, regardless of cognitive acceptance, provides context for dealing with people in ambiguous situations. This narrative—crime being Black—also forms the basis for racial bias, racial prejudice and racism,

61 *Jones v. Alfred H. Mayer Co.*, 392 U.S. 409 (1968): 441–443.

TABLE 1.1 *FBI 2019 Crime In the United States*

ARRESTS BY RACE AND ETHNICITY

	TOTAL ARRESTS											
	RACE						PERCENT DISTRIBUTION[1]					
OFFENSE CHARGED	TOTAL	WHITE	BLACK OR AFRICAN AMERICAN	AMERICAN INDIAN OR ALASKA NATIVE	ASIAN	NATIVE HAWAIIAN OR OTHER PACIFIC ISLANDER	TOTAL	WHITE	BLACK OR AFRICAN AMERICAN	AMERICAN INDIAN OR ALASKA NATIVE	ASIAN	NATIVE HAWAIIAN OR OTHER PACIFIC ISLANDER
TOTAL	6,816,975	4,729,290	1,815,144	164,852	86,733	20,956	100.0	69.4	26.6	2.4	1.3	0.3
Murder and nonnegligent manslaughter	7,964	3,650	4,078	125	83	28	100.0	45.8	51.2	1.6	1.0	0.4
Rape[3]	16,599	11,588	4,427	249	276	59	100.0	69.8	26.7	1.5	1.7	0.4
Robbery	56,305	25,143	29,677	635	568	282	100.0	44.7	52.7	1.1	1.0	0.5
Aggravated assault	274,376	169,467	91,164	7,192	4,902	1,651	100.0	61.8	33.2	2.6	1.8	0.6
Burglary	118,843	81,104	34,188	1,728	1,464	359	100.0	68.2	28.8	1.5	1.2	0.3
Larceny-theft	592,679	393,226	178,937	11,718	7,133	1,665	100.0	66.3	30.2	2.0	1.2	0.3
Motor vehicle theft	57,278	38,719	16,409	1,213	721	216	100.0	67.6	28.6	2.1	1.3	0.4
Arson	6,291	4,453	1,553	121	125	39	100.0	70.8	24.7	1.9	2.0	0.6
Violent crime[4]	**355,244**	**209,848**	**129,346**	**8,201**	**5,829**	**2,020**	**100.0**	**59.1**	**36.4**	**2.3**	**1.6**	**0.6**
Property crime[4]	775,091	517,502	231,087	14,780	9,443	2,279	100.0	66.8	29.8	1.9	1.2	0.3
Other assaults	703,534	455,901	219,400	16,037	9,907	2,289	100.0	64.8	31.2	2.3	1.4	0.3

Source: Federal Bureau of Investigation.

Forgery and counterfeiting	32,100	21,537	9,668	338	501	56	100.0	67.1	30.1	1.1	1.6	0.2
Fraud	78,698	51,861	24,041	1,424	1,208	164	100.0	65.9	30.5	1.8	1.5	0.2
Embezzlement	9,886	5,983	3,587	114	179	23	100.0	60.5	36.3	1.2	1.8	0.2
Stolen property; buying, receiving, possessing	63,035	38,751	21,998	1,108	825	353	100.0	61.5	34.9	1.8	1.3	0.6
Vandalism	126,161	86,360	34,670	3,198	1,598	335	100.0	68.5	27.5	2.5	1.3	0.3
Weapons; carrying, possessing, etc.	108,847	60,494	45,530	1,129	1,247	447	100.0	55.6	41.8	1.0	1.1	0.4
Prostitution and commercialized vice	19,811	10,074	8,370	73	1,205	89	100.0	50.9	42.2	0.4	6.1	0.4
Sex offenses (except rape and prostitution)	28,627	21,360	5,903	596	668	100	100.0	74.6	20.6	2.1	2.3	0.3
Drug abuse violations	1,052,101	748,874	274,670	14,098	11,857	2,602	100.0	71.2	26.1	1.3	1.1	0.2
Gambling	1,895	1,081	553	13	214	34	100.0	57.0	29.2	0.7	11.3	1.8
Offenses against the family and children	58,042	38,196	16,454	2,821	493	78	100.0	65.8	28.3	4.9	0.8	0.1
Driving under the influence	646,607	526,928	90,888	12,373	13,071	3,347	100.0	81.5	14.1	1.9	2.0	0.5

Source: Federal Bureau of Investigation.

(Continued)

TABLE 1.1 ***FBI 2019 Crime In the United States (Continued)***

ARRESTS BY RACE AND ETHNICITY

	TOTAL ARRESTS											
	RACE						PERCENT DISTRIBUTION[1]					
OFFENSE CHARGED	TOTAL	WHITE	BLACK OR AFRICAN AMERICAN	AMERICAN INDIAN OR ALASKA NATIVE	ASIAN	NATIVE HAWAIIAN OR OTHER PACIFIC ISLANDER	TOTAL	WHITE	BLACK OR AFRICAN AMERICAN	AMERICAN INDIAN OR ALASKA NATIVE	ASIAN	NATIVE HAWAIIAN OR OTHER PACIFIC ISLANDER
Liquor laws	109,887	85,350	17,077	5,657	1,651	152	100.0	77.7	15.5	5.1	1.5	0.1
Drunkenness	218,095	164,797	32,255	18,238	2,431	374	100.0	75.6	14.8	8.4	1.1	0.2
Disorderly conduct	208,690	132,676	64,049	9,811	1,820	334	100.0	63.6	30.7	4.7	0.9	0.2
Vagrancy	15,952	10,763	4,497	473	201	18	100.0	67.5	28.2	3.0	1.3	0.1
All other offenses (except traffic)	2,192,791	1,532,998	577,689	54,049	22,248	5,807	100.0	69.9	26.3	2.5	1.0	0.3
Suspicion	1,316	1,008	257	49	2	0	100.0	76.6	19.5	3.7	0.2	0.0
Curfew and loitering law violations	10,565	6,948	3,155	272	135	55	100.0	65.8	29.9	2.6	1.3	0.5

[1] Because of rounding, the percentages may not add to 100.0.

[2] The ethnicity totals are representative of those agencies that provided ethnicity breakdowns. Not all agencies provide ethnicity data; therefore, the race and ethnicity totals will not equal.

[3] The rape figures in this table are aggregate totals of the data submitted based on both the legacy and revised Uniform Crime Reporting definitions.

[4] Violent crimes are offenses of murder and nonnegligent manslaughter, rape, robbery, and aggravated assault. Property crimes are offenses of burglary, larceny-theft, motor vehicle theft, and arson.

Source: Federal Bureau of Investigation.

Arrest rate statistics are not synonymous with and do not explain criminal behavior

Disproportionate Arrest data measures the percentage of Blacks in the overall U.S. population (13%) and the percentage of arrests that are Black (27% in 2016). **UCR Arrest data** reports crimes known to the police and on persons arrested. **Disproportionate criminal behavior** is the relationship between proportion of Blacks (13%) and actual Black criminal behavior in the total of all criminal behavior. *These concepts are not the same although they are discussed as if they are.*

1. *UCR Arrest data is a proxy for crime occurrence. Data does not reflect crimes not reported and unknown to the police.*
2. *UCR data is subject to crime coding manipulation, police non-reporting of crimes, and it only lists street level crime.*
3. *Arrest data is the result of police activity and its' relation to police attention to crime occurrence.*
4. *Arrest data is the result of police policy determinations on what offenses will and will not result in arrests.*
5. *Arrest data is an aggregate of outcomes of police saturation of specific locations & communities (i.e., over policing).*

Disproportionate criminal behavior is a complicated mix of external and individual structural, societal, and ecological factors.

1. *Individual factors*
    a. *Mental health disorders and learning disabilities & misdiagnosis*
    b. *Emotional /mental /psychological disability & misdiagnosis*
    c. *Physical health and lack of quality and consistent medical care*
    d. *Development of defiant moral values & behaviors*
    e. *Lack of physical and emotional security or maladaptive reactions to stress (PTSD)*
2. *Social factors*
    a. *Lack of quality of school education*
    b. *Negative/deviant family dynamics*
    c. *Abusive/neglective parental behavior*
    d. *Negative social peer associations*
    e. *Social/political isolation*
    f. *Systemic racism*
    g. *Exposure to structural poverty (compared to enduring periodic lack of finances)*

Source: Federal Bureau of Investigation.

3. *Economic factors*
    a. *Lack of employment opportunities*
    b. *Lack of availability of public transportation*
    c. *Lack of quality healthy fresh food*
4. *Environmental factors*
    a. *Types of crime in the community*
    b. *Level of chronic fear of crime/violence*
    c. *Police saturation*
    d. *Police over-enforcement vs. under protection*
    e. *Lack of availability of mental health services*
    f. *Sociology & psychology of concentrated community poverty*

Poor and structurally deficient communities have social, economic, and environmental problems. These problems cause crime (these are criminogenic factors). In today's society, Blacks are disproportionately concentrated in such communities. Race is not a cause or explanation of crime. Race is incorrectly used as a proxy for crime and a political shorthand description of criminogenic factors. Explanations of societal/group level crime are ecological and structural not racial.

both implicit and explicit. These variations on how Blacks are perceived (negative stereotype, racial bias, racial prejudice, implicit racism, and explicit racism) are not the same and they manifest themselves differently in social, political, and criminal justice policy.

The disproportionality argument is intentionally rigged to the detriment of Blacks and creates the false narrative that crime is not committed by Whites because of the way disproportionality statistics are discussed. Whites make up most of the U.S. population. As the FBI reports show, Whites account for 70% of crime arrests and Blacks account for 27%, while Whites account for 77% of the population. Thus, by the disproportionate arrest narrative, Whites are under-represented as offenders (based on arrest statistics) even while making up the majority of those who are arrested (70%). Although Whites commit most of the crime in America, Blacks are disproportionately arrested compared to Whites. The disproportionate arrest rate of Blacks is translated, in political terms, into disproportionate criminal activity making the face of crime Black. The disproportionate arrest/crime commission narrative involves racism because "anytime the behavior of a few members of a racial group is projected onto the entire group, that is racism. Racism denies the individuality of people."[62]

62 Correspondence with Dr. Delores Jones-Brown, Professor of Criminal Justice, John Jay College (Retired) February 2018.

Because Whites are underrepresented, White crime is supplanted in political consciousness for the popular narrative of Black crime. In the popular narrative, when social conservatives and commentators talk about violent crime or gun violence, they example Chicago and Baltimore or some other city (code word for Black). They don't example Wyoming, Kansas, or rural areas of gun violence or drug crimes because those areas are examples of White crime. When White (and Black) social conservatives talk about Black crime it's coached in group descriptions and generalities regarding Black behavior. But when White crime is discussed, it's couched in individualistic language. The racism is in the language of the narrative. Consider school shootings vs. shootings in Chicago dynamic. The later are urban and Black and the explanations include deviant Black culture, lack of discipline in the schools, and lack of fathers. The former are rural, suburban, and White and the explanations include individual victimization due to school bullying, individual mental health needs that are not addressed, and White avoidance of disproportionate suspension of Blacks and other minorities from schools. The subtle narrative of White avoidance of disproportionality is that if schools would suspend all violent kids regardless of disproportionate impact, the few White violent students who commit the school shootings would be suspended as well. Consider the questions not asked during a school mass shooting. The questions are not "what is the state of the White families or White culture in the schools that are resulting in these shootings?" But when discussing urban crime, Black culture is always discussed. Policy questions are birthed by political questions. Crime committed by Whites is seen as generic or individual, but crime committed by Blacks is seen as general social disorder. Thus, White crime is made politically and rhetorically invisible.

"Anytime the behavior of a few members of a racial group is projected onto the entire group, that is racism. Racism denies the individuality of people. But, conservative criminologists like to talk about 'individual responsibility' and reject structural and community explanations EXCEPT when they want to talk about racial disproportionality in offending (as measured by arrest rates)."[63] On the political level, "what is the result of the 'disproportionality' discussion? White criminals will be suspected and surveilled less and innocent Blacks will be suspected and surveilled more."[64] The disproportionality debate diverts attention from the fact that "structural and individual factors are driving criminal activity in both groups not skin-color/racial identity."[65]

If crime is explained and caused by racial identity—Blackness—then arguably there would be no arrests of White people at all. Rather than focusing attention on race as a tool for understanding crime patterns or behaviors, the focus should be on what arrestees, regardless of race,

63 Jones-Brown.

64 Jones-Brown.

65 Jones-Brown.

"have in common INSTEAD of comparing arrestees to the general population, because the overwhelming majority of both racial groups are NOT getting arrested."[66]

As discussed in later chapters, popular culture and political discourse not only assume the criminal Black man but discounts the criminal White man. This narrative that crime is Black leads to policy outcomes and outputs that focus crime policy on surveillance and incarceration of Blacks to the exclusion of Whites. The point is criminal justice policy is defined by how crime is represented. Because crime is couched in race, even when race-neutral criminogenic factors are discussed to explain crime, they are perceived within a racial context. This context is made all the worse when many of those criminogenic factors are structurally imbedded in communities that house a significant Black population. The racialization of crime also prevents policy from being developed to focus of the sociological, psychological, and economic factors that create environments that foster crime that is committed regardless of race.[67]

In summation, there are multiple explanations for the disproportionate involvement of Blacks within the criminal justice system. These include poverty, educational failure, lack of economic opportunity, single female head of households, the fall of the importance and significance of the Black male within the Black family,[68] the use of prisons as a method of addressing social inequalities, inequality in criminal sanctions of crimes committed by Blacks, aggressive and militaristic police crime suppression and neighborhood patrol operations in Black neighborhoods, as well as historical overt racism. These social and political factors were supplemented by judicial support of overt racism.[69] Another explanation is the use of extralegal factors within the operation of the criminal justice system, specifically in criminal sentencing. One of those factors being the use of prior criminal history. For example, a committee commissioned by the Pennsylvania Supreme Court concluded that "after controlling for legally proscribed factors and mode of conviction, the study found that the defendant status characteristics of race, ethnicity, gender, and age definitely affect sentencing outcomes of all kinds." The committee further concluded:

> 1. Courts rely primarily on the legally prescribed factors, i.e., the type and seriousness of offenses and the defendant's prior criminal record, in determining sentences for defendants.

---

66 Jones-Brown.

67 For additional discussion on the use of crime statistics and race see, Katheryn Russell, *The Color Of Crime*, 110–129 (1998), Matthew Robinson, "The construction and reinforcement of myths of race and crime," *Journal of Contemporary Criminal Justice* 16, no. 2 (2000): 133, Khalil Gibran Muhammad, *The Condemnation of Blackness: Race, Crime and the Making of Modern Urban American* (2011), Robert J. Sampson and William Julius Wilson, "Toward a Theory of Race, Crime and Urban Inequality" (37–54) in *Crime and Inequality* John Hagan and Ruth Peterson (Eds.) (1995).

68 Daniel Moynihan, *The Negro Family: The Case for National Action* (1965).

69 See *Dred Scott v. Sandford*, 60 US 393 (1857).

> 2. In sentencing, the mode of conviction matters. Defendants who were convicted following a trial—especially a jury trial—were substantially more likely to be incarcerated and received substantially longer prison terms than those who entered guilty pleas.
> 3. Race affects sentencing outcomes. Overall, African Americans are slightly more likely to be incarcerated that Whites and receive slightly higher sentences. African Americans had a 1.2 percent greater probability of incarceration and received sentences that were, on average, 1.3 months longer than Whites. Young African American males, age 18–29, had a 4.8 percent greater probability of incarceration and received sentences that were, on average, 4.3 months longer that Whites. Older African American males, ages 30 and over, had a 4.1 percent greater probability of incarceration and received sentences that were, on average, 3 months longer than Whites.[70]
>
> The observation that the courts "rely primarily on the legally prescribed factors, i.e., the type and seriousness of the offenses and the defendant's prior criminal record, in determining sentences for defendants" is important in understanding how legally acceptable distinguishing factors can have a disparate impact. For as more African Americans, especially African American men, are more likely to be arrested and come into the system and thus develop more numerous criminal histories (through plea agreements); they are more likely to be incarcerated and for longer periods of times than whites. Thus although racial bias may not be driving the incarceration it is subtly impacting incarceration by disparately developing the very factors that result in the overrepresentation of African American males at the sentencing stage. If more African Americans are taking pleas, in part, because "defendants who are convicted following a trial—especially a jury trial—are substantially more likely to be incarcerated and receive substantially longer prison terms than those who entered guilty pleas" the result of more developed criminal histories through plea agreements impacts later sentencing decisions, disparately impacting African Americans.[71]

Overt and covert legal and political discrimination, as discussed in Chapters Four, Five, and Seven, also plays a role. Consider a subtle example of implicit racism. On his radio show,[72] Bill Bennett, a White social conservative and former cabinet secretary in the Reagan Administration, entertained a caller from Texas whom he welcomed enthusiastically. The caller relayed

70 Pennsylvania Supreme Court Committee on Racial and Gender Bias in the Justice System (2003). *Final Report of the Pennsylvania Supreme Court Committee on Racial and Gender Bias in the Justice System* at 129, 130.

71 Arthur Garrison, "Disproportionate Incarceration of African Americans: What History and the First Decade of Twenty-First Century Has Brought", 11 *Institute of Justice and International Studies* 87, 103 (2011).

72 Bill Bennett, *Morning In America Radio Show* (January 28, 2014).

the story in the *Washington Post*[73] of the Vatican releasing two white doves as a symbolic gesture for peace. Upon the release of the doves, a Black crow and a seagull attacked the doves in mid-flight. The *Washington Post* article specifically identified the attacking crow as Black while not identifying that the attacking seagull was White. The caller remarked that *what was newsworthy was that the newspaper article on the incident reported on the rarely reported incidents of Black-on-White crime*! To which Bill Bennett and his producer laughed but said they did not want to get into the Zimmerman case again.

We will return to the socio-historical political examination of race and social policy as a method of understanding race and criminal justice policy in Chapters Four, Five, and Seven. In Chapter Two, attention will shift to constitutional law and the authority of the police to use force.

KEY DISCUSSION CONCEPTS

- Black personal dysfunction and criminality
- *The Moynihan Report* (1965)
- Social Conservatives' explanation for crime
    - Bill O'Reilly
- Disproportionate Minority Confinement
- "Dog whistle" politics and criminal justice policy
- Criminological explanations for crime
- Political defense of police use of force
- Blacks are criminogenic
- Crime as code for racism
- Black conservatives
- Black Codes and Jim Crow laws, policies, and practices
    - Pig Laws
    - Anti-vagrancy laws
    - Peonage
    - Convict-lease system
    - Racial neighborhood exclusion laws
    - Legal restrictive covenants
    - Red lining
    - White only suburbs
    - G.I. Bill

73 Charity Brown, "Peace doves come under attack at the Vatican," *Washington Post* (Jan. 27, 2014), http://www.washingtonpost.com/national/health-science/peace-doves-come-under-attack-at-the-vatican/2014/01/27/bb0362d0-876a-11e3-916e-e01534b1e132_story.html.

  - Blockbusting
  - Racial steering
- Physical, social, economic, psychological concentration of poverty
- Racial profiling
- The Great Society
- Politics of the 1960s
- Slave laws and policies
  - Fugitive Slave Acts (1793 and 1850)
  - Negro Seaman's Acts (1820s)
- Race and American politics 1950s–1990s
- Urban riots 1964–1968
- War on Drugs (1970s)
- War on poverty (1964–1968)
- Systematic and systemic racism

DISCUSSION QUESTIONS

1. What is the relationship between the modern criminal justice system policies of the 1980s-1990s and the politics of the 1950s–1960s? This chapter proposes that the Black Codes and Jim Crow laws of the 1860s have a direct relation to the operation of the criminal justice system and how it is perceived by Blacks today. Compare on contrast the Black Codes and Jim Crow laws with the laws of the 1980s-1990s and discuss differences in purpose and result of these laws?
2. How do the Heritage Foundation, Bill O'Reilly, and Sheriff Clarke explain the relationship between race, poverty, and crime? How does Bob Woodson explain poverty and what makes his views different from O'Reilly and the Heritage Foundation?
3. John Derbyshire, the New Century Foundation, and Taylor and Whitney assert that police *should* focus on Blacks more than Whites when trying to identify criminals, because Blacks are simply more criminal than Whites. If police follow this advice, will it reduce crime? Why, or why not?
4. What social, societal, structural, and sociological factors explain crime? How does chronic stress impact mental health in poor communities and how does the lack of mental health services explain deviant/self-destructive and criminal behavior?
5. Do arrest rates and crime rates measure the same thing? How are arrest rates used in political and academic discourse? Is this discourse detrimental to Blacks on a political level? What is the social and political result of the narrative that Blacks are criminogenic?
6. Who is Patrick Moynihan, and why does he matter to discussions of race, poverty, and crime in America? What is the political and policy significance of his report

and the 1965 "freedom is not enough" speech that he wrote for President Johnson in 1965?

7. What is the difference between systematic racism and systemic racism? Do you think the distinction matters? Why, or why not? Do you think either concept is relevant to understanding the American criminal justice system in the American twenty-first century?
8. Is crime explained by individual choices or is it the result of environmental factors or is crime a combination of these two? Explain and discuss.

CHAPTER TWO

Police Shootings and Limitations of the Law

THE FOURTH AMENDMENT AND POLICE USE OF DEADLY FORCE

STUDENT LEARNING OBJECTIVES

1. Students will be able to explain the relationship between the Fourth Amendment and police use of force.
2. Students will be able to explain how the U.S. Supreme Court has applied the Fourth Amendment to police use of force and how it determines if the police use of force was reasonable.
3. Students will be able to explain police provocation theory (police-created danger) and how the Supreme Court and lower judicial courts have applied this concept to police use of force.
4. Students will be able to explain federal law that imposes criminal culpability and civil liability upon police officers and police agencies for violation of federal civil rights.
5. Students will be able to explain the limits of Fourth Amendment protection and remedies for police use of force.
6. Students will be able to explain how a municipality can be held liable for policies and decisions that are made by its agents.
7. Students will be able to explain what limitations the Fourth Amendment places on police and municipal civil liability and criminal culpability.

A FOURTH AMENDMENT STORY

On November 22, 2014, two Cleveland, Ohio police officers were called to investigate a "man with a gun" in the park. The caller told the 911 dispatcher that there was a juvenile in the park flashing a toy gun. The juvenile was later identified as 12-year-old Tamir Rice. The police were only told by the dispatcher that there was an active shooter in the park. The police officers arrived at the park and as they stopped, opened their car doors, one of the officers shot and killed Tamir. The film of the shooting showed that Timothy Loehmann, one of the officers in the car, fired his weapon within two seconds of arriving on the scene. On December 28, 2015, the grand jury impaneled by Cuyahoga County prosecutor Tim McGinty, following his recommendation, determined that the two police officers should not be charged with the death of Rice.[1]

The police department and McGinty explained that the officers were not told they were being called to a juvenile holding a toy gun, they were told that a man with a gun was in the park. McGinty explained in his statement, "the Code One, high-priority call about a possible active shooter next to a rec center was based on inaccurate information" because the 911 dispatcher, "passed along detailed information about the 'guy' outside the rec center's clothing, including the colors of his coat and his camouflage hat, but not the all-important facts that the 9-1-1 caller said the gunman was 'probably a juvenile' and the gun might not be real. Had the officers been aware of those qualifiers, the training officer who was driving might have approached the scene with less urgency." McGinty concluded that, the "police officers and the police department must live with the awful knowledge that their mistakes—however unintentional—led to the death of a 12-year-old boy. So will the police radio personnel whose errors were a substantial contributing factor to the tragic outcome." In addition to the failure of the 911 staff to properly relay the full facts to the police, McGinty commented, "If the color and design of Tamir's pellet gun had screamed "Toy" then the call that set this tragedy in motion might never have been made."

According McGinty, the "police were prepared to face a possible active shooter in a neighborhood with history of violence. There are in fact memorials to two slain Cleveland Police officers in that very park. And both had been shot to death nearby in the line of duty. Police are trained that it takes only a third of a second to draw and fire a weapon at them—and therefore they must react quickly to any threat. Officer Loehmann had just seen Tamir put an object into his waist as he stood up in the gazebo and started walking away. A moment later, as the car slid toward him, Tamir drew the replica gun from his waist and the officer fired. Believing he was about to be shot was a mistaken—yet reasonable—belief given the high-stress circumstances and his police training. He had reason to fear for his life."

McGinty stated that although, "The death of Tamir Rice was an absolute tragedy. It was horrible, unfortunate and regrettable. But it was not, by the law that binds us, a crime." He explained that "to charge police ... the State must be able to show that the officers acted outside the constitutional boundaries set forth by the Supreme Court of the United States. Simply put ... human error, mistakes and miscommunication ... [does] not indicate criminal conduct by police." Upon "close examination [of the] enhance[d] surveillance video ... it is now indisputable that Tamir was drawing his gun from his waist as the police car slid toward him and Officer Loehmann exited the vehicle. ... [I]t is likely that Tamir ... either intended

1 Statement from County Prosecutor Timothy J. McGinty on the decision of the Grand Jury in the Tamir Rice case 12/28/2015 at http://ftpcontent4.worldnow.com/woio/pdf/McGintyRemarks.pdf

to hand it to the officers or to show them it wasn't a real gun. But there was no way for the officers to know that because they saw the events rapidly unfolding in front of them from a very different perspective." McGinty asserted that the video clearly established self-defense and reasonableness of action at the moment the police arrived on the scene.

McGinty's analysis of parameters of the Fourth Amendment law was, of course, correct. Police accountability in use of force is not governed or defined by mistake, incompetence, poor police tactics, miscommunication or stupidity. Police use of force is governed, as far as criminal culpability and civil liability are concerned, by the Fourth Amendment to the U.S. Constitution. The law under the Fourth Amendment regarding police use of force is very narrow and so is its protection. Fourth Amendment analysis does not focus on the injury sustained by the person shot or the motive of the officer. A Fourth Amendment inquiry only seeks to determine if the police, without the help of hindsight, acted reasonably under the facts known to them at the time of the use of force. Federal criminal civil rights law in police shootings is even more restrictive because it requires proof that the police intentionally and knowingly acted to violate the civil rights of the person killed. In cases of ambiguity, the officer gets the benefit of the doubt.

Tamir Rice was killed because the police did not utilize distance, cover, and assessment upon entering an ambiguous situation. But the broader point is that the failure of the police to use proper tactics is irrelevant to Fourth Amendment analysis. What matters is whether what the police did, with what they knew at the time, was reasonable. Police tactical error notwithstanding, it was objectively reasonable for the police to fear for their lives when confronted with a person pointing a gun at them. It was reasonable to use deadly force. The fact that the police were wrong in their assessment of danger, with the use of hindsight, does not change the reasonableness of the action under the Fourth Amendment.

Not every moral wrong is a legal wrong and not every legal wrong has a criminal sanction as a remedy. What is lawful is not always just and what is just is not always required by the law. As the Rice case shows, a dead child due to government incompetence and overreaction does not automatically equal constitutional and criminal illegality.

INTRODUCTION

The United States Constitution was ratified June 21, 1788, with a promise to those who feared that the national government created by the new constitution would not and could not abuse the rights of American citizens. The promise made between those who supported the Constitution—Alexander Hamilton and James Madison, among others—and those who opposed it was that the First Congress would pass a list of amendments to the constitution that made clear that the national government could not abridge certain rights. This promise was fulfilled by the passage of ten amendments, the *Bill of Rights*, which were ratified on December 15, 1791. These amendments were to limit the power of the new national government. They were not intended to be applied to the states. The application of the Bill of Rights to the states developed through history, which included the passage of the Fourteenth Amendment and the Supreme Court acceptance of the theory of incorporation, which led to the due process cases in the 1960s, which applied the First, Second, Fourth, Fifth, Sixth, Eighth Amendment protections to the states.

The text of the Fourth Amendment is as follows:

> The right of the people to be secure in their persons, houses, papers, and effects, against unreasonable searches and seizures, shall not be violated, and no Warrants shall issue, but upon probable cause, supported by Oath or affirmation, and particularly describing the place to be searched, and the persons or things to be seized.

The Fourth Amendment protects people from—and here is the key point—"unreasonable" search and seizure of their "persons, houses, papers and effects." This means the police have the power to search and seize your house, papers, and property. The only limit on that power is whether they do it reasonably. The police can seize you. The only limit on that power is whether they do it reasonably. By seizure, the courts have held that the police have the power to stop you and make you remain under their authority. This power also allows them to use force to make you comply with their demands. This power functions on a continuum. A continuum that ranges from the power to yell at you to make you stop to the power to beat you with physical force to the power to shoot you dead in the street. The sole limitation on this power is whether it is used reasonably. This chapter examines what is "reasonable" use of force under the Fourth Amendment. What are the limits to that protection? This chapter provides a legal background for the broader question of police use of force and race.

There is a political, constitutional, and sociological history that places negative connotations on Blacks, in general, and specifically conflates Black males and criminality in the mind of America. As discussed in Chapter Three, the perception of race and criminality is reflected in the behavior of police and societal (political) protection of the police when they use deadly force on young Black males. Although these perceptions, and the history that created them, are complicated and are full of nuances, the authority, power, and legality of the police to use force and deadly force is much less complex. The Supreme Court held in *Monell v. Department of Social Services* (1978), *Harlow v. Fitzgerald (1982)*, *Tennessee v. Garner* (1985), and *Graham v. Connor* (1989) collectively that the right against unreasonable search and seizure, seizure being use of force, can be enforced under the Civil Rights Act of 1871 (The Ku Klux Klan Act). Local government agencies, including police departments and police officers, are subject to civil liability for violating individual constitutional rights. The complexity of understanding police use of force becomes much more complicated when, as discussed in Chapters Three and Six, the use of force is examined within the context of race and prevalence of police using deadly force on unarmed young Black men or stopping them on the street because they look suspicious.

THE SUPREME COURT AND POLICE USE OF FORCE

The Fourth Amendment protects against unreasonable use of force and the question of whether the force was unreasonable is judged from the perspective of what the officer knew and believed when use of force is applied.[2] The Court has held that the Fourth Amendment is only invoked upon the specific intention of the police to seize. As the Court defined a seizure in *Brower v. County of Inyo* (1989), "a Fourth Amendment seizure does not occur whenever there is a governmentally caused termination of an individual's freedom of movement (the innocent passerby), nor even whenever there is a governmentally caused and governmentally *desired* termination of an individual's freedom of movement (the fleeing felon), but only when there is a governmental termination of freedom of movement *through means intentionally applied*."[3] Establishing a "[v]iolation of the Fourth Amendment requires an intentional acquisition of physical control. A seizure occurs even when an unintended person or thing is the object of the detention or taking ... This is implicit in the word "seizure," which can hardly be applied to an unknowing act."[4] Thus a seizure occurs when the officer intends to impede freedom of movement.

The Supreme Court in its seminal case, *Tennessee v. Garner* (1985), established the following regarding the constitutional limitations of police use of deadly force:

> ***Whenever an officer restrains the freedom of a person to walk away, he has seized that person.*** *United States v. Brignoni-Ponce,* 422 U. S. 873, 878 (1975). While it is not always clear just when minimal police interference becomes a seizure, *see United States v. Mendenhall,* 446 U. S. 544 (1980), there can be no question that apprehension by the use of deadly force is a seizure subject to the reasonableness requirement of the Fourth Amendment.[5]

The Court held that the police are governed not only as to whether an officer has probable cause to make the seizure (use of force justification) but how that seizure was conducted (method of use of force).

---

2 For example see, Dowling v. City of Philadelphia, 855 F.2d 136, 141 (3rd Cir. 1988) ("The proper inquiry in a section 1983 claim based on false arrest or misuse of the criminal process is not whether the person arrested in fact committed the offense but whether the arresting officers had probable cause to believe the person arrested had committed the offense.") and Doherty v. Haverkamp, No. 93-5256, 1997 U.S. Dist. LEXIS 7547, at *17-8 (E.D. Pa. May 27, 1997) ("Thus, the determination of a Fourth Amendment violation for false arrest depends, first and last, upon whether the arresting officers acted reasonably under all of the circumstances existing at the time and place of the arrest or detention.").

3 Brower v. County of Inyo, 489 US 593, 596–597 (1989).

4 Brower v. County of Inyo, 596.

5 Tennessee v. Garner, 471 U.S. 1, 7 (1985)

> A police officer may arrest a person if he has ***probable cause to believe that person committed a crime.*** *E.g., United States v. Watson,* 423 U.S. 411 (1976). Petitioners and appellant argue that, if this requirement is satisfied, the Fourth Amendment has nothing to say about how that seizure is made. This submission ignores the many cases in which ***this Court***, by balancing the extent of the intrusion against the need for it, ***has examined the reasonableness of the manner*** in which a search or ***seizure is conducted.*** To determine the constitutionality of a seizure, "[w]e must balance the nature and quality of the intrusion on the individual's Fourth Amendment interests against the importance of the governmental interests alleged to justify the intrusion."[6]

The legality of use of force involves two separate questions. Even if the use of force was justified, the Fourth Amendment requires that the level of force and the intensity of the force must be reasonable. The Court specifically rejected the assertion that the Fourth Amendment is only concerned with the legal justification of the use of force. Civil liability and criminal culpability can be established by the method of the use of force alone. Unreasonable application of force is liable or culpable even if it was legally justified in being applied.

The facts of *Tennessee v. Gardner* involved a botched burglary and the shooting of the suspected burglar as he attempted to escape arrest. Elton Hymon, of the Memphis, Tennessee, police department, responded to a possible burglary call.[7] Upon entering the house of the suspected burglary, the officer heard a back door slam and, upon investigation, saw Edward Garner running away towards a fence and, upon seeing Garner stopped at the fence and about to escape over the fence, Officer Hymon shot him in the back of the head, killing him.[8] Tennessee law authorized police officers to shoot escaping felons, and the constitutionality of the statute was appealed to the Supreme Court resulting from a section 1983 civil rights law suit filed by Garner's father.[9]

Justice White, writing for the Court, asserted that under Fourth Amendment analysis the constitutionality of any seizure by the police or state policy governing that seizure, "the question [is] whether the totality of the circumstances justified a particular sort of search or seizure."[10] In regard to the use of deadly force by police to secure a suspect, the Court held that, "notwithstanding probable cause to seize a suspect, an officer may not always do so by killing him. The intrusiveness of a seizure by means of deadly force is unmatched. The suspect's fundamental interest in his own life need not be elaborated upon."[11] Justice White explained that the interest against shooting a suspect also includes the requirement of the

6 Tennessee v. Garner at 7–8. Citing, United States v. Place, 462 U. S. 696, 703 (1983).

7 Tennessee v. Garner, 471 U.S. at 3.

8 Tennessee v. Garner at 3–4.

9 Tennessee v. Garner at 4–5.

10 Tennessee v. Garner at 8–9.

11 Tennessee v. Garner at 9.

judiciary to determine guilt and apply suitable sanction, rather than have the death penalty imposed upon the suspect without trial right in the street by the police. Justice White stated that both of these interests are to be weighed against the needs for effective law enforcement and reduction of violence during arrests because "suspects know that they may be shot if they flee."[12] The Court rejected the contention that fear of being shot is an effective law enforcement tool to prevent escape.[13]

Having made clear that, "Petitioners and appellant have not persuaded us that shooting nondangerous fleeing suspects is so vital as to outweigh the suspect's interest in his own life,"[14] the Court settled the base question of the case: Can the police shoot an unarmed, non-violent suspect felon for fear of his escape? The Court ruled in the negative.

> ***The use of deadly force to prevent the escape of all felony suspects, whatever the circumstances, is constitutionally unreasonable.*** It is not better that all felony suspects die than that they escape. ***Where the suspect poses no immediate threat*** to the officer and no threat to others, ***the harm resulting from failing to apprehend him does not justify the use of deadly force*** to do so. It is no doubt unfortunate when a suspect who is in sight escapes, but the fact that the police arrive a little late or are a little slower afoot does not always justify killing the suspect. A police officer may not seize an unarmed, nondangerous suspect by shooting him dead. The Tennessee statute is unconstitutional insofar as it authorizes the use of deadly force against such fleeing suspects.[15]

But the Court made equally clear that

> ***Where the officer has probable cause to believe that the suspect poses a threat of serious physical harm***, either to the officer or to others, ***it is not constitutionally unreasonable to prevent escape by using deadly force.*** Thus, if the suspect threatens the officer with a weapon or there is probable cause to believe that he has committed a crime involving the infliction or threatened infliction of serious physical harm, deadly force may be used if necessary to prevent escape, and if, where feasible, some warning has been given.[16]

The presence of a weapon or a suspect's actions that leads a police officer be believe the suspect has a weapon and posses a threat to the police officer will justify deadly use of force.

All Fourth Amendment analysis of police use of force involves the determination of whether the actions of the police are objectively reasonable from the perspective of the officer

12 Tennessee v. Garner

13 Tennessee v. Garner at 10.

14 Tennessee v. Garner at 11.

15 Tennessee v. Garner.

16 Tennessee v. Garner, 471 U.S. at 11–12.

at the time of the action.[17] To test the reasonableness of the action of the officer, the law requires that the officer articulate reasons to justify the action taken, and then, the court determines if those reasons were, under the totality of the circumstances, reasonable for the officer to make.[18]

The Court held in *Garner* that the District Court and the Court of Appeals found that Officer Hymon did not think or believe that Gardner was armed; in fact, Officer Hymon stated that he did not believe Garner was armed. "Restated in Fourth Amendment terms," the Court concluded, "this means Hymon had no articulable basis to think Garner was armed."[19] Thus, approvingly citing the Court of Appeals, "the facts, as found, did not justify the use of deadly force."[20] The legal conclusion being, "Hymon did not have probable cause to believe that Garner, whom he correctly believed to be unarmed, posed any physical danger to himself or others."[21] This lack of probable cause made his seizure unconstitutional, and the Tennessee statute that authorized such a seizure was also unconstitutional.

Four years later in *Graham v. Connor*, the Court affirmed its decision in *Gardner* and settled that all police use of force cases are subject to Fourth Amendment analysis, but only the Fourth Amendment. In the *Graham* case, Dethorne Graham was suffering from a diabetic insulin reaction and was acting uncooperative when encountered by the police who thought he had robbed a grocery store. He was subsequently beaten by the police but was released when they discovered the store had not been robbed. The Court held that the Fourth Amendment governed both deadly and non-deadly use of force by police cases. Specifically, the Court held that

> (1) ***Police use of force—deadly or not—are subject to the "reasonableness" standard*** against physically intrusive governmental conduct;
> (2) In ***Determining whether the force used to effect a particular seizure is "reasonable"*** the Fourth Amendment requires ***careful attention to the facts*** and circumstances of ***each particular case***, including
> A. *the* ***severity of the crime*** *at issue.*
> B. *whether the suspect poses an* ***immediate threat to the safety of the officers or others.***
> C. *whether he is* ***actively resisting arrest or attempting to evade arrest by flight.***
> (3) Reasonableness is determined by looking at the ***totality of the circumstances and whether they justify the use of force.***
> (4) The "reasonableness" of a particular use of force must be ***judged from the perspective of a reasonable officer on the scene***, rather than with the 20/20 vision of hindsight. The

---

17 See Ryburn v. Huff 565 U.S. ______, ______ (2012) (Slip Op., at 8) (emphasis added). See also *Infra* notes 19–21, 24–27.

18 Terry v. Ohio, 392 U.S. 1 (1968).

19 Tennessee v. Garner, 471 U.S. at 20.

20 Tennessee v. Garner.

21 Tennessee v. Garner at 21.

> Fourth Amendment is not violated by an arrest of the wrong person nor by the mistaken execution of a valid search warrant on the wrong premises.
> (5) ***The "reasonableness" test is an objective one.*** The question is whether the officers' actions are "objectively reasonable" in light of the facts and circumstances confronting them, ***without regard to their underlying intent or motivation.*** An officer's evil intentions will not make a Fourth Amendment violation out of an objectively reasonable use of force; nor will an officer's good intentions make an objectively unreasonable use of force constitutional.
> (6) With respect to a claim of excessive force, not every push or shove, even if it may later seem unnecessary in the peace of a judge's chambers violates the Fourth Amendment. ***The calculus of reasonableness must embody allowance for the fact that police officers are often forced to make split-second judgments***—in circumstances that are tense, uncertain, and rapidly evolving—about the amount of force that is necessary in a particular situation.[22]

CIVIL LIABILITY: PROSECUTOR AND POLICE IMMUNITY

One remedy for violations of constitutional rights is the filing of civil liability law suits against the police. In civil liability law, government officials enjoy a heightened level of protection from civil liability claims. Prosecutors, for example, enjoy absolute immunity from claims of malicious prosecution relating to their responsibilities in determining what charges to file and the presenting of evidence during a judicial proceeding, and police officers and other government officials enjoy qualified immunity. In explaining the justification for absolute immunity for prosecutor determinations regarding the filing and pursuing cases in court, the Supreme Court wrote in *Imbler v. Pachtman:*

> The question presented in this case is whether a state prosecuting attorney who acted within the scope of his duties in initiating and pursuing a criminal prosecution is amenable to suit under 42 U.S.C. § 1983 for alleged deprivations of the defendant's constitutional rights.
> ...
> We granted certiorari to consider the important and recurring issue of prosecutorial liability under the Civil Rights Act of 1871.
> Title 42 U.S.C. § 1983 provides that "[e]very person" who acts under color of state law to deprive another of a constitutional right shall be answerable to that person in a suit for damages.
> ...

22 Graham v. Connor, 490 U.S. 386, 395–397 (1989) (emphasis added).

> The function of a prosecutor that most often invites a common law tort action is his decision to initiate a prosecution, as this may lead to a suit for malicious prosecution if the State's case misfires.
>
> ...
>
> The common law immunity of a prosecutor is based upon the same considerations that underlie the common law immunities of judges and grand jurors acting within the scope of their duties. These include concern that harassment by unfounded litigation would cause a deflection of the prosecutor's energies from his public duties, and the possibility that he would shade his decisions instead of exercising the independence of judgment required by his public trust. ...
>
> ...
>
> If a prosecutor had only a qualified immunity, the threat of § 1983 suits would undermine performance of his duties no less than would the threat of common law suits for malicious prosecution.
>
> ...
>
> We conclude that the considerations outlined above dictate the same absolute immunity under § 1983 that the prosecutor enjoys at common law. To be sure, this immunity does leave the genuinely wronged defendant without civil redress against a prosecutor whose malicious or dishonest action deprives him of liberty. But the alternative of qualifying a prosecutor's immunity would disserve the broader public interest. It would prevent the vigorous and fearless performance of the prosecutor's duty that is essential to the proper functioning of the criminal justice system.[23]

The Court has held that there are limits to the application of *Imbler.* The Court has held that it is the function of the office that caries absolute immunity protection, not the person who performs the act. In *Connick v. Thompson* (2011), the Court held a Prosecutor's office can be held liable under failure-to-train theory if defendant can establish (1) the policymaker for the district attorney's office was "deliberately indifferent" to the need to train the prosecutors about their Brady disclosure obligation with respect to evidence and (2) that the lack of training actually caused the Brady violation. Liability is established if failure to train amounts to deliberate indifference to the rights of persons with whom the untrained prosecutor will come into contact and the lack of training amounts to a "policy or custom" to violate constitutional rights, which is actionable under §1983.

---

23 Imbler v. Pachtman, 424 U.S. 409, 410, 417, 421–424, 427–430 (1976) respectively (Internal footnotes omitted). See also Rehberg v. Paulk, 566 U.S. ____ (2012) in which the Court held that a police officer who lied during his grand jury testimony had absolute immunity when the officer testifies as a witness at the grand jury. The Court affirmed the principle that a witness enjoys absolute immunity from liability regarding testimony given to a grand jury. But a police officer has qualified immunity when he is the complaining witness and has initiated the prosecution of the case. See, Messerchmidt v. Millender, 556 U.S. ____ (2012).

To establish deliberate indifference, the defendant must establish the agency was put on actual notice that the failure to train was causing the same specific constitutional violation prior to the violation that is alleged in the complaint. The Court held that the need for better training or training that would have addressed the alleged violation will not establish deliberate indifference and the office of a prosecutor is entitled to the assumption that its line prosecutors, being trained in the law, will properly apply *Brady* evidence requirements without subsequent training by the office. The Court held that to prove deliberate indifference, a plaintiff must prove that the office was on actual notice that, absent additional specified training, it is "highly predictable" that the prosecutors would be confounded by the law regarding Brady and make incorrect decisions. Failure-to-train will result in violations which are so highly predictable that the failing to train amounted to a policy of inaction equivalent to a conscious policy to disregard the defendants' Brady rights.

The Court has also held that absolute immunity is limited to the actions of prosecutors regarding trial and performance in trial. Prosecutors acting outside of these areas enjoy only qualified immunity. In *Buckley v. Fitzsimmons* (1993) the Court held that actions by prosecutors outside of advocacy and preparation of a case—criminal investigation, legal advice to police, and statements made to the press—enjoy qualified and not absolute immunity. The Court affirmed that prosecutors have absolute immunity, because the function the prosecutor has is an integral part of the judicial process. If prosecutors could be sued for actions taken in the performance of that fundamental function, the judicial process could not achieve its goals. Because of this vital function, the prosecutor has, in the judicial process, the absolute immunity of a prosecutor, but this is limited to the prosecutor's fundamental function—trial preparation (the decision to charge and prosecute) and advocacy (what is done in court).

Police officers enjoy similar protections but not complete protection from civil liability. In explaining the justification for qualified immunity for police and other government officials the Court held in *Anderson v. Creighton:*

> (1) The Fourth Amendment allows for a balancing between the need for individuals to use the courts and constitutional guarantees to vindicate violations of induvial rights with the need for government officials to operate within their assigned duties without fear of being sued for those decisions.
>
> (2) The law has accommodated these conflicting concerns by generally providing government officials performing discretionary functions with a *qualified immunity*, shielding them from civil damages liability as long as their *actions could reasonably have been thought consistent with the rights they are alleged to have violated. Qualified immunity protects 'all but the plainly incompetent or those who knowingly violate the law'.*

> (3) Officials are immune from being sued unless "the law clearly proscribed the actions" they committed and the law must be "clearly established" at the time the actions were committed.[24]

To prevail in a civil law suit against the police for excessive use of force, both lethal and non-lethal, the Court established in *Anderson v. Creighton* that the plaintiff must prove that the police use of force (1) violated the Fourth Amendment and (2) the Fourth Amendment violation, in the situation that the police used force, was clearly established in law when the police action occurred.[25]

The Court held in *San Francisco v. Sheehan* that to establish civil liability the illegality of the actions by the officer (1) are not open to serious debate regarding the unreasonableness of the actions and (2) must be such that only a "plainly incompetent" police officer or one who "knowingly violates clearly established law" would commit.[26]

In *Tolan v. Cotton*, the Court held that qualified immunity requires the court to determine, (1) whether the evidence presented in the best light of the plaintiff (2) established the officer violated clearly established law.[27] The Court made this clear seven years earlier in *Scott v. Harris* in 2007.[28] *Harris* involved a case in which Victor Harris was rendered a quadriplegic

---

24 Anderson v. Creighton, 483 U.S. 635, 638–639, 643–644 (1987) respectively (internal citation omitted) (emphasis added). See also Malley v. Briggs, 475 U.S. 335 (1986) and *Supra* note 22.

25 The Court defined liability as requiring that "the right the official is alleged to have violated must have been 'clearly established' … the contours of the right must be sufficiently clear that a reasonable official would understand that what he is doing violates that right. This is not to say that an official action is protected by qualified immunity unless the very action in question has previously been held unlawful, *see Mitchell[v. Forsyth], supra,* at 472 U. S. 535, n. 12; but it is to say that, in the light of preexisting law, the unlawfulness must be apparent." Anderson v. Creighton, 483 U.S. at 640.

26 "Public officials are immune from suit under 42 U. S. C. §1983 unless they have violated a statutory or constitutional right that was clearly established at the time of the challenged conduct. An officer cannot be said to have violated a clearly established right unless the right's contours were sufficiently definite that any reasonable official in his shoes would have understood that he was violating it, meaning that existing precedent ... placed the statutory or constitutional question beyond debate. This exacting standard gives government officials breathing room to make reasonable but mistaken judgments by protecting all but the plainly incompetent or those who knowingly violate the law." San Francisco v. Sheehan, 575 US ___, (slip op, 10–11) (2015) (Internal citations omitted). Taylor v. Barkes, 575 U.S. ___, ___ (2015) (Slip op., at 3–4). See also, Stanton v. Sims, 571 U.S. ___, ___ (2013) (Slip op., 3, 8) See also Department of Justice Report, *Infra* note 62 and 63, 18 U.S.C. § 242—Deprivation of Rights Under the Color of Law for discussion of a similar standard for federal criminal liability.

27 Tolan v. Cotton, 572 U.S. ___, (Slip Op at 6–7) (2014).

28 Scott v. Harris, 550 U.S. ___, ___ (Slip Op., at 3–4) (2007).

after an attempted police seizure.[29] Harris was injured in a car crash caused by the police forcing his car off the road after a high speed car chase in which Harris refused to stop upon the police orders and their determination that Harris' driving was causing a danger to the public. The Court in *Harris* held that *Garner* did not establish a *per se* rule regarding the use of deadly force, and the issue in the case was whether officer Scott acted reasonably[30] when he used force against Harris' car, which resulted in the accident. The Court concluded that (1) "it is clear from the videotape that respondent posed an actual and imminent threat to the lives of any pedestrians who might have been present, to other civilian motorists, and to the officers involved in the chase,"[31] (2) "Second, we are loath to lay down a rule requiring the police to allow fleeing suspects to get away whenever they drive *so recklessly* that they put other people's lives in danger,"[32] and (3) "we lay down a more sensible rule: A police officer's attempt to terminate a dangerous high-speed car chase that threatens the lives of innocent bystanders does not violate the Fourth Amendment, even when it places the fleeing motorist at risk of serious injury or death."[33]

The Court held in *Garner* that while it is reasonable to shoot an escaping violent felon, it was not reasonable to shoot an unarmed nonviolent escaping felon. But, the simplicity of the rule in *Garner* is limited to the specific facts and the conclusion of the case. In applying the principle of *Garner*, the Court in *Mullenix v. Luna* addressed a case in which a Texas Department of Public Safety Trooper Chadrin Mullenix killed Israel Leija Jr. when Mullenix attempted to shoot out Leija's tires but shot Leija in the chest instead. The Court held that the question of the use of force must be defined by the specific facts of the incident as they were known to Mullenix.

> Put simply, qualified immunity protects "all but the plainly incompetent or those who knowingly violate the law." *Malley* v. *Briggs*, 475 U. S. 335, 341 (1986).
>
> "We have repeatedly told courts ... not to define clearly established law at a high level of generality." The dispositive question is "whether the violative nature of *particular* conduct is clearly established." This inquiry "must be undertaken in light of the specific context of the case, not as a broad general proposition."
>
> ...
>
> In this case, Mullenix confronted a reportedly intoxicated fugitive, set on avoiding capture through high-speed vehicular flight, who twice during his flight had threatened to shoot police officers, and who was moments away from encountering an officer at Cemetery Road. The relevant inquiry is whether existing precedent placed the conclusion

29 The question we need to answer is whether Scott's actions were objectively reasonable." Scott v. Harris, 550 U.S. ____, ____(2007) (Slip Op., at 8).

30 Scott v. Harris at ____, (Slip Op., at 10–11).

31 Scott v. Harris at ____, (Slip Op., at 11).

32 Scott v. Harris at ____, (Slip Op., at 12–13).

33 Scott v. Harris at ____, (Slip Op., at 13).

> that Mullenix acted unreasonably in these circumstances "beyond debate." The general principle that deadly force requires a sufficient threat hardly settles this matter. ("[I]t would be unreasonable to expect a police officer to make the numerous legal conclusions necessary to apply *Garner* to a high-speed car chase … ").
>
> By the time Mullenix fired, Leija had led police on a 25-mile chase at extremely high speeds, was reportedly intoxicated, had twice threatened to shoot officers, and was racing towards an officer's location …
>
> The Court has thus never found the use of deadly force in connection with a dangerous car chase to violate the Fourth Amendment, let alone to be a basis for denying qualified immunity. … Given Leija's conduct, we cannot say that only someone "plainly incompetent" or who "knowingly violate[s] the law" would have perceived a sufficient threat and acted as Mullenix did. …
>
> The fact is that when Mullenix fired, he reasonably understood Leija to be a fugitive fleeing arrest, at speeds over 100 miles per hour, who was armed and possibly intoxicated, who had threatened to kill any officer he saw if the police did not abandon their pursuit, and who was racing towards Officer Ducheneaux's position. Even accepting that these circumstances fall somewhere between the two sets of cases respondents discuss, qualified immunity protects actions in the "'hazy border between excessive and acceptable force.'" [34]

The Court further clarified the standard for determining how the courts were to apply the Fourth Amendment in cases in which police assert qualified immunity in *District of Columbia v. Wesby* (2018).

In the *Wesby* case, the police were confronted with a riotous house party and the issue was whether the police had probable cause to believe that the occupants of the house were trespassing—had entered the house without permission of the owner—when the occupants claimed that they had permission. The Court held that the police had probable cause to believe the occupants were trespassing. The Court held that even if the officers were wrong in not believing the occupants they had a right to be in the apartment, the officers did not act in a way that was clearly prohibited by the law. That lack of clarity prevented civil liability. The Court held that the officers were immune from civil liability on the alternative ground that the officer's mistake was reasonable. Mistaken belief that probable cause existed does not establish civil liability.[35] In the recent case of *Kisela v. Hughes*, the Court in a *Per Curium* opinion, held that in regard to the "clearly established" requirement

> the focus is on whether the officer had fair notice that her conduct was unlawful, reasonableness is judged against the backdrop of the law at the time of the conduct. … An officer

34 *Mullenix v. Luna*, 577 U.S. ____ (2015) (Slip. Op. 5–8, 12) (internal citations omitted) (emphasis added).

35 District of Columbia v. Wesby, 583 U. S. ____ (2018) (Slip op., 13–16) (internal citations and quotation marks omitted).

> cannot be said to have violated a clearly established right unless the right's contours were sufficiently definite that any reasonable official in the defendant's shoes would have understood that he was violating it. That is a necessary part of the qualified-immunity standard.[36]

Collectively, the Court held in *Garner, Graham, Harris, Luna, Tolan, Wesby,* and *Hughes* that

> (1) The intent of the officer is not relevant to the reasonableness analysis.
> (2) The fact that, in hindsight, the officer was wrong does not create civil liability.
> (3) The force must be reasonable under the circumstances and facts known to the officer at the time.
> (4) How the force is utilized/imposed must be reasonable under the circumstances and facts known to the officer at the time.
> (5) Reckless and violent behavior that puts the police or the public in danger can justify the use of force and deadly force.
> (6) Only established law, that is law beyond dispute and clearly established, can form the basis for civil liability.
> (7) Clearly established law exists when the law is beyond debate regarding what the police are prohibited from doing.
> (8) Clearly established law requires that the facts of previous cases are similar enough to inform or give fair warning to a police officer that the facts he/she is confronted with prohibit specific action.
> (9) Although police can be on notice that certain actions violate the law because the actions taken by the police are self-evident that they were unlawful; generally to establish "clearly established law" prior decisions must establish "reasonable" or "fair warning" that the police conduct at issue violates constitutional rights. But in defining fair warning the Court has specifically rejected the assertion that the "clearly established" standard requires prior cases to be "fundamentally similar" or have "materially similar" facts to the case at issue.[37]
> (10) The fact that the police were factually wrong in their assessment that they can use force does not establish civil liability if the mistake was reasonable under the circumstances.

---

36 Kisela v. Hughes 584 U. S. ___ (2018) (Slip, Op., 4–5) (internal citations and quotation marks omitted). Hughes involved a police officer, Kisela, who shot Hughes who was walking towards another woman with a knife and failed to stop and drop the knife upon police commands. Kisela asserted that he shot Hughes to defend the woman. The Court held that even if the facts are viewed most favorably to Hughes and that Kisela did not have probable cause to shot Hughes, Kisela was entitled to qualified immunity. The Court concluded that "This is far from an obvious case in which any competent officer would have known that shooting Hughes to protect Chadwick would violate the Fourth Amendment." Id at 6. Justice Sotomayor issued a dissenting opinion joined by Justice Ginsberg.

37 Hope v. Pelzer, 536 U.S. 730 (2002).

(11) Qualified immunity protects all but the plainly incompetent police officer or an officer who knowingly violates established law when the use of force occurs.

Qualified immunity will protect police action if their actions violate constitutional rights at a high level of generality, such as the right to be free "unreasonable search and seizure" under the Fourth Amendment or the right "not be punished prior to an adjudication of guilt in accordance with due process of law" under the Fifth Amendment substantive due process clause.[38] In cases of dubious case law, the police officer enjoys the benefit of the doubt even if the court finds the specific actions of the officer violated constitutional rights.

The Court has made clear that these high burdens are established to make sure that only clearly unreasonable police actions are subjected to civil liability and as discussed below, police incompetence or disregard for procedure, alone, does not establish violation of established law, but it can help establish that the actions of an officer were unreasonable.

THE CIRCUIT COURTS AND POLICE USE OF FORCE: POLICE LIABILITY ESTABLISHED BY PRE-SEIZURE CONDUCT

Introduction on Police Liability Causation

In the literature on police use of force, *officer-created jeopardy* (*state-created danger*) refers to the actions of police prior to the situation that results in the need to use of force. State-created danger occurs when the action of that state or its agent, the police officer, creates a danger of injury to the plaintiff. In the jurisprudence on police use of force, this officer-created jeopardy is referred to as *pre-seizure conduct* or *provocation*. In other words, the police action before the use of force (pre-seizure conduct) provoked or created the situation in which police use

38 Bell v. Wolfish, 441 U.S. 520, 535 (1979). As the Second Circuit recently held, "Having decided that Allah's substantive due process rights were violated, we nonetheless conclude that Defendants are entitled to qualified immunity. ... We agree that *Wolfish* and its progeny put prison officials on notice that pretrial detainees have a substantive due process right not to be subjected to restrictions amounting to punishment. But just as the general proposition, for example, that an unreasonable search or seizure violates the Fourth Amendment is of little help in determining whether the violative nature of particular conduct is clearly established the general principle articulated in *Wolfish* does not clearly establish that a substantive due process violation would result from Allah's placement in Administrative Segregation based solely on his prior assignment to (and failure to complete) that program. Nor does Allah identify any other case law that would have placed Defendants on notice that their conduct violated substantive due process. Rather, as the district court noted, the evidence shows that the defendants, though mistaken, were simply trying to fulfill their professional duties." *Allah v. Milling*, 16-1443-pr Second Circuit Court of Appeals (November 22, 2017) at 23–24 (internal citation and quotation marks omitted).

of force or deadly force became necessary. Provocation by a police officer resulting in injury can sustain a civil liability case.

To sustain a claim of constitutional injury (i.e., police use of force resulting in injury or death) based on police provocation, the plaintiff must establish a chain of events from the initial police behavior (the pre-seizure conduct—officer-created jeopardy) to the police use of force unbroken by the behavior of the plaintiff. In other words, the plaintiff's actions must not result or cause the officer's use of force.

In all civil liability cases, the plaintiff must establish both factual causation ("but for") and proximate cause (legal responsibility). Factual causation is the factual link between an act and a resulting harm. In other words, "but for" the police action the plaintiff would not have suffered injury. Once factual causation is established, the plaintiff must also establish proximate cause, which defines legal responsibility for a harm based on one's actions. Proximate cause speaks to whether the harm was objectively reasonably foreseeable from the action taken. Proximate cause is a legal question of whether the defendant is lawfully responsible for the harm, and factual causation is whether in fact the action of the defendant led to the harm. Factual causation is broken by an intervening factual event, and proximate cause is broken by the absence of a reasonable foreseeable result recognized in law to be directly attached to an act.

In police use of force cases, the courts will look at the behavior of the plaintiff and determine if the use of force by the police and the resulting injury was the result of the plaintiff's actions and not the initiating police behavior that was in violation of the Fourth Amendment. "In other words, as long as the officer's use of force was reasonable given the plaintiff's acts, then despite the [police creation of danger or jeopardy], the plaintiff's own conduct would be a superseding cause that limited the officer's liability."[39] The police officer creation of the danger and the harm (the police use of force and the injury due to the force) is factual causation. The plaintiff's behavior can be an intervening event and/or a superseding cause. As the Third Circuit Court held in explaining intervening event, if the officers' use of force was reasonable given the plaintiff's acts (the intervening event), then despite the illegal entry, the plaintiff's own conduct would be an superseding cause of the injury.[40]

Put another way, proximate cause is established in a police use-of-force case when the police violate a legal standard, and it is foreseeable that the breaking of that legal standard

---

39 Lamont v. New Jersey, 637 F. 3d 177, 186 (3d Cir 2011) (Internal citation and quotation brackets omitted).

40 Hector v. Watt, 235 F. 3d 154, 160 (CA3 2001) "A suspect's threatening movements [is] a superseding cause that [breaks] the causal chain between the initial stop and the shooting." Lamont v. New Jersey, 637 F. 3d 177, 186 citing *Hundley v. District of Columbia*, 494 F. 3d 1097, 1104–1105 & n.5 (D.C. Cir. 2007).

> We conclude that the troopers' decision to enter the woods did not proximately cause Quick's death. Rather, Quick's noncompliant, threatening conduct in the woods was a superseding cause that served to break the chain of causation between the entry and the shooting. Holding otherwise would, as noted in Hundley, tend to deter police officers "from approaching and detaining potentially violent suspects." [Hundley], 494 F.3d at 1105.

will result in a specific harm. The mere violation of a legal standard by the police will not establish proximate cause unless the suffered harm is the foreseeable result of the specific violation of the legal standard. For example, the police failure to knock and announce by itself, for example, can create liability when the result of the entry is the police shooting the defendant. The reason being that it is foreseeable that when a homeowner feels threatened by the unknown entry, arms himself and confronts the "intruder," and is shot in the process by the police because they did not give notice that they were police not an intruder.[41]

If the police unlawfully entered by not knocking and announcing themselves at the door but when inside announced their presence and then were faced with a defendant with a gun resulting in the defendant being shot, the defendant with the gun failure will break the proximate cause link. If the police, in violation of knock and announce, announce themselves after the initial entry, the subsequent announcement and the defendant approaching them with a gun would be an intervening event that would establish a superseding cause that break the proximate cause and relieves the officer of civil liability.

Not every intervening event will result in the creation of superseding cause that breaks proximate cause. If the occurrence of an intervening event is clearly foreseeable from the action of the police, it will not break proximate cause. The point is this: if the intervening event (action) is due to the intentional, negligent, or reckless behavior of the plaintiff and that action factually resulted in the harm, then the police officer will not be liable. But if the intervening event (action) of the plaintiff is a reasonably foreseeable result from the defendant's actions, then the intervening event (action) is considered within the risk of harm created by the police officer, and proximate cause is maintained, because the intervening event did not create a superseding cause. Whether liability can be maintained will be totally fact specific to the specific case.

Judicial Application of Provocation and Police Pre-Seizure Conduct

As shown in table one below a majority of the federal circuit courts that have adopted the pre-seizure conduct or provocation approach to determining if police use of force is reasonable. The courts have utilized provocation as a way to determine whether the force was reasonable under the totality of the circumstances or if proximate cause is established or both. As the First Circuit explained in *Lockhart-Bembery v. Sauro* (2007), to establish civil liability the plaintiff must be able to prove (1) the officer "affirmatively act[ed] to increase the threat of harm to the claimant or affirmatively prevents the individual from receiving assistance," (2) "[a] proximate causal link between a government agent's actions and a personal injury" and (3) the [the officer's

41 See Wilson v. Arkansas, 514 U. S. 927 (1995). See also Hudson v. Michigan, 547 U. S. ____ (2006), Slip Op. at 7. ("The interests protected by the knock-and-announce requirement are quite different—and do not include the shielding of potential evidence from the government's eyes. One of those interests is the protection of human life and limb, because an unannounced entry may provoke violence in supposed self-defense by the surprised resident.")

action] ... shock[s] the conscience of the court." The police behavior must be "manifestly outrageous' behavior [to] qualif[y] as conscience-shocking."[42] Shocking the conscience can be established when police conduct proves deliberately indifferent to a known risk under circumstances when police officers "have an opportunity to reflect and make reasoned and rational decisions."[43] But the Supreme Court has made clear that the law must be clearly established that the behavior complained of by the plaintiff, if true, rises to the level of shocking the conscience.

One way to establish a case based on pre-seizure conduct or provocation is to focus on the tactics and decisions the police utilized before applying the actual use of force. For example, in *Estate of Smith v. Marasco* (2005) the Third Circuit addressed a case in which the state police utilized a Special Emergency Response Team (SERT) Team, otherwise known as a Special Weapons And Tactics Team (SWAT) team, on a Vietnam veteran suffering from PTSD, held

> As the Supreme Court has observed:
> Whether the point of the conscience-shocking is reached when injuries are produced with culpability falling within the middle range, following from something more than negligence but less than intentional conduct, such as recklessness or `gross negligence, is a matter for closer calls.
>
> [Yet the qualified immunity jurisprudence teaches us that "closer calls" are usually to be resolved in favor of the officer.]
>
> ...
>
> Still, our decisions do give us some guidance as to how to determine whether a given action "shocks the conscience." ... In particular, we must determine whether the officer is confronted with a "hyperpressurized environment" such as a high-speed chase, or, in the alternative, has "the luxury of proceeding in a deliberate fashion." In the latter case, "deliberate indifference" may be sufficient to "shock the conscience," in the former, it is usually necessary to show that the officer deliberately harmed the victim. ... The question we must address, of course, is not simply whether the behavior of the troopers "shocks the conscience" under the applicable standard, but whether a reasonable officer would have realized as much. In this regard, "the salient question" we must ask is whether the law, as it existed in 1999, gave the troopers "fair warning" that their actions were unconstitutional. It is not necessary for the plaintiffs to identify a case presenting analogous factual circumstances, but they must show that the contours of the right at

42 Lockhart-Bembery v. Sauro, 498 F.3d 69, 77 (1st Cir. 2007) citing Frances-Colon v. Ramirez, 107 F.3d 62 (1st Cir.1997), Rivera v. Rhode Island, 402 F.3d 27, 35 (1st Cir.2005); County of Sacramento v. Lewis, 523 U.S. 833, 846–850, 118 S.Ct. 1708, 140 L.Ed.2d 1043 (1998) and Hasenfus v. LaJeunesse, 175 F.3d 68, 73 (1st Cir.1999).

43 Melendez-Garcia v. Sanchez 629 F.3d at 36 citing County of Sacramento v. Lewis, 523 U.S. 833, 851–852 (1998).

> issue were "sufficiently clear that a reasonable official would understand that what he is doing violates that right."[44]

Even though the failure to use proper police tactics is not, *per se*, unreasonable; some courts have held that such failure is relevant to the reasonableness inquiry.[45] For example, in *Moody v. Philadelphia Housing Authority*, the Pennsylvania Commonwealth Court affirmed the trial court and held that failure to comply with clear police policy and procedures, along with established case law, can negate qualified immunity.[46]

The Pennsylvania court concluded that officer-created jeopardy occurs when the officer makes a conscious decision to disregard standard established police tactics, policies, and/or procedures, which then places the officer in a greater risk of harm to himself or others and his/her actions lead to the need to use force.[47] When a police officer violates standard, written, and known operational tactics, which creates a situation that results in the use of force, the use of force can be found to be unreasonable, because the officer created a risk that results in the need to use deadly force. This theory of police liability is very limited. The police officer's action, the disregarding of policy, must be more than mistake or poor police work. As the Tenth Circuit Court held, "An officer's pre-seizure conduct can be part of the reasonableness inquiry, but only if the officer's own 'reckless or deliberate conduct during the seizure unreasonably created the need to use such force.'"[48] The disregard of constitutional rights, the action of the police, must rise to the level of reckless disregard or behavior as those of a "plainly incompetent" police officer or those of an officer who "knowingly violated the law."[49]

Unlawful Use of Force and Time of Event Distinction

---

44 Estate of Smith v. Marasco, 430 F.3d 140, 153–155 (3rd Cir. 2005) (Internal citations and quotation marks omitted). See also, Melendez-Garcia v. Sanchez 629 F.3d 25, 37 (1st Cir. 2010) (Internal citation and quotation marks omitted) which held, the burden of "shocks the conscience is extremely high, requiring stunning evidence of arbitrariness and caprice that extends beyond mere violations of state law, even violations resulting from bad faith to something more egregious and more extreme."

45 For example, see Gilmore v. City of Atlanta, 774 F.2d 1495 (11th Cir. 1985) and Estate of Starks v. Enyart, 5 F.3d 320 (7th Cir. 1993) but to the contrary see, *Drewitt v. Pratt*, 999 F 2d 774 (4th Cir. 1993), Fraire v. City of Arlington, 957 F 2d 1268 (5th Cir. 1992) which held that failure to comply with police procedures does not establish liability or unreasonableness.

46 Moody v. Philadelphia Housing Authority, 673 A.2d 14, 18–19 (1996) (Emphasis added).

47 Moody v. Philadelphia Housing Authority. See also, Jeffrey J. Noble & Geoffrey P. Alpert, "State-Created Danger Should Police Officers Be Accountable for Reckless Tactical Decision Making?" in *Critical Issues in Policing*, eds. Roger G. Dunham and Geoffrey P. Alpert (2015), 567–583.

48 Pauly v. White, 2016 U.S. App. LEXIS 2184 at 32 (February 9, 2016) (10th Cir. 2016). See also, U.S. v. Bradley, 196 F.3d 762 (7th Cir. 1999).

49 See *Supra* notes 23, 24 and Malley v. Briggs, 475 U. S. 335, 341 (1986) respectively.

The Supreme Court has held that the standard for civil liability under Fourth Amendment focuses on the objective reasonableness of the police action, and this has been interpreted by some circuit courts to only require police use of force to be reasonable, as defined by the totality of the circumstances *at the moment the force is used.*[50] Other circuit courts have interpreted the reasonableness inquiry to include pre-seizure conduct of the police[51] with focus on *the events that led up to the moment the use of force was used.* As the Third Circuit held, "we want to express our disagreement with those courts which have held that analysis of "reasonableness" under the Fourth Amendment requires excluding any evidence of events preceding the actual "seizure."[52] The court inquired, "How is the reasonableness of a bullet striking someone to be assessed if not by examining preceding events?" The court answered its own rhetorical question by holding that all of the events that lead to a police use of deadly force are to be considered in evaluating the reasonableness of the use of force.

The Seventh Circuit in *Williams v. Indiana* (2015) came to a similar conclusion. The case involved a fatal shooting of John Brown by Indiana State Police Officer Blanchard who responded to Brown's attempted suicide. Blanchard kicked in the door and found Brown with a knife in his hand. There was dispute whether Brown came at Blanchard when Blanchard shot and killed him. It was open to debate whether Blanchard's kicking of the door created the situation that lead to him shooting Brown. On that dispute, the district court denied summary judgment, because there was a dispute in the facts, which are for a jury to settle. The Court of Appeals affirmed the denial of summary judgement.[53]

The Tenth Circuit in *Holland v. Harrington* (2001) similarly held that when the issue involves the decision to use force, in this case a SWAT team to execute a misdemeanor warrant, the court would look at the reasons that underlined the application for the use of force. The Tenth Circuit concluded that, although the decision to use overwhelming force implicates the reasonableness requirement of the Fourth Amendment, the decision to use such force, *per se*, does not create a Fourth Amendment violation.[54]

Although the Supreme Court has made clear that the courts are to keep in mind that "the 'reasonableness' of a particular use of force must be judged from the perspective of a reasonable officer on the scene [and the] calculus of reasonableness must embody allowance for the fact that police officers are often forced to make split-second judgments—in circumstances that are tense, uncertain, and rapidly evolving—about the amount of force that is necessary in a

50 See Salam v. Proulx, 93 F.3d 86, 91 (2nd Cir. 1996). See also Cole v. Bone, 993 F.2d 1328 (8th Cir. 1993), Rollins v. Smith, 106 Fed. Appx. 513, (8th Cir. Ark. 2004), Carter v. Buscher, 973 F.2d 1328 (7th Cir. 1992), and Bella v. Chamberlain, 24 F.3d 1251(10th Cir. 1994).

51 See Abraham v. Raso 183 F.3d 279 (3d Cir. 1999), St. Hilaire v. City of Laconia 71 F3d 20 (1st Cir 1995), Rowland v. Perry 41 F3d 167 (4th Cir. 1994), and Grazier v. Philadelphia, 328, 126 F.3d 120, 126–127 (3rd Cir. 2011).

52 Abraham v. Raso 183 F.3d 279, 291 (3rd Cir. 1999).

53 Abraham v. Raso at 485.

54 Holland v. Harrington, 268 F.3d 1179, 1189–1191 (10th Cir. 2001).

particular situation"[55] lower courts have also observed that "since the victim of deadly force is unable to testify, courts should be cautious on summary judgment to "ensure that the officer is not taking advantage of the fact that the witness most likely to contradict his story—the person shot dead—is unable to testify."[56]

Summary: Police Provocation in the Courts

To summarize, the legal question of officer created jeopardy (provocation) is whether the police can unreasonably create a situation which results in the officer being confronted with a deadly threat resulting in the use of deadly force and the enjoy qualified immunity from civil liability. Various state and six circuit courts have adopted the provocation rule.

Circuit courts that accept the police-created jeopardy (provocation) rule

YES	NO
The First Circuit—*St. Hilaire v. City of Laconia* (1995) "[T]he question in [Hodari] was not whether the seizure was reasonable, which requires an examination of the totality of the circumstances, but whether there had been a seizure at all. We do not read this case as forbidding courts from examining circumstances leading up to a seizure, once it is established that there has been a seizure." The First Circuit—*Lockhart-Bembery v. Sauro* (2007) "The plaintiff must be able to prove the officer "affirmatively act[ed] to increase the threat of harm to the claimant ... "	**The Second Circuit**—*Salam v. Proulx* (1996) "Plaintiff additionally contends that Officer Proulx is liable for using excessive force because he created a situation in which the use of deadly force became necessary. ... However, Officer Proulx's actions leading up to the shooting are irrelevant to the objective reasonableness of his conduct at the moment he decided to employ deadly force. The reasonableness inquiry depends only upon the officer's knowledge of circumstances immediately prior to and at the moment that he made the split-second decision to employ deadly force."

55 Graham v. Connor, *Supra* note 18.

56 Abraham v. Raso 183 F.3d 279, 294 (3rd Cir. 1999).

YES	NO
The Third Circuit—*Abraham v. Raso* (1999) "[W]e want to express our disagreement with those courts which have held that analysis of "reasonableness" under the Fourth Amendment requires excluding any evidence of events preceding the actual "seizure." Third Circuit—*Lamont v. New Jersey* (2011) "In other words, as long as the officer's use of force was reasonable given the plaintiff's acts, then despite the [police creation of jeopardy] the plaintiff's own conduct would be a superseding cause that limited the officer's liability." See also *Hector v. Watt* (2001)	**The Fourth Circuit**—*Gandy v. Virginia* (2013) "In determining whether an officer was justified in using deadly force ... we must focus on the moment when such force was employed. See *Elliott v. Leavitt* (4th Cir. 1996) ("Graham requires us to focus on the moment force was used; conduct prior to that moment is not relevant in determining whether an officer used reasonable force.") ... A police officer's pre-seizure conduct, regardless of whether it was ill-advised or violative of law enforcement protocol, is generally not relevant for purposes of an excessive force claim under the Fourth Amendment which looks only to the moment force is used. See *Greenidge v. Ruffin*, 927 F.2d 789, 791 (4th Cir. 1991) (explaining that "evidence of the officer's alleged violation of police procedures immediately preceding the arrest" was irrelevant to whether officer's use of deadly force was constitutionally excessive). Thus, the mere decision itself to make a surprise entry as opposed to other alternatives affords no basis for liability against Sergeant Pittman."
The Seventh Circuit— *Williams v. Indiana State Police* (2015) "That does not mean that Blanchard's pre-seizure conduct is irrelevant to the Fourth Amendment claim. The sequence of events leading up to the seizure is relevant because the reasonableness of the seizure is evaluated in light of the totality of the circumstances. The sequence of events leading up to the seizure is relevant because the reasonableness of the seizure is evaluated in light of the totality of the circumstances. For instance, the short period of time that elapsed from Blanchard's arrival to the confrontation, and his abrupt action in kicking in the door, give context to John's possession of the knife that might be different if John had himself opened the door holding the knife.	**The Fifth Circuit**—*Rockwell v. Brown* (2011) "Lastly, the Rockwells, relying on case law from other circuits, urge this Court to examine the circumstances surrounding the forced entry, which may have led to the fatal shooting, in evaluating the reasonableness of the officers' use of deadly force. This argument is unavailing. It is well-established that '[t]he excessive force inquiry is confined to whether the [officer or another person] was in danger *at the moment of the threat* that resulted in the [officer's use of deadly force].'"

(Continued)

Circuit courts that accept the police-created jeopardy (provocation) rule (Continued)

YES	NO
The circumstances known by Blanchard, or even created by him, inform the determination as to whether the lethal response was an objectively reasonable one. But our case law does not clearly establish that an officer may be liable under the Fourth Amendment solely for his pre-seizure conduct that led to the encounter. See Graham … We are aware that officers responding to a scene in which a suicidal person is locked in a room are faced with the difficult determination as to whether delay in responding will allow the person to further harm himself or to become aggressive toward others. It is clearly established, however, that officers cannot resort as an initial matter to lethal force on a person who is merely passively resisting and has not presented any threat of harm to others."	
The Ninth Circuit—*Billington v. Smith* (2002)* "[W]here an officer intentionally or recklessly provokes a violent confrontation, if the provocation is an independent Fourth Amendment violation, he may be held liable for his otherwise defensive use of deadly force." The Ninth Circuit citing Smith held in *Sheehan v. City of San Francisco* (2014) "Under our case law, however, officers may be held liable for an otherwise lawful defensive use of deadly force when they intentionally or recklessly provoke a violent confrontation by actions that rise to the level of an independent Fourth Amendment violation." *Supreme Court reversed the Ninth in *Los Angeles v. Mendez* (2017)—"We hold that the Fourth Amendment provides no basis for such a rule. A different Fourth Amendment violation cannot transform a later, reasonable use of force into an unreasonable seizure." But "All we hold today is that once a use of force is deemed reasonable under *Graham*, it may not be found unreasonable by reference to some separate constitutional violation."	**The Sixth Circuit**—*Livermore v. Lubelan* (2007) "Livermore points to *Billington v. Smith* (9th Cir. 2002), in which the Ninth Circuit held that a plaintiff's Fourth Amendment claim against police officers who used deadly force may survive summary judgment, even where the particular seizure is reasonable, if the defendant police officers acted recklessly in creating the circumstances which required the use of deadly force. … [W]e have rejected such an analysis. The proper approach under Sixth Circuit precedent is to view excessive force claims in segments. That is, the court should first identify the "seizure" at issue here and then examine "whether the force used to effect that seizure was reasonable in the totality of the circumstances, not whether it was reasonable for the police to create the circumstances. … Livermore argues that Lt. Ellsworth acted negligently by increasing the likelihood that Rohm would be shot. … All of the actions concerning Lt. Ellsworth,

Circuit courts that accept the police-created jeopardy (provocation) rule (Continued)

YES	NO
	however, occurred in the hours and minutes leading up to Rohm's killing; *Dickerson* instructs us to disregard these events and to focus on the "split-second judgments" made immediately before the officer used allegedly excessive force. … Under Dickerson, the preceding decisions made by Lt. Ellsworth are immaterial and not a sufficient basis for a claim under the Fourth Amendment."
The Tenth Circuit—*Pauly v. White* (2016)* "Since at least 2006 … in this circuit … the requisite causal connection for establishing a Section 1983 violation "is satisfied if the defendant[s] set in motion a series of events that the defendant[s] knew or reasonably should have known would cause others to deprive the plaintiff of [his] constitutional rights. Likewise, it has been clearly established since 2006 that for an officer to be liable under Section 1983, the officer's conduct must be both a but-for and proximate cause of the plaintiff's constitutional harm. Accepting as true plaintiffs' version of the facts, a reasonable person in the officers' position should have understood their conduct would cause Samuel and Daniel Pauly to defend their home and could result in the commission of deadly force against Samuel Pauly by Officer White. … An officer's pre-seizure conduct can be part of the reasonableness inquiry, but only if the officer's own reckless or deliberate conduct during the seizure unreasonably created the need to use such force." *The Supreme Court vacated this decision on alternative grounds in *White v. Pauly* (2017) holding, "the panel majority misunderstood the "clearly established" analysis: It failed to identify a case where an officer acting under similar circumstances as Officer White was held to have violated the Fourth Amendment. Instead, the majority relied on Graham, Garner, and their Court of Appeals progeny [to] lay out excessive-force principles at only a general level. Of course, "general	**The Eighth Circuit**—*Cole v. Bone* (1993) "The Fourth Amendment prohibits unreasonable seizures, not unreasonable or ill-advised conduct in general. Consequently, we scrutinize only the seizure itself, not the events leading to the seizure, for reasonableness under the Fourth Amendment. … The district court seemingly believed that Rice's conduct was legally unreasonable because it was not authorized under the policies of the Missouri Highway Patrol. We need not determine whether Trooper Rice violated Missouri Highway Patrol policy, however, for under section 1983 the issue is whether the government official violated the Constitution or federal law, not whether he violated the policies of a state agency. Conduct by a government official that violates some state statutory or administrative provision is not necessarily constitutionally unreasonable. … It could be argued, of course, that Trooper Rice's decision to use deadly force might not have been the most prudent course of action; other courses of action, such as another stationary roadblock, might conceivably have been available. The Constitution, however, requires only that the seizure be objectively reasonable, not that the officer pursue the most prudent course of conduct as judged by 20/20 hindsight vision."

(Continued)

Circuit courts that accept the police-created jeopardy (provocation) rule (Continued)

YES	NO
statements of the law are not inherently incapable of giving fair and clear warning" to officers, *United States v. Lanier,* 520 U. S. 259, 271 (1997), but "in the light of pre-existing law the unlawfulness must be apparent" *Anderson v. Creighton* [(1987)]. For that reason we have held that Garner and Graham do not by themselves create clearly established law outside "an obvious case." *Brosseau v. Haugen*, 543 U. S. 194, 199 (2004) (per curiam); see also *Plumhoff v. Rickard*, 572 U. S. ____, ____ (2014) (slip op., at 13) (emphasizing that Garner and Graham "are 'cast at a high level of generality' "). Regarding police created jeopardy claim by the plaintiffs that "the conduct of Officers Truesdale and Mariscal did not adequately alert the Paulys that they were police officers" resulting in the Paulys use of force to defend their home and "respondents suggest that a reasonable jury could infer that White witnessed the other officers' deficient performance and should have realized that corrective action was necessary before using deadly force" the Court had no opinion. But it held that the court of appeals "majority did not conclude that White's conduct—such as his failure to shout a warning—constituted a run-of-the-mill Fourth Amendment violation. Indeed, it recognized that 'this case presents a unique set of facts and circumstances' in light of White's late arrival on the scene. This alone should have been an important indication to the majority that White's conduct did not violate a "clearly established" right. Clearly established federal law does not prohibit a reasonable officer who arrives late to an ongoing police action in circumstances like this from assuming that proper procedures, such as officer identification, have already been followed. No settled Fourth Amendment principle requires that officer to second-guess the earlier steps already taken by his or her fellow officers in instances like the one White confronted here."	

Circuit courts that accept the police-created jeopardy (provocation) rule (Continued)

YES	NO
The Eleventh Circuit—*Gilmere v. Atlanta* (1985) "The district court found that Sampson's purported fear of bodily injury was subjectively reasonable, given that at the time of the shooting the decedent was apparently free and moving toward him. The court declared, however … that Officer Sampson's belief that his life was in danger was not objectively reasonable and could not justify the killing. In another context we might have difficulty concluding that these findings establish a constitutional violation sufficiently egregious to "shock the conscience" as required by Rochin. Here, however, any fear on the officer's part was the fear of retaliation against his own unjustified physical abuse. We conclude that a moment of legitimate fear should not preclude liability for a harm which largely resulted from his own improper use of his official power. For this reason, we affirm this portion of the district court's holding as well."	
The District of Columbia Circuit—*Barrett v. United States* (1933) "Appellant, [is] a detective sergeant of the Metropolitan police department [and] was convicted [for] assault [resulting from an arrest]. Manifestly, appellant should have been allowed to prove facts and circumstances leading up to the arrest. … [I]n order to determine [if the force used in the arrest was justified] it is necessary to look at all the surrounding circumstances. In making an arrest the measure of necessary force is that which an ordinarily prudent and intelligent person, with the knowledge and in the situation of the arresting officer, would have deemed necessary. [The jury instruction the defendant requested] read as follows: '(5) The court instructs the jury that in determining what force the defendant had a right to use in arresting Baber they should take into consideration the information which was in the possession of the defendant [and]	

(Continued)

Circuit courts that accept the police-created jeopardy (provocation) rule (Continued)

YES	NO
(7) The jury are instructed that a police officer may use such force as a reasonable and prudent man would use under all the circumstances in making an arrest and ... in considering whether the officer acted as a reasonable man would act, you may take into consideration every circumstance leading up to and surrounding the arrest and also any knowledge which the officer may possess concerning the danger of effecting the arrest.' These prayers state the law and were applicable under the facts of the case. It was prejudicial error not to give them."	

As summarized in table one, the First, Third, Seventh, Ninth, Tenth, and Eleventh Circuit courts have adopted the provocation approach. The D.C. Circuit has not directly ruled on the adoption of the provocation approach but has held that police use of force cases require "consideration [of] every circumstance leading up to and surrounding" the use of force including "any knowledge which the officer may possess concerning the danger" the officer was faced with. The Second, Fourth, Fifth, Sixth, and Eighth circuit courts have rejected the provocation approach.

POLICE USE OF FORCE, SELF-DEFENSE, AND FEDERAL CRIMINAL CULPABILITY

More recent issues of police shootings have shifted to the question of officer safety and officer-perceived threats as justification for the use of deadly and non-deadly force. If the officer reasonably believes that his life or the life of another officer is in danger, the officer can use deadly force. Under the Fourth Amendment, the officer must be able to articulate reasons for that belief, which resulted in the use of force. This raises two issues. First, what is the law of self-defense, and second, how does unconscious or implicit racial bias impact how an officer perceives actions by Blacks—whether they are threatening enough to justify the use of deadly force. The second question is the subject we will discuss in Chapter Three.

General Self-Defense Law

Self-defense law, though varied among the fifty states, all share the basic requirements to justify self-defense. These include (1) the nature of the threat, (2) the totality of the circumstances regarding the threat, and (3) the reasonableness of the force used. Regarding the use of deadly force, the person using the force (1) must believe that deadly force or force that can cause serious bodily harm is imminently threatened, (2) did not initiate the confrontation, and (3) must believe that the deadly force used was needed to prevent deadly force from being inflicted upon him/her. Deadly force, generally, is limited to repelling a threat or imposition of deadly force, kidnapping, or rape. States vary on the ability to use force or deadly force to prevent theft in a home or destruction of property in a home. The right to self-defense includes the right to defend oneself in one's home and at work, without the requirement of retreat, with some states providing the same right to any place a person has a legal right to be, known as "stand your ground" laws. Depending on the jurisdiction, there may be a requirement for retreat (if, under the circumstances, it can be done with safety) before force or deadly force can be used. State law may also require the lack of viable options to the person threatened with force. In other words, there is no other level of force available other than deadly force to respond to the immediate force being used against the person who is claiming self-defense. While it is a general rule that self-defense cannot be used to repel force used by the police, some courts have held that self-defense can be utilized against the police. For example, the Supreme Court of Pennsylvania in *Commonwealth v. French*[57] and *Commonwealth v. Biagini*[58] held that a citizen can use force when the police use unreasonable force to effect an arrest when the force used rises to aggravated assault.[59]

In a self-defense case, the self-defense analysis focuses on whether the use of force was reasonable. States vary as to definition of reasonableness. The test can be objective or subjective. The objective test is whether a reasonable person in the situation would believe deadly force was required. The subjective test is whether the person who used the force (1) reasonably believed deadly force was required, *and* (2) that belief was reasonable for that person to have. The objective test does not focus on what the actual person believed but rather on what a reasonable person in that situation would have believed. An individual who uses deadly force is more likely to escape criminal/civil responsibility if the test is subjective, whether he/she actually believed deadly force was necessary and was that person's belief reasonable to have; rather than if the test is objective, would a reasonable person in the accused position have used deadly force. Regardless of whether the test is objective or subjective, the assessment of the facts and circumstances regarding the use of force are not retroactive with the use of hindsight. The assessment of the facts are as the person believed them to be at the time (subjective) or what a reasonable person would have believed them to be at the time (objective) the deadly force was used.

Police Shootings and Federal Criminal Culpability

Police shootings, which are governed by the Fourth Amendment, are assessed under the objective test. Another distinction between police and civilian use of force analysis is that the requirement that the person using deadly force did not start the altercation, by definition,

57 Commonwealth v. French, 531 Pa. 42; 611 A.2d 175, 177–179 (1992).

58 Commonwealth v. Biagini 540 Pa. 22, 655 A.2d 492, 459–500 (1995).

59 Aggravated assault occurs if force used causes serious bodily injury which is bodily injury which creates a substantial risk of death or which causes serious, permanent disfigurement or protracted loss or impairment of the function of any bodily member or organ. 18 PA. CONS. STAT. § 2602, 2702 (2016).

does not apply in police shootings. Regardless of whether the use of force is committed by a police officer or a private person, the use of force event and its legality must be determined reasonable under the totality of circumstances test. In terms of the police, the totality of the circumstances test is utilized to determine if the use of force was reasonable under the Fourth Amendment. Civil liability for the officer can only be established if the facts are such that the officer did not act reasonably. Criminal liability requires not only that the officer acted unreasonably but also that the use of deadly force by the officer had no legal justification. While criminal culpability requires lack of legal justification on the state level, under federal criminal law, culpability requires that the officer act with willful intent to violation established law.[60] The federal law makes it unlawful for anyone

> under color of any law, statute, ordinance, regulation, or custom, [to] willfully subject[] any person in any State, Territory, Commonwealth, Possession, or District to the deprivation of any rights, privileges, or immunities secured or protected by the Constitution or laws of the United States.[61]

According to the Justice Department "Section 242 of Title 18 makes it a crime for a person acting under color of any law to willfully deprive a person of a right or privilege protected by the Constitution or laws of the United States [and] [i]t is not necessary that the crime be motivated by animus toward the race, color, religion, sex, handicap, familial status or national origin of the victim."[62] To prove a violation of section 242, the Justice Department must prove "beyond a reasonable doubt: (1) that the defendant was acting under color of law, (2) that he deprived a victim of a right protected by the Constitution or laws of the United States, (3) that he acted willfully, and (4) that the deprivation resulted in bodily injury and/or death."[63] Under the color of law, is a term of art, which means acting under authority granted by statutory law. The willfully requirement requires proof that the officer who uses force or deadly force must have done so with, "the purpose to deprive a person of a right which has been made specific either by the express terms of the Constitution or laws of the United States or by decisions interpreting them. While the officer need not be thinking in Constitutional terms when deciding to use force, he must know what he is doing is wrong and decide to do

---

60 See 18 U.S.C. § 242—Deprivation of Rights Under the Color of Law. See generally, federal criminal law protection of civil rights under 18 U.S.C. § 241–249.

61 18 U.S.C. § 242

62 Department of Justice web page on 18 U.S.C. § 242—Deprivation of Rights Under the Color Of Law at http://www.justice.gov/crt/deprivation-rights-under-color-law. See also, Alison M Smith, "Overview of Selected Federal Criminal Civil Rights Statutes," Congressional Research Service (December 16, 2014).

63 "Department of Justice Report Regarding the Criminal Investigation into the Shooting Death of Michael Brown by Ferguson, Missouri Police Officer Darren Wilson," Department of Justice (March 4, 2015) at 9.

it anyway. Mistake, panic, misperception, or even poor judgment by a police officer does not provide a basis for prosecution under Section 242."[64]

While proper police tactics suggest that a police officer should utilize time, distance, and cover to control and assess the situation before utilizing deadly force, the Fourth Amendment has no such requirement. All that is required under the Fourth Amendment is that it was reasonable for the police officer to conclude that there was a threat worthy of the use of deadly force at the point the deadly force was used.[65] Because of the nature of a confrontation between a police officer and a possible assailant, the officer receives great deference and the benefit of the doubt under the Fourth Amendment and Section 242.[66]

Even if the prosecution can prove that it was objectively unreasonable for the officer to have used deadly force, i.e., a reasonable officer in that situation would not have used deadly force or would have perceived the situation to require such force, the government must prove beyond a reasonable doubt that the officer, "acted willfully, that is, with the purpose to violate the law. Proof of willful intent can be proved two ways: (1) the officer directly with purposeful intent decided to violate the law or (2) the officer acted with the highest level of negligence which is equal with a direct decision. The Supreme Court has held that an act is done willfully if it was 'committed' either 'in open defiance or in reckless disregard of a constitutional requirement which has been made specific and definite.' The government need not show that the defendant knew a federal statute or law protected the right with which he intended to interfere [but only that the officer's aim was] to deprive a citizen of a right and that right was protected [or] the defendant intended to engage in the conduct that violated the Constitution and that he did so knowing that it was a wrongful act."[67] Willfulness to deprive a person of constitutional and/or state rights can be inferred from conduct, and reckless disregard for the law establishes willful intent to deprive those rights.[68]

Under federal law, police error in the perception of the behavior of a person confronted, which results in the use of force or deadly force, does not carry criminal or civil liability if the error is reasonable and/or devoid of willful intent to violate the law. One cannot establish a Section 242 case even, "if [the officer] was mistaken in his interpretation of [the] conduct

---

64 Department of Justice Report, *Supra* note 63 at 79 (internal citation and quotation omitted). The Justice Department cited, United States v. Lanier, 520 U.S. 259, 267 (1997), citing Screws v. United States, 325 U.S. 91 (1945) and United States v. McClean, 528 F.2d 1250, 1255 (2nd Cir. 1976).

65 Department of Justice Report, Supra note 63 at 84.

66 Department of Justice Report, Supra note 63 at 85.

67 Department of Justice Report, Supra note 63 at 85–86 (internal citation and quotation omitted). The Department report cited, Screws v. United States, 325 U.S. 91, 101–107 (1945) and United States v. Walsh, 194 F.3d 37, 52–53 (2d Cir. 1999). See also, United States v. Reese, 2 F.3d 870, 881 (9th Cir. 1993), United States v. Dise, 763 F.2d 586, 592 (3d Cir. 1985), United States v. McClean, 528 F.2d 1250, 1255 (2nd Cir. 1976).

68 Department of Justice Report, Supra note 63 at 11. See *supra* notes 22, 25 and 26 for similar standard for federal civil liability.

[of the person shot], the fact that others [could] interpret[] that conduct the same way as [the officer] precludes a determination that he acted with a bad purpose to disobey the law. The same is true even if [the officer] could be said to have acted with poor judgment in the manner in which he first interacted with [the person shot], or in pursuing [the person] after the [beginning of the] incident."[69] Police error, without more, precludes a federal criminal civil rights charge.

LIMITATIONS TO FOURTH AMENDMENT PROTECTIONS

Fourth Amendment analysis does not focus on the injury sustained by the person shot or the motive of the officer. Because of the limited scope of the Fourth Amendment regarding police use of force its inquiry only seeks to determine if the police, without the help of hindsight, acted reasonably. Federal criminal civil rights law in police shootings is even more restrictive, because it requires proof that the police intentionally (knowingly) or recklessly acted to violate the civil rights of a person subjected to police use of force. The Fourth Amendment does not require professionalism, the intelligent use of force, or even compliance with department policy that establishes the restrained and gradual elevation of force in a given situation. The Fourth Amendment does not focus on subjective mental decision making, nor does it consider how race impacts the decision making or processing of a police officer.

The Supreme Court has made clear that the standard for police action is always whether the action is objectively reasonable. The officer's subjective intent is not relevant. Regarding judicial review of police action, the Court has also made clear that, "*judges should be cautious about second-guessing a police officer's assessment*, made on the scene, of the danger presented by a particular situation. ... [We] have instructed that *reasonableness "must be judged from the perspective of a reasonable officer on the scene*, rather than with the 20/20 vision of hindsight" and that "[t]he calculus of reasonableness must embody allowance for the fact that police officers are often forced to make split-second judgments—in circumstances that are tense, uncertain, and rapidly evolving."[70]

Under Fourth Amendment analysis, it does not matter whether the behavior of a person subjected to police use of force is in fact innocent or non-threatening. The legal question is the perception and actions of the police officer and whether the officer thought the behavior of the person was threatening. As an Ohio court made clear, "[The] relevant legal consideration is not what this defendant-officer 'should have' known or done, but rather what the reasonable officer, placed in his shoes, 'could have believed' about the situational need for deadly force in reacting to an imminent threat. The objectively reasonable officer can be mistaken. What is a 'reasonable' belief in light of the officer's perceptions could also be a mistaken belief, and the

---

69 Department of Justice Report, Supra note 63 at 86.

70 See, Ryburn v. Huff, 565 U.S. ____, ____ (2012) (Slip Op., at 8) (emphasis added).

fact that it turned out to be mistaken does not detract from its reasonableness when considered within the factual context and compressed time-frame of his decision to act."[71]

The U.S. Supreme Court came to the same conclusion regarding reasonable mistake in *Heien v. North Carolina* which involved a police officer incorrectly believing a state law required both brake lights to be operational when, in fact, only one brake light was required.[72] The Court held that

> The Fourth Amendment prohibits "unreasonable searches and seizures." Under this standard, a search or seizure may be permissible even though the justification for the action includes a reasonable factual mistake. ... Because the officer's mistake about the brake-light law was reasonable, the stop in this case was lawful under the Fourth Amendment.
>
> ...
>
> To be reasonable is not to be perfect, and so the Fourth Amendment allows for some mistakes on the part of government officials.[73]

In an effort to place some limitation on the assertion that the Court's decision will encourage police to allow themselves to be ignorant of the law to get around being required to be correct in knowing and enforcing the law, the Court held,

> Contrary to the suggestion of Heien and *amici*, our decision does not discourage officers from learning the law. The Fourth Amendment tolerates only *reasonable* mistakes, and those mistakes—whether of fact or of law—must be *objectively* reasonable. We do not examine the subjective understanding of the particular officer involved. And the inquiry is not as forgiving as the one employed in the distinct context of deciding whether an officer is entitled to qualified immunity for a constitutional or statutory violation. Thus, an officer can gain no Fourth Amendment advantage through a sloppy study of the laws he is duty bound to enforce.[74]

A reasonable mistake of law analysis assumes that the law is clearly established. Individual ignorance of clearly established law will not be found objectively reasonable. But that is all the Fourth Amendment protects against. The amendment finds no violation in mistakes, *per se*.

In summary, only police action without objectively reasonable explanation or action done with purposeful and flagrant intent to violate the Fourth Amendment will invoke a violation of the Fourth Amendment prohibition against unreasonable seizure. Simple mistake

---

71 Ohio v. White, 988 N.E.2d 595, 618–619 (2013). See also, U.S. Supreme Court opinions, Saucier v. Katz, 533 U.S. 194, 121 S.Ct. 2151, 150 L.Ed.2d 272 (2001) and *Pearson v. Callahan*, 555 U.S. 223, 129 S.Ct. 808, 172 L.Ed.565 (2009).

72 Heien v. North Carolina, 574 U.S. ____ (2014) (Slip op).

73 Heien v. North Carolina, 574 U.S. ____ (2014) (Slip op). at 1–2, 5.

74 Heien v. North Carolina, 574 U.S. ____ (2014) (Slip op). at 11–12.

(reasonable error) of law and/or fact will not invoke the Fourth Amendment. Fourth Amendment jurisprudence is defined by the reasonableness of why (justification) the police used force and how much (method/manor) force is used at the moment, not whether it was correctly determined to be necessary to be used in the light of all the facts in calmness of reflection.

The Fourth Amendment right against unreasonable seizure covers the entire continuum of police use of force, from a verbal command to stop to the use of deadly force. The Court has also made clear that the police are allowed a certain latitude in the use of force before such force is found to implicate a Fourth Amendment violation. The Supreme Court has held that the decision to use force (justification) and the level of force (method/manor) are two different legal questions, and the later does not change the analysis of whether the decision to use force to impose the seizure was unreasonable. Civil liability and criminal culpability can be established by either the unjustified decision to use force or the unreasonable method (manor) or level of force used. Judged by the totality of the circumstances, a mistake of fact or law by the officer resulting in the decision to use force or the level of force used will not be converted into civil liability or criminal culpability if the mistake was objectively reasonable under the circumstances as known to the officer. The mistake must rise to the level of recklessness to create civil liability or criminal culpability.

CUSTOM, POLICY, OR PRACTICE: MUNICIPAL AND POLICE AGENCY LIABILITY

In the seminal case *Monell v. Department of Social Services* (1978) the Supreme Court held that civil liability can also be established against a police department or city government due to the behavior of individual police officer actions under a §1983 Civil Rights claim.[75] The Court ruled that mere employment by the municipality will not establish liability.[76] The Court subsequently held in *Harlow v. Fitzgerald* (1982), that

> Our decisions have recognized immunity defenses of two kinds. For officials whose special functions or constitutional status requires complete protection from suit, we have recognized the defense of "absolute immunity." The absolute immunity of legislators, in their legislative functions, and of judges, in their judicial functions, now is well settled. Our decisions also have extended absolute immunity to certain officials of the Executive Branch. These include prosecutors and similar officials, executive officers engaged in adjudicative functions, and the President of the United States.
>
> For executive officials in general, however, our cases make plain that qualified immunity represents the norm. [H]igh officials require greater protection than those with less

75 Monell v. Department of Social Services of the City of New York, 436 US 635, 690 (1978).

76 Monell v. Department of Social Services of the City of New York at 691.

> complex discretionary responsibilities. Nonetheless, we held that a governor and his aides could receive the requisite protection from qualified or good faith immunity.[77]

The Court explained that government officials, due to the nature of their work, are entitled to a "good faith" or qualified immunity from the burdens of defending a law suit for the decisions they make in the performance of their duties. Civil liability only attaches when an official "*knew or reasonably should have known that the action he took within his sphere of official responsibility would violate the constitutional rights of the [plaintiff], or if he took the action with the malicious intention to cause a deprivation of constitutional rights or other injury ...* "[78] The Court made clear that decisions made by government officials due to choice of available options (discretionary) enjoys qualified protection from litigation, while actions that are taken as required by law (Ministerial) are not covered by qualified immunity.[79]

Qualified immunity will not protect government action that, on its face, is unconstitutional. The Court held in *Groh v. Ramirez* (2004) that an Alcohol, Tobacco, and Firearms agent executing a warrant that was clearly unconstitutional on its face was not entitled to qualified immunity even though a magistrate had signed the warrant.[80] Qualified immunity will cover simple negligence or error in judgement, blatant violation of law is outside of its protection. But to be outside, it must be blatant.

Applying these cases to police agencies under a section 1983 lawsuit, under *Monell*, a police department does not have absolute immunity but is not liable under *respondeat superior*; and under *Harlow*, individual employees and leaders of the police agency can claim qualified immunity from the burden of the lawsuit if they acted in good faith and did not violate clearly established law in forming or implementing policies or customs through the use of their discretionary power to act within their official duties. The Court held, three years after it decided *Harlow*, that government officials are liable when they make policy that violates constitutional rights. But, the focus is on policy, not on single event violations.[81]

Under *Monell*, "there must be an affirmative link between the policy and the particular constitutional violation alleged."[82] The Court made clear that an unconstitutional act of an employee, senior or not, does not create an unconstitutional decision by the municipality *per se*. A causal link is required between the employee and a decision made by the municipality. A constitutional injury caused by a policy requires a direct link to the official policy maker under local or state law that is responsible for making the policy or by subordinates who are directly authorized by that policy maker to make or enforce the policy claimed to have caused

77 Harlow v. Fitzgerald, 457 US 800, 807 (1983).

78 Harlow v. Fitzgerald at 815 (Internal citation omitted).

79 Harlow v. Fitzgerald at 816, 818.

80 Groh v. Ramirez, 540 U.S. 551, (2004).

81 Oklahoma City v. Tuttle, 471 US 808 (1985).

82 Oklahoma City v. Tuttle

the injury. The Court clarified this point in *Ashcroft v. Iqbal* (2009), when it held not only that a supervisor is not liable for the acts of a subordinate, but that in claims of discrimination or violation of constitutional rights, a specific intent to violate rights is required.[83] The Court, in reviewing the law of municipal liability, summarized the case law in *Collins v. City of Harker Heights* (1992) holding that

> The city is not vicariously liable under 1983 for the constitutional torts of its agents: it is only liable when it can be fairly said that the city itself is the wrongdoer.
>
> . . .
>
> > "In *Monell v. New York City Dept. of Social Services*, 436 U.S. 658 (1978), we decided that a municipality can be found liable under 1983 only where the municipality itself causes the constitutional violation at issue. Respondeat superior or vicarious liability will not attach under 1983. 'It is only when the "execution of the government's policy or custom ... inflicts the injury" that the municipality may be held liable under 1983.' *Springfield v. Kibbe* (1987) (quoting *Monell*).
> >
> > "Thus, our first inquiry in any case alleging municipal liability under 1983 is the question whether there is a direct causal link between a municipal policy or custom and the alleged constitutional deprivation."
>
> We did not suggest that all harm-causing municipal policies are actionable under 1983 or that all such policies are unconstitutional. Moreover, we rejected the city's argument that only unconstitutional policies can create municipal liability under the statute. Instead, we concluded that, if a city employee violates another's constitutional rights, the city may be liable if it had a policy or custom of failing to train its employees, and that failure to train caused the constitutional violation. In particular, we held that the inadequate training of police officers could be characterized as the cause of the constitutional tort if—and only if—the failure to train amounted to "deliberate indifference" to the rights of persons with whom the police come into contact.
>
> Although the term "deliberate indifference" has been used in other contexts to define the threshold for finding a violation of the Eighth Amendment, see *Estelle v. Gamble*, (1976), as we have explained, that term was used in the *Canton* case for the quite different purpose of identifying the threshold for holding a city responsible for the constitutional torts committed by its inadequately trained agents.[84]

The Court made clear deliberate indifference is the level of burden of proof to establish liability. It is not a state of mind establishing intent to commit a constitutional tort. Deliberate indifference allows for municipal civil liability to be established on a level higher than *respondeat superior.*

---

83 Ashcroft v. Iqbal, 556 U.S. 662 (2009)

84 Collins v. City of Harker Heights, 503 US 115, 122–124 (1989).

In *Will v. Michigan Department of State Police* (1989) the Court held that while a locality can be sued under § 1983 a state cannot.[85] The Court reasoned that "it does not follow that, if municipalities are persons, then so are States. States are protected by the Eleventh Amendment, while municipalities are not."[86] "[A] suit against a state official in his or her official capacity is not a suit against the official, but rather is a suit against the official's office. As such, it is no different from a suit against the State itself. [Thus we] hold that neither a State nor its officials acting in their official capacities are 'persons' under § 1983."[87] The Court subsequently held in *McMilligan v. Monroe County, Alabama* (1997) that state law governs whether an official is a state or county official.[88]

Eight years after the Court issued its decision in *Will v. Michigan*, the Court held in *Board of County Commissioners v. Brown* (1997) that "it is not enough for a § 1983 plaintiff merely to identify conduct properly attributable to the municipality. The plaintiff must also demonstrate that, through its deliberate conduct, the municipality was the "moving force" behind the injury alleged. That is, a plaintiff must show that the municipal action was taken with the requisite degree of culpability and must demonstrate a direct causal link between the municipal action and the deprivation of federal rights."[89]

The Court held that when a case involves a facially lawful policy or practice, but it is claimed that the result was a violation of a constitutional right caused by the implementation of the policy, the showing of a constitutional injury alone will not establish liability. Only "deliberate indifference" to a known or obvious consequence of the policy implementation will create liability. A showing of simple or even heightened negligence will not suffice."[90] Thus, to establish liability, the plaintiff must establish that not only was the policy or custom the result of a constitutional injury, the plaintiff must show that the decision maker knew and/or had actual notice that the policy would result in constitutional injury.

The requirement that "'deliberate indifference' [only] exists where adequate scrutiny ... would lead a reasonable supervisor to conclude that the plainly obvious consequences of the decision to hire would be the deprivation of a third party's constitutional rights"[91] and that the plaintiff must establish "a strong connection between the background of the particular applicant and the specific violation alleged such that the hired officer was highly likely to

---

85 Will v. Michigan Department of State Police, 491 US 58, 66 (1989).

86 Will v. Michigan Department of State Police at 70.

87 Will v. Michigan Department of State Police at 71.

88 McMilligan v. Monroe County, Alabama, 520 US 112 (1997).

89 Board of County Commissioners of Bryan County, Oklahoma v. Brown, 520 US 397, 404 (1997).

90 Board of County Commissioners of Bryan County, Oklahoma v. Brown at 406–407.

91 Board of County Commissioners of Bryan County, Oklahoma v. Brown at 433–434

inflict the particular type of injury suffered [and a] showing of simple or even heightened negligence will not suffice"[92] has led to some absurd results.

For example, the Fifth Circuit explained that "[W]hen the State takes a person into its custody and holds him there against his will, the Constitution imposes upon it a corresponding duty to assume some responsibility for his safety and general well-being. Indeed, detainees in jails and prisons are restricted in their ability to fend for themselves ... officers in detention facilities are often able to exercise almost complete control over detainees, which creates real risks that officers will sexually assault the people in their care. These risks [are] well-known to corrections officials. Accordingly, when hiring officers for detention facilities, officials must be careful to thoroughly examine applicants' backgrounds and diligently inquire about the conduct underlying any prior offenses."[93] In the same case the Fifth Circuit explained that "[e]ven if the County had done a thorough job of investigating the jailer's background, it would have required an enormous leap to connect 'improper advances' towards female [high school] students to the sexual assault. Consequently, there were no grounds to find that the alleged rape in question was a plainly obvious consequence of hiring him." [94]

In *Rivera v. Mull*, the Fifth Circuit held that the municipality, that hired a guard, with an arrest history involving unlawful sexual contact with a girl under the age of consent, who raped a female detainee, was not liable for the assault due to the hiring. The court concluded that the arrest for the sexual assault occurred when the guard was a minor himself at the time and thus the case could have involved two juveniles in non-coercive sexual contact. Because the juvenile record was "vague and inconclusive" as to the facts and details of the incident, the court concluded that as a matter of law, "a jury could not find that a plainly obvious consequence of hiring Fierros was that he would sexually assault a detainee."[95] The "specific circumstances of this case, the connection between Fierros's prior arrests and the injury to Rivera is not strong enough to show that Appellees were deliberately indifferent in hiring him."[96] In other words, proximate cause was not established enough to defeat the municipalities qualified immunity.

The court concluded that the absolute power of guards leaves female detainees defenseless to rape, added to a prior incident of sexual abuse committed by the hired guard, and the failure

---

92 Rivera v. Mull, Fifth Circuit Court of Appeals No. 16–10675 (July 6, 2017) at 5 (internal citation and quotation marks omitted).

93 Rivera v. Mull, Fifth Circuit Court of Appeals at 7–8 citing DeShaney v. Winnebago Cty. Dep't of Soc. Servs., 489 U.S. 189, 199–200 (1989) and Hare v. City of Corinth, 74 F.3d 633, 639 (5th Cir. 1996) (internal quotation marks omitted).

94 Rivera v. Mull, Fifth Circuit Court of Appeals at 7 (internal citation and quotation marks omitted and added). Citing Hardeman v. Kerr County, 244 F. App'x 593, 596 (5th Cir. 2007).

95 Rivera v. Mull, Fifth Circuit Court of Appeals at 9.

96 Rivera v. Mull, Fifth Circuit Court of Appeals at 8.

of the county to fully develop a history of the prior incident did not establish liability due to deliberate indifference to the threat that the guard would commit rape. An absurd result.

In regard to failure to train and supervise as a means to establish civil liability, the plaintiff must establish (1) that training and supervision is required, (2) the municipality knew its training was inadequate, (3) that failure was deliberately indifferent to the risk of constitutional injury, and (4) the deliberate indifference directly resulted in the constitutional injury asserted by the plaintiff. In *Rivera v. Mull* the court held that although the jail offered some level of training regarding the prohibition of sexual contact between detainees and guards, after a prior incident of sexual assault that occurred in the jail in a surveillance camera observed area, the sexual assault asserted by the plaintiff occurred in non-surveillance camera area used for attorney advising and mental health counseling, and prior case law could have left an impression with the jail administration that a prior incident of abuse did not require changes to prison operations. The result being, "we conclude that it was not clearly established at the time of the alleged misconduct that Appellees needed to make significant changes to their training, supervision, and policies in response to the July 2014 incident of sexual abuse."[97]

*****

The Fourth Amendment only protects against unreasonable use of force and the question of whether the force was unreasonable. The focus is on what the officer believed and perceived and whether it was reasonable. Returning to the issue of criminal justice and race, it is important to understand Fourth Amendment analysis and its application does not address or consider historical racism by the police or the social issue and policy debates involved in the dynamics of race and criminal justice. Fourth Amendment analysis narrows to a specific dynamic: what the officer thought at the time of force and whether what the officer did was objectively reasonable. This issue of what the police officer believed and how he/she perceived the situation that results in the use of force or deadly force becomes more completed when placed within the context of police interaction with young Black men. Police interaction with Blacks raises the more complicated issues of unconscious or implicit racial bias, the perceptions of Blacks as criminals, and how the behavior of a Black man relates to the fear of an individual police officer for his/her safety. How these perceptions of threats and fear of Blacks and how they dictate behavior of the police is the topic of Chapter Three.

KEY COURT CASES

1 *Imbler v. Pachtman* (1976)
2 *Monell v. Department of Social Services* (1978)

---

97 Id at 9–15

3 *Harlow v. Fitzgerald* (1982)
4 *Tennessee v. Garner* (1985)
5 *Anderson v. Creighton* (1987)
6 *Graham v. Connor* (1989)

KEY CONCEPTS

1 Qualified immunity
2 Absolute immunity
3 Police pre-seizure conduct/provocation (officer created jeopardy)
4 Civil liability and causation
5 Self-defense justification
6 Federal crime: Deprivation of rights under color of law
7 Agency civil liability: Custom, policy, or practice

KEY STATUTES

1 Civil Rights Act of 1871 (the Ku Klux Klan Act)
2 18 U.S.C. § 242

DISCUSSION/CLASS EXERCISES

1. The plaintiffs, two women, claim that Rogers, a police officer, sexually assaulted them during two separate traffic stops. The plaintiffs sued Crum, the chief of police. In reviewing the officer's record in his prior department, it was found that he used excessive force; was determined by a psychologist to be inflexible, defensive, and unwilling to take direction; received a letter of reprimand for insubordination; received a complaint for being harassing and overbearing during a traffic stop; was threatening and unprofessional; drew a weapon during a traffic stop; was unable to take criticism; aggravated situations; and other similar complaints but had no allegations of sexual misconduct.
   a. What are the legal issues raised by this case?
   b. Is the department liable for hiring the officer?
2. A young Black male broke into the home of a 77-year-old woman in a college town. The town is an almost all-White college town where about 2% of the college population is composed of Black youth. The police obtained a list of all Black students at the college, approximately 450. After attempts to question all of them failed to produce a suspect, the police conducted a sweep of the entire town, stopping and questioning

more than 200 non-white persons who fit the description of the suspect—race, gender, and an injury to the hand.

a. What are the legal issues raised by this case?
b. Is this a case of racial profiling? Why or why not?
c. Do the facts of this case establish a seizure?
d. When the police stopped and examined the hands of 450 Black students, was this an unlawful seizure? Why or Why not?

3. Officer Jane Becky, a patrol officer, stopped Susan Cindy for speeding on a busy intersection at 2:30 p.m. The dispatcher notified Becky that a person with the same name, date of birth, and general description with a tattoo on her chest was wanted on a felony warrant. The officer explained that the wanted person had a tattoo on her breast and asked Cindy if she had a tattoo. Cindy, who had her two nine-year-old sons in the car, informed the officer that she had not been in any trouble and that she did not have any tattoos. She was told by Becky that she could take her down to the station to prove she did not have any tattoos. Cindy refused to go to the station, and Becky insisted that she would need to see her chest in order to confirm that she did not have a tattoo. Cindy, under her perception that she was obligated to prove she did not have a tattoo, exposed herself to Officer Becky.
   a. Was this a seizure? Was this a search?
   b. Did the officer violate Cindy's Fourth Amendment rights? Why or why not?
4. What is Police pre-seizure conduct/provocation (officer created jeopardy) and how is it related to civil liability? Why have some courts allowed this rule while others have not?
5. In what situations can a prosecutor claim absolute immunity from a civil law suit, and when can the prosecutor claim qualified immunity? Why are police officers only entitled to qualified immunity?
6. This chapter asserts that, in regard to police use of force, the Fourth Amendment provides very limited opportunities to sue the police and the Fourth Amendment provides the benefit of the doubt to the police. Explain the constitutional and legal basis for the assertion. Do you agree or disagree? Why?
7. What is required to prove a criminal civil rights violation? What is the law regarding self-defense claimed by a civilian and claimed by a police officer. What are the differences?
8. What must be proven to establish municipal liability for the actions of an employee of the agency that violate the constitutional rights of another.

CHAPTER THREE

Race, Implicit Biases, and the Social Psychology of Fear of Blacks as Criminogenic

STUDENT LEARNING OBJECTIVES

1. Students will be able to explain and define the different types or racism and how social psychology has explained how each type operates within social dynamics.
2. Students will be able to define how social media in terms of television, movies, and crime reporting defines and supports negative images of blacks, specifically defining Black males as criminals.
3. Students will be able to explain how negative perceptions of Blacks affects police perceptions of Black behavior and how these perceptions provides an explanation for disproportionate contact between police and Blacks.
4. Students will be able to apply social psychology theory to the issue of police use of force and race and explain how negative perceptions of Blacks affects police decisions to use force.
5. Students will be able to apply social psychology literature to social discourse and narratives regarding Blacks and crime and be able to differentiate different types of racism within political discourse and narratives.

INTRODUCTION: THE SCIENCE OF FEAR AND RACE

As reviewed in Chapter Two, the Fourth Amendment is a minimalist standard which only requires police use of force to be reasonable, as defined by the totality of the circumstances as the officer knew them, when force is used. Only intentional or reckless behavior can support civil liability under the Fourth Amendment and only when the force used is objectively unreasonable *and* without legal justification or with intent to violate the law (under federal law) can criminal culpability be established. In most instances police shootings involve use of deadly force due to a police officer belief that a threat of death or serious bodily injury is being threatened against him/her or to others which required the officer to shoot the person making the threat. The Fourth

Amendment does not consider police officer mistake, panic, misperception, failure to follow department policy, failure to use proper police tactics, or even poor judgment as foundations for criminal culpability or civil liability. More broadly, Fourth Amendment analysis does not address or consider historical racism by the police or the social issue and policy debates involved in the dynamics of race and criminal justice. More importantly, the Fourth Amendment does not consider research on how police perceptions of the inherent dangerousness of young Black males influences police interactions.

The criminal justice and psychology literature is anything but sparse on the question of how police use force, specifically on how police use force against Blacks.[1] The research on this subject began in the early 1980s and has continued to develop for more than thirty years. The first two decades of academic research reflected the social, societal and political temperament of the 1980s and 1990s. The research, like society as a whole, concluded that in regard to police shootings in general and police shootings of Blacks in particular, (1) racism had no impact on the police decision to shoot or not to shoot Blacks and (2) Blacks were disproportionately arrested and involved in being subjected to police use of force because they are disproportionally involved in criminal activity.[2] The research reflected the politics of the fall of 1960s liberalism and the idea of rehabilitation of criminals, along with the political reaction to the rise of crime and violence due to the rise of crack cocaine, the rise of conservative politics in the 1980s all of which resulted in the assertion that Blacks were disproportionally represented in all aspects of the criminal justice system because they were disproportionately criminal. Beginning in the early twenty-first century, psychology and modern criminal justice research suggested an opposite view with focus on how people think and perceive information on a conscious and subconscious level, and how police perceive threats and criminality to the detriment of Black people in general and young Black males specifically.[3]

---

1 For example see, Charles F. Klahm IV and Rob Tillyer, "Understanding Police Use of Force: A Review of the Evidence," *Southwest Journal of Criminal Justice* 7, no. 2 (2010): 214, Cynthia Lee, "'But I Thought He Had a Gun'—Race and Police Use of Deadly Force," *Hastings Race and Poverty Law Journal* 2 (2004): 1, Jennifer L. Eberhardt et al., "Seeing Black: Race, Crime, and Visual Processing," *Journal of Personality and Social Psychology* 87, no. 6 (2004): 876, Steven G. Brandl and Meghan S Stroshine, "The Role of Officer Attributes, Job Characteristics, and Arrest Activity in Explaining Police Use of Force," *Criminal Justice Policy Review* 20, no. 10(2012): 1, Melody S. Sadler, Joshua Correll, Bernadette Park, and Charles M. Judd, "The World is Not Black and White: Racial Bias in the Decision to Shoot in a Multiethnic Context," *Journal of Social Issues* 68, no. 2 (2012): 286, and Phillip Atiba Goff and John F. Dovidio, "Contemporary Racial Bias and Law Enforcement: A Report Prepared for the New York State Task Force on Police-on-Police Shooting," In *New York State Task Force on Police-on-Police Shootings* (2010): 92–99.

2 John S. Goldkamp, "Minorities as Victims of Police Shootings: Interpretation of Racial Disproportionality and Police Use of Deadly Force," *Justice Systems Journal* 2 (1976): 169, Cynthia Lee, "'But I Thought He Had a Gun,' Race and Police Use of Deadly Force," *Hastings Race and Poverty Law Journal* 2 (2005): 1.

3 *Supra* note 1 and *Infra* note 4.

Police interactions with the public in general and specifically with Blacks within the criminal justice literature have focused on suspect characteristics (race/ethnicity, gender, age, suspect demeanor, suspect class, suspect level of intoxication), encounter characteristics (suspect threat of weapons, how the contact is initiated, suspect resistance, reason for arrest, presence of other officers or bystanders, level of conflict), and officer characteristics (race/ethnicity, gender, age, experience, education), all of which have some explanatory power but none are exclusively determinative in explaining the disproportionate impact on Blacks.[4] Quantitative research has also found support for non-criminal activity, race-based explanations for police stops and use of force. These explanations include ***Minority Threat Theory, Out of Place Theory, Status of Offender/Officer Theory*** and ***Black's Theory of Law***. For example, research by Joseph Ferrandino on the "out of place" theory posits that police stop Blacks when they are in predominantly White neighborhoods regardless of criminal activity, but also posits that Whites in predominantly Black neighborhoods are also stopped by police because they are "out of place."[5] Police behavior is not static and the purpose of the police agency can influence how racial bias is operationalized. For example, Patricia Warren et al. reported that

> Status characteristics appear to influence stop decisions made by local police. In all local police models, race, age, and age of the vehicle are significant predictors. Highway patrol officers' stop decisions-, on the other hand, appear to be influenced more by driving behaviors than status characteristics. … We expected this, for two reasons. First is that the [state police officer] generally does not do the type of routine police work traditionally associated with the local police. Second is that it is difficult for the highway patrol to identify the race of drivers because cars are moving at fairly high speeds.[6]

Jeff Rojek et al., research also found support for the "out of place" theory to explain White police officers searching of Blacks during stops as well as for Donald Black's Theory of Law.

> That the decision to invoke the law depends on the relative social position of the parties involved in a given case as well as on the technical merits of the legal violation. … [T] he decisions of legal agents to invoke the law (e.g., detain, investigate, search, cite, and

4 Charles F. Klahm IV and Rob Tillyer, "Understanding Police Use of Force: A Review of the Evidence," *Southwest Journal of Criminal Justice* 7, no. 2 (2010): 214. See also, Bennett I. Cappers, "Policing, Race, and Place," *Harvard Civil Rights-Civil Liberties Law Review* 44 (2008): 43.

5 Joseph Ferrandino, "Minority Threat Hypothesis and NYPD Stop and Frisk Policy," *Criminal Justice Review* 40, no. 2 (2014):209. See also, Malcolm D. Holmes, "Minority Threat and Police Brutality: Determinants of Civil Rights Criminal Complaints in U.S. Municipalities," *Criminology* 38, no. 2 (2000): 343, Robert M. Fogelson, "From Resentment to Confrontation: The Police, the Negroes, and the Outbreak of the Nineteen-Sixties Riots," *Political Science Quarterly* 83, no. 2(1968): 217, and Sandra Bass "Policing space, Policing Race: Social Control Imperatives and Police Discretionary Decisions," *Social Justice* 28, no. 1 (2001):156.

6 Patricia Warren, Donald Tomaskovic-Devey, William Smith, Matthew Zingraff, and Marcinda Mason, "Driving While Black: Bias Processes and Racial Disparity in Police Stops," *Criminology* 44, no. 3 (2006): 709, 731.

> arrest) can be explained by the agent's social position relative to that of the citizen in a given incident. Black's theory has special relevance to the disparate treatment of racial minorities by legal authorities."[7]

Donald Black asserts that the application of the law and the use of formal legal processes, police, courts, attorneys, etc., are utilized only when people believe and define an incident as a crime or more specifically, is serious enough to be worthy of police action. In other words not every incident is worthy of police attention. The police are called only when people believe they should be called. That belief is governed by two factors. First, the level of intimacy or relationship between people in a dispute or conflict and how the nature of that relationship factors in—whether it is a relationship between intimates, whether the dispute involves social superiors to inferiors, or from inferiors to superiors. Secondly, the social geography in the relationship. The social geography is defined by the social location (the location of the conflict) and the direction of the incident (the relationship between parties—the victims, perpetrators, and agents of formal governmental control—and how each defines the conflict and how each determines whether formal social control, the criminal justice system, is required to address the conflict). Black asserts that "equality before the law does not exist. The reality is legal relativity, not legal universalism: Law varies with its social geometry its location and direction in social space" and being a sociologist, he asserts that crime, the definition of crime, and treatment of an incident as crime is a system of social structure and cultural similarities and differences.[8] The limitation to this theory, of course, is that the law is not relative, the enforce-

---

7 Jeff Rojek, Richard Rosenfeld, and Scott Decker, "Policing Race: The Racial Stratification of Searches in Police Traffic Stops," *Criminology* 50, no. 4 (2012)993-994. See, Donald Black, *The Behavior of Law* (1976), and Donald Black, *The Manners and Customs of the Police* (1980). See also, David E. Barlow and Melissa Hickman Barlow, "Racial Profiling: A Survey of African American Police Officers," *Police Quarterly* 5, no. 3 (2002):334.

8 See, Donald Black, "How law behaves: An interview with Donald Black," *International Journal of Law, Crime and Justice* 38, no. 1 (2010): 40–41. Black argues that how the parties to a conflict are socially located defines the development and use of the law.

For example, the social stratification of a society is relevant to the handling of an individual case primarily when the case is stratified as well, such as when it has a downward direction (from a social superior against an inferior)—a case structure that attracts more law.

In regard to the "relevance of third parties such as judges, jury members, lawyers, and witnesses," Black asserts that these third parties to conflict define and explain different results with the same facts. He asserts that the result of the O.J. Simpson case in which the criminal trial resulted in an acquittal, was because nine out of the twelve jurors were Black while the civil trial had no Black jurors and that jury found O.J. Simpson civilly liable on the same evidence as was presented at the criminal trial. Black concludes this proves his theory of partisanship—"Partisanship is a direct function of social closeness to one side and social remoteness from the other. The jury culturally closer to Simpson thus acquitted him while the jury culturally closer to the victims found him liable for the killings." Black, "How law behaves ... " at 44.

ment of it is. What the law requires is not synonymous with how it is enforced and how its agents actualize what the law requires and does. Black's observation that enforcement of the law is influenced by how its agents (generally the criminal justice system and specifically the police) treat those who are perceived as inferior or in need of social control (Blacks in general and specifically young Black males) is one explanation of how police treat Black males regardless of the race of the police officer. As discussed in Chapter One and later in this chapter, Black police officers can be just as racially prejudiced against young Black males, if not even more so, than White police officers.

SOCIAL PSYCHOLOGY: DEFINING AND EXPLAINING IMPLICIT BIAS AND PERCEPTIONS OF BLACKS

While criminal justice research on race and police has focused on suspect characteristics, or, encounter and officer characteristics, the science of psychology and social psychology focuses on the emotional and social dynamics of human interaction. This field of study has provided additional understanding on how police perceive people and act according to these explicit and implicit mental dynamics.

Research on how people view Blacks is almost universal in finding that Blacks tend to invoke concepts of danger or at least suspicion. Social psychology research focuses on how these perceptions develop and function in decision making even if they are cognitively

---

The problem with his explanation is that it discounts entirely the impact of the differential in the burden of proof in a civil vs. a criminal case. He also discounts the lack of skill in the presentation of the evidence in the two cases by the prosecution vs. the plaintiff's attorneys. He also discounts the law that governs the two types of cases which prevent O.J. from taking the witness stand in a criminal case while in a civil case O.J. was required to testify. These legal distinctions between the two cases affected the difference in jury outcomes.

There is no doubt that race had a serious impact on the criminal case both on the jury and on society as a whole, but simply saying the jurors identified with Simpson because he is Black and the civil jury identified with the Goldmans because they were White oversimplifies the dynamics of both cases. Black's theory is also an example of infrahumanization/dehumanization of Blacks regarding their ability to comprehend and process evidence in an objective and professional manner regarding criminal culpability. O.J. was found not guilty because the prosecutors botched the case while the plaintiff's attorneys in the civil case were much more skilled.

An additional limitation to Black's theory is that he assumes the law is relative and socially defined at the micro level. He conflates legal decision-making by various parties to conflict with the behavior or the nature of the law itself. What the law is and what it requires is different than how people view and use the law in specific conflicts. The former is macro while the latter is micro. His theory is also limited because he asserts that his theory maintains that the only way to secure a neutral jury is to have one that is socially identical. Black, "How law behaves ... " at 44. Of course, the intentional formation of a jury that is socially and racially identical to the defendant is both socially and legally prohibited.

rejected. Research literature on visual processing, assessing threat, and determining responsive behavior based on initial observations by society in general, and police, in particular, when viewed from the perspective of race has observed that

> The mere presence of a Black man, for instance, can trigger thoughts that he is violent and criminal. Simply thinking about a Black person renders these concepts more accessible and can lead to misremembering the Black person as the one holding the razor. Merely thinking about Blacks can lead people to elevate ambiguous behavior as aggressive, to miscategorize harmless objects as weapons, or to shoot quickly, and, at times, inappropriately.[9]

This is what is called in the social psychology literature ***Implicit Bias***.[10] In a summary report to the New York State Task Force on police use of force, scholars from Yale University and UCLA explained that bias or social (cultural) stereotypes (note, not racism) is the result of a psychological process created through

> historical cultural associations, ingroup affinities, and self- and group interests, the majority of White Americans still harbor negative feelings and beliefs about Blacks, which are implicit— frequently unconscious and typically automatically activated.
>
> . . .
>
> Researchers have demonstrated that officers often evidence similar forms of bias in their willingness to shoot Black armed suspects more quickly than White armed suspects.
>
> . . .
>
> The implicit association between Blacks and criminality has also led officers to incorrectly identify darker-skinned Blacks as criminal suspects. … Similarly, the emerging field of racial dehumanization has used implicit bias paradigms to demonstrate that ***the implicit association between Blacks and apes leads both to citizens' increased endorsement of anti-Black violence by police and to an increased use of the death penalty for convicted Back felons.*** Taken together, this research suggests that implicit bias may be a subtle, uncontrolled, and unintentional mechanism through which individual officer attitudes may result in racially disparate outcomes.[11]

---

9 Jennifer L. Eberhardt, Supra 1 at 768.

10 Phillip Atiba Goff and John F. Dovidio, *New York State Task Force on Police-on-Police Shootings* at 93, Supra note 1. See also, R. Richard Banks, Jennifer L. Eberhardt, and Lee Ross, "Discrimination and Implicit Bias in a Racially Unequal Society," *California Law Review* 94, no. 4 (2006): 1169, and *Infra* note 129.

11 Goff and Dovidio at 93–94 (emphasis added). See also, Dora Apel, "Just joking? Chimps, Obama and racial stereotype," *Journal of Visual Culture* 8, no. 2 (2009), Dora Capozza, Giulio Boccato, Luca Andrighetto, and Rossella Falvo "Categorization of Ambiguous Human/Ape Faces: Protection of Ingroup but Not Outgroup Humanity," *Group processes & intergroup relations* 12, no. 6 (2009): 777, and Infra note 81.

The associating apes with Blacks is not new. It is reminiscent of Lord Chief Justice Mansfield in ***The Zong Massacre Case*** (*Gregson v. Gilbert*) in 1783 in which he equated the value of the lives of Black slaves with horses when both are thrown overboard by the crew. It was reflected in the opinion by Chief Justice Taney in the ***Dred Scott*** decision in 1857 when the Court said there is no law regarding the protection of Blacks that the White man need respect.[12] It is reflected in modern racial politics, as discussed in Chapter Ten, when Roseanne Barr tweeted that a senior Obama Advisor was the baby of an ape, fathered by a member of the Muslim Brotherhood.

Social Psychology: Defining and Explaining Perceptions of Blacks: Stereotypes and Police Decision-making

The presence of Blacks, fear of crime, and the factor environmental ambiguity and bidirectional stereotyping

Social psychological research focuses on how stereotypes can affect the initial decision to shoot a suspect and the time that an officer takes in deciding to shoot a Black or White unarmed suspect as well as the accuracy in making the decision to shoot. A ***stereotype*** is a category of expected values, beliefs or expectations that are applied to a group and then applied to a person who is a member of that group. The stereotype helps people organize expectations of new people or situations. Stereotypes are descriptive. Stereotypes can be confirmed or abandoned upon addition information within a new encounter or experience. They are initial ways to relate to something or someone. ***Racial bias*** is more complicated because it can hold negative stereotypes that define how a new relationship should occur or how certain people should be treated regardless of the correctness or incorrectness of an initial stereotype of a group or an individual.

Research has shown that racial bias affects the speed with which a police officer will decide to shoot or not shoot, because the officer is mentally processing his/her racial bias in assessing the situation and the decision to shoot.[13] Using a video game showing Black and White suspects both armed and unarmed, researchers found that police officers, "seemed to have greater difficulty (indexed by longer latencies) responding to stereotype-incongruent targets (unarmed Black targets and armed White targets), rather than to stereotype-congruent targets" which were armed Black targets and unarmed White targets.[14] The study found that, "Accurate responses to targets congruent with culturally prevalent stereotypes (i.e., armed Black targets and unarmed White targets) required less time than did responses to stereotype-incongruent targets (i.e., unarmed Black targets and armed White targets)."[15] In other words, when the

12 See discussion in Chapter Five.

13 Joshua Correll et al., "Across the Thin Blue Line: Police Officers and Racial Bias in the Decision to Shoot," *Journal of Personality and Social Psychology* 92, no. 6(2007): 1006.

14 Correll et al. 1015

15 Correll et al. at 1020.

target was White and armed police reacted slower in shooting than when the target was Black and armed. The implicit bias of Black criminality prevented police from reacting when the armed suspect did not match the stereotype of the typical armed suspect.[16] Put simply, "we found that officers orient more quickly to Black people when processing danger-related stimuli."[17] As partial explanation for this result, researchers found that the "[b]ias increased as a function of the community's size, crime rate, and the proportion of Black residents and other ethnic minority residents. Police in larger, more dangerous and more racially diverse environments are presumably much more likely to encounter Black criminals, reinforcing the stereotypic association between race and crime. By contrast, officers with little exposure to Black people may be less likely to rehearse this association."[18]

One factor that social science provides in explaining police bias is the nature of the perception of the presence of Blacks in an environment. ***Minority threat theory*** in general is a conflict theory which asserts that as the political, social, economic strength of a minority group increases, the dominant social group will react with social control measures to stem the increase of power by the minority group. Minority threat theory research has shown that there is a ***tipping point*** in the percentage of Blacks in a neighborhood, after which when reached, the presence of Blacks creates a fear of lack of safety and the presence of social disorder.[19] In other words, the presence of Blacks *per se* increases White perceptions and fears of lack of safety and the presence of social disorder. This fear is manifested in political and criminal justice policies in general and specifically the behavior of the police. Both negatively impact Blacks. The political significance of the tipping point and perceptions of Black criminality with increased Blacks in neighborhoods is not whether in fact the presence and percentage of Blacks in a neighborhood brings an increase in criminal activity; it's the belief that it does in the minds of the police and the community that matters.[20]

---

16 "To the extent that longer latencies reflect difficulty, the persistent bias in reaction times suggests that even experts have some trouble processing stereotype-incongruent targets." Id at 1020.

17 Correll et al.

18 Correll et al. at 1020, "[O]fficers from urban, high-crime, predominantly minority districts (environments likely to reinforce stereotypes about Black people) showed greater racial bias in their latencies."

19 See, Ted Chiricos, Michael Hogan, and Marc Gertz, "Racial Composition of Neighborhood and Fear of Crime," *Criminology* 35, no. 1 (1997): 107; Ralph Taylor and Jeanette Covington, "Community structural change and fear of crime," *Social Problems* 40, no. 3 (1993): 374; Wesley Skogan, "Fear of Crime and Neighborhood Change," *Crime and Justice* (1986): 203; Jeanette Covington and Ralph B. Taylor, "Fear of Crime in Urban Residential Neighborhoods," *The Sociological Quarterly* 32, no. 2 (1991): 231; Wesley Skogan, "Crime and the Racial Fears of White Americans," *The Annals of the American Academy of Political and Social Science* 539 (1995): 59; and *Supra* note 5.

20 Chiricos, Hogan, and Gertz. See also, Joshua Correll et al., "Across the Thin Blue Line: Police Officers and Racial Bias in the Decision to Shoot," at 1022, *Supra* note 13.

The political, societal and historical explanations for why Blacks are *per se* dangerous are discussed in Chapters One, Four and Seven in this book, but this fear is not only intellectually or politically determined. This fear of the Black man is also the result of subconscious psychological processing within society and individuals. Social psychology explains that as social beings we all make "quick and almost effortless classifications of a unique individual into broad social categor[ies] [which] lead people to assume that traits generally associated with the category also apply to this particular member."[21]

> Either in the absence of individual information or in spite of it, stereotypic associations can influence an observer's perceptions in a top-down fashion. A stereotype, in essence, can function as a schema to help clarify or disambiguate an otherwise confusing situation. Of particular interest [regarding the police decision to shoot] is the possibility that the officers' decision to fire was influenced by the stereotypic association between African Americans and violence.[22]

This line of research is significant since police encounters with unknown suspects, by definition, involve "ambiguity," which includes the fact that the police do not have all of the information regarding the situation and the unknown subject. This "ambiguity" can "set the stage for bias, prompting the officers to draw on other sources of information, including stereotypes, in an effort to understand what is happening"[23] and for making the determination if the unknown person should be shot.

Social psychology has established that individuals activate concepts of social groups to help define the visual environment they are in and in the process, individual "social group members bring to mind the concepts with which those social groups are associated [and] concepts bring to mind the social groups with which those concepts are associated."[24] This process is called ***bidirectional stereotyping***. This process helps to explain why the presence of Blacks *per se* induces negative reactions. Bidirectional stereotyping occurs when "[s]ocial categories (e.g. Black Americans) tend to be strongly associated with [certain] concepts (e.g., aggressive, musical, poor)" and "the Black racial category functions … for a number of ostensibly race-neutral concepts, such as crime, jazz, basketball, and ghetto. These concepts may trigger clear, visual images of Black Americans."[25] This process of stereotyping is bidirectional because "the social category [Black Americans] influence[s] the likelihood that the category will be activated by the concept, the activism of the concept may bring to mind prototypical

---

21 Joshua Correll et al., "The Police Officer's Dilemma: Using Ethnicity to Disambiguate Potentially Threatening Individuals," *Journal of Personality and Social Psychology*, 83, no. 6 (2002): 1314.

22 Correll et al., "The Police Officer's Dilemma … "

23 Correll et al., "The Police Officer's Dilemma … "

24 Jennifer L. Eberhardt et al., "Seeing Black: Race, Crime, and Visual Processing," *Journal of Personality and Social Psychology* 87, no. 6 at 889, *Supra* note 1.

25 Eberhardt et al. at 877.

category members. Crime, for example, may trigger images of those Black Americans who seem most physically representative of the Black racial category (i.e., those who look highly stereotypical)."[26] Put simply when the concept—crime—is psychologically considered, a specific category is "uploaded" into the unconscious mind—Blacks; and when an individual Black man is viewed, he is categorized with a concept—criminal. Crime and race are psychologically linked. When a police officer is confronted with a situation that does not provide enough information for cognitive level determinations, the ambiguity causes the officer to "upload" information to fill the ambiguity. This subconscious emotional/psychological thinking allows negative perceptions of Blacks to define or provide a context for the actual situation the officer is in and then psychologically the officer acts in accordance with these negative perceptions. The actual negative stereotype does not need to reach conscious cognitive level thinking for the stereotypes to influence the behavior of the officer.

The significance of this bidirectional stereotyping is that "it functions as visual tuning devices—directing people's eyes, their focus, and their interpretations of the stimuli with which they are confronted. To a large extent, these associations cause people to see (and not see) in similar ways, despite individual differences in explicit racial attitudes."[27] "[B]idirectional associations … guide how people process stimuli in their visual environment."[28] Thus when a police officer observes a Black man and the category of criminal is uploaded, the dynamics of the definition of criminal makes the officer more inclined to view and process the observed behavior of the Back man as criminal which leads to police contact. Bidirectional association of crime and race "determine[s] which information is important and worthy of attention and which is not. So, for example, the association of Blacks with crime renders crime objects relevant in the context of Black faces and Black faces relevant in the context of crime."[29] This explains the psychology of what a police officer will consider reasonable articulable suspicion (RAS) evidence of criminality worthy of a Terry Stop and worthy of a Terry Frisk. As discussed in Chapter Six, the Fourth Amendment only requires a police officer to have RAS. Social psychology research provides insight into how an officer initially focuses on Blacks and then forms RAS. The literature explains that the police attention is initiated by bidirectional stereotype bias of Black criminality, and that processing influences how the officer establishes RAS in his mind.

Research has found that this bidirectional stereotype bias against Blacks has allowed police officers to more quickly identify Blacks with crime-related objects in their hands (i.e., weapons). Research has found police officers had the reverse reaction in that they have delayed response to Whites with crime-related objects.[30] Because of racial bias, police don't see White

---

26 Eberhardt et al., "Seeing Black … " at 877.

27 Eberhardt et al., "Seeing Black … " at 877.

28 Eberhardt et al., "Seeing Black …" at 889.

29 Eberhardt et al., "Seeing Black …" at 889.

30 Eberhardt et al., "Seeing Black …" at 890.

criminality because they perceive and define criminality with Black faces. Put another way, when police look for crime and recognize it, they expect it to be Black, not White. Thus, Black crime is more recognized and pursued. People tend to see what they expect to see, how they expect to see it. The problem with this psychological process is that police officers with

> delayed response to White suspects with guns or knives ... may be more likely to get hurt, shot, or killed when confronting White armed suspects in comparison with Black armed suspects. In contrast, unarmed, innocent Blacks may easily become the targets of intense visual surveillance by both police officers and the lay public. With their eyes, perceivers may tie individual Black targets to a group-based suspicion—and sadly, Black people who appear highly stereotypically Black may be the most likely of all to feel the tug. Such processes could indicate that racial profiling may be rooted in more fundamental perceptual processes that previously recognized.[31]

The problem of racial profiling is exacerbated by the fact that "notions of race are so powerful because they can operate through ostensibly race-neutral concepts (such as crime)."[32] The problem is also subtle because "racial stereotyping strongly condemns linking Black people to crime, but not linking crime to Black people. Thus, opposition to stereotyping tends to condemn one aspect of the association, even as it exempts the other" from condemnation.[33] In other words it is racist (with all the negative social and political implications attached) to say Blacks are criminals, but it's socially acceptable (within social conservative circles and politics at the very least) to say criminals are Black.

Police Shoot-and-Don't-Shoot Research: Measuring Impact of Implicit Bias, Blacks, and Police Decisionmaking

Much of the social psychology research on racial bias in police decisionmaking to shoot or not shoot are based on laboratory experiments in which police and non-police participants are provided situations in which a quick decision is required to shoot or not shoot using push buttons to simulate shooting.[34] More recent research has asserted that the push button research methodology to test decision making to shoot or not shoot and the nature of how

---

31 Eberhardt et al., "Seeing Black ..." at 890.

32 Eberhardt et al., "Seeing Black," ... at 890.

33 Eberhardt et al., "Seeing Black," ... at 891.

34 See, Jennifer L. Eberhardt, Phillip Atiba Goff, Valerie J. Purdie, and Paul G. Davies, "Seeing Black: Race, Crime, and Visual Processing," *Journal of Personality and Social Psychology* 87, no. 6 (2004): 876, Joshua Correll, Bernadette Park, Charles M. Judd, Bernd Wittenbrink, Melody S. Sadler, and Tracie Keesee "Across the Thin Blue Line: Police Officers and Racial Bias in the Decision to Shoot," *Journal of Personality and Social Psychology* 92, no. 6 (2007): 1006, Lois James, David Klinger, and Bryan Vila, "Racial and ethnic bias in decisions to shoot seen through a stronger lens: experimental results from high-fidelity laboratory simulations," *Journal of Experimental Criminology* 10, no. 3 (2014): 323, and Joshua Correll, Bernadette Park, Charles M. Judd, and Bernd Wittenbrink,

those decisions are made "are not very well-suited to uncover behavioral biases that operate in the real world."[35] The more recent shoot / don't shoot laboratory experiments use real life simulations through the use of life size video simulations with filmed actors of various races portraying armed and unarmed suspects with participants responding with a real gun.[36] This new research has produced some contrary results to push button picture shoot / don't shoot experiment results. For example, push button experiments found that

> Participants fired at an armed target more quickly of he was an African American than if he was White and they decided not to shoot an unarmed White target more quickly than an unarmed African American target.
>
> . . . .
>
> [W]hereas participants tended to shoot unarmed targets more frequently than they decided not to shoot armed targets, in general, this tendency was stronger when the target was African American than when the target was White.
>
> . . . .
>
> [T]he responses of participants to those stimuli depended at some level on the ethnic category of the target, with potentially hostile targets identified as such more quickly if they were African American rather than White and benign targets identified as such more quickly if they were White rather than African American.[37]

The researchers using the push button method concluded that race was used to "interpret an ambiguously threatening target. When ambiguous behavior is performed by an African American, it seems more hostile, more mean, and more threatening than when it is performed by a White person. Participants also recognize a weapon more quickly and more accurately after seeing an African American face rather than a White face."[38] Researchers using the life size video simulations experiments found that "participants took longer to shoot Black suspects

---

"The Police Officer's Dilemma: Using Ethnicity to Disambiguate Potentially Threatening Individuals," *Journal of Personality and Social Psychology* 83, no. 6 (2002): 1314.

35 Lois James, David Klinger and Bryan Vila, "Racial and ethnic bias in decisions to shoot seen through a stronger lens: Experimental results from high-fidelity laboratory simulations," *Journal of Experimental Criminology* 10, no. 3 (2014): 323, 337.

36 James et al., "Racial and ethnic bias in decisions to shoot," ... See also, Lois James, Bryan Vila, and Kenn Daratha, "Results from experimental trials testing participant responses to White, Hispanic and Black suspects in high-fidelity deadly force judgment and decision-making simulations," *Journal of Experimental Criminology* 9, no. 2 (2013): 189.

37 Joshua Correll et al., "The Police Officer's Dilemma: Using Ethnicity to Disambiguate Potentially Threatening Individuals," *Journal of Personality and Social Psychology* 83, no. 6. Supra note 34 at 1317, 1318.

38 Id at 1320. See also, Jennifer L. Eberhardt et al., "Seeing Black: Race, Crime, and Visual Processing," *Journal of Personality and Social Psychology* 87, no. 6, and Joshua Correll et al., "Across the Thin Blue Line: Police Officers and Racial Bias in the Decision to Shoot," *Journal of Personality and Social Psychology* 92, no. 6. Supra note 34.

than White or Hispanic suspects [and] participants were more likely to shoot unarmed White suspects than unarmed Black or Hispanic suspects. Participants were also more likely to fail to fire at armed Black suspects than armed White or Hispanic suspects. In other words, there was a significant bias favoring Blacks where decisions to shoot were concerned"—a ***reverse racism effect***.[39]

The social psychology literature also investigates how involuntary biochemical reaction to stimuli (i.e., Blacks) involves a heightened level of fear regardless of the behavior of the stimuli. For example, Lois James and her colleagues measured the physiological and brain wave patterns of participants during the life size situations. She measured the decrease in alpha waves of her participants, which are indicative of participants' fear for their safety when they were placed in certain situations. She found that the presence of Blacks, *per se*, caused an increase fear and the depression alpha waves. While the life size video method produced findings that "are contrary to the findings from researchers using button-pushing experimental design" the research results were "[c]onsistent with findings from the button-pushing experiments [that] suspect race significantly predicted threat arousal; participants exhibited greater alpha suppression when facing armed Black as compared to armed White or Hispanic suspects. [T]here was no significant difference in alpha suppression among participants when they faced Hispanic vs. White suspects armed with deadly weapons."[40]

James and her colleagues found that the appearance of Blacks created a psychological fear response regardless of whether the Black suspect was guilty (armed) or innocent (unarmed).[41] "[B]lack suspects elicited a stronger threat response across all levels of difficulty in scenarios that

---

39 Lois James, Bryan Vila, and Kenn Daratha, "Results from experimental trials testing participant responses to White, Hispanic and Black suspects in high-fidelity deadly force judgment and decision-making simulations," Supra note 35 at 328–329. See also, Lois James, Stephen M. James, and Bryan J. Vila, "The Reverse Racism Effect: Are Cops More Hesitant to Shoot Black Than White Suspects?" *Criminology & Public Policy* 15, no. 2 (2016): 1. See also, Infra notes 137–141 and accompanying text for similar results that race was not significantly significant to the decision to shoot Blacks. But see Aaron Roussell, Kathryn Henne, Karen S. Glover and Dale Willits, "Impossibility of a 'Reverse Racism' Effect: A Rejoinder to James, James, and Vila," *Criminology & Public Policy* (January 2017) at http://onlinelibrary.wiley.com/doi/10.1111/1745-9133.12289/full

40 Lois James, Bryan Vila, and Kenn Daratha, "Results from experimental trials testing participant responses to White, Hispanic and Black suspects in high-fidelity deadly force judgment and decision-making simulations," *Supra* note 35 at 335. "Alpha brain waves occur when individuals are relaxed, and tend to be lower in magnitude when individuals are aroused by some external stimuli. The reduction of alpha waves when individuals are exposed to stimuli, often called 'alpha suppression,' can thus be taken as an indicator of arousal provoked by the stimuli. Such neurophysiological arousal has been associated with a threat response so alpha suppression as measured by the difference between alpha waves during rest periods and when research subjects are participating in scenarios can provide an indication of the subconscious component of participants' threat responses." Id. at 331 (internal citations omitted)

41 James et al., "Racial and ethnic bias in decisions to shoot," … at 335–336. Supra note 35.

involved weapons."[42] There was no alpha suppression, enhanced fear response, when faced with Hispanics or Whites with weapons.[43] The authors concluded that "participants' subconscious bias that blacks were more threatening resulted in behaviors that favored blacks over White or Hispanic suspects [and in regard to the] subconscious bias against blacks it had an inverse effect on the speed with which they pulled the trigger . . . ."[44] The authors provided the following as an explanation.

> [T]here is some evidence from the field to support the proposition that an officer's threat bias could cause him or her to tend to take more time to make decisions to shoot people whom they subconsciously perceived as more threatening because of race or ethnicity. This behavioral "counter-bias" might be rooted in people's concerns about the social and legal consequences of shooting a member of a historically oppressed racial or ethnic group.[45]

The proposition is that police will hesitate in using deadly force when encountering Blacks because of the political and social backlash to the use of such force. But the authors found that even accepting this reverse racism effect as true, their results were in line with the push button method research that regardless of the difficulty in the simulation in order to determine guilt or innocence or the time restrictions imposed to make the determination; Blacks were perceived to be more dangerous than Whites and Hispanics *per se.*

Although interesting, the premise of the reverse racism effect has limited credibility due to the lack of criminal sanctions in police shooting cases. As discussed in Chapter Two, fourth amendment jurisprudence is very constraining in finding police use of force subject to criminal culpability or civil liability. There is a difference between police officer culpability or civil liability, which can affect police officer behavior, and the political backlash to police use of force. Political backlash will only affect the individual officer when laws or policies are broken. If the backlash is based on negative optics of a unarmed Black man dead in the street, the individual officer will not be affected, but the police chief may be negatively affected, i.e., fired. The lack of criminal culpability or civil liability and the exclusive province of political backlash make the theory of reverse racism effect theoretically and practically untenable.

Social Psychology: Defining and Explaining Perceptions of Blacks: Police Decision-Making—Why and How it Matters

Police Use of Force Decisionmaking: The Psychology of Pattern Recognition and Threat Assessment and How Race as a Proxy for Crime Explains Racial Perceptions and Decisionmaking

It is important to understand why this research is significant in understanding police shootings. Police are tasked with making assessments of possible crime commission situations,

---

42 James et al., "Racial and ethnic bias in decisions to shoot," . . . at 335

43 James et al., "Racial and ethnic bias in decisions to shoot,". . .

44 James et al., "Racial and ethnic bias in decisions to shoot," . . . at 336.

45 James et al., "Racial and ethnic bias in decisions to shoot," . . . Supra note 35.

interpreting the behavior of people and possible suspects in ambiguous situations, and taking actions to maintain safety and order. Police officers, like all people, develop patterns of thinking through their experiences and expectations and they use those patters to assess new and ambiguous situations. Because human assessments of ambiguous situations are not complete, prior experience and preconceived notions—biases—are used to "fill in the gaps" between what is known and what is not known.

> Cognitive theorists recognize that learning involves the acquisition or reorganization of information or observations and that the relative power of learning varies according to the degree of familiarity with the subject and the number of repeated associations with that subject to which one is exposed. From this perspective, scripts, or cognitive schema, develop as shorthand for categorizing events in memory. They often start as simple and loosely organized networks but can evolve into systematic and complex relationships. Research findings provide evidence that these schemas form a mental model that plays a key role in predicting a person's responses to other individuals, places, and things in future encounters or events. Once formed, persons, places, or things that have familiar characteristics or properties activate these cognitive schemas. For example, it is likely that these schemas or biases will be triggered when judging the behavior of a person that accords with one's preexisting mental image for the group to which the person belongs, especially when the observed behavior is ambiguous. An individual may, therefore, respond in a learned way to another individual who is a member of a particular group with which he or she has experiences or a history. Once a person has identified another individual or a group by an assumed role, future behavioral patterns will be predicted on the previously developed schema. In other words, otherwise-unbiased police officers can "learn" to be biased and acquire and accumulate prejudicial attitudes and beliefs.[46]

Police officers, like all people, use ***pattern recognition* or *schema motor learning*** to make asscssments about their environment.

> Schemas are mental maps people rely on to classify incoming information almost effortlessly and make quick interpretations—sometimes without conscious thought. Consider this situation: An off-duty officer and his/her significant other walk into a coffee shop. The officer's attention is immediately drawn to a heavily tattooed male wearing all red sitting at a table. After the couple exits the shop, the officer says to his/her mate, "I wouldn't expect to see a gang member in this place?" The companion replies, "What gang member?" The officer wonders why he/she is so incredibly perceptive to the surrounding

---

46 Michael R. Smith, and Geoffrey P. Alpert, "Explaining police bias a theory of social conditioning and illusory correlation," *Criminal Justice and Behavior* 34, no. 10 (2007): 1262, 1271–1272. See also, Dennis A. Gioia, and Charles C. Manz, "Linking cognition and behavior: A script processing interpretation of vicarious learning," *Academy of Management Review* 10, no. 3 (1985): 527.

environment while his/her mate seems so clueless. The difference is that the officer has an internal mental model or schemata for a gang member that allows the officer to effectively and internally match patterns of gang member physical characteristics and behaviors to what is seen while moving through one's environment. This perception allows the officer to make a rapid judgment of the individual and assessment of his threat level.[47]

In applying *pattern recognition* or *schema motor learning*

In a law enforcement context, the premise of the theory can by synthesized to this: In order for police officers to be effective and safe, they must learn to recognize certain movements, behaviors, objects and scenario characteristics as being potentially or immediately threatening. Through training and experience, they must develop a list of criteria that when met, call for prompt, definitive action. Depending on the circumstances of the encounter that response can range from seeking cover to create more options, the issuance of additional verbal commands or in the most extreme situations, the delivery of deadly force.[48]

However, when making these assessments, it is important to consider that these quick, often unconscious, judgments could be wrong. The supposed gang member might have been a tourist who is unfamiliar with the city's gang culture, or just a guy who likes to wear red. All humans, not just officers, develop schema to reduce the effort it takes to assess their environments and navigate the countless decisions they face each

---

47 Laura Zimmerman and David Blake, "Officers Facing Criminal Charges: Faulty Decision Making?" *Police Forum* 25, no. 2 (2015): 12, 13. See also, William J. Lewinsky, "Letter to the Task Force" (101–102) In *New York State Task Force on* Police-on-*Police Shootings* (2010). Supra note 1.

48 William J. Lewinsky, "Letter to the Task Force," in *New York State Task Force on* Police-on-*Police Shootings* (2010): 101–102. Supra note 1 at 102. See also, Richard Schmidt, "A schema theory of discrete motor skill learning," *Psychological Review* 82, no. 4 (1975): 225, Seth D. DuCharme, "The Search for Reasonableness in Use-of-Force Cases: Understanding the Effects of Stress on Perception and Performance," *Fordham Law Review* 70, no. 6 (2002): 2515, Richard Schmidt and Timothy Donald Lee, *Motor Control and Learning: A Behavioral Emphasis* (Human Kinetics, 2005). Dennis A. Gioia and Charles C. Manz, "Linking cognition and behavior: A script processing interpretation of vicarious learning," *Academy of Management Review* 10, no. 3 (1985): 527, Charles F. Klahm and Rob Tillyer, "Rethinking the Measurement of Officer Experience and Its Role in Traffic Stop Searches," *Police Quarterly* 18, no. 4 (2015): 343, Leo Carroll and Lilliana Gonzalez, "Out of Place: Racial Stereotypes and the Ecology of Frisks and Searches Following Traffic Stops," *Journal of Research in Crime and Delinquency* 51 (2014): 559, Brad W. Smith and Malcolm D. Holmes, "Police Use of Excessive Force in Minority Communities: A Test of the Minority Threat, Place, and Community Accountability Hypotheses," *Social Problems* 61, (2014): 83, George E. Higgins, Gennaro F. Vito, and Elizabeth L. Grossi, "The Impact of Race on the Police Decision to Search During a Traffic Stop: A Focal Concerns Theory Perspective," *Journal of Contemporary Criminal Justice* 28 (2012): 166, and Christopher Barnum and Robert L. Perfetti, "Race-Sensitive Choices by Police Officers in Traffic Stop Encounters," *Police Quarterly* 13 (2010): 180.

> day. Everyone views the world with some bias, mainly because biases are extremely difficult to recognize and mitigate. Police officers develop biases based on the amount and type of crime they see every day and who they see committing the crimes. The challenge is in not letting bias override assessment of the unique characteristics of each individual event.[49]

If the police officer, through experience and psychological predetermination—or bias—perceives Blacks as criminal and dangerous, the officer is more likely to use non-deadly or deadly force as a preconditioned response. The point of schema motor learning and police quick acting upon these scheme is how the quick recognition of a pending event and how the resulting pre-conditioned response (learned behavior) to the event, as it is enfolding, are operationalized within the officer's reaction and decision to shoot or not to shoot a Black man perceived, *per se*, as criminal and violent.

As discussed later in this chapter, it matters how the social culture, media and society as a whole portrays Blacks. Negative portrayals of Blacks as criminals in fiction and in political discourse influence how society and its protectors—the police—perceive innocent but ambiguous behaviors of Blacks. If a police officer acts through pre-categorized behavior assessments which have attached to them pre-determined responses—the implicit bias that Blacks are criminal and their actions tend to reflect both criminal behavior and danger to the police officer when engaged with Blacks—it becomes more likely Blacks will suffer force at the hands of police.

It should be clear that acting under stereotypes or implicit bias are not the same as acting under prejudice or racism. ***Stereotypes*** are a subconscious tool to make sense of the world in ambiguous situations and "although people often personally disavow negative stereotypes about African Americans, they are well aware that those stereotypes exists [and] this knowledge represents a psychological link between the social category and the trait [which] predispose[s] a participant to make use of the stereotypic trait in interpretations of an ambiguous target—even if he or she does not personally endorse the stereotype."[50] This means that the racial "stereotype measure is not a simple proxy for personal prejudice levels."[51] ***Prejudice or racism*** is the personal acknowledgement of racial bias and accepting them as true with personal moral approval. Racial stereotypes and racial prejudice are strongly correlated only with "lower motivation to control prejudice."[52] Research has shown that Blacks can share

49 Laura Zimmerman and David Blake, "Officers Facing Criminal Charges: Faulty Decision Making?" *Police Forum* 25, no. 2. Supra note 47 at 13.

50 Joshua Correll et al., "The Police Officer's Dilemma: Using Ethnicity to Disambiguate Potentially Threatening Individuals," *Journal of Personality and Social Psychology* 83, no. 6 Supra note 34 at 1321.

51 Correll et al. at 1323.

52 Correll et al. at 1323.

the same racial stereotypic perspectives as Whites.[53] ***Cultural stereotypes*** create a cultural perception of Blacks and they "can be automatically activated even when a perceiver does not endorse them."[54] The point being, police don't consciously decide to shoot an unarmed Black man because he is Black, but that lack of explicit desire is beside the point. The problem is that the police will act upon the cultural stereotype that Blacks are dangerous and, in an ambiguous situation, the police will approach the individual Black man with an assumption that he is a threat to be controlled.

For example, a dark-skinned man from Guinea is chased into his apartment complex by a group of men. The man retreats because these men just came upon him without warning in the dark. When cornered, he turns and shows his wallet with ID when the men yell, "Police!" Upon showing his wallet, he is shot by multiple police officers. Because he looked like a Black rape suspect, the police were prone to use deadly force in the confrontation. Such was the case of Amadou Diallo. The fact that he was innocent of any crime was of no consequence to the jury that found the officers not guilty of all charges.[55] Diallo was Black, afraid, running away from a group of unidentified men who were aggressively chasing him because they believed he was a rape suspect. The police responded to his escape and he was literally, not figuratively, shot dead in the street. As previously discussed in Chapter Two, if the police officer's belief was that Diallo was violent and posed a threat and if the jury believes that the belief was objectively reasonable for the officer to make, there is neither criminal culpability nor civil liability. In the case of Diallo, the jury thought it was reasonable to initially suspect him as a wanted rapist as opposed to being a man on his way home who had a right to avoid a group of White men swooping down upon him in the night. The jury determined it was reasonable for the police to initiate the contact with force of arms and an attitude to match to secure Diallo rather than approach him as a citizen worthy of the assumption of innocence until proven otherwise and fully entitled to his liberty but obligated to answer police questions. Implicit bias occurred in choosing the former attitude and approach. The point is the attitude of the approach, not that the approach was made. Note, Diallo looked like a suspect—he was not determined to be the suspect before the police approached him with force. But he was treated like the suspect nonetheless.

Implicit bias that Blacks are violent and criminal in police perception and decision-making is not the only manifestation of the history of race in America. The theory of ***aversive racism*** explains a more subtle but subversive process. Aversive racism combines implicit bias with *the desire to be seen as not having racial biases.*

> Aversive racism is a specific type of contemporary racism held by people who (a) endorse egalitarian values and beliefs, (b) believe themselves to be unprejudiced, but (c)

53 Correll et al. at 1325.

54 Correll et al. at 1323.

55 Jane Fritsch, "The Diallo Verdict: The Overview; 4 Officers in Diallo Shooting Are Acquitted of All Charges," *New York Times* Feb. 26, 2000.

> unconsciously hold negative beliefs about Blacks and other out-groups, and (d) subtly discriminate in ways that are ambiguous and indirect and that can be rationalized as something other than racial discrimination …
>
> Aversive racism is not considered pathological. Rather, people are predisposed through the normal psychological process of categorization—placing people into known and understandable groups or categories. These group identities are created and reinforced through interpersonal and macro-level social and cultural messages. Through social cues we categorize people as belonging to "our" group or to "other" groups; race is a frequent form of categorization in the United States. Social cues for aversive racism surround us daily within our routine daily lives. Though overt racism has declined, aversive racism is estimated to affect a "substantial portion of well-educated and liberal whites in the United States."[56]

The theory asserts that, "because most Americans now consciously want not only to appear but also to be nonprejudiced yet also possess implicit bias (the defining characteristic of an aversive racist), contemporary racism is expressed in more subtle ways than old-fashioned racism."[57] This type of bias, aversive racism, allows a person to maintain egalitarian values and as such will not directly discriminate against Blacks, but will express bias or racism in subtle and indirect ways through justifying racist ideas "on the basis of some factor other than race. [Aversive racism utilizes] behaviors that ultimately harm Blacks but in ways that allow Whites to maintain their self-image as nonprejudiced and that insulate[s] them from recognizing that their behavior is not colorblind."[58]

---

56 Nancy Rodenborg, Laura A. Boisen, "Aversive Racism and Intergroup Contact Theories: Cultural Competence in a Segregated World," *Journal of Social Work Education* 49, no. 4 (Fall 2013)564-579, 566.

57 Phillip Atiba Goff and John F. Dovidio, *New York State Task Force on Police-on-Police Shootings* at 94. Supra note 1. See also, John F. Dovidio and Samuel L. Gaertner, "Aversive racism and selection decisions: 1989 and 1999," *Psychological Science* 11, no. 4(2000): 315, John F. Dovidio and Samuel L. Gaertner, "Aversive Racism," *Advances in Experimental Social Psychology* 36 (2004): 1, and John F. Dovidio, "The aversive form of racism," (p. 61–89), *Prejudice, Discrimination, and Racism*, ed. Samuel L. Gaertner (Academic Press, 1986).

58 Phillip Atiba Goff and John F. Dovidio, *New York State Task Force on Police-on-Police Shootings* at 94. Supra note 1. See also, Ann V. McGillicuddy-De Lisi, Melissa Daly, and Angela Neal, "Children's Distributive Justice Judgments: Aversive Racism in Euro-American Children?" *Child Development* 77, no. 4 (2006): 1063, Adam R. Pearson, John F. Dovidio, and Samuel L. Gaertner, "The Nature of Contemporary Prejudice: Insights from Aversive Racism," *Social and Personality Psychology Compass* 3, no. 3 (2009): 314, Anish Bavishi, Juan M. Madera, and Michelle R. Hebl, "The effect of professor ethnicity and gender on student evaluations: Judged before met," *Journal Of Diversity In Higher Education* 3, no. 4 (2010): 245, Eric Swank, Hideko Asada, and John Lott, "Student Acceptance of a Multicultural Education: Exploring the Role of a Social Work Curriculum, Demographics, and Symbolic Racism," *Journal of Ethnic and Cultural Diversity in Social Work* 10, no. 2 (2001): 85, Jane Mildred and Ximena Zúñiga "Working with resistance to diversity issues in the classroom: Lessons from teacher training and

Because aversive racism is not explicit, a police officer, for example, does not decide to abuse the rights of Blacks or intend to use force when in contact with Blacks—but if spontaneous behavior is required, unconscious attitudes will be utilized, making the officer "more likely to falsely perceive a gun" when dealing with someone who is Black.[59] Aversive racism allows an officer to utilize negative racial bias and assert that he/she acted without bias by focusing on behavior that on its face may be race-neutral but the bias is what made the behavior appear criminal in the first place—thus initiating a *Terry* Stop and the need to perform a *Terry* Frisk. For example, the officer will say, "I thought he had a gun," which was in fact a wallet. The officer will assert "race had nothing to do with it, I shot a man, not a Black man, I thought he had a gun." The gun, or belief there was one, is a non-racial category worthy of police response—deadly force. But the police officer's subconscious processing (implicit bias/ cultural stereotyping) filtered what the officer saw; a Black man—who is likely (presumed) to be armed and dangerous—and as such, the schema of the officer resulted in the use of force in an ambiguous situation. The Black man is dead because the officer was psychologically prone to be ready to use deadly force. The bias that young Black men are armed and dangerous provides a filter through which the wallet is turned into the gun. Discussed later in this chapter, this error in identifying objects due to racial bias is called discriminability error.

When discussing police action, research has shown that attitudes are not the entire explanation, because less than 10% of all behavior is explained by attitudes.[60] The point is that situations and how they are created—in other words, the social context of an interaction between police and Blacks—can "produce racial inequality even absent racial bias. This is the theory of *racism without racists*—that racial discrimination can occur absent malicious intent."[61] In its broader application and definition, ***racism without racists theory*** proposes that

---

multicultural education," *Smith College Studies in Social Work* 74, no. 2 (2004): 359, Su L. Boatright-Horowitz and Sojattra Soeung, "Teaching White Privilege to White Students Can Mean Saying Good-bye to Positive Student Evaluations," *American Psychologist* 64, no. 6 (2009): 574, Kamilla L. Venner and Steven P. Verney, "Motivational Interviewing: Reduce Student Reluctance and Increase Engagement in Learning Multicultural Concepts," *Professional Psychology: Research and Practice* 42, no. 6 (2015): 116, and Shaun L. Gabbidon, "Exploring the role of race and course content in criminal justice course evaluation: A case study," *Journal of Criminal Justice Education* 13, no. 1 (2002): 101.

59 Phillip Atiba Goff and John F. Dovidio, *New York State Task Force on Police-on-Police Shootings* at 95. *Supra* note 1.

60 Goff and Dovidio citing, J.F. Dovidio, "On the Nature of Contemporary Prejudice: The Third Wave," *Journal of Social Issues* 57 (2001): 829, R. LaPierre, "Attitude vs. Action," *Social Forces* 13 (1934): 230, and A.W. Wicker, "Attitudes vs. Actions: The Relationship of Verbal and Overt Behavioral Responses to Attitude Objects," *Journal of Social Issues* 25, no. 4 (1969): 41.

61 Phillip Atiba Goff and John F. Dovidio, *New York State Task Force on Police-on-Police Shootings, Supra* note 1 at 95. See also the discussion of systemic racism and the *Moynihan Report* in Chapter One and Eduardo Bonilla-Silva, *Racism Without Racists*, Second Edition (Rowman & Littlefield, 2006).

the conception of colorblindness supports the subjugation of Blacks structurally and socially as a replacement for the abandoned system of legal subjugation by Jim Crow.

> [W]hites have developed powerful explanations—which have ultimately become justifications—for contemporary racial inequality that exculpate them from any responsibility for the status of people of color. These explanations emanate from a new racial ideology that I label colorblind racism. This ideology, which acquired cohesiveness and dominance in the late 1960s, explains contemporary racial inequality as the outcome of nonracial dynamics. Whereas Jim Crow racism explained blacks' social standing as the result of their biological and moral inferiority, color-blind racism avoids such facile arguments. Instead, whites rationalize minorities' contemporary status as the product of market dynamics, naturally occurring phenomena, and blacks' imputed cultural limitations.
>
> ...
>
> Color-blind racism is racism without racists! Minimization of racism is a frame that suggests discrimination is no longer a central factor affecting minorities' life chances ("It's better now than in the past" or "There is discrimination, but there are plenty of jobs out there"). This frame allows whites to accept facts [of racial inequality and injustice] and still accuse minorities of being "hypersensitive," of using race as an "excuse," or of "playing the infamous race card." More significantly, this frame also involves regarding discrimination exclusively as all-out racist behavior ... [62]

This more radical application of racism-without-racists theory proposes that modern racism is manifested through benign social and political concepts like favoring "equal opportunity" as opposed to "equal outcomes" and asserts that Whites who support the former have "ignored the effects of past and contemporary discrimination on the social, economic, and educational status of minorities. Therefore, by supporting equal opportunity for everyone without a concern for the savage inequalities between whites and blacks, [support for equal opportunity] safeguards White privilege."[63]

Racism without racists is part of the larger ***critical race theory*** (CRT) scholarship. Critical race theory has been defined as asserting the following regarding race and racism:

> First, racism is ordinary, not aberrational ... Second, most would agree that our system of white-over-color ascendancy serves important purposes, both psychic and material, for the dominant group. ...
>
> The second feature, sometimes called "interest convergence" or material determinism, adds a further dimension. Because racism advances the interests of both white elites (materially) and working-class Caucasians (psychically), large segments of society have little incentive to eradicate it ...

---

62 Eduardo Bonilla-Silva, *Racism Without Racists* at 2, 29 respectively, *Supra* note 61.

63 Bonilla-Silva at 31.

> A third theme of critical race theory, the "social construction" thesis, holds that race and races are products of social thought and relations. [R]aces are categories that society invents, manipulates, or retires when convenient …
>
> Another, somewhat more recent, development concerns differential racialization and its many consequences. Critical writers in law, as well as in social science, have drawn attention to the ways the dominant society racializes different minority groups at different times, in response to shifting needs such as the labor market. … Popular images and stereotypes … shift over time, as well. …
>
> [A] second signature [of] CRT [is] revisionist history. Revisionist history reexamines America's historical record, replacing comforting majoritarian interpretations of events with ones that square more accurately with minorities' experiences.[64]

The ***classical or "idealist" CRT*** approach asserts that racism is a way of thinking, a way to mentally categorize a group of people, or a way to engage in discourse with people. Racism is an attitude and race is a social construction. While ***CRT realists*** assert that racism is a power dynamic in which the dominate race uses racism to maintain dominance in society. Racism is a means to an end—not an actual belief. ***CRT materialists*** maintain that prejudice rather than racism is what is important because prejudice allows for the racialization of unjust treatment of the minority group.[65] CRT presumes that the dynamics of social organization is race domination to some level. CRT asserts that racism is found in the denial of race dominance. CRT asserts that the mere skin color of White provides a social, structural, cultural, political, and economic expectation of superiority to those with Black skin. CRT asserts that words like objectivity, neutrality, color-blindness, meritocracy, and equality under law are used to protect discriminatory results and to maintain White dominance in race-neutral terms.[66]

A full debate on this field of research is outside of the focus of this book. But the observation that certain behaviors and attitudes are connected to race, as discussed in this chapter, is both established in the social psychology literature and, as discussed in Chapters One, Four, Seven, and Eight, these behaviors and attitudes have been detrimental to Blacks—both historically and contemporaneously.

Police Use of Force and Race: Racism Without Racists, Situational Bias, Stereotype Threat, and Other Nuanced Explanations

Racism without racists theory is useful for purposes of understanding police and race interactions, less on the theory of race conflict, but more on the explanation of structural situational

---

64 Richard Delgado and Jean Stefancic, *Critical Race Theory: An Introduction,* Second Edition (NYU Press, 2012), 7–10, 20.

65 Delgado and Stefancic at 17–18.

66 Amy Rector-Aranda, "School Norms and Reforms, Critical Race Theory, and the Fairytale of Equitable Education," *Critical Questions in Education* 7, no. 1 (2016): 1–3 (internal citation omitted).

dynamics of the theory. Police don't consciously determine to oppress or otherwise discriminate against Blacks, *per se*, at the beginning of each shift, but the conception that Black males are more criminal than the White males they encounter colors their perception of Black male behavior, and colors lawful behavior into suspect or criminal behavior in non-racial terms that the officer can assert when making a *Terry* Stop. Thus the result is racist but the situation and the individual officer is not *per se*. The racism without racist theory explains the result of structural and situational dynamics independent of the good faith of the officer making a stop. That is where the focus should be rather than on a theory of White supremacy which politically will never be settled and is counterproductive in social discourse and problem solving.

Just as a side note, as discussed in the introduction of the book, it is plain error to equate the desire for equal opportunity and the rewards of success with protecting White supremacy or to imply that life in America today is little better than life in the early and middle twentieth century for Blacks. Nor is the valuing of individual achievement supportive of White supremacy. The problem with lower Black achievement compared to Whites is multifaceted, complicated, and nuanced and it's no more answered by the assertion earned success is protecting. White supremacy than it is answered by the theory of individual Black social and genetic inferiority. But we digress.

Consider the following in understanding how situational bias and racism without racists occurs: the police initially perceive and take notice of four Black men in a car or a Black man on the street and their blackness uploads, unconsciously, an image of crime or criminality. The police begin processing the actual observed behavior through the lens of racial bias and perceive it as criminal behavior. The officer processes the behavior and mentally creates race-neutral suspicious behavior that he can articulate, which creates a race-neutral reason to engage in the confrontation. This bias can be compounded by the officer mistaking irritation of the driver or the man on the street (the irritation stemming from the belief they were stopped because of their race) with criminal attempt to evade guilt by failing to answer simple and ordinary police stop questions. Racism without racists and aversive racism is also exampled by the politics of social conservatives who *in toto* reject any and all assertions that the initial police attention, which leads to police stops, is explained, in part, by racial prejudice or biased perceptions of Blacks.

The racism-without-racists theory has been linked with the concept of ***stereotype threat***, which can manifest itself when Whites psychologically utilize implicit biases or racial defenses because of fear of being considered overt racists when they perceive themselves as not racists.[67] The reaction to the fear of being stereotyped as overtly racist can produce behavior that in fact is discriminatory. For example, police officers or social conservatives assert that disproportionate incarceration is not caused by police racist behavior or social policies—it's because "you Blacks, as a group, commit more crime than Whites and have poor family structure

---

67 Goff and John F. Dovidio, New York State Task Force on Police-on-Police Shootings Supra note 1 at 96 and *Infra* note 69.

and values. Your criminality causes your incarceration." Thus, they engage in the very racial stereotyping and prejudice they initially propose they do not have.

Research on stereotype threat and police perceptions of Blacks has shown that "officers concerned with being stereotyped as prejudiced are most likely to engage in disparate use of force towards Blacks as opposed to White suspects. Nearly as important, ***implicit bias seems to be less predictive of racially disparate use of force than is the fear of seeming prejudice.***"[68] Research has shown that regarding the dynamic of behavior, (1) the activation of negative stereotypes of an out group is psychologically and physiologically unintentional, unconscious, and automatic, (2) only 10% of behavior is explained by attitudes, but (3) while activation of stereotypes may be unintentional and socially hardwired into human beings as a way to understand their environments, determined self-regulation can reduce prejudice and stereotype uploading and develop unintentional, unconscious, and automatic uploading of non-stereotype processes.[69]

More recent research on stereotype threat has focused on how Blacks react to fears of being labeled as criminal by police and how that belief can create behavior that is considered criminal by the police.[70] "Stereotype threat is a situational threat, based on situational cues and the risk of being stereotyped in a specific situation."[71] Stereotype threat theory on the macro level focuses on the creation of social and political criminal justice policy that works to the detriment of Blacks through the various stages of the criminal justice system.[72]

---

68 Goff and John F. Dovidio, New York State Task Force on Police-on-Police Shootings Supra note 1 at 97 (emphasis added).

69 Supra note 60. See also, Pei Wang, Ya-Ping Yang, Chen-Hao Tan, Xiang-Xia Zhao, Yong-He Liu, and Chong-De Lin. "Stereotype activation is unintentional: Behavioural and event-related potenials evidence," *International Journal of Psychology* 51, no. 2 (2016): 156, Lisa Legault, Isabelle Green-Demers, and Allison L. Eadie. "When internalization leads to automatization: The role of self-determination in automatic stereotype suppression and implicit prejudice regulation," *Motivation and Emotion* 33, no. 1 (2009): 10, and Tiffany A. Ito, Naomi P. Friedman, Bruce D. Bartholow, Joshua Correll, Chris Loersch, Lee J. Altamirano, and Akira Miyake, "Toward a comprehensive understanding of executive cognitive function in implicit racial bias," *Journal of Personality and Social Psychology* 108, no. 2 (2015): 187.

70 Cynthia J. Najdowski, Bette L Bottoms, and Phillip Atiba Goff, "Stereotype Threat and Racial Differences in Citizens' Experiences of Police Encounters," *Law and Human Behavior* 39, no. 5 (2015):463.

71 Najdowski, Bottoms, and Goff at 474.

72 Christina Mancibi, Daniel P. Mears, Eric A. Stewart, Kevin M. Beaver and Justin T. Pickett, "Whites' Perceptions About Black Criminality: A Closer Look at Contact Hypothesis," *Crime and Delinquency* 61, no. 7 (2015): 996, Cynthia J. Najdowski, "Stereotype Threat in Criminal Interrogations: Why Innocent Black Suspects are at Risk for Confessing Falsely," *Psychology, Public Policy, and Law* 17, no. 4 (2011): 562, Ryan J. Hurley, Jakob Jensen, Andrew Weaver, and Travis Dixon, "Viewer Ethnicity Matters: Black Crime in TV News and Its Impact on Decisions Regarding Public Policy," *Journal of Social Issues* 171, no. 1 (2015): 55, and Vesla M. Weaver, "Frontlash: Race and the Development of Punitive Crime Policy," *Studies in American Political Development* 21 (Fall 2007): 230.

Stereotype threat theory on the micro level focuses on how Blacks perceive and react to pre- and post-police presence and initial contact and how Black fear of police is interpreted by White police regarding possible criminal activity.

Stereotype threat theory on the macro level regarding police interactions involves how police perceive Blacks and criminality.[73] "Blacks are concerned they will be judged and treated unfairly by police, in line with those stereotypes. This is concerning because stereotype threat has been shown to have ironic effects on performance and behavior, which inadvertently increase an individual's likelihood of confirming the stereotype."[74]

Najdowski and her colleagues provided college students with situations in which they had to describe what a police officer would do to determine the extent to which the students showed concern about police perception of their behavior unfairly. They provided the participants with a brief story in which they were asked to imagine they were alone at night and saw a police officer in front of them and when they saw the officer looking at them, they were asked what they would think the officer would think of them.[75] Specifically, participants were asked if they thought the officer would think "they were doing something wrong." In other words did they think the officer would think about their behavior unjustly. They were also asked what behaviors they would exhibit when looking at the officer.

The researchers found that Black participants scored higher on the fear that the police officer would think they were doing something wrong than Whites, Blacks scored higher on anticipated anxiety than Whites, and that Blacks would engage in self-regulatory behavior in the presence of police more than Whites. The point being that Blacks, knowing that police have biased perceptions of them, ac differently than Whites when confronted by the police regardless of actual behavior of the police or their own behavior. "Stereotype threat is the concern one experiences when at risk of being perceived in light of a negative stereotype that applies to one's group" and an individual Black male will act in realization of how police see his group, Blacks, as criminals. The problem with this race based anxiety created behavior in Blacks is that it produces the very behavior that looks criminal to police and judges.[76] Najdowski and her colleagues found when Blacks came into contact with police, all three stereotype threat behaviors—anticipated anxiety, self-regulatory efforts (avoidance) and suspicious behavior (viewed from the perspective of the police)—were significantly and positively correlated.[77]

---

73 Cynthia J. Najdowski, Bette L Bottoms, and Phillip Atiba Goff "Stereotype Threat and Racial Differences in Citizens' Experiences of Police Encounters," at 463–464. Supra note 70.

74 Najdowski, Bottoms, and Goff at 464

75 Najdowski, Bottoms, and Goff at 467

76 Najdowski, Bottoms, and Goff at 464 (internal citation omitted). See also, Cynthia J. Najdowski, "Stereotype Threat in Criminal Interrogations: Why Innocent Black Suspects are at Risk for Confessing Falsely." Supra note 72.

77 Cynthia J. Najdowski, Bette L Bottoms, and Phillip Atiba Goff "Stereotype Threat and Racial Differences in Citizens' Experiences of Police Encounters," at 469 Supra note 70.

The reason understanding stereotype threat is significant is that Blacks, being psychologically predisposed to being afraid that the police will suspect them as criminal because of their race, will change their behavior to escape the notice of the police. The problem is that such behavior looks suspicious to police and provides justification for a *Terry* Stop. As discussed in Chapter Six, suspicious evasion of the police creates reasonable articulable suspicion under Supreme Court jurisprudence. When a Black male is observed by the police and he fails to look the officer in the eye, fidgets or otherwise fails to give clear answers or retreats from an area so as not to further interact with the police due to his fear of being treated unjustly (i.e., suspected of being criminal due to racial bias); from the perspective of the officer, the Black male is being avoidant and is being suspicious, i.e., criminal. The resulting police assumption of guilt is the result of the stereotype threat reaction of the Black male. The Black male is stopped because of his fear of police stereotyping, not because of actual criminal behavior. The police officer is not racist *per se*, but the Jim Crow level policy and historical abuse of Blacks, although ended, has created a psychological dynamic in which the interaction between the Black male and the police officer results in racist outcomes—i.e., racism without racists theory.

Najdowski and her colleagues' study found that White males significantly disagreed that police would judge them unfairly and did not fear the police would engage them. This differential between White and Black expectations, the researchers hypothesized, is explained by the difference in experience with police between Blacks and Whites. Whites don't have the historical experience of negative encounters with police and thus even if they fear that the police may engage them unjustly, they don't believe that it was due to their race nor do they believe that negative consequences may occur as a result of the contact. ***This difference in life experience explains why Blacks and Whites perceive the police and the criminal justice system so diametrically differently and why Blacks behave with trepidation when confronted by police in situations of isolation and police hegemony over them.***

White young men don't fear the police because, as Najdowski and her colleagues explain, they don't need to because their experiences have not made them fear the police. This lack of fear of police by Whites because they are White was described by Najdowski and her colleagues as ***stereotype lift***.[78] An example of the phenomenon of stereotype lift, the lack of fear of police because of the ***privilege of Whiteness***, was the case of Caren Turner in March 2018. Turner was a commissioner on the New York New Jersey Port Authority. Turner got a call from her daughter who was a passenger in car with four of her friends and she told her mother that the Tenafly, New Jersey, police had stopped the car and was having it towed. Turner drove to the scene and verbally attacked the police officers, demanded that they refer to her as commissioner, informed them that New Jersey police were under her jurisdiction, that the officers had to report to her why the car was stopped, that she was friend with the mayor, and

78 Najdowski et al., "Stereotype Threat and Racial Differences," ... at 472 (internal citation omitted).

after demanding explanation told the officers that they acted shamefully and walked away telling the officers to "shut the fuck up."[79]

The stereotype lift is in the fact that she thought she had the right and power, and that she acted in accordance with that thought, to verbally berate three police officers on the highway while they were conducting a lawful traffic stop without the fear of ending up face down on the hood of the police car in handcuffs or worse. Turner's behavior is also an example of White privilege. The privilege, as discussed below, was manifested in two way. First, Turner had no fear to speak to the police and she believed she could do so as she did. Second, the privilege is reflected by the fact that no Black woman—and certainly no Black male—would have felt free to drive up upon a police action, insert herself into it, demand to be spoken to by her title, and curse the officers to their faces without fear of being arrested. In fact, a Black woman would not entertain the idea that such behavior would not result in arrest. Consider when basketball star Sterling Brown was confronted by a police officer in January 2018 due to Brown's illegal parking of his car in an empty parking lot at two in the morning.[80] Upon telling the officer not to push him, the officer called for backup. When Sterling responded to the officer "you don't own me" when the officer told him "I own this" the officer, backed by four other officers, tased Sterling after he was forced to the ground by the four officers. Upon publication of the incident the mayor and police chief stated at a press conference that the officers acted inappropriately and they were being disciplined.

The social fact of White privilege (stereotype lift) was manifested in the ability of Turner to berate the officers in broad daylight and being able to walk away; while Sterling alone in a deserted parking lot at night after defending his right not to be pushed and not accepting being told by the officer "I own this" found himself face down in the street and then tased.

Stereotype lift allows Whites to feel safe around police, when isolated, because the stereotype they have (non-criminal and due of respect) allows them not to fear police negative criminal stereotypes that are inflicted on Blacks. Stereotype lift can also lead to aggressive or assertive behavior of Whites in the presence of police due to the lack of fear that police will respond violently towards them. This dynamic of dehumanization and infrahumanization, discussed below, in which White men are inoculated from the fear of being judged and

---

79 See video, Port Authority Commissioner Telling Cops: 'You may shut the f*** up!' at https://www.youtube.com/watch?v=1xjwZ110WBY (March 31, 2018) and Alexandra Faul, "Transit official's videotaped berating of police ends with her resignation" ABC News (April 25, 2018) at http://abcnews.go.com/US/transit-officials-videotaped-berating-police-ends-resignation/story?id=54720268

80 Body cam shows the violent arrest of NBA's Sterling Brown—Daily Mail at (https://www.youtube.com/watch?v=pTMKEntV9xc), Milwaukee police chief apologizes for treatment of Bucks' Sterling Brown (https://www.youtube.com/watch?v=dI4vSdAirj4) and Milwaukee chief apologizes for arrest of Bucks guard Brown (https://www.youtube.com/watch?v=aoZxaCpqbvY). See also, discussion of police training officer who discusses why the police aggravated the situation "Police instructor analyzes Sterling Brown taser video" (https://www.youtube.com/watch?v=2KtI7ex1Xeo)

treated as criminal due to their membership of being in the in-group (White) and feeling invulnerable to police suspicions, in other scholarship is called ***White privilege***. White privilege encompasses what Whites don't have to think about or consider regarding their safety or belonging in America. White privilege is the enjoyment of being perceived and treated as good, just, nonthreatening, and worthy of being left alone. It's the right to be assumed to deserve the benefits of being assumed law abiding and the curtesy that comes with it. All of these benefits are based on nothing more than mere existence. All of these assumptions are respected and expected from the social, political, and law enforcement agencies with the power to treat people conversely. The privilege is in the enjoyment of these assumptions and benefits without action or the need to assert them. White privilege encompasses the fact that Blacks, on various personal, social, political, societal, and rhetorical levels, are obligated to affirmatively assert and demand these assumptions and benefits. They have to demand them against the social and societal suspicion or hesitation of applying them to Blacks without debate, as they are applied to Whites in America.

Recent research makes the research on the psychology of race perception even more multivariate by considering the concept of ***dehumanization***[81] which is different than racism or prejudice/implicit bias. Dehumanization is different than racism or racial bias in that dehumanization ascribes less humanity to a group while racism or bias ascribes negative behaviors or attributes to a group. Racism is the conscious acceptance of negative racial biases of a certain group (Blacks) and intentionally treating individual members of that group with those biases. Prejudice is knowledge of having those negative racial biases and being influenced by them in interactions with individual members of that group. Dehumanization differs from both in that it removes from a group (Blacks) humanness or ascribes to Blacks the level of animal.[82]

---

81 For example see, Phillip Atiba Goff, Matthew Christian Jackson, Brooke Allison Lewis Di Leone, Carmen Marie Culotta and Natalie Ann DiTomasso, "The Essence of Innocence; Consequences of Dehumanizing Black Children," *Journal of Personality and Social Psychology* 106, no. 4 (2014): 526, Naira Delgado, Armando Rodríguez-Pérez, Jeroen Vaes, Jacques-Philippe Leyens, and Verónica Betancor, "Priming Effects of Violence on Infrahumanization," *Group Processes & Intergroup Relations* 12, no. 6 (2009): 699, Emanuele Castano and Roger Giner-Sorolla, "Not quite human: Infrahumanization in response to collective responsibility for intergroup killing," *Journal of Personality and Social Psychology* 90, no. 5 (2006): 804, Lasana T. Harris and Susan T. Fiske "Dehumanizing the Lowest of the Low: Neuroimaging Responses to Extreme Out-Groups," *Psychological Science* 17, no. 10 (2006): 847, Stephen Loughnan and Nick Haslam, "Animals and Androids: Implicit Associations between Social Categories and Nonhumans," *Psychological Science* 18, no. 2 (2007): 116, and Friederike Eyssel and Xanthula Ribas. "How to be good (or bad): On the fakeability of dehumanization and prejudice against outgroups." *Group Processes & Intergroup Relations* 15, no. 6 (2012): 804.

82 Id. See also, Flavia Albarello and Monica Rubini, "Reducing dehumanisation outcomes towards Blacks: The role of multiple categorisation and of human identity," *European Journal of Social Psychology* 42, no. 2 (2012): 875.

While dehumanization reduces the out-group to less-than-human or animal-level significance, ***infrahumanization*** looks at value imputation, both within a group and between groups. Because "people tend to reserve human essence for their in group … humanity is operationalized in terms of secondary emotions, which are differentially attributed to social groups."[83] Infrahumanization allows members of the in-group (Whites) to hold positive attributes. Those within the group tend to be recognized as holding those attributes of humanity that are positive and they are associated with infra-members of the group. Those who are not within the group (the out group) tend to enjoy lowered attribution of the same positive attributes associated with the in-group. Thus "infrahumanization has characterized the phenomenon as a mild and subtle form of emotional prejudice."[84] Both dehumanization and infrahumanization is a process of thinking about ones' own group and members of another group. Dehumanization is about seeing members of another group as not being human at all and thus immune from moral codes of treatment held by ones' group, but infrahumanization involves seeing the out-groups as human, thus deserving of a minimal level of moral treatment, but it elevates the humanity of the in-group while reducing the positive human values of the outgroup.[85] The significance of the process of infrahumanization is that it is emotional and

---

83 Friederike Eyssel and Xanthula Ribas, "How to be good (or bad): On the fakeability of dehumanization and prejudice against outgroups," *Group Processes & Intergroup Relations* 15, no. 6 at 804. Supra note 81.

84 Friederike Eyssel and Xanthula Ribas at 809. See also, Verónica Betancor Rodriguez, Alexandra Chas Villar, Armando Rodríguez-Pérez, and Naira Delgado Rodríguez, "Infrahumanization in children: An evaluation of 70 terms relating to humanity," *Psicothema* 28, no. 1 (2016): 53, Naira Delgado Rodríguez, Armando Rodríguez-Pérez, Jeron Vaes, Verónica Betancor Rodríguez, and Jacques-Philippe Leyens, "Contextual Variations of Infrahumanization: The Role of Physical Context and Territoriality," *Basic and Applied Social Psychology* 34, no. 5 (2012): 456, Jacques-Philippe Leyens, "Retrospective and Prospective Thoughts about Infrahumanization," *Group Processes & Intergroup Relations* 12, no. 6 (2009): 807, John Martin, Mark Bennett, and Wayne S. Murray "A developmental study of the infrahumanization hypothesis," *British Journal of Developmental Psychology* 26, no. 2 (2008): 153, Brezo P. Cortes, Stéphanie Demoulin, Ramon T. Rodriguez, Armando P. Rodriguez, and Jacques-Philippe Leyens, "Infrahumanization or Familiarity? Attribution of Uniquely Human Emotions to the Self, the Ingroup, and the Outgroup," *Personality and Social Psychology Bulletin* 31, no. 2 (2005): 243, and Jeroen Vaes, Maria Paola Paladino, Luigi Castelli, Jacques-Philippe Leyens, and Anna Giovanazzi, "On the Behavioral Consequences of Infrahumanization: The Implicit Role of Uniquely Human Emotions in Intergroup Relations," *Journal of Personality and Social Psychology* 85, no. 6 (2003): 1016.

85 Jacques-Philippe Leyens, Stephanie Demoulin, Jeroen Vaes, Ruth Gaunt and Maria Paola Paladino, "Infra-humanization: The Wall of Group Differences," *Social Issues and Policy Review* 1, no. 1 (2007): 139–172, 142–144. See also, Friederike Eyssel and Xanthula Ribas, "How to be good (or bad): On the fakeability of dehumanization and prejudice against outgroups," *Group Processes & Intergroup Relations* 15, no. 6 at 810, Supra note 81. See also, *Group Processes & Intergroup Relations* Special Issue: Dehumanization: Humanity and its Denial 12, no. 6 (2009).

people may not be aware of the distinction in the lack of positive emotional attributions they are making to an outgroup, but those attributions can be affected by cognitive influences.

Infrahumanization is exampled in an emotional reaction to behavior that is cruel or evil against an out-group which is justified or otherwise discounted of negativity when committed by fellow members of the in-group. In other words, people can emotionally and then cognitively justify observed cruelty if committed by members of one's own group.[86] This ability to justify cruelty or discount it as not cruel in the first place can also explain why an individual who has not committed the cruelty will be prone not to perceive the out-group as worthy of the kindness that would be expected for the in-group; as well as being more prone to condone or even participate in the cruelty or at the very least not perceive the treatment of the out group as cruelty.

The post-Jim Crow manifestation of infrahumanization, backed by implicit racism, is the idea that Blacks need to be socially controlled because they are criminal. Blacks are criminal, so they receive less sympathy for injustice they may suffer at the hands of the police or criminal justice system. An example of infrahumanization occurs when young Black men complain of being stopped and frisked when they have done nothing wrong or worthy of police attention and the response is "Well, it stops crime" or "Blacks disproportionately commit crime, so police disproportionate stopping of Blacks is normal." The infrahumanization is in the callous disregard or lack of sensitivity to the experiences of Blacks by Whites and social conservatives. Infrahumanization is the willful ignorance and blindness to the difference in treatment by police of Blacks in poor and less politically and economically stable communities and the treatment by police in more affluent and politically assertive communities. Infrahumanization is reflected in White privilege when ***White privilege*** is defined by ***the right and ability not to see, experience, or care about the historical and contemporary Black experience with the police.***

Research on racial prejudice focuses on the attributes imposed on the out group. Classical research on dehumanization and infrahumanization originated in the 1950s when Blacks were perceived as lazy and Jews were perceived as overly ambitious and both were not to be trusted.[87] But not all infrahumanization emotional prejudices are the same, rather they are on a continuum. The most extreme dehumanize the out-group in total and result in the German camps of the 1940s while less extreme levels simply impute lower levels of respectability. The less extreme levels can be consciously and unconsciously. There is content to stereotypes that tend to dehumanize the out-group as well as attribute positive perceptions to the in-group. For example, the in-group can be the police, and the society the police protect and the out-group can be criminals, or those who oppose police abuse. In this dynamic, the

---

86 Emanuele Castano and Roger Giner-Sorolla, "Not quite human: Infrahumanization in response to collective responsibility for intergroup killing," *Journal of Personality and Social Psychology* 90, no. 5. Supra note 81.

87 Lasana T. Harris and Susan T. Fiske, "Dehumanizing the Lowest of the Low: Neuroimaging Responses to Extreme Out-Groups," *Psychological Science* 17, no. 10 at 847. Supra note 81.

in-group dehumanizes those who make assertions of abuse by police as being pro-criminal by discounting their complaints as being false or encouraging lawlessness.

Dehumanization occurs cognitively and infrahumanization occurs emotionally and both utilize stereotypes as well as minority threat theory to reduce the out-group both on a macro (group) and micro (individual) level. Infrahumanization places groups in levels of social and emotional acceptance and those levels help explain how each group receives or is deprived of imputed human warmth from other groups. Thus there is logic to cognitive dehumanization and emotional infrahumanization. People look at characteristics of people within a group and apply them to all members of the group and to individuals within a group. People are humanized or dehumanized based on group membership and the imputed characteristics of that group. It is through this emotional and psychological process that people are seen as more or less than.

This process is explanative of research that has found that police misperceive Black children as older than they are, more responsible for their actions, less deserving of the presumption of childlike innocence, more likely to be treated as adults within the criminal justice system, and more likely to suffer use of force by police than White children of the same age.[88]

Social psychology and criminal justice research on police perceptions have shown that police, like the general population, hold negative implicit and unconscious biases about Blacks. But more recent research has shown that these biases may not be predictive of negative treatment of Blacks but what is predictive is the dehumanization of Blacks.[89] Goff and his colleagues conducted a study of sixty urban police officers in which the officers were provided with twelve scenarios of male perpetrators of different races and they were asked to determine the age and culpability of each target male. Further, the officers were asked to complete racial bias determinative tests and the internal affairs department provided the researchers with service and psychological backgrounds of each officer and their history of incidents in their use-of-force reports. Thus the researchers were able to match actual police officer histories with psychological evaluations and laboratory experimentation. The research sought to determine if "implicit dehumanization facilitate[s] racial disparities in the perception of child suspects in real world policing contexts" through the hypothesis that "dehumanization would predict racial disparities in the amount of force used against Black children ... participants would overestimate the age of Black male children [and] participants would rate Black suspects as more culpable (i.e., lacking in innocence) than White and Latino suspects."[90]

Dehumanization is manifested when Black children are perceived less childlike in age and not enjoying the same deference in their behavior, being accorded as childlike indiscretions,

---

88 Phillip Atiba Goff, Matthew Christian Jackson, Brooke Allison Lewis Di Leone, Carmen Marie Culotta and Natalie Ann DiTomasso, "The Essence of Innocence; Consequences of Dehumanizing Black Children," *Journal of Personality and Social Psychology* 106, no. 4. Supra note 81.

89 Goff et al. at 532–533.

90 Goff et al.

but rather being perceived as older, more responsible for their actions, and being treated more as adults (with the corresponding sanctions) than White children of the same age and behavior. In other words, Black children are seen more as adults than little children and they are not perceived as childlike or given the same treatment of innocence and deference that White children are given. The dehumanization is the difference between the two treatments. This type of dehumanization can result in police seeing a Black child with a toy gun as a threat to be shot rather than as a child to be tempered. The former being evidenced in the shooting of Tamir Rice in Columbus, Ohio, in November, 2014. Tamir was 12 years old and 195 pounds, but the officers thought he was over 18 years old and 185 pounds.[91]

Goff and his colleagues found that police, as did other non-police participants in similar study groups,[92] (1) "overestimated the age of Black felony suspects to a greater degree than that of Black misdemeanor suspects as well as all other suspects," (2) "Black 13-year-olds were miscategorized as adults by police officers (average age error = 4.59)" years, (3) "[t]here were no differences in age overestimations between White felony suspects and White misdemeanor suspects," (4) "White felony suspects were rated as significantly younger than both Black felony suspects and Latino suspects," (5) "Black felony suspects were also rated as older than Latino felony suspects," (6) "White misdemeanor suspects were also rated younger than both Black misdemeanor suspects and Latino misdemeanor suspects," (7) "White targets were rated as less culpable when associated with felonies, whereas Black targets were rated as significantly more culpable when associated with felonies," and (8) "a moderately strong relationship between age errors and ratings of culpability such that the older an officer thought a child was, the more culpable that child was rated for their suspected crime."[93]

Because "we were able to link our attitude measures to disparities in use of force toward citizens of different races" by comparing police psychological and use of force records, they found "evidence that anti-Black dehumanization predicts racially disparate treatment of Black children in contexts where measures of racial bias do not."[94] In other words, while measures of racism did not explain behavior, measures of implicit dehumanization process (measured by

---

91 See police officers' statements at http://i2.cdn.turner.com/cnn/2015/images/12/01/officer.loehmann.statement.pdf and http://i2.cdn.turner.com/cnn/2015/images/12/01/officer.garmback.statement.pdf. See also FBI final investigation report, at http://prosecutor.cuyahogacounty.us/pdf_prosecutor/en-US/Tamir%20Rice%20Investigation/Crawford-Review%20of%20Deadly%20Force-Tamir%20Rice.pdf, and the final investigation report from the County Prosecutor at https://assets.documentcloud.org/documents/2657234/Rice-Case-Report-FINAL-FINAL-12-28a.pdf. See also CNN reports on the shooting at http://www.cnn.com/2015/12/01/us/tamir-rice-investigation-officer-timothy-loehmann-statement/ and http://www.cnn.com/2015/06/13/us/tamir-rice-report/

92 Phillip Atiba Goff, Matthew Christian Jackson, Brooke Allison Lewis Di Leone, Carmen Marie Culotta and Natalie Ann DiTomasso, "The Essence of Innocence; Consequences of Dehumanizing Black Children," *Journal of Personality and Social Psychology* 106, no. 4. Supra note 81 at 529–532, 535–539.

93 Goff et al. at 534–535

94 Goff et al. at 535

the level of associating Blacks with apes) were predictive of use of force on Black child suspects, the overestimating age of Blacks children and perceptions of culpability even controlling for racial bias.[95] These results have a policy impact on how the criminal justice system in general, and how the police on the street specifically, interact with Blacks children. They are perceived more adult-like than they should be, they are more likely to be treated as adults by the police, and more likely to be arrested, and these results disparities are less the result of overt racism than the dehumanizing of Blacks over time.[96]

Goff and his colleagues in a separate study used a larger group of one hundred police officers in an urban police department to replicate the results of the previous study. The same results were found in the larger group.[97] The research concluded that the more Blacks were associated with apes the more likely the police would have violent encounters with Black youth.[98]

As discussed in Chapter Five, in 1783 the great Chief Justice Mansfield wrote that there was no difference between Black slaves and horses regarding the killing of either of them, and in 1857 the Chief Justice of the United States Supreme Court held that there was no law regarding Blacks that a White man is bound to respect. More than three hundred years later, research[99] has shown that the association of Blacks with apes is still contemporary[100] and results in less sympathy for Blacks when subjected to use of force.

> Contemporary approaches to racial prejudice suggest that these more egregious forms of racial bias have been relegated to the past. It is commonly thought that old-fashioned prejudice has given way to a modern bias that is implicit, subtle, and often unintended. This new understanding of racial bias may have led researchers and laypeople alike to believe that the dehumanization and subjugation of Blacks was primarily a historical phenomenon. However, as recently as the early 1990s, California state police euphemistically referred to cases involving young Black men as N.H.I.—No Humans Involved. One of the officers who participated in the Rodney King beating of 1991 had just come from

95 Goff et al.

96 Goff et al.

97 Goff et al. at 536

98 Goff et al.

99 .Phillip Atiba Goff, Matthew Christian Jackson, Brooke Allison Lewis Di Leone, Carmen Marie Culotta and Natalie Ann DiTomasso, "The Essence of Innocence; Consequences of Dehumanizing Black Children" 106 (4) *Journal of Personality and Social Psychology* at 527, 532 Supra note 81.

100 Dora Capozza, Giulio Boccato, Luca Andrighetto, and Rossella Falvo "Categorization of Ambiguous Human/Ape Faces: Protection of Ingroup but Not Outgroup Humanity" at 778 Supra note 11 citing Phillip Atiba Goff, Jennifer L. Eberhardt, Melissa J. Williams, and Matthew Christian Jackson. "Not yet human: implicit knowledge, historical dehumanization, and contemporary consequences" 94(2) *Journal of personality and social psychology* 292 (2008).

> another incident in which he referred to a domestic dispute involving a Black couple as "something right out of Gorillas in the Mist." ...
>
> A series of six studies provide evidence of a bidirectional association between Blacks and apes that can operate beneath conscious awareness yet significantly influence perception and judgments. ... This is consistent with prior research showing that, whereas Blacks and crime were positively associated, Whites and crime were negatively associated. That Whites and apes are negatively associated is also consistent with early biologically racist accounts of evolution that rendered Blacks as least evolved (ergo closest to apes) and Whites as most evolved (ergo farthest from apes).
>
> ... [E]ven controlling for implicit anti-Black prejudice, the implicit association between Blacks and apes can lead to greater endorsement of violence against a Black suspect than against a White suspect. [101]

It is a general human characteristic to treat children in a different manor than adults. Children are, by definition, perceived and treated as innocent and not as culpable as adults and certain attributes of childhood—childlike behavior and immaturity—mitigate culpability for actions. The dehumanization factor is that Black children are not afforded these protections compared to White children.[102] They are perceived as more culpable, thus less innocent or at least less deserving of non-punitive treatment, and older than they are.

Again, the point being, the ***differentials in treatment are not based on racism.*** The differentials in treatment, as the field social psychology reveals, are more complicated. But ***the impact of dehumanization, infrahumanization, racial stereotyping, bidirectional stereotyping, and aversive racism can put police use of force—due to pattern recognition and motor-learning responses to fear of Blacks—in a racial context outside of explicit racism.*** Social psychology provides a context to understand how Blacks are perceived and treated by the criminal justice system and the disparities that occur outside of and exclusive of assertions of racism.

The significance of dehumanization and infrahumanization, compared to racism or stereotype bias, is they involve cognitive and emotional perception and imputed value on out-groups. Both dehumanization and infrahumanization mitigate the human value of people and allow out-groups to be perceived as less-than. The process of racism and prejudice is the stereotyping of the out-group into categories with negative social connotations and treatment. The significance of infrahumanization research is that it establishes that racism is not always the

---

101 Phillip Atiba Goff, Jennifer L. Eberhardt, Melissa J. Williams, and Matthew Christian Jackson, "Not Yet Human: Implicit Knowledge, Historical Dehumanization, and Contemporary Consequences," *Journal of Personality and Social Psychology* 94, no. 2 at 292, 304. Supra note 100 (internal citation omitted).

102 Phillip Atiba Goff, Matthew Christian Jackson, Brooke Allison Lewis Di Leone, Carmen Marie Culotta and Natalie Ann DiTomasso, "The Essence of Innocence; Consequences of Dehumanizing Black Children," *Journal of Personality and Social Psychology* 106, no. 4 at 539–541. Supra note 81.

determinative factor in explaining disproportionate treatment of Blacks. The infrahumanization or the emotional detachment of the in-group to the experience of Blacks and their pain regarding that experience is independent of classical racism or prejudice as an explanation of negative disproportionate treatment and outcomes of Blacks within the criminal justice system in general and specifically, police encounters resulting in deadly and non-deadly use of force.

One aspect of dehumanization and racial threat scholarship is the study of how images of Black people, and specifically Black males, are cognitively portrayed in society. Consider how Blacks are portrayed in news stories,[103] T.V. shows, and in movies, as criminal or otherwise socially suspect. In commercials that portray the American middle-class ethic, are the actors more likely to be White than Black? Commercials that portray less-than-flattering dynamics of life in America, are the actors more likely to be Black? In police T.V. episodes in which the focus is on a violent criminal (rapist or murderer) is the victim more likely to be White and then is the criminal more likely to be Black?

> Over the last two decades, perceptions about crime and offending have been studied under the context of what scholars have designated as the "racialization of crime"—that is, the increasingly prominent emphasis of race in discussions about offending. Much of this work has centered on examining the extent to which minorities are linked with accounts of crime. Findings from several studies indicate that the news media disproportionately report on crimes that involve African American offenders. For example, one study of local news media crime reporting found that African Americans were twice as likely as Whites to be depicted as perpetrators, 6 times more likely to be portrayed as perpetrators than as law enforcement officers, and overrepresented as criminals, representing close to 37% of the perpetrators depicted whereas comprising only one fifth of those arrested according to official crime reports.
>
> A similar line of research has found that in addition to this "prototypical" offender depiction, African Americans, as compared with other races, are also more likely to be portrayed as violent and threatening criminals in the news media. [Research has] found that among the crime stories featured during a 6-months sample period in Chicago, 84% of news reports about Black perpetrators involved violent offenses (e.g., homicide) rather than nonviolent crimes; in comparison, only 71% of crime stories about White perpetrators involved violent crimes. In this same study ... Black suspects were significantly more likely to be featured being physically held or restrained by officers (38%) compared with White offenders (18%).[104]

103 Ryan J. Hurley, Jakob Jensen, Andrew Weaver, and Travis Dixon, "Viewer Ethnicity matters: Black Crime in TV News and Its Impact on Decisions Regarding Public Policy." Supra note 72.

104 Christina Mancibi, Daniel P. Mears, Eric A. Stewart, Kevin M. Beaver and Justin T. Pickett, "Whites' perceptions About Black Criminality: A Closer Look at Contact Hypothesis," at 998–999. Supra note 72 (internal citation omitted).

"A substantial body of content analytic work has demonstrated that news and entertainment programming offer largely negative depictions of diverse groups, varying based on the type of content and the particular group. Moreover, a growing number of studies have documented adverse effects of exposure to stereotypical portrayals on both ethnic minority and majority audiences."[105]

For example, consider how positive versus negative images of Black males are portrayed in movies. Consider all the positive Black male roles Denzel Washington has made over his career, yet of his five Best Actor Oscar nominations his only win came from when he portrayed a psychopathic homicidal police officer in *Training Day*. Consider the 2017 movie, *Hidden Figures*, based on the true story about three Black women who were responsible for the successful orbital flight of John Glenn in 1962 as well as designing computer programs to make various NASA computers function together despite being victims of serious overt racism. The movie also portrayed the husband of one of the women, a Black Lt. Colonel in the U.S. Army, with positive family values that would have made Jerry Falwell and any member of the Christian Coalition of the 1980s bow in respect. That movie was nominated for best movie in 2017 but lost to a movie, *Moonlight*, which was about the pains and sufferings of a Black man dealing with his drug-addicted mother and how that experience led him to sell drugs when he grew up. My point is look at what is portrayed as the best story of the year. A story of intergenerational drug use and crime by Blacks is honored over a story of three family-oriented, highly educated Black women being responsible for America's first successful space flight in the face of overt racism. The portrayal of Blacks as drug dealers and criminals had more salience than the portrayal of the true story of Blacks being at the forefront of advanced mathematics and computer science in the early 1960s. Conservatives have their racism, but Hollywood liberals have their own.

The point is that human beings understand the world through their own experiences and then by social and media portrayals of the world outside of their personal experiences. Both create subconscious and conscious perceptions and definitions of the world. If Blacks are portrayed by the media and political discourse as violent and criminal, this helps conflate crime and Blacks in the collective mind of society.

As any advertising executive will tell you, television can shape your positive or negative perceptions of things. The whole point of commercial advertising is to get people to have a positive desire for some product, whether they actually need it or not. Political advertising is about creating negative perceptions of an opponent, regardless of whether it's true or not. Political advertising also is about creating positive perceptions of one self, also regardless of whether it is true or not.

In both commercial and political advertising, the goal is to create and/or change how a person or product is viewed both long and short term, and how emotional and/or cognitive

105 Ryan J. Hurley, Jakob Jensen, Andrew Weaver, and Travis Dixon, "Viewer Ethnicity Matters: Black Crime in TV News and Its Impact on Decisions Regarding Public Policy," 156–157. Supra note 72 (internal citation omitted).

opinions can be invoked upon viewing or considering a product and/or person. This is called ***cognitive accessibility***.[106] Cognitive accessibility is the ability of an opinion or perception to be invoked without independent cognitive thinking or processing. It allows for automatic association between concepts or individuals. For example, you are told a candidate is a Democrat and you upload negative perceptions of the party and connect them to the candidate regardless of the fact that you know nothing about the individual candidate or his/her ideas.

Cognitive accessibility occurs when mental shortcuts connecting race and crime are created and activated by the media and political discourse. Research has shown that "activation occurs outside of the perceiver's conscious awareness, which is why suppression efforts by participants might be unsuccessful when prior news viewing is assessed."[107] The reporting of news stories in which the criminals are Black reinforces the perceptions that Blacks are criminal. This reinforcement is called ***confirmation bias*** of racial stereotypes.

Confirmation bias is the process of information gathering in which either (1) a person interprets information in order to come to a desired conclusion about something or (2) selectively collects data and/or places undue and biased weight on some information to the exclusion of others to support a predetermined conclusion or to oppose a conflicting conclusion.[108] Confirmation bias can be conscious as well as unconscious or a process of unwittingly selecting information that sustains preconceived notion of an event or group.[109] Confirmation bias occurs by the active seeking of support of a conclusion or receiving it passively. Confirmation bias of negative assertions find support and confirmation by what is passively observed and affirmed to the holder of the biased ideas when these negative racial biases are operationalized.

Social conservatives utilize confirmation bias of racial stereotypes when they focus on Black on Black crime to reinforce the fear of Blacks by Whites. As discussed in Chapter One, the subtle, and sometimes explicit, message is if these Black people are so violent to their own, how much more will they do to Whites if given the chance. Not all Blacks are criminal,

---

106 Travis L. Dixon, "Psychological Reactions to Crime News Portrayals of Black Criminals: Understanding the Moderating Roles of Prior News Viewing and Stereotype Endorsement," *Communication Monographs* 73, no. 2 (2006): 162–187.

107 Travis L. Dixon, "Psychological Reactions to Crime News Portrayals of Black Criminals: Understanding the Moderating Roles of Prior News Viewing and Stereotype Endorsement," at 183.

108 Nickerson, Raymond S. "Confirmation bias: A ubiquitous phenomenon in many guises." 2(2) *Review of general psychology* 175 (1998).

109 For example, see Id., Susan T. Fisk, "Stereotyping, prejudice, and discrimination at the seam between the centuries: Evolution, culture, mind, and brain." 30(3) *European Journal of Social Psychology* 299 (2000), John M. Darley, and Paget H. Gross. "A hypothesis-confirming bias in labeling effects." 44(1) *Journal of Personality and Social Psychology* 20 (1983), John F. Dovidio, Kerry Kawakami, and Samuel L. Gaertner. "Implicit and explicit prejudice and interracial interaction." 82(1) *Journal of personality and social psychology* 62 (2002), and Mark Chen and John A. Bargh, "Nonconscious behavioral confirmation processes: The self-fulfilling consequences of automatic stereotype activation." 33(5) *Journal of Experimental Social Psychology* 541 (1997).

conservatives will gladly admit, but they will defend the "truth" that most criminals are Black. More significantly, they are criminal not due to societal injustices but due to a lack of moral clarity. These narratives have consequences in political discourse and policy determination. "In summary, multiple exposures to Black criminals via prior news viewing leads to repeated cognitive activation of the stereotype which in turn strengthens its use in race and crime judgments."[110]

Similar research on exposure to racial stereotypes focuses on how stereotypes affect discriminability. ***Discriminability*** is "the ability to respond based on the objective features of the stimulus. That is, discriminability is the ability to respond "gun" to guns and "tool" to tools, corrected for systematic biases."[111] Payne and his colleagues sought to determine if the race of a subject influenced the ability to correctly determine if an object was a gun or some type of tool.

> The present research asked two main questions. First, can people control at will their tendency to stereotypically misidentify objects as guns when paired with Black racial cues, and to misidentify objects as "not guns" when paired with White racial cues? Second, in conditions where this stereotypical tendency is reduced or exacerbated, how do the processes of stimulus discrimination and accessibility bias mediate those changes?
>
> Regarding the first question, participants' explicit goals did not effectively regulate their stereotypical pattern of misidentifications. This bias appears to be very difficult to control. It is not only "unintentional" in the sense that it occurs in the absence of a specific intention; it appears to be "unintentional" in the sense that the bias operates even against the express will of participants.

Use of bias is hard-wired into the process of human social thinking even when the bias is cognitively rejected. This is why racism is not prejudice and neither is bias. But use of bias unprocessed can produce negative results. As Payne and his colleagues explain,

> The failure of conscious goals to regulate participants' stereotypical misidentifications of objects as weapons is unlikely to be the result of insensitive measures. Both accessibility bias and discriminability estimates were demonstrated to be sensitive to manipulations expected to affect them. Discriminability was sensitive to limits on processing time, and accessibility was sensitive to racial cues.

Discriminability is related to time to act or react and correctly discern risk or danger while accessibility of bias and stereotypes is related to race observed and what is attached to the race observed. Thus a police officer in an ambiguous situation with a Black youth under time

---

110 Travis L. Dixon *Supra* note 106 at 183.

111 B. Keith Payne, Alan J. Lambert, and Larry L. Jacoby, "Best laid plans: Effects of goals on accessibility bias and cognitive control in race-based misperceptions of weapons," *Journal of Experimental Social Psychology* 38, no. 4 (2002): 386, 394–395.

pressure can't tell a gun from a wallet (discriminability) and uploads Black criminal (cognitive accessibility). The officer under trained behavior schema acts accordingly. Both, the point should be clear, are not explained by explicit racism. The results of the research by Payne and his colleagues found that

> Regardless of the participants' goals, they made few stereotypical misidentifications when ample processing time was available …
>
> The second suggestion, to ignore race, may be equally impractical. A growing body of research shows that suppressing particular thoughts can be quite difficult, and even result in "rebound effects" in which the unwanted thought becomes more influential than it would have been without suppression attempts.

As discussed later in this chapter, some propose that police training to discount race is a solution to problematic police encounters. Although such training is important, social psychology literature provides caution in discounting race altogether. Forcing police not to see race makes them see it all the more. Such training can also build resentment and support stereotype threat theory, discussed earlier in this chapter. The point being, to tell

> police officers that they should not pay attention to race may be as ineffective as asking readers not to think of a [thing, resulting in them thinking of what you asked them not to think about]. Although our results yielded no direct evidence of a rebound effect, the fact that "avoid bias" instructions make salient the very information that one is imploring participants to ignore similarly highlights the difficulties inherent in successful inhibition of stereotypical processing.[112]

This research confirmed prior research on how negative stereotypes affect the ability to tell a tool from a gun. "The race of the faces selectively influenced the accessibility bias parameter, but not discriminability, suggesting that the stereotypical pattern of errors was driven by automatic racial bias."[113]

Implicit Bias and Stereotype Threat: Policy Implications and Street Level Outcomes for Blacks

The significance of social psychology research is that it provides another explanation of how Whites and Blacks perceive crime, race and police in America. The point, not surprising, is that both Whites and Blacks have stereotypes regarding crime and police. These stereotypes are invoked and utilized differentially by race because of the historical and contemporary experiences and perceptions each has.

---

112 Payne, Lambert, and Jacoby, "Best laid plans: Effects of goals on accessibility bias and cognitive control in race-based misperceptions of weapons," at 394–395.

113 Payne, Lambert, and Jacoby at 396.

Research has shown that these stereotypes are created, in part, by negative portrayals of Blacks in the media.[114] The impact of conflating crime and race, as previously discussed, manifests itself in promoting harsher guilt attributions to Blacks, increased support for law enforcement, conservative political positions on non-criminal justice topics that are linked to race (i.e., welfare, affirmative action), more harsh punishments for certain types of crimes, and support for the Republican Party—all of which have been linked to exposure of stereotypical crime reports and stereotypical media depictions of Blacks.[115] While the research on media influence is clear that it does influence perceptions and stereotypes, which results in policy preferences, more recent research is focusing on how this influence is differentiated by race and what stereotypes are primed by stereotypical media reports. Hurley and his colleagues hypothesized that "certain kinds of policy judgments related to stereotype activation might affect ethnic minority and majority groups similarly (e.g., those about crime and criminality); whereas, other decisions (e.g., those about public law enforcers) might not function in the same manner."[116] Specifically they focused on how media stories can create differential differences in how Blacks and Whites view the police and individual criminal culpability.

The researchers theorized that because public policy analysis requires a higher level of thinking, differences between Whites and Blacks, can't be explained by racial stereotypes alone; thus ethnicity plays a role outside of exposure to stereotypical media exposure.[117] Participants were exposed to news stories in which Whites and Blacks were shown to be suspects in the crimes reported. Participants were divided into two classifications, White (n=117) and racial/ethnic (20 Blacks and 16 Hispanic). Researchers hypothesized that exposure to stereotypical news stories would affect Whites' policy decisions but would not affect racial/ethnic groups' policy decisions. Participants were then given a story regarding an unidentified inmate who was eligible for probation for manslaughter (measure of guilt attribution—individual responsibility) as well as being asked general questions regarding support for the police (support for police).[118] "As predicted, participants who viewed a majority of Black suspects claimed that a nondescript inmate was less likely to be able to be rehabilitated than those in the control condition"[119] and those who were exposed to media stories with no mention of crime. As expected, exposure to stereotypical news stories did not impact the relationship

---

114 Travis L. Dixon, "Psychological Reactions to Crime News Portrayals of Black Criminals: Understanding the Moderating Roles of Prior News Viewing and Stereotype Endorsement," *Communication Monographs* 73, no. 2. Supra note 106.

115 Ryan J. Hurley, Jakob Jensen, Andrew Weaver, and Travis Dixon, "Viewer Ethnicity Matters: Black Crime in TV News and Its Impact on Decisions Regarding Public Policy," 157–158. Supra note 72.

116 Ryan Hurley et al. at 159

117 Ryan Hurley et al. at 159.

118 Ryan Hurley et al. at 161–162.

119 Ryan Hurley et al. at 163.

between guilt attribution measurements by the racial/ethnic members.[120] The research found that the race of the suspect can affect support for police in Blacks not necessarily for Whites.

> [R]acial/ethnic minorities who viewed Black crime showed significantly less support for the police than White participants. White's support for the police appears to have been unaffected by viewing predominantly White versus predominantly Black criminal suspects in these data. On the other hand, racial/ethnic participants revealed significant differences in police support depending upon the treatment condition such that police support was higher when viewing White criminals and significantly lower after viewing a majority of Black criminals. … . Conservatives were also found to be more supportive of the police than liberals. [121]

These results are in line with dehumanization research discussed above in which qualities of the in group are attributed to individual members of the same group and negative qualities attributed to the out group are transferred to individuals who may be members of the out group. In their study, Hurley and his colleagues, contended that negative conceptions of rehabilitation and individual culpability were imposed on an unidentified inmate by participates after being exposed to negative stereotypes of Black criminality when compared to the control group (non-exposure to stereotype stories). The results that only the racial/ethnic group showed significant change regarding support of the police and that the change was dictated by exposure to White or Black criminality was not surprising because Blacks and Whites, both historically and contemporarily, have different experiences with the police and each have different beliefs as a preliminary matter on whether law enforcement treats Blacks and Whites equally. The researchers' results reflected the difference. Racial minorities, when viewing the news stories showing Blacks as criminals invoked latent distrust, which was reflected in significant reduction in police support. Racial minorities when viewing the news stories showing Whites as criminals invoked support for law and order, which was reflected in significant increase in police support. The result that Whites showed no significant change in support of the police regardless of the suspect being Black or White is not surprising because Whites tend to see police action with support and assumption of fair treatment.

Whites tend to assume that if the police have arrested a person, he/she did something worthy of arrest and that the police don't arrest the innocent because that would be a waste of time and resources—Crime control theory (discussed in Chapter Seven). Blacks hold no such assumption that police don't arrest the innocent and thus hold skepticism when the police arrest Blacks. Because the Black experience is that Whites are not policed and not arrested for the crimes they commit because police are detailed to Black communities to arrest Blacks for the crimes they commit, when a White is arrested the assumption made is that he/she must have been guilty to catch the otherwise non-attention of the police. We will return to

120 Ryan Hurley et al. at 164.

121 Ryan Hurley et al.

the argument of crime commission vs. police deployment in regard to crime statistics and disproportionate arrests in Chapter Six.

The impact of conflating Blacks with crime and violence in America has consequences. Increased support for crime-control-theory[122] oriented social policy, social acceptance of police use of force, social expectation of disproportionate minority confinement and involvement with police, and generally less sympathy or acceptance of Black claims and complaints of injustice at the hands of the criminal justice system are significantly associated with perceptions of Black criminality. As ***racial threat theory*** proposes, "Whites are more supportive of punitive sanctions because they perceive an increasing threat to their economic, political, and social hegemony in the presence (or assumed presence) of large numbers of minorities and the concomitant belief that Blacks are a violent and threatening population. … [R]esearch has shown that racial attitudes generally, and racialized views of crime specifically, are among the most consistent and strongest predictors of Whites' attitudes toward crime policies."[123] Whites that hold racialized views of crime are more likely to support the death penalty, increased spending in criminal justice (police and prisons), and more inclined to support increased penalties for violent crime.[124] White acceptance of these policies, in part, is popular because of the lack of fear that these policies will be imposed on them. As dehumanization and infrahumanization theory explains, harsh punishment is acceptable to the in group since they believe such punishment is only applicable to the out group because only the out group commits the crimes that the sanctions would be applicable too.

As social psychology, criminal justice, and public policy research shows, Whites believe the majority of violent crime is committed by Blacks. The result of this perception is insensitivity to the outcome of disproportionate application of harsh sanctions, police brutality and disproportionate incarceration of Blacks. Conservative middle-class Whites *and Blacks* don't view these outcomes, especially disproportionate incarceration, as unjust, but rather they see them as expected. For example, in a panel discussion on gun control, a middle-class White conservative Christian male minister was asked why there was a clear disagreement between White and Black evangelical Christians on the issues of gun control and ownership and he answered, "Well it's simple. It's simple, White middle-class evangelicals use guns for protection and unfortunately the people on the lower social economic rung of the ladder are victims of gun violence." When challenged, he responded, "It's the truth. Look, where is the gun violence happening? It's happening in the inner cities … It's the result of gang violence

122 See discussion in Chapter Seven. See also, Vesla M. Weaver, "Frontlash: Race and the Development of Punitive Crime Policy," *Studies in American Political Development* 21. Supra note 72.

123 Christina Mancibi, Daniel P. Mears, Eric A. Stewart, Kevin M. Beaver and Justin T. Pickett, "Whites' perceptions About Black Criminality: A Closer Look at Contact Hypothesis" at 997. Supra note 72 (internal citation omitted).

124 Mancibi et al. at 999–1000, 1014–1015.

... Why is this a Black and White issue?"[125] When asked if White middle-class people kill themselves or about mass shootings that are committed by Whites, he was perplexed as to what the point was. He answered, sure Whites shoot themselves and are involved in mass shootings but the majority of gun violence incidents are committed by those in the inner city. The implicit racism in saying, "White middle-class evangelicals use guns for protection" but "the people on the lower social economic rung of the ladder" don't, and defining violent crime as "It's happening in the inner cities," totally escaped him. The implicit racism is in the description of crime and gun violence in one dimensional terms of White middle-class law-abiding fear of crime vs. inherent urban Black criminality. The implicit racism is in the conception that White men only want guns to protect their families and Black men want guns to commit homicides and other crimes, both in urban areas and perhaps in suburban neighborhoods where White law-abiding men live.

The discounting of crime committed by Whites for the more public violence that occurs in the inner city, whether the minister realizes it or not, leads him to believe White middle-class Christian evangelicals need guns for protection—not from Whites, but from inner city Blacks that are committing the violence. The fear, unconscious or not, is in the fear that Blacks may move from the inner city to where he lives. But to be fair to the White minister, he was seated next to a Black minister who was in complete agreement with him, or at the very least voiced no dissent. Thus, the complexity of racial dynamics becomes more complicated and nuanced when considering Black middle-class perceptions compared to non-middle-class Black perceptions. The Black minister did not want inner-city Blacks to move where he lived either. Class is an independent factor to explain racial bias of Blacks. A bias middle–class, educated Blacks can share with middle and working-class suburban Whites.

Implicit Bias, the Stereotyping of Blacks as Criminals, and Police Psychology: Police Policy and Program Implications

The psychology of perceptions of race and police use of force involves a complicated combination of factors. These include (1) implicit bias of Blacks as criminals and dangerous, (2) racial depictions of Blacks as criminal in various media outlets (T.V., movies, news reporting, and music), (3) unconscious dehumanization of Blacks in general and young Black men in particular, (4) racial stereotyping, (5) bidirectional stereotyping, (6) aversive racism, (7) police psychology of schema, pattern recognition, and motor learning responses, and (8)

125 Panel discussion, "Armed in America: Faith and Guns," PBS (May 10, 2016). The panel discussion was a live discussion after the premier of the airing of the documentary, *The Armor of Light* published by Independent Lens, PBS (May 10, 2016). *The Armor of Light* is a documentary featuring the conversion of a pro-life evangelical preacher, Robert Schenck, to the gun control movement and his approach to gun control from an evangelical Christian theological perspective and his work with Lucy McBath, the mother of Jordan Davis, who was shot and killed by a White male, Michael Dunn, who was later convicted in Florida of first degree murder.

Social psychology descriptions of race and racism

Racism---------Implicit Bias--------Bidirectional Stereotyping----Averse Racism----Racism--------Stereotype Threat-----Dehumanization

Without Racists

Klan thinking

Fear or suspicion of Blacks because they are Black—uploading and processing unconscious negative stereotypes.

Applying observed individual characteristics to the general group and applying stereotype group characteristics to an observed individual. Example: See an individual Black male and perceive crime, think about crime and perceive Black males

Having racial biases but claiming (both, emotionally and cognitively) not to have biases—the Two are aversive to each other. Also involves emotional rejecting of being confronted with having biases. Example: "I am not racists! How dare you! I did not stop those Black males in the car because they were Black, they were driving erratically."

Personal interactions or social policies when implemented result in a racist result when neither party or the social policy have racial intent or implementation. The focus is on racial outcome not malicious racial intent. Theory assumes outcome occurred without malicious racial intent.

Behavior or reaction to the fear of being stereotyped. Manifested in cognitive defense of racial biases with non-racial justifications ("you Blacks, as a group, commit more crime than Whites and have poor family structure and values. Your criminality causes your incarceration") or Blacks avoiding the police because of fear of being perceived as criminal and police perceiving the avoidance as indicative of criminal activity.

Ascribes less humanity to a group, while racism or bias ascribes negative behaviors or attributes to a group, or ascribes to group the level of an animal. Dehumanization removes or reduces from a group (Blacks) the benefits of humanness. Example of removing or reducing humanness—Black children are perceived older and bigger than they actually are and they are perceived as less innocent and more culpable for their actions than White children.

neurophysiological threat arousal on sight of Black males as a physical threat to personal safety as evidenced by alpha wave suppression which uploads fear responses to the presence of Blacks. The neurophysiological threat arousal supplements (9) cognitive accessibility of stereotypes of Blacks to "fill in the blanks" in situations of ambiguity which (10) provides the context and ability of the police failure to correctly discriminate between a Black man with a wallet and a gun.

All of these dynamics exist within a historical context dating back to slavery and the devaluation of Black life and they all function outside of explicit racism.

What is the solution?

There are various suggestions in the criminological, criminal justice, social psychology and sociological literature on how to deal with racial bias and racism in policing and society as a whole. They include programs and initiatives that produce positive community police interactions. These include soft police community programs like "Coffee with a Cop, Shop with a Cop, community police academies, liaisons with specific communities, advisory councils, police-sponsored movie nights, or block parties,"[126] police emotional processing and stress reduction meditation training,[127] and tabletop bias situational decision-making training.[128] In addition the abandonment of certain aggressive and militarized policing including implementation of broken windows theory of policing communities, zero-tolerance policing, utilization of drug/violent crime suppression task forces, and unconstitutional use of stop-and-frisk as a violent crime reduction strategy.

More importantly, aside from these types of initiatives and programs, there also needs to be an end to social conservative and police leadership automatic defense of police use of force or deadly force and the automatic assumption of guilt of those who suffer police use of force and their deserving of such force. The value of the life taken by a police officer must be respected by the department and society as a whole by having some skepticism of a police officer who is armed and trained in the use of deadly or non-deadly force who asserts he was in fear of his life, especially when the officer was aided by fellow police officers at the scene when the deadly or non-deadly force was used. In a recent article on deadly force it was concluded that,

> irrespective of the legality of police use-of-force decisions (good or bad), one must be ever cognizant that citizen perceptions and experiences matter. When everyday citizens view a video of police behavior (or witness it in person) and consider it a questionable application of force, police officials need to recognize such perception. Too often, officials hunker

---

126 Lorie A. Fridell, "Racial Aspects of Police Shootings," *Criminology & Public Policy* 15, no. 2 (2016): 481, 483–484.

127 For example, see Matthias Berking, Caroline Meier, and Peggilee Wupperman. "Enhancing Emotion-Regulation Skills in Police Officers: Results of a Pilot Controlled Study," *Behavior Therapy* 43, no. 3 (2010): 329, Michael S. Christopher, Richard J. Goerling, Brant S. Rogers, Matthew Hunsinger, Greg Baron, Aaron L. Bergman, and David T. Zava, "A pilot study evaluating the effectiveness of a mindfulness-based intervention on cortisol awakening response and health outcomes among law enforcement officers," *Journal of Police and Criminal Psychology* 31, no. 1 (2016): 15, and Alberto Chiesa and Alessandro Serretti, "Mindfulness-based stress reduction for stress management in healthy people: a review and meta-analysis," *The Journal of Alternative and Complementary Medicine* 15, no. 5 (2009): 593.

128 Laura Zimmerman and David Blake, "Officers Facing Criminal Charges: Faulty Decision Making," *Police Forum* 25, no. 2(2015): 12–13. See also, *Supra* note 10.

> down into defense mode seeking to justify the behavior, which causes the citizenry to become even more distrustful of the police, and thus, the cycle continues benefitting no one.[129]

Other suggestions include focusing on police legitimacy and procedural justice theory[130] and organizational justice theory.[131] ***Organizational justice theory*** proposes that the more the police officer perceives his own agency as respectful to him and is fair to him, the more the more likely the officer will do the same for members of the community.[132] ***Police legitimacy and procedural justice theory*** suggests that the more police personally interact and get to know the individuals living in a community and treat members of the community with respect, the more the police will be perceived as legitimate by the community.[133] Both theories focus on how the police department treats individuals. Organizational justice theory focuses on how individual police officers perceive the legitimacy of their treatment by the police department and police legitimacy theory focuses on how individual community members, and by extension how the community as a whole, are treated by the individual police officer. Police legitimacy theory is about how the community perceives the legitimacy of police interactions and the use of force utilized by the police regardless of whether that interaction leads to an arrest. Police legitimacy theory also emphasizes the principles of Sir Robert Peel and the origin of modern policing in the western world.

Advanced police racial biased training has also been suggested to be a tool to introduce of officers to their own subconscious biases and through counter-bias training, introduce

---

129 William Terrill, "Deadly Force: To shoot or not to shoot," *Infra* note 147 at 495.

130 For example, see Tom R. Tyler, "Enhancing police legitimacy," *The Annals of the American Academy of Political and Social Science* 593, no. 1 (2004): 84, Tom R. Tyler and Cheryl J. Wakslak, "Profiling and Police Legitimacy: Procedural Justice, Attributions of Motive, and Acceptance of Police Authority," *Criminology* 42, no. 2 (2004): 253, and Lyn Hinds and Kristina Murphy, "Public Satisfaction with Police: Using Procedural Justice to Improve Police Legitimacy," *Australian & New Zealand Journal of Criminology* 40, no. 1 (2007): 27.

131 Jerald Greenberg, "A taxonomy of organizational justice theories," *Academy of Management Review* 12, no. 1 (1987): 9.

132 Scott E. Wolfe, and Alex R. Piquero, "Organizational Justice and Police Misconduct," *Criminal Justice and Behavior* 38, no. 4 (2011): 332.

133 For example, see Tom R. Tyler and Jeffrey Fagan, "Legitimacy and cooperation: Why Do People Help the Police Fight Crime in Their Communities?" *Ohio State Journal of Criminal Law* 6(2008): 231, Jacinta M. Gau, Nicholas Corsaro, Eric A. Stewart, and Rod K. Brunson, "Examining macro-level impacts on procedural justice and police legitimacy," *Journal of Criminal Justice* 40, no. 4 (2012): 333, James E. Hawdon, John Ryan, and Sean P. Griffin, "Policing Tactics and Perceptions of Police Legitimacy," *Police Quarterly* 6, no. 4 (2003): 469, and Jason Sunshine and Tom R. Tyler, "The Role of Procedural Justice and Legitimacy in Shaping Public Support for Policing," *Law & society review* 37, no. 3 (2003): 513.

officers to counter narratives and experiences to negate the racial biases that they have.[134] Some research has shown that police officers who were exposed to "counter-stereotypes reduced the biased application of force" by reducing the effect of bias-aggravating power of ambiguity.[135]

> Biases and stereotypes are most likely to impact us when we are facing ambiguous stimuli. This concept can be applied to ambiguous people and ambiguous situations. Applied to people, it makes sense that we are most likely to "fill in" with stereotypes a person whom we do not know. They are a "blank slate," and so we are inclined to add information; the science shows we add information related to the stereotypes associated with their group(s). The bias-aggravating potential of ambiguous situations is directly related to use-of-force video scenarios. Stereotypes are least likely to impact police who are facing an unambiguous threat. For instance, the officer who enters a scene (in real life or in a video) where a person is pointing a gun at him or her is unlikely to be impacted by that person's demographics. In contrast, if the officer enters a scene where a person is engaging in ambiguous "furtive" movements, the science indicates that stereotypes about which groups are dangerous (or are not) will impact the interpretation of that ambiguous scene.[136]

As previously discussed in this chapter, racial bias affects how the police officer deals with ambiguity. In theory police anti-bias training will make racial demographics irrelevant to police use-of-force decisions and will replace stereotypical with counter-stereotypical perceptions in ambiguous-threat situations.[137] The issue is not explicit but implicit racism and how it operates through activation and application.

> Activation refers to the existence of the stereotype in an individual's head; a person sees another person from a particular group (e.g., gender group or racial group) and associates that person with a stereotype that is associated with that group. But, importantly, this activation does not necessarily impact behavior. A person could have an implicit bias activation but not apply that activation to behavior.[138]

Police use of force based on implicit stereotyping against Blacks indicates activation and application has occurred[139] but activation does not automatically involve application of the stereotype to actual police behavior. A stop-and-frisk can be the result of the activation and

---

134 Lorie A. Fridell, "Racial Aspects of Police Shootings," *Criminology & Public Policy* 15, no. 2. Supra note 127 at 485. See also, Ashby E. Plant and B. Michelle Peruche, "The consequences of race for police officers' responses to criminal suspects," *Psychological Science* 16, no. 3 (2005): 180–183.

135 Lorie A. Fridell, "Racial Aspects of Police Shootings," *Criminology & Public Policy* 15, no. 2. Supra note 127 at 485.

136 Fridell.

137 Fridell.

138 Fridell at 482.

139 Fridell at 482.

application of implicit bias but the implicit bias that caused the officer to place attention on the Black individual in the first place is activation alone.

> These two processes are linked to two sets of interventions to address implicit biases, and these interventions can help us further understand the disparate findings and the implications of them for police. First, there are ways that individuals can reduce their biases; that is, there are mechanisms that can reduce the activation of the stereotypes. Second, there are ways that individuals can manage their biases; that is, even if activation occurs, people can still thwart the application of bias to behavior.
>
> Two key mechanisms for reducing the activation of biases are the "contact theory" and "exposure to counter-stereotypes."[140]

Use of force and race dynamics becomes even more nuanced when considering that research has shown that there are different types of police use of force, and deadly and non-deadly use of force should be independently studied and addressed by policy. Additional to the research in the social sciences of psychology and criminology, the discipline of economics and theories of law and economics provide additional perspectives on the types of police use of force. For example, research that applied empirical economic analysis to police decisions to use force, both deadly and non-deadly, in relation to racial bias concluded that

> On non-lethal uses of force, there are racial differences—sometimes quite large—in police use of force, even after accounting for a large set of controls designed to account for important contextual and behavioral factors at the time of the police-civilian interaction. Interestingly, as use of force increases from putting hands on a civilian to striking them with a baton, the overall probability of such an incident occurring decreases dramatically but the racial difference remains roughly constant. Even when officers report civilians have been compliant and no arrest was made, blacks are 21.3 2 (0.04) percent more likely to endure some form of force in an interaction. Yet, on the most extreme use of force—officer-involved shootings—we are unable to detect any racial differences in either the raw data or when accounting for controls.
>
> We argue that these facts are most consistent with a model of taste-based discrimination in which police officers face discretely higher costs for officer-involved shootings relative to non-lethal uses of force.[141]

Taste-based discrimination theorizes that people have biases or "tastes" that they will indulge in but only if the benefit of indulging the taste is more than the cost for engaging in enjoying the taste. This is classical economics theory of human behavior; human decision-making is

140 Fridell at 482–483.

141 Roland G. Fryer Jr., "An Empirical Analysis of Racial Differences in Police Use of Force," National Bureau of Economic Research Working Papers Series (2016) at 35. See also supra note 39 for similar results that police take longer to shoot Black suspects than White suspects.

regulated by the benefit of having something vs. the cost of having it. People seek what they enjoy but only to the level that the cost is not more than the enjoyment. Taste-based discrimination occurs when "biased police officers interact with B[lack] civilians [and] they derive psychic pleasure from using force, independent of whether they are compliant or not."[142] What Professor Fryer found in his research was that

> even when we take perfectly compliant individuals and control for civilian, officer, encounter and location variables, black civilians are 21.1 (0.041) percent more likely to have any force used against them compared to white civilians with the same reported compliance behavior.[143]

Thus perfect compliance by a Black citizen does not eliminate the likelihood of being subjected to police use of force if the officer has determined to indulge a taste for doing so.

> Taste-based discrimination is consistent with ... non-lethal uses of force if, among those who discriminate, the preference for discrimination is greater than the expected costs of wrongly using force. In other words, the expected price of discrimination is not large enough—either through low penalties or low probabilities of detection—to alter behavior of those who have biased preferences. This model is also consistent with the lack of racial differences in officer-involved shooting if there is a discrete increase in the costs of being deemed a discriminator, relative to the costs incurred with non-lethal uses of force.[144]
>
> As police departments across America consider models of community policing such as the Boston Ten Point Coalition, body worn cameras, or training designed to purge officers of implicit bias, our results point to another simple policy experiment: increase the expected price of excessive force on lower level uses of force. To date, very few police departments across the country either collect data on lower level uses of force or explicitly punish officers for misuse of these tactics. The appealing feature of this type of policy experiment is that it does not require officers to change their behavior in extremely high-stakes environments. Many arguments about police reform fall victim to the "my life versus theirs, us versus them" mantra. Holding officers accountable for the misuse of hands or pushing individuals to the ground is not likely a life or death situation and, as such, may be more amenable to policy change.[145]

When this ***Harvard study*** was published, social conservatives focused on the conclusion that police shootings were not affected by race and the conclusion was a surprise to the researchers. But they failed to acknowledge the conclusion that non-deadly use of force or low-force

---

142 Roland G. Fryer Jr., "An Empirical Analysis of Racial Differences in Police Use of Force," ... at 27.

143 Roland G. Fryer Jr., "An Empirical Analysis of Racial Differences in Police Use of Force," ... at 31.

144 Roland G. Fryer Jr., "An Empirical Analysis of Racial Differences in Police Use of Force," ... 31–32.

145 Roland G. Fryer Jr., "An Empirical Analysis of Racial Differences in Police Use of Force at 35–36

aggressive handling of Blacks was disproportionate even when holding behavior of Blacks constant. Thus they found that race did not influence the use of deadly force but it did influence manhandling of Blacks.

Considering this research, one additional solution to police use of force should be considered. Because "the police ultimately draw on their coercion power as a means of control, whether it be for legitimate (e.g., maintain order, ensure safety, or enforce the law) or illegitimate purposes (e.g., to harass, punish, or denigrate)"[146] and because this power is exclusively given to the police by society, unjust application of this power should be condemned. Note, I said "unjust" not "unlawful," for the legality of use of force, as discussed in Chapter Two, is balanced in the police officer's favor. The use of force, when considered in the history of race and policing in America, must be constrained by more than the law. Society must show universal disdain for the use of force that is unfair and unjust, not simply for force unreasonably used from the perspective of a reasonable police officer under the circumstances. In other words, the use of unjust deadly force and non-deadly force against Blacks must involve a moral contempt to supplement the Fourth Amendment analysis to determine if the force was legal in application.

Independent from Fourth Amendment analysis, America, especially White middle-class suburban conservatives who enjoy positive and respectful engagement with police must abandon the admiration of police ***noble-cause corruption***[147] which allows for the acceptance of police use of unlawful force or the misuse lawful tactics upon those they (the police) believe are guilty in order to bring them to justice and protect society. An example of this, as discussed in Chapter Six, is the use of stop-and-frisk, a criminal investigation technique, as a crime-suppression technique to reduce homicides in specific neighborhoods. The impact of the policy was the unlawful stopping and searching of Black males through the justification that it reduced the number of guns and homicides. The insidious nature of the racism in the debate over the NYPD stop-and-frisk policy was in the distinction in treatment and the justification for the distinction. ***The noble cause (reduction of homicides) justified the corruption (violation of individual constitutional fourth amendment rights of Black males).*** The NYPD and the Mayor asserted stop-and-frisk brought down homicides in the Black community and the inconvenience and humiliation of being stopped and searched in the street like a criminal (standing up handcuffed or spread out on the hood of a police car, or face down in the dirt) is minimal compared to the deaths that were prevented. Treatment that would not be tolerated in White middle-class neighborhoods. Thus the constitutional rights of Blacks in Black neighborhoods are not as absolute as those who live in White neighborhoods. Noble cause corruption, as does dehumanization, supports implicit bias and the belief that Blacks are supposed to be reflected disproportionately in

146 William Terrill, "Deadly Force: To shoot or not to shoot," *Criminology and Public Policy* 15, no. 2 (2016): 491.

147 William Terrill, "Deadly Force: To shoot or not to shoot ," at 492

arrest and incarceration because as Harry Houck, former NYPD police detective and CNN Law Enforcement Analyst, said, "they are" prone to criminality, "the statistics say this."[148]

Societal rejection of police noble-cause corruption needs to be operationalized in effective and uncompromised criminal and civil consequences for police misconduct and the abandonment of the social assumption that police misconduct does not exist as a problem. There needs to be an abandonment of the idea that police that violate the law and abuse the rights of Blacks are just "bad apples." Police abuse is not incongruity within policing, a reflection of the belief in both society and policing as a whole or within a specific police department that Blacks are the face of crime. Police abuse reflects a societal acceptance of Blacks not having the same right to enjoy the presumption of non-criminality and the constitutional protection that accompany that assumption. The assumption that Blacks are criminogenic leads to police scrutiny and physical control until proven non-threatening.

Police officers who are prone to believe young Black males are more likely to be armed and criminal do not appear from outside of the society to protect it from criminals, i.e., Blacks. As Patrick Spradlin, a White Austin, Texas police officer, said to a Black woman, Breaion King, who was arrested for resisting arrest,

> Why are so many people afraid of black people? I can give you a really good—a really good idea of why it might be that way, violent tendencies. I want you to think about that, I'm not saying anything. I'm not saying it's true. I'm not saying that I can prove it or nothing. But 99 percent of the time, when you hear about stuff like that, it is the black community that's being violent. That's why a lot of the white people are afraid of them, and I don't blame them. There are some guys I look at it, I, yeah, I know it's my job to deal with them and I know it's probably going to be ugly, but that's the way it goes. But yeah, some of them, because of their appearance and what not. Some of them are very intimidating."[149]

Implicit racism in policing originates only from only one source, society itself. Society must admit that the social history and politics of racism in America has long term and systemic impact. Racism is not a static belief, it's a process of thinking based on experience and perceptions. In trying to understand police psychology, Ms. King discussed racism with officer Spradlin while in the back of a police car handcuffed after being thrown to the ground by

---

148 *CNN panel goes off the rails when* ex-cop *claims black people are 'prone to criminality'* (July 11, 2016) at https://www.youtube.com/watch?v=q8sbqjGtTTY

149 *Austin police officer discusses racism with Breaion King after her arrest* at https://www.youtube.com/watch?v=4cLXk_F5KQw. See discussion and press conference by Austin Police Department Chief of Police on the incident, *Cop To African American Woman: Blacks Have "Violent Tendencies"* at https://www.youtube.com/watch?v=UyrXmTId1sc, *Violent Austin police arrest of teacher caught on dashcam* at https://www.youtube.com/watch?v=PwdRPqWRpEo and *Police chief Acevedo apologizes and condemns Breaion King's violent arrest* at https://www.youtube.com/watch?v=9ALdQ6w-UM4

another officer. Officer Spradlin admitted that racism existed but racism was in the eyes of the beholder and he said that police officers had to take a four-hour psychological exam to weed out racists before they become police officers. Ms. King, a third-grade school teacher, then asked Officer Spradlin if experiences of police can build a racist image of Blacks and change a person into a racist, to which officer Spradlin said sure, absolutely. The Austin, Texas police chief disavowed both the police officer who used force on Ms. King and the comments by officer Spradlin, and put out a statement that racism does exist and impacts how Blacks are perceived by police. The Chief said during the press conference, "For those that think that life is perfect for people of color, I want you to listen to that conversation and tell me that we don't have social issues in this nation, issues of bias, issues of racism, issues of people being looked at differently because of their color."[150]

Officer Brian Richter, who slammed Ms. King to the ground, was subsequently fired in January 2018 for an unrelated excessive use of force incident and the filing of a false statement regarding that force during an arrest in July 2017.

Recent research has shown that police abuse is situational based on police resentment of Black crime. Comparing police use of force against Blacks both before and after incidents of police being shot by Blacks, "in 2007 and 2011, the use of physical force by police officers against blacks increased substantially by 16.0% and 13.3%, respectively, in the days after the shootings" but incidents of Whites and Hispanics shooting police showed no change. "The race-specific nature of the response whether driven by perceptions of threat, concerns about officer safety, or implicit stereotypes indicates racial bias."[151]

Police use of force—either deadly or non-deadly—has an impact on perceptions of American justice. Blacks who observe police use minimal use of force without justification are more prone to assume more levels of force are also without justification. But, as discussed in Chapter Seven, the problem is that if only Blacks witness unjustified use of force while Whites never see or experience use of force by police or enjoy positive and respectful initiated contact with police, the distinction between treatments is manifested in the political and policy arguments regarding policing. But the difference in treatment has even broader impacts within society. As recent research has concluded,

> Much more troubling, due to their frequency and potential impact on minority belief formation, is the possibility that racial differences in police use of non-lethal force have spillovers on myriad dimensions of racial inequality. If, for instance, blacks use their lived experience with police as evidence that the world is discriminatory, then it is easy

150 Christopher Mele, Niraj Chokshi, and Christine Hauser, "Texas Investigates Violent Traffic Arrest of Black Teacher," *New York Times* July 22, 2016. at http://www.nytimes.com/2016/07/23/us/texas-investigates-violent-traffic-arrest-of-black-teacher.html?_r=0 and *Cop To African American Woman: Blacks Have "Violent Tendencies"* at https://www.youtube.com/watch?v=UyrXmTId1sc

151 Joscha Legewie, "Racial profiling and use of force in police stops: How local events trigger periods of increased discrimination," *American Journal of Sociology* 122, no. 2 (2016): 379, 381.

> to understand why black youth invest less in human capital or black adults are more likely to believe discrimination is an important determinant of economic outcomes. Black Dignity Matters.[152]

As discussed in this chapter, the dispute in the literature is not whether Blacks suffer from a bias of presumed and perceived criminality and danger in the eyes of society in general or by the police specifically, but only on how this bias manifests itself in the use of deadly force. Race may or may not be statistically significant in the police officer's decision to shoot a Black man, but it is almost universally established in the literature that race is statically significant in the police officer's initial decision to approach, detain, and enforce physical control of Blacks using non-deadly force. Racial bias is more complicated because it's no longer exclusively defined and operationalized by open and dominative racism—the KKK, neo-Nazi type—which until recently has been universally condemned without thought or hesitation. See Chapter Nine, President Trump and the Charlottesville incident for discussion on the debatability of universal and unconditional condemnation of KKK-level racism.

In any event modern American racism, as discussed in this chapter, is more explained by aversive racism than the KKK kind. Aversive racism involves holding in one's mind the contradictory rejection of racist ideas and sympathizing with past victims of racism and supporting racial justice but "at the same time possess conflicting, often non-conscious, negative feelings and beliefs about Blacks that are rooted in basic psychological processes that promote racial bias" while believing and wanting to be perceived as non-prejudiced.[153] Aversive racism manifests itself in anger when the aversive racists is challenged regarding his beliefs about Blacks, especially when discussing code concepts like police brutality and holding police responsible for abuse or whether Blacks are criminogenic. "The negative feelings that aversive racists have toward Blacks typically do not reflect open antipathy, but rather consist of more avoidant reactions of discomfort, anxiety, or fear. That is, they find Blacks 'aversive', while at the same time find any suggestion that they might be prejudiced 'aversive' as well." Aversive racism is the result of the "conflict between the denial of personal prejudice and underlying unconscious negative feelings and beliefs [and those] unconscious negative feelings and beliefs

152 Roland G. Fryer Jr., "An Empirical Analysis of Racial Differences in Police Use of Force," ... Supra note 142 at 36.

153 Adam R. Pearson, John F. Dovidio, and Samuel L. Gaertner, "The Nature of Contemporary Prejudice: Insights from Aversive Racism," *Social and Personality Psychology Compass* 3, no. 3 (2009): 314,

get expressed in subtle, indirect, and often rationalizable ways."[154] Aversive racism is similar to stereotype threat theory in that it's a reaction to being confronted with biases ideas one holds and/or advocates. Aversive racism goes to the emotional reaction and opposition to the confrontation while stereotype threat explains the cognitive and intellectual justification for the racial biased ideas.

Aversive racism is fostered by racial mistrust, media portrayals of Blacks as criminals and violent to Whites specifically, and violent in general, as well as the differential in White and Black experiences with the police and the criminal justice system. Research is without serious dissent that Blacks and White perceive the criminal justice system and the treatment of Blacks by police differently. The reason for this differential in opinion about police treatment is largely explained by the fact that police in actuality treat Blacks and Whites differently. The debate is in why and how they are treated differently.

Even universally recognized White social conservative political leaders, in rare moments of clarity and honesty, admit that Whites don't share the same experiences with police, and these divergent experiences between Blacks and Whites complicate and dictate various political perspectives on policing in America. In a conversation, former Speaker of the House Newt Gingrich, an unquestioned White Reagan/Goldwater social conservative political leader, concluded

> It is more dangerous to be black in America. It's both more dangerous because of crime—and which is the Chicago story—but it is more dangerous in that it's substantially more likely to end up in a situation where the police don't respect you and where you could easily get killed. I think sometimes for whites it's difficult to appreciate how real that is, and how that is an everyday danger. … It took me a long time—and a number of people talking to me over the years—to begin to get a sense of this. If you are a normal white American, the truth is you don't understand being black in America and you instinctively underestimate the level of discrimination and the level of additional risk. … To the degree

316–317. See also, John F. Dovidio, Louis A. Penner, Terrance L. Albrecht, Wynne E. Norton, Samuel L. Gaertner, and J. Nicole Shelton, "Disparities and distrust: The implications of psychological processes for understanding racial disparities in health and health care," *Social science & medicine* 67, no. 3 (2008): 478, John F. Dovidio and Samuel L. Gaertner. "Aversive racism," *Advances in Experimental Social Psychology* 36 (2004): 1, Patricia G. Devine, "Stereotypes and prejudice: Their automatic and controlled components," *Journal of Personality and Social Psychology* 56, no. 1 (1989): 5, Ann Berlak, "CHAPTER TWO: Challenging the Hegemony of Whiteness by Addressing the Adaptive Unconscious," *Counterpoints: Undoing Whiteness in the Classroom: Critical educultural teaching approaches for social justice activism* 321 (2008): 47, Kevin Durrheim. "Implicit prejudice in mind and interaction," in *Beyond Prejudice: Extending the Social Psychology of Conflict, Inequality and Social Change*, eds. John Dixon and Mark Levine (Cambridge University Press, 2012), 179–199, and Geoffrey Beattie, *Our Racist Heart?: An Exploration of Unconscious Prejudice in Everyday Life*, (Routledge, 2013).

154 Adam R. Pearson, John F. Dovidio, and Samuel L. Gaertner, "The Nature of Contemporary Prejudice: Insights from Aversive Racism," *Social and Personality Psychology Compass* 3, no. 3 (2009): 314, 316–317.

> that you are an African American, you are raising your teenage boys to be very careful in obeying the police because literally their lives are at risk and they can see it on television. At the same time, if you're a normal Caucasian, you don't see that, that's not part of your experience.[155]

As Rand Paul, a White Republican and leader of the libertarian wing of conservative politics, wrote regarding police shootings of Blacks and how police treatment of Blacks is different than police treatment of Whites,

> If I had been told to get out of the street as a teenager, there would have been a distinct possibility that I might have smarted off. But, I wouldn't have expected to be shot.
>
> . . . .
>
> When you couple this militarization of law enforcement with an erosion of civil liberties and due process that allows the police to become judge and jury—national security letters, no-knock searches, broad general warrants, pre-conviction forfeiture—we begin to have a very serious problem on our hands.
>
> Given these developments, it is almost impossible for many Americans not to feel like their government is targeting them. Given the racial disparities in our criminal justice system, it is impossible for African-Americans not to feel like their government is particularly targeting them.
>
> . . . .
>
> Anyone who thinks that race does not still, even if inadvertently, skew the application of criminal justice in this country is just not paying close enough attention. Our prisons are full of black and brown men and women who are serving inappropriately long and harsh sentences for non-violent mistakes in their youth.[156]

As Charles Koch, a chief financial supporter of the Republican Party and various libertarian and social conservative think tanks, reflected in an interview on America and the principles of its founding philosophical document and truthfully admitted that Blacks were not included in the proposition that all men are created equal at the founding of America.

> The promise in the Declaration of Independence [is that it asserted that all people are created equal and that the sole role and purpose of government was to protect individual rights of life, liberty and pursuit of happiness]. But the tragedy was that it wasn't fully applied. For example it was not applied to Blacks. They were treated as not fully human and made slaves. ... And so wherever this promise of the Declaration of Independence

---

155 Van Jones and Newt Gingrich Facebook conversation (https://www.youtube.com/watch?v=ooOlwf3F07Y) (July 8, 2016)

156 Rand Paul, "We Must Demilitarize the Police," (Op Ed) *Time Magazine*, August 4, 2014. (http://time.com/3111474/rand-paul-ferguson-police/?utm_source=twitterfeed&utm_medium=twitter)

> that everyone had these rights was not applied we had monstrous injustices and problems affecting the whole country.[157]

Newt Gingrich came to similar conclusions regarding American history and the politics of America reaching up to its values when he became Speaker of House in the historic 1994 elections in which the Republicans ended the 40 year rule of the House by the Democrats. In his acceptance speech on the floor of House January 4, 1995, Gingrich said

> I do want to pick up directly on what Dick Gephardt said, because he said it right. No Republican here should kid themselves about it. The greatest leaders in fighting for an integrated America in the 20th century were in the Democratic Party. The fact is, it was the liberal wing of the Democratic Party that ended segregation. The fact is that it was Franklin Delano Roosevelt who gave hope to a Nation that was in distress and could have slid into dictatorship. Every Republican has much to learn from studying what the Democrats did right.

Race has always been a factor in American political discourse and race has always been a mitigator in the response to Black oppression of suffering. Reconsider the discussion of infrahumanization in light of a conversation on the *Bill O'Reilly Show*. O'Reilly was interviewing a reoccurring guest on his show, Lt. Col. Ralph Peters. The interview topic was President Trump and his bombing of Syria in response to the president of Syria using sarin gas on rebels in an ongoing civil war in which children were shown dying of the gas. The context of the conversation turned to the atrocities in Nigeria committed by the terrorist group Boko Haram. O'Reilly asked his guest why action has not been taken to address the children in Nigeria that have been burned and killed equally if not more than in Syria. O'Reilly asked why the western powers and the North Atlantic Treaty Organization (NATO) under the U.N. flag hadn't sent a military force into Nigeria to end the slaughter of children. Lt. Col. Peters, without any hesitation and with total exactitude, simply answered, "Because they're black. And the lighter the skin the more apt we are to engage." O'Reilly responded, "Do you really think it's a racial thing?" To which his guest explained through analogy, "We were much more concerned about the Balkans in the 90s than we were about an immense war going on in central Africa that killed millions."[158]

As refreshing as Col. Peters' blunt honesty is, infrahumanization of Blacks which produces insensitivity to Black suffering is usually much more subtle. Infrahumanization of Blacks provides a way to categorize the competence of Blacks in ways that support the emotional and cognitive beliefs of Whites. Infrahumanization can allow for high positive (warm) acceptance

---

157 Interview with Bill Bennett, Segment 6: Charles explains why Koch Industries actively promotes the principles of a free and open society (June 15, 2016) at http://news.kochind.com/news/2016/bill-bennett-interview-with-charles-koch,-part-(1)

158 *The O'Reilly Factor* (https://www.youtube.com/watch?v=7zR5_3a8DrI) (7:54-8:22) (Tuesday, April 11, 2017)

of Blacks as people and members of the community while imputing on them low professional or lifestyle competency, or at least lower competency than Whites.[159]

Consider the episode "Dark Sage" in the television series *Little House on the Prairie*.[160] In the episode the town doctor hired a Black doctor as his assistant. The Black doctor was well trained and had served as a surgeon in the civil war. The town doctor, who was White, sent the Black doctor to care for farm animals and gave him other seemingly demeaning tasks. When the doctor protested, the White doctor told him that's what country doctors do, they care for sick farm animals as well as the people of the town. He said, as a country doctor you should have known that. The episode climaxes when the husband of a White woman who is about to die in childbirth is knocked unconscious, so the Black doctor could perform surgery to save the woman and the baby. The husband said no Black man is touching his wife. After saving the woman, the Black doctor tells his wife they are leaving because the racism is too much.

The next day at church the White doctor gets up and confesses his prejudice to the whole town in attendance at church. He said that he had always thought he did not indulge in racism and that he always thought that a Black man could be a good man, a good farmer, and good blacksmith—but a doctor! No! He could not be his intellectual equal. He could not be his professional peer. Even worse, a Black man could not be his professional superior! The doctor admitted that he did not have the medical skill and knowledge that the Black doctor had. He admitted that the White woman would have died under his care. She would have died not due to his misconduct as a doctor but due to his lack of knowledge that the Black doctor had. Emotional infrahumanization of Blacks provides a way to categorize them into acceptable and unacceptable social status. Aversive treatment occurs when a Black man steps outside of the acceptable status made for him.

BLACK DEHUMANIZATION AND WHITE INFRAHUMANIZATION: THOMAS JEFFERSON, JEFFERSON DAVIS, AND THE IDEAS IN THE FOUNDING OF AMERICA

As previously discussed, dehumanization is a process in which members of the in-group ascribe negative characteristics (not human) to members of the out-group. Infrahumanization explains emotional insensitivity to the abuse suffered by the out-group by members of the in-group. Both concepts allow members of the out-group to be seen as "less than" human or "less deserving of" than members of the in-group. Infrahumanization supports the dehumanization of the out-group and provides members of the in-group the ability to hold biases without them believing that in fact they hold prejudices and racist ideals.

---

159 Lasana T. Harris and Susan T. Fiske, "Dehumanizing the lowest of the low neuroimaging responses to extreme out-groups," *Psychological Science* 17, no. 10 at 847–848. Supra note 81.

160 *Little House on the Prairie,* season 8, episode 4, "Dark Sage," aired October 26, 1981, NBC. TV series.

As detailed in later chapters of this book, Blacks have historically been dehumanized as chattel and were denied freedom and were used as animals for service before the civil war. After the war Blacks were denied constitutional and social rights of citizenship. After the fall of Jim Crow the infrahumanization that supported Jim Crow manifested itself into social acceptance or rationalization of Black incarceration and harsh treatment by police. This social acceptance or rationalization reduces sympathy or aversion to police use of force when it involves Blacks who are perceived as a social threat.

Dehumanization and infrahumanization differ from implicit racial bias in that the latter proposes that social and societal and political discourse has created a negative image and perception of Blacks and this bias or prejudice influences decisions regarding Blacks. The negative perceptions, even when rejected when consciously considered, are still uploaded into conscious thinking when exposed to ambiguous situations in which decisions regarding the situations do not provide time for higher-level thinking and decision-making. These conscious and unconscious perceptions are socially transmitted.

Long before the signing of the Declaration of Independence it was settled under colonial law that citizenship was not intended for Blacks to enjoy. At the signing of the Declaration of Independence it was settled politically, socially, legally, and religiously that Blacks were not included in the proposition that all men were equal. The beneficiaries of the purpose of government—the protection of equality and liberty of all people—did not include Blacks. The purpose of government, especially in the South, as discussed in Chapters Five and Seven, was to make sure Whites enjoyed these rights at the expense of Blacks and to make sure Blacks did not enjoy these rights at all.

To quote the writer of the Declaration of Independence, Thomas Jefferson, the hero and sage of White social conservatives and social conservative thought regarding individual liberty from government, Jefferson famously wrote regarding slavery and how it affects human behavior,

> It is difficult to determine on the standard by which the manners of a nation may be tried ... There must doubtless be an unhappy influence on the manners of our people produced by the existence of slavery among us. The whole commerce between master and slave is a perpetual exercise of the most boisterous passions, the most unremitting despotism on the one part, and degrading submissions on the other. Our children see this, and learn to imitate it; for man is an imitative animal. This quality is the germ of all education in him. From his cradle to his grave he is learning to do what he sees others do. If a parent could find no motive either in his philanthropy or his self-love, for restraining the intemperance of passion towards his slave, it should always be a sufficient one that his child is present. But generally it is not sufficient. The parent storms, the child looks on, catches the lineaments of wrath, puts on the same airs in the circle of smaller slaves, gives a loose to his worst of passions, and thus nursed, educated, and daily exercised in tyranny, cannot but be stamped by it with odious peculiarities. The man must be a prodigy who can retain his manners and morals undepraved by such circumstances. And with what execration

> should the statesman be loaded, who permitting one half the citizens thus to trample on the rights of the other … For in a warm climate, no man will labour for himself who can make another labour for him. … Indeed I tremble for my country when I reflect that God is just: that his justice cannot sleep forever … [161]

Jefferson makes the point plain. Racism and racial stereotypes are transferred from one generation to another and people operationalize and justify the racism they are exposed to. As Jefferson explains, a society defined by slavery and racism and "thus nursed, educated, and daily exercised in tyranny, cannot but be stamped by it with odious peculiarities [and the person] must be a prodigy who can retain his manners and morals undepraved by such circumstances." Implicit bias explains all those who are not prodigies.

Thomas Jefferson was not immune from the results of being nursed in the tyranny of slavery. But Jefferson was more than simply tainted with racism regarding Blacks, he was the unparalleled intellectual of his day and he set the tone for making racism socially and scientifically acceptable. His arguments in *Notes on the State of Virginia, Query XIV: The administration of justice and description of the laws?* pre-dated by almost a century the ideas of Social Darwinism and late nineteenth and early twentieth century genetic explanations for human behavior. The man who wrote that all men are created equal and endowed by their creator with the right to life, liberty and happiness made clear Blacks were inferior to Whites in all things. This inferiority required the separation of Blacks from Whites.

> It will probably be asked, Why not retain and incorporate the blacks into the state, and thus save the expense of supplying, by importation of white settlers, the vacancies they will leave? Deep rooted prejudices entertained by the whites; ten thousand recollections, by the blacks, of the injuries they have sustained; new provocations; the real distinctions which nature has made; and many other circumstances, will divide us into parties, and produce convulsions which will probably never end but in the extermination of the one or the other race.[162]

Jefferson reflects why Black and White integration was opposed both during his time and would be opposed well into the twentieth century—White fear that Blacks will seek revenge and will attack Whites for their mistreatment. Thus Blacks must be kept under social control. The debate until Appomattox was whether that social control was achieved through slavery or repatriation to Africa. After Appomattox the answer to that debate was Jim Crow. After the 1960s the answer to that debate was the utilization of the criminal justice system.

---

161 Thomas Jefferson, "Notes on the State of Virginia, Query XVIII: Manners, The particular customs and manners that may happen to be received in that state?" (1781)

162 Thomas Jefferson, "Notes on the State of Virginia, Query XIV: The administration of justice and description of the laws?"

Jefferson explains the need for social control is simple; Blacks are inferior by design of nature which is made clear by their physical and behavioral attributes.

> To these objections, which are political, may be added others, which are physical and moral. The first difference which strikes us is that of colour ... the difference is fixed in nature ... The circumstance of superior beauty, is thought worthy attention in the propagation of our horses, dogs, and other domestic animals; why not in that of man? Besides those of colour, figure, and hair, there are other physical distinctions proving a difference of race. They have less hair on the face and body. They secrete less by the kidnies, and more by the glands of the skin, which gives them a very strong and disagreeable odour. This greater degree of transpiration renders them more tolerant of heat, and less so of cold, than the whites ... They seem to require less sleep. A black, after hard labour through the day, will be induced by the slightest amusements to sit up till midnight, or later, though knowing he must be out with the first dawn of the morning. They are at least as brave, and more adventuresome. But this may perhaps proceed from a want of forethought, which prevents their seeing a danger till it be present. When present, they do not go through it with more coolness or steadiness than the whites.[163]

Blacks may have the ability to be brave but that is because Blacks lack the ability to think with forethought. Jefferson explains that socially Blacks are present oriented, they play when they should rest and they are more apt to play than work. As Jefferson explained, they are sexual but not loving and family oriented. They breed and procreate, they do not form family bonds as White people do.

> They are more ardent after their female: but love seems with them to be more an eager desire, than a tender delicate mixture of sentiment and sensation. Their griefs are transient. Those numberless afflictions, which render it doubtful whether heaven has given life to us in mercy or in wrath, are less felt, and sooner forgotten with them. In general, their existence appears to participate more of sensation than reflection. To this must be ascribed their disposition to sleep when abstracted from their diversions, and unemployed in labour. An animal whose body is at rest, and who does not reflect, must be disposed to sleep of course.

As to intellectual abilities Blacks are inferior on all levels of scientific and poetic creation or understanding.

> Comparing them by their faculties of memory, reason, and imagination, it appears to me, that in memory they are equal to the whites; in reason much inferior, as I think one could scarcely be found capable of tracing and comprehending the investigations of Euclid [a Greek mathematician]; and that in imagination they are dull, tasteless, and anomalous.

---

163 Thomas Jefferson, "Notes on the State of Virginia, Query XIV: The administration of justice and description of the laws?"

> … Many millions of them have been brought to, and born in America. … But never yet could I find that a black had uttered a thought above the level of plain narration; never see even an elementary trait of painting or sculpture. In music they are more generally gifted than the whites with accurate ears for tune and time … Misery is often the parent of the most affecting touches in poetry. —Among the blacks is misery enough, God knows, but no poetry. … But his imagination is wild and extravagant, escapes incessantly from every restraint of reason and taste, and, in the course of its vagaries, leaves a tract of thought as incoherent and eccentric, as is the course of a meteor through the sky.[164]

Jefferson then explains that the ignorant condition of Blacks is not due to slavery but by the fact that by nature and creation they are inferior. Jefferson compares slavery in the United States to slavery by the Romans and concludes slavery does not suppress the nature of the slave.

> The improvement of the blacks in body and mind, in the first instance of their mixture with the whites, has been observed by everyone, and proves that **their inferiority is not the effect merely of their condition of life.** We know that among the Romans, about the Augustan age especially, the condition of their slaves was much more deplorable than that of the blacks on the continent of America. The two sexes were confined in separate apartments, because to raise a child cost the master more than to buy one. … But in this country the slaves multiply as fast as the free inhabitants. Their situation and manners place the commerce between the two sexes almost without restraint. … With the Romans, the regular method of taking the evidence of their slaves was under torture. Here it has been thought better never to resort to their evidence. When a master was murdered, all his slaves, in the same house, or within hearing, were condemned to death. Here punishment falls on the guilty only, and as precise proof is required against him as against a freeman.[165]

Here Jefferson provides another foundation for the idea that protection and equality under the law does not apply to Blacks. He justifies the lack of torture of Black slaves in criminal trials with the statement that testimony of Blacks is of no value at all in the courts of justice. This idea that Blacks have no role in criminal trials outside of defendant would last well into the twentieth century. Jefferson continued,

> Yet notwithstanding these and other discouraging circumstances **among the Romans, their slaves *were*** often their rarest artists. They excelled too in science, insomuch as to be usually employed as tutors to their master's children. … But they were **of the race of whites. It is not their condition then, but nature, which has produced the distinction.**

164 Thomas Jefferson, "Notes on the State of Virginia, Query XIV: The administration of justice and description of the laws?"

165 Thomas Jefferson, "Notes on the State of Virginia, Query XIV: The administration of justice and description of the laws?"

> — Whether further observation will or will not verify the conjecture, that nature has been less bountiful to them in the endowments of the head, I believe that in those of the heart she will be found to have done them justice.[166]

After concluding that nature was not unjust in making Blacks inferior, Jefferson deals with the social results of nature's decision. He focused on the distinction on how government must apply the law to Blacks and Whites and concludes that equality is not required.

> That disposition to theft with which they have been branded, must be ascribed to their situation, and not to any depravity of the moral sense. The man, in whose favour no laws of property exist, probably feels himself less bound to respect those made in favour of others. When arguing for ourselves, we lay it down as a fundamental, that laws, to be just, must give a reciprocation of right: that, without this, they are mere arbitrary rules of conduct, founded in force, and not in conscience:

His conclusion, the law must not be arbitrary when it comes to Whites, but the law is whatever the White master says it is when it comes to Blacks. Jefferson continued, regarding the treatment of Blacks under the law,

> it is a problem which I give to the master to solve, whether the religious precepts against the violation of property were not framed for him as well as his slave? And whether the slave may not as justifiably take a little from one, who has taken all from him, as he may slay one who would slay him? That a change in the relations in which a man is placed should change his ideas of moral right and wrong, is neither new, nor peculiar to the colour of the blacks. Homer tells us it was so 2600 years ago.[167]

Jefferson explained that the moral and philosophical question over the treatment of slaves and the protection of the law being applied to the slave and slave master is an old debate. Jefferson explained that it was true that in Rome slaves had status in the home of their masters and enjoyed legal protections,

> But the slaves of which Homer speaks were whites. Notwithstanding these considerations which must weaken their respect for the laws of property, we find among them numerous instances of the most rigid integrity, and as many as among their better instructed masters, of benevolence, gratitude, and unshaken fidelity.[168]

---

166 Thomas Jefferson, "Notes on the State of Virginia, Query XIV: The administration of justice and description of the laws?" (1781)

167 Thomas Jefferson, "Notes on the State of Virginia, Query XIV: The administration of justice and description of the laws?" (1781)

168 Thomas Jefferson, "Notes on the State of Virginia, Query XIV: The administration of justice and description of the laws?" (1781)

Thomas Jefferson then concludes with his most famous statement regarding Blacks,

> **The opinion, that they are inferior in the faculties of reason and imagination** ... requires many observations ... To our reproach it must be said, that though for a century and a half we have had under our eyes the races of black and of red men ... **I advance it therefore** as a suspicion only, that **the blacks, whether originally a distinct race, or made distinct by time and circumstances, are inferior to the whites in the endowments both of body and mind.**

The conclusion he draws from Black inferiority, regarding race mixing on a social level without slavery, would provide support for social policies in America that would last for more than a hundred and eighty years.

> This unfortunate difference of colour, and perhaps of faculty, is a powerful obstacle to the emancipation of these people. Many of their advocates, while they wish to vindicate the liberty of human nature, are anxious also to preserve its dignity and beauty. Some of these, embarrassed by the question "What further is to be done with them?" join themselves in opposition with those who are actuated by sordid avarice only. Among the Romans emancipation required but one effort. The slave, when made free, might mix with, without staining the blood of his master. But with us a second is necessary, unknown to history. When freed, he is to be removed beyond the reach of mixture.[169]

"Blacks, whether originally a distinct race, or made distinct by time and circumstances, are inferior to the whites in the endowments both of body and mind." So said the writer of "all men are created equal." The discontinuity of these two principles would be exposed by the fathers of the confederacy and states' rights, Senators John Calhoun and Jefferson Davis. They would assert, as discussed in Chapter Four, that Jefferson was wrong in his second premise and was correct in the first.

Senator **Jefferson Davis**, the future President of the Confederacy, would invoke the scriptures, a strategy for supporting slavery discussed in Chapter Five, to justify the dehumanization of Blacks and their enslavement as well as assert that the system of slavery elevates the White man regardless of his economic position. On March 2, 1859, on the floor of the U.S. Senate, Davis stated,

> I reply to the statement, and I reply in no offensive sense. The Senator makes a statement that the white laborers of the South are degraded. I say there was never anything less true, either in the Senate or out of it. I say that ***the lower race*** of human beings that constitute

---

169 Thomas Jefferson, Notes on the State of Virginia, Query XIV: "The administration of justice and description of the laws?" (1781)

> the substratum of ***what is termed*** **the slave population of the South, elevates every white man in our community.**[170]

This part of Davis' response was to the general argument of the South that their slaves were treated better than free laborers in the North. The South argued that their slaves were cared for outside of labor, and when they were old, were economically supported. They asserted that in the North a worker was paid for their service in jobs that were life threatening. And when injured or too old to work they were discarded for a new worker. The South asserted that slavery was the more humane system.

Davis then argued that unlike the North, the South had no social caste system among Whites based on employment.

> I say it is there true that every mechanic assumes among us the position which only a master workman holds among you. Hence it is that mechanic in our southern states is admitted to the table of his employer, converses with him on terms of equality—not merely political equality, but an actual equality—wherever the two men come in contact. The white laborers of the South are all of them men who are employed in what you would term the higher pursuits of labor among you.[171]

Whites, according to Davis, regardless of economic or work status, were unified by the proposition that all Whites were better than Blacks. Blackness was attached not only to slavery but whiteness was attached to Black inferiority.

> It is the presence of a lower caste, those lower by their mental and physical organization, controlled by the higher intellect of the white man, that gives this superiority to the white laborer. Menial services are not there performed by the white man. **We have none of our brethren sunk to the degradation of being menials. That belongs to the lower race**—the descendants of Ham, who, under the judgement of God speaking to the prophet Noah, were condemned to be servants. **To propose that** we should change our industrial system, that **we should bring negroes up to a level with the white man**, would be such **an offense** that the lecturer who would come to teach such philosophy would be fortunate indeed if he should escape without some public indignity.[172]

Dehumanization and infrahumanization allows people to elevate the emotional value of Whites and to justify the negative treatment of Blacks without seeing a contradiction.

---

170 Jefferson Davis, "Speech in U.S. Senate," in *The Essential Writings of Jefferson Davis*, ed. William Cooper (New York: Modern Library, 2004), 159.

171 Jefferson Davis, "Speech in U.S. Senate," in *The Essential Writings of Jefferson Davis*, ed. William Cooper (New York: Modern Library, 2004), 159.

172 Jefferson Davis, "Speech in U.S. Senate," in *The Essential Writings of Jefferson Davis* (New York: Modern Library, 2004): 159–160.

Slavery, according to Davis, not only puts Blacks in their place but elevates all Whites to a higher place regardless of the individual worth of Whites or Blacks. Davis concluded his defense of slavery with the following:

> **One of the reconciling features in the existence of that particular institution called domestic slavery of African bondsmen, is the fact that it raises white men to the same general level, that it dignifies and exalts every white man by the presence of a lower race.**
>
> I say it in no terms of disparaging comparison with others. I say but what has been with me a deliberate conviction, that it is promotive of, if not essential to, the preservation of the higher orders of republican civilization.[173]

The premise of the pre-revolutionary era was that the law attached blackness to slavery and detached slavery or indentured servitude from whiteness. The status of free and slave, the status between being protected by the law and being outside of the protection of the law, the status of full citizenship and being a second-class citizen, was based solely on skin color. From the distinction based on skin color came the social beliefs of inferiority that Jefferson, Calhoun and Davis—later by post-bellum America—so clearly annunciated. Being White made Whites better. Being Black made Blacks inferior. As discussed in the remaining chapters of this book, blackness being negative fostered systematic policies of social control—slavery, Black Codes and Jim Crow—followed by systemic policies of social control through the criminal justice system post Jim Crow. Both the systematic and systemic social control of Blacks has been a constant historical theme in American political rhetoric and policy.

To summarize, implicit racial bias proposes that societal and political discourse has created a negative image and perception of Blacks, and this bias or prejudice influences decisions regarding Blacks. The negative perceptions, even when rejected when consciously considered, are still uploaded into conscious thinking when exposed to ambiguous situations in which decisions regarding the situations do not provide time for higher-level thinking and decision-making. These conscious and unconscious perceptions are socially transmitted. Long before the signing of the Declaration of Independence and the ratification of the U.S. Constitution, it was settled politically, socially, legally, and religiously that Blacks were not included in the proposition that all men were equal. Long after the signing of the Declaration of Independence and the ratification of the U.S. Constitution, it was settled that it was not intended for Blacks to enjoy the protection of government, which was purposed to ensure the rights of equality and liberty of all people. The purpose of government, especially in the South, as discussed in Chapters Five and Seven, was to

---

173 Jefferson Davis, "Speech in U.S. Senate," in (*The Essential Writings of Jefferson Davis* (New York: Modern Library, 2004): 159–160.

make sure Whites enjoyed these rights at the expense of Blacks and to make sure Blacks did not enjoy these rights at all.

*****

The fact that the days of George Wallace and Strom Thurmond (the significance of both men in American policy and modern political history regarding race is discussed in Chapters Four and Seven) are over does not mean that the racism that defined them is over. Racism has many forms—the death of KKK-level racism does not mean the problem of racism has been eradicated. Although racism is not—post the 1960s and 1970s—the single explanation of the disparities within the criminal justice system, racism was at the beginning of those disparities. As discussed in Chapter Four, negative perceptions of Blacks were developed within the American political and social culture through more than a century of politics. The development of this political and social culture further helps place in context the dynamics of race and criminal justice.

KEY TERMS AND CONCEPTS

1. Minority threat theory
2. Out of place theory
3. Status of offender / officer theory
4. Black's theory of law
5. Social geography and utilization of the police
6. Social psychology
7. Cultural stereotypes
8. Implicit bias
9. Prejudice and racism
10. Aversive racism
11. Stereotype threat theory
12. Cognitive accessibility
13. Discriminability
14. Dehumanization and Infrahumanization
15. Stereotype Lift / White privilege
16. Shoot / don't shoot research
17. Police ambiguity
18. Reverse racism effect
19. Involuntary bio-chemical and brain wave reaction (fear) to stimuli (race)
20. Pattern recognition (schema motor learning)
21. Racism without racists
22. Critical Race Theory (CRT)
23. Racial Threat Theory / Tipping Point Theory

DISCUSSION QUESTIONS

1. In this chapter it is argued that when looking at police behavior in relation to race, various factors should be considered. How does the character of suspects, the encounter, and the police officer interact in light of threat theories?
2. What is implicit bias?
3. Explain and define shoot/don't shoot research and why police and civilians in experiments are more likely and quicker to shoot Blacks than Whites. What are the strengths and weaknesses of this research? What are the two types of methodologies for this research? Do you agree with the conclusions of this research? Why or why not?
4. In Chapter Two the law regarding the Fourth Amendment asserts that police work in situations in which they have to make decisions without calm reflection and some situations require decisionmaking within seconds. How does the field of social psychology address the problem of ambiguity and the utilization of stereotype?
5. How do bidirectional stereotyping and the "uploading" of stereotypes affect police decision-making? How does the process work? What is the relationship between bidirectional stereotyping and racial profiling? Do you agree with the theory of bidirectional stereotyping as an explanation for police encounters with Blacks? Why or why not?
6. What is pattern recognition (schema motor learning), and how does it explain police behavior? Do you think it explains behavior in relation to the decision to shoot when engaging a young Black male?
7. What is the distinction between cultural stereotypes, implicit bias, and aversive racism? How can aversive racism be used to explain police behavior? How can aversive racism provide an explanation to a Terry Stop and police use of force? How does aversive racism relate to stereotype threat theory? How does stereotype threat theory affect the behavior of both Blacks and Whites?
8. What is critical race theory and what does it offer in understanding police behavior and police encounters with Blacks? Does it provide a positive or negative explanation?
9. What is the difference between dehumanization, infrahumanization, racism, and prejudice? How does dehumanization and infrahumanization affect the level of sympathy to Black suffering? How do dehumanization, infrahumanization, and racial threat theory explain the politics of and distinctions between liberal and conservative reactions to police shootings?
10. How does social psychology use cognitive accessibility and discriminability to explain how police reaction and correct perception of threats? How are these concepts related to implicit bias, stereotype, and pattern recognition (schema motor learning)?
11. How is the treatment of police officers in their department related to how Blacks perceive police officers on the street? What is organizational justice theory and Police legitimacy and procedural justice theory? Discuss what policy implications are made in this chapter regarding police use of force based on social psychology literature.

12. Social conservatives often quote Jefferson and the Declaration of Independence as the foundation of American moral and political purpose. Should Jefferson's views on race in Query XIV and slavery in Query XVIII be equally quoted as part of American moral and political history? Does it matter in the twenty-first century what Jefferson thought about race? Are his thoughts on race and social control still reflected in social and criminal justice policy and politics today?

CHAPTER FOUR

The Foundations of Racism in America

A REVIEW OF PRE- AND POST-CIVIL WAR RACE POLITICS

STUDENT LEARNING OBJECTIVES

1. Students will be able to put criminal justice policy and political perspectives in the larger context of American political history and the rhetoric regarding race.
2. Students will be able to link the development of the criminal justice system with the politics and policies of pre- and post-civil war America and why these social political contexts matter in understanding the formation of the contemporary criminal justice system.
3. Students will know who John Calhoun, Alexander Stephens, Jefferson Davis, Abraham Lincoln, James Garfield, Harry Truman, Orval Faubus, Strom Thurmond, George Wallace, Dwight D. Eisenhower, Barry Goldwater, John F. Kennedy, and Lyndon Johnson are and will be able to place these political figures in context with American political history and criminal justice history and explain their significance to both.
4. Students will be able to explain the link between rhetorical defenses of slavery and the inferiority of Blacks with rhetorical defenses of Jim Crow and how both were defended by the political argument of states' rights.
5. Students will be able to explain the link between the politics of civil rights, states' rights, and the criminal justice policies of the 1960s.
6. Students will be able to explain the political rhetoric of the Republican and Democratic parties in social, political, and historical context.

*****

This chapter begins with a brief summary of American politics from the rise of the Great Depression through the 1960s. This history starts with a broader view of American political thought that begins with the antebellum period—the 1840s through to 1861—and then the postbellum period—1865 through the 1890s. These periods are significant to the history of how race was perceived and what role the national government had regarding slavery and, a century later, Jim Crow. The politics and narratives of states' rights and the tyranny of the federal government when attempting to control slavery and then end Jim Crow forms the background for the criminal justice policies of the 1960s through the first decade of the twenty-first century. The meaning of the rule of law, Black incarceration, the justifications for that incarceration, the rhetoric of law and order, and the role of government to deal with crime all find their origins in the rhetoric of the antebellum, postbellum, and civil rights eras.

THE RISE OF MODERN POLITICAL SOCIAL CONSERVATISM IN AMERICA: AN OVERVIEW

In 1929, the New York Stock Market crashed, and the resulting worldwide depression brought a worldwide debate on the value of capitalism and the role of government to control capitalism and provide financial security for its citizens. The debate led to the rise of Hitler, Stalin, Mussolini, and Franco in Europe, and Roosevelt in the United States. While the former four brought Nazism, Communism, and Fascism as an answer, Roosevelt brought the New Deal. Franklin D. Roosevelt, first elected in 1932, asserted that the purpose of the federal government was to provide a minimal level of financial security for all Americans while supporting the operation and individual ideals of free market capitalism. Traditional values and economic conservatives opposed Roosevelt and the philosophy behind the New Deal programs from its inception. President Roosevelt prevailed in three subsequent elections (1936, 1940, and 1944), and the programs became a staple of modern American life.

After World War II, the nation had not only defeated Nazism and Fascism; it had defeated the Great Depression and had emerged as a world superpower with an economic and industrial base that was second to none. But more importantly, Americans developed the worldview that American dominance in the world, *Pax Americana*, and economic security from depression was the norm, not the exception. More importantly, the Roosevelt years had built into the American political system the idea that the national government was the primary governmental institution. In 1946, the federal government assumed responsibility for maintaining full employment and maintaining economic stability. By the end of World War II, all political and economic roads led to Washington, D.C. The federal government was no longer first among equals, it was first with no equals, and the state governments were secondary, if not subservient, in the new federalism. By 1946 the federal government had put its weight behind economic fairness, if not equality, the limitation on laissez faire capitalism and ending state Jim Crow. The rejection of this new reality is the foundational definition of modern social and economic conservativism.

Social conservatives in the 1950s were convinced that America was moving in the wrong direction for a multitude of reasons. The post-depression policies of Roosevelt, which had supplanted classical Republican perspectives on the role of government, were compounded by social and political change. The rise of the supremacy of the federal government at the expense of state government continued during the civil rights movement in the 1950s with its the goal of causing the fall of the one-hundred-year-old social/political system of segregation. The federal government supported the end of Jim Crow with military troops and U.S. Marshalls to bring the Southern states to heel in 1957 (the Little Rock Nine), 1962 (James Meredith), 1963 (integration of University of Alabama), and 1965 (protection of the second Selma Edmund Pettus Bridge march). The Supreme Court's support of the rising civil rights movement was made all the worse in conservative eyes by the Court not only requiring the states to allow Black children to be seated with White children, because we (the Supreme Court) say so, but while doing so, the states cannot force those children to say the Lord's Prayer in school.

During the 1950s and early 1960s, conservatives as a group united in their opposition of the growing federal government and the social changes occurring in society. These conservatives included William F. Buckley and his magazine the *National Review*, Ronald Reagan, Richard Nixon, Milton Friedman, the editors of the *Wall Street Journal*, Strom Thurmond, and George Wallace, just to name a few. The rhetoric of Thurmond and Wallace is significant. These conservatives came onto the political and social stage with conservative principles that attacked not only the liberalism of the 1960s (and the civil rights acts of the 1960s), but both political parties, which supported and/or tolerated these movements rather than opposing them at all costs. During this period, conservatives led by Thurmond and Wallace and followed by Goldwater and Reagan established a unifying theory of what American conservatism should and would be. They united under the banner of states' rights, opposition to the Civil Rights Acts of 1964 and 1968, forced integration, limited government, and individual economic and social responsibility.

By 1964, White flight from the cities had begun, and the rise of the suburbs like Levittown, New York, began the social and political separation that would later create the silent majority (and the Southern strategy) that elected Nixon in 1968. By the time of the ascent of Johnson and his election in 1964, America was adopting liberal policies on every sphere of society, but there had also developed a growing backlash to those very policies. That backlash would center conservatism into the Republican Party in the 1964, 1966, and 1968 elections.

In 1964, Barry Goldwater won the Republican nomination for president. His nomination established the control of the party by free market, anti–great society, personal responsibility, crime control model, limited federal government, strong military, low taxes, anti–integration and socially conservative, traditional family values-oriented voters. In 1966, conservative White middle-class blowback gave the Republicans a significant victory in the midterm elections and foreshadowed the fall of President Johnson and the Great Society. In the midterm elections of 1966,

> Republicans were revivified and on the brink of an era of increasing political success, including near-domination of presidential elections that Democrats have occasionally overcome but have not yet ended four decades later.
>
> A number of events took a toll on Johnson's popularity by late 1966, including lack of demonstrable success in Vietnam, race riots and other civil disturbances at home, and

> an increasing sense that the Great Society was running amok, spending too much and centralizing too much.
>
> When all was said and done, the GOP gained 47 House seats, three Senate seats, eight governorships, and 557 state legislative seats. Republican governors controlled 25 states, the most since the early 1950s. Republicans actually won a majority of the aggregated national vote for U.S. Senate. Of the 38 House districts where Democrats had replaced Republicans in 1964, only 14 remained in Democratic hands in 1966.[1]

By 1968 (especially after the urban riots of 1967) politics in America abandoned the hopeful and optimistic ideals of the early 1960s and became more hostile to the policies of President Johnson and the social policies of the left. By 1968, both the left and the right of the political spectrum opposed the Vietnam War, and support for civil rights was being abandoned by both White middle-class suburban voters and Black urban youth. The civil rights movement merged with civil disobedience, both of which merged with White middle-class fear of crime, which merged with Blacks in general and Black males specifically within the American political and social mind. By the end of 1968, the nation turned away from the optimism of the early 1960s. By 1968, John F. Kennedy, Martian Luther King Jr., and Robert F. Kennedy had been assassinated, and the civil rights movement took a militant approach to American society. The promises of the Johnson Administration had not come to fruition, and Blacks were beginning to abandon the integration non-violent perspective of King as a method to achieve economic success. The social fabric of the nation changed not only because of the civil rights movement, it changed, because the middle and late 1960s witnessed the dawn of the second wave of the women's movement and the gay rights movements. President Richard Nixon took office in 1969 on a law and order platform in which the silent majority sought to turn back America and American society from the influence of the 1960s, the counterculture and the decade of Woodstock.

The re-election of Nixon in 1972 continued to centralize conservatism in the Republican Party, because that election solidified liberal control of the Democratic Party. As the 1964 election gave traditional conservatives control of the Republican Party during their convention, the 1972 divided and cantankerous Democratic convention established control of the Democratic Party to the social liberals. The nomination of McGovern split the Democratic Party and forced out many conservative Democrats (foreign policy conservatives/ Wilsonians (neo-cons), the Nixon "hard hats" (urban and suburban non–college educated working class White males) and middle-class educated White males all of which joined the Republican Party.

By the election of Reagan in 1980, a coalition of the various strands of conservative thought found a unifying figure in Reagan and found a figure who could win. To this day, all

---

1 Andrew E. Busch, *1966 Foreshadows Republican Era* (2006) at http://ashbrook.org/publications/oped-busch-06-1966/.

conservatives, regardless of stripe, revere Reagan because of his accomplishment in 1980 and his reelection in 1984 (winning 49 out of 50 states).

The strategy that carried the Republican Party from a devastating loss in 1964 to dominance in the 1980s has been called the *Southern Strategy.* The southern strategy is built on the proposition that in American politics the goal is to achieve political power to make policy and elections are won or lost on group conflicts. Put another way, elections are not won by voting for what you like but rather by voting against what you hate. If a voter is convinced the nation is moving in the wrong direction, that voter will vote against the party that is in power that is linked with that wrong direction. In politics, hate is a stronger motivator than love. Voters vote against what they hate more than vote for what they love.

Voting is also explained by the fact that that people vote based on the group they are in and the values that are attached to the group they are in. The group can be religious, cultural, gender, class (economic) or racial. By 1964 the New Deal coalition of southern poor whites, urban whites, and Blacks to a limited extent, which had dominated the politics of the Democratic Party was breaking up over the adoption of civil rights by the northern states under the Democratic Party. With the Democrats adopting policies that increased the number of Blacks in the party, southern Democrats and then Republicans—lead by Wallace, Thurmond, Goldwater and Nixon—sought to dislodge southern White democrats from the party in order to convert them into Republicans. By the election of Nixon in 1968 and 1972 the strategy included the use of dog whistle politics of tough on crime and by the 1980s opposition to affirmative action and abortion to hold White voters. The southern strategy sought to create a new republican majority by combining White and middle-class voters in the south, west and in suburbia.[2]

The southern strategy between 1964 and 1972 took advantage of White resentment and unease of (1) Black advancement—which many believed occurred at their expense—and (2) the general cultural changes in America—the rise of women's rights, Gay rights, integration, liberal moral sexual behavior and attitudes, and the general abandonment of the 1930s and 1940s vision of the role of women and men in society. The southern strategy bonded these voters into a voting majority that took hold with Nixon and bore full fruit with the election of Reagan.

The southern strategy in the late 1960s through the early 1970s, aside from fighting integration and the agenda of the post 1968 civil rights movement, translated segregationist racism into conservative politics of states' rights and law and order. Defense of segregation gave way in the early 1970s to opposition to bussing and affirmative action. The rhetoric of Wallace and Thurmond in the 1940s through the early 1960s was replaced by the rhetoric of Wallace,

---

2 Ian Haney Lopez, *Dog Whistle Politics: How Coded Racial Appeals have Reinvented Racism and Wrecked the Middle Class* (2014) at 26–34. See also, Kevin Phillips, *The Emerging Republican Majority,* 1st ed. (1969), Dan T. Carter, *The Politics of Rage: George Wallace, The Origins of the New Conservatism and the Transformation of American Politics,* second ed. (LSU Press, 2000) and Dan T. Carter, *From George Wallace to Newt Gingrich: Race in the Conservative Counterrevolution 1963–1994* (LSU Press, 1996).

Thurmond, Nixon, and Reagan in the late 1960s through the 1980s of law and order, limited government, the war on drugs and crime, opposition to affirmative action, and reverse discrimination. Republican politics took advantage of resentment among southern democrats that the Democratic Party was no longer a "White man's party." The campaign of Wallace in 1968 injected into conservative rhetoric and orthodoxy a resentment of social and political elites in both parties and the narrative of the forgotten man in the political discourse in both parties. Nixon in a 1968 radio address would mirror this narrative with his assertion of the "salient center" which the following year became the "silent majority"[3] which in 1980 under Jerry Farwell became the "moral majority." All of these brand names represented the same type of voter. They were the people of Middle America, living in Middle America, who do not demonstrate, who do not picket or protest, who did not riot, who respected authority, and were the people who were open to being convinced to vote for either party. These were also the voters who resented the speed of change in society (end of segregation and imposed integration) and the hippie protesters of 1968. They were the people who supported law enforcement, feared urban crime and riots, resented the conclusions of the Kerner Commission that blamed Black violence and riots on White America, and were voters who both resented the protesters of the Vietnam War and resented the failures in the war in Vietnam. They were the voters who believed America was moving down the wrong track, both morally and socially. Nixon and Wallace both realized that if the rhetoric of raw racism could be substituted for law and order and removed from arguments defending states' rights and conservatism in general, these White voters (in the North, South, and Midwest) could be tipped into the Republican Party. They were in 1968 and 1972 and have not left since.

By the second decade of the new century, discussed in Chapters Nine and Ten, the southern strategy had evolved into republican White voters resenting social elites— in both parties and in the media—who they perceived as looking down upon them. These voters of the South and Midwest turned on the "Republican Establishment" which they perceived as selling out working class White voters, who had supported them for decades, for social and corporate elites who supported international trade that produced wealth in New York and political power in Washington but had failed to make life better for the White middle class. In this rebellion, birthed by the resentment of a Black man elected as president, non-college educated White men and women and Whites in general turned on the Republican Party and produced the election of Donald Trump.

This political history of the parties provides a background for understanding the resulting criminal justice policies introduced in Chapter One and discussed in detail in Chapter Seven. The remainder of this chapter will begin to explain how these policies developed by examining the historical political rhetoric within American political discourse regarding the protection

---

3 For further discussion on the origin of the silent center and silent majority rhetoric, see interview with Nixon speech writer Richard Whalen at http://weekendamerica.publicradio.org/display/web/2008/05/16/silent_center.html

of the liberty and freedom of Blacks in America. How presidents and party leaders spoke regarding whether Blacks, as people, had a right or did not have a right to equal justice under the law has defined how Blacks, over time, are negatively perceived; a phenomenon that was discussed in Chapter Three. The rhetorical political history of race in America, like all race history, is a very complicated and evolving subject.

THE POLITICAL RHETORIC OF RACE AND THE POLITICIANS OF THE ANTEBELLUM AND POSTBELLUM PERIODS: THE ORIGINS OF POLITICAL SOCIAL CONSERVATISM AND RACE POLITICS IN THE REPUBLICAN AND DEMOCRATIC PARTIES

The same nation that was built on the idea that all men are created equal established slavery based on the proposition that Blacks were inferior to Whites and that slavery was their natural state.[4] That same nation endured a Civil War at the cost of 620,000 lives to settle the debate on whether slavery was a "great institution [and was] the most safe and stable basis for free institutions in the world" as Senator John Calhoun of South Carolina asserted (on the floor of the U.S. Senate) on January 10, 1838.[5] The 1838 speech, *On The Importance Of Domestic Slavery*, was in support of a document, *The Calhoun Resolutions, w*hich proposed six resolutions on states' rights and limited powers of the national government. During this period of time, states' rights and defiance of the federal government and subjugation of Blacks merged. This is where states' rights, being the rhetorical code for the protection of segregation and limiting the federal government power to govern how states treat the civil rights of minorities, finds its roots.

The *Calhoun Resolutions asserted* six principles,

> ***Resolved***, That in the adoption of the Federal Constitution, the States adopting the same acted severally, as free, independent, and sovereign States; and that each, for itself, by its own voluntary assent, entered the Union with the view to its increased security against all dangers, domestic as well as foreign, and the more perfect and secure enjoyment of its advantages, natural, political, and social.
> ***Resolved***, That in delegating a portion of their powers to be exercised by the Federal Government, the States retained, severally, the exclusive and sole right over their own domestic institutions and police, and are alone responsible for them is an assumption of superiority not warranted by the Constitution …
> ***Resolved***, That this Government was instituted and adopted by the several States of this Union … and … this Government is bound so to exercise its powers [for the] increased stability and security to the domestic institutions of the States that compose the Union;

4 *Infra* notes 5–13.

5 John Calhoun, "On the Importance of Domestic Slavery" Speech in the U.S. Senate on January 10, 1838.

> and that it is the solemn duty of the Government to resist all attempts by one portion of the Union to use it as an instrument to attack the domestic institutions of another, or to weaken or destroy such institutions, instead of strengthening and upholding them, as it is in duty bound to do.
> ***Resolved***, That domestic slavery, as it exists in the Southern and Western States of this Union, composes an important part of their domestic institutions, inherited from their ancestors, and existing at the adoption of' the Constitution, by which it is recognized as constituting an essential element in the distribution of its powers among the States; and that no change of opinion, or feeling, on the part of the other States of the Union in relation, to it, can justify them or their citizens in open and systematic attacks thereon, with the view to its overthrew; and that all such attacks are in manifest violation of the mutual and solemn pledge to protect and defend each other, given by the States, respectively, on entering into the Constitutional compact, which formed the Union, and as such is a manifest breach of faith, and a violation of the most solemn obligations, moral and religious.
> ***Resolved***, That the intermeddling of any State or States, or their citizens, to abolish slavery ... is immoral or sinful; or the passage of any act or measure of Congress, with that view, would be a direct and dangerous attack on the institutions of all the slaveholding States.
> ***Resolved***, ... it is the solemn duty of all, and more especially of this body, which represents the States in their corporate capacity, to resist all attempts to discriminate between the States in extending the benefits of the Government to the several portions of the Union; and that to refuse to extend to the, Southern and Western States ... the institution of slavery, as it exists among them, is immoral or sinful, or otherwise obnoxious, would be contrary to that equality of rights and advantages which the Constitution was intended to secure alike to all the members of the Union, and would, in effect, disfranchise the slaveholding States, withholding from them the advantages, while it subjected them to the burthens, of the Government.

Calhoun's document defined states' rights in the first two resolutions. In the remaining four resolutions he made clear that the context for the assertion and defense of states' rights is the protection of slavery and opposing the federal government's attempts to limit the growth and spread of slavery.

Calhoun argued that the federal government was one of limited powers; that it was formed by the states, not "We the people;" that it was the abolition of slavery, not slavery itself that was evil; and that the federal government should seek to protect, not interfere, with the Southern and Western states' implementation of slavery. In support of the six resolutions, Calhoun asserted that the issue of slavery was more than an issue of master and slave but was an issue of the plan of God and nature and how free men govern themselves under the Constitution.

> He saw (said Mr. C.) in the question before us the fate of the South. It was a higher than the mere naked question of master and slave. It involved a great political institution, essential to the peace and existence of one-half of this Union. A mysterious Providence

> had brought together two races, from different portions of the globe, and placed them together in nearly equal numbers in the Southern portion of this Union. They were there inseparably united, beyond the possibility of separation. Experience had shown that the existing relation between them secured the peace and happiness of both. Each had improved; the inferior greatly; so much so, that it had attained a degree of civilization never before attained by the black race in any age or country. Under no other relation could they coexist together. To destroy it was to involve a whole region in laughter, carnage, and desolation; and, come what will, we must defend and preserve it.
>
> This agitation has produced one happy effect at least; it has compelled us to the South to look into the nature and character of this great institution, and to correct many false impressions that even we had entertained in relation to it, *Many in the South once believed that it was a moral and political evil; that folly and delusion are gone; we see it now in its true light, and regard it as the most safe and stable basis for free institutions in the world.*[6]

In his February 6, 1837, *Slavery a Positive Good* speech on the floor of the U.S. Senate Calhoun defended the economic, social, political, and natural order of life regarding slavery in the South.

> But I take a higher ground. I hold that in the present state of civilization, where two races of different origin, and distinguished by color, and other physical differences, as well as intellectual, are brought together, *the relation now existing in the slaveholding States between the two, is, instead of an evil, a good, a positive good.* I feel myself called upon to speak freely upon the subject where the honor and interests of those I represent are involved. I hold then, that there never has yet existed a wealthy and civilized society in which one portion of the community did not, in point of fact, live on the labor of the other. Broad and general as is this assertion, it is fully borne out by history ... But I will not dwell on this aspect of the question; I turn to the political; and here *I fearlessly assert that the existing relation between the two races in the South, against which these blind fanatics are waging war, forms the most solid and durable foundation on which to rear free and stable political institutions.* It is useless to disguise the fact. There is and always has been in an advanced stage of wealth and civilization, a conflict between labor and capital. The condition of society in the South exempts us from the disorders and dangers resulting from this conflict; and which explains why it is that the political condition of the slaveholding States has been so much more stable and quiet than that of the North ... Surrounded as the slaveholding States are with such imminent perils, I rejoice to think that our means of defense are ample, if we shall prove to have the intelligence and spirit to see and apply them before it is too late. All we want is concert, to lay aside all party differences and unite

6 John Calhoun, "On the Importance of Domestic Slavery" (emphasis added).

> with zeal and energy in repelling approaching dangers. *Let there be concert of action, and we shall find ample means of security without resorting to secession or disunion.*[7]

On February 19, 1847, Calhoun again asserted that the federal government was the creation of the states not the people and would prophesy the assertions made by the Confederate South less than two decades later. In his *Speech on the Importance of His Resolutions on the Slave Question*, Calhoun said on the floor of the U.S. Senate,

> I rise to offer a set of resolutions in reference to the various resolutions from the State legislatures upon the subject of what they call the extension of slavery. ... Sir, the day that the balance between the two sections of the country—the slaveholding States and the non-slaveholding States-is destroyed, is a day that will not be far removed from political revolution, anarchy, Civil War, and widespread disaster. ... *Ours is a Federal Constitution. The States are its constituents, and not the people.* The twenty-eight States—the twenty-nine States (including Iowa)—stand under this Government as twenty-nine individuals ... it was so formed that every State, as a constituent member of this Union of ours, should enjoy all its advantages, natural and acquired, with greater security, and enjoy them more perfectly. The whole system is based on justice and equality—perfect equality between the members of this republic. ...
>
> Mr. President, not only is that proposition grossly inconsistent with the constitution, but the other, which undertakes to say that no State shall be admitted into this Union, which shall not prohibit by its constitution the existence of slaves, is equally a great outrage against the constitution of the United States. Sir, I hold it to be a fundamental principle of our political system that the people have a right to establish what government they may think proper for themselves; that every State about to become a member of this Union has a right to form its government as it pleases; and that, in order to be admitted there is but one qualification, and that is, that the Government shall be Republican.[8]

This apostasy that the states, not the people, established the constitution would find echo in the mouth of President Reagan at his inaugural address in January 1981, when he said, "It is my intention to curb the size and influence of the Federal establishment and to demand recognition of the distinction between the powers granted to the Federal Government and

---

7 John Calhoun Speech, "Slavery a Positive Good" at http://teachingamericanhistory.org/library/document/slavery-a-positive-good/ (Emphasis added). See generally, Thomas G. West, *Vindicating the Founders: Race, sex, Class, and Justice in the Origins of America* (1977) for the proposition that the Founders, specifically Jefferson, recognized slavery as an evil but admitted that it was an evil that could not be separated from the good in forming the United States under the Constitution or for that matter forming the alliance among the colonies to fight for independence from Great Britain.

8 John Calhoun Speech, "Speech On The Introduction Of His Resolutions On The Slave Question" (February 19, 1847) at http://www.founding.com/founders_library/pageID.2283/default.asp.

those reserved to the States or to the people. All of us need to be reminded that the Federal Government did not create the States; the States created the Federal Government." This appeal and assertion of states' rights should always be considered within the origin of the concept. The moral underpinnings and history asserted by Calhoun, the father of states' rights theory, is the rejection of the federal government having influence and authority over how the states treated Blacks. In 1860, the issue was slavery; in the 1960s the issue was segregation; and today, it's about police use of force against Blacks.

On June 7, 1848 Calhoun gave his *speech on the Oregon Bill* which prevented the expansion of slavery into the Oregon territory. In his speech he made two main arguments. The first argument was that Blacks and Whites were not equal and second, the assertion by the founding generation that "all men and created equal" was factually and philosophically false. As to the first premise, the context is Northern assertions that the South opposes free labor in favor of slave labor. Calhoun asserted that

> There is no part of the world were agricultural, mechanical, and other descriptions of labor are more respected than in the South, with the exception of two descriptions of employment—that of menial and body servants. No Southern man—not the poorest or the lowest—will, under any circumstance, submit to perform either of them. He has too much pride for that, and I rejoice that he has. They are unsuited to the spirit of a freeman. But the man who would spurn them feels not the least degradation to work in the same field with his slave; or to be employed to work with them in the same field or in any mechanical operation; and, when so employed, they claim the right,—and are admitted, in the country portion of the South—of sitting at the table of their employers. Can as much, on the score of equality, be said of the North? With us the two great divisions of society are not the rich and poor, but white and black; and all the former, the poor as well as the rich, belong to the upper class, and are respected and treated as equals, if honest and industrious; and hence have a position and pride of character of which neither poverty nor misfortune can deprive them.[9]

As discussed in Chapter Three, the future President of the Confederacy, Jefferson Davis, would say the same thing a decade later at the dawn of the American Civil War.

Both asserted that the poor White man can work on the same level as the slave, but the poor White man can and does enjoys a seat at the table of the slave master and eats at that table as an equal. The Black slave does not. Calhoun made clear that the poor White man may be poor, but he is not a nigger and cannot be treated as such. This dehumanization of Blacks and infrahumanization of Whites, as discussed in Chapter Three, is significant in explaining the fall of Reconstruction and the rise of Jim Crow policies after the Civil War and southern

---

9 John Calhoun Speech on the Oregon Bill June 27, 1848 athttp://www.constitutionreader.com/reader/chapter.engz?doc=constitution&chapter=OEBPS/Text/ch76.xhtml

White voters' rejection of the Democratic Party after its adoption of the civil rights movement in the 1960s.

Calhoun's second point in his *speech on the Oregon Bill* was that the founding generation was wrong about slavery as evil and that all men were created equal, thus slavery can be opposed under the Declaration of Independence and the Constitution. It was this belief in the north that Calhoun said would break the Union and one the South had a right to break the Union over. He said,

> Now is the time to take the step, and bring about a result so devoutly to be wished. I have believed, from the beginning, that this was the only question sufficiently potent to dissolve the Union . . . .
>
> Now, let me say, Senators, if our Union and system of government are doomed to perish, and we to share the fate of so many great people who have gone before us, the historian, who, in some future day, may record the events ending in so calamitous a result, will devote his first chapter to the ordinance of 1787, lauded as it and its authors have been, as the first of that series which led to it. His next chapter will be devoted to the Missouri compromise, and the next to the present agitation. Whether there will be another beyond, I know not. It will depend on what we may do.

On this point Calhoun was right. As Jefferson said before him and Lincoln would say after him, America cannot exist half-free and half-slave and that because God is just a reckoning over slavery would come upon America. Calhoun complained that federal laws that prevented the spread of slavery in America would force the South to ask itself,

> If neither the barriers of the constitution nor the high sense of right and justice should prove sufficient to protect you, are you prepared to sink down into a state of acknowledged inferiority; to be stripped of your dignity of equals among equals, and be deprived of your equality of rights in this federal partnership of States? If so, you are woefully degenerated from your sires, and will well deserve to change condition with your slaves;—but if not, prepare to meet the issue. The time is at hand, if the question should not be speedily settled, when the South must rise up, and bravely defend herself, or sink down into base and acknowledged inferiority . . .

But Calhoun was much more interested in the political and philosophical basis for Americanism: The theory of America, social conservatives assert, from its inception is written in the first paragraph of the Declaration of Independence—"We hold these truths to be self-evident, that all men are created equal, that they are endowed by their Creator with certain unalienable Rights, that among these are Life, Liberty and the pursuit of Happiness." *Calhoun, the father of states' rights, asserted that this premise and assertion was false.* Calhoun said in his Oregon speech, regarding what the historian will conclude regarding the break-up of the Union,

> [i]f he should possess a philosophical turn of mind, and be disposed to look to more remote and recondite causes, he will trace it to a proposition . . . which, as now expressed

> and now understood, is the most false and dangerous of all political errors. The proposition to which I allude … that "all men are born free and equal." …
>
> [he argued men are not born, babies are born, and they are not born free but born under the control of their parents and they are not born equal in abilities or status]
>
> If we trace it back, we shall find the proposition differently expressed in the Declaration of Independence. That asserts **that "all men are created equal."** The form of expression, though less dangerous, **is not less erroneous.** … It was inserted in our Declaration of Independence without any necessity. It made no necessary part of our justification in separating from the parent country, and declaring ourselves independent.

Note his point. The father of states' rights asserts that the assertion that the famous phrase of the Declaration of Independence was a political throwaway line that had nothing to do with why the colonies declared independence. He continued,

> Nor had it any weight in constructing the governments which were substituted in the place of the colonial. …
>
> If the proposition be traced still further back, it will be found to have been adopted from certain writers on government … Among these, Locke … According to their expression, **"all men in the state of nature were free and equal."** From this the others were derived; and it was this to which I referred when **I called it a hypothetical truism;**—to understand why, will require some explanation.

Calhoun proceeded to agree with basic Lockean theory that man is a social creature and needs government to enjoy liberty. Affirming Locke, Calhoun concluded and asserted the American concept of republican government.

> Such being the case, it follows that any, the worst form of government, is better than anarchy; and that individual liberty, or freedom, must be subordinate to whatever power may be necessary to protect society against anarchy within or destruction without; for the safety and well-being of society is as paramount to individual liberty, as the safety and well-being of the race is to that of individuals; and in the same proportion the power necessary for the safety of society is paramount to individual liberty.
>
> On the contrary, government has no right to control individual liberty beyond what is necessary to the safety and well-being of society. Such is the boundary which separates the power of government and the liberty of the citizen or subject in the political state, which, as I have shown, is the natural state of man—the only one in which his race can exist, and the one in which he is born, lives, and dies.

But he adds that government is not designed to make that which is unequal equal. Further, *individual liberty under government assumes inequality between subjects and citizens under government.* He asserted what is now orthodoxy of conservative rhetoric that as government grows the individual is reduced, especially when government seeks to make that which is unequal equal. Calhoun laid the foundation for modern conservative thought when he asserted that liberty is not given but earned and the more the induvial is allowed to live independently of government and can develop whatever skills he has, the smaller the government will need to be. But the reverse, making all men equal regardless of their place in life, will result in anarchy and the need for bigger and more powerful government.

> It follows from all this that the quantum of power on the part of the government, and of **liberty** on that of individuals, **instead of being equal in all cases, must necessarily be very unequal among different people, according to their different conditions.**
>
> For just in proportion as a people are ignorant, stupid, debased, corrupt, exposed to violence within, and danger from without, **the power necessary for government** to possess, in order to preserve society against anarchy and destruction, **becomes greater and greater, and individual liberty less and less, until the lowest condition is reached,—when absolute and despotic power becomes necessary on the part of the government, and individual liberty extinct.**
>
> So, on the contrary, just as a people rise in the scale of intelligence, virtue, and patriotism, and the more perfectly they become acquainted with the nature of government, the ends for which it was ordered, and how it ought to be administered, and the less the tendency to violence and disorder within, and danger from abroad,—the power necessary for government becomes less and less, and individual liberty greater and greater.
>
> Instead, then, of all men having the same right to liberty and equality, as is claimed by those who hold that they are all born free and equal, **liberty is the noble and highest reward bestowed on mental and moral development**, combined with favorable circumstances. Instead, then, of liberty and equality being born with men,—instead of all men and all classes and descriptions being equally entitled to them, **they are high prizes to be won**, and are in their most perfect state, not only the highest reward that can be bestowed on our race, but the most difficult to be won,—and when won, the most difficult to be preserved.

Life, Liberty and the pursuit of Happiness are not unalienable rights that one is born with but are rewards to be earned. Rejection of this truth in pre-civil war America, Calhoun asserted, was compounded by the error that Blacks who are born inferior should enjoy the rights of Whites who are their superior. Regarding the first error with the second, Calhoun concluded his speech asserting that,

> the dangerous error I have attempted to expose,—that all men are born free and equal,—as if those high qualities belonged to man without effort to acquire them, and to all equally alike, regardless of their intellectual and moral condition. … . We now begin to experience the danger of admitting so great an error to have a place in the declaration of our independence. For a long time it lay dormant; but in the process of time it began to germinate, and produce its poisonous fruits.
>
> It had strong hold on the mind of **Mr. Jefferson**, the author of that document, which caused him to take an **utterly false view** of the subordinate relation of the **black** to the

> white race in the South; and to hold, in consequence, that the latter, though utterly unqualified to possess liberty, were as **fully entitled to both liberty and equality** as the former; **and that to deprive them of it was unjust and immoral.**
>
> **To this error, his proposition to exclude slavery from the territory northwest of the Ohio may be traced,**—and to that the ordinance of 1787,—and through it the deep and dangerous agitation which now threatens to engulf, and will certainly engulf, if not speedily settled, our political institutions, and involve the country in countless woes.

States' rights was built on two premises, first all men are not born equal and second, Blacks are not equal to whites. Regarding slavery, Blacks do not have a right to liberty and freedom protected by the federal government.

The advocacy of Calhoun, followed by the defenders of the confederacy and secession, established and created the concept of states' rights. The opposition was both moral (the defense of slavery) and political. Calhoun's arguments on the moral opposition to the North was that Blacks were inferior and the attempts by the North to make Blacks equal with Whites had to be opposed at all costs. Calhoun's political arguments were simply about voting power. Because of the bicameral design of Congress, population governed membership in the House of Representatives, but it did not matter in the membership of the Senate. All states had two votes regardless of population. The south knew it would lose control of the House so all battles over slavery were settled in the Senate where the south could maintain a majority of slave states. Thus how states were admitted into the Union—slaver or free—was the defining political issue in the 1840s and 1850s. Calhoun explained that his opposition to Northern assertions, "that there should be no further admission of any States into this Union which permitted, by their constitutions, the existence of slavery [and] that slavery shall not hereafter exist in any of the territories of the United States; the effect of which would be to give to the non-slaveholding States the monopoly of the public domain, to the entire exclusion of the slaveholding States."[10]

By the election of Lincoln, the time for political debate was over. More importantly, the idea that the slave states defined Blacks as inferior by definition was also a debate that had ended, as far as the South was concerned. Confederate Vice President **Alexander Stephens**, in the ***Corner-Stone Speech*** on March 21, 1861, echoed the views of Calhoun, one score and three years later, on the Founders' false proposition that all men are created equal and that slavery was evil.

> **Our new government is founded upon exactly the opposite idea; *its corner-stone, rests upon the great truth, that the negro is not equal to the white man; that slavery—subordination to the superior race—is his natural and normal condition. This, our new government, is the first, in the history of the world, based upon this great physical, philosophical, and moral truth.*** This truth has been slow in the process of its development,

10 John Calhoun Speech, "Speech On The Introduction Of His Resolutions On The Slave Question" (February 19, 1847) at http://www.founding.com/founders_library/pageID.2283/default.asp

like all other truths in the various departments of science. It has been so even amongst us. Many who hear me, perhaps, can recollect well, that this truth was not generally admitted, even within their day. The errors of the past generation still clung to many as late as twenty years ago. Those at the North, who still cling to these errors, with a zeal above knowledge, we justly denominate fanatics. All fanaticism springs from an aberration of the mind from a defect in reasoning. It is a species of insanity. One of the most striking characteristics of insanity, in many instances, is forming correct conclusions from fancied or erroneous premises; so with the anti-slavery fanatics. Their conclusions are right if their premises were. They assume that the negro is equal, and hence conclude that he is entitled to equal privileges and rights with the white man. If their premises were correct, their conclusions would be logical and just but their premise being wrong, their whole argument fails. ... They [are] attempting to make things equal which the Creator had made unequal. ...

It is upon this, as I have stated, our social fabric is firmly planted; and I cannot permit myself to doubt the ultimate success of a full recognition of this principle throughout the civilized and enlightened world. ...

Many governments have been founded upon the principle of the subordination and serfdom of certain classes of the same race; such were and are in violation of the laws of nature. Our system commits no such violation of nature's laws. **With us, all of the white race, however high or low, rich or poor, are equal in the eye of the law. Not so with the negro.** ***Subordination is his place. He, by nature, or by the curse against Canaan, is fitted for that condition which he occupies in our system.***

The architect, in the construction of buildings, lays the foundation with the proper material-the granite; then comes the brick or the marble. The substratum of our society is made of the material fitted by nature for it, and by experience we know that it is best, not only for the superior, but for the inferior race, that it should be so. ***It is, indeed, in conformity with the ordinance of the Creator. It is not for us to inquire into the wisdom of His ordinances, or to question them. For His own purposes, He has made one race to differ from another,*** as He has made "one star to differ from another star in glory." **The great objects of humanity are best attained when there is conformity to His laws and decrees,** in the formation of governments as well as in all things else. **Our confederacy is founded upon principles in strict conformity with these laws.** This stone which was rejected by the first builders "is become the chief of the corner" the real "corner-stone" in our new edifice. I have been asked, what of the future? It has been apprehended by some that we would have arrayed against us the civilized world. I care not who or how many they may be against us, when we stand upon the eternal principles of truth, if we are true to ourselves and the principles for which we contend, we are obliged to, and must triumph.[11]

---

11 Alexander Stephens Corner-Stone Speech at http://teachingamericanhistory.org/library/document/cornerstone-speech/ (Emphasis added).

Stephens made clear that the Confederacy was built upon the rejection of various principles and beliefs of the founding generation—both in constitutional structure and regarding slavery. Stephens explained,

> But not to be tedious in enumerating the numerous changes for the better, allow me to allude to one other though last, not least. The new constitution has put at rest, forever, all the agitating questions relating to our peculiar institution African slavery as it exists amongst us the proper status of the negro in our form of civilization. This was the immediate cause of the late rupture and present revolution. Jefferson in his forecast, had anticipated this, as the "rock upon which the old Union would split." He was right. What was conjecture with him, is now a realized fact. But whether he fully comprehended the great truth upon which that rock stood and stands, may be doubted. ***The prevailing ideas entertained by him and most of the leading statesmen at the time of the formation of the old constitution, were that the enslavement of the African was in violation of the laws of nature; that it was wrong in principle, socially, morally, and politically. It was an evil they knew not well how to deal with, but the general opinion of the men of that day was that, somehow or other in the order of Providence, the institution would be evanescent and pass away.*** This idea, though not incorporated in the constitution, was the prevailing idea at that time. The constitution, it is true, secured every essential guarantee to the institution while it should last, and hence no argument can be justly urged against the constitutional guarantees thus secured, because of the common sentiment of the day. ***Those ideas, however, were fundamentally wrong. They rested upon the assumption of the equality of races. This was an error.*** It was a sandy foundation, and the government built upon it fell when the "storm came and the wind blew."[12]

Stephens' statement, "It was a sandy foundation, and the government built upon it fell when the "storm came and the wind blew," was an allusion to the book of Matthew 7: 24–27.

The first and only President of the Confederacy came to the same conclusion as his future Vice President when he resigned from the U.S. Senate after Mississippi seceded from the Union. In his January 1861 Farewell Address to the U.S. Senate speech, Jefferson Davis asserted that the states had a right to secede from the Union when it did not relent from seeking to limit the expansion of the social and political institution of slavery. He agreed with Calhoun and Stephens that the issue of the conflict was whether the founding generation in the Declaration of Independence and the Constitution meant to include Blacks within the idea that all men are created equal. He asked rhetorically in his farewell address

> How happened it that among the items of arraignment made against George III was that he endeavored to do just what the North has been endeavoring of late to do—to stir up insurrection among our slaves? *Had the Declaration announced that the negroes were free*

12 Alexander Stephens Corner-Stone Speech at http://teachingamericanhistory.org/library/document/cornerstone-speech/ (Emphasis added).

> *and equal, how was the Prince to be arraigned for stirring up insurrection among them? And how was this to be enumerated among the high crimes which caused the colonies to sever their connection with the mother country?*

Davis alluded to the original draft of the Declaration of Independence in which Jefferson listed the unlawful enslavement of Blacks, imposing slavery on the colonies, and then inciting rebellion among the slaves against the colonies as reasons for demanding independence. Jefferson's slave clause was abandoned in the final draft of the document upon Southern slave state opposition. The point being, of course, Davis asked rhetorically how the North could claim incitement against slavery as a good when it was listed among the sins of England. As to the Constitution, Davis asserted

> When our Constitution was formed, the same idea was rendered more palpable, for there we find provision made for that very class of persons as property; they were not put upon the footing of equality with white men—not even upon that of paupers and convicts; but, so far as representation was concerned, were discriminated against as a lower caste, only to be represented in the numerical proportion of three fifths.[13]

In an example of original intent and strict construction, Davis argued that the Declaration of Independence declared all political men within the politics of governance were equal, not that all men were morally and ethnically equal.

> It has been a conviction of pressing necessity, it has been a belief that we are to be deprived in the Union of the rights which our fathers bequeathed to us, which has brought Mississippi into her present decision. She has heard proclaimed the theory that all men are created free and equal, and this made the basis of an attack upon her social institutions; and the sacred Declaration of Independence has been invoked to maintain the position of the equality of the races. *That* ***Declaration of Independence is to be construed by the circumstances and purposes for which it was made.*** *The communities were declaring their independence*; the people of those communities were asserting that no man was born—to use the language of Mr. Jefferson—booted and spurred to ride over the rest of mankind; *that* ***men were created equal—meaning*** *the men of the political community;* ***that there was no divine right to rule;*** that no man inherited the right to govern; that there were no classes by which power and place descended to families, but that all stations were equally within the grasp of each member of the body-politic. ***These were the great principles*** they announced; these were the purposes for which they made their declaration; these were the ends to which their enunciation was directed. ***They have no reference to the slave.***[14]

---

13 Jefferson Davis, Farewell Address to the U.S. Senate (January 21, 1861) (emphasis added) https://jefferson-davis.rice.edu/Content.aspx?id=87.

14 Jefferson Davis, Farewell Address to the U.S. Senate (January 21, 1861) (emphasis added) https://jefferson-davis.rice.edu/Content.aspx?id=87

As discussed in Chapter Five, the U.S. Supreme Court, four years before Davis's speech, came to the same conclusion in *Dred Scott v. Sandford* in 1857.

> The question is simply this: ***Can a negro, whose ancestors were imported into this country, and sold as slaves, become a member of the political community formed and brought into existence by the Constitution of the United States***, and as such become entitled to all the rights, and privileges, and immunities, guaranteed by that instrument to the citizen? One of which rights is the privilege of suing in a court of the United States in the cases specified in the Constitution. … [W]hether the descendants of such slaves, when they shall be emancipated, or who are born of parents who had become free before their birth, are citizens of a State, in the sense in which the word citizen is used in the Constitution of the United States. And this being the only matter in dispute on the pleadings, the court must be understood as speaking in this opinion of that class only, that is, of those persons who are the descendants of Africans who were imported into this country, and sold as slaves.
>
> …
>
> The words "people of the United States" and "citizens" are synonymous terms, and mean the same thing. They both describe the political body who, according to our Republican institutions, form the sovereignty, and who hold the power and conduct the Government through their representatives. They are what we familiarly call the "sovereign people," and every citizen is one of this people, and a constituent member of this sovereignty. The question before us is, whether [those who are African slaves and decedents of African slaves] are constituent members of this sovereignty? ***We think they are not, and that they are not included, and were not intended to be included, under the word "citizens" in the Constitution, and can therefore claim none of the rights and privileges which that instrument provides for and secures to citizens of the United States.*** On the contrary, they were at that time considered as a subordinate and inferior class of beings, who had been subjugated by the dominant race, and, whether emancipated or not, yet remained subject to their authority, and had no rights or privileges but such as those who held the power and the Government might choose to grant them.[15]

Such was the law until the fall of slavery and the rise of the Fourteenth Amendment in 1868.

President Jefferson Davis and Vice President Alexander Stephens were not the only voices explaining the secession of the South. The Southern States of the Confederacy were equally direct and clear on the purpose, justification, and moral certitude of why they were seceding from the Union. Their official declarations of secession were based on two overarching ideas: first, the protection of slavery as an economic and social institution, along with the moral truth about the inferiority of those that were enslaved; second, the rejection of anti-slavery abolitionists' politics of the North and claims of universal failure of the federal government

15 *Dred Scott v. Sandford*, 60 US 393, 403, 404–405 (1857).

and the Northern states to enforce the fugitive slave clause of the Constitution and supporting legislation. Consider the major declarations and documents of the Confederate states:

- ***The Declaration of the Immediate Causes Which Induce and Justify the Secession of South Carolina from the Federal Union*** (December 24, 1860)
  - [T]he non-slaveholding States … have assume the right of deciding upon the propriety of our domestic institutions; and have denied the rights of property … they have denounced as sinful the institution of slavery; they have permitted open establishment among them of societies ... They have encouraged and assisted thousands of our slaves to leave their homes; and those who remain, have been incited by emissaries, books and pictures to servile insurrection.

    ... A geographical line has been drawn across the Union, and all the States north of that line have united in the election of a man to the high office of President of the United States, whose opinions and purposes are hostile to slavery. He is to be entrusted with the administration of the common Government, because he has declared that that "Government cannot endure permanently half slave, half free," and that the public mind must rest in the belief that slavery is in the course of ultimate extinction.

    ...This sectional combination for the submersion of the Constitution, has been aided in some of the States by elevating to citizenship, persons who, by the supreme law of the land, are incapable of becoming citizens; and their votes have been used to inaugurate a new policy, hostile to the South, and destructive of its beliefs and safety.

    ...We, therefore, the People of South Carolina, by our delegates in Convention assembled, appealing to the Supreme Judge of the world for the rectitude of our intentions, have solemnly declared that the Union heretofore existing between this State and the other States of North America, is dissolved ...
- ***Governor Isham G. Harris Speech to the General Assembly Regarding a Referendum Calling for a Tennessee Secession Convention*** (January 7, 1861)
  - The systematic, wanton, and long continued agitation of the slavery question, with the actual and threatened aggressions of the Northern States and a portion of their people, upon the well-defined constitutional rights of the Southern citizen; the rapid growth and increase, in all the elements of power, of a purely sectional party, whose bond of union is uncompromising hostility to the rights and institutions of the fifteen Southern States, have produced a crisis in the affairs of the country, unparalleled in the history of the past, resulting already in the withdrawal from the Confederacy of one of the sovereignties which composed it, while others are rapidly preparing to move in the same direction. ...

    The Constitution distinctly recognizes property in slaves—makes it the duty of the States to deliver the fugitive to his owner, but contains no grant of power to the

Federal Government to interfere with this species of property … [T]he Supreme Court of the United States in the case of *Dred Scott vs. Sandford* … said:

> "Now, as we have already said in an earlier part of this opinion upon a different point, the right of property in a slave is distinctly and expressly affirmed in the Constitution. And no word can be found in the Constitution which gives Congress a greater power over slave property, or which entitles property of that kind to less protection than property of any other description. The only power conferred, is the power coupled with the duty, of guarding and protecting the owner in his rights."

This decision of the highest judicial tribunal, known to our Government, settles the question, beyond the possibility of doubt, that slave property rests upon the same basis, and is entitled to the same protection, as every other description of property; that the General Government has no power to circumscribe or confine it within any given boundary; to determine where it shall, or shall not exist, or in any manner to impair its value … Hence, there is no power on earth which can rightfully determine whether slavery shall or shall not exist within the limits of any State, except the people thereof acting in their highest sovereign capacity.

The attempt of the Northern people, through the instrumentality of the Federal Government—their State governments, and emigrant aid societies—to confine this species of property within the limits of the present Southern States—to impair its value by constant agitation and refusal to deliver up the fugitive ... is justly regarded by the people of the Southern States as a gross and palpable violation of the spirit and obvious meaning of the compact of Union. ... It claims the constitutional right to abolish slavery in the District of Columbia ... It proposes a prohibition of the slave trade between the States ... It has, by the deliberate Legislative enactments of a large majority of the Northern States, openly and flagrantly nullified ... the fugitive slave law ... with impunity defies the Government, tramples upon our rights, and plunders the Southern citizen. ... It has, by its John Brown and Montgomery raids, invaded sovereign States and murdered peaceable citizens. It has justified and "exalted to the highest honors of admiration, the horrid murders, arsons, and rapine of the John Brown raid, and has canonized the felons as saints and martyrs. ... It has, in the person of the President elect, asserted the equality of the black with the white race ... To evade the issue thus forced upon us at this time, without the fullest security for our rights, is, in my opinion, fatal to the institution of slavery forever. The time has arrived when the people of the South must prepare either to abandon or to fortify and maintain it.

- ***The Ordinance of Secession of Alabama*** (January 11, 1861)
  - An Ordinance to dissolve the union … .

  Whereas, the election of Abraham Lincoln and Hannibal Hamlin to the offices of president and vice-president of the United States of America, by a sectional party, avowedly hostile to the domestic institutions and to the peace and security of the people of the State of Alabama, preceded by many and dangerous infractions of the constitution of the United States by many of the States and people of the Northern section, is a political wrong of so insulting and menacing a character as to justify the people of the State of Alabama in the adoption of prompt and decided measures for their future peace and security, therefore:

. . . .

And as it is the desire and purpose of the people of Alabama to meet the slave-holding States of the South, who may approve such purpose, in order to frame a provisional as well as permanent Government upon the principles of the Constitution of the United States,

Be it resolved by the people of Alabama in Convention assembled, That the people of the States of Delaware, Maryland, Virginia, North Carolina, South Carolina, Florida, Georgia, Mississippi, Louisiana, Texas, Arkansas, Tennessee, Kentucky and Missouri, be and are hereby invited to meet the people of the State of Alabama, by their Delegates, in Convention, on the 4th day of February, A.D., 1861, at the city of Montgomery, in the State of Alabama, for the purpose of consulting with each other as to the most effectual mode of securing concerted and harmonious action in whatever measures may be deemed most desirable for our common peace and security.

- ***The Declaration of Secession of Georgia*** (January 29, 1861)
  - A brief history of the rise, progress, and policy of anti-slavery and the political organization into whose hands the administration of the Federal Government has been committed will fully justify the pronounced verdict of the people of Georgia. The party of Lincoln, called the Republican Party, under its present name and organization, is of recent origin. It is admitted to be an anti-slavery party …

    … While the subordination and the political and social inequality of the African race was fully conceded by all, it was plainly apparent that slavery would soon disappear from what are now the non-slave-holding States of the original thirteen ... The material prosperity of the North was greatly dependent on the Federal Government; that of the South not at all.

    In the first years of the Republic the navigating, commercial, and manufacturing interests of the North began to seek profit and aggrandizement at the expense of the agricultural interests. ... The Presidential election of 1852 resulted in the total overthrow of the advocates of restriction and their party friends. Immediately after this result the anti-slavery portion of the defeated party resolved to unite all the elements in the North opposed to slavery and to stake their future political fortunes upon their hostility to slavery everywhere. This is the party two whom the people of the North have committed the Government. They raised their standard in 1856 and were barely defeated. They entered the Presidential contest again in 1860 and succeeded.

The prohibition of slavery in the Territories, hostility to it everywhere, the equality of the black and white races, disregard of all constitutional guarantees it its favor, were boldly proclaimed by its leaders and applauded by its followers ... For twenty years past the abolitionists and their allies in the Northern States have been engaged in constant efforts to subvert our institutions and to excite insurrection and servile war among us. They have sent emissaries among us for the accomplishment of these purposes.

- ***The Ordinance of Secession of Texas*** (February 1, 1861)
  - To dissolve the Union between the State of Texas and the other States united under the Compact styled "the Constitution of the United States of America."
    WHEREAS, The Federal Government has failed to accomplish the purposes of the compact of union between these States, in giving protection either to the persons of our people upon an exposed frontier, or to the property of our citizens, and
    . . . .
    WHEREAS, The recent developments in Federal affairs make it evident that the power of the Federal Government is sought to be made a weapon with which to strike down the interests and property of the people of Texas, and her sister slave-holding States, instead of permitting it to be, as was intended, our shield against outrage and aggression; THEREFORE,
    . . . .We, the People of the State of Texas, by Delegates in Convention assembled, do declare and ordain, that the Ordinance adopted by our Convention of Delegates, on the Fourth day of July, A.D. 1845, and afterwards ratified by us, under which the Republic of Texas was admitted into Union with other States and became a party to the compact styled "The Constitution of the United States of America" be, and is hereby repealed and annulled. . . .
- ***A Declaration of the Causes which Impel the State of Texas to Secede from the Federal Union*** (February 2, 1861)
  - Texas abandoned her separate national existence and consented to become one of the Confederated States ... She was received as a commonwealth holding, maintaining and protecting the institution known as negro slavery—the servitude of the African to the white race within her limits—a relation that had existed from the first settlement of her wilderness by the white race, and which her people intended should exist in all future time. Her institutions and geographical position established the strongest ties between her and other slave-holding States of the confederacy. Those ties have been strengthened by association. But what has been the course of the government of the United States, and of the people and authorities of the non-slave-holding States, since our connection with them?

    The controlling majority of the Federal Government, under various pretenses and disguises, has so administered the same as to exclude the citizens of the Southern States, unless under odious and unconstitutional restrictions, from all the immense territory owned in common by all the States on the Pacific Ocean, for the avowed purpose of ... destroying the institutions of Texas and her sister slave-holding States.

By the disloyalty of the Northern States and their citizens and the imbecility of the Federal Government ... permitted in those States and ... Kansas to trample upon the ... lives and property of Southern citizens in that territory, and finally, by violence and mob law to usurp the possession of the same as exclusively the property of the Northern States.

The Federal Government, while but partially under the control of these our unnatural and sectional enemies, has for years almost entirely failed to protect the lives and property of the people of Texas against the Indian savages on our border, and more recently against the murderous forays of banditti from the neighboring territory of Mexico; and ... when our State government has expended large amounts for such ... the Federal Government has refused reimbursement...

....

In all the non-slave-holding States, in violation of that good faith and comity which should exist between entirely distinct nations, the people have formed themselves into a great sectional party ... based upon the unnatural feeling of hostility to these Southern States and their beneficent and patriarchal system of African slavery, proclaiming the debasing doctrine of the equality of all men, irrespective of race or color—a doctrine at war with nature, in opposition to the experience of mankind, and in violation of the plainest revelations of the Divine Law. They demand the abolition of negro slavery throughout the confederacy, the recognition of political equality between the white and the negro races, and avow their determination to press on their crusade against us, so long as a negro slave remains in these States.

....

By consolidating their strength, they have placed the slave-holding States in a hopeless minority in the federal Congress, and rendered representation of no avail in protecting Southern rights against their exactions and encroachments.

....

And, finally, by the combined sectional vote of the seventeen non-slave-holding States, they have elected as president and vice-president of the whole confederacy two men whose chief claims to such high positions are their approval of these long continued wrongs, and their pledges to continue them to the final consummation of these schemes for the ruin of the slave-holding States.

In view of these and many other facts, it is meet that our own views should be distinctly proclaimed.

We hold as undeniable truths that the governments of the various States, and of the confederacy itself, were established exclusively by the white race, for themselves and their posterity; that the African race had no agency in their establishment; that they were rightfully held and regarded as an inferior and dependent race, and in that condition only could their existence in this country be rendered beneficial or tolerable.

That in this free government all white men are and of right ought to be entitled to equal civil and political rights; that the servitude of the African race, as existing in these States, is mutually beneficial to both bond and free, and is abundantly authorized and justified by the experience of mankind, and the revealed will of the Almighty Creator, as recognized by all Christian nations; while the destruction of the existing relations between the two races, as advocated by our sectional enemies, would bring inevitable calamities upon both and desolation upon the fifteen slave-holding States. By the secession of six of the slave-holding States, and the certainty that others will speedily do likewise, Texas has no alternative but to remain in an isolated connection with the North, or unite her destinies with the South.

For these and other reasons, solemnly asserting that the federal constitution has been violated and virtually abrogated by the several States named, seeing that the federal government is now passing under the control of our enemies to be diverted from the exalted objects of its creation to those of oppression and wrong, and realizing that our own State can no longer look for protection, but to God and her own sons—We the delegates of the people of Texas, in Convention assembled, have passed an ordinance dissolving all political connection with the government of the United States of America and the people thereof and confidently appeal to the intelligence and patriotism of the freeman of Texas to ratify the same at the ballot box, on the 23rd day of the present month.

- ***A Declaration of the Immediate Causes which Induce and Justify the Secession of the State of Mississippi from the Federal Union*** (Not Dated)
    - Our position is thoroughly identified with the institution of slavery—the greatest material interest of the world. Its labor supplies the product which constitutes by far the largest and most important portions of commerce of the earth. These products are peculiar to the climate verging on the tropical regions, and by an imperious law of nature, none but the black race can bear exposure to the tropical sun. These products have become necessities of the world, and a blow at slavery is a blow at commerce and civilization. That blow has been long aimed at the institution, and was at the point of reaching its consummation. There was no choice left us but submission to the mandates of abolition, or a dissolution of the Union, whose principles had been subverted to work out our ruin. [The North] advocates negro equality, socially and politically, and promotes insurrection and incendiarism in our midst. It has enlisted its press, its pulpit and its schools against us, until the whole popular mind of the North is excited and inflamed with prejudice.
- ***The Constitution of the Confederate States Article I*** (March 11, 1861)
    - The importation of negroes of the African race from any foreign country other than the slaveholding States or Territories of the United States of America, is

hereby forbidden ... Congress shall also have power to prohibit the introduction of slaves from any State not a member of, or Territory not belonging to, this Confederacy ... No … law denying or impairing the right of property in negro slaves shall be passed.

- ***The Constitution of the Confederate States Article IV*** (March 11, 1861)
    - The citizens of each State ... shall have the right of transit and sojourn in any State of this Confederacy, with their slaves and other property; and the right of property in said slaves shall not be thereby impaired ... No slave … escaping shall, in consequence ... be discharged from such service or labor; but shall be delivered up on claim of the party to whom such slave belongs ... The Confederate States may acquire new territory ... In all such territory the institution of negro slavery, as it now exists in the Confederate States, shall be recognized and protected be Congress and by the Territorial government; and the inhabitants of the several Confederate States and Territories shall have the right to take to such Territory any slaves lawfully held by them in any of the States or Territories of the Confederate States.
- ***President Jefferson Davis Message to Congress Regarding the Ratification of the Constitution of the Confederate States*** (April 29, 1861)
    - When the several States delegated certain powers to the United States Congress, a large portion of the laboring population consisted of African slaves imported into the colonies by the mother country. In twelve out of the thirteen States negro slavery existed, and the right of property in slaves was protected by law. This property was recognized in the Constitution, and provision was made against its loss by the escape of the slave. The increase in the number of slaves by further importation from Africa was also secured by a clause forbidding Congress to prohibit the slave trade anterior to a certain date, and in no clause can there be found any delegation of power to the Congress authorizing it in any manner to legislate to the prejudice, detriment, or discouragement owners of that species of property, or excluding it from the protection of the Government.

      ...The climate and soil of the Northern States soon proved unpropitious to the continuance of slave labor, whilst the converse was the case at the South ... [T]he constitutional provision for their rendition to their owners was first evaded, then openly denounced as a violation of conscientious obligation and religious duty; men were taught that it was a merit to elude, disobey, and violently oppose the execution of the laws enacted to secure the performance of the promise contained in the constitutional compact; owners of slaves were mobbed and even murdered in open day solely for applying to a magistrate for the arrest of a fugitive slave.

      ... In the meantime ... the African slaves ... In moral and social condition they had been elevated from brutal savages into docile, intelligent, and civilized agricultural laborers, and supplied not only with bodily comforts but with careful religious instruction. Under the supervision of a superior race their labor had been so directed as not only to allow a gradual and marked amelioration of their own condition" their labor undergirded "the productions of the South in cotton, rice, sugar, and tobacco, for the full development and continuance of which the labor of African slaves was and is indispensable, had swollen to an amount which formed nearly three-fourths of the exports of the whole United States and had become absolutely necessary to the wants of civilized man.

- ***John Wilkes Booth "To Whom it May Concern" Letter*** (1864)
    - Right, or wrong, God, judge me, not man. For be my motive good or bad, of one thing I am sure, the lasting condemnation of the North. ... The very nomination of Abraham Lincoln four years ago, spoke plainly—war—war upon Southern rights and institutions, his election proved it. ... This country was formed for the white not for the black man. And looking upon African slavery from the same stand-point, held by those noble framers of our Constitution, I for one, have ever considered it, one of the greatest blessings (both for themselves and us,) that God ever bestowed upon a favored nation. Witness heretofore our wealth and power, witness their elevation in happiness and enlightenment above their race, elsewhere.

So much for the assertion that the Civil War was not a war to protect the institution of slavery.

As Lincoln said at his second inaugural address, "[F]our years ago ... [w]hile the inaugural address was being delivered ... insurgent agents were in the city seeking to destroy ... seeking to dissolve the Union [, and they] would make war rather than let the nation survive, [we] would accept war rather than let it perish, and the war came." As Lincoln said, one-eighth of the whole U.S. population was composed of slaves and the South was not going to surrender the institution of slavery. "All knew that this interest was somehow the cause of the war."

But more importantly the Civil War was about the eradication of slavery, not eradicating the racism (the belief in the inferiority of Blacks) that undergirded it. The latter was shared by both the North and South. This distinction is key in understanding the policies of America both before and after the Civil War.

But the same nation that produced Calhoun, Stephens, and Davis and the Southern ordinances of secession also produced Abraham Lincoln and James Garfield. Lincoln said America would not remain half slave and half free.[16] He answered Southern secession and its use of force against the Union with the assertion that

> Our popular government has often been called an experiment. Two points in it, our people have already settled,—the successful establishing and the successful administering of it. One still remains,—its successful maintenance against a formidable internal attempt to overthrow it. It is now for them to demonstrate to the world that those who can fairly carry an election can also suppress a rebellion; that ballots are the rightful

16 Abraham Lincoln, "House Divided," Speech (June 1858).

> and peaceful successors of bullets; and that when ballots have fairly and constitutionally decided, there can be no successful appeal back to bullets; that there can be no successful appeal, except to ballots themselves, at succeeding elections. Such will be a great lesson of peace; teaching men that what they cannot take by an election, neither can they take it by a war; teaching all the folly of being the beginners of a war.[17]

Twenty years after Lincoln stood before Congress and defended the primacy of the Constitution and rejected the appeal to bullets after the appeal of ballots, another president would stand before the nation and, during his inaugural address, reflect on the primacy of the Constitution, law, and justice in the American republic. President James Garfield said in 1881,

> The supreme trial of the Constitution came at last under the tremendous pressure of Civil War. We ourselves are witnesses that the Union emerged from the blood and fire of that conflict purified and made stronger for all the beneficent purposes of good government.
>
> ...
>
> The supremacy of the nation and its laws should be no longer a subject of debate. That discussion, which for half a century threatened the existence of the Union, was closed at last in the high court of war by a decree from which there is no appeal—that the Constitution and the laws made in pursuance thereof are and shall continue to be the supreme law of the land, binding alike upon the States and the people. This decree does not disturb the autonomy of the States nor interfere with any of their necessary rights of local self-government, but it does fix and establish the permanent supremacy of the Union.[18]

Although Lincoln always believed that the ballot must overcome the bullet in American politics, the issue of slavery was an evolving issue with him. To Lincoln, before the attack on Fort Sumter, the Civil War was about his election, not the abolition of slavery. Lincoln was clear that if he could save the Union and maintain slavery, he would, and if he could maintain the Union without slavery, he would.

> My paramount object in this struggle *is* to save the Union, and is *not* either to save or to destroy slavery. If I could save the Union without freeing *any* slave I would do it, and if I could save it by freeing *all* the slaves I would do it; and if I could save it by freeing some and leaving others alone I would also do that. What I do about slavery, and the colored race, I do because I believe it helps to save the Union; and what I forbear, I forbear because I do *not* believe it would help to save the Union.[19]

---

17 Abraham Lincoln, "Letter to James C. Conkling" (August 26, 1963) and Abraham Lincoln, "First Message to Congress, Special Session" (July 4, 1861), respectively.

18 James Garfield, "Inaugural Address," March 4, 1881.

19 Abraham Lincoln, "Letter to Horace Greeley" (August 22, 1862).

At a peace conference in which he debated with some Southern and Northern attendees, Lincoln made clear that he was prepared to discuss all issues of slavery, so long as the Constitution was obeyed. As Lucius E. Chittenden reported the discussion of the conference,

> A delegate from New Jersey asked Mr. Lincoln pointedly if the North should not make further concessions to avoid Civil War? For example, consent that the people of a territory should determine its right to authorize slavery when admitted into the Union? "It will be time to consider that question when it arises," he replied. "Now we have other questions which we must decide. In a choice of evils, war may not always be the worst. Still I would do all in my power to avert it, except to neglect a Constitutional duty. As to slavery, it must be content with what it has. The voice of the civilized world is against it; it is opposed to its growth or extension. Freedom is the natural condition of the human race, in which the Almighty intended men to live. Those who fight the purposes of the Almighty will not succeed. They always have been, they always will be, beaten."[20]

For Lincoln, the moral issue of slavery was not enough to go to war over, while preserving the Union was. The significance of the Civil War was the fact that the moral issue of maintaining and protecting slavery was significant enough for the South to go to war over, regardless of maintaining the Union. Only after two years of war did Lincoln come to understand that the war was not simply over the dispute of his election, but it was over a fundamental debate—was America a nation of freedom and liberty for all, or only for White men? At Gettysburg, he said of the American system based on liberty, "we are engaged in a great Civil War, testing whether that nation, or any nation so conceived and so dedicated, can long endure." In answering his own question, Lincoln asserted, "that we here highly resolve that these dead shall not have died in vain—that this nation, under God, shall have a new birth of freedom—and that government of the people, by the people, for the people, shall not perish from the earth."

Four years into the war, Lincoln considered the carnage, sacrifice, and cost endured by the Union and reflected in his *Second Inaugural Address* that the war was not a challenge he wanted but a challenge he had to answer. But, the four years had humbled him in that he now understood that the war was about more than just enforcing his election or defending the nature of American democracy, the war was about the evil of slavery and the ideals it was built upon. Lincoln answered Stephens and Calhoun, both of whom defended and asserted the moral righteousness and validity of slavery by asserting that the judgment of a just and righteous God had come upon the nation that indulged in slavery; the day of reckoning, the Civil War, had come.

> Both read the same Bible and pray to the same God, and each invokes His aid against the other. It may seem strange that any men should dare to ask a just God's assistance in wringing their bread from the sweat of other men's faces, but let us judge not, that we be not judged. The prayers of both could not be answered. That of neither has been answered

---

20 *Infra* note 48 at 76.

> fully. The Almighty has His own purposes. "Woe unto the world because of offenses; for it must needs be that offenses come, but woe to that man by whom the offense cometh." ***If we shall suppose that American slavery is one of those offenses*** which, ***in the providence of God***, must needs come, but which, having continued through His appointed time, ***He now wills to remove***, and that ***He gives to both North and South this terrible war*** as the woe due to those by whom the offense came, shall we discern therein any departure from those divine attributes which the believers in a living God always ascribe to Him? Fondly do we hope, fervently do we pray, that this mighty scourge of war may speedily pass away. Yet, ***if God wills that it continue until all the wealth piled by the bondsman's two hundred and fifty years of unrequited toil shall be sunk, and until every drop of blood drawn with the lash shall be paid by another drawn with the sword***, as was said three thousand years ago, so still it must be said "***the judgments of the Lord are true and righteous altogether.***" [21]

The proposition that both the North and South were responsible for the plague of slavery and that both must deal with the vestiges of it was echoed by President Garfield in his Inaugural address. As Lincoln admitted in 1865, President Garfield asserted in 1881 that the

> responsibility for the existence of slavery did not rest upon the South alone. The nation itself is responsible for the extension of the suffrage, and is under special obligations to aid in removing the illiteracy which it has added to the voting population. For the North and South alike there is but one remedy. All the constitutional power of the nation and of the States and all the volunteer forces of the people should be surrendered to meet this danger by the savory influence of universal education.
>
> It is the high privilege and sacred duty of those now living to educate their successors and fit them, by intelligence and virtue, for the inheritance which awaits them.
>
> …
>
> My countrymen, we do not now differ in our judgment concerning the controversies of past generations, and fifty years hence our children will not be divided in their opinions concerning our controversies. ***They will surely bless their fathers and their fathers' God that the Union was preserved, that slavery was overthrown, and that both races were made equal before the law.*** We may hasten or we may retard, but we cannot prevent, the final reconciliation. Is it not possible for us now to make a truce with time by anticipating and accepting its inevitable verdict?[22]

---

21 Abraham Lincoln, "Second Inaugural Address" (March 4, 1865) (emphasis added). Lincoln cited Matthew 7:1, 18:7 and Psalms 19:9 (KJV) respectively.

22 James A. Garfield "Inaugural Address" (March 4, 1881) at http://www.presidency.ucsb.edu/ws/?pid=25823 (emphasis added)

The truce Garfield anticipated and hoped to bring about would require more than a century to be fully embraced and manifested in American society.

The meaning of the war and the higher American values that justified it were not lost on those soldiers who fought for the Union. To them, the war was to maintain a nation and to rid that nation of its greatest sin, slavery. The perspective of Lincoln and his view of the significance of the war were shared by the future President James Garfield. Before he rose to national prominence, Garfield served as a major general in the Civil War. The war instilled in him a disdain for slavery, admiration for Blacks who fought in the Union effort, and a strong sense of union and republic under the constitution and law. During his presidential campaign in 1880, he gave a speech in New York City in which he reflected on the ideals of Alexander Hamilton and Lincoln. In his August 1880 *Boys in Blue* speech, James Garfield spoke of the war and the freeing of the slaves as a noble cause that was in line with the greatness of America. But more importantly, he spoke of Blacks as people equal to Whites both as human beings and citizens, rather than as a post–Civil War social and societal problem to endure. He said Blacks had a right to live under the "sun of liberty."

> Gentlemen, ideas outlive men; ideas outlive all earthly things. You who fought in the war for the Union fought for immortal ideas, and by their might you crowned the war with victory. [Great applause.] But victory was worth nothing except for the truths that were under it, in it, and above it. We meet tonight as comrades to stand guard around the sacred truths for which we fought. [Loud and prolonged cheers.] And while we have life to meet and grasp the hand of a comrade, we will stand by the great truths of the war. ["Good," "good," and loud cheers.] Many convictions have sunk so deep into our hearts that we can never forget them. Think of the elevating spirit of the war itself. ...
>
> Another thing we will remember: we will remember our allies who fought with us. Soon after the great struggle began, we looked behind the army of white rebels, and saw 4,000,000 of black people condemned to toil as slaves for our enemies; and we found that the hearts of these 4,000,000 were God-inspired with the spirit of Liberty, and that they were all our friends. [Applause.] ***We have seen the white men betray the flag and fight to kill the Union; but in all that long, dreary war we never saw a traitor in a black skin.*** [Great cheers.] *Our comrades escaping from the starvation of prison, fleeing to our lines by the light of the North star, never feared to enter the black man's cabin and ask for bread.* ["Good, good," "That's so," and loud cheers.] In all that period of suffering and danger, ***no Union soldier was ever betrayed by a black man or woman.*** [Applause.] And now that we have made them free, so long as we live we will stand by these black allies. [Renewed applause.] *We will stand by them until the sun of liberty, fixed in the firmament of our Constitution, shall shine with equal ray upon every man, black or white, throughout the Union.* [Cheers.] Fellow-citizens, fellow-soldiers, in this there is the beneficence of eternal justice, and by it we will stand forever. [Great applause.] A poet has said that in individual life we rise, "On stepping-stones of our dead selves to higher things," and the Republic rises on the glorious achievements of its dead and living heroes to a higher and nobler national

> life. [Applause.] We must stand guard over our past as soldiers, and over our country as the common heritage of all. [Applause.][23]

At the June 1880 Republican convention, **Garfield** delivered a speech extolling that the party of Lincoln **stood for the correctness of the Union cause** during the Civil War. **That cause was liberty, justice, the rule of law, and freedom for both Blacks and Whites.** At the convention, he said of the party,

> Twenty-five years ago, this Republic was bearing and wearing a triple chain of bondage. Long familiarity with traffic in the bodies and souls of men had paralyzed the consciences of a majority of our people; the narrowing and disintegrating doctrine of State-sovereignty had shackled and weakened the noblest and most beneficent powers of the National Government; and the grasping power of slavery was seizing upon the virgin Territories of the West, and dragging them into the den of eternal bondage.
>
> At that crisis the Republican party was born. It drew its first inspiration from that fire of liberty which God has lighted in every human heart, and which all the powers of ignorance and tyranny can never wholly extinguish. The Republican party came to deliver and to save. It entered the arena where the beleaguered and assailed Territories were struggling for freedom, and drew around them the sacred circle of liberty, which the demon of Slavery has never dared to cross. It made them free forever. Strengthened by its victory on the frontier, the young party, under the leadership of that great man who, on this spot, twenty years ago, was made its chief, entered the national capitol and assumed the high duties of government. The light which shone from its banner illumined its pathway to power. Every slave-pen and the shackles of every slave within the shadow of the capitol were consumed in the re-kindled fire of freedom.
>
> ...
>
> It confronted a Rebellion of unexampled magnitude, with slavery behind it, and, under God, fought the final battle of Liberty until the victory was won.
>
> Then, after the storms of battle, were heard the calm words of peace spoken by the conquering nation, saying to the foe that lay prostrate at its feet: "This is our only revenge—that you ***join us in lifting into the serene firmament of the Constitution***, to shine like stars for ever and ever, ***the immortal principles of truth and justice: that all men, white or black, shall be free, and shall stand equal before the law.***"
>
> ...
>
> ***The Republican party offers to our brethren of the South the olive branch*** of Peace, and invites them to renewed brotherhood, ***on this supreme condition: That it shall be admitted, forever, that in the War for the Union we were right and they***

23 James A. Garfield, "Boys in Blue" Speech, (New York, August 6, 1880) (Emphasis added). American Experience, *Murder of a President James Garfield* (2016) http://www.pbs.org/wgbh/americanexperience/features/primary-resources/garfield-campaign-speech/.

> ***were wrong.*** On that supreme condition we meet them as brethren, and ask them to share with us the blessings and honors of this great Republic.[24]

As Garfield said in his 1881 *Inaugural Address* regarding the significance of the accomplishments of the Civil War,

> The will of the nation, speaking with the voice of battle and through the amended Constitution, has fulfilled the great promise of 1776 by proclaiming "liberty throughout the land to all the inhabitants thereof."
>
> The elevation of the negro race from slavery to the full rights of citizenship is the most important political change we have known since the adoption of the Constitution of 1787. No thoughtful man can fail to appreciate its beneficent effect upon our institutions and people. It has freed us from the perpetual danger of war and dissolution. It has added immensely to the moral and industrial forces of our people. It has liberated the master as well as the slave from a relation which wronged and enfeebled both. It has surrendered to their own guardianship the manhood of more than 5,000,000 people, and has opened to each one of them a career of freedom and usefulness. It has given new inspiration to the power of self-help in both races by making labor more honorable to the one and more necessary to the other. The influence of this force will grow greater and bear richer fruit with the coming years.
>
> No doubt this great change has caused serious disturbance to our Southern communities. This is to be deplored, though it was perhaps unavoidable. But those who resisted the change should remember that under our institutions ***there was no middle ground for the negro race between slavery and equal citizenship.*** There can be no permanent disfranchised peasantry in the United States. ***Freedom can never yield its fullness of blessings so long as the law or its administration places the smallest obstacle in the pathway of any virtuous citizen.***
>
> The emancipated race has already made remarkable progress. With unquestioning devotion to the Union, with a patience and gentleness not born of fear, they have "followed the light as God gave them to see the light." They are rapidly laying the material foundations of self-support, widening their circle of intelligence, and beginning to enjoy the blessings that gather around the homes of the industrious poor. They deserve the generous encouragement of all good men. So far as my authority can lawfully extend they shall enjoy the full and equal protection of the Constitution and the laws.

Advocacy against the evil of racial discrimination was not silent in the last decades of the nineteenth century within American political discourse. Garfield exemplified the difference

---

24 James A. Garfield, "Nomination of John Sherman" Speech, (Chicago, June 5, 1880) from American Experience, *Murder of a President James Garfield* (2016). Film. http://www.pbs.org/wgbh/americanexperience/features/primary-resources/garfield-nomination-sherman/.

between being against slavery and not believing that Blacks were equal to Whites under the law, as well as socially and politically. There is a distinction. While the Northern abolitionists opposed the South on the institution of slavery, they did not oppose the underlying idea supporting slavery, that Blacks were socially and legally inferior to Whites. Slavery was simply the logical conclusion to the inferiority of Blacks. The distinction between the North and South was that the South was willing to accept the logical conclusion of inferiority of Blacks, while the North was not, and the South was prepared to defend the rightness of slavery at the expense of the Union, while the North was not willing to accept slavery at the expense of the Union. Garfield, while seeking the presidency, recognized the humanity of Blacks, and when a group of Black students from Fisk College came to sing for him at his house, he said to them, "I tell you now, in the closing days of this campaign, that I would rather be with you and defeated than against you and victorious."[25] The nature of slavery had made an impression on him, and he wrote to his wife, "Slavery may have great charms for the rich, but no one can fail to see that it is the poor man's bane."[26] He later wrote, "This is my hope, that when we shall return to civil life, there shall go up an unrelenting cry for freedom. If this shall ever be realized, the thousands who have fallen on the bloody field, or in the fever wards of the hospitals, will not have died in vain."[27] The humanity of Blacks and the determination to ensure their liberty and equality in American society was voiced but sadly rejected soon after the Civil War. Upon the death of Lincoln, Garfield reflected upon the reason for his death and the significance of what he had died for, when he wrote his wife,

> My Dear Lucretia: My heart is so broken with our great national loss that I can hardly think or write or speak. It remains for us to keep that faith, to go forward in the great work until it shall be completed. This nation shall be saved from its enemies; its glory shall be restored. On the ruins of slavery and treason, the temples of freedom and justice shall be built, and shall survive forever.[28]

President Garfield was assassinated four months into his administration. In his short administration, he implored America, in 1881, to realize, "there was no middle ground for the negro race between slavery and equal citizenship ... Freedom can never yield its fullness of blessings so long as the law or its administration places the smallest obstacle in the pathway of any virtuous citizen." He said of the character of Blacks in 1880, "In all that period of suffering and danger, no Union soldier was ever betrayed by a black man or woman." As a General in the Civil War, he could testify that, "We have seen the white men betray the flag and fight to kill the Union; but in all that long, dreary war we never saw a traitor in a black skin. Our

---

25 American Experience, *Murder of a President James Garfield* (2016) http://www.pbs.org/wgbh/americanexperience/features/transcript/garfield-transcript/.

26 American Experience, *Murder of a President James Garfield* (2016)

27 American Experience, *Murder of a President James Garfield* (2016)

28 American Experience, *Murder of a President James Garfield* (2016)

comrades escaping from the starvation of prison, fleeing to our lines by the light of the North Star, never feared to enter the black man's cabin and ask for bread." The vision he proposed for America was that, "We will stand by them until the sun of liberty, fixed in the firmament of our Constitution, shall shine with equal ray upon every man, black or white, throughout the Union." History would show that America would not heed his words or accept his vision. It would be almost seven decades before America would again hear a president publicly defend the ideals of equal freedom and justice for Blacks.

Rather than adopting the values of President Garfield, America chose to adopt the values of what has been called the second great corrupt bargain[29] in American political history, the compromise of 1877. With the compromise of 1877, America would complete the national government abandonment of Blacks to the mercies of those White men who President Garfield said had betrayed the flag and fought to kill the Union; the Southern Democrats and the states of the confederacy. The compromise of 1877 resulted from the election of 1876 between Rutherford B. Hayes (R) and Samuel Tilden (D), which the House of Representatives decided in spring 1877. Southern Democrats agreed to support the election of Hayes with his promise to remove federal troops from the South. The result of the bargain was the establishment of home rule in the South, the complete decimation of the economic and political gains made by former slaves during the First Reconstruction, the rise of Jim Crow, and the criminalization of Blacks as a means of social control. This bargain also resulted in the death of the Republican Party having any significant political influence in the South until the rise of Strom Thurmond, Barry Goldwater, and George Wallace nine decades later.

Sixteen years before Garfield became president and two days after Lee surrendered to Grant, Lincoln commented on an issue that would vex the nation for a century thereafter. He said, regarding the new constitution and the admittance of the State of Louisiana, "[i]t is also unsatisfactory to some that the elective franchise is not given to the colored man. I would myself prefer that it were now conferred on the very intelligent, and on those who serve our cause as soldiers."[30] It was not the end of the war and Lincoln being victorious in it that John Wilkes Booth resented. What Booth resented was Lincoln supporting what he called the outrage of "nigger suffrage," to which Booth said at Lincoln's speech, "That is the last speech he will make." It would take a century for what Lincoln only began to support to become a reality—a reality he was killed for supporting.

---

29 The first great corrupt bargain being the election of 1824 when the House of Representatives voted for John Quincy Adams over Andrew Jackson, who had won the popular vote. Henry Clay, who did not have enough electoral votes to be considered by the House, is believed to have supported Adams in return for a cabinet position which in fact he received—the position of Secretary of State. Neither Adams nor Clay ever lived down accusations of a stolen election and Jackson defeated Adams in the 1828 election ushering in the Age of Jackson and Jacksonian Democracy.

30 Abraham Lincoln, "Last Public Address" (April 11, 1865).

THE POLITICAL RHETORIC OF RACE AND THE POLITICIANS OF THE MODERN CIVIL RIGHTS ERA: THE RISE OF MODERN POLITICAL SOCIAL CONSERVATISM AND RACE POLITICS IN THE REPUBLICAN AND DEMOCRATIC PARTIES IN AMERICAN SOCIAL AND POLITICAL HISTORY

At the dawn of the twentieth century, the American century, the federal government was embroiled in the question of whether lynching should be outlawed. The issue of lynching in America has always been race based and a tool of extrajudicial punishment of Blacks in general but, more specifically, for Black men accused of sexual transgressions involving White women. President Theodore Roosevelt in his December 3, 1906, Annual Address to Congress said regarding lynching,

> The members of the white race on the other hand should understand that every lynching represents by just so much a loosening of the bands of civilization; that the spirit of lynching inevitably throws into prominence in the community all the foul and evil creatures who dwell therein. No man can take part in the torture of a human being without having his own moral nature permanently lowered.
>
> Every lynching means just so much moral deterioration in all the children who have any knowledge of it, and therefore just so much additional trouble for the next generation of Americans.
>
> Let justice be both sure and swift; but let it be justice under the law, and not the wild and crooked savagery of a mob.

Consider the point the president made. White men should not engage in lynching, because it represents the breakdown of civilization and the moral nature of White men. The fact that in a lynching a Black man has been murdered is a superfluous point. After admitting that lynch mobs arise over the issue of White rage at the rape of White women by Black men, he explained,

> In connection with the delays of the law, I call your attention and the attention of the Nation to the prevalence of crime among us, and above all to the epidemic of lynching and mob violence that springs up, now in one part of our country, now in another ... It is necessary to have an awakened public conscience, and to supplement this by whatever legislation will add speed and certainty in the execution of the law. ... A great many white men are lynched, but the crime is peculiarly frequent in respect to black men. The greatest existing cause of lynching is the perpetration, especially by black men, of the hideous crime of rape—the most abominable in all the category of crimes, even worse than murder. Mobs frequently avenge the commission of this crime by themselves torturing to death the man committing it; thus avenging in bestial fashion a bestial deed, and reducing themselves to a level with the criminal.

> Lawlessness grows by what it feeds upon; and when mobs begin to lynch for rape they speedily extend the sphere of their operations and lynch for many other kinds of crimes, so that two-thirds of the lynchings are not for rape at all; while a considerable proportion of the individuals lynched are innocent of all crime ...

Although lynch mobs arise when the crime of rape of White women by Blacks occurs, the president asserted that the illegality and immorality of lynching was in the fact that the justification of the practice devolves into extrajudicial punishment for other crimes. True as this may be, note how the president bypasses the truth behind lynching; it occurs against Black men, because they are Black and because they are accused of touching White women. He whitewashed the truth of lynching; that it is murder of Black men by White men, because they are Black, by focusing on the more general moral argument that lynching is extrajudicial and punishes innocent victims of the mob. When the president did acknowledge race, he asserted that Blacks need to see Black rapists as people not worthy of protection. He said,

> Every colored man should realize that the worst enemy of his race is the negro criminal, and above all the negro criminal who commits the dreadful crime of rape; and it should be felt as in the highest degree an offense against the whole country, and against the colored race in particular, for a colored man to fail to help the officers of the law in hunting down with all possible earnestness and zeal every such infamous offender ...

Wait a moment. The "worst enemy of his race is the negro criminal," not criminals in general but the negro criminal. Not Ku Klux Klan members but the negro criminal. In a time of White lynch mobs, the national political acceptance of the Ku Klux Klan, and the illegal southern system of peonage supplementing the system of convict leasing in the South; the president told Blacks, regarding Blacks accused of raping White women, that it is the "highest degree of offense for the colored man to fail to help the officers of the law in hunting down ... such [an] infamous offender." This was the advice President Roosevelt gave Blacks when it was common knowledge and experience that a Black man accused of raping of a White woman would not receive a fair trial, if a trial at all! In such cases he is more likely to receive adjudication in the night, under a tree, by the knot of a rope to the cheers of many. Leaving that aside, consider the president's focus: you Blacks lose more when Blacks act criminally—a theme that has never left political discourse on Black criminality.

The president concluded his remarks on lynching by admonishing that those who raise up lynch mobs increase Black criminal behavior.

> Be it remembered, furthermore, that the **individuals who**, whether from folly, from evil temper, from greed for office, or in a spirit of mere base demagogy, indulge in the inflammatory and incendiary speeches and writings which tend to **arouse mobs and to bring about lynching**, not only thus excite the mob, but also tend by what criminologists call "suggestion," **greatly to increase the likelihood of a repetition of the very crime against which they are inveighing**. When the mob is composed of the people of one race and the

> man lynched is of another race, **the men who** in their speeches and writings either **excite** or justify the action tend, of course, to excite a bitter race feeling and to **cause the people** of the opposite race **to lose sight of the abominable act of the criminal** himself; **and** in addition, by the prominence they give to the hideous deed they undoubtedly tend to **excite** in other brutal and depraved natures **thoughts of committing it**. Swift, relentless, and orderly punishment under the law is the only way by which criminality of this type can permanently be suppress.

Really! The more lynching of Blacks for raping White women you have, the more Blacks will get angry and go out and find White women to rape. Only in the total dehumanization of Blacks to the level of the ape could this logic make sense. But this was the logic of early twentieth century progressivism and its adoption of social Darwinism within the Gilded Age.

Roosevelt's speech is an example of the whitewashing of the evil of White racism perpetrated on Blacks. He asserted that lynching is evil, but that it affected all people—not just Blacks; "a great many white men are lynched" the president explained. The evil of lynching is that it was done by Whites to Blacks because they were Black. Lynching was a tool of social control and power. The fact that on rare occasions White men were lynched does not change the nature of lynching, the purpose of it, the target of it, or the perpetrators of it.

Political rhetoric has policy implications. There is a difference between saying lynching is generally wrong vs. asserting it is wrong for White men to lynch Black men when they are accused of raping White women. The former is an example of overgeneralizing to facilitate the avoidance of acknowledging specific racial injustice. Lynching in America has no history of White men catching the end of the rope for raping Black women. Lynching has no history of White men being hung for raping other White women. For that matter, no Black man has been lynched by a White mob for raping a Black woman.

Roosevelt was wrong. The crime of rape did not awaken the lynch mob; the crime of Black men raping White women woke the lynch mob. The history and crime of lynching is not general, it's specific. The president was right that lynching is an abomination under a society that claims it functions under the rule of law. But that's not the point when dealing with lynching in America. Historically, when lynching was not about the accusation of a Black man raping a White woman, it was used as a tool to keep Blacks in their place and prevent them from asserting their rights under the constitution—either in the 1870s or the 1950s. These facts were not lost on Blacks nor was the fact that federal legislation to outlaw lynching was opposed by Southern Democrats for decades. Because of Southern Democrats opposition, federal legislation prohibiting lynching never survived the Senate filibuster. On December 19, 2018 after more than a century from the first attempt, the Senate passed a federal anti-lynching bill.

One hundred years to the month after Lincoln issued the *Emancipation Proclamation*, the same nation that he died preserving produced a Governor, George C. Wallace, who, before a praising crowd as Calhoun and Stephens did before him, asserted that

> Today I have stood, where once Jefferson Davis stood, and took an oath to my people. It is very appropriate then that from this Cradle of the Confederacy, this very Heart of the Great Anglo-Saxon Southland, that today we sound the drum for freedom as have our generations of forebears before us done, time and time again through history. Let us rise to the call of freedom-loving blood that is in us and send our answer to the tyranny that clanks its chains upon the South. In the name of the greatest people that have ever trod this earth, I draw the line in the dust and toss the gauntlet before the feet of tyranny. ***And I say segregation today segregation tomorrow segregation forever.***[31]

Although George Wallace and his "segregation today, segregation tomorrow, segregation forever," speech in 1963 are famous and infamous for displaying the position of Southern Democrats' rejection of civil rights, the rebellion of the Southern Democrats from the pro-civil rights position of the national Democratic Party began with Harry Truman and Strom Thurmond in 1948.

Strom Thurmond v. Harry Truman: States' Rights and the Republicans Seek the South

In 1947, echoing his statement six months before when he issued his executive order creating the President's Committee on Civil Rights discussed in Chapter One, Truman in a speech at the National Association for the Advancement of Colored People (NAACP) convention stated

> I should like to talk to you briefly about civil rights and human freedom. It is my deep conviction that we have reached a turning point in the long history of our country's efforts to guarantee a freedom and equality to all our citizens ...
>
> As Americans, we believe that every man should be free to live his life as he wishes. He should be limited only by his responsibility to his fellow countrymen. If this freedom is to be more than a dream, each man must be guaranteed equality of opportunity. The only limit to an American's achievement should be his ability, his industry and his character. The rewards for his effort should be determined only by these truly relevant qualities.
>
> Our immediate task is to remove the last remnants of the barriers, which stand between millions of our citizens and their birthright. There is no justifiable reason for discrimination because of ancestry, or religion. Or race, or color.
>
> We must not tolerate such limitations on the freedom of any of our people and on their enjoyment of the basic rights, which every citizen in a truly Democratic society must possess.
>
> Every man should have the right to a decent home, the right to an education, the right to adequate medical care, the right to a worthwhile job, the right to an equal share in the making of public decisions through the ballot, and the right to a fair trial in a fair court.
>
> We must insure that these rights—on equal terms are enjoyed by every citizen.
>
> To these principles I pledge my full and continued support.

31 George C. Wallace, "Inaugural Address" as Governor of Alabama (January 14, 1963) (Emphasis added).

> Many of our people still suffer the indignity of insult, the harrowing fear of intimidation, and, I regret to say, the threat of physical injury and mob violence. The prejudice and intolerance in which these evils are rooted still exist. The conscience of our nation, and the legal machinery which enforces it, have not yet secured to each citizen full freedom from fear.
>
> We cannot wait another decade or another generation to remedy those evils. We must work, as never before, to cure them now. The aftermath of war and the desire to keep faith with our nation's historic principles make the need a pressing one. …
>
> This is a difficult and complex undertaking. Federal laws and administrative machineries must be improved and expanded. We must provide the government with better tools to do the job. As a first step, I appointed an Advisory Committee on Civil Rights last December. Its members, fifteen distinguished private citizens, have been surveying our civil rights difficulties and needs for several months. I am confident that the product of their work will be a sensible and vigorous program for action by all of us.[32]

Eight months later, Truman, in a special message to Congress citing the Declaration of Independence, asserted that the meaning of the document can be distilled to the following principles,

> We believe that all men are created equal and that they have the right to equal justice under law.
>
> We believe that all men have the right to freedom of thought and of expression and the right to worship as they please. We believe that all men are entitled to equal opportunities for jobs, for homes, for good health and for education. We believe that all men should have a voice in their government and that government should protect, not usurp, the rights of the people. These are the basic civil rights which are the source and the support of our democracy.
>
> …
>
> We shall not, however, finally achieve the ideals for which this Nation was founded so long as any American suffers discrimination as a result of his race, or religion, or color, or the land of origin of his forefathers.
>
> …
>
> The protection of civil rights is the duty of every government which derives its powers from the consent of the people. This is equally true of local, state, and national governments. There is much that the states can and should do at this time to extend their protection of civil rights. Wherever the law enforcement measures of state and local governments are inadequate to discharge this primary function of government, these measures should be strengthened and improved.

---

32 Harry S. Truman, "Address to the NAACP Convention" (June 28, 1947). http://www.pbs.org/wgbh/americanexperience/features/primary-resources/truman-naacp47/.

> The Federal Government has a clear duty to see that Constitutional guarantees of individual liberties and of equal protection under the laws are not denied or abridged anywhere in our Union. That duty is shared by all three branches of the Government, but it can be fulfilled only if the Congress enacts modern, comprehensive civil rights laws, adequate to the needs of the day, and demonstrating our continuing faith in the free way of life.[33]

Not since President Garfield, almost seven decades before, had a president stated that the protection of Black civil rights is the duty of the federal government under the constitution. Truman proceeded to recommend to Congress a sweeping set of proposals to address discrimination, including the passage of an anti-lynching law, the creation of the President's Commission on Civil Rights; along with legislation protecting the right vote and home rule with the right to vote for residents in Washington D.C., fair housing and interstate transportation legislation and the establishment of a civil rights division within the U.S. Justice Department. All of which was passed by Congress between 1957 and 1968.

Truman's assertion that, "The Federal Government has a clear duty to see that Constitutional guarantees of individual liberties and of equal protection under the laws are not denied or abridged anywhere in our Union" was tantamount to a declaration of war to Southern Democrats as Congressman William M. Colmer of Mississippi made clear.

> Mr. Speaker, not since the first gun was fired on Fort Sumter, resulting as it did in the greatest fratricidal strife in the history of the world, has any message of any President of these glorious United States provoked so much controversy, and resulted in the driving of a schism in the ranks of our people, as did President Truman's so-called civil-rights message, sent to the Congress several weeks ago. Not only did that message provoke serious racial controversies, but it raised anew the issue of the rights of the sovereign States as against a strong centralized government and drove a devastating wedge into the unity of the Democratic Party at a time when that party was riding high on a wave of popularity in the entire country.
>
> It revived the age-old controversy which flourished at the very beginning of our Government, the controversy of a strong centralized government as advocated by Alexander Hamilton on the one hand, and a government of the people as opposed to a government by the rulers, as advocated by the greatest of all exponents of civil rights, possibly the greatest Democrat of them all, Thomas Jefferson. For, after all, it was Jefferson's theory that that people is best governed who is least governed, and the closer the government is to the people, the better the government is.
>
> ...

33 Harry S. Truman, "Special Message to the Congress on Civil Rights," February 2, 1948. http://www.presidency.ucsb.edu/ws/?pid=13006.

> For, if the Federal Government can repeal the poll tax in Mississippi and several other Southern States, regulate employment under the FEPC, punish innocent taxpayers under the Anti-Lynch Bill, and abolish segregation in the several States by usurpation of the sovereign rights of the several States of the Union, then we have indeed witnessed an end of constitutional government as conceived by the founding fathers.
>
> ...
>
> Does any fair-minded American find amazement, however, that the people of the South are in revolt against the leadership of the Democratic Party? It is necessary to remind any student of political history in this country that it was the section from which I hail that has cradled, nourished, and sustained the Democratic Party throughout its lean as well as its prosperous years? The South has ever been a strong believer in and contender for the Jeffersonian theory of democracy. It has ever been ready to fight for those principles. Many of its most gallant sons shed their precious blood upon the altar of States' rights. Certainly it is not surprising, therefore, that it should take the lead in the battle against this program, which would destroy the last vestige of the rights of the sovereign States....
>
> ...
>
> And what, I ask you, my colleagues, has this message of our President, calling for the enactment of this program, accomplished to date? ... it has encouraged the arrogant demands of these minority groups to whom it was designed to appeal. Witness, Mr. Speaker, the sorry spectacle of an erstwhile pullman porter, William Randolph, a Negro labor leader, defiantly telling the membership of a committee of this Congress that unless segregation in the armed forces should be abolished that he would call upon the Negroes of this country to ignore the call of their country in the event of a war with Russia. Such ingratitude, such arrogance, such treason can only be attributed to such political bargaining as this proposed program.[34]

The final die was cast during the Democratic Convention in July 1948 when the party placed in its platform that the federal government should outlaw poll taxes, integrate the armed forces, and end racial discrimination in federal employment. To make matters worse for Southern Democrats, Senator Hubert Humphrey, in his speech on the floor of the convention,[35] said the following.

> Friends, delegates, I do not believe that there can be any compromise on the guarantees of the civil rights which we have mentioned in the minority report. In spite of my desire for unanimous agreement on the entire platform, in spite of my desire to see everybody here in honest and unanimous agreement, there are some matters which I think must be stated

---

34 William M. Colmer, "Remarks in the House of Representatives" (April 8, 1948). http://www.pbs.org/wgbh/americanexperience/features/primary-resources/truman-south48/.

35 Hubert Humphrey, Speech at the Democratic Party Convention, July 14, 1948. http://www.americanrhetoric.com/speeches/huberthumphey1948dnc.html

> clearly and without qualification. There can be no hedging—the newspaper headlines are wrong. There will be no hedging, and there will be no watering down—if you please—of the instruments and the principles of the civil-rights program.
>
> My friends, to those who say that we are rushing this issue of civil rights, I say to them we are 172 years late. To those who say that this civil-rights program is an infringement on states' rights, I say this: The time has arrived in America for the Democratic Party to get out of the shadow of states' rights and to walk forthrightly into the bright sunshine of human rights. People—human beings—this is the issue of the 20th century. People of all kinds—all sorts of people—and these people are looking to America for leadership, and they're looking to America for precept and example.

With the Democratic Party adopting civil rights and supporting the end of Jim Crow without concern for states' rights and with the assertion the federal government has the responsibility to enforce the principles of the Declaration of Independence, the Southern Democrats with the leadership of Strom Thurmond, Senator from South Carolina, abandoned the party and formed The States' Rights Democratic Party (the Dixiecrats) to run against Truman in November 1948. The South in 1948 rebelled, seceded, and fractured their party over whether Blacks were to be treated equal under the law and as social equals. Thurmond and the election of 1948 was the beginning of contemporary race politics and the realigning of the policies of both parties for the rest of the century.

In 1847, John Calhoun opposed the federal government opposition to the spread of slavery in the West and the admission of any non-slave state into the Union. To defend this opposition Calhoun asserted states' rights and local control of domestic affairs as a right embodied the Constitution and the natural order of individual liberty that the Constitution was created to protect. On the floor of the U.S. Senate he stated,

> Sir, I hold it to be a fundamental principle of our political system that the people have a right to establish what government they may think proper for themselves; that every State about to become a member of this Union has a right to form its government as it pleases.[36]

One century later, Strom Thurmond stood at a podium in Texas and asserted that same theory and explanation for why the States' Rights Party opposed federal anti-lynching, employment discrimination, and desegregation laws supported by the Democratic, Republican, and Progressive party platforms. In his acceptance speech at the States' Rights Democratic Party convention on August 11, 1948, Strom Thurmond made clear what the party stood for and why. He defined states' rights as the

> Right of the people to govern themselves ... The preservation of the prerogatives of the people of a sovereign state, their right to deal exclusively with domestic problems, and the absolute and unqualified denial of a totalitarian state in the United States ... the right

36 *Supra* note 8.

> to rule and govern ourselves [in] such domestic matters as voting and qualifications in voting, segregation, law enforcement and private employment ... [I]f we lose states rights, which safeguard the most precious of all human rights-the right to control and govern ourselves at home, the right to life, liberty and the pursuit of happiness-then may we ask, "For what is a man profited if he shall gain the whole world and lose his own soul?"

To be clear, the policies that Thurmond said would destroy the nature of American government were outlawing lynching and racial discrimination in voting and employment.

Regarding those who supported the rights of Blacks to vote and have equal employment and to have the federal government enforce that right with legislation, he said, "it is a fraud on the American people to pretend that human rights can long endure without constitutional restraint on the power of government." Why? Because, according to Thurmond and states' rights advocates, Hitler proved that! At the States' Rights Democratic Party convention Thurmond said, "Hitler offered the people of Germany a shortcut to human progress. He gained power by advocating human rights for minority groups. Under his plan, the constitutional rights of the people were destroyed." He noted that Hitler and Mussolini, as well as Stalin, advocated for human and equal rights for all. They sought to protect minority rights by federal law enforcement power. He asked what the result was of these policies. He replied, "tears, blood, disillusionment and tragedy."

> The proposal to take from you your right to deal with your local problems in a way that is satisfactory to you and to invest the right to deal with those problems in Washington in a way that is wholly unsatisfactory to you, is so antagonistic to our form of government ... that it is obligated to be communistic in concept, un-American in principle, and un-Democratic in execution.
>
> Now let me examine this so-called Civil Rights program ...

In regard to the federal law outlawing the poll tax, he said, "[b]y this bill, Congress invades the power of the state to elect their own officials and would control elections within the states by taking this power from the people." This is an abomination, because "if liberty is to be retained in this country, the control of our elections must remain at home." This is the states' rights response to a federal law that outlaws requiring people to pay to have a right to vote. That the poll tax law was used to make sure Blacks could not vote was irrelevant to the right of the people to make such a law.

As to the federal anti-lynching law, Senator Thurmond made clear that the law was communistic and totalitarian in nature and purpose.

> Of course, everyone is against lynching. The reds, the Pinks and the subversive are making use of this horror which American people hold for this form of murder to try to change our system of government.
>
> If the anti-lynching Bill were enacted, the Congress would seize the power to punish for crimes committed within a state.

> ... Local control of the police power [is] deliberately and intentionally denied to the federal government ... because ... concentration of police power is the certain road to dictatorship, to tyranny, and to oppression. Without exception, every country which the communists have taken over from "within," and every country which has come under control of a dictator, has lost its freedom through central control of the police powers and the creation of a centralized police system.
>
> In the anti-lynching bill the federal government, under the guise of preventing lynching, is trying to take their police power from the states ... Federal Police! What could be more un-American? When this occurs, the last vestige of ... a free people will have been destroyed.

According to Thurmond, not only did the federal government want to create a federal police force to control every citizen, but it wanted to use that force to help Blacks. This made the policies of Truman all the more intolerable, because it was not the role of the federal government to tell the states and the people in the states how to treat their niggers. Thurmond's campaign remarks soon after the 1948 States' Rights Democratic Party convention, discussed below, will explain why I used that word.

Strom Thurmond and his defense of segregation and opposition to federal anti-lynching legislation made clear that the decision to segregate or not is for the states to decide. As Calhoun said before him, Thurmond said that the states that have chosen segregation are not trying to impose it on the states that do not have segregation, and as such, the states that don't have segregation should not try to impose their policies on those that do. In his 1948 acceptance speech he made clear that those who want to end segregation, like those who sought the end of slavery, were not noble but rather "agitators and socially maladapted persons who do not care about or understand the conditions existing in the many communities in the United States where people of different races work and live together." In many places, he said, "the people voluntarily establish segregation."

As to anti-employment discrimination, such laws were not only "patterned after a Russian law written by Joseph Stalin about 1929," but "he used it as a means of advancing himself to supreme dictator of Soviet Russia." Equal employment was a tool of those who were seeking a utopia in which all were equal, but such a utopia, he asserted, would be at the price of liberty and the freedom of the employer to hire who he pleased and fire who he pleased, and for the worker it came at the price of his ability to choose who he would work for and who he would not. Thurmond made clear in his acceptance speech that the support of federal legislation to create equal employment, "illustrates the extent to which communistic ideas and cooperative comrades have infiltrated into the United States." Returning to the states' rights assertion that to enforce such laws, he complained that, a national police force implemented through the Civil Rights section of the Justice Department would engulf and invade all areas of private life. Government influence and control of decisions within the workplace, Thurmond concluded, is the road to dictatorship. Such was the goal "in Germany and Italy by the dictator to destroy the liberties of those people."

The platform of the States' Rights Party reflected the views of Thurmond and made clear,

> We stand for the segregation of the races and the racial integrity of each race; the constitutional right to choose one's associates; to accept private employment without governmental interference, and to earn one's living in any lawful way. We oppose the elimination of segregation, the repeal of miscegenation statutes, the control of private employment by Federal bureaucrats called for by the misnamed civil rights program. We favor home-rule, local self-government and a minimum interference with individual rights.
>
> We oppose and condemn the action of the Democratic Convention in sponsoring a civil rights program calling for the elimination of segregation, social equality by Federal fiat, regulations of private employment practices, voting, and local law enforcement.
>
> We affirm that the effective enforcement of such a program would be utterly destructive of the social, economic and political life of the Southern people, and of other localities in which there may be differences in race, creed or national origin in appreciable numbers.
>
> We demand that there be returned to the people to whom of right they belong, those powers needed for the preservation of human rights and the discharge of our responsibility as Democrats for human welfare. We oppose a denial of those by political parties, a barter or sale of those rights by a political convention, as well as any invasion or violation of those rights by the Federal Government. We call upon all Democrats and upon all other loyal Americans who are opposed to totalitarianism at home and abroad to unite with us in ignominiously defeating Harry S. Truman, Thomas E. Dewey and every other candidate for public office who would establish a Police Nation in the United States of America.[37]

Although Strom Thurmond discussed his opposition to civil rights law and the civil rights movement in classical state's rights scholarly race neutral tones, he revealed the truth behind states' rights theory in American politics when he said a few weeks after the convention, "I wanna tell you, ladies and gentlemen, that there's not enough troops in the army to force the Southern people to break down segregation and admit the nigger race into our theatres, into our swimming pools, into our homes and into our churches."[38] During a campaign stop in the 1948 election, Thurmond repeated his contempt for the civil rights proposals of the Truman Administration regarding anti-lynching legislation and his defense of the state's rights position to maintain segregation in a speech in Dallas,

37 Platform of the States' Rights Democratic Party (August 14, 1948).

38 Strom Thurmond, speaking at a States' Rights Democratic Party campaign event on September 8, 1948 at Dallas, Texas, "Strom Thurmond's Infamous 'Swimming Pool' Speech" at https://www.youtube.com/watch?v=SG-clHmRqo0

Texas.[39] At the September 8, 1948, campaign event, Thurmond diverted from his prepared text and said,

> Remember, not only did the report of the Truman Committee Civil Rights contain the anti-lynching law, the anti-poll tax law, and the FEPC. It contained, as well, demands for the complete elimination of segregation: the abolition of segregation in the schools as to pupils and teachers: in the buses and trains: in the beauty parlors, and swimming pools and restaurants, in the union halls and bar associations and medical associations, in business and social clubs: in private and denominational schools: in all the angles and facets of private life, as well as public activities. It condemned the thought of segregation, and advocated the creation of thought police, charged with the education of the people.[40]

At this point, Thurmond continued *ad libitum from his prepared speech* and made his famous "swimming pool" statement.[41]

The assertion of local control and states' rights has never been invoked in American political discourse outside of opposition of federal government protection of Black civil rights. States' rights were used in 1860 to oppose abolition of slavery, it was used in 1948 to oppose abolition of segregation, and it is used today to oppose federal investigations of police abuse of power in the Black community.

Strom Thurmond and George Wallace: Desegregation, Race, States' Rights, and Southern Democrats Move to the Republican Party

While the states' rights politics and rhetoric of 1948 were reemerging through the Southern Democrats, they were not taking hold of the Republican Party after World War II. The Republicans still viewed themselves as the party of Lincoln and supported the power of the national government to enforce the law, even in the South. In 1954 the Supreme Court ruled, in *Brown v. Board of Education*, that segregation in the public schools on the basis of race was unconstitutional. The South reacted in outrage and defiance. On March 12, 1956, on the floor of the House of Representatives, Howard Smith of Virginia, chairman of the House Rules Committee, read a speech that has come to be known as the "Southern Manifesto," which declared Southern opposition of the Supreme Court and its *Brown* decision. The Southern Manifesto was formally titled *the 'Declaration of Constitutional Principles*, and "it was signed by 82 Representatives and 19 Senators—roughly one-fifth of the membership of Congress and

39 Infra note 41. See also the official campaign released speech with Senator Thurmond's handmade notations. Address by J. Strom Thurmond September 8, 1948, Binder #II, Special Collections and Archives, Manuscript 100, Strom Thurmond Collection Gubernatorial Series 1948 States Rights Campaign Speeches September 8, 1948.

40 Id.

41 Correspondence with Alan Burns, Associate Librarian and Political Archivist, Special Collections, Strom Thurmond Papers Depository, Clemson University Library Special Collections Department.

all from states that had once composed the Confederacy."[42] The Manifesto was signed by delegations from Alabama, Arkansas, Florida, Georgia, Louisiana, Mississippi, North Carolina, South Carolina, Tennessee, Texas, and Virginia.

Senator Strom Thurmond, the author of the Manifesto, read it on the floor of the United States Senate on the same day. The Manifesto made clear, as follows, that the South would resist the *Brown* decision with all lawful means.

> The Decision of the Supreme Court in the School Cases—Declaration of Constitutional Principles
>
> Mr. President, the increasing gravity of the situation following the decision of the Supreme Court in the so-called segregation cases, and the peculiar stress in sections of the country where this decision has created many difficulties, unknown and unappreciated, perhaps, by many people residing in other parts of the country, have led some Senators and some Members of the House of Representatives to prepare a statement of the position which they have felt and now feel to be imperative.
>
> I now wish to present to the Senate a statement on behalf of 19 Senators, representing 11 States, and 77 House Members, representing a considerable number of States likewise.
>
> **Declaration of Constitutional Principles**
>
> The unwarranted decision of the Supreme Court in the public school cases is now bearing the fruit always produced when men substitute naked power for established law. The Founding Fathers gave us a Constitution of checks and balances because they realized the inescapable lesson of history that no man or group of men can be safely entrusted with unlimited power. They framed this Constitution with its provisions for change by amendment in order to secure the fundamentals of government against the dangers of temporary popular passion or the personal predilections of public officeholders.
>
> We regard the decisions of the Supreme Court in the school cases as a clear abuse of judicial power. It climaxes a trend in the Federal Judiciary undertaking to legislate, in derogation of the authority of Congress, and to encroach upon the reserved rights of the States and the people.

Thurmond complained of a lawless Supreme Court that was threating the system of federalism, amending the constitution by fiat, and exercising unlimited power in a representative democracy, complaints about the Court that are staples in Republican and social conservative orthodoxy to this day. It was in reaction to the *Brown* decision and the due process revolution that would follow that Southern Democrats, social conservatives, and later, the Republican Party made attacking the "liberal Court" and "liberal judges" who "legislated from the bench" political orthodoxy to this day. This political orthodoxy has been implemented first, rhetorically in the 1960s and later in the 1980s and 1990s, with seeking to control the membership

---

42 Historical Highlights, "The Southern Manifesto of 1956," History, Art & Archives: United States House of Representatives at http://history.house.gov/Historical-Highlights/1951-2000/The-Southern-Manifesto-of-1956/.

of the Court through presidential appointments. The politics of both parties trying to control the Court crystalized in the seminal appointment battles of Robert Bork (October 1987) and Clarence Thomas (October 1991).

As discussed in Chapter Seven, the jurisprudence of the Court from *Brown* through the due process cases in the 1960s "gave conservatives politicians a villain to rail against—and run against. The Court's controversial decisions spurred a generation-long anticrime backlash"[43] as well as a social conservative backlash against the civil rights movement policies of the late 1960s and 1970s. The Court was seen as a protector of Blacks and criminals, and by the end of the 1960s, the rhetorical language changed from the indignation of the Court putting "niggers" in local elementary and high schools and swimming pools to protecting criminals. Southern democrats, now moving to the Republican Party, changed their election rhetoric in 1968 from "segregation, segregation tomorrow, segregation forever" to the rhetoric of law and order and protecting law-abiding citizens.

Here is where race code and dog whistle rhetoric developed. Conservatives assert that they don't oppose equality for Blacks but they oppose affirmative action, support local police, oppose forced busing, support local control of schools, and support states' rights, federalism, and strict constructionist judges. The reason this is code is because social conservative attacks on the Court only began when it embraced civil rights. The same voters that opposed civil rights in the 1940s and 1950s were the ones who now wanted strict scrutiny judicial nominees and control of criminals, and who demanded law and order in the streets in the 1960s through the 1990s. The segregationists of the 1950s would become the opponents of busing and the Great Society and the proponents of local control of criminal justice. Social conservatives changed their rhetoric from being proponents of Jim Crow to supporting limited government. Limited government means limited federal protection from local policing. Both Blacks and social conservative voters know what that means in fact.

After asserting that the *Brown* decision was a lawless decision, Thurmond asserted in his 1956 Senate speech defending the **Southern Manifesto** that the text of the Constitution takes no position on schools and definitely does not require that they be integrated.

> The original Constitution does not mention education. Neither does the 14th Amendment nor any other amendment. The debates preceding the submission of the 14th Amendment clearly show that there was no intent that it should affect the system of education maintained by the States.
>
> The very Congress which proposed the amendment subsequently provided for segregated schools in the District of Columbia.
>
> When the amendment was adopted in 1868, there were 37 States of the Union. Every one of the 26 States that had any substantial racial differences among its people, either approved the operation of segregated schools already in existence or subsequently

43 Radley Balko, *Rise of the Warrior Cop: The Militarization of America's Police Forces* (PublicAffairs, 2013), 56.

> established such schools by action of the same law-making body which considered the 14th Amendment.
>
> As admitted by the Supreme Court in the public school case (*Brown v. Board of Education*), the doctrine of separate but equal schools "apparently originated in Roberts v. City of Boston (1849), upholding school segregation against attack as being violative of a State constitutional guarantee of equality." This constitutional doctrine began in the North, not in the South, and it was followed not only in Massachusetts, but in Connecticut, New York, Illinois, Indiana, Michigan, Minnesota, New Jersey, Ohio, Pennsylvania and other northern states until they, exercising their rights as states through the constitutional processes of local self-government, changed their school systems.
>
> In the case of *Plessy v. Ferguson* in 1896 the Supreme Court expressly declared that under the 14th Amendment no person was denied any of his rights if the States provided separate but equal facilities. This decision has been followed in many other cases. It is notable that the Supreme Court, speaking through Chief Justice Taft, a former President of the United States, unanimously declared in 1927 in *Lum v. Rice* that the "separate but equal" principle is "within the discretion of the State in regulating its public schools and does not conflict with the 14th Amendment."
>
> This interpretation, restated time and again, became a part of the life of the people of many of the States and confirmed their habits, traditions, and way of life. It is founded on elemental humanity and commonsense, for parents should not be deprived by Government of the right to direct the lives and education of their own children.

Notice how smoothly discrimination and racism can be defended in non-racist language. As discussed in Chapter Five, *Plessy* and the post-Reconstruction cases are premised on the fact that segregation was built on the "fact" that Blacks were inferior. Yet, Thurmond places separate but equal in such non-racist and constitutional legal terms, that the policy sounds benevolent and the result of unanimous agreement among Blacks and Whites after equal political discourse. The policy of segregation is not about keeping Blacks in their place, he explains, but rather it's the result of mutual acceptance of the natural order of things. As Southern Democrats said segregation is the natural order of things in 1948, social conservatives say today Black disproportionate incarceration is the natural order of things. As both assert, only liberal communist leftists in their utopian worldview of equality think otherwise.

Thurmond made clear separate but equal is "founded on elemental humanity and commonsense, for parents ... to direct the lives and education of their own children." Thurmond continued,

> Though there has been no constitutional amendment or act of Congress changing this established legal principle almost a century old, the Supreme Court of the United States, with no legal basis for such action, undertook to exercise their naked judicial power and substituted their personal political and social ideas for the established law of the land.

> This unwarranted exercise of power by the Court, contrary to the Constitution, is creating chaos and confusion in the States principally affected. It is destroying the amicable relations between the white and Negro races that have been created through 90 years of patient effort by the good people of both races. It has planted hatred and suspicion where there has been heretofore friendship and understanding.
>
> Without regard to the consent of the governed, outside mediators are threatening immediate and revolutionary changes in our public schools systems. If done, this is certain to destroy the system of public education in some of the States.

After all, who does the Supreme Court think it is upending almost a century of discrimination and Jim Crow just because a few malcontents think Blacks are equal! This aggression by outside meddlers who seek to upend the "amicable relations between the White and Negro races that have been created through 90 years of patient effort by the good people of both races" cannot go unanswered or opposed. As such, Thurmond concluded his speech with a declaration of defiance to *Brown*.

> With the gravest concern for the explosive and dangerous condition created by this decision and inflamed by outside meddlers:
>
> We reaffirm our reliance on the Constitution as the fundamental law of the land.
>
> We decry the Supreme Court's encroachment on the rights reserved to the States and to the people, contrary to established law, and to the Constitution.
>
> We commend the motives of those States which have declared the intention to resist forced integration by any lawful means.
>
> We appeal to the States and people who are not directly affected by these decisions to consider the constitutional principles involved against the time when they too, on issues vital to them may be the victims of judicial encroachment.
>
> Even though we constitute a minority in the present Congress, we have full faith that a majority of the American people believe in the dual system of government which has enabled us to achieve our greatness and will in time demand that the reserved rights of the States and of the people be made secure against judicial usurpation.
>
> We pledge ourselves to use all lawful means to bring about a reversal of this decision which is contrary to the Constitution and to prevent the use of force in its implementation.
>
> In this trying period, as we all seek to right this wrong, we appeal to our people not to be provoked by the agitators and troublemakers invading our States and to scrupulously refrain from disorder and lawless acts.[44]

Calhoun's 1838 six resolutions defending slavery, through the theory of states' rights, could not have said it better. Senator Thurmond's *Southern Manifesto* made clear that the South would

44 Strom Thurmond, "Southern Manifesto" Congressional Record, 84th Congress, Second Session. Vol. 102, part 4, March 12, 1956, 4515–4516 and 4459–4460.

resurrect Calhoun's theory of nullification with the policy of interposition; the South would oppose forced integration of its schools and, by extension, society as a whole.

The first act of defiance by the South occurred in Arkansas when Governor Orval Faubus, on September 2, 1957, ordered the National Guard to block the entrance to the Little Rock High School to prevent nine Blacks teenagers from integrating the school as ordered by the federal district court. In his televised address,[45] he explained his actions. Faubus first gave a long dissertation on how Arkansas was a progressive Southern state in which "negroes" were never denied the right to vote, they were integrated in high school athletic teams, "negro" teachers were paid equal to White teachers, that "negros" were admitted into the University of Arkansas, and they were hired in state government positions, and were elected to state offices. He then concluded,

> These facts are given as irrefutable proof that the citizens of Arkansas have been mindful of their problems as they relate to the good relations of the races, that the citizenry as a whole have met their responsibilities in this and other fields, and that improvements and progress have been made in an orderly and peaceful manner.

But

> We are now faced with a far different problem, and that is the forcible integration of the public schools of Little Rock against the overwhelming sentiment of the people of the area. This problem gives every evidence and indication that the attempt to integrate forcibly will bring about widespread disorder and violence.
>
> There is another aspect which I must recognize, and that is the fact that this particular problem and its solution is not only State-wide, but nation-wide in scope. This, of course, is most unfortunate, but it is a situation not of my making.
>
> The plan of integration now being forced upon us by the Federal Courts was set up by the Little Rock School Board and its Superintendent, and approved by a Federal Court prior to expressions of the people, which have been made manifest since that time. These expressions of the people have been clearly indicated by the greatest, time-honored principles of Democracy—by the exercise of the franchise at the ballot box, and the expressions of the members of the Legislature who are elected by and are the representatives of the people.

Like Calhoun and Thurmond before him and Wallace after him, Faubus defined the issue in states' right terms and resistance of the formation of a national police to enforce the will of the national government on a free people. But, he also used rhetoric that would later be adopted by Wallace and Goldwater, by conflating the desire for civil rights with Black criminal violence.

> Now that a Federal Court has ruled no further litigation is possible before the forcible integration of Negroes and Whites in Central High School tomorrow, the evidence of

45 Gov. Orval E. Faubus, "Television and Radio Address" (September 2, 1957) at http://www.southerncolloqrhetoric.net/resources/Faubus570902.pdf.

> discord, anger and resentment has come to me in a deluge from many, many sources. There is evidence of disorder and threats of disorder which could have but one inevitable result—that is, violence, which can lead to injury and harm to persons and property.
>
> A police check has revealed a sale of unusually large numbers of weapons in the Little Rock area. The check reveals that some stores have completely sold out their stocks of knives. These sales have been mostly to Negro youths, but many have been sold to Whites as well.
>
> One store reported that a gang of Negro youths came as a group, and every one of its members purchased knives while another group waited outside. When the first group went out, the second group entered for the same purpose, whereupon the owner took his remaining stock of knives, locked it up, and declined to make further sales.
>
> ...
>
> I have undeniable reports of a telephone campaign of massive proportions going on in the City of Little Rock at this time, calling upon the mothers of White children to assemble peaceably upon the school grounds at 6:00 A. M. tomorrow, the opening day of school.

The governor was making clear that, as a result of the integration of Central High School, hordes of knife-wielding Black youths were going to run wild on peace-loving White mothers who opposed the integration of their children's school. Because of the threat of violence due to the forced integration by the federal court in defiance state appeals to litigate the matter further Faubus asserted that,

> I must state here, in all sincerity, it is my firm conviction that it will not be possible to restore or to maintain order and protect the lives and property of the citizens, if forcible integration is carried out tomorrow in the schools of this community. The inevitable conclusion, therefore, must be that the schools in Pulaski County, for the time being, must be operated on the same basis as they have been operated in the past.

While Faubus, in 1957, claimed that he unleashed the National Guard and the State Police to prevent the Little Rock Nine from entering the school was due to the need to protect property and prevent physical violence and not to protect segregation in the schools, the following year he disclosed his true beliefs on the issue of integration of the public schools. In September 1958, Faubus signed legislation that closed all the public schools in the Little Rock School District, which was later approved by a statewide referendum.

On September 18, 1958, Faubus dropped his pretense of preventing violence and explained his support for the legislation in clear opposition to integration in classical states' rights terms.

> Those who would integrate our schools at any price are still among us. They have seized upon the present situation to promote and foment concern and discontent, because of the temporary closing of the schools. They have spread wild rumors and attempted to

> organize demonstrations. These are the same people and the same forces who have all along been opposed to the majority will of the people of Little Rock and Arkansas.
>
> Last year, I stated during the September crisis that I was not elected Governor of Arkansas to surrender all our rights as citizens to an all-powerful federal autocracy. It is my responsibility, and it is my purpose and determination, to defend the constitutional rights of the people of Arkansas to the full extent of my ability.
>
> ...
>
> To the students who are concerned, I say that in the years to follow, when you have come to realize the importance of maintaining our form of government, and the importance of preserving the great freedoms and privileges which we have known, you will be happy and proud to remember that you suffered inconvenience and personal sacrifice, and thereby made a worthwhile contribution to the maintenance of our dual system of government.
>
> In this dual system of government, with its checks and balances, lies the strength of the United States of America. To you people in this struggle who seek to preserve our form of government, I am proud of my role as a leader in the fight. I did not seek this role. It was thrust upon me in the course of events. I did not, nor do I now, shrink from my responsibilities in what is perhaps the greatest struggle for constitutional government during this century.
>
> To you who oppose the great majority of Arkansas people in this fight, I urge you to think—lest in your consuming desire to gain your ends, among them the destruction of Orval Faubus, you destroy also the very principles of government that enable you and all others to live as a free people, and to rear your children under the high standards of living and freedom which prevail in this state and nation.
>
> It was with a heavy heart that I found it necessary to sign the bills of the Extraordinary Session of the General Assembly and to close the High Schools in the City of Little Rock. I took this action only after the last hope of relief from an intolerable situation had been exhausted.
>
> The Supreme Court shut its eyes to all the facts, and in essence said—integration at any price, even if it means the destruction of our school system, our educational processes, and the risk of disorder and violence that could result in the loss of life—perhaps yours. [46]

If there was any doubt as to what the real issue was, Faubus settled the doubt when he concluded his speech with the following statement.

> Some people dread, shrink from, and grow weary of the struggle in which we are now engaged. I grow weary, also, but is there any choice? Once integration is effected totally and completely, will the peace and harmony you desire be attained? *If we are to judge by the results*

---

46 Orval E. Faubus, "Speech on School Integration" (September 18, 1958) at http://www.blackpast.org/1958-governor-orval-e-faubus-speech-school-integration.

> *elsewhere, anywhere, once total, or near total integration is effected, the peace, the quiet, the harmony, the pride in our schools, and even the good relations that existed heretofore between the races here, will be gone forever.*

Integration does not bring peace, order, or justice. Integration, he made clear, means the destruction of good education. A theme advanced in the 1970s to oppose school bussing as a tool for school integration discussed in Chapter Eight.

> In conclusion, to you citizens of Little Rock, I must warn that you will be subjected to a terrific propaganda campaign from now until September 27th. This barrage of slanted, distorted, and even false versions, will emanate—yes, is already emanating, from the same sources as before—both inside and outside the city and the state. I know you, the people, will understand.
>
> This issue is now where all public issues belong—in your hands, the hands of the people.
>
> The decision is yours to make. Your decision will be my decision, as I am your public servant.
>
> Public sentiment is with you in this struggle to preserve our legal and time-honored rights.
>
> If you stand fast, we can win!

President Dwight D. Eisenhower was not impressed by the arguments of Faubus and was inclined to enforce federal law.

After Faubus unleashed the National Guard and state police to prevent the Little Rock Nine from entering the school, President Eisenhower detached the 101st Airborne Division to enforce the federal district court order. In his speech Eisenhower asserted, as Lincoln stated and as Kennedy would later proclaim, that the states will be made to comply with federal law. "I have come to the President's office in the White House ... speaking from the house of Lincoln, of Jackson and of Wilson ... [to] better convey ... the action I was compelled today to take and the firmness with which I intend to pursue this course until the orders of the Federal Court at Little Rock can be executed without unlawful interference."[47]

Eisenhower was not the first Republican to assert the primacy of the law and the Constitution over the states. Lincoln came to the same conclusion on the eve of his being sworn in as President of the United States. While in New York before his inauguration, Lincoln debated the passions of slavery and whether the North was obeying the law that required the return of slaves and was inciting war in its newspapers. After Lincoln denied both charges, he was confronted by William E. Dodge, who said that the whole country was in great anxiety over the possibility of war over slavery and, "It is for you, sir, to say whether the whole nation shall be plunged into bankruptcy; whether the grass shall grow in the streets of our commercial

---

47 President Dwight D. Eisenhower, "Address on Little Rock," Arkansas (September 24, 1957) at http://historymatters.gmu.edu/d/6335/.

cities." To which Lincoln responded, "Then I say it shall not. If it depends upon me, the grass will not grow anywhere except in the fields and the meadows." Thinking he had Lincoln in the debate, Dodge quickly responded, "Then you will yield to the just demands of the South. You will leave her to control her own institutions. You will admit slave states into the Union on the same conditions as free states. You will not go to war on account of slavery!" Lincoln responded,

> I do not know that I understand your meaning, Mr. Dodge. Nor do I know what my acts or my opinions may be in the future, beyond this. If I shall ever come to the great office of President of the United States, I shall take an oath. I shall swear that I will faithfully execute the office of President of the United States, of all the United States, and that I will, to the best of my ability, preserve, protect, and defend the Constitution of the United States. This is a great and solemn duty. With the support of the people and the assistance of the Almighty I shall undertake to perform it. I have full faith that I shall perform it. ***It is not the Constitution as I would like to have it, but as it is, that is to be defended. The Constitution will not be preserved and defended until it is enforced and obeyed in every part of every one of the United States. It must be so respected, obeyed, enforced, and defended, let the grass grow where it may.***[48]

Dodge did not respond. As Lincoln would not yield to the demands of the South to spread the plague of slavery across the entire United States and would force the South to respect the results of the 1860 election, Eisenhower would not yield to the demands of the South to keep Jim Crow in the schools against the Constitution and the Supreme Court.

On September 2, 1957, Faubus said he would stand in defiance of a federal district court order and would not allow the Little Rock Nine to enter the school. On September 24, 1957, he received an answer to his challenge to the federal government from President Eisenhower. In a television address to the nation, Eisenhower, as did Lincoln, defended the responsibility of the national government and the president to make sure the law is faithfully executed and that the states are subservient to the supremacy of the law and the Constitution as decided by the Supreme Court; personal views of the law and states' rights notwithstanding. He stated,

> The very basis of our individual rights and freedoms rests upon the certainty that the President and the Executive Branch of Government will support and insure the carrying out of the decisions of the Federal Courts, even, when necessary with all the means at the President's command.
>
> Unless the President did so, anarchy would result.
>
> There would be no security for any except that which each one of us could provide for himself.

---

48 Lucius E. Chittenden, *Recollections of President Lincoln and His Administration* (1891) (BiblioBazaar, 2009), 73–75. (Emphasis added). See also discussion at *supra* note 20 at 76.

> The interest of the nation in the proper fulfillment of the law's requirements cannot yield to opposition and demonstrations by some few persons.
>
> Mob rule cannot be allowed to override the decisions of our courts.
>
> Now, let me make it very clear that Federal troops are not being used to relieve local and state authorities of their primary duty to preserve the peace and order of the community ... In the present case the troops are there, pursuant to law, solely for the purpose of preventing interference with the orders of the Court.
>
> The proper use of the powers of the Executive Branch to enforce the orders of a Federal Court is limited to extraordinary and compelling circumstances. Manifestly, such an extreme situation has been created in Little Rock. This challenge must be met and with such measures as will preserve to the people as a whole their lawfully-protected rights in a climate permitting their free and fair exercise. The overwhelming majority of our people in every section of the country are united in their respect for observance of the law—even in those cases where they may disagree with that law.

Eisenhower referred to Little Rock as a "city, under the leadership of demagogic extremists, disorderly mobs [that] have deliberately prevented the carrying out of proper orders from a Federal Court" and "Local authorities have not eliminated that violent opposition ..." He explained,

> This morning the mob again gathered in front of the Central High School of Little Rock, obviously for the purpose of again preventing the carrying out of the Court's order relating to the admission of Negro children to that school.
>
> Whenever normal agencies prove inadequate to the task and it becomes necessary for the Executive Branch of the Federal Government to use its powers and authority to uphold Federal Courts, the President's responsibility is inescapable. In accordance with that responsibility, I have today issued an Executive Order directing the use of troops under Federal authority to aid in the execution of Federal law at Little Rock, Arkansas. This became necessary when my Proclamation of yesterday was not observed, and the obstruction of justice still continues.
>
> It is important that the reasons for my action be understood by all our citizens. As you know, the Supreme Court of the United States has decided that separate public educational facilities for the races are inherently unequal and therefore compulsory school segregation laws are unconstitutional.
>
> Our personal opinions about the decision have no bearing on the matter of enforcement; the responsibility and authority of the Supreme Court to interpret the Constitution are very clear. Local Federal Courts were instructed by the Supreme Court to issue such orders and decrees as might be necessary to achieve admission to public schools without regard to race—and with all deliberate speed.
>
> ...

> Proper and sensible observance of the law then demanded the respectful obedience which the nation has a right to expect from all its people. This, unfortunately, has not been the case at Little Rock. Certain misguided persons, many of them imported into Little Rock by agitators, have insisted upon defying the law and have sought to bring it into disrepute. The orders of the court have thus been frustrated.

As Kennedy would later say, Eisenhower put the enforcement of the law and defending the American way of life in international Cold War terms.

> A foundation of our American way of life is our national respect for law.
>
> In the South, as elsewhere, citizens are keenly aware of the tremendous disservice that has been done to the people of Arkansas in the eyes of the nation, and that has been done to the nation in the eyes of the world.
>
> At a time when we face grave situations abroad because of the hatred that Communism bears toward a system of government based on human rights, it would be difficult to exaggerate the harm that is being done to the prestige and influence, and indeed to the safety, of our nation and the world.
>
> Our enemies are gloating over this incident and using it everywhere to misrepresent our whole nation. We are portrayed as a violator of those standards of conduct which the peoples of the world united to proclaim in the Charter of the United Nations. There they affirmed "faith in fundamental human rights" and "in the dignity and worth of the human person" and they did so "without distinction as to race, sex, language or religion."
>
> And so, with deep confidence, I call upon the citizens of the State of Arkansas to assist in bringing to an immediate end all interference with the law and its processes. If resistance to the Federal Court orders ceases at once, the further presence of Federal troops will be unnecessary and the City of Little Rock will return to its normal habits of peace and order and a blot upon the fair name and high honor of our nation in the world will be removed.
>
> Thus will be restored the image of America and of all its parts as one nation, indivisible, with liberty and justice for all.

While Eisenhower was not in complete support of the *Brown* decision, what was more important was that the law had to be obeyed. While the Southern Democrats and states' rights advocates dating back to Calhoun's focus on the right of the South to treat its slaves and then its' negroes as they saw fit under the concept of states' rights; Lincoln, Eisenhower, and the Congress of 1964 asserted that federal law would prevail on the issue of civil rights. The elections of 1948 would begin the debate in modern American politics regarding the legitimacy of national power to protect the rights of minorities who suffered under the hand of local government in open defiance of the Constitution. The election of 1948 would also begin the transition of states' rights ideology from the

Southern Democratic wing of the Democratic Party to the Republican Party, which would be complete by 1968.

Strom Thurmond and George Wallace: States' Rights, the Politics of Social Conservatism, and the Republicans Take the South

In the three-candidate race of 1948, Truman won, but Thurmond won South Carolina, Alabama, Mississippi, and Louisiana. The rhetoric and politics of opposing civil rights and protecting Jim Crow under the banner of states' rights would shift from the Democratic to the Republican Party as the Southern Democrats abandoned the party and joined the Republicans in the South. As discussed in Chapter Seven, this transition would solidify under the rhetoric of George Wallace and the formal adoption of opposition to civil rights legislation by conservatives who took control of the Republican Party through the politics of Barry Goldwater and the advocacy of Ronald Reagan[49] in 1961 and in the elections of 1964–1968.

After Wallace proclaimed his famous promise regarding segregation, he also foreshadowed the linking in the American political mind of civil rights and integration with crime with the desire to create White fear of Black crime. In his famous January 1963 speech[50] Wallace also said,

> The Washington, D.C. school riot report is disgusting and revealing. We will not sacrifice our children to any such type school system—and you can write that down. The federal troops in Mississippi could be better used guarding the safety of the citizens of Washington, D.C., where it is even unsafe to walk or go to a ballgame—and that is the nation's capitol. I was safer in a B-29 bomber over Japan during the war in an air raid, than the people of Washington are walking to the White House neighborhood. A closer example is Atlanta. The city officials fawn for political reasons over school integration and THEN build barricades to stop residential integration—what hypocrisy!
>
> Let us send this message back to Washington by our representatives who are with us today—that from this day we are standing up, and the heel of tyranny does not fit the neck of an upright man that we intend to take the offensive and carry our fight for freedom across the nation, wielding the balance of power we know we possess in the Southland that WE, not the insipid bloc of voters of some sections will determine in the next election who shall sit in the White House of these United States. That from this day, from this hour from this minute we give the word of a race of honor that we will tolerate their boot in our face no longer and let those certain judges put that in their opium pipes of power and smoke it for what it is worth.

49 See Ronald Reagan, "A Time for Choosing" (October 27, 1964) and "Encroachment Control" (March 30, 1961).

50 George Wallace Gubernatorial Inaugural Address.

In line with Thurmond, Wallace said,

> We can no longer hide our head in the sand and tell ourselves that the ideology of our free fathers is not being attacked and is not being threatened by another idea for it is. We are faced with an idea that if a centralized government assume enough authority, enough power over its people, that it can provide a utopian life that if given the power to dictate, to forbid, to require, to demand, to distribute, to edict and to judge what is best and enforce that will produce only "good" and it shall be our father and our God.
>
> ...
>
> As the national racism of Hitler's Germany persecuted a national minority to the whim of a national majority ... so the international racism of the liberals seek to persecute the international white minority to the whim of the international colored majority ... so that we are footballed about according to the favor of the Afro-Asian bloc.
>
> ...
>
> It is this theory of international power politic that led a group of men on the Supreme Court for the first time in American history to issue an edict, based not on legal precedent, but upon a volume, the editor of which said our Constitution is outdated and must be changed and the writers of which, some had admittedly belonged to as many as half a hundred communist-front organizations. It is this theory that led this same group of men to briefly bare the ungodly core of that philosophy in forbidding little school children to say a prayer.

In his speech, Wallace, like Thurmond before him and Calhoun before him, asserted that the use of national power to protect Blacks and end Jim Crow was equal to tyranny and the imposition of communist dictatorship by those who were against both the Constitution and God Himself.

> It is a system that is the very opposite of Christ for it feeds and encourages everything degenerate and base in our people as it assumes the responsibilities that we ourselves should assume. Its psuedo-liberal spokesmen and some Harvard advocates have never examined the logic of its substitution of what it calls "human rights" for individual rights, for its propaganda play on words has appeal for the unthinking. Its logic is totally material and irresponsible as it runs the full gamut of human desires including the theory that everyone has voting rights without the spiritual responsibility of preserving freedom.
>
> ...
>
> [After the Civil War] There were no government handouts, no Marshall Plan aid, no coddling to make sure that our people would not suffer; instead the South was set upon by the vulturous carpetbagger and federal troops, all loyal Southerners were denied the vote at the point of bayonet, so that the infamous, illegal 14th Amendment might be passed. There was no money, no food and no hope of either. But our grandfathers bent their knee only in church and bowed their head only to God.

Wallace and Thurmond before him advocated the current conservative Republican Party proposition that the national government, under the control of so-called civil rights leaders and Democrats, seek to create a utopia that, by definition, is detrimental to individual liberty. Note: not freedom, but liberty.

Conservatives define freedom as liberty. To conservatives, the Constitution protects liberty to be free from government. Civil rights advocates and liberals defined freedom in terms of enforced laws to prevent discrimination in the 1960s and for the demand for social and economic justice. Liberals define freedom in terms of being free from economic inequality, chronic poverty, and structural social problems that arise from them. The best tool for that is government. This desire to equalize human inequality is what Wallace and Thurmond and social conservatives called government created utopia. This utopia, by definition, creates a powerful government and reduces citizens to the level of subjects, serfs, and slaves.

As Wallace made clear, this goal of perfection and release from economic fear is a desire for a communistic utopia, not a free society under the law. A utopia, he explained, makes mankind dependent on government, not free from it, and it makes government the source of life, not the protector of individual liberty.

> In encouraging our fears of economic insecurity it demands we place that economic management and control with government; in encouraging our fear of educational development it demands we place that education and the minds of our children under management and control of government, and even in feeding our fears of physical infirmities and declining years, it offers and demands to father us through it all and even into the grave. It is a government that claims to us that it is bountiful as it buys its power from us with the fruits of its rapaciousness of the wealth that free men before it have produced and builds on crumbling credit without responsibilities to the debtors our children. It is an ideology of government erected on the encouragement of fear and fails to recognize the basic law of our fathers that governments do not produce wealth people produce wealth free people; and those people become less free as they learn there is little reward for ambition that it requires faith to risk and they have none as the government must restrict and penalize and tax incentive and endeavor and must increase its expenditures of bounties then this government must assume more and more police powers and we find we are become government-fearing people not God-fearing people.

Thus, opposition to civil rights and the end to Jim Crow is hidden within and papered over under the assertions of states' rights which protects against government tyranny. This is how states' rights became code in political discourse through the rest of twentieth century. When social conservatives in the 1960s and 1970s opposed laws protecting Blacks, women, and other political minorities they are reaching out to voters who wished for a return to the great days of Calhoun, Thurmond, and Wallace. The opposition to civil rights rhetorically changed to opposition of creating a liberal utopia in which men became government fearing not God fearing.

The reason all this is code is because these fears of a government-enforced communist utopia originated with federal government opposition to Jim Crow by law. Only when the rights of Blacks are at issue does states' rights become a rallying cry.

John F. Kennedy: Desegregation, Race, States' Rights, and Blacks Move to the Democratic Party

Racial prejudice in American presidential politics was so intense that it manifested itself in ways in which Blacks were not the main focus. But even in those situations, race was still invoked. When John F. Kennedy ran for the Democratic nomination, anti-Catholic sentiments were raised to derail his nomination. Protestant preachers said his election would elect the Pope to the White House and that the American civilization was at risk with Kennedy running for president. The Ku Klux Klan joined the Christian Anti-Communist Crusade in opposition to him. To help allay protestant fears that Kennedy would be a stooge for the Pope, protestant Pastor Herbert Meza invited Kennedy to speak at a special meeting of the Association of Ministers of Greater Houston on September 12, 1960. Meza recounted that, when he announced that he was hosting Kennedy to speak to a group of about 400 protestant ministers, the protestant blowback was intense. In recounting the reaction, he said he got the following letter from a woman living in New Orleans; "I am 65 years old, I have been teaching Sunday school for 20 years, I hope your daughter marries a nigger." He said that was the climate of the 1960 presidential election.[51] The way to curse a White Protestant who supported a White Catholic candidate for President was to curse him with a prayer that his daughter would marry a nigger. When it came to race, the climate in the 1960 election was little better than the election climate of 1948.

In political policy development, rhetoric precedes policy. As the Jim Crow policy protecting rhetoric of Strom Thurmond was answered by President Truman and Senator Humphrey in the 1940s, similarly the rhetoric of Governor Wallace was answered by two presidents in the 1960s, Presidents John F. Kennedy and Lyndon Johnson. ***But between rhetoric and policy lay the politics of getting elected.*** In the election of 1960, the Democrats sought to take Black voters from the Republican Party, which had enjoyed the Black vote from the days after the Civil War. Although the Democrats began to secure Black votes with the depression policies of Franklin D. Roosevelt and desegregation policies of Truman, the Republicans still had a foothold in the Black vote. Kennedy, in 1960, continued to pursue the transfer of Black voter support to the Democratic Party when he used his influence in Alabama and got the local authorities to release Dr. King after he was arrested after failure to leave an all-White restaurant on October 16, 1960. Both Kennedy and Nixon were made aware of the arrest. Both Nixon and Kennedy could have acted to ensure the safety of Dr. King. The point is that Kennedy (through his brother Bobby) made the call to the local authorities, and Nixon did not. That decision helped solidify the perception that the Democratic Party was supportive of civil rights. Dr. King was released on

---

51 CNN *Race for the White House* series, Episode One, "JFK vs. Nixon." (Aired March 6, 2016).

October 28th, eleven days before the election, and Kennedy secured the majority of the Black vote and the election. The move not only made Kennedy look like he supported civil rights but implied that Nixon did not. To this day, that political move by the Kennedys infuriates many Republicans who knew that John F. Kennedy was no great supporter of civil rights in 1960.

Three years later, in the same year of Wallace's famous declaration, President Kennedy, in his famous speech, spelled out the moral issue of Jim Crow operating in a nation premised on freedom. Kennedy, from the Oval Office in the White House, announced

> This afternoon ... the presence of Alabama National Guardsmen was required on the University of Alabama [to allow] the admission two clearly qualified young Alabama residents who happened to have been born Negro.
>
> ...
>
> Today, we are committed to a worldwide struggle to promote and protect the rights of all who wish to be free. And when Americans are sent to Vietnam or West Berlin, we do not ask for whites only. It ought to be possible, therefore, for American students of any color to attend any public institution they select without having to be backed up by troops. It ought to be possible for American consumers of any color to receive equal service in places of public accommodation, such as hotels and restaurants and theaters and retail stores, without being forced to resort to demonstrations in the street, and it ought to be possible for American citizens of any color to register and to vote in a free election without interference or fear of reprisal. It ought to be possible, in short, for every American to enjoy the privileges of being American without regard to his race or his color. In short, every American ought to have the right to be treated as he would wish to be treated, as one would wish his children to be treated. But this is not the case.
>
> ...
>
> We are confronted primarily with a moral issue. It is as old as the Scriptures and is as clear as the American Constitution.
>
> The heart of the question is whether all Americans are to be afforded equal rights and equal opportunities, whether we are going to treat our fellow Americans as we want to be treated. If an American, because his skin is dark, cannot eat lunch in a restaurant open to the public, if he cannot send his children to the best public school available, if he cannot vote for the public officials who will represent him, if, in short, he cannot enjoy the full and free life which all of us want, then who among us would be content to have the color of his skin changed and stand in his place? Who among us would then be content with the counsels of patience and delay?
>
> One hundred years of delay have passed since President Lincoln freed the slaves, yet their heirs, their grandsons, are not fully free. They are not yet freed from the bonds of injustice. They are not yet freed from social and economic oppression. And this Nation, for all its hopes and all its boasts, will not be fully free until all its citizens are free.
>
> ...

> This is one country. It has become one country because all of us and all the people who came here had an equal chance to develop their talents. We cannot say to ten percent of the population that you can't have that right; that your children cannot have the chance to develop whatever talents they have; that the only way that they are going to get their rights is to go in the street and demonstrate. I think we owe them and we owe ourselves a better country than that.[52]

His speech echoed President Garfield, more than eight decades before, who, in his inaugural address in 1881, concluded,

> The free enjoyment of equal suffrage is still in question, and a frank statement of the issue may aid its solution. It is alleged that in many communities negro citizens are practically denied the freedom of the ballot. In so far as the truth of this allegation is admitted, it is answered that in many places honest local government is impossible if the mass of uneducated negroes are allowed to vote. These are grave allegations. So far as the latter is true, it is the only palliation that can be offered for opposing the freedom of the ballot. Bad local government is certainly a great evil, which ought to be prevented; but to violate the freedom and sanctities of the suffrage is more than an evil. It is a crime which, if persisted in, will destroy the Government itself. Suicide is not a remedy. If in other lands it be high treason to compass the death of the king, it shall be counted no less a crime here to strangle our sovereign power and stifle its voice.
>
> It has been said that unsettled questions have no pity for the repose of nations. It should be said with the utmost emphasis that this question of the suffrage will never give repose or safety to the States or to the nation until each, within its own jurisdiction, makes and keeps the ballot free and pure by the strong sanctions of the law.[53]

After the assassination of President Kennedy on November 22, 1963, President Lyndon B. Johnson said of civil rights before a joint session of Congress,

> Our most immediate tasks are here on this Hill. First, no memorial oration or eulogy could more eloquently honor President Kennedy's memory than the earliest possible passage of the Civil Rights Bill for which he fought so long. We have talked long enough in this country about equal rights. We have talked for a hundred years or more. It is time now to write the next chapter, and to write it in the books of law. I urge you again, as I did in [1957] and [1960], to enact a civil rights law so that we can move forward to eliminate from this nation every trace of discrimination and oppression that is based upon race or color. ...
>
> The time has come for Americans of all races and creeds and political beliefs to understand and to respect one another. So let us put an end to the teaching and the

52 John F. Kennedy "Civil Rights Address" (address from Oval Office, June 1963).

53 President Garfield, "Inaugural Address" (1881).

> preaching of hate and evil and violence. Let us turn away from the fanatics of the far left and the far right, from the apostles of bitterness and bigotry, from those defiant of law, and those who pour venom into our nation's bloodstream.[54]

The Southern Democrat position of states' rights would be adopted by the Republican Party with the defection of the Southern Democrats beginning in 1948. In his speech on his decision to vote against the Civil Rights Act 1964, which prohibited and ended a century of racial discrimination in public accommodations (Title II) and employment discrimination based on race (Title VII), Goldwater, reflecting the principles of Calhoun, Thurmond, and Wallace, claimed that the bill violated states' rights and that the implementation of the bill would create oppression through the creation of massive national police force.

> I wish to make myself perfectly clear. The two portions of this bill to which I have constantly and consistently voiced objections, and which are of such overriding significance that they are determinative of my vote on the entire measure, are those which would embark the federal government on a regulatory course of action with regard to private enterprise in the area of so-called public accommodations and in the area of employment—to be more specific, titles II and VII of the bill. I find no constitutional basis for the exercise of federal regulatory authority in either of these areas; and I believe the attempted usurpation of such power to be a grave threat to the very essence of our basic system of government; namely, that of a constitutional republic in which fifty sovereign States have reserved to themselves and to the people those powers not specifically granted to the central or federal government.
>
> If it is the wish of the American people that the federal government should be granted the power to regulate in these two areas and in the manner contemplated by this bill, then I say that the Constitution should be so amended by the people as to authorize such action in accordance with the procedures for amending the Constitution which that great document itself prescribes.
>
> ...
>
> My basic objection to this measure is, therefore, constitutional. But, in addition, I would like to point out to my colleagues in the Senate and to the people of America, regardless of their race, color, or creed, the implications involved in the enforcement of regulatory legislation of this sort. To give genuine effect to the prohibitions of this bill will require the creation of a federal police force of mammoth proportions. It also bids fair to result in the development of an "informer" psychology in great areas of our national life—neighbors spying on neighbors, workers spying on workers, businessmen spying on businessmen-where those who would harass their fellow citizens for selfish and narrow purposes will have ample inducement to do so. These, the federal police force and an "informer" psychology, are the hallmarks of the police state and landmarks in the destruction of a free society.

---

54 President Lyndon B. Johnson, "Let Us Continue" speech before Joint Session of Congress (November 27, 1963).

> I repeat again: I am unalterably opposed to discrimination of any sort and I believe that though the problem is fundamentally one of the heart, some law can help-but not law that embodies features like these, provisions which fly in the face of the Constitution and which require for their effective execution the creation of a police state. And so, because I am unalterably opposed to any threats to our great system of government and the loss of our God-given liberties, I shall vote "no" on this bill.[55]

The tyranny of Jim Crow and its effects on Blacks for a century, although evil, are acceptable compared to the tyranny of a federal government growing in power to rectify the former evil. So said Calhoun (in the defense of slavery), so said Thurmond (in the use of federal troops to enforce court orders), so said Wallace (in school house door opposition integration), and so said Goldwater. Barry Goldwater explained his opposition to federal government enforcement of civil rights in the high tones of a Jeffersonian, but in fact, they were in line with the Confederate South, Strom Thurmond, and George Wallace. Goldwater's approach established Republican Party orthodoxy on civil rights.

Although Goldwater was handily defeated in 1964, as was Thurmond in 1948, both of their candidacies established the political and policy fault lines of the two political parties, defined modern American politics, and shaped the policies of both parties. The Republican Party opposed civil rights on states' rights grounds and the policies of the Great Society on individual liberty grounds. The Democrat Party supported civil rights and the Great Society. The fault lines were set for party policy and election battles for decades thereafter.

Beginning in 1964, President Johnson instituted a series of national policies that not only sought to end the century-old system of Jim Crow with condemnation but sought to rectify its consequences. Ten years after the beginning of the modern civil rights movement, with the Supreme Court decision of *Brown v. Board of Education* in 1954 and culminating in the landmark passage of the Civil Rights Acts of 1964 and 1965, policy attention shifted from ending racial Jim Crow and segregation to economic disparities and the failure of Blacks to attain the American Dream. In his famous *Freedom is Not Enough* speech at Howard University on June 4, 1965, President Johnson said,

> In far too many ways American Negroes have been another nation: deprived of freedom, crippled by hatred, the doors of opportunity closed to hope.
>
> In our time change has come to this Nation, too. The American Negro, acting with impressive restraint, has peacefully protested and marched, entered the courtrooms and the seats of government, demanding a justice that has long been denied. The voice of the

55 Barry Goldwater, Speech on the Floor of the U.S. Senate in opposition to the Civil Rights Act of 1964 on June 18, 1964 Congressional Record, 88th Cong., 2nd Sess., June 18, 1964, 14318–19; New York Times, June 19, 1964 reprinted in *The Political Principles of Senator Barry Goldwater as Revealed in His Speeches and Writings: A Source Book*, eds. Leonard Schlup and James Manley (2012): 202–204.

Timeline of American Politics

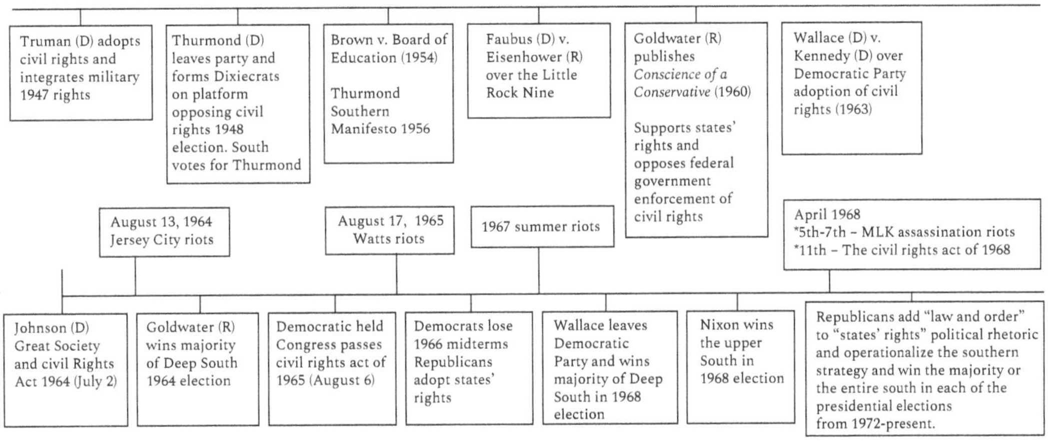

Negro was the call to action. But it is a tribute to America that, once aroused, the courts and the Congress, the President and most of the people, have been the allies of progress.

Thus we have seen the high court of the country declare that discrimination based on race was repugnant to the Constitution, and therefore void. We have seen in 1957, and 1960, and again in 1964, the first civil rights legislation in this Nation in almost an entire century.

...

The voting rights bill will [establish the freedom to vote]. ... But freedom is not enough. You do not wipe away the scars of centuries by saying: Now you are free to go where you want, and do as you desire, and choose the leaders you please.

You do not take a person who, for years, has been hobbled by chains and liberate him, bring him up to the starting line of a race and then say, "you are free to compete with all the others," and still justly believe that you have been completely fair.

Thus it is not enough just to open the gates of opportunity. All our citizens must have the ability to walk through those gates.

This is the next and the more profound stage of the battle for civil rights. We seek not just freedom but opportunity. We seek not just legal equity but human ability, not just equality as a right and a theory but equality as a fact and equality as a result.

...

Its object will be to help the American Negro fulfill the rights which, after the longtime of injustice, he is finally about to secure. To move beyond opportunity to achievement. To shatter forever not only the barriers of law and public practice, but the walls which bound the condition of many by the color of his skin. To dissolve, as best we can, the antique enmities of the heart which diminish the holder, divide the great democracy, and do wrong—great wrong—to the children of God.

> And I pledge you tonight that this will be a chief goal of my administration, and of my program next year, and in the years to come. And I hope, and I pray, and I believe, it will be a part of the program of all America.[56]

This speech, along with Johnson's War on Poverty speech before Congress in January, 1964,[57] began four years of social programs, which resulted in Medicare, Medicaid, federal school loans, food stamps, and a host of other programs between 1964 and 1968. With the passage of the Civil Rights Act of 1968, Jim Crow died. Its death was not without cost. As Johnson said with passage of the Civil Rights Act on 1964, "we just delivered the South to the Republican Party for a long time to come."[58]

Barry Goldwater, The Father of Modern Political Conservatism: The Defining of the Republican Party

In 1960, Goldwater published *The Conscience of a Conservative* in which he laid out the principles that would form the modern Republican Party. Modern American thinking and conservatism, on a policy and political level, cannot be understood without reading Goldwater's 1960 book. It's a short book of 127 pages, but its significance lies in it clarifying what conservatism is and how conservatives perceive the purpose and role of the national government. A full review of the book cannot be done here, but a brief review allows the reader to understand how the conservative view of the federal protection of Blacks and the attack on segregation by the Democratic Party gave rise to the mutiny of Southern Democrats to the Republican Party. Goldwater gave cover to the states' rights of Calhoun, Thurmond, and Wallace and gave it a "noble" and "race-neutral" intellectual standing that was politically adopted and implemented by Reagan in 1980.

Goldwater begins with a defense of conservative thinking and defends that it's not only a theory of economics, but is a theory that opposes both "autocrats with 'Democratic Jacobins' [and] the tyranny of the French monarchy. [The conservative is] equally revolted at the attempt to solve [the problem of the monarchy] by a mob tyranny ... under the banner of egalitarianism. ... Today, therefore, he is at odds with dictators who rule by terror, and equally with those gentler collectivists who ask our permission to play God with the human race."[59] Goldwater explained that conservative theory is based on two propositions, that man is an economic

---

56 President Lyndon B. Johnson, Commencement speech at Howard University, June 4, 1964. Public Papers of the Presidents of the United States: Lyndon B. Johnson, 1965. Volume II, Entry 301, pp. 635–640. Washington, D. C.: Government Printing Office, 1966.

57 President Lyndon B. Johnson, Annual Message to Congress, January 8, 1964.

58 See Chapter One. Some assert that Johnson did not say this. Regardless of that debate, the point is he was right. The Democrats suffered a string of losses from 1966 through 1980 in the South and from 1980s to present no Democrat presidential candidate for the presidency has won the South.

59 Barry Goldwater, *The Conscience of a Conservative* (Victor Publishing Co., 1960): 13.

and spiritual creature. Man has desires both for economic success but also spiritual success. But while socialists focus only on the economic needs and desires of man,

> It is Conservatism that puts material things in their proper place—that has a structured view of the human being and of human society, in which economics plays only a subsidiary role.
>
> The root difference between the Conservatives and the Liberals of today is that Conservatives take account of the whole man, while the Liberals tend to look only at the material side of man's nature. The Conservative believes that man is, in part, an economic, an animal creature; but that he is also a spiritual creature with spiritual needs and spiritual desires. What is more, these needs and desires reflect the superior side of man's nature, and thus take precedence over his economic wants. Conservatism therefore looks upon the enhancement of man's spiritual nature as the primary concern of political philosophy. Liberals, on the other hand,—in the name of a concern for "human beings"—regard the satisfaction of economic wants as the dominant mission of society. They are, moreover, in a hurry. So that their characteristic approach is to harness the society's political and economic forces into a collective effort to compel "progress." In this approach, I believe they fight against Nature.[60]

This last point, "a collective effort to compel 'progress' [which is a] fight against nature" is nothing new. As discussed in Chapter Five, the Supreme Court in 1883 came to the same conclusion in the Civil Rights Cases. Conservatives don't oppose federal government action per se; they oppose federal government action to quicken the achievement of freedom of individuals from societal and social injustice or oppression. It does not matter if the federal action seeks a just result; the problem is that it seeks to make a change in the first place.

Conservatives, by definition, despise quick social change and, specifically, social change created by national government policies. Recall the speeches by Thurmond in 1948 and Wallace in 1963, which equated national government social and economic equality with Hitler, Stalin, and Mussolini. Because these tyrants implemented federal programs like social security, Medicare and social programs like those of the Great Society. The role of the federal government, as Calhoun explained in his defense of slavery manifesto in 1843, is to support the states and leave social policy to them. Goldwater was in complete agreement. In regard to social programs to address social poverty and discrimination in several states, Goldwater wrote,

> Now the point is not that Congress failed to act ... but rather that the federal government had no business entering these fields in the first place, and thus had no business taking upon itself the prerogative of judging the States' performance ...
>
> The Tenth Amendment is *not* "a general assumption," but a prohibitory rule of law. The Tenth Amendment recognizes the states' jurisdiction in certain areas. States' Rights

---

60 Barry Goldwater, *The Conscience of a Conservative* (Victor Publishing Co., 1960): 10–11.

> means that the States have a right to act or *not to act*, as they see fit, in the areas reserved to them. The States may have duties corresponding to the people of the states, not to the federal government. Therefore, the recourse lies not with the federal government, which is not sovereign, but with the people who are, and who have full power to take disciplinary action ... The Constitution, I repeat, draws a sharp and clear line between federal jurisdiction and state jurisdiction.[61]

Conservatives, the Civil War notwithstanding, think the Constitution created a national government with no independent sovereignty that the people can appeal to and use for their welfare. The Federal government has a purpose and role in protecting freedom and the general welfare but in only a very limited area.

> The *legitimate* functions of government are actually conductive to freedom. Maintaining internal order, keeping foreign foes at bay, administering justice, removing obstacles to the free interchange of goods—the exercise of these powers makes it possible for men to follow their chosen pursuits with maximum freedom.[62]

Anything outside of these specific objectives belongs to the states through the Tenth Amendment. When conservatives complain of governmental power being abused, by definition, this does not apply to the states. Goldwater ideology, in application, results in the assertion that the people of America have no appeal to the federal government as a separate sovereign to seek redress of social grievances. Only the federal government is subject to the possibility of

> the corrupting influence of power, the natural tendency of men who possess *some* power to take unto themselves *more* power. The tendency leads eventually to the acquisition of all power—whether in the hands of one or many makes little difference to the freedom of those left on the outside.
>
> ...
>
> The framers of the Constitution had learned the lesson. They were not only students of history, but victims of it: they knew from vivid, personal experience that freedom depends on effective restraints against the accumulation of power in a single authority. And this is what the Constitution is: *a system of restraints against the natural tendency of government to expand in the direction of absolutism.*[63]

Goldwater completely ignored the fact that slavery, Black Codes, Jim Crow, and the use of the criminal justice system to keep Blacks in a near state of slavery (discussed in Chapter Seven) occurred under state, not federal, government authority and policy. From Calhoun through Goldwater, tyranny only occurs when the federal government acts to stop states from abusing Blacks. It is this lesson of history that Blacks instinctively understand when listening to social

---

61 Barry Goldwater, *The Conscience of a Conservative* (Victor Publishing Co., 1960): 28–30

62 Barry Goldwater, *The Conscience of a Conservative* (Victor Publishing Co., 1960): 17.

63 Barry Goldwater, *The Conscience of a Conservative* (Victor Publishing Co., 1960): 17–18.

conservatives who expose the values of states' rights. Blacks know what states' rights means and has always meant.

Goldwater decried that, although the federal government can do good things, the same power can be used for evil and it's the chance of evil that must be controlled and focused on, not the good that could be done. He warned that,

> But note that the very instrument by which these desirable ends are achieved *can* be the instrument for achieving undesirable ends—that government can, instead of extending freedom, restrict freedom. And note, secondly, that the "can" quickly becomes "will" the moment the holders of government power are left to their own devices.[64]

Goldwater concludes that individual freedom is always under threat in society.

> The delicate balance that ideally exists between freedom and order has long since tipped against freedom practically everywhere on earth. In some countries, freedom is altogether down and order holds absolute sway. In our country the trend is less far advanced, but it is well along and gathering momentum every day. Thus, for the American Conservative, there is no difficulty in identifying the day's overriding political challenge: it is *to preserve and extend freedom.* As he surveys the various attitudes and institutions and laws that currently prevail in America, many questions will occur to him, but the Conservative's first concern will always be: *Are we maximizing freedom?* I suggest we examine some of the critical issues facing us today with this question in mind.[65]

Blacks can't travel on buses or eat and find lodging in American hotels and restaurants because they are Black; and laws to rectify this lack of freedom according to Goldwater conservativism threaten the extension of freedom. The real question, of course, was whose freedom Goldwater was concerned about.

In 1960, only six years after *Brown v. Board of Education*; three years before Wallace said a Black man could not enter the University of Alabama, because he was Black; and three years after Faubus sent an army to prevent nine children from going into a high school because they were Black; Goldwater said the goal of conservatives and Republicans should be to preserve and extend freedom from the power of national government to act! Why? Because education and the policies of education are none of the national government's business.

As Goldwater made clear, "I am here concerned [that] the cornerstone of the Republic, our chief bulwark against the encroachment of individual freedom by Big Government, is fast disappearing."[66] To conservatives, the big government was the federal government, and only the federal government. He never considered that to the nine children, the state was the big government preventing them from enjoying the preservation and extension of freedom he

---

64 Barry Goldwater, *The Conscience of a Conservative* (Victor Publishing Co., 1960): 17.

65 Barry Goldwater, *The Conscience of a Conservative* (Victor Publishing Co., 1960): 14.

66 Barry Goldwater, *The Conscience of a Conservative* (Victor Publishing Co., 1960): 25–26.

advocated. Freedom to conservatives is freedom from the national government action (abuse); it does not mean freedom from government abuse. Goldwater bemoaned, "I regret to say that in actual practice, the Republican Party, like the Democratic Party, summons the coercive power of the federal government whenever national leaders conclude that the States are not performing satisfactorily."[67] According to Goldwater, the states are free to abuse the rights of whomever they choose.

Goldwater concluded that there is a reason the Constitution "draws a sharp and clear line between federal jurisdiction and state jurisdiction ... There is a reason for its reservation of States' Rights. Not only does it prevent the accumulation of power in the central government that is removed from the people and relatively immune from popular restraints; it also recognizes the principle that essentially local problems are best dealt with by the people most directly concerned."[68] This last point that local problems should be handled by local government—the government closest to the people and the problem—is the foundation of modern social conservative rhetoric, especially when it comes to federal investigations of chronic police abuse of Black communities. Local problems belong to the local people and only them. As Goldwater asserted, "If the people are unhappy with [their state policy] they can bring pressure to bear on their state officials and, if that fails, they can elect a new set of officials. And if, in the unhappy event they should wish to divest themselves of this responsibility, they can amend the Constitution."[69] Note that only in the states does this system of democracy of voting and removing officials and putting new ones in to meet the needs of the people exist. On the federal level, Goldwater wrote, we have people in government who are "immune from popular restraints." What conservatives and Goldwater, by design, fail to consider is that when you take high political philosophy and apply it to the world in operation, you create politics. Note the political result of the idea of leaving the ending segregation and racism to the states. From 1877 to 1960—for more than eight decades—Black people remained in the back of the bus. And if Calhoun, the father of states' rights theory, had his way, the back of the bus would have been a great leap forward.

If conservatives had prevailed in 1860, slavery would have endured for at least the remainder of the nineteenth century. Leaving Lincoln's victory aside, if conservative theory had prevailed in the 1940s and 1950s the American Apartheid would have continued with nothing to oppose it. American Apartheid had fully functioned for almost a century unabated when the Court ruled in *Brown*. There is no reason it would have ended if the conservative theory had prevailed. The reason Blacks left the Republican Party is because they correctly perceived conservative policy of opposing the federal government's use of governmental power to end the vestiges of slavery as supporting those vestiges. The result of nuanced and abstract conservative political theoretical conversations about constitutional interpretation

---

67 Barry Goldwater, *The Conscience of a Conservative* (Victor Publishing Co., 1960): 26.

68 Barry Goldwater, *The Conscience of a Conservative* (Victor Publishing Co., 1960): 30.

69 Barry Goldwater, *The Conscience of a Conservative* (Victor Publishing Co., 1960): 30.

and the protection of rights of all Americans that resulted in protecting the rights of Whites to segregate Blacks to secondhand status was not lost on Blacks. The result of conservative theory—maintaining Jim Crow to maintain control of the federal government—was acceptable to White conservatives but it was not acceptable to segregated Blacks.

Nevertheless, Goldwater defended states' rights with a clarity that has formed the foundation for modern politics. Goldwater faced the segregation issue head-on when he said "An attempt has been made in recent years to disparage the principle of States' Rights by equating it with defense of the South's position on racial integration. I have already indicated that the reach of States' Rights is much broader than that[!]"[70] Goldwater made clear that Black civil rights may be important, but there are more important issues at play than their rights when considering federal government powers under the constitution. The freedom of Blacks from discrimination is not the point. The rights of states involve higher issues and higher principles. Easy for him to say, he could stay at any hotel and eat at any restaurant of his choosing when he traveled. It took the Civil Rights Act of 1964 and the Supreme Court in *Katzenbach v. McClung* (1964) to provide those basic civil rights to Blacks.

This aside, Goldwater provided another concept that conservatives have maintained for decades. Goldwater wrote that conflict between states' rights and civil rights was, in fact, not real, but imagined!

> I say an imagined conflict because I deny that there can be a conflict between States' Rights, properly defined—and civil rights, properly defined. If States' "Rights" are so asserted as to encroach upon individual rights that are protected by valid federal laws, then the exercise of state power is a nullity. Conversely, if individual "rights" are asserted as to infringe upon valid state power, then the assertion of those "rights" is a nullity. The rights themselves do not clash. The conflict arises from a failure to define the two categories of rights correctly, and to assert them lawfully.
>
> States' Rights are easy enough to define. The Tenth Amendment does it succinctly ...
>
> A civil right is a right that is asserted and is therefore protected by some valid law. It may be asserted by the common law, or by local or federal statutes, or by the Constitution; *but unless a right is incorporated in the law, it is not a civil right and is not enforceable by the instruments of the civil law ...*
>
> In the field of racial relations, there are some rights that are clearly protected by valid laws and are therefore "civil" rights. One of them is the right to vote. ... The Fourteenth Amendment ... makes it clear ... that people of all races shall be equally entitled [to all the economic rights in a capitalist and property oriented society]. It is otherwise let us note, with education. For the federal Constitution does not require the States to maintain racially mixed schools. Despite the recent holding of the Supreme Court, I am firmly convinced-not only that integrated schools are not required-but that the Constitution does not permit any interference whatsoever by the federal government in the field of

70 Barry Goldwater, *The Conscience of a Conservative* (Victor Publishing Co., 1960): 32.

> education. It may be just or wise or expedient for negro children to attend the same schools as white children, but they do not have a civil right to do so which is protected by the federal constitution, or which is enforceable by the federal government.
>
> ... Consequently, under the Tenth Amendment, jurisdiction over the entire field was reserved to the States ...
>
> The intentions of the Fourteenth Amendment's authors are perfectly clear. ... The amendment was not intended to, and therefore it did not outlaw racially separate schools. It was not intended to, and therefore it did not, authorize any federal intervention on the field of education.[71]

Goldwater was not only unimpressed with the Supreme Court saying otherwise, he established a cornerstone concept regarding conservatives' general distain for "activists" on the Court. Activists being those who create a right in the Constitution that is not in the text. The distain for the Court in conservative political theory and politics starts with the *Brown* case in 1954. Of the *Brown* decision, Goldwater wrote, "it was only by engrafting its own views onto the established law of the land that the Court was able to reach the decision it did."[72] His attack on the Court established another concept within social conservative and Republican orthodoxy—advocacy of original intent interpretation of the Constitution.

> I am therefore not impressed by the claim that the Supreme Court's decision on school integration is the law of the land. The Constitution, and the laws "made in pursuance thereof," are the "supreme law of the land." The Constitution is what its authors intended it to be and said it was—not what the Supreme Court says it is. If we condone the practice of substituting our own intentions for those of the Constitution's framers, we reject, in effect, the principles of Constitutional Government: we endorse a rule of men, not of laws.[73]

Hamilton wrote on the issue of constitutional interpretation and the Supreme Court,

> I admit, however, that the Constitution ought to be the standard of construction for the laws, and that wherever there is an evident opposition, the laws ought to give place to the Constitution. But this doctrine is not deducible from any circumstance peculiar to the plan of the convention, but from the general theory of a limited Constitution; and as far as it is true, is equally applicable to most, if not to all the State governments.[74]

On the principle of judicial review, Alexander Hamilton, one of the three chief defenders and architects of the Constitution and the key writer on the judiciary, would disagree with Goldwater on the role of the judiciary. He wrote in 1788,

---

71 Barry Goldwater, *The Conscience of a Conservative* (Victor Publishing Co., 1960).

72 Barry Goldwater, *The Conscience of a Conservative* (Victor Publishing Co., 1960), 36.

73 Barry Goldwater, *The Conscience of a Conservative* (Victor Publishing Co., 1960), 37.

74 Alexander Hamilton, *Federalist* No. 81, in *The Federalist Papers* (1788).

> Some perplexity respecting the rights of the courts to pronounce legislative acts void, because contrary to the Constitution, has arisen from an imagination that the doctrine would imply a superiority of the judiciary to the legislative power. It is urged that the authority which can declare the acts of another void, must necessarily be superior to the one whose acts may be declared void. As this doctrine is of great importance in all the American constitutions, a brief discussion of the ground on which it rests cannot be unacceptable.
>
> There is no position which depends on clearer principles, than that every act of a delegated authority, contrary to the tenor of the commission under which it is exercised, is void. No legislative act, therefore, contrary to the Constitution, can be valid. To deny this, would be to affirm, that the deputy is greater than his principal; that the servant is above his master; that the representatives of the people are superior to the people themselves; that men acting by virtue of powers, may do not only what their powers do not authorize, but what they forbid.
>
> If it be said that the legislative body are themselves the constitutional judges of their own powers, and that the construction they put upon them is conclusive upon the other departments, it may be answered, that this cannot be the natural presumption, where it is not to be collected from any particular provisions in the Constitution. It is not otherwise to be supposed, that the Constitution could intend to enable the representatives of the people to substitute their will to that of their constituents. *It is far more rational to suppose, that the courts were designed to be an intermediate body between the people and the legislature*, in order, among other things, *to keep the latter within the limits assigned to their authority. The interpretation of the laws is the proper and peculiar province of the courts.* A constitution is, in fact, and must be regarded by the judges, as a fundamental law. *It therefore belongs to them to ascertain its meaning, as well as the meaning of any particular act proceeding from the legislative body. If there should happen to be an irreconcilable variance between the two, that which has the superior obligation and validity ought, of course, to be preferred; or, in other words, the Constitution ought to be preferred to the statute, the intention of the people to the intention of their agents.*
>
> Nor does this conclusion by any means suppose a superiority of the judicial to the legislative power. It only supposes that the power of the people is superior to both; and that *where the will of the legislature, declared in its statutes, stands in opposition to that of the people, declared in the Constitution, the judges ought to be governed by the latter rather than the former.* They ought to regulate their decisions by the fundamental laws, rather than by those which are not fundamental.[75]

So much for the assertion by many social conservative commentators that the Supreme Court created the concept of judicial review.

---

75 Alexander Hamilton, *Federalist* No. 78, in *The Federalist Papers* (1788) (emphasis added).

Both Hamilton and Madison in the *Federalists Papers*[76] and John Marshall in *Marbury v. Madison* (1801) ("It is emphatically the province and duty of the Judicial Department to say what the law is. Those who apply the rule to particular cases must, of necessity, expound and interpret that rule")[77] made clear that the Constitution is a law and, as such, it was open to interpretation as to its meaning. The final determination regarding its meaning and the agency of government that determines the meaning of the law is the judiciary, not in the elected branches of government. To the idea that determination of the constitutionality of the laws should be placed in the same body as those who make the laws, Hamilton wrote,

> The members of the legislature will rarely be chosen with a view to those qualifications which fit men for the stations of judges; …
>
> These considerations teach us to applaud the wisdom of those States who have committed the judicial power, in the last resort, not to a part of the legislature, but to distinct and independent bodies of men. Contrary to the supposition of those who have represented the plan of the convention, in this respect, as novel and unprecedented, it is but a copy of the constitutions of New Hampshire, Massachusetts, Pennsylvania, Delaware, Maryland, Virginia, North Carolina, South Carolina, and Georgia; and the preference which has been given to those models is highly to be commended. [78]
>
> It equally proves, that though individual oppression may now and then proceed from the courts of justice, the general liberty of the people can never be endangered from that quarter; I mean so long as the judiciary remains truly distinct from both the legislature and the Executive. For I agree, that "there is no liberty, if the power of judging be not separated from the legislative and executive powers." And it proves, in the last place, that as liberty can have nothing to fear from the judiciary alone, but would have everything to fear from its union with either of the other departments ...
>
> The complete independence of the courts of justice is peculiarly essential in a limited Constitution. By a limited Constitution, I understand one which contains certain specified exceptions to the legislative authority; such, for instance, as that it shall pass no bills of attainder, no *ex post facto* laws, and the like. Limitations of this kind can be preserved in practice no other way than through the medium of courts of justice, whose duty it must be to declare all acts contrary to the manifest tenor of the Constitution void. Without this, all the reservations of particular rights or privileges would amount to nothing.[79]

---

76 *Federalist Papers* 78 and 81 by Hamilton and *Federalist Papers* 51 by Madison (1788).

77 *Marbury v. Madison*, 5 U.S. 137, 177 (1801).

78 Alexander Hamilton, *Federalist* No. 81, in *The Federalist Papers* (1788).

79 Alexander Hamilton, *Federalist* No. 78, in *The Federalist Papers* (1788).

The founding generation, as voiced by Hamilton, clearly intended the Supreme Court to be an independent body and have the authority to determine the legality of laws passed by Congress and to make sure all laws passed by the states or by Congress were subservient to the Constitution. He made clear that liberty gives way to tyranny when the legislative power enjoys judicial power concurrently. More significantly to Goldwater, Hamilton made clear that the structure of the Constitution is such that the Supreme Court, the judicial department, is the agency tasked with constitutional interpretation and that power is specifically deprived from Congress. This truth should not be confused with legitimate principles on how the Court should exercise this power. For Hamilton also made clear that

> [i]n the first place, there is not a syllable in the plan under consideration which *directly* empowers the national courts to construe the laws according to the spirit of the Constitution, or which gives them any greater latitude in this respect than may be claimed by the courts of every State.[80]
>
> It can be of no weight to say that the courts, on the pretense of a repugnancy, may substitute their own pleasure to the constitutional intentions of the legislature. This might as well happen in the case of two contradictory statutes; or it might as well happen in every adjudication upon any single statute. The courts must declare the sense of the law; and if they should be disposed to exercise WILL instead of JUDGMENT, the consequence would equally be the substitution of their pleasure to that of the legislative body. The observation, if it prove any thing, would prove that there ought to be no judges distinct from that body.[81]

Hamilton and the founders clearly rejected the Court exercising will, rather than judgment, and asserted that the power of the Court is limited to making sure that all laws were subservient and in compliance with the Constitution and the laws passed thereof. The Court is to interpret the law and determine its compliance with the Supreme Law, not substitute its view on what the law should be under the Supreme law. But this question is a different issue than the question of whether the power to be the final arbiter of what the Constitution means exclusively belongs to the Supreme Court. The former is a subject for perpetual debate, but the latter is not. The power to determine the meaning of the Constitution does not extend to the elective branches of government. Goldwater was not correct that "Congress and the states, equally with the Supreme Court, are obligated to interpret and comply with the Constitution according to their own lights."[82] As John Locke and Charles Montesquieu, the intellectual Founding Fathers of republican government theory and western common law, made clear in their writings — the king can't be a judge in his own case. The people may have to obey

80 Alexander Hamilton, *Federalist* No. 81, in *The Federalist Papers* (1788).

81 Alexander Hamilton, *Federalist* No. 78, in *The Federalist Papers* (1788).

82 Barry Goldwater, *The Conscience of a Conservative* (1960), 36.

the king, but the king must obey the law, both as it is written and as it's interpreted by the judiciary—the guardians of the law.[83]

Leaving Goldwater's error on constitutional structural historical origins aside, he made very clear his policy view on the decision of the *Brown* decision, "[T]he court said that what matters is not the ideas of the men who wrote the Constitution, but the *Court's* ideas. ... I therefore support all efforts by the States, excluding violence of course, to preserve their rightful powers over education."[84] This is exactly what they did for decades! To this day, full integration of our schools has not been accomplished.

In defense of *Brown*, the Court was not presented with the legal question of whether the writers of the Fourteenth Amendment intended the amendment to apply to public education, although they considered the question—but the legal question they were presented with was whether the principle of "separate but equal" under *Plessy v. Fergson* (1896) applied to public education. When Goldwater quoted the Court stating what the question was, he did not do so completely.[85] The Court defined the legal question as follows,

> We must look instead to the effect of segregation itself on public education.
> In approaching this problem, we cannot turn the clock back to 1868, when the Amendment was adopted, or even to 1896, when *Plessy v. Ferguson* was written. We must consider public education in the light of its full development and its present place in American life throughout the nation. Only in this way can it be determined if segregation in public schools deprives these plaintiffs of the equal protection of the laws. [86]

To which the Court concluded,

> We come then to the question presented: does segregation of children in public schools solely on the basis of race, even though the physical facilities and other "tangible" factors may be equal, deprive the children of the minority group of equal educational opportunities? We believe that it does.
>
> ...
>
> We conclude that, in the field of public education, the doctrine of "separate but equal" has no place. Separate educational facilities are inherently unequal. Therefore, we hold that the plaintiffs and others similarly situated for whom the actions have been brought are, by reason of the segregation complained of, deprived of the equal protection of the laws guaranteed by the Fourteenth Amendment. This disposition makes unnecessary

---

83 Arthur Garrison, "The Traditions and History of the Meaning of the Rule of Law" *Georgetown Journal of Law & Public Policy* 12, no. 2 (2014): 565.

84 Barry Goldwater, *The Conscience of a Conservative* at 36–37.

85 Barry Goldwater at 36.

86 *Brown v. Board of Education*, 347 U.S. 483, 492–493 (1954).

> any discussion whether such segregation also violates the Due Process Clause of the Fourteenth Amendment. [87]

The Court reasoned that, because education has such a significant impact on society and the opportunities that education provides to all Americans, segregation by race clearly imputes a badge of inferiority on Blacks that will travel with them for life. It will interfere with the social, economic, and professional opportunities that are not interfered with when considering White children. Thus, the unequal treatment in school, created by the application of the "separate but equal" doctrine, creates an equal protection violation of the Fourteenth Amendment. The functional result of *Brown* was not integration of schools, for the Southern states fought tooth and nail to obstruct the Court for more than two decades. The functional result of *Brown* was it ushered in the rise of the civil rights movement, the fall of Jim Crow, and the rise of the federal government as the protector of individual rights from the states. To Goldwater conservatives, a result that was an oxymoron and an act of tyranny at the same time.

Truth be told, what conservatives truly reject is not judicial review and the power of the Court to declare legislation unconstitutional because social conservative have no problems using the Court to secure conservative policy objectives like opposition to affordable government supported healthcare, unrestricted rights to carry guns, and interstate reciprocity of state concealed carry gun permits. What they oppose are the political results of Supreme Court decisions they don't support. The objections are political not constitutional. Conservative outcries of violations to the structure of the Constitution and the individual freedoms that the Constitution is designed to protect have historically only been voiced when the results liberate Blacks from slavery and later from Jim Crow. In the case of *Brown*, what Goldwater resented was the imposition of integration and the dismantling of segregation and White supremacy—first with education and then in society as a whole—at the command of the federal courts enforced by the federal government. The resentment of Supreme Court decisions has not changed. Now, conservatives reject the Supreme Court producing "liberal" social policy results—legalized abortion, affirmative action, and homosexual marriage, just to name a few.

Goldwater made clear that modern American conservative theory asserts that the "Congress and the states, equally with the Supreme Court, are obligated to interpret and comply with the Constitution according to their own lights."[88] Calhoun said that the states had the power to nullify federal government action under the Constitution. Wallace said the states have a right to interpose themselves between the people and the federal government. Goldwater said the states and the Congress are equal and independent of the Supreme Court in

---

87 *Brown v. Board of Education*, 347 U.S. at 493, 495.

88 Barry Goldwater, *The Conscience of a Conservative* (1960), 37.

interpreting the Constitution, and the former are not subject to the latter. This has been conservative orthodoxy ever since. Goldwater, four years after he published his book, took control of the Republican Party with these principles and ran for president of the United States. Although he lost, he changed American politics forever. The politics and presidential campaign of Goldwater papered over social conservative opposition to the disposing of Jim Crow laws and the racism undergirding it and made such opposition respectable by invoking theories of government that were disavowed by the writers of the Constitution and the *Federalist Papers.* Goldwater defended ideas that were defeated at the constitutional convention and on the fields of the American Civil War.

In explaining the significance of modern conservative thought in America and the rise of conservatism in the Republican Party, much credit is rightly given to Goldwater and *The Conscience of a Conservative.* As Matthew Dalleck writes,

> [b]y the late 1950s conservatives had established a strong base of support in the growing Southwest. For much of the century wealthy easterners had controlled the Republican Party, but in the postwar years a growing number of businessmen and political leaders from the Sunbelt, many of whom had prospered in the postwar industrial boom, began playing a greater role in national politics. Stressing individual initiative, free enterprise, and a militant anti-communism, conservatives formed a variety of single-interest groups to challenge the ideas and programs of the liberal eastern establishment.
>
> In the early 1960s conservatives continued to benefit from large-scale social and demographic changes. In the South the growth of the civil-rights movement, industrial expansion, and the rise of an urban middle class revitalized the Republican party. The policies of the Kennedy Administration also helped the conservative cause. As President, Kennedy courted many eastern business leaders, drawing their support away from liberal Republicans. He also undercut much of the appeal of moderate Republicans: his position on civil rights, for example, was virtually indistinguishable from theirs. As conservatives began to develop positions on key issues which increasingly appealed to voters, liberal Republicans had trouble distinguishing themselves from Kennedy-style liberals.
>
> …
>
> At the beginning of the 1960s conservatives were in a better position than at any time since the 1930s to challenge moderate Republicans for control of the party. But large obstacles remained. Not only were conservatives widely viewed as wild-eyed fanatics but they squabbled among themselves, had trouble articulating a positive program of reform, had few grassroots organizations, and lacked the funding to make the movement a serious political force.
>
> The year 1960, though, brought a turning point for the conservative movement. That year Barry Goldwater published *The Conscience of a Conservative.* Generally dismissed in the national media, the book stands today as one of the most important political tracts in modern American history.

> ...
>
> But perhaps the greatest achievement of Goldwater's book—and the reason for its startling success with the right—was that it gave conservatives, for the first time, a blueprint for translating their ideas into political action.
>
> ...
>
> > "It contained the core beliefs of our political faith, it told us why we had failed, what we must do. We read it, memorized it, quoted it. ... For those of us wandering in the arid desert of Eisenhower Republicanism, it hit like a rifle shot."
>
> ...
>
> By 1968 conservatives dominated the Republican Party. In 1960 Nixon had wooed those on his left; eight years later he employed the conservative speechwriter Pat Buchanan, chose the fiery Spiro Agnew as his running mate, and trumpeted his anti-Communist credentials and his opposition to busing to win southern delegates. Nixon was not an ideological conservative, but to gain the nomination he had to appeal to the party's new conservative majority.[89]

As the Heritage Foundation, the chief think tank for American conservatism, observed[90] regarding the significance of *The Conscience of a Conservative* and Goldwater's campaign in 1964,

> On November 3, 1964, President Lyndon B. Johnson was re-elected by the largest popular vote margin in U.S. history, crushing his conservative opponent, Republican Barry Goldwater. Johnson received 61 percent of the vote, topping the previous record set by Franklin D. Roosevelt, and carried 44 states for a total of 486 electoral votes. The election also produced the biggest Democratic majority in the House of Representatives since 1936. *The New York Times* summed up that "Barry Goldwater not only lost the presidential election yesterday but the conservative cause as well." At the time, most political analysts agreed with these declarations.
>
> Yet, just two years later, the GOP, led by Goldwater-inspired conservatives, made a remarkable comeback, gaining 47 seats in the House, four seats in the Senate, and eight governorships. Moreover, just 16 years after the Goldwater debacle, Republican Ronald Reagan, running as an unapologetic conservative, won the first of two landslide presidential elections. As columnist-commentator George Will put it, Barry Goldwater lost 44 states but won the future.
>
> Paradoxically, Goldwater's monumental loss marked the beginning of a shift to the Right that would eventually end 50 years of liberal dominance in American politics. Goldwater shaped the Republican Party's positions on limited government, welfare, and

---

89 Matthew Dalleck, "The Conservative 1960s," *The Atlantic Monthly* 276, no. 6(December 1995): 130–135. http://www.theatlantic.com/magazine/archive/1995/12/the-conservative-1960s/376506/

90 See *Infra* note 103.

> defense, which would carry the United States into the 21st century. Goldwater revived our constitutional heritage, placing it at the center of popular political discussion when the conservative cause seemed lost.
>
> ...
>
> He constantly defended the independent entrepreneur and the small businessman, warning that "any government big enough to give you everything you want is big enough to take away everything you have."[91]

The significance of Goldwater, in 1964, was that he opened a divide between liberals and conservatives and defined how that divide would result in policy. Goldwater lost in 1964, but the ideals of Goldwater prevailed in 1966 and 1968, providing the path for 1980.

On issues of race, Goldwater papered over the racism and principles of Calhoun, Thurmond, and Wallace and their protection of slavery and Jim Crow under the banner of states' rights with the concept of limited government and the freedom of the individual. Goldwater defined and established the rhetorical conservative answer to institutional and legal segregation and discrimination more than a century old, as follows:

> It so happens that I am in agreement with the objectives of the Supreme Court as stated in the Brown decision. I believe that it is both wise and just for Negro children to attend the same schools as whites, and that to deny them this opportunity carries with it strong implications of inferiority. *I am not prepared, however, to impose that judgment of mine on the people of Mississippi or South Carolina, or tell them what methods should be adopted and what pace should be kept in striving toward that goal. That is their business, not mine.* I believe that the problem of race relations, like all social and cultural problems, is best handled by the people directly concerned. Social and cultural change, however desirable, should not be effected by the engines of national power. Let us, through persuasion and education, seek to improve institutions we deem defective. But let us, in doing so, respect the orderly processes of the law. Any other course enthrones tyrants and dooms freedom.[92]

As Calhoun, Thurmond, and Wallace said before him, Goldwater, with a little more tact, made equally clear; it's none of the federal government's business how the states treat its Blacks. Goldwater, modernizing the states' rights views of Calhoun, Thurmond, and Wallace, recognized the evil of discrimination and even said it should not be so, but he made clear as the champions of states' rights before him asserted, the federal government is not the agency to rectify the evil. Blacks, Goldwater and modern conservatives argued, were to be left to the mercies of the segregationists and time. Persuasion and education over time, Goldwater

---

91 Lee Edwards, *Barry M. Goldwater: The Most Consequential Loser in American Politics* (July 2014) at http://www.heritage.org/research/reports/2014/07/barry-m-goldwater-the-most-consequential-loser-in-american-politics#_ftn22

92 Barry Goldwater, *The Conscience of a Conservative* (1960), 27–28 (emphasis added).

asserted, are the only constitutional ways to end Jim Crow. To put an end to Jim Crow would immediately enthrone tyrants. Calhoun would be in total agreement.

In 1964, in his *Civil Rights and the Common Good*[93] speech, Goldwater asserted,

> [b]ut the fundamental issue of our day—the new area into which the act of 1964 dangerously treads—is a different one. It is the issue of *unfair discrimination in the private affairs of men. Here government can provide no lasting solution.* No law can make one person like another if he doesn't want to. Government can do little more than offer moral leadership and persuasion. The ultimate solution lies in the hearts of men.

As discussed in Chapter Five, the Supreme Court would say the same thing in *Plessy v. Ferguson* in 1896. Goldwater explained,

> ... [t]his is a moral problem, and local leadership is needed to make headway in solving it. The best thing the President can do is to use his office to persuade and encourage localities to take up the task of leadership.
>
> ...
>
> In a free society, government is by consent—hence by the *opinion*—of the governed. Law as an expression of opinion cannot be more enlightened than the opinion it expresses. Political leadership must always work first for the enlightenment of hearts and minds—for the opinions which enable men to understand each other and respect their differences.
>
> ...
>
> The forces working for true equality and true justice lie in the heart of this great American people. Let us place a more patient confidence in their ultimate triumph.

This sentiment of "wait" and let persuasion change hearts, and society should refrain from using coercive laws to end racial discrimination was shared by many Americans during the early civil rights era. Goldwater, unlike Wallace, asserted states' rights did not mean that governmental and social racial discrimination should not be ended, but that it was not the federal government's role to end it. Individual freedom, the cornerstone of conservatism, includes the right to choose when and how individuals associate. As Goldwater made clear in his speech,

> [o]ur aim, as I understand it, is neither to establish a segregated society nor to establish an integrated society. It is to preserve a *free* society.

What Goldwater attempted to paper over was the facts that American history had proven that a free society can fully function while enslaving and/or racially discriminating against a portion of its citizens and not violate the principles of liberty. With this truth papered over, Goldwater could easily propose,

93 Barry Goldwater, "Civil Rights and the Common Good" (speech at the Conrad Hilton Hotel October 16, 1964) (emphasis added).

> It is often said that only the freedom of a member of a minority is violated when some barrier keeps him from associating with others in his society. But this is wrong. Freedom of association is a double freedom or it is nothing at all. It applies to both parties who want to associate with each other. And so the barriers infringe the freedom of everybody in the society, not just the minorities.
>
> Now, the removal of such barriers enhances freedom. That is clear. But it is equally clear that freedom is diminished when barriers are raised against the freedom *not* to associate. We must never forget that the freedom to associate means the same thing as the freedom not to associate. It is wrong to erect legal barriers against either side of this freedom.
>
> We are forced to only one conclusion. As far as the government is concerned, it must ensure freedom of association, but it cannot and should not ensure association itself. That is a matter that must be mutually and freely decided by the individuals involved. It is a matter of the heart and conscience.

It is easy for those who do not feel the sting of discrimination to assert that segregation nonetheless affects everyone equally. But the more significant aspect of Goldwater's speech is that it established the idea that the focus of conservatism is not ending discrimination and its effects, but rather it focuses on establishing freedom of opportunity regardless of the results. Goldwater also reduced Jim Crow, and the effects of slavery before it, to the simple issue of integration—not the human, social, and political value and equality of Blacks in America. It was to this blind spot of conservative theory and the American social perspective of law and order over justice that Dr. Martin Luther King Jr. wrote to address from inside a jail cell.

In 1963, Dr. Martin Luther King Jr. wrote his famous letter[94] from inside of a Birmingham Jail to Protestant church leaders who asserted that he was inciting violence, that his protests were not "well timed" to end discrimination and racial injustice, and that he was violating the law and threatening peace and order. To the assertion that freedom will come through persuasion and that Blacks should wait for it to produce consensus against racial segregation and injustice, Dr. King famously wrote,

> We know through painful experience that freedom is never voluntarily given by the oppressor; it must be demanded by the oppressed. Frankly I have never yet engaged in a direct action movement that was "well timed," according to the timetable of those who have not suffered unduly from the disease of segregation. For years now I have heard the word "Wait!" It rings in the ear of every Negro with a piercing familiarity. This "wait" has almost always meant "never." It has been a tranquilizing thalidomide, relieving the emotional stress for a moment, only to give birth to an ill-formed infant of frustration. We must come to see with the distinguished jurist of yesterday that "justice too long delayed is justice denied."

94 Dr. Martin Luther King Jr., "Letter from a Birmingham Jail" (April 16, 1963).

> We have waited for more than three hundred and forty years for our constitutional and God-given rights. The nations of Asia and Africa are moving with jet-like speed toward the goal of political independence, and we still creep at horse and buggy pace toward the gaining of a cup of coffee at a lunch counter.
>
> I guess it is easy for those who have never felt the stinging darts of segregation to say wait. But when you have seen vicious mobs lynch your mothers and fathers at will and drown your sisters and brothers at whim; when you have seen hate filled policemen curse, kick, brutalize, and even kill your black brothers and sisters with impunity; when you see the vast majority of your twenty million Negro brothers smothering in an air-tight cage of poverty in the midst of an affluent society; when you suddenly find your tongue twisted and your speech stammering as you seek to explain to your six-year-old daughter why she can't go to the public amusement park that has just been advertised on television, and see tears welling up in her little eyes when she is told that Funtown is closed to colored children, and see the depressing clouds of inferiority begin to form in her little mental sky, and see her begin to distort her little personality by unconsciously developing a bitterness toward white people; when you have to concoct an answer for a five-year-old son asking in agonizing pathos: "Daddy, why do white people treat colored people so mean?"; when you take a cross-country drive and find it necessary to sleep night after night in the uncomfortable corners of your automobile because no motel will accept you; when you are humiliated day in and day out by nagging signs reading "white" men and "colored"; when your first name becomes "nigger" and your middle name becomes "boy" (however old you are) and your last name becomes "John," and when your wife and mother are never given the respected title "Mrs."; when you are harried by day and haunted by night by the fact that you are a Negro, living constantly at tip-toe stance never quite knowing what to expect next, and plagued with inner fears and outer resentments; when you are forever fighting a degenerating sense of "nobodiness"—then you will understand why we find it difficult to wait. There comes a time when the cup of endurance runs over, and men are no longer willing to be plunged into an abyss of injustice where they experience the bleakness of corroding despair. I hope, sirs, you can understand our legitimate and unavoidable impatience.

Social conservative theory had no answer for Dr. King then, as they have no answer for police shooting young Black men or disproportionate Black incarceration today, except that Blacks are disproportionately criminal and systemic racism in American policing is a figment of the imagination of the progressive left.

As Goldwater, in his 1964 acceptance speech at the Republican convention, asserted, "We Republicans seek a government that attends to its inherent responsibilities of maintaining a stable monetary and fiscal climate, encouraging a free and a competitive economy and enforcing law and order." Goldwater conservatism puts a primacy on obedience to the law, because only through obedience can order be maintained, and order allows individuals to enjoy liberty. Individual enjoyment of liberty, under conservative theory, is the sole justification for government. Goldwater made clear in his speeches that, as to the issue of changing unjust laws, the only appeal to changing them is through political persuasion and that appeal should occur at the most local level of government. In his acceptance speech, he said,

> Our towns and our cities, then our counties, then our states, then our regional contacts—and only then, the national government. That, let me remind you, is the ladder of liberty, built by decentralized power. On it also we must have balance between the branches of government at every level.

Dr. King countered with the proposition that maintaining individual liberty was not the sole purpose of government but rather the protection and advancement of justice is the defining obligation of government. Although the states and local governments have a responsibility to end the structural evils of Jim Crow, the federal government has an independent role, being an independent sovereign authority under the constitution, to ensure that law and justice are provided to any group of citizens under the Constitution, within any of the states who are also under the Constitution. With an echo of Lincoln, as to the issue of law and obedience to unjust laws, Dr. King wrote in his letter from jail,

> You express a great deal of anxiety over our willingness to break laws. This is certainly a legitimate concern. Since we so diligently urge people to obey the Supreme Court's decision of 1954 outlawing segregation in the public schools, it is rather strange and paradoxical to find us consciously breaking laws. One may well ask: "How can you advocate breaking some laws and obeying others?" The answer is found in the fact that there are two types of laws: There are just laws and there are unjust laws. I would be the first to advocate obeying just laws. One has not only a legal but moral responsibility to obey just laws. Conversely, one has a moral responsibility to disobey unjust laws. I would agree with Saint Augustine that "An unjust law is no law at all."
>
> ...
>
> I must make two honest confessions to you, my Christian and Jewish brothers. First, I must confess that over the last few years I have been gravely disappointed with the white moderate. I have almost reached the regrettable conclusion that the Negroes' great stumbling block in the stride toward freedom is not the White Citizen's "Counciler" or the Ku Klux Klanner, but the white moderate who is more devoted to "order" than to justice; who prefers a negative peace which is the absence of tension to a positive peace which is the presence of justice; who constantly says "I agree with you in the goal you seek, but I can't agree with your methods of direct action"; who paternalistically feels that he can set the timetable for another man's freedom; who lives by the myth of time and who constantly advises the Negro to wait until a "more convenient season." Shallow understanding from people of good will is more frustrating than absolute misunderstanding from people of ill will. Lukewarm acceptance is much more bewildering than outright rejection.

> I had hoped that the white moderate would understand that law and order exist for the purpose of establishing justice, and that when they fail to do this they become dangerously structured dams that block the flow of social progress ...
> Oppressed people cannot remain oppressed forever.

Dr. King was correct. A distinction exists between law and order versus law and order under justice.[95] The distinction lies in the fact that "law and order can produce a perverse outcome when the letter of the law is pursued without justice and mercy. Injustice can occur when the process is lawful."[96] The demand for law and order being a primary objective of Goldwater conservatism in the face of century's old injustice—slavery first, Jim Crow segregation second—is what diffuses states' rights of any morality or viability in American political theory and history.

Nevertheless, Goldwater established conservative orthodoxy that asserts that if the federal government is given the power to end discrimination and prohibit legal enforcement of Black second-class status, it is also given the power to take away individual liberty. Put simply, conservatives considered the cure worse than the disease. Social change takes time and in a choice between change imposed by the federal government and change imposed by time for the South to see the error of its ways; in such a choice, Blacks must suffer the pain of waiting for time. The pain of waiting for change is palatable over the tyranny of White America being forced to see Blacks as equals before the law and in society under the forceful hand of federal law.

Calhoun made clear that the right of the South to hold slaves in the Union is higher than the right of those who wish to maintain the Union without slavery. One hundred years later, Goldwater said it was tyranny for federal government to enforce the right of Blacks to be recognized as equal citizens under the Constitution and to be free from being discriminated against on the basis of race at the expense of the right of the people of the South to refuse to treat Blacks as equal under the law and in society, because they are inferior to Whites. To Calhoun, union without slavery established by the coercive hand of the national government upon the states was tyranny. To Goldwater, union without Jim Crow, established by the coercive hand of the national government upon the states, was tyranny. Goldwater social conservative theory, regardless of the issue, opposes federal government intervention into local issues. In the days of Calhoun, the issue was opposition and limitations on the spread of slavery. In the days of Thurmond and Wallace, the issue was protection of Jim Crow. In both the dispute was over the federal government coming to the aid of Blacks under abuse by state and local

---

95 Arthur H. Garrison, "The Traditions and History of the Meaning of the Rule of Law," *Georgetown Journal of Law & Public Policy* 12, no. 2 (2014): 565.

96 Arthur H. Garrison, "The Traditions and History of the Meaning of the Rule of Law," *Georgetown Journal of Law & Public Policy*, at 595. See also, Arthur H. Garrison, "The Rule of Law and the Rise of Control of Executive Power," *Texas Review of Law & Politics* 18, no. 2 (2014): 304.

government. In the politics of today, the issue is social conservative opposition to federal oversight of local police who have been found to discriminate or otherwise violate the rights of people in minority communities. A century separated Calhoun from Goldwater and yet they said the same thing.

The idea of states' rights, as Goldwater made clear, is the operational theory of making government benign to individual liberty, which is the goal and purpose of government. In his 1964 election pamphlet, *Barry Goldwater Speaks out for a Stronger America,* Goldwater summarized the principles of his campaign and the principles that would form the philosophical base of the Republican Party from 1966–1968 and in 1980 under Reagan. In his pamphlet he stated

> There is a reason for (the Constitution's) reservation of States' Rights.
>
> Not only does it prevent the accumulation of power in a central government that is remote from the people and relatively immune from popular restraints; it also recognizes the principle that essentially local problems are best dealt with by the people most directly concerned. Who knows better than New Yorkers how much and what kind of publicly-financed slum clearance in New York City is needed and can be afforded? Who knows better than Nebraskans whether that State has an adequate nursing program? Who knows better than Arizonans the kind of school program that is needed to educate their children?
>
> The people have long since seen through the spurious suggestion that federal aid comes free. They know that the money comes out of their own pockets, and that it is returned to them minus a broker's fee taken by the federal bureaucracy. They know, too, that the power to decide how that money shall be spent is withdrawn from them and exercised by some planning board deep in the caverns of one of the federal agencies. They understand this represents a great and perhaps irreparable loss-not only in their wealth, but in their priceless liberty.
>
> [Liberty is defined as] equal treatment for all Americans, but preferential treatment for none.
>
> The right to vote, to equal treatment before the law, to hold property, and to the protection of contracts are clearly guaranteed by the 14th and 15th Amendments to the Constitution. These rights should be rigorously enforced. Existing law demands it.
>
> In the schools, the Attorney General already has the authority through court decrees to effect integration. But if more authority must be granted, we should write a law that is tightly drawn, that can be used like a rifle, not a shotgun.
>
> As for the proposed public accommodations law, it is unconstitutional and a clear example of a new law which will only hinder, not help the cause of racial tolerance. Such a law could even open the door to a police-state system of enforcement that would eventually threaten the liberty of us all.

Just to be clear, Goldwater campaigned under the assertion that federal laws that allowed Blacks to live anywhere they could afford would "open the door to a police-state system." He also established social conservative rejection of anti-poverty funding. His election pamphlet made clear,

> No matter how we try, we cannot pass a law that will make you like me or me like you. The key to racial and religious tolerance lies not in laws alone but, ultimately, in the hearts of men.
>
> He is a staunch defender of personal freedom and the rights of every individual. Unenforceable government edicts benefit no one. Continued public attention and moral persuasion, I believe, will do more, in the long run to create the good will necessary to the acceptance of decent racial relations in all segments of our society.
>
> Our people must not be herded into the streets for the redress of their grievances. We have better ways, more lasting and more honest ways. [97]

Barry Goldwater, The Father of Modern Political Conservatism: The Political Rhetoric of Law and Order Through the Conflating of Crime and Race in the Republican Party

In addition to adopting the views of Southern Democrats, Goldwater also infused into Republican political orthodoxy the politics of White fear of Black crime and the responsibility of the national government to maintain law and order. The politics of White fear of crime in general and Black urban crime in particular would establish how and why social conservatives considered it tyranny for the federal government to address the injustice of Jim Crow, but support the federalization of crime control. The politics of crime would shift the Republican party from the purity of Goldwater theory. But Goldwater would seed the ground for the federalization when he added fear of crime to his acceptance speech at the Republican Convention on July 16, 1964.

> *The growing menace in our country tonight, to personal safety, to life, to limb and property, in homes, in churches, on the playgrounds, and places of business, particularly in our great cities, is the mounting concern, or should be, of every thoughtful citizen in the United States.*
>
> *Security from domestic violence,* no less than from foreign aggression, *is the most elementary and fundamental purpose of any government,* and a government that cannot fulfill that purpose is one that cannot long command the loyalty of its citizens. History shows us—demonstrates that nothing—*nothing prepares the way for tyranny more than the failure of public officials to keep the streets from bullies and marauders.* …

---

97 "Barry Goldwater Speaks out for a Stronger America" Barry Goldwater for President 1964 Campaign Brochure http://www.4president.org/brochures/goldwater1964brochure.htm. See also, Barry Goldwater, "Civil Rights and the Common Good" (Speech delivered in Chicago on October 16, 1964) and "Republican Principles Address Before the 1968 Republican National Convention in Convention Hall, Miami Beach, Florida August 5, 1968" *The Political Principles of Senator Barry Goldwater as Revealed in His Speeches and Writings: A Source Book*, eds. Leonard Schlup and James Manley (2012) (242–253).

> *We Republicans seek a government that attends to its inherent responsibilities* of maintaining a stable monetary and fiscal climate, encouraging a free and a competitive economy and *enforcing law and order ...*
>
> Our towns and our cities, then our counties, then our states, then our regional contacts—and only then, the national government. That, let me remind you, is the ladder of liberty, built by decentralized power. On it also we must have balance between the branches of government at every level.

In the law and order section of Nixon's acceptance speech for the Republican nomination for president in August 1968, Nixon was in line with the Goldwater assertion that one of the primary objectives of government is to maintain law and order. But, he finessed it within a broader argument that a great nation is not great if it can't keep order in its own streets, and a nation that can't command respect in its streets can't command respect in the world. This approach to law and order would become a staple in Republican rhetoric for decades.

In the first part of the law and order speech, Nixon conflates lawlessness with national weakness and asserts that the cause of the weakness is the Johnson Administration's failure to seek and maintain simple law and order.

> When the nation with the greatest tradition of the rule of law is plagued by unprecedented lawlessness;
>
> ...
>
> And when the President of the United States cannot travel abroad or to any major city at home without fear of a hostile demonstration—then it's time for new leadership for the United States of America.
>
> ...
>
> The American Revolution was and is dedicated to progress, but our founders recognized that the first requisite of progress is order. Now, there is no quarrel between progress and order—because neither can exist without the other.
>
> So let us have order in America—not the order that suppresses dissent and discourages change but the order which guarantees the right to dissent and provides the basis for peaceful change.
>
> And tonight, it is time for some honest talk about the problem of order in the United States.

Then Nixon supplements his assertion that President Johnson is weak on crime with what had become standard Republican and social conservative orthodoxy that the federal courts lead by the Supreme Court, were handcuffing the police and were letting criminals roam free on technicalities.

> Let us always respect, as I do, our courts and those who serve on them. But let us also recognize that some of our courts in their decisions have gone too far in weakening the peace forces as against the criminal forces in this country and we must act to restore that balance.

> Let those who have the responsibility to enforce our laws and our judges who have the responsibility to interpret them be dedicated to the great principles of civil rights.
>
> But let them also recognize that the first civil right of every American is to be free from domestic violence, and that right must be guaranteed in this country.

Nixon asserted, as Johnson did in 1966, that the role of the federal government is to maintain law and order. This rhetoric would form the beginning of the modern federalization of criminal justice and crime prevention policy. Nixon asserted in 1968 at the Republican national convention,

> And if we are to restore order and respect for law in this country there is one place we are going to begin. We are going to have a new Attorney General of the United States of America.
>
> I pledge to you that our new Attorney General will be directed by the President of the United States to launch a war against organized crime in this country. I pledge to you that the new Attorney General of the United States will be an active belligerent against the loan sharks and the numbers racketeers that rob the urban poor in our cities. I pledge to you that the new Attorney General will open a new front against the filth peddlers and the narcotics peddlers who are corrupting the lives of the children of this country.
>
> Because, my friends, let this message come through clear from what I say tonight. Time is running out for the merchants of crime and corruption in American society. The wave of crime is not going to be the wave of the future in the United States of America. We shall re-establish freedom from fear in America so that America can take the lead in re-establishing freedom from fear in the world.

By 1968 the law and order rhetoric was recognized as the Republican dog whistle for White Northern working class and Southern Democrat voters—a fact that Nixon recognized and tried to finesse in the concluding section of his speech.

> And to those who say that law and order is the code word for racism, there and here is a reply:
>
> Our goal is justice for every American. If we are to have respect for law in America, we must have laws that deserve respect. Just as we cannot have progress without order, we cannot have order without progress, and so, as we commit to order tonight, let us commit to progress.

George Wallace, in his campaign for president in 1968, also acknowledged the problem of law and order in Republican politics being considered code for race, and in his speech at Madison Square Garden on October 24, 1968, he argued that the loss of law and order was not due to Blacks in general or linking of Blacks to criminals. The same man who said "segregation

Excerpts from Richard Nixon, "Address Accepting the Presidential Nomination at the Republican National Convention in Miami Beach, Florida." 1968.

today, segregation tomorrow, and segregation forever" was evolving his rhetoric and said in New York City,

> I am very grateful for the fact that in 1966 my wife received more black votes in Alabama than did either one of her opponents. We are proud to say that they support us now in this race for the presidency, and we would like to have the support of people of all races, colors, creeds, religions, and national origins in the state of New York.
>
> Our system is under attack: the property system, the free enterprise system, and local government. Anarchy prevails today in the streets of the large cities of our country, making it unsafe for you to even go to a political rally here in Madison Square Garden, and that is a sad commentary. Both national parties in the last number of years have kowtowed to every anarchist that has roamed the streets.
>
> I want to say before I start on this any longer, that I'm not talking about race. The overwhelming majority of all races in this country are against the breakdown of law and order as much as those who are assembled here tonight. It's a few anarchists, a few activists, a few militants, a few revolutionaries, and a few Communists.
>
> ...
>
> Now what are some of the things we are going to do when we become president? We are going to turn back to you, the people of the states, the right to control our domestic institutions. Today you cannot even go to the school systems of the large cities of our country without fear. This is a sad day ... I can assure you of this that there's not ten cents worth of difference with what the national parties say ... I remember six years ago when this anarchy movement started, Mr. Nixon said: "It's a great movement" and Mr. Humphrey said, "It's a great movement." Now when they try to speak and are heckled down, they stand up and say: "we've got to have some law and order in this country." They ought to give you law and order back for nothing, because they have helped to take it away from you, along with the Supreme Court of our country that's made up of Republicans and Democrats.

Note the subtlety of the conservative populist wing of conservative ideology. The threat to law and order in the context of 1968 is that both parties have kowtowed to anarchists. Not civil rights advocates or the NAACP, but to "a few anarchists, a few activists, a few militants, a few revolutionaries, and a few Communists." In 1968, Congress passed the Civil Rights Act of 1968 (the Fair-Housing Act of 1968) that outlawed discrimination in housing. This law, passed with support by both Northern Democrats and Republicans over the votes of Southern Democrats, Wallace described in his 1968 Madison Square Garden speech as follows.

> Every year on the federal level we have passed a law that would jail you without a trial by jury about the sale of your own property. Mr. Nixon and Mr. Humphrey, both three or four weeks ago, called for the passage of a bill on the federal level that would require you to sell or lease your own property to whomsoever they thought you ought to least it to. I say that when Mr. Nixon and Mr. Humphrey succumb to the blackmail of a few anarchists in the streets who said we're going to destroy this country if you do not destroy that adage

> that a man's home is his castle, they are not fit to lead the American people during the next four years in our country.

According to Wallace, the agreement to ending housing discrimination based on race was succumbing to blackmail to a few anarchists. With this as background, Wallace returned to the tradition of states' rights and blaming the Supreme Court for handcuffing the police in dealing with protesters, which results in the lack of law and order.

> When I become your president, I am going to ask that Congress repeal this so-called open occupancy law and we're going to, within the law, turn back to the people of every state their public school system. Not one dime of your federal money is going to be used to bus anybody any place that you don't want them to be bussed in New York or any other state.
>
> Yes, the theoreticians and the pseudo-intellectuals have just about destroyed not only local government but the school systems of our country. That's all right. Let the police handle it. So let us talk about law and order. We don't have to talk about it much up here. You understand what I'm talking about in, of course, the City of New York, but let's talk about it.
>
> Yes, the pseudo-intellectuals and the theoreticians and some professors and some newspaper editors and some judges and some preachers have looked down their nose long enough at the average man on the street: the pipe-fitter, the communications worker, the fireman, the policeman, the barber, the white collar worker, and said we must write you a guideline about when you go to bed at night and when you get up in the morning. But there are more of us than there are of them because the average citizen of New York and of Alabama and of the other states of our union are tired of guidelines being written, telling them when to go to bed at night and when to get up in the morning.
>
> I'm talking about law and order. The Supreme Court of our country has hand-cuffed the police, and tonight if you walk out of this building and are knocked in the head, the person who knocks you in the head is out of jail before you get in the hospital, and on Monday morning, they'll try a policeman about it. I can say I'm going to give the total support of the presidency to the policemen and the firemen in this country, and I'm going to say, you enforce the law and you make it safe on the streets, and the president of the United States will stand with you. My election as president is going to put some backbone in the backs of some mayors and governors I know through the length and breadth of this country.
>
> You had better be thankful for the police and the firemen of this country. If it were not for them, you couldn't even ride in the streets, much less walk in the streets, of our large cities. Yes, the Kerner Commission Report, recently written by Republicans and Democrats, said that you are to blame for the breakdown of law and order, and that the police are to blame. Well, you know, of course, you aren't to blame. They said we have a sick society. Well, we don't have any sick society. We have a sick Supreme

> Court and some sick politicians in Washington, that's who's sick in our country. The Supreme Court of our country has ruled that you cannot even say a simple prayer in a public school, but you can send obscene literature through the mail, and recently they ruled that a Communist can work in a defense plant. But when I become your president, we're going to take every Communist out of every defense plant in the United States, I can assure you.

Wallace merged the fear of crime with those who supported civil rights and labeled them as communists and anarchists. At a campaign speech at the 1968 Fraternal Order of Police National Convention in Chicago, he told the police audience, "If the police of this country, could just run it for about two years, then we could walk in the parks and on the streets in safety. And you are doing a magnificent job. Thank you very much."[98]

It has been Republican orthodoxy, even in the populist wing, to support the police at all costs and to label those who question the police or assert that the police are abusive as "the left" or anti–law and order or "weak on crime." According to social conservatives, the left are

Timeline of Race, Political Rhetoric, and Politics in America

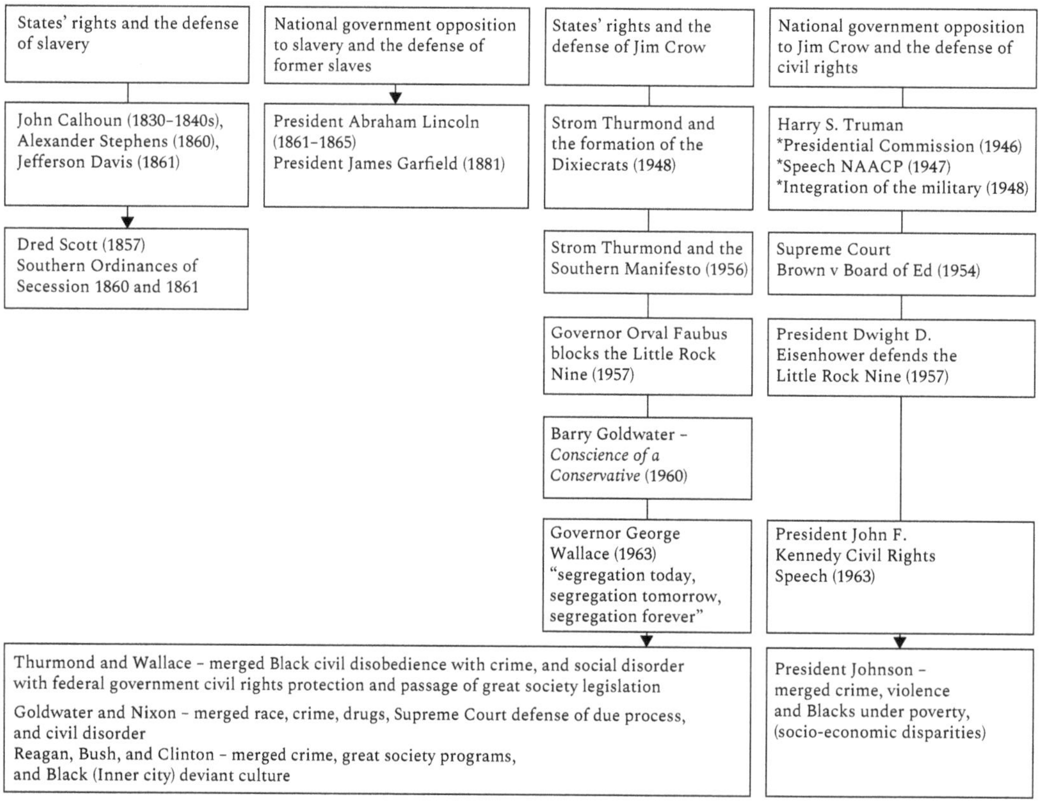

98 CNN Documentary *1968: The Year That Changed America* part 1 (Aired May 27, 2018)

those who hate America and its principles of individual responsibility, capitalism, individual liberty and limited government, and want to replace Americanism with a utopian society that can't exist in the real world. Republicans for decades have asserted that "the left" have subjected "ordinary" citizens to the mercies of criminal coddling liberal courts. By describing those who sought the end of Jim Crow and have the Bill of Rights apply to state criminal trials as anti-American, the Republicans formed a voting constituency that became the Nixon "silent majority," then the Reagan "hard hats," then the Jerry Farwell "moral majority" voters who later became the Buchanan "brigade" and, later, the "Tea Party" voters in 2008 after Barack Obama was elected. These voters, Wallace said, are "the average man on the street: the pipe-fitter, the communications worker, the fireman, the policeman, the barber, the white collar worker" who resent the political and social elites in both parties, the media, and the courts who tell these voters how to live, who to live next to and "when you [are to] go to bed at night and when you get up in the morning." Add to this the politics of resentment of the White "average man on the street" regarding quotas and affirmative action programs for Blacks and forced integration through bussing and housing laws. All this combined to create the modern political base voter of the Republican Party, and as discussed in Chapter Seven, this base provided support for crime-control criminal justice policies that have had a discriminatory impact on Blacks.

Ronald Reagan actualized and implemented crime-control criminal justice policies early in his presidency when he proposed major criminal justice legislation in 1982.[99] As Goldwater, Nixon, and Wallace first asserted, Reagan continued to assert that law and order and the fear of crime was a subject that demanded federal attention. Not civil rights, not removing the systemic results of Jim Crow and slavery, not police brutality. The federal government has no role with these issues. To do so is tyranny. But crime control in urban cities in the 1980—that deserves federal government attention.

That federal attention begins with uncompromising support of the local urban police and affirming the fear people have of urban crime and the lack of law and order in the streets. Reagan continued in the Republican tradition that one of the few social matters, unlike poverty, that social conservatives believed should be addressed on the federal level is crime.

In his radio Address to the Nation on Crime and Criminal Justice Reform in September 1982 Reagan said,

> Today I want to talk with you about a subject that's been very much on my mind, even as we've been busy with budgets, interest rates, and legislation. It's a subject I know you've been thinking about too—crime in our society.
>
> Many of you have written to me how afraid you are to walk the streets alone at night. We must make America safe again, especially for women and elderly who face so many moments of fear.

99 Ronald Reagan, "Radio Address to the Nation on Crime and Criminal Justice Reform" September 11, 1982 at http://www.presidency.ucsb.edu/ws/?pid=42952

After making clear that the national government had a role in making make sure women and the elderly could walk the streets at night in safety, Reagan proposed that part of that role is to put the courts back in their proper place by making them focus on victims and not due process of the accused.

> I want you to know that this administration, even as it has been battling our economic problems, is taking important action on the Federal level to fight crime.
> As Attorney General Smith pointed out recently, an important part of the problem is that Americans are losing faith in our courts and our entire legal system ...
> We can and must make improvements in the way our courts deal with crime ...
> These will include suggested revisions of the exclusionary rule. Now, this is the rule that can force a judge to throw out of court on the basis of a small technicality an entire case, no matter how guilty the defendant or how heinous the crime. Our bill would stop this grievous miscarriage of justice by allowing evidence to be introduced where the police officer was acting in good faith. This position has already been taken by some enlightened Federal judges, and I'm asking the Congress to make it the law of the land.
> ...
> I hope we can count on your support in our war on crime and our efforts to protect the innocent and put the professional criminals in jail where they belong. Working together we can make America safe again for all our people.

One month later, Reagan, in his remarks on the unveiling of new legislative initiatives to deal with drug trafficking, continued to focus on fear of crime, distrust of and attacks on the courts, and rejection of the Great Society conception that crime is related to poverty.[100] The orthodoxy of social conservatives and the Republican Party dating back to 1964 is the rejection of the proposition that crime has a social link to poverty. Standing on the "get tough on urban crime" foundation laid by Wallace, Goldwater, and Nixon, the mantle was taken up by Reagan. Reagan said at speech before the employees of the U.S. Justice Department in October 1982,

> The perception is growing that the crime problem stems from the emergence of a new privileged class in America, a class of repeat offenders and career criminals who think they have a right to victimize their fellow citizens with virtual impunity. They're openly contemptuous of our way of justice. They don't believe they'll be caught, and if they are caught, they're confident that once their cases enter our legal system, the charges will be dropped, postponed, plea-bargained away, or lost in a maze of legal technicalities that make a mockery of our legitimate and honorable concern with civil liberties.
> ... This rise in crime, this growth of a hardened criminal class, has partly been the result of misplaced government priorities and a misguided social philosophy.

---

100 Ronald Reagan, "Remarks Announcing Federal Initiatives Against Drug Trafficking and Organized Crime" October 14, 1982 at *The American Presidency Project* http://www.presidency.ucsb.edu/ws/?pid=43127

Reagan spoke in concurrence with Goldwater's *Conscience of a Conservative*, as well as cultivated and seeded the foundation for the rhetoric of "super predators" and the crime control policies that would be advocated by Bill Clinton in the 1990s. Reagan said to the Justice Department employees,

> At the root of this philosophy lies utopian presumptions about human nature that see man as primarily a creature of his material environment. By changing this environment through expensive social programs, this philosophy holds that government can permanently change man and usher in an era of prosperity and virtue. In much the same way, individual wrongdoing is seen as the result of poor socioeconomic conditions or an underprivileged background. This philosophy suggests in short that there is crime or wrongdoing, and that society, not the individual, is to blame.
>
> But what has also become abundantly clear in the last few years is that a new political consensus among the American people utterly rejects this point of view. The increase in citizen involvement of the crime problem and the tough new State statutes directed at repeat offenders make it clear that the American people are reasserting certain enduring truths—the belief that right and wrong do matter, that individuals are responsible for their actions, that evil is frequently a conscious choice, and that retribution must be swift and sure for those who decide to make a career of preying on the innocent.

SUMMARY

The significance of the history of the development of modern conservative thought is that it explains the conservativisation of American social and criminal justice policy during the presidencies of Reagan, Bush, and Clinton during the 1980s and 1990s. Social conservatives are interested in individual liberty, small government, social order, and the protection of private property, not the achievement of equal justice or the protection of due process.

> As members of the nation's conservative movement, we strongly support constitutionally limited government, transparency, individual liberty, personal responsibility, and free enterprise. *We believe public safety is a core responsibility of government* because the establishment of a well-functioning *criminal justice system enforces order* and respect for every person's right to property and life, *and ensures that liberty does not lead to license.*
>
> ...
>
> *Crime victims, along with the public and taxpayers, are among the key "consumers" of the criminal justice system*; the victim's conception of justice, public safety, and the offender's risk for future criminal conduct should be prioritized when determining an appropriate punishment.
>
> ...

> These principles are grounded in time-tested conservative truths—constitutionally limited government, transparency, individual liberty, personal responsibility, free enterprise, and the centrality of the family and community. All of these are critical to addressing today's criminal justice challenges. It is time to apply these principles to the task of delivering a better return on taxpayers' investments in public safety. Our security, prosperity, and freedom depend on it.[101]

As this consortium of conservative criminal justice policy-makers made clear, conservatives assert that the purpose of the criminal justice system is safety, not ensuring due process of the accused. "*A timeless conservative idea is that the interests of crime victims and public safety always take precedence over the interests of the criminal defendant and presumably due process.* To conservatives, *crime control trumps due process* and it should be the criminal justice system, not the criminal's justice system."[102] Understanding the impact of race within criminal justice requires understanding the broader discourse on how conservatives define human nature. As discussed in Chapter Seven, from Goldwater through Reagan, Republican and social conservative orthodoxy asserts crime is the result of individual choice and that choice explains crime. The politics of crime in the late 1960s shifted Republicans from the orthodoxy of Goldwater to supporting aggressive national government involvement in the lives of its citizens when it comes to punishing criminals.

There is a difference in how conservatives and liberals perceive human behavior and the role of government to constrain negative human behavior. Social conservatives explain the difference as follows:

> In essence liberals believe that man is naturally good; that there is no absolute standard of morality to be taught and adhered to by citizens; and that crime is a product of poverty and deprivation. Thus, society is held responsible for criminal behavior in supposedly having failed to provide for the material needs of the individual who commits crimes, and thereby having engendered the conditions that brought about the corruption of a naturally-good person.
>
> In contrast, social conservatives believe that man is born with a natural capacity for good or evil; that there are absolute moral values (based on traditional religious beliefs and teaching) that need to be inculcated through the family, church, and school, to form an individual of good character and moral values; and that individuals of ill-formed character and defective moral values are responsible for crime, not socio-economic conditions. Conservatives believe that the poor and deprived are not predestined to criminality by their condition; and that individuals have free will and freedom of choice regardless of

101 Right on Crime (n.d.) at http://rightoncrime.com/the-conservative-case-for-reform/statement-of-principles/ (emphasis added)

102 John Paul Wright and Matt DeLisi, *Conservative Criminology: A call to Restore Balance to the Social Sciences* 66 (2016) (emphasis added)

> their particular personal circumstances. Thus, for conservatives, the individual is responsible for his or her criminal acts, and needs to be held accountable for them by society.
>
> ...
>
> In sum, with respect to the application of criminal law there is an undeniable and fundamental difference between liberals and conservatives. Ultimately it derives from their differing views of human nature, the nature of moral values, and their resultant differing beliefs as to where responsibility lies for criminal behavior.[103]

Conservative theory rejects the proposition that social injustice, the history of Jim Crow, and the impact of historical racism on the development of American society serve as explanations for poverty or crime. Discussed in detail in Chapter Eight, conservative theory, which supports the crime control model over the due process model, supplemented with the assumption of criminality in Black males helps to explain the disproportionate incarceration of Blacks in federal and state prisons.

As the President of the Heritage Foundation made clear in his 2004 annual President's Essay on Goldwater and *The Conscience of a Conservative*,

> As the author of *The Conscience of a Conservative* and then as a presidential candidate, Barry Goldwater insisted on addressing the key issues that have dominated the national debate for the past four decades: taxes (flatten them); government spending (work toward reducing and even eliminating subsidies, as in agriculture); Social Security (it is in actuarial trouble—strengthen it by introducing a voluntary option); *law and order (the right of victims should take precedence over those of criminals)*; and morality in government (the president and all in public office must avoid scandal and corruption and set a good example for society).[104]

Take note of the second to last assertion, "law and order (the right of victims should take precedence over those of criminals)" in the American context of race and criminal justice. Conservatives reject the use of governmental power, (i.e., police power) with the exception of that power being implemented through the criminal justice system and its agents. The question to be considered is who suffers under that government power as a historical matter? Who is that government power directed upon? Why is that government force, which interferes with individual liberty, acceptable when its application is through the criminal justice system? Social conservatives since Thurmond assert government power that affects individual liberty is tyranny by definition. So why do they allow the complete unleashing of that power upon whomever the criminal justice system choses? As discussed in Chapters Seven through Nine,

103 "Crime and Punishment—Liberal vs. Conservative" (Blog, June 8, 2010) at http://passrobcp-lc.blogspot.com/2010/06/crime-and-punishment-liberal-vs.html

104 Edwin J. Feulner, "The 2004 Essay: The Conscience of a Conservative by Barry Goldwater" (2004), 13. at http://www.heritage.org/about/speeches/president-essays (emphasis added)

the answer is in who that government power is unleashed upon and who is perceived to be protected by that power.

The conservative coalition that Barry Goldwater infused into the Republican Party came into full fruition under the Reagan coalition in 1980. One aspect of that coalition is the law and order wing, as reflected by the Heritage Foundation President. In Chapter Three, we discussed how police and Whites are more supportive of police use of force when utilized on the "out group," which is historically Black. This dynamic allows for the conservative support of governmental power, criminal justice, and the police, when in theory, they oppose the growth of governmental power. Conservatives defend local police but oppose the rise of federal law enforcement. Why the dichotomy?

The answer to this dichotomy is simple; police use of force is unidirectional. On the local level, the criminal justice system with all its coercive power, is supported and enlarged under conservative presidents, because its purpose is to deal with suppression of urban crime, which means Blacks in certain neighborhoods. Criminal justice and social psychology literature is ubiquitous with research that Blacks and Whites see local police differently. Whites have positive and supportive perceptions of city police, and they believe the police only interfere with the guilty, while Blacks know better due to their historical and contemporary experience. Whites support local police, because they perceive their personal safety as directly linked to support of local police. Whites don't fear police abuse, because the power and activity of police in urban areas is pointed at Black neighborhoods. Local police, in conservative and White American perspectives, are not abusive. After all, the police only use force upon the guilty criminal, and when they apply force to Blacks, as we discussed in Chapter Three, that's what is supposed to occur, because Blacks are criminal and they should face the force of the police. Thus, local police are efficient and non-abusive of their power.

But, federal law enforcement does not enjoy this perception from social conservatives. The reason being that unlike Blacks, Whites are more likely to suffer the sting of forced obedience to the law from federal law enforcement, rather than city police. The federal government delivers the sting to White America. The purpose of government, in conservative theory, is to keep the "them" in line, not to apply force to keep the "us" in line. Governmental force on the "us" is tyranny. Government force on the "them" is effective maintenance of law and order. Federal law enforcement agencies are not supported by social conservatives and states' rights advocates on the same level that urban police receive, because in the eyes of conservatives, federal law enforcement (the civil rights division of the U.S. Justice Department, the Equal Employment Opportunity Commission, Occupational Safety and Health Administration, Internal Revenue Service, and other financial and public health and safety agencies) unconstitutionally interferes with local matters—like local police operations that Blacks assert are discriminatory. Today, city police departments and individual police officers are subject to the power of federal law enforcement through the U.S. Justice Department Civil Rights and Criminal Divisions. Conservatives have always held resentment for federal interference with local police agency matters. Such interference or oversight is *per se* tyranny; so say Calhoun,

Thurmond, Wallace, Goldwater, and Reagan—the fathers of the modern social conservatism and the Republican Party.

*****

Criminal justice literature asserts that Blacks are disproportionately represented in arrest and incarceration rates. The more complicated and disputed issue is why this is. This chapter focused on the history of American political rhetoric that supported the practice of social control of Blacks, first as slaves and, then, as second-class citizens after the Civil War. This chapter introduced the political leaders of the antebellum, postbellum, and civil rights movement periods of America that created the political environment for the "get tough on crime" policies of the 1970s through the 1980s. The insensitivity to the results of those policies on the Black community, which will be discussed in Chapter Seven.

The political history of the two parties in America and the policies that each party supported regarding race and the politics of law and order in the 1960s in America resulted in policies that continued the incarceration of Blacks. This political development forms the context for understanding the chronic incarceration of Blacks, which as discussed in Chapter Seven, pre-date the dawn of the twentieth century, much less the dawn of the Great Society. The incarceration rate of Blacks did not begin with the rise of President Johnson and the Great Society and social welfare programs as social conservatives have advocated for more than fifty years. As seen in this chapter, racism in the postbellum era along with the racism of Strom Thurmond and George Wallace and the politics that inspired the criminal justice policies of the 1960s. This history provides the background for understanding the psychological racism discussed in Chapter Three.

The incarceration rate of Blacks is a problem resulting from systematic and systemic policies and historical development. Although the current dynamics of Black incarceration are not explained by overt and conscious racism, the origin of the problem of disproportionate incarceration is racism. As discussed throughout this book, the disproportionate involvement of Blacks in the criminal justice system is the result of a combination of social, political, historical, and legal events, along with various social, societal, and individual factors. To the legal history of the rise and fall of judicial support of Jim Crow the next chapter turns.

KEY PEOPLE

1. John Calhoun
2. Alexander Stephens
3. Jefferson Davis
4. Abraham Lincoln
5. James Garfield
6. Harry Truman
7. Orval Faubus

8. Strom Thurmond
9. George Wallace
10. Dwight D. Eisenhower
11. Barry Goldwater
12. John F. Kennedy
13. Lyndon Johnson

KEY SPEECHES AND DOCUMENTS

1. Slavery a Positive Good (1837)
2. The Importance of Slavery: The Calhoun Resolutions (1838)
3. *Speech on the Importance of His Resolutions on the Slave Question* (1847)
4. *Dred Scott v. Sanford* (1857)
5. *The House Divided* Speech (1858)
6. *The Cornerstone Speech* (1861)
7. Jefferson Davis speech in the Senate (1861)
8. *Letter to Horace Greeley* (1862)
9. Lincoln Second Inaugural Address (1865)
10. *Boys in Blue* Speech (1880)
11. *Nomination of John Sherman* Speech (1880)
12. James Garfield Inaugural Speech (1881)
13. Truman Speech to the NAACP (1947)
14. Special Message to Congress on Civil Rights (1948)
15. Strom Thurmond Address and Acceptance of the Nomination for President at the States' Rights Democratic (Dixiecrats) Party (1948)
16. The Southern Manifesto (1956)
17. Orval Faubus Television and Radio Address (1957)
18. Orval Faubus speech on School Integration (1957)
19. Eisenhower Speech on Little Rock (1957)
20. *Conscience of a Conservative* (1960)
21. Declaration of the Immediate Causes Which Induce and Justify the Secession of South Carolina from the Federal Union (1860)
22. Governor Isham G. Harris Speech to the General Assembly Regarding a Referendum Calling for a Tennessee Secession Convention (1861)
23. Declaration of Secession of Georgia (1861)
24. A Declaration of the Causes which Impel the State of Texas to Secede from the Federal Union (1861)
25. A Declaration of the Immediate Causes which Induce and Justify the Secession of the State of Mississippi from the Federal Union (Not Dated)
26. The Constitution of the Confederate States Articles I and IV (March 11, 1861)

27. President Jefferson Davis Message to Congress Regarding the Ratification of the Constitution of the Confederate States (1861)
28. Governor of Alabama Inaugural Address (1963)
29. Kennedy Civil Rights Speech (1963)
30. Johnson "Let us continue" Speech (1963)
31. *Letter from a Birmingham Jail* (1963)
32. Barry Goldwater Speech on Civil Rights Act (1964)

DISCUSSION QUESTIONS

1. This chapter asserts that understanding American criminal justice policy requires an understanding of American political history in general and that history in regards to race. Do you agree? What is the purpose of history, and why does it aid the criminal justice student?
2. What is the significance of slavery to the modern Republican and Democratic parties? What is the significance of Jim Crow to states' rights and the civil rights movement? How does the rhetoric regarding these relate to the study of criminal justice?
3. What is the significance of John Calhoun and his defense of slavery to the purpose of the national government and the primacy of Constitutional law? What is the role of the national government under Calhoun's defense of states' rights?
4. What is the significance of Alexander Stephens' "Corner-Stone" speech and the speech by Jefferson Davis, both in 1861? How do both relate to the theory or original intent and the Supreme Court opinion in *Dred Scott*?
5. What was Abraham Lincoln's and James Garfield's answer to the issue of race, and what American principles were defended in the Civil War? Why does this matter in relation to Blacks and how they are perceived? How does this matter in regard to the protection of the law for Blacks? Is their rhetoric relevant to the nature of American politics regarding race today?
6. What is the significance of the rhetoric of Strom Thurmond and Harry S. Truman on the rise of the modern Republican and Democratic parties and their social policies on race and the rule of law? How did the rhetoric of both men change the politics of the Democratic and Republican parties?
7. Why did Strom Thurmond, George Wallace, and Barry Goldwater oppose the civil rights laws to prevent lynching and discrimination? What was the relationship between preventing the national government from enforcing those laws and race? Why did they support law and order policies in the inner city? Explain how they made the distinction?
8. What is the significance of the rhetoric of Dwight D. Eisenhower and Oval Faubus on the rise of the modern Republican and Democratic parties and their social policies on race and the rule of law? How did the rhetoric of both men change the politics of the

Democratic and Republican parties? How did their actions affect the defining of the rule of law and constitutional law for both parties? Why are their actions significant to the enforcement of federal law?

9. What is the significance of the rhetoric of George Wallace and John F. Kennedy on the rise of the modern Republican and Democratic parties and their social policies on race and the rule of law? How did the rhetoric of both men change the politics of the Democratic and Republican parties?
10. What events caused Southern Democrats to abandon the Democratic Party for the Republican Party? How did the Supreme Court get involved in this change, and what did the Court do that caused George Wallace, Strom Thurmond, and Barry Goldwater to accuse it of being lawless and establishing the tyranny of the federal government? What significance does this event have to modern discussions on the role of government? How does the debate and rhetoric of the role of government impact criminal justice policy?
11. It has been argued that to understand the Republican Party and conservative rhetoric and politics, all roads lead from Barry Goldwater and his book the *Conscience of a Conservative*. What were the main arguments in the book? How to they pertain to modern ideas of justice, the rule of law, the role of the federal government, and constitutional law? Do you agree or disagree with his arguments? Why, or why not?
12. What is the southern strategy and how does it fit within American historical, political, rhetorical, and policymaking regarding Blacks in America?

CHAPTER FIVE

The Foundations of Racism in America

A BRIEF REVIEW OF THE LEGAL HISTORY OF RACE

******

> But religion cannot be the only guardian of our morality. Of course not—there is self-responsibility. And failing that, does the law not have a duty? Does the bench and parliament not have a duty to uphold and create the laws, to set the precedents that progress our morality, not retard it! If not to protect us from others, then to protect us from ourselves! Laws that allow us to diminish the humanity of anybody, are not laws—they are frameworks for crime. A constitution can never be finite—surely as humanity evolves so too must its laws. And frankly I really do not care if you as an individual are without character or conscience—But a land whose laws contain neither—whose laws sanction not control the barbarous among its citizens—that is a country whose hope is lost.[1]

STUDENT LEARNING OBJECTIVES

1. Students will be able to explain how White Christians, both in Europe and in America, who were involved in the African slave trade and who owned slaves, justified their actions with the Bible, as well as explain how slavery abolitionists used the Bible to assert that slavery was evil. Students will be exposed to both arguments and will be able to explain why the former was due to manipulation and false interpretation of the Bible and the principles of Christianity.
2. Students will be able to explain why it matters that Christianity was used to place Blacks in an inferior position to Whites and how that belief survived slavery to form the foundation for Jim Crow laws and the adoption of second-class status for Blacks under the law enforced by the Supreme Court.
3. Students will be able to put the Civil War and the rise of Jim Crow in context with the idea of Black inferiority and the need for social control of Blacks.

1 *Belle,* directed by Amma Asante (2013; released 2014), Film.

4. Students will be able to explain Supreme Court jurisprudence supporting both the rise and fall of Jim Crow laws.

BACKGROUND: THE CONGRUENCE OF EUROPEAN CHRISTIANITY, THE VALUE OF BLACK BODIES, AND SLAVERY

In the movie *Belle,* regarding the transatlantic slave trade and the law allowing insurance companies to provide financial insurance against losses of the cargo of slave ships, it was observed that "It is the utter injustice ... the industrial slaughter of so many. No. It is more than that. It's the shame of a law that would uphold a financial transaction upon that atrocity."[2] The movie centered on the life of Dido Elizabeth Lindsey, the grandniece of Lord Chief Justice William Mansfield. The time period for the movie was 1783 when Lord Mansfield decided *The Zong Massacre Case.*[3] The case involved an incident in which slave traders threw live slaves overboard and then claimed they had to save the lives of the crew due to lack of water for both the slaves and the crew. During the trial, Mansfield accepted this argument of necessity and informed the jury that slaves, like other property aboard a ship, could be thrown overboard and be under insurance protection. Mansfield held that evidence discovered after the trial showed that the ship was not in distress, as claimed, and that it had rained before the slaves were thrown overboard. Mansfield ordered the jury verdict for the ship owners to be overturned for a new trial. The reporter of the case wrote that this case probably led to the law that prevented insurance companies from being required to pay for the loss of slaves based on their death due to natural causes, ill-treatment by the crew, or being thrown overboard for any reason.[4]

Mansfield has been criticized for equating the lives of slaves with the lives of horses when he wrote that, "The matter left to the jury, was whether it was from necessity: for they had no doubt (though it shocks one very much) that the Case of Slaves was the same as if Horses had been thrown overboard," as well as equating the financial compensation value of slaves with horses; "I was informed if they die a Natural Death they did not pay, but in an Engaged if they are attacked and the Slaves are kill'd they will be paid for them as much as for Damages done for goods and it is frequently done, just as if horses were kill'd they are paid for in the gross, just as well as for Horses killed but you don't pay for Horses that die a Natural Death."[5]

---

2 *Belle,* directed by Amma Asante (2013; Released 2014), Film.

3 Gregson v. Gilbert (1783) (3 Doug. KB 232).

4 James Walvin, *The Zong: A Massacre, The Law and the End of Slavery* (2011) and Jeremy Krikler, Jeremy, "A Chain of Murder in the Slave Trade: A Wider Context of the *Zong* Massacre" *International Review of Social History* 57, no. 3 (2012): 393.

5 James Walvin, *The Zong: A Massacre, The Law and the End of Slavery* at 153.

But, what Mansfield said regarding the value of Black lives, that they were equal, at best, to the lives of horses, was true under the law!

This was not the first slave case in which Mansfield, one of the more significant legal and judicial minds in Western legal jurisprudence history, would opine upon. Mansfield held that the practice of slavery in England was illegal in *The Somerset Case* (1772), in which he famously held

> [t]he state of slavery is of such a nature that it is incapable of being introduced on any reasons, moral or political; but only by positive law, which preserves its force long after the reasons, occasions, and time itself from whence it was created, is erased from memory: it's so odious, that nothing can be suffered to support it, but positive law. Whatever inconveniences, therefore, may follow from the decision, I cannot say this case is allowed or approved by the law of England; and therefore the black must be discharged.[6]

Somerset ended the practice of slavery in England, and it was one of the key reasons the colonies moved to gain independence from England—the reason being Lord Mansfield's decision was binding on the entire British Kingdom, which included the colonies. The case was seen by many in the colonies as a threat to the legality and the support of the institution of slavery within the British Kingdom and the colonies.[7]

Here begins the objective of this chapter. The idea that Blacks were little more than property and were treated as such allowed for their dehumanization and need to be controlled. The principle of Black inferiority under the law survived slavery and formed the foundation for the system of discrimination in America based on race that formed the passage of Jim Crow laws in America. With the subsequent fall of Jim Crow after the civil rights movement, the idea of Black inferiority and need for social control survived and found implementation through the criminal justice system. There is a continuity of social control based on inferiority of Blacks that runs from slavery through the crime control policies of today. One of the factors underlying this continuity is one of the original justifications for slavery—biblical assent, if not Bible command, that Blacks were intended by God to be servants of Whites.

Slavery and its Justification Under Christianity

The European slave trade of Africa and the Caribbean is not the origin of slavery. Islamic conquests of North Africa, shortly after the death of Muhammad in 632 AD, between the middle seventh and early eighth centuries (647–709 AD) and inter-tribal warfare on the continent had established slavery in Africa centuries before the first Europeans (the Portuguese in 1526 AD) landed on the African shores and bought slaves on the beach. Historically, slavery served

---

6 Somerset v. Stewart, 98 *ER* 499, 510, 20 *Howell's State Trials* Cols1–6, 79–82, 82 (1772).

7 For discussion of the history of slavery in the colonies from a legal and political perspective and the impact of *The Somerset Case* see, Alfred W. Bumrosen and Ruth G. Bumrosen, *Slave Nation: How Slavery United the Colonies & Sparked the American Revolution* (2005).

as a tool of the victor over the defeated in times of war. Ancient Hebrew, Greek, Roman, and Islamic slavery was based on conquest, not race or ethnicity; slavery was the price of defeat in war. A person captured or defeated in war was not considered subhuman or equal to animals when enslaved. European enlightenment and American Christianity changed the nature of slavery by justifying it through the belief that Africans were supposed to be slaves, because they were inferior to Whites by civilization achievement (European justification) or because they were the sons of Ham, and thus, Africans were slaves by the design and will of God (American Christian justification).

The belief of American Christian slave owners that Africans were slaves by divine decree was supported by two propositions. First, the puritan settlers of the North America were the new chosen people of God, and they were entitled to treat the indigenous peoples of North America and Africans brought to North America as the Hebrews of the Old Testament treated the indigenous peoples found on the other side of the Jordan. They read in the Bible that God said to Moses, "Completely destroy them—the Hittites, Amorites, Canaanites, Perizzites, Hivites and Jebusites" and "the Israelites captured the Midianite women and children and took all the Midianite herds, flocks and goods as plunder. They burned all the towns where the Midianites had settled, as well as all their camps. They took all the plunder and spoils, including the people and animals."[8] American Christian slave owners reasoned, as Moses acted in the land of the Jordan, so can we in Africa. Second, the Old Testament allowed the children of Israel to hold and take slaves from the conquered nations and God specifically blessed the patriarch of the Old Testament, Abraham, who owned slaves. American slave Christian theology asserted that in the New Testament God commanded that slaves were to obey their masters not as eye-pleasers but as unto God. Although Paul asked Philemon for the freedom of the slave Onesimus and admonished Philemon that because Onesimus was a brother in Christ and he should be treated as such, the point is Paul sent the slave back to his master. They pointed to the fact that Paul offered to

---

8 Deuteronomy 20:17 and Numbers 31:9–11) (NIV). See also Numbers 31:17–18, 32–35 (NIV) respectively regarding the war with the Midianites ("Now kill all the boys. And kill every woman who has slept with a man, but save for yourselves every girl who has never slept with a man." "The plunder remaining from the spoils that the soldiers took was 675,000 sheep, (33) 72,000 cattle, (34) 61,000 donkeys (35) and 32,000 women who had never slept with a man.")

In defense of the law allowing the taking of young women authorized in the Bible, the Midianites and Moabites and others that God commanded to be destroyed practiced various types of abominations and idol worship and human sacrifices. God wanted those practices whipped off the face of the earth. As for the young women, because they were too young to have participated in the abominations they could not be punished with death. Furthermore, upon capture by the soldiers of Israel, the young girls were not to be mistreated, they were not to be raped and sold into slavery, but rather married to the soldiers as wives and if not married they were to be freed unharmed as required by the command of God in Deuteronomy 21:10–14 (NIV). Historically, at the time, such a command was without equal.

pay for his freedom and specifically did not command that his freedom be given.[9] American White Christians reasoned that the Bible itself, both in the Old and New Testaments, not only did not prohibit slavery, but it acknowledged and approved of the practice of owning slaves and required slaves to comply with their status. They reasoned that, since the Bible condoned slavery and since it did not condemn the practice, it was not immoral or prohibited for Christians to kidnap, buy, and hold African slaves.

White Christendom also used the Bible to justify seeing Africans and other people of color as inferior and subject to the will of Whites by divine design. In the book of Genesis Noah, his wife, his three sons (Ham, Shem, and Japheth), and their wives were rescued from the flood. After the family found solid land Noah got drunk and passed out naked. The scriptures report that Ham saw Noah naked and looked upon him, but when Shem and Japheth knew of their father's position, they covered him without looking at his nakedness. When Noah woke up and knew what Ham had done, he cursed Ham's son Canaan with the curse that he shall serve the sons of Shem and Japheth. The sons of Shem led to Abraham, the patriarch of the Jewish nation. The sons of Japheth include Europeans and Asians. The sons of Canaan are the colored peoples of the world, including those of Africa and the Middle East.[10] This story, along with the fact that God gave the land of Canaan to the Jews both before and after they were delivered from Egypt, buttressed the belief that God had made his choice between the children of Noah; Shem first, Japheth second, and Ham to serve both. Blacks were, by God's will, cursed to the status of slaves to the descendants of Japheth. White Europeans, the sons of Japheth, were within their rights by God to take African slaves and sell them to White Christians in the colonies in North America at will and at their mercy with no concern of the judgment of God.[11]

But as Lincoln and Jefferson and the abolitionists would observe, that judgement would come. The consequences in using the name of God to justify the evils of kidnapping (man-stealing) and racial slavery were inflicted upon America as Lincoln said in his address to Congress in March 1865. Decades before, one of the fathers of American social conservative thought, Thomas Jefferson, came to the same conclusion when he wrote that he feared for America when he considered God and that His justice will not be stayed forever.

---

9 See Colossians 3:22, Ephesians 6:5–9, 1 Peter 2:18–20, and Philemon 8–21(NKJV)

10 See, Genesis 9:18–27; 10:2,5:11:26.

11 For additional scholarship on Christian justification of slavery see, Larry R. Morrison, "The Religious Defense of American Slavery Before 1830," *Journal of Religious Thought* 37 (1980): 16, Larry E. Tise, *Proslavery: A History of the Defense of Slavery in America, 1701–1840* (University of Georgia Press, 1990), Stephen R. Haynes, *Noah's Curse: The Biblical Justification of American Slavery* (2002), David M. Goldenberg, *The Curse of Ham: Race and Slavery in Early Judaism, Christianity, and Islam* (2009), John Coffey, "Evangelicals, Slavery & the Slave Trade: From Whitefield to Wilberforce," *Anvil-Bristol* 24, no. 2 (2007): 97, David Meager, "Why Did Christians Justify African Slavery," *Cross Way* 104 (Spring 2007) and Ibram X. Kendi, *Stamped from the Beginning: The Definitive History of Racist Ideas in America* (2016).

Lincoln's belief that the Civil War had divine consequences began to take form after the first two years of the war and the death of his eleven-year-old son William on February 20, 1862. At his son's funeral, the eulogy by Rev. Phineas Gurley had a great impact on Lincoln as he tried to make sense of both the death of his son and the war that already had cost thousands of lives and had no end in sight. The meaning Lincoln looked for was impressed upon him after reflection on the last paragraphs of Rev. Gurley's eulogy.

> What we need in the hour of trial, and what we should seek by earnest prayer, is confidence in Him who sees the end from the beginning and doeth all things well.
> Only let us bow in His presence with an humble and teachable spirit; only let us be still and know that He is God; only let us acknowledge His hand, and hear His voice, and inquire after His will, and seek His holy spirit as our counsellor and guide, and all, in the end, will be well. In His light shall we see light; by His grace our sorrows will be sanctified—they will be made a blessing to our souls—and by and by we shall have occasion to say, with blended gratitude and rejoicing, "It is good for us that we have been afflicted."

Lincoln asked for a copy of the eulogy, and after pondering the meaning of Rev. Gurley's observation that, "What we need in the hour of trial, and what we should seek by earnest prayer, is confidence in Him who sees the end from the beginning and doeth all things well," he penned, in September 1862, his thoughts on the meaning of the war and the nature of the presence of God in the affairs of men. Lincoln wrote,

> The will of God prevails. In great contests each party claims to act in accordance with the will of God. Both may be, and one must be, wrong. God cannot be for and against the same thing at the same time. In the present Civil War it is quite possible that God's purpose is something different from the purpose of either party—and yet the human instrumentalities, working just as they do, are of the best adaptation to effect His purpose. I am almost ready to say that this is probably true—that God wills this contest, and wills that it shall not end yet. By his mere great power, on the minds of the now contestants, He could have either saved or destroyed the Union without a human contest. Yet the contest began. And, having begun He could give the final victory to either side any day. Yet the contest proceeds.

Lincoln's thoughts and writing were preserved by John Hay, a White House secretary, who entitled the writing "Meditation on the Divine Will," and although it was unpublished and not intended to be read by anyone, parts of it are found in Lincoln's second inaugural address. The Christian foundation of America was on Lincoln's mind, and he saw the war as God's statement and judgment on slavery. He believed God's position on slavery was confirmed when the Union Army won the battle of Antietam on September 17, 1862, which in time, turned out to be a turning point of the war, which would lead to the final defeat of the Confederate South and slavery.

According to the notes taken by Secretary of the Navy Gideon Welles, Lincoln announced to his cabinet, after the victory at Antietam, that "God had decided this question in favor of the slaves." That as far as the war was concerned, Lincoln was determined to fight it and win it, for God had made His decision. Welles wrote, "He was satisfied that it was right, was confirmed and strengthened in his action by the vow and the results."[12] On April 16, 1862—nine months before the ***Emancipation Proclamation*** (January 1, 1863)—Lincoln signed the ***District of Columbia Emancipation Act*** which not only freed the slaves in Washington D.C. but Congress authorized the expenditure of one million dollars of reparations to provide compensation to the slave masters for the loss of the value of their emancipated slaves.

On January 1, 1863, Lincoln issued the ***Emancipation Proclamation***. Although the *Emancipation Proclamation* was a war measure to confiscate the "contraband" of the South and did not technically free the slaves, it clarified the explanation for the war. There was now no doubt what each side was fighting for. As the ordinances of secession, discussed in Chapter Four, made clear, the south was never unsure what the war was about; but now the north was sure.

The emancipation proclamation was the enforcement and culmination of two prior acts of Congress. It followed the passage of the ***Militia Act of 1862*** and the ***Second Contraband Act of 1862***, both passed on July 17, 1862. Section 12 of the *Militia Act* allowed Blacks to serve in the Union Army as soldiers. Section 9 of the *Second Contraband Act* stated that

> And be it further enacted, That all slaves of persons who shall hereafter be engaged in rebellion against the government of the United States … escaping from such persons and taking refuge within the lines of the army; and all slaves captured from such persons. … and all slaves of such person found on [or] being within any place occupied by rebel forces and afterwards occupied by the forces of the United States, shall be deemed captives of war, and shall be forever free of their servitude, and not again held as slaves.

Section 11 further authorized the president to "employ as many persons of African descent as he may deem necessary and proper for the suppression of this rebellion, and for this purpose he may organize and use them in such manner as he may judge best for the public welfare." Both pieces of legislation provided the legal basis for the emancipation proclamation of 1863. Two years later, the Thirteenth Amendment settled the issue, Blacks were not slaves but were citizens of the Union.

Although the *Second Contraband Act* established that Blacks were free in any slave state *in rebellion* to the Union in which the Union army took control, the bottom line was that this approach was about winning the war not about freeing the slaves *in toto*. But the winning of the war was the required prerequisite to freeing the slaves *in toto*. It's on that basis that the *Militia Act*, the *Second Contraband Act* and the *Emancipation Proclamation* deserve their place of respect in the history of Black freedom in the United States. As abolitionists knew,

---

12 See Rev. Phineas Gurley, "The Death of Willie Lincoln" at http://www.abrahamlincolnonline.org/lincoln/education/williedeath.htm, Abraham Lincoln, "Meditation on the Divine Will" at http://www.abrahamlincolnonline.org/lincoln/speeches/meditat.htm, PBS, *People and ideas: Abraham Lincoln* at http://www.pbs.org/wgbh/pages/frontline/godinamerica/people/abraham-lincoln.html and (cont.) Ronald C. White Jr., *God in America part three Transcript* at http://www.pbs.org/godinamerica/transcripts/hour-three.html.

The Emancipation Proclamation (1863)
By the President of the United States of America:

A Proclamation.

Whereas, on the twenty-second day of September, in the year of our Lord one thousand eight hundred and sixty-two, a proclamation was issued by the President of the United States, containing, among other things, the following, to wit:

"That on the first day of January, in the year of our Lord one thousand eight hundred and sixty-three, *all persons held as slaves within any State or designated part of a State, the people whereof shall then be in rebellion against the United States, shall be then, thenceforward, and forever free; and the Executive Government of the United States, including the military' and naval authority thereof, will recognize and maintain the freedom of such persons, and will do no act or acts to repress such persons, or any of them, in any efforts they may make for their actual freedom.*

"That the Executive will, on the first day of January aforesaid, by proclamation, designate the States and parts of States, if any, in which the people thereof, respectively, shall then be in rebellion against the United States; and the fact that any State, or the people thereof, shall on that day be, in good faith, represented in the Congress of the United States by members chosen thereto at elections wherein a majority of the qualified voters of such State shall have participated, shall, in the absence of strong countervailing testimony, be deemed conclusive evidence that such State, and the people thereof, are not then in rebellion against the United States."

Now, therefore I, Abraham Lincoln. President of the United States, by virtue of the power in me vested as Commander-in-Chief, of the Army and Navy of the United States in time of actual armed rebellion against the authority and government of the United States, and as a fit and necessary war measure for suppressing said rebellion, do, on this first day of January, in the year of our Lord one thousand eight hundred and sixty-three, and in accordance with my purpose so to do publicly proclaimed for the full period of one hundred days, from the day first above mentioned, order and designate as the States and parts of States wherein the people thereof respectively, are this day in rebellion against the United States, the following, to wit:

[List of states and areas in rebellion]

And by virtue of the power, and for the purpose aforesaid, I do order and declare that all persons held as slaves within said designated States, and parts of States, are, and henceforward shall be free; and that the Executive government of the United States, including the military and naval authorities thereof, will recognize and maintain the freedom of said persons.

And I hereby enjoin upon the people so declared to be free to abstain from all violence, unless in necessary self-defence; and I recommend to them that, in all cases when allowed, they labor faithfully for reasonable wages.

And I further declare and make known, that such persons of suitable condition, will be received into the armed service of the United States to garrison forts, positions, stations, and other places, and to man vessels of all sorts in said service.

And upon this act, sincerely believed to be an act of justice, warranted by the Constitution, upon military necessity, I invoke the considerate judgment of mankind, and the gracious favor of Almighty God.

In witness whereof, I have hereunto set my hand and caused the seal of the United States to be affixed.

Done at the City of Washington, this first day of January, in the year of our Lord one thousand eight hundred and sixty three, and of the Independence of the United States of America the eighty-seventh.

By the President: ABRAHAM LINCOLN

as Frederick Douglass would advocate, and as Lincoln would be humbled to admit; only war would remove slavery from the America. The war was about slavery and settling whether it or the union would prevail. As discussed throughout this book, removing racism from America is a whole other issue.

The Complicated Integration of Slavery, Black Inferiority, and Freedom Within American Christian Heritage

The end of the Civil War settled whether God had put his imprimatur on slavery, but the idea that Blacks are inferior to Whites survived the Civil War, and the idea of Black inferiority has been a plague in American society to this day. The carnage of the Civil War, the injustice of the

Black Codes and Jim Crow, the racial riots of Whites attacking Blacks in the 1920s through 1930s followed by urban riots in the 1960s and later in the twenty-first century all resulted from the misuse of the name and the word of God to justify slavery and racial discrimination. After the Civil War, Southern states passed miscegenation laws, which were defended as laws in line with scripture for more than a century. In 1965, Judge Leon M. Bazile affirmed the conviction of Mildred and Richard Loving for breaking Virginia's miscegenation law in 1958 and justified his decision by evoking the authority of God. He wrote in his opinion that the "Almighty God created the races white, black, yellow, malay and red, and he placed them on separate continents. And but for the interference with his arrangement there would be no cause for such marriages. The fact that he separated the races shows that he did not intend for the races to mix."[13] Two years later, the Supreme Court ruled in *Loving v. Virginia* that laws prohibiting interracial marriages were unconstitutional.

The reason slave owner assertions that Christianity supported slavery of Africans is significant is because America is built on a Christian heritage and the misuse of the Bible to justify slavery and racism provides both a historical and contemporary explanation for American political rhetoric and policy development. America's legal, political, and social structures *are* founded on Western classical Judeo-Christian principles.[14] A change occurred in America in the 1960s. At the beginning of the 1960s, the generation of Dr. King entered the decade asserting that the Bible and the Constitution agreed that Jim Crow was evil. By the time of his death, the baby boom generation entered the beginning of the abandonment of the Bible as the exclusive source of the definition of right and wrong. This post-1960s America, regarding the significance of the Bible, has been referred to as the making of post-Christian America.

In the pre-1960s America, the country *was* perceived, and it perceived itself, as a Christian nation, meaning that it was acknowledged within society that there was a God, and right and wrong was defined significantly by His word—the Bible. It was upon the Bible and its principles that political and social debate of whether something was just would be determined. The debate over slavery and later segregation was whether the Bible allowed it, not whether it mattered what the Bible said on the subject. Because the Bible said, "you shall not use the name of God in vain" as far back as President Lincoln and even before him, it was recognized by many that it was evil and not acceptable to God to use His name to justify slavery or racial discrimination and injustice. As previously discussed, others thought the Bible made clear

---

13 Opinion of Judge Leon M. Bazile Caroline County Circuit Court, Virginia (January 22, 1965) at https://www.encyclopediavirginia.org/Opinion_of_Judge_Leon_M_Bazile_January_22_1965

14 For discussion of Western legal traditions based on Christian principles, see Augusto Zimmermann, "God, Locke and Montesquieu: Some Thoughts Concerning the Religious Foundations of Modern Constitutionalism," *The Western Australian Jurist* 1 (2010): 1–13, Arthur H. Garrison, "The Traditions and History of the Meaning of the Rule of Law," *Georgetown Journal of Law & Public Policy* 12, no. 2 (2014): 565, and Arthur H. Garrison, "The Rule of Law and the Rise of Control of Executive Power," *Texas Review of Law & Politics* 18, no. 2 (2014): 304.

that the sons of Ham were to serve the sons of Japheth. The point being that both sides of the war, as Lincoln observed in his *Second Inaugural Address*, called upon the same God to prove the justice of their positions. As Lincoln concluded, God had made his choice.

In 1947, Jackie Robinson broke the color barrier in major league baseball by signing with the Brooklyn Dodgers. In the 2013 movie *42*, based on the lives of Jackie Robinson and Branch Rickey, the manager of the Brooklyn Dodgers, a fictional conversation occurred between Rickey and another team manager who stated that he would not field his team if Robinson played in the game. To which Rickey asked, "You think God likes baseball, Herb?" The owner asked "What—what the hell is that supposed to mean?" To which Rickey responded, "It means someday you're gonna meet God! And when He inquires as to why you didn't take the field against Robinson in Philadelphia, and you answer that it's because he was a Negro! It may not be a sufficient reply!"[15] In the post-Christian America, this conversation could not occur. In post-Christian America, right and wrong is determined by subjective belief. In America today, to invoke the name of God and the Bible as absolute and determinative in social debate on policy, is considered offensive. In contemporary societal debates over whether something is right and wrong, it is assumed that the Bible has nothing to offer and it is not the final standard to which actions must be defined and must be in compliance with.

Although it is true that in America, from the colonial period through the antebellum period, the scriptures of the Bible were manipulated to justify slavery and, a hundred years after that, to justify Jim Crow, the point is the Bible was used in the debate in the first place. While it is not within the scope of this book to fully refute the intentional misrepresentations and violations of scriptural interpretation by White Christendom to achieve their desired outcome—the justification of the slave trade and holding slaves—the misrepresentations can be answered as follows.

First, the history of slavery in the world is one in which "man took dominion over man. The conquered were made serve the conqueror. The weak were made to serve the strong. And freedom was gone from the world. *God made men, men made slaves*!"[16]

Second, the Old Testament makes kidnapping a death penalty offense while allowing the enslavement of captured enemies in war:[17] "He that stealeth a man and selleth him, or if he be found in his hand, he shall surely be put to death."[18] Thus, as Jefferson wrote in the slave clause of the Declaration of Independence—which was removed by Southern threats of revolt and refusal to sign the document—the imposition of slavery on the colonies was a crime committed by the King because it involved the kidnapping of Africans, not the taking of men in war.

---

15 *42*, directed by Brian Helgeland (Warner Bros., 2013), Film. See "Do You Think God Likes Baseball?" at https://www.youtube.com/watch?v=2jtJ1yo8uQ4

16 *The Ten Commandments* directed by Cecil B. DeMille (1956), Film.

17 Arthur H. Garrison, "Defining the Meaning and Purpose of Justice, Law, and Criminal Justice: A Hermeneutical Judeo-Christian Biblical Perspective" *Journal of Catholic Legal* Studies 55, no. 1 (2016): 1.

18 Exodus 21:16 (KJV).

Third, Noah, not God, cursed the son of Ham! Nor is it recorded in scripture that God affirmed Noah's curse. *Fourth*, as a hermeneutical matter,[19] the curse did not establish a spiritual or biblical tradition upon succeeding generations. The curse is not mentioned post-Noah, and Noah, unlike Abraham and Moses, is not a prophet or a patriarch of the scriptures.

Fifth, the curse was issued by a drunk who cursed his grandson for the sin of his son. *Sixth*, even if one assumes that the curse of Noah has biblical/spiritual intergenerational status or approval from God, all curses under the Old Testament were atoned[20] for under the New Testament.[21]

Seventh, the New Testament, when slavery was mentioned, required masters to be just to their slaves, for it reminded them that they were slaves to Christ. Although the scriptures make clear, as White Christians proclaimed, that slaves were to obey their masters; the context of the scripture is that they were to obey and serve their masters as Jesus served God and they should do all things for God as He watches all. The obedience was not obedience based on slavery itself. In context, the New Testament says, regarding slaves,

> Bondservants, be obedient to those who are your masters according to the flesh, with fear and trembling, in sincerity of heart, as to Christ; not with eye service, as men-pleasers, but as bondservants of Christ, doing the will of God from the heart, with goodwill doing service, as to the Lord, and not to men, knowing that whatever good anyone does, he will receive the same from the Lord, whether *he is* a slave or free.
>
> And you, masters, do the same things to them, giving up threatening, knowing that your own Master also is in heaven, and there is no partiality with Him.[22]

The corruption of this scripture regarding slave obedience was compounded by the fact that slaves were to be treated as brothers of the faith without threatening or harshness, something White Christian slave owners were known not to do. God's word was clearly violated by the sale of family members and the rape of Black women by slave owners and overseers for the purposes of personal pleasure and increasing the population of slaves.

Eighth, there is a difference between saying White Christians corrupted scripture and saying the scripture is corrupt. The former is true, not the latter. Consider that Jesus was placed on the cross not because he disputed "thus saith the Lord," for He was in agreement with the Jewish priests that "thus saith the Lord" is definitive. He was placed on the cross,

---

19 For an example of the application of the science of hermeneutics to the Bible, see Arthur H. Garrison, "A Hermeneutical Proof of the Bible" *Journal of Grace Theology* 5, no 1 (2018); 3

20 See 1 John 2:2, Ephesians 1:7 (NKJV).

21 See 1 John 2:2, Ephesians 1:7 (NKJV).

22 Ephesians 6:5–9 (NKJV). See also Colossians 3:22 and 1 Peter 2:18 (NKJV) in which the instruction of slaves obey your masters is written within the context of how Christian homes can maintain order, peace and love between members. It was not written within a context of domination.

because He opposed the corrupt interpretation and application of "thus saith the Lord" by deceitful priests who used the scriptures for their own benefit and social positions.

Lastly, the New Testament makes clear that the heart of God on the matter of Christians owning slaves was that He desired them to be freed and accepted as brothers of the faith.[23] Christianity is about redemption from sin through Jesus. Christianity redeems, not condemns; it makes one free; it does not enslave one to another, "It was for this freedom that Christ set us free [completely liberating us]; therefore keep standing firm and do not be subject again to a yoke of slavery [which you once removed]."[24] Christianity brought this truth to the American slave: the knowledge that he was a child of God and, as such, had to be treated that way. This truth emboldened the abolitionist movement in the North. In the face of this truth, as discussed in Chapter Three, Jefferson said, "I tremble for my country when I reflect that God is just: that his justice cannot sleep forever," and in the face of this truth Lincoln concluded in his *Second Inaugural Address* regarding the carnage of the American Civil War that, "the judgments of the Lord are true and righteous altogether."

In his book, *Narrative of An American Slave*, Frederick Douglass wrote of the cruelty of slavery and how that cruelty was justified through the corruption of Christianity. On reflection of these two truths, Frederick Douglass wrote about a slave girl, Henny, who, when a child, burned her hands to the point of having no use of them.

> I have said my master found religious sanction for his cruelty. As an example, I will state one of many facts going to prove the charge. I have seen him tie up a lame young woman, and whip her with a heavy cowskin upon her naked shoulders, causing the warm red blood to drip; and, in justification of the bloody deed, he would quote this passage of Scripture—"He that knoweth his master's will, and doeth it not, shall be beaten with many stripes."
>
> . . .
>
> The secret of master's cruelty toward "Henny" is found in the fact of her being almost helpless. When quite a child, she fell into the fire, and burned herself horribly. Her hands were so burnt that she never got the use of them. She could do very little but bear heavy burdens. She was to master a bill of expense; and as he was a mean man, she was a constant offence to him. He seemed desirous of getting the poor girl out of existence. He gave her away once to his sister; but, being a poor gift, she was not disposed to keep her. Finally, my benevolent master, to use his own words, "set her adrift to take care of herself." Here was a recently-converted man, holding on upon the mother, and at the same time turning out her helpless child, to starve and die! Master Thomas was one of the many pious slaveholders who hold slaves for the very charitable purpose of taking care of them.[25]

---

23 See generally, The Book of Philemon (NKJV).

24 Galatians 5:1 (AMP).

25 Frederick Douglass, *Narrative of the Life of Frederick Douglass: An American Slave* (1845) at 48–49, (emphasis in original) at https://www.ibiblio.org/ebooks/Douglass/Narrative/Douglass_Narrative.pdf

In his slave narrative, Douglass goes out of his way to make a distinction between slavery and Christianity and defends the latter, claiming to be a Christian himself, while providing an impassioned attack on the former and its use of the Bible as justification. He makes clear the hypocrisy and evil was in the Christian slave owner, not in the Bible itself.

> I FIND, since reading over the foregoing Narrative, that I have, in several instances, spoken in such a tone and manner, respecting religion, as may possibly lead those unacquainted with my religious views to suppose me an opponent of all religion. To remove the liability of such misapprehension, I deem it proper to append the following brief explanation. What I have said respecting and against religion, I mean strictly to apply to the *slaveholding religion* of this land, and with no possible reference to Christianity proper; for, between the Christianity of this land, and the Christianity of Christ, I recognize the widest possible difference—so wide, that to receive the one as good, pure, and holy, is of necessity to reject the other as bad, corrupt, and wicked. ... I love the pure, peaceable, and impartial Christianity of Christ: I therefore hate the corrupt, slaveholding, women-whipping, cradle-plundering, partial and hypocritical Christianity of this land. Indeed, I can see no reason, but the most deceitful one, for calling the religion of this land Christianity. ... We have men-stealers for ministers, women-whippers for missionaries, and cradle-plunderers for church members ... The man who robs me of my earnings at the end of each week meets me as a class-leader on Sunday morning, to show me the way of life, and the path of salvation. He who sells my sister, for purposes of prostitution, stands forth as the pious advocate of purity. He who proclaims it a religious duty to read the Bible denies me the right of learning to read the name of the God who made me. He who is the religious advocate of marriage robs whole millions of its sacred influence, and leaves them to the ravages of wholesale pollution. The warm defender of the sacredness of the family relation is the same that scatters whole families,—sundering husbands and wives, parents and children, sisters and brothers,—leaving the hut vacant, and the hearth desolate. We see the thief preaching against theft, and the adulterer against adultery. We have men sold to build churches, women sold to support the gospel, and babes sold to purchase Bibles for *poor heathen! all for the glory of God and the good of souls!* ... . The dealer gives his blood-stained gold to support the pulpit, and the pulpit, in return, covers his infernal business with the garb of Christianity.[26]

His point was ***slavery as practiced by White Christians is neither an example nor a reflection of what Christianity itself requires and justifies.***

A story is told of a runaway slave who was asked, "Are you a nigger?" The man responded no, I am not. I am free man. When asked why, he responded, "because you cannot own a child of God." To which the questioner responded, "No, you cannot, can you? You can own

---

26 Frederick Douglass, *Narrative of the Life of Frederick Douglass: An American Slave* (1845) at, 101–2 at https://www.ibiblio.org/ebooks/Douglass/Narrative/Douglass_Narrative.pdf (emphasis in original)

a horse, you can own a mule, or cow, or an ox. But you cannot own a child of God."[27] That is the truth of the Bible, and the Bible is true.[28] Manipulation of the Bible for evil purposes will not go unpunished forever. A story[29] is told of an evil mayor who risked his life, limb, and fortune and those of his men to get a copy of the Bible. In justifying the risk to his men, he said of the Bible,

> It's a weapon! A weapon that aims right at the hearts and minds of the weak and desperate. It will give us control of them! If we wanna rule more than one small fucking town we have to have it. People will come from all over and do exactly what I tell them if the words are from the book. It's happened before, and it will happen again. All we need is that book.

After securing the Bible the mayor finds that he can't read it or use it. It was said to the mayor,

> You worked so hard for that book. You sacrificed so much, so many men. More than you could spare. Now, all those people who were too scared to even say your name. They're downstairs, tearing up the bar right now, did you know that? And there's no one there to stop them. And you are feverish. I can't imagine what it must feel like to have what you want so close and it might as well be a million miles away.

At the end of the story, the mayor lost all his men and fortune, and like the South and its evil use of the Bible to justify slavery and racism, he was found decimated sitting in rubble.

The corruption of the scriptures by White American Christianity occurred both in the antebellum and postbellum periods. The split in American society over the plight of Blacks was limited in scope. *The split between the Northern and Southern Christians was not over the social and political equality of Blacks with Whites or the belief that they were inferior to Whites, the split was only over the issue of slavery.* This distinction over the Civil War is important to understand when viewing American social history when it comes to Blacks.

After the Civil War, the Black Codes and Jim Crow found support in both Northern and Southern Christianity. Although the Methodists and Baptists, which split over the issue of slavery, remained split after the Civil War, both, along with the Protestant, Lutheran, and Mormon churches, supported racism and racial segregation in their churches and as social policy well past the middle of the twentieth century. Racial segregation in American Christendom, as a matter of church policy, didn't end until the late 1970s.

The result of the corruptions and violations of scriptural interpretation by White American Christians was the rise of the Black Christian Church theology. The Black Christian Church became a distinct separate branch of American Christianity based on a rejection of the American protestant theology presented by slave owners that separated the quality of spiritual life

---

27 *The Free State of Jones*, directed by Gary Ross (2016), Film.

28 See, Arthur H. Garrison, "A Hermeneutical Proof of the Bible" *Journal of Grace Theology* 5, no 1 (2018); 3

29 *The Book of Eli*, directed by The Hughes Brothers (2010), Film.

from the quality of physical life.[30] This division of the spiritual life of a slave from the physical/ societal injustice suffered by the slave, of course, served the slave owners interests. This theology allowed the slaves to be Christianized and allowed them to be slaves nonetheless, because only the saving of their souls had eternal or practical significance. Once saved, the nature of their bodies—life as a slave—was of no comparable consideration to White Christian slave owners or American society.

The Black Christian Church's rejection of the corruption and violations of scriptural interpretation by White American Christians and the resulting devaluation and the demarcation between the spiritual and physical pre-dates the Civil War. The misrepresentation of Christianity was not lost on Northern abolitionists and men like Frederick Douglass who traveled within the United States and Great Britain and made clear that there was a distinction between Christianity and the "White Man's religion." Douglass, in his travels, writings, and oratory, chided European missionary churches for accepting money from Southern slave owners. In his history of Douglass, Dr. Nathan Huggins wrote that, according to Douglass,

> Slavery, rather than being a means of civilizing and Christianizing backward and pagan Africans, was shown to keep slaves unschooled and unlettered and ignorant of Christianity, except as a it might serve the master and the institution. Slaveowners, rather than being gentle, Christian folk, were coarse men and women who dared not follow truly Christian teachings or their own humane and civilizing instincts.
>
> . ...
>
> Even more pernicious than the Free Church's acceptance of money from an evil source was their recognition of slaveholders as fellow Christians. Slavery existed in the United States, Douglass insisted, because it was respectable. The slaveholder was respectable, holding important officers in the government and the church. Men "are sold to build churches, women to support missionaries, and children to send Bibles to the heathen." The main goal of abolitionists in the United States was to make the slaveholder disrespectable. The surest way was to deny them the name Christian. That Christian churches and their clergy would extend fellowship to slaveholders countered the whole thrust of the American antislavery movement. Like other Garrisonians, Douglass insisted that a Christian could find no neutral ground on slavery.[31]

Douglass urged the merging of the Christian faith with Christian behavior. He advocated that the Christian faith required the Christian church to behave in a certain manner and that manner required the rejection of slavery as an institution endorsed by Christianity. His

---

30 For discussion see, lecture by David H. Healey, "The Paradox of the Two Christian Faiths" (2000) at https://scholarworks.iu.edu/journals/index.php/iusburj/article/view/19832/25909 and Raphael Warnock, *The Divided Mind of the Black Church* (NYU Press, 2013)

31 Nathan Irvin Huggins, *Slave and Citizen: The Life of Frederick Douglass* (1980) at 21, 29–30

approach would find resonance with both Christian and non-Christian abolitionists in both America and Great Britain.

Eventually, Douglass prevailed regarding slavery, but the devaluation of the treatment of Black bodies in America operated in American political, societal, social, and cultural history long after slavery. A century later, the Black Christian Church rejection of the devaluation and the demarcation between the spiritual and physical provided the foundation for the pursuit of the dismantling of Jim Crow and legalized systematic racism during the civil rights movement of the 1950s and 1960s, and it guides calls for social justice and addressing systemic racism in the Post-Civil Rights Era. As discussed in Chapters Three, Six, Seven, Eight, and Nine, this systemic racism is manifested (1) in the expectation of discriminatory results of Black incarceration in the criminal justice system in general and, specifically, how police perceive and treat Blacks in relation to use of force; (2) in how both disproportionate incarceration and police use of force have been described, defended, and justified by social conservatives; and (3) in the history and policies of the crime control model politics of the 1980s and 1990s.

Europe, over time, abandoned its cultural inferiority theory of colored people when it adopted the system of European colonization of Africa and the idea that it was the obligation of Whites to rule but also to look after the needs of these inferior peoples. European colonists sought to make their colonies part of their empire both culturally and legally. They adopted what the French called *Noblesse Oblige* or the "White Man's Burden" in Rudyard Kipling's famous 1899 poem. Through this approach, they would "civilize" the peoples in their colonies and make them part of European tradition. The assumption within this approach was that the peoples of the colonies could be made equal, and the historical result was that they would be treated equally before the law. This approach separated the experiences of people under European slavery and colonization and those under American slavery. The former allowed for the development of proposition that colored people were equals, and the later rejected that proposition.

European slavery of Africa and the Caribbean, in general, and American slavery, in particular, as abominable as it was, was not America's original sin. Slavery of Africans was well established on the face of the earth long before the American colonies got involved in it in 1619. The original sin in America is racism and the proposition that Black people were not equal to Whites either on a social or genetic level.

After the Civil War, and with the fall of the institution of slavery, the justification for slavery—secular-based racism and inferiority of Blacks to Whites—remained and became the foundation for Jim Crow. Racism was adopted by both the North and South, and its manifestation—Jim Crow—lasted for the next century. This is what President Obama meant when he said, as discussed in the introduction, that racism is in America's DNA.

THE ANTEBELLUM PERIOD: THE DRED SCOTT DECISION

Slavery was not only sanctioned by politics in America, as discussed in Chapter Four, the industrialization of the atrocity of slavery was sanctioned by law and protected by America's courts. John Calhoun, Alexander Stephens, and the South found support from the Supreme Court when it said in *Dred Scott* (1857) that Blacks, who were slaves long before the Declaration of Independence and the U.S. Constitution were written, as a group were not citizens of the United States and had no rights that the White man was bound to respect and, as a race, Blacks were, by definition, inferior to Whites. The Court held that the *Missouri Compromise of 1820* was an unconstitutional violation of the Due Process Clause of the Fifth Amendment, because the *Missouri Compromise of 1820* limited the ability of a citizen to move freely in the United States with his property (slaves) between free and slave states. The *Dred Scott case,* along with the *Kansas-Nebraska Act of 1854,* which asserted popular sovereignty in determining if Kansas and Nebraska would allow or prohibit slavery, destroyed the last political compromise over slavery. The hard feelings over the repeal of the *Missouri Compromise of 1820* by the passage of the *Kansas-Nebraska Act of 1854* along with the *Dred Scott* decision and the sectional division of the North and South over the meaning of the election of Lincoln in 1860 made the Civil War inevitable.

The significance of the *Dred Scott* decision is the Court's infamous conclusion on the status of Blacks under law.

> It is difficult at this day to realize the state of public opinion in relation to that unfortunate race, which prevailed in the civilized and enlightened portions of the world at the time of the Declaration of Independence, and when the Constitution of the United States was framed and adopted. But the public history of every European nation displays it in a manner too plain to be mistaken.
>
> ***They had for more than a century before been regarded as beings of an inferior order***, and altogether ***unfit to associate with the white race***, either in social or political relations; *and so far inferior*, that ***they had no rights which the white man was bound to respect***; and that the negro might justly and lawfully be reduced to slavery for his benefit. He was bought and sold, and treated as an ordinary article of merchandise and traffic, whenever a profit could be made by it. This opinion was at that time fixed and universal in the civilized portion of the white race. It was regarded as an axiom in morals as well as in politics, which no one thought of disputing, or supposed to be open to dispute; and men in every grade and position in society daily and habitually acted upon it in their private pursuits, as well as in matters of public concern, without doubting for a moment the correctness of this opinion.
>
> And in no nation was this opinion more firmly fixed or more uniformly acted upon than by the English Government and English people. …
>
> The opinion thus entertained and acted upon in England was naturally impressed upon the colonies they founded on this side of the Atlantic. And, accordingly, a negro of the

> African race was regarded by them as an article of property, and held, and bought and sold as such, in every one of the thirteen colonies which united in the Declaration of Independence, and afterwards formed the Constitution of the United States. The slaves were more or less numerous in the different colonies, as slave labor was found more or less profitable. But no one seems to have doubted the correctness of the prevailing opinion of the time.[32]

Lincoln disagreed. During the famous Lincoln-Douglass debates, ***Lincoln*** delivered his ***Speech on the Dred Scott Decision*** and asserted that under the *Declaration of Independence* Blacks were equal to Whites. In answering Douglass who supported the logic of *Dred Scott*, Lincoln said on June 26, 1857 that the writers of the declaration intended all men to be equal in their pursuit of life, liberty and happiness because that would create a society free from despotism and would protect America from "the proneness of prosperity to breed tyrants. I have now briefly expressed my view of the *meaning* and *objects* of that part of the Declaration of Independence which declares that 'all men are created equal.'"

Lincoln was right morally on what the *Declaration of Independence* could be used for and was used for in the advocacy of those who opposed slavery, but as a legal issue Taney was correct.[33] Dating before the beginning of the founding, slavery was an institution well established within the legal, social, economic, and constitutional structure of the colonies. As a matter of original intent and strict construction of the history of the *Declaration of Independence* and the Constitution as of 1857, Blacks were slaves and property and were never intended to be citizens under the Constitution, and the phrase "all men are created equal" was understood not to include Blacks but to include only Whites.

But Lincoln's speech regarding *Dred Scott* involved more than the dispute over the meaning of the declaration or legal analysis of the decision itself. It was also a political speech to counter the politics of the Democratic party. The political dispute around the legal issues of the *Dred Scott* decision was the White fear that Black equality under the law equaled Blacks marrying Whites. As Lincoln stated, "There is a natural disgust in the minds of nearly all white people, to the idea of an indiscriminate amalgamation of the white and black races" and Douglass was seeking to use this disgust to his advantage in the election. Lincoln's arguments

---

32 Dred Scott v. Sandford, 60 U.S. 393, 407–8 (1857).

33 "[T]he Dred Scott case was 'a reasonable decision given the moment.' The historical fact is that in '1857 as it had been since 1788 ... the United States was a slave holder's republic.' Dred Scott correctly concluded that blacks as a group had no rights which the white man was bound to respect and were deemed inferior to whites because 'if you look at the laws of the United States, whether in 1788, 1789, or 1857 you find for vast majority of African Americans that was their legal status'" Arthur H. Garrison, "Disproportionate Incarceration of African Americans: What History and the First Decade of Twenty-First Century Have Brought," *Journal of the Institute of Justice & International Studies* 11 (2011): 87, 108 (quotations citing Paul Finkelman, panelist on *Dred Scott v. Sandford* session in the Pepperdine Law School Symposium "Supreme Mistakes: Exploring the Most Maligned Decisions in Supreme Court History," April 1, 2011).

were designed to counter Douglas. The use of White resentment and fear of Black equality and Black miscegenation to win elections in the twentieth century did not originate in that century. It was fully functioning years before Lincoln took the oath of office as president.

Douglass sought to secure White votes by asserting that the reason Republicans assert that Blacks are included in "all men are created equal" under the declaration was "because they want to vote, and eat, and sleep, and marry with negroes!" Lincoln's answer was to be insulted by the proposition. Lincoln said, "Now I protest against that counterfeit logic which concludes that, because I do not want a black woman for a *slave* I must necessarily want her for a *wife*. I need not have her for either." He concluded that although in "some respects she certainly is not my equal" the *Declaration of Independence* required the conclusion that "in her natural right to eat the bread she earns with her own hands without asking leave of any one else, she is my equal, and the equal of all others."

THE POSTBELLUM PERIOD: THE SUPREME COURT AND ITS SUPPORT OF THE RISE OF JIM CROW

It was only after the Civil War and the passage of the Thirteenth, Fourteenth, and Fifteenth Amendments that the Constitution was changed to include Blacks as citizens and legal persons worthy to stand before the bar of justice to seek redress of their grievances. But it must be understood that the dispute and battle between abolitionists and pro-slavery forces was over the morality and existence of Black slavery in the United States, not whether Blacks were socially and legally equal to Whites in the United States. The Civil War settled the former in the negative, and the rise of Jim Crow settled the latter also in the negative. Only a century after the end of the Civil War, was the later changed to the affirmative.

As with the nation, the Supreme Court tired of addressing the purpose of Civil War Amendments, and in little more than a decade after the end of the Civil War and the passage of the Civil War Amendments, the Supreme Court added its voice and support to the history of Jim Crow and the systematic racism that replaced slavery. The process of the Supreme Court adding its voice to this process began in 1873.

In *The Slaughter-House Cases* (1873), the Court held that the privileges and immunities clause of the Fourteenth Amendment only protects rights of United States citizenship, and the amendment does not affect the police powers of the state to govern individual rights under state law.[34] In March 1876, the Court reviewed criminal indictments under the Enforcement Act of 1870, also known as the *Civil Rights Act of 1870* and the Ku Klux Klan Act, which made the following a federal crime:

> That if two or more persons shall band or conspire together, or go in disguise upon the public highway, or upon the premises of another, with intent to violate any provision of

---

34 The Slaughter-House Cases 83 U.S. 36 (1873).

> this act, or to injure, oppress, threaten, or intimidate any citizen, with intent to prevent or hinder his free exercise and enjoyment of *any right or privilege granted or secured to him by the Constitution or laws of the United States*, or because of his having exercised the same, such persons shall be held guilty of felony, and, on conviction thereof, shall be fined or imprisoned, or both, at the discretion of the court—the fine not to exceed $5,000, and the imprisonment not to exceed ten years—and shall, moreover, be thereafter ineligible to, and disabled from holding, any office or place of honor, profit, or trust created by the Constitution or laws of the United States.[35]

The Court held in *United States v. Cruikshank*, in a detailed strict scrutiny and original intent format, that the key phrase of the Civil Rights Act of 1870 statute was "any right or privilege granted or secured to him by the Constitution," and proceeded to hold that the First Amendment right to peaceably assemble predated the Constitution; it "was not, therefore, a right granted to the people by the Constitution" and more significantly, the protection of the right under the divided government and limited powers design of the American federal system put "the obligation on the part of the States to afford [the right of peaceful assembly] protection."[36] Thus, as a practical matter the Court's decision eviscerated the federal authority to protect the rights of the former slaves.

In *United States v. Cruikshank*, the Court set the stage for the death of federal enforcement of civil rights with the following statement,

> The particular amendment now under consideration assumes the existence of the right of the people to assemble for lawful purposes, and protects it against encroachment by Congress. The right was not created by the amendment; neither was its continuance guaranteed, except as against congressional interference. For their protection in its enjoyment, therefore, the people must look to the States.
>
> ...
>
> The right there specified is that of "bearing arms for a lawful purpose." This is not a right granted by the Constitution. Neither is it in any manner dependent upon that instrument for its existence. The second amendment declares that it shall not be infringed, but this, as has been seen, means no more than that it shall not be infringed by Congress. This is one of the amendments that has no other effect than to restrict the powers of the national government, leaving the people to look for their protection against any violation by their fellow citizens of the rights it recognizes, to what is called, in *The City of New York v. Miln*, 11 Pet. 139, the "powers which relate to merely municipal legislation, or what was, perhaps, more properly called internal police," "not surrendered or restrained" by the Constitution of the United States.
>
> ...

35 *United States v. Cruikshank*, 92 U.S. 542 (1876).

36 *United States v. Cruikshank*, 92 U.S. at 551.

> In *Minor v. Happersett,* 21 Wall. 178, we decided that the Constitution of the United States has not conferred the right of suffrage upon anyone, and that the United States have no voters of their own creation in the States. In *United States v. Reese et al.*[92 U. S. 214 (1875)], we hold that the Fifteenth Amendment has invested the citizens of the United States with a new constitutional right, which is, exemption from discrimination in the exercise of the elective franchise on account of race, color, or previous condition of servitude. From this, it appears that the right of suffrage is not a necessary attribute of national citizenship, but that exemption from discrimination in the exercise of that right on account of race, &c., is. The right to vote in the States comes from the States, but the right of exemption from the prohibited discrimination comes from the United States. The first has not been granted or secured by the Constitution of the United States, but the last has been.[37]

The background for this case was the famous ***Colfax Massacre*** of three White Republicans and more than a hundred Black Union Soldiers in Colfax, Louisiana, on April 13, 1873, by a mob of White Democrats to prevent a political meeting of the freemen at the Colfax Courthouse. The federal government proceeded to try various members of the riot under the Enforcement Act. The Court held that the various charges, based on violation of rights granted by the Constitution, including the right to assemble for political purposes, were violations of state laws and only state prosecution could address the violations, because the Constitution does not grant any of these rights. The Court made clear that the federal government did not have general police powers and that the Civil War Amendments did not grant the power to prosecute violations of rights between citizens. Those powers belonged to the state. As the Court reasoned,

> The very highest duty of the States, when they entered into the Union under the Constitution, was to protect all persons within their boundaries in the enjoyment of these "unalienable rights with which they were endowed by their Creator." Sovereignty, for this purpose, rests alone with the States. It is no more the duty or within the power of the United States to punish for a conspiracy to falsely imprison or murder within a State, than it would be to punish for false imprisonment or murder itself.
>
> ***The Fourteenth Amendment prohibits a State from depriving any person of life, liberty, or property without due process of law, but this adds nothing to the rights of one citizen as against another.*** It simply furnishes an additional guaranty against any encroachment by the States upon the fundamental rights which belong to every citizen as a member of society.
>
> ...
>
> ***The Fourteenth Amendment prohibits a State from denying to any person within its jurisdiction the equal protection of the laws***; but this provision does not, any more than

37 *United States v. Cruikshank*, 92 U.S. at 552–53,555–56.

> the one which precedes it, and which we have just considered, ***add anything to the rights which one citizen has under the Constitution against another.*** The equality of the rights of citizens is a principle of Republicanism. Every Republican government is in duty bound to protect all its citizens in the enjoyment of this principle, if within its power. That duty was originally assumed by the States, and it still remains there. The only obligation resting upon the United States is to see that the States do not deny the right. This the amendment guarantees, but no more. The power of the national government is limited to the enforcement of this guaranty.[38]

The practical effect of the decision was that national government had no power to protect Blacks from White mobs that conspired to commit murder and interfere with rights listed in the Constitution, because those violations are simple criminal matters that are left to the states alone.

As to the applicability of the *Civil Rights Act of 1866*, the Court held that it could only be violated if it is alleged and proven that a violation of rights occurred with the specific intent to violate the rights of a person based on their race.[39] Mere political violence with a political goal does not invoke federal government protection, because such crimes are simple crimes that are for the state governments to prosecute. The conviction of the defendants was reversed by the trial court, and the decision was affirmed by the Supreme Court. It would take a century of lynching, rape, murder, and violence before Blacks would be protected by federal criminal justice.

The significance of the Colfax Massacre and the subsequent decision by the Supreme Court eliminating the power of the national government to address race-based crimes, is that it makes clear that justice is not guaranteed without federal oversight of states. Although the Court dismissed the indictments and affirmed the circuit court in reversing the convictions of the members of the mob, what is significant is that a trial occurred in the first place and the trial occurred in federal court. As the New Orleans riot of July 30, 1866, made clear, without federal presence, there is no accountability at all. On July 30th a force of New Orleans police officers, at the order of Southern Democrats, attacked a detachment of Black union soldiers who had marched to the Mechanics Institute where Republican freedmen were meeting to discuss establishing the right to vote for freed Blacks. The New Orleans police force killed more than a hundred Black soldiers and the Republican politicians at the meeting. Unlike those of the Colfax Massacre, the members of the police force and the local politicians that ordered the attack were not arrested or brought to trial.

---

38 *United States v. Cruikshank*, 92 U.S. at 553–55.

39 *United States v. Cruikshank*, 92 U.S. at 555–56.

In October 1883, in the *Civil Rights Cases*,[40] the Court held that section one of the Civil Rights Acts of 1875,[41] which outlawed discrimination in public accommodations[42] on the basis of prior servitude, was unconstitutional, because the Thirteenth and Fourteenth Amendments didn't apply to private action.[43] The Court held,

> [a]nd so, in the present case, until some State law has been passed, or some State action through its officers or agents has been taken, adverse to the rights of citizens sought to be protected by the Fourteenth Amendment, no legislation of the United States under said amendment, nor any proceeding under such legislation, can be called into activity, for the prohibitions of the amendment are against State laws and acts done under State authority.

The Court held the Act unconstitutional because it did not focus on state action.

> *An inspection of the law shows that it makes no reference whatever to any supposed or apprehended violation of the Fourteenth Amendment on the part of the States.* It is not predicated on any such view. It proceeds *ex directo* to declare that certain acts committed by individuals shall be deemed offences and shall be prosecuted and punished by proceedings in the courts of the United States. It does not profess to be corrective of any constitutional wrong committed by the States; it does not make its operation to depend upon any such wrong committed. It applies equally to cases arising in States which have the justest laws respecting the personal rights of citizens, and whose authorities are ever ready to enforce such laws, as to those which arise in States that may have violated the prohibition of the amendment. *In other words, it steps into the domain of local jurisprudence, and lays down rules for the conduct of individuals in society towards each other, and imposes sanctions for the enforcement of those rules, without referring in any manner to any supposed action of the State or its authorities.*
>
> ...
>
> [I]t is clear that the law in question cannot be sustained by any grant of legislative power made to Congress by the Fourteenth Amendment. That amendment prohibits the States from denying to any person the equal protection of the laws.

---

40 Civil Rights Cases, 109 U.S. 3 (1883).

41 "An Act to protect all citizens in their civil and legal rights" The Civil Rights Act (March 1, 1875) 18 Stat. 335.

42 Section One reads as follows:

That all persons within the jurisdiction of the United States shall be entitled to the full and equal enjoyment of the accommodations, advantages, facilities, and privileges of inns, public conveyances on land or water, theatres, and other places of public amusement, subject only to the conditions and limitations established by law and applicable alike to citizens of every race and color, regardless of any previous condition of servitude.

43 *Civil Rights Cases*, 109 U.S. at 13,14,18 (emphasis added).

The Court made clear that only state action could be prevailed upon by Congressional power. So long as discrimination and abuse imposed on the former slaves is conducted by private individuals, federal law has no application.

> ***In this connection, it is proper to state that civil rights, such as are guaranteed by the Constitution against State aggression, cannot be impaired by the wrongful acts of individuals, unsupported by State authority in the shape of laws, customs, or judicial or executive proceedings.*** The wrongful act of an individual, unsupported by any such authority, is simply a private wrong, or a crime of that individual; an invasion of the rights of the injured party, it is true, whether they affect his person, his property, or his reputation; but if not sanctioned in some way by the State, or not done under State authority, his rights remain in full force, and may presumably be vindicated by resort to the laws of the State for redress. An individual cannot deprive a man of his right to vote, to hold property, to buy and sell, to sue in the courts, or to be a witness or a juror; he may, by force or fraud, interfere with the enjoyment of the right in a particular case; he may commit an assault against the person, or commit murder, or use ruffian violence at the polls, or slander the good name of a fellow citizen; but, unless protected in these wrongful acts by some shield of State law or State authority, he cannot destroy or injure the right; he will only render himself amenable to satisfaction or punishment, and amenable therefore to the laws of the State where the wrongful acts are committed. Hence, in all those cases where the Constitution seeks to protect the rights of the citizen against discriminative and unjust laws of the State by prohibiting such laws, it is not individual offences, but abrogation and denial of rights, which it denounces and for which it clothes the Congress with power to provide a remedy.[44]

The Court made clear the protection of the former slaves by the federal government was over. As discussed in Chapter Four, states' rights and home rule was now the new policy. Protection of Black civil rights was defined by the states alone. The Court also made clear that although the Thirteenth Amendment ended slavery; it did not end the Black inferiority or the second-class status of Blacks. The Court wrote

> ***Congress did not assume, under the authority given by the Thirteenth Amendment, to adjust what may be called the social rights of men and races in the community***, but only to declare and vindicate those fundamental rights which appertain to the essence of citizenship, and the enjoyment or deprivation of which constitutes the essential distinction between freedom and slavery.[45]

Blacks were no longer slaves. That's all the Thirteenth Amendment offers. Congress, the Court held, did not alleviate the nature of slavery from the necks of the former slaves.

---

44 *Civil Rights Cases*, 109 U.S. at 17–18 (emphasis added).

45 *Civil Rights Cases*, 109 U.S. at 22 (emphasis added).

The Court subsequently held that private discrimination and prohibition of Blacks from public accommodations carried no negative vestiges of slavery, prohibited by the Thirteenth Amendment.[46] Justice Bradley concluded with his infamous summary of the case and the use of the law to protect former slaves:

> When a man has emerged from slavery, and, by the aid of beneficent legislation, has shaken off the inseparable concomitants of that state, ***there must be some stage in the progress of his elevation when he takes the rank of a mere citizen and ceases to be the special favorite of the laws***, and when his rights as a citizen or a man are to be protected in the ordinary modes by which other men's rights are protected. There were thousands of free colored people in this country before the abolition of slavery, enjoying all the essential rights of life, liberty and property the same as white citizens, yet no one at that time thought that it was any invasion of his personal status as a freeman because he was not admitted to all the privileges enjoyed by white citizens, or because he was subjected to discriminations in the enjoyment of accommodations in inns, public conveyances and places of amusement. ***Mere discriminations on account of race or color were not regarded as badges of slavery.***[47]

The Civil Rights Cases were built upon an earlier case in the same year, January 1883, in which the Court held in *Unites States v. Harris* that the text of the Thirteenth, Fourteenth, and Fifteenth Amendments doesn't provide positive rights to any citizen and that any level of enforcement of those rights belongs to the states, not to Congress. Further, the Thirteenth, Fourteenth, and Fifteenth Amendments do not provide Congress with the authority to criminalize violations of the Amendments. The Court concluded,

> [t]he language of the amendment does not leave this subject in doubt. ***When the state has been guilty of no violation of its provisions; when it has not made or enforced any law abridging the privileges or immunities of citizens of the United States***; when no one of its departments has deprived any person of life, liberty, or property without due process of law, or denied to any person within its jurisdiction the equal protection of the laws; ***when, on the contrary, the laws of the state***, as enacted by its legislative and construed by its judicial and administered by its executive departments ***recognize and protect the rights of all persons, the amendment imposes no duty*** and confers no power upon Congress.[48]

The Court consequently held a federal statute that made it unlawful for an individual to conspire to deprive a person of the equal protection of the laws as unconstitutional.

> Section 5519 of the Revised Statutes is not limited to take effect only in case the state shall abridge the privileges or immunities of citizens of the United States or deprive any person

46 *Civil Rights Cases*, 109 U.S. at 21–23.

47 *Civil Rights Cases*, 109 U.S. at 25 (emphasis added).

48 *United States v. Harris*, 106 U.S. 629, 639 (1883).

> of life, liberty, or property without due process of law or deny to any person the equal protection of the laws. It applies no matter how well the state may have performed its duty. Under it, private persons are liable to punishment for conspiring to deprive anyone of the equal protection of the laws enacted by the state.
>
> ...
>
> As, therefore, the section of the law under consideration is directed exclusively against the action of private persons, without reference to the laws of the states or their administration by the officers of the state, we are clear in the opinion that it is not warranted by any clause in the Fourteenth Amendment to the Constitution.
>
> ...
>
> [As to the inquiry does the] Thirteenth Amendment warrant the enactment of sec. 5519 of the Revised Statutes. We are of opinion that it does not. Our conclusion is based on the fact that the provisions of that section are broader than the Thirteenth Amendment would justify. Under that section, it would be an offense for two or more white persons to conspire, etc., for the purpose of depriving another white person of the equal protection of the laws. It would be an offense for two or more colored persons, enfranchised slaves, to conspire with the same purpose against a white citizen or against another colored citizen who had never been a slave. Even if the amendment is held to be directed against the action of private individuals as well as against the action of the states and United States, the law under consideration covers cases both within and without the provisions of the amendment. It covers any conspiracy between two free white men against another free white man to deprive the latter of any right accorded him by the laws of the state or of the United States. A law under which two or more free white private citizens could be punished for conspiring or going in disguise for the purpose of depriving another free white citizen of a right accorded by the law of the state to all classes of persons—as, for instance, the right to make a contract, bring a suit, or give evidence—clearly cannot be authorized by the amendment which simply prohibits slavery and involuntary servitude. [49]

The Court argued the law failed because of its statutory overbreadth because the law could cover two Whites conspiring against another White, as well as to two Whites conspiring against a Black. The Court rejected the law, because it applied to all criminal conspirators, and that was beyond the scope of the Thirteenth Amendment. Put simply, the Court held that Congress does not have general police power. The Court wrote that Congress, through the Thirteenth Amendment to end slavery, cannot enact general criminal statutes outlawing traditional crimes outlawed by state law.

The Court, in *Harris*, in an example of states' rights orthodoxy and a staple of what would be conservative Republican federalism protection politics from the 1950s to present, reasoned

---

49 *Civil Rights Cases*, 109 U.S. at 639–40, 641.

> [i]f Congress has constitutional authority under the Thirteenth Amendment to punish conspiracy between two persons to do an unlawful act, it can punish the act itself, whether done by one or more persons. A private person cannot make constitutions or laws, nor can he with authority construe them, nor can he administer or execute them. The only way, therefore, in which one private person can deprive another of the equal protection of the laws is by the commission of some offense against the laws which protect the rights of persons, as by theft, burglary, arson, libel, assault, or murder. If, therefore, we hold that section 5519 is warranted by the Thirteenth Amendment, we should by virtue of that amendment, accord to Congress the power to punish every crime by which the right of any person to life, property, or reputation is invaded. Thus, under a provision of the Constitution which simply abolished slavery and involuntary servitude, we should, with few exceptions, invest Congress with power over the whole catalogue of crimes. A construction of the amendment which leads to such a result is clearly unsound.[50]

The Court also concluded that under Article Four of the Constitution, the Privileges and Immunities Clause, it "was never supposed that the section under consideration conferred on Congress the power to enact a law which would punish a private citizen for an invasion of the rights of his fellow citizen conferred by the State of which they were both residents; on all its citizens alike."[51] The Court would affirm *Harris* in its decision in *United States v. Morrison* more than a century later.

> The Constitution requires a distinction between what is truly national and what is truly local. ... The regulation and punishment of intrastate violence ... has always been the province of the States. Congress has no general right to punish murder committed within any of the States, and that it is clear ... that Congress cannot punish felonies generally. Indeed, we can think of no better example of the police power, which the Founders denied the National Government and reposed in the States, than the suppression of violent crime and vindication of its victims. The Constitution ... withholds from Congress a plenary police power.[52]

After the Court made clear in *Harris* that Congress was without power to criminally punish Whites who openly conspired to deprive Blacks of their rights under the Civil War Amendments, the Court held that two Blacks could be tried and convicted in all-White juries in *Virginia v. Rives*.[53] The Court held that a federal statute that allowed for a citizen to have a case transferred to federal court when the state courts cannot or will not enforce a citizens constitutional rights does not apply when the constitutional violation occurs due to the action

---

50 *United States v. Harris* at 642–43

51 *Civil Rights Cases*, 109 U.S. at 644.

52 *United States v. Morrison*, 529 U.S. 598, 617–618 (2000) (internal quotation marks and citation omitted)

53 *Virginia v. Rives*, 100 U.S. 313 (1880).

of a state official and not the court. The Court concluded that when a state official—in this case the sheriff—fails to secure an integrated jury pool as required by state law, the federal removal statute does not apply because the trial court itself is not refusing to comply with constitutional requirements.[54] The Court held that

> [n]or did the refusal of the court and of the counsel for the prosecution to allow a modification of the venire, by which one-third of the jury, or a portion of it, should be composed of persons of the petitioners own race, amount to any denial of a right secured to them by any law providing for the equal civil rights of citizens of the United States. The privilege for which they moved, and which they also asked from the prosecution, was not a right given or secured to them, or to any person, by the law of the State, or by any act of Congress, or by the Fourteenth Amendment of the Constitution. ***It is a right to which every colored man*** is entitled that, in the selection of jurors to pass upon his life, liberty, or property, ***there shall be no exclusion of his race***, and no discrimination against them because of their color. ***But this is a different thing from the right which it is asserted*** was denied to the petitioners by the state court, *viz.*, ***a right to have the jury composed in part of colored men. A mixed jury in a particular case is not essential to the equal protection of the laws, and the right to it is not given by any law of Virginia or by any Federal statute. It is not, therefore, guaranteed by the Fourteenth Amendment.***[55]

The proposition that the trial court is not responsible for maintaining a fair jury pool creation and that a fair trial can occur when Blacks are excluded from a jury pool or from being seated in specific case because of race would prevail until the Court overruled *Rives* in *Norris v. Alabama* (1935) and *Batson v. Kentucky* (1986).[56]

In *Plessy v. Ferguson (1896)*, the South, having lost the war and the debate on whether Blacks were citizens and had the right to sue before the bar of justice, found support for their social and racial separation policies when the Court ruled, regarding the Fourteenth Amendment, that the

> object of the amendment was undoubtedly to enforce the absolute equality of the two races before the law, but, ***in the nature of things, it could not have been intended to abolish distinctions based upon color, or to enforce social, as distinguished from political, equality, or a commingling of the two races upon terms unsatisfactory to either.*** Laws permitting, and even requiring, their ***separation, in places where they are liable to be brought into contact, do not necessarily imply the inferiority of either race*** to the other, and have been generally, if not universally, recognized as within the competency of the state legislatures in the exercise of their police power. The most common instance

54 *Virginia v. Rives*. at 322.

55 *Virginia v. Rives* at 322–23.

56 *Norris v. Alabama*, 294 U.S. 587 (1935) and *Batson v. Kentucky*, 476 U.S. 79 (1986).

> of this is connected with the establishment of separate schools for white and colored children, which have been held to be a valid exercise of the legislative power even by courts of states where the political rights of the colored race have been longest and most earnestly enforced.
>
> ...
>
> ***We consider the underlying fallacy of the plaintiff's argument to consist in the assumption that the enforced separation of the two races stamps the colored race with a badge of inferiority. If this be so, it is not by reason of anything found in the act, but solely because the colored race chooses to put that construction upon it.***[57]

Thirteen years after the Court invalidated the Thirteenth Amendment as a tool to protect Blacks from racial discrimination by invalidating the Civil Rights Act of 1875, the Court invalidated the Fourteenth Amendment as a tool for the same purpose. According to the Court, racial discrimination did not mean racial inferiority.

Separate but equal was based on race, and the Court concluded that the stamp of inferiority from the hand of racism is a figment of Black people's imagination. This social and political attitude of insensitivity and discounting of Black concerns regarding disparate impact of government action has found modern application, as discussed in Chapters Eight and Nine, in the disproportionate punishment between crack and powder cocaine, the expectation that Blacks are supposed to be disproportionately arrested and incarcerated, the disproportionate police shootings of Blacks, and the lack of criminal sanctions being applied to police for those deaths.

The Court, in *Plessy*, made an interesting and very familiar social conservative argument regarding the difference between political and social equality.

> The argument also assumes that social prejudices may be overcome by legislation, and that equal rights cannot be secured to the negro except by an enforced commingling of the two races. We cannot accept this proposition. If the two races are to meet upon terms of social equality, it must be the result of natural affinities, a mutual appreciation of each other's merits, and a voluntary consent of individuals. ... Legislation is powerless to eradicate racial instincts, or to abolish distinctions based upon physical differences, and the attempt to do so can only result in accentuating the difficulties of the present situation. If the civil and political rights of both races be equal, one cannot be inferior to the other civilly or politically. ***If one race be inferior to the other socially, the constitution of the United States cannot put them upon the same plane.***[58]

Barry Goldwater, as discussed in Chapter Four, could not have said it better when he said the same in 1964 at the Hilton Hotel.

---

57 *Plessy v. Ferguson*, 163 U.S. 537, 544, 551 (1896) (emphasis added).

58 *Plessy v. Ferguson*, 163 U.S. at 551–52.

The Court in *Plessy* made clear that slavery was over, but Black inferiority was now assumed to be true, and Black treatment based on that inferiority was without legal remedy. To which Justice Harlan answered in his famous lone dissent that

> [t]he destinies of the two races, in this country, are indissolubly linked together, and the interests of both require that the common government of all shall not permit the seeds of race hate to be planted under the sanction of law. What can more certainly arouse race hate, what more certainly create and perpetuate a feeling of distrust between these races, than state enactments which, in fact, proceed on the ground that colored citizens are so inferior and degraded that they cannot be allowed to sit in public coaches occupied by white citizens? That, as all will admit, is the real meaning of such legislation as was enacted in Louisiana.
>
> ...
>
> ***The arbitrary separation of citizens, on the basis of race, while they are on a public highway, is a badge of servitude wholly inconsistent with the civil freedom and the equality before the law established by the constitution. It cannot be justified upon any legal grounds.***[59]

The significance of the *Civil Rights Cases*, *U.S. v. Cruikshank*, and *Plessy v. Ferguson*, along with *United States v. Harris*, *Virginia v. Rives*, and *The Slaughter-House Cases*, which held the Civil Rights Act of 1875 and the Privileges and Immunities Clause of the Fourteenth Amendment did not apply to individual discrimination but only to state action is that *in toto* these cases rejected the proposition that the Thirteenth and Fourteenth Amendments were sources of protection from the vestiges of slavery and racism. These cases solidified the abandonment of the former slaves in the late nineteenth century in an effort to "bind the nations' wounds" for the benefit of sectional reconciliation.[60] As Woodward points out,

> since the Negro was the symbol of sectional strife, the liberals joined in deprecating further agitation of his cause and in defending the Southern view of race in its less extreme forms. It was quite common in the 'eighties and 'nineties to find ... Northern liberals and former abolitionists mouthing the shibboleths of white supremacy regarding the negro's innate inferiority, shiftlessness, and hopeless unfitness for full participation in the white man's civilization. Such expressions doubtless did much to add to the reconciliation of North and South, but they did so at the expense of the Negro. Just as the Negro gained his emancipation and new rights through a falling out between white men, he now stood to lose his rights through the reconciliation of white men.
>
> The cumulative weakening of resistance to racism was expressed also in a succession of decisions by the United States Supreme Court between 1873 and 1898 ... the court

59 *Plessy v. Ferguson*, 163 U.S. at 560, 562 (emphasis added).

60 C. Vann Woodward, *The Strange Career of Jim Crow* (Oxford University Press, 1955) at 70.

> drastically curtailed the privileges and immunities recognized as being under federal protection. It continued the trend in its decision on the *Civil Rights Cases* of 1883 by virtually nullifying the restrictive parts of the Civil Rights Act ... [T]he court held that the Fourteenth Amendment gave Congress power to restrain states but not individuals from acts of racial discrimination and segregation ... [In *Hall v. de Cuir*, 1877 the Supreme Court ruled] that a state could not *prohibit* segregation on a common carrier, the Court in 1890 (*Louisville, New Orleans, and Texas Railroad v. Mississippi*) ruled that a state could constitutionally *require* segregation on carriers. In *Plessy v. Ferguson*, decided in 1896, the Court subscribed to the doctrine that "legislation is powerless to eradicate racial instincts" and laid down the "separate but Equal" rule for the justification of segregation. Two years later, in 1898, in *Williams v. Mississippi* the Court completed the opening of the legal road to proscription, segregation, and disfranchisement by approving the Mississippi plan for depriving Negroes of the franchise. ... Throughout the North there was not only acquiescence among the white population in the "Southern Way" of solving the race problem but a tendency to imitate it in practice.[61]

THE SUPREME COURT AND ITS ACQUIESCENCE TO JIM CROW: RACISM IS NOT UNCONSTITUTIONAL

As *Dred Scott* made clear in 1857, Blacks were surely not equal to whites under the law. The original sin of America was the belief that Blacks, by the hand and will of God, were intended to be slaves of Whites. This belief, which was imbedded into the economic justification of slavery in the late eighteenth and early nineteenth century, was not excised from the American heart after the Civil War. Although slavery was abandoned, racism was embraced into the American political and historical landscape for the next century. The ideals of Lincoln and Garfield, as discussed in Chapter Four, regarding the meaning of the Civil War, were abandoned. The Court, as did the nation, abandoned the purpose of three Civil War Amendments and asserted neither the war nor the amendments were about eradicating the underpinnings of slavery—racism—or making the Black man equal under the law, but rather the war occurred to settle what Lincoln made clear.

> A house divided against itself cannot stand. I believe this government cannot endure, permanently, half slave and half free. I do not expect the Union to be dissolved—I do not expect the house to fall—but I do expect it will cease to be divided. It will become all one thing or all the other. Either the opponents of slavery will arrest the further spread of it, and place it where the public mind shall rest in the belief that it is in the course of ultimate

61 C. Vann Woodward, *The Strange Career of Jim Crow* (Oxford University Press, 1955) at 70–72.

> extinction; or its advocates will push it forward, till it shall become lawful in all the States, old as well as new—North as well as South.[62]
>
> . ... [F]our years ago all thoughts were anxiously directed to an impending Civil War. ... While the inaugural address was being delivered from this place. ... agents were in the city seeking to destroy ... seeking to dissolve the Union ... [they] would make war rather than let the nation survive, and [we] would accept war rather than let it perish, and the war came.
>
> One-eighth of the whole population were colored slaves, not distributed generally over the Union, but localized in the southern part of it. These slaves constituted a peculiar and powerful interest. All knew that this interest was somehow the cause of the war.[63]

If the war was nothing more than a violent settling of the political and legal debate of whether the Constitution had primacy over all the states and whether America could be a nation of half free labor and half slave labor, then it would be easy for both the North and South to embrace the inferiority of Blacks as a theory of the American social order during the period of reconciliation of the nation—which is what occurred. This belief that Black lives are inferior to White lives when they come into conflict, as discussed in Chapters Four, Seven, and Eight, is a curse that has plagued the politics and policies of the United States to this day and is reflected in use of force and treatment of Blacks by the police and the disproportionate incarceration of Blacks by the criminal justice system as discussed in Chapters Three, Six, and Seven.

Before the abandonment of the true reason for the amendments, the Court, in a moment of clarity, provided an honest summation of the Civil War Amendments. In the *Slaughter House Cases* (1873), the Court explained

> [t]he institution of African slavery, as it existed in about half the States of the Union, and the contests pervading the public mind for many years between those who desired its curtailment and ultimate extinction and those who desired additional safeguards for its security and perpetuation, culminated in the effort, on the part of most of the States in which slavery existed, to separate from the Federal government and to resist its authority. This constituted the war of the rebellion, and whatever auxiliary causes may have contributed to bring about this war, undoubtedly the overshadowing and efficient cause was African slavery.
>
> In that struggle, slavery, as a legalized social relation, perished. It perished as a necessity of the bitterness and force of the conflict. When the armies of freedom found themselves upon the soil of slavery, they could do nothing less than free the poor victims whose enforced servitude was the foundation of the quarrel. And when hard-pressed in the contest, these men (for they proved themselves men in that terrible crisis) offered their services and were accepted by thousands to aid in suppressing the unlawful rebellion,

62 Abraham Lincoln, "House Divided Speech," (speech, Illinois Republican State Convention, June 16, 1858).

63 Abraham Lincoln, "Second Inaugural Address," (Washington DC, March 4, 1865).

> slavery was at an end wherever the Federal government succeeded in that purpose. The proclamation of President Lincoln expressed an accomplished fact as to a large portion of the insurrectionary districts when he declared slavery abolished in them all. But the war being over, those who had succeeded in reestablishing the authority of the Federal government were not content to permit this great act of emancipation to rest on the actual results of the contest or the proclamation of the Executive, both of which might have been questioned in after times, and they determined to place this main and most valuable result in the Constitution of the restored Union as one of its fundamental articles. Hence, the thirteenth article of amendment of that instrument.

In regard to the Thirteenth Amendment (1865), which ended "involuntary servitude," the Court held

> [t]he word servitude is of larger meaning than slavery, as the latter is popularly understood in this country, and the obvious purpose was to forbid all shades and conditions of African slavery. It was very well understood that, in the form of apprenticeship for long terms, as it had been practiced in the West India Islands, on the abolition of slavery by the English government, or by reducing the slaves to the condition of serfs attached to the plantation, the purpose of the article might have been evaded if only the word slavery had been used.

In regard to the justification and need for the Fourteenth Amendment (1868), the Court observed that

> notwithstanding the formal recognition by those States of the abolition of slavery, the condition of the slave race would, without further protection of the Federal government, be almost as bad as it was before. Among the first acts of legislation adopted by several of the States in the legislative bodies which claimed to be in their normal relations with the Federal government were laws which imposed upon the colored race onerous disabilities and burdens and curtailed their rights in the pursuit of life, liberty, and property to such an extent that their freedom was of little value, while they had lost the protection which they had received from their former owners from motives both of interest and humanity.
>
> They were in some States forbidden to appear in the towns in any other character than menial servants. They were required to reside on and cultivate the soil without the right to purchase or own it. They were excluded from many occupations of gain, and were not permitted to give testimony in the courts in any case where a white man was a party. It was said that their lives were at the mercy of bad men, either because the laws for their protection were insufficient or were not enforced.
>
> These circumstances, whatever of falsehood or misconception may have been mingled with their presentation, forced upon the statesmen who had conducted the Federal government in safety through the crisis of the rebellion, and who supposed that, by the thirteenth article of amendment, they had secured the result of their labors, the conviction

> that something more was necessary in the way of constitutional protection to the unfortunate race who had suffered so much. They accordingly passed through Congress the proposition for the fourteenth amendment ...

The Court finished its review of the Civil War Amendments by observing that the purpose of the Fifteenth Amendment (1870) became clear when

> [a] few years' [of] experience satisfied the thoughtful men who had been the authors of the other two amendments that, notwithstanding the restraints of those articles on the States and the laws passed under the additional powers granted to Congress, these were inadequate for the protection of life, liberty, and property, without which freedom to the slave was no boon. They were in all those States denied the right of suffrage. The laws were administered by the white man alone. It was urged that a race of men distinctively marked, as was the negro, living in the midst of another and dominant race, could never be fully secured in their person and their property without the right of suffrage.
> Hence, the fifteenth amendment ... .

As to the application and meaning of the Civil War Amendments, the purpose and history of all three amendments, the Court concluded

> no one can fail to be impressed with the one pervading purpose found in them all, lying at the foundation of each, and without which none of them would have been even suggested; we mean the freedom of the slave race, the security and firm establishment of that freedom, and the protection of the newly made freeman and citizen from the oppressions of those who had formerly exercised unlimited dominion over him.[64]

The Court in 1873 wrote emphatically that the Civil Rights Amendments were intended to protect the former slave and to address the "oppressions of those who had formerly exercised unlimited dominion over him" by prohibiting involuntary servitude, which meant making unlawful any action that had the effect of "reducing the slaves to the condition of serfs attached to the plantation" after the war. Nevertheless, the Court ruled in the *Slaughter Houses Cases* that the amendments did not reach private discrimination, private discrimination being the true venue and vector of being reduced to the condition of serfs. Private discrimination along with allowing states, by statute, to enforce individual discrimination was the death of what presidents Lincoln and Garfield advocated for. It would be almost a century before Black legal and social equality would return as a goal of presidential rhetoric and government policy. As the nation tired of the Reconstruction years (1865–1877)[65] and the problem of the former slaves, so did the Court. In 1883 in the *Civil Rights Cases*, the Court held that Blacks must

---

64 *The Slaughter-House Cases*, 83 U.S. 36, 68–71 (1873). The Court affirmed the historical purpose of the Civil War Amendments in *Jones v. Alfred H. Mayer Co.*, 392 U.S. 409, 422–37 (1968).

65 The exact date of the beginning of Reconstruction has been subject to scholarly debate in which some date the beginning with Emancipation Proclamation issued by President Lincoln on January 1, 1863, or when the

"cease to be the special favorite of the laws and mere discriminations on account of race or color are not regarded as badges of slavery," and by 1896, the Court said in *Plessy*

> [w]e consider the underlying fallacy of the plaintiff's argument to consist in the assumption that the enforced separation of the two races stamps the colored race with a badge of inferiority. If this be so, it is not by reason of anything found in the act, but solely because the colored race chooses to put that construction upon it.

Racism was the underpinning of the *American* brand of slavery. When slavery ended, racism remained. When Northern tempers cooled after Reconstruction—coupled with the rise of the Southern "Lost Cause of the Confederacy Theory" during Reconstruction and the adoption Social Darwinism and Scientific Racism by American political and social elites in the late nineteenth century—there was a total abandonment of federal power to protect the rights of the former slaves, of whom the Court said in *Dred Scott*, Blacks "***had no rights which the White man was bound to respect.***"[66] Racism has a long and evolving consistent history, from the *Zong Massacre Case* (1783), ("[if] the Slaves are kill'd they will be paid for them as much as for Damages done for goods and it is frequently done, just as if horses")[67] to *Dred Scott* (1857) to the *Civil Rights Cases* (1883) ("Mere discriminations on account of race or color were not regarded as badges of slavery")[68] to *Plessy v. Ferguson* (1896) ("enforced separation of the two races stamps the colored race with a badge of inferiority. If this be so, it is ... but solely because the colored race chooses to put that construction upon it").[69]

Even the great dissenter, Justice Harlan, was in line with the approach of Social Darwinism and the inherent inferiority of Blacks—as he wrote in his famous dissent in *Plessy*, "***The white race deems itself to be the dominant race in this country. And so it is in prestige, in achievements, in education, in wealth and in power. So, I doubt not, it will continue to be***

North won the Civil War and the South formally surrendered on April 9, 1865, or when the radical Republicans took control of the House and Senate in March 1867 after the elections of 1866. See Michelle Alexander, *The New Jim Crow*, at 35 (2010), Douglas A. Blackmon, *Slavery by Another Name: The Re-Enslavement of Black Americans from the Civil war to World War II* (2008) and C. Vann Woodward, *The Strange Career of Jim Crow* at 6 (1955).

But the end of Reconstruction is uniformly defined by scholars as March 2, 1877, when the Republicans promised Southern Democrats that they would withdrew federal troops from the South if they would support the election of Hayes. Such was the Compromise of 1877 which allowed Republican Rutherford B. Hayes to ascend to the presidency on March 4, 1877, after the disputed election of 1876. See Roy Morris Jr., *Fraud of the Century: Rutherford B. Hayes, Samuel Tilden, and the Stolen Election of 1876* (2004), Eric Foner, *Reconstruction: America's Unfinished Revolution, 1863–1877* (1988), and Lloyd Robinson, *The Stolen Election: Hayes versus Tilden–1876* (1968).

66 The *Dred Scott Case*, 60 U.S. 393, 407 (1857).

67 *Gregson v. Gilbert* (1783) (3 Doug. KB 232).

68 *Civil Rights Cases*, 109 U.S. 3, 25 (1883).

69 *Plessy v. Ferguson*, 163 U.S. 537, 544, 551 (1896).

for all time."[70] Harlan's dissent on this point is telling, for he believed that that the White race was superior to the Black race on social and political levels and that White superiority would be maintained, in part, by its fidelity to equality before the law. His point was that the recognition and assertion of Whites being superior belongs to social interaction, but not to the operation of justice and equality under the law in the courts. Harlan wrote,

> ***The white race deems itself to be the dominant race in this country. And so it is* in prestige, in achievements, in education, in wealth and in power. So, I doubt not, it will continue to be for all time if it remains true to its great heritage and holds fast to the principles of constitutional liberty.** But in view of the Constitution, in the eye of the law, there is in this country no superior, dominant, ruling class of citizens. There is no caste here. *Our Constitution is color-blind*, and neither knows nor tolerates classes among citizens. In respect of civil rights, all citizens are equal before the law. The humblest is the peer of the most powerful. The law regards man as man, and takes no account of his surroundings or of his color when his civil rights as guaranteed by the supreme law of the land are involved. It is therefore to be regretted that this high tribunal, the final expositor of the fundamental law of the land, has reached the conclusion that it is competent for a State to regulate the enjoyment by citizens of their civil rights solely upon the basis of race.
>
> In my opinion, the judgment this day rendered will, in time, prove to be quite as pernicious as the decision made by this tribunal in the *Dred Scott Case*. ... But it seems that we have yet, in some of the States, a dominant race—a superior class of citizens, which assumes to regulate the enjoyment of civil rights, common to all citizens, upon the basis of race. The present decision ... will encourage the belief that it is possible, by means of state enactments, to defeat the beneficent purposes which the people of the United States had in view when they adopted the recent amendments of the Constitution, by one of which the blacks of this country were made citizens of the United States and of the States in which they respectively reside, and whose privileges and immunities, as citizens, the States are forbidden to abridge. ... What can more certainly arouse race hate, what more certainly create and perpetuate a feeling of distrust between these races, than state enactments which, in fact, proceed on the ground that colored citizens are so inferior and degraded that they cannot be allowed to sit in public coaches occupied by white citizens. That, as all will admit, is the real meaning of such legislation as was enacted in Louisiana.[71]

This conception of the law only requiring equality in process, not outcome in the application of the law, would form the basis for the modern arguments on the meaning of due process of law and equal protection of the law in both government regulation of business in the late nineteenth and early twentieth centuries, as well as in the modern civil rights movement in

70 *Plessy v. Ferguson*.at 559.

71 *Plessy v. Ferguson* at 559–60 (emphasis added).

the 1960s and arguments over affirmative action in the 1970s through the early twenty-first century.[72]

The social and racial inferiority of Blacks notwithstanding, Harlan argued that under the law, Blacks and Whites were equal, because that was what the Civil War and the Civil War Amendments established.

> The sure guarantee of the peace and security of each race is the clear, distinct, unconditional recognition by our governments, National and State, of every right that inheres in civil freedom, and of the equality before the law of all citizens of the United States, without regard to race. State enactments regulating the enjoyment of civil rights upon the basis of race, and cunningly devised to defeat legitimate results of the war under the pretence of recognizing equality of rights, can have no other result than to render permanent peace impossible and to keep alive a conflict of races the continuance of which must do harm to all concerned. This question is not met by the suggestion that social equality cannot exist between the white and black races in this country. That argument, if it can be properly regarded as one, is scarcely worthy of consideration, for social equality no more exists between two races when traveling in a passenger coach or a public highway than when members of the same races sit by each other in a street car or in the jury box, or stand or sit with each other in a political assembly, or when they use in common the street of a city or town, or when they are in the same room for the purpose of having their names placed on the registry of voters, or when they approach the ballot box in order to exercise the high privilege of voting.
>
> There is a race so different from our own that we do not permit those belonging to it to become citizens of the United States. Persons belonging to it are, with few exceptions, absolutely excluded from our country. I allude to the Chinese race. But, by the statute in question, a Chinaman can ride in the same passenger coach with white citizens of the United States, while citizens of the black race in Louisiana, many of whom, perhaps, risked their lives for the preservation of the Union, who are entitled, by law, to participate in the political control of the State and nation, who are not excluded, by law or by reason of their race, from public stations of any kind, and who have all the legal rights that belong to white citizens, are yet declared to be criminals, liable to imprisonment, if they ride in a public coach occupied by citizens of the white race. It is scarcely just to say that a colored citizen should not object to occupying a public coach assigned to his own race. He does not object, nor, perhaps, would he object to separate coaches for his race if his rights under the law were recognized. But he objecting, and ought never to cease objecting, to the proposition that citizens of the white and black race can be adjudged criminals because they sit, or claim the right to sit, in the same public coach on a public highway.

---

72 For discussion on the historical development on the meaning of the rule of law see, Arthur H. Garrison, "The Traditions and History of the Meaning of the Rule of Law," *Georgetown Journal of Law & Public Policy* 12 no. 2 (2014): 565.

> The arbitrary separation of citizens on the basis of race while they are on a public highway is a badge of servitude wholly inconsistent with the civil freedom and the equality before the law established by the Constitution. It cannot be justified upon any legal grounds.[73]

THE SUPREME COURT AND ITS ABANDONMENT OF JIM CROW: THE RISE OF CONSTITUTIONAL RIGHTS AND THE RESURRECTION OF THE CIVIL WAR AMENDMENTS

The Supreme Court, like American politics, would eventually change and find room for Blacks under the Constitution. The Court initiated its defense of Black rights with its famous holding in *Brown v. Board of Education* in 1954.[74] *Plessy* established separate but equal, which had become a foundational concept for Jim Crow laws. After fifty-eight years, Thurgood Marshall and lawyers from the National Association for the Advancement of Colored People Legal Defense Fund launched a direct assault on the concept by arguing to the Supreme Court that separate but equal had no place in education, that separate but equal was a violation of due process and equal protection of law under the Fourteenth Amendment, and separate but equal was solely based on the idea of inferiority of Blacks compared to Whites.

The Court originally heard arguments in December 1952, and Marshall argued that *Plessy* should be overruled and that the Court hold that the Fourteenth Amendment prohibits segregated schools based on race. The Court ordered that rearguments be submitted in December 1953 on the question of whether the drafters of the Fourteenth Amendment intended the amendment to prohibit segregated schools based on race. The Court issued its opinion on May 17, 1954.

The Court concluded that its requested research and argument on the question provided no clear cut answer. The Court explained that,

> Reargument was largely devoted to the circumstances surrounding the adoption of the Fourteenth Amendment in 1868. It covered exhaustively consideration of the Amendment in Congress, ratification by the states, then-existing practices in racial segregation, and the views of proponents and opponents of the Amendment. This discussion and our own investigation convince us that, although these sources cast some light, it is not enough to resolve the problem with which we are faced. At best, they are inconclusive.[75]

The Court further explained that history was of little help, because public education was, at best, in its infancy and had no status in the South at the time the Fourteenth Amendment was

---

73 *Plessy v. Ferguson*, 162 U.S. at 560–62.

74 Brown v. Board of Education, 347 U.S. 483 (1954).

75 *Brown v. Board of Education* at 489.

drafted and ratified by the states. Having found that legal history provided no clear answer as to whether the Fourteenth Amendment prohibited segregation in schools based on race, the Court wrote that

> In approaching this problem, we cannot turn the clock back to 1868, when the Amendment was adopted, or even to 1896, when *Plessy v. Ferguson* was written. We must consider public education in the light of its full development and its present place in American life throughout the Nation. Only in this way can it be determined if segregation in public schools deprives these plaintiffs of the equal protection of the laws.[76]

The Court asserted that education was foundational to citizenship and the success of all children. The Court explained that,

> [t]oday, education is perhaps the most important function of state and local governments. Compulsory school attendance laws and the great expenditures for education both demonstrate our recognition of the importance of education to our democratic society. It is required in the performance of our most basic public responsibilities, even service in the armed forces. It is the very foundation of good citizenship. Today it is a principal instrument in awakening the child to cultural values, in preparing him for later professional training, and in helping him to adjust normally to his environment. In these days, it is doubtful that any child may reasonably be expected to succeed in life if he is denied the opportunity of an education. Such an opportunity, where the state has undertaken to provide it, is a right which must be made available to all on equal terms.
>
> We come then to the question presented: does segregation of children in public schools solely on the basis of race, even though the physical facilities and other "tangible" factors may be equal, deprive the children of the minority group of equal educational opportunities? We believe that it does.[77]

In *Plessy*, the Court held that to place a meaning of imposed Black inferiority on "separate but equal" policies was a decision made by Blacks not Whites. The significance of the *Brown* decision is the that the Court abandoned *Plessy* and held regarding Black and White children in public school, "To separate them from others of similar age and qualifications solely because of their race generates a feeling of inferiority as to their status in the community that may affect their hearts and minds in a way unlikely ever to be undone."[78] Justice Harlan's dissent in *Plessy* found affirmance in *Brown* when Chief Justice Warren affirmed that separate but equal was based on the idea that the Black race was too inferior to be allowed to sit with the White race in the same classroom. Chief Justice Warren affirmed the district court in Kansas and its conclusion that

---

76 *Brown v. Board of Education* at 492–93.

77 *Brown v. Board of Education* at 493.

78 *Brown v. Board of Education* at 494.

> [s]egregation of white and colored children in public schools has a detrimental effect upon the colored children. The impact is greater when it has the sanction of the law; for the policy of separating the races is usually interpreted as denoting the inferiority of the negro group. A sense of inferiority affects the motivation of a child to learn. Segregation with the sanction of law, therefore, has a tendency to [retard] the educational and mental development of negro children and to deprive them of some of the benefits they would receive in a racial[ly] integrated school system.[79]

The Court famously concluded,

> [w]hatever may have been the extent of psychological knowledge at the time of *Plessy v. Ferguson*, this finding is amply supported by modern authority. Any language in *Plessy v. Ferguson* contrary to this finding is rejected.
>
> We conclude that, in the field of public education, the doctrine of "separate but equal" has no place. Separate educational facilities are inherently unequal. Therefore, we hold that the plaintiffs and others similarly situated for whom the actions have been brought are, by reason of the segregation complained of, deprived of the equal protection of the laws guaranteed by the Fourteenth Amendment. This disposition makes unnecessary any discussion whether such segregation also violates the Due Process Clause of the Fourteenth Amendment.
>
> ... On reargument, the consideration of appropriate relief was necessarily subordinated to the primary question—the constitutionality of segregation in public education. We have now announced that such segregation is a denial of the equal protection of the laws.[80]

The Court ordered additional argument on how the *Brown* decision should be implemented, and as discussed in Chapter Four, Southern Democrats and Republicans fought the full implementation of *Brown* for more than twenty years. Nevertheless, *Brown* ushered in the rise of the modern civil rights movement and, within a decade, Congress passed legislation that broke the back of Jim Crow.

Brown notwithstanding, *United States v. Harris* and *Civil Rights Cases* are still valid case law regarding the meaning of the Fourteenth Amendment and that it only applies to government discrimination and not to private discrimination and that Congress has no authority to prevent private discrimination based on race under the Fourteenth Amendment. In *United States v. Morrison* (2000), the Court wrote regarding *United States v. Harris*,

> the Court considered a challenge to § 2 of the Civil Rights Act of 1871. That section sought to punish 'private persons' for 'conspiring to deprive anyone of the equal protection of the laws enacted by the State.' 106 U. S., 4. at 639. We concluded that this law exceeded Congress' § 5 power because the law was 'directed exclusively against the action of private

79 *Brown v. Board of Education*.

80 *Brown v. Board of Education* at 494–95.

> persons, without reference to the laws of the State, or their administration by her officers.' *Id.*, at 640. In so doing, we reemphasized our statement from *Virginia* v. *Rives,* 100 U. S. 313, 318 (1880), that 'these provisions of the fourteenth amendment have reference to State action exclusively, and not to any action of private individuals.[81]

In *Morrison*, the Court affirmed *Harris* and held that

> the language and purpose of the Fourteenth Amendment place certain limitations on the manner in which Congress may attack discriminatory conduct. These limitations are necessary to prevent the Fourteenth Amendment from obliterating the Framers' carefully crafted balance of power between the States and the National Government. ... Foremost among these limitations is the time-honored principle that the Fourteenth Amendment, by its very terms, prohibits only state action. ... Shortly after the Fourteenth Amendment was adopted, we decided [in] ... the *Civil Rights Cases* ... that the public accommodation provisions of the Civil Rights Act of 1875, which applied to purely private conduct, were beyond the scope of the § 5 [of the Fourteenth Amendment] enforcement power. ... "The fourteenth amendment prohibits a state from depriving any person of life, liberty, or property, without due process of law; but this adds nothing to the rights of one citizen as against another. It simply furnishes an additional guaranty against any encroachment by the States upon the fundamental rights which belong to every citizen as a member of society." [*United States v. Cruikshank*, 92 U. S. 542, 554 (1876)]. ... We believe that the description of the § 5 power contained in the *Civil Rights Cases* is correct [82]

But, the Court found a way to affirm the limitations of the Fourteenth Amendment and still provide Congress with the power to break Jim Crow. Ten years after *Brown*, the Court limited the impact of the conclusion in *Harris* by holding Congress has the authority to implement modern civil rights laws based on the commerce clause of the Constitution. In the famous case of Ollie's Barbeque, *Heart of Atlanta Motel v. United States* in 1964, the Court held,

> In light of our ground for decision, it might be well at the outset to discuss the *Civil Rights Cases, supra,* which declared provisions of the Civil Rights Act of 1875 unconstitutional. 18 Stat. 335, 336. We think that decision inapposite and without precedential value in determining the constitutionality of the present Act. Unlike Title II of the present legislation, the 1875 Act broadly proscribed discrimination in "inns, public conveyances on land or water, theaters, and other places of public amusement," without limiting the categories of affected businesses to those impinging upon interstate commerce. In contrast, the applicability of Title II is carefully limited to enterprises having a direct and substantial relation to the interstate flow of goods and people, except where state action is involved. Further, the fact that certain kinds of businesses may not in 1875 have been

81 *United States v. Morrison*, 529 U.S. 598, 621 (2000).

82 *United States v. Morrison* at 620–22, 624 (2000).

> sufficiently involved in interstate commerce to warrant bringing them within the ambit of the commerce power is not necessarily dispositive of the same question today.[83]

The Court in *Morrison*, which affirmed *Harris*, affirmed that Congress can regulate private behavior through the Commerce Clause under three categories.

> First, Congress may regulate the use of the channels of interstate commerce. (citing *Heart of Atlanta Motel, Inc. v. United States*, 379 U. S. 241, 256 (1964); *United States v. Darby*, 312 U. S. 100, 114 (1941)). Second, Congress is empowered to regulate and protect the instrumentalities of interstate commerce, or persons or things in interstate commerce, even though the threat may come only from intrastate activities. Finally, Congress' commerce authority includes the power to regulate those activities having a substantial relation to interstate commerce ... i.e., those activities that substantially affect interstate commerce.[84]

Because racial discrimination in hotel lodging touches interstate commerce—the flow of people between states and the ability to travel and have a place to stay at night during that travel—Congress through the commerce clause had the ability to regulate individual behavior.

In 1968 the Court, without specifically reversing the *Civil Rights Cases*, held in *Jones v. Alfred H. Mayer Co.*(1968) that Congress can prohibit private housing discrimination under the Thirteenth Amendment.[85] This case, along with the Civil Rights Act of 1968 marked the end of systematic Jim Crow as a matter of law.

The Court held (see appendix) in *Jones* that section 42 U.S.C. § 1982 (Civil Rights Act of 1866) in its original form paraphrased the Fourteenth Amendment ("All persons born or naturalized in the United States, and subject to the jurisdiction thereof, are citizens of the United States"), which is applicable to the states and that the modern draft of section 1982 ("All citizens of the United States shall have the same right, in every State and Territory, as is enjoyed by white citizens thereof to inherit, purchase, lease, sell, hold, and convey real and personal property") can be enforced under section 2 of the Thirteenth Amendment. What distinguished the *Civil Rights Cases* from *Jones* was that the former was based on interpretation of section 1 of the Thirteenth Amendment. Section 1 focused on meaning and applicability of ending "involuntary servitude." *Jones* involved the interpretation and application of section 2 and Congressional power "to enforce this article by appropriate legislation."

The Court in *Jones* held that Congress could prohibit racial discrimination in housing, although private individuals were imposing the discrimination, by affirming the purpose of the Thirteenth Amendment in the *Slaughter House Cases*—"The word servitude is of

---

83 Heart of Atlanta Motel v. United States, 379 U.S. 241, 250–51 (1964).

84 *United States v. Morrison*, 529 U.S. 598, 609 (2000).

85 *Jones v. Alfred H. Mayer Co. at* 437–44 (1968). For further discussion, see Darrell A. H. Miller, "White Cartels, the Civil Rights Act of 1866, and the History of Jones v. Alfred H. Mayer Co," *Fordham L. Rev.* 77 (2008): 999.

larger meaning than slavery … the obvious purpose was to forbid all shades and conditions of African slavery … reducing the slaves to the condition of serfs attached to the plantation. … " The Court in *Jones* held that Congress has broad latitude in interpreting the meaning of the phrase "involuntary servitude" under section 1 and, as such, under section 2 ("Congress shall have power to enforce this article") Congress can prohibit what constitutes badges of slavery. The Court concluded that Congress had the authority under section 2 to determine that racial discrimination in housing constitutes an act of involuntary servitude.

****

Justice Brown's opinion in *Plessy* (1896) that segregation by law had nothing to do with enforced views of inferiority, and Justice Bradley's opinion in the *Civil Rights Cases* (1883) that the federal government had no power to prohibit private discrimination based on race would prevail for more than half a century until Thurgood Marshall challenged the assertion in *Brown v. Board of Education* in 1954, in which Chief Justice Warren held that *separate but equal* had no place in American education,[86] and Congress passed the Civil Rights Act of 1964.

While facial Jim Crow discrimination was wiped from the books of American statutory and constitutional law by the end of the 1960s, the effect of being Black within the functioning of American criminal justice has been more intractable. As discussed in Chapter Three, the concept of race and racism has influenced how police treat Blacks. In Chapter Six, we return to race and policing and look at a case study of this interaction in New York City regarding the use of the police tactic of stop and frisk.

KEY CONCEPTS, CASES AND DOCUMENTS

1. The Zong Massacre case (*Gregson v. Gillbert*) (1783)
2. *Somerset v. Stewart* (1772)
3. The Genesis story of Noah and his sons
4. The eulogy by Rev. Phineas Gurley (1862)
5. Abraham Lincoln's "Meditation on the Divine Will" (1862)
6. Post-Christian America
7. Black Christian Church theology
8. Narrative of An American Slave (1845)
9. Nobles Oblige and White Man's Burden
10. *Dred Scott Case* (1857)
11. Abraham Lincoln speech on *Dred Scott* (1857)

86 *Brown v. Board of Education*, 347 U.S. 483 (1954).

12. The Missouri Compromise (1850)
13. The Kansas-Nebraska Act of 1854
14. House Divided Speech (1858)
15. Lincoln Second Inaugural Address (1865)
16. The Civil War Amendments: Thirteenth, Fourteenth and Fifteenth
17. *The Slaughterhouse Cases* (1873)
18. *United States v. Cruikshank* (1876)
19. The Civil Rights Act of 1866
20. *The Civil Rights Cases* (1883)
21. *United States v. Harris* (1883)
22. *Virginia v. Rives* (1880)
23. *Plessy v. Ferguson* (1896)
24. *Brown v. Board of Education* (1954)
25. *Heart of Atlanta Motel v. United States* (1964)
26. *Jones v. Alfred H. Mayer* (1968)
27. *United States v. Morrison* (2000)

KEY PEOPLE

1. Lord Chief Judge William Mansfield
2. Frederick Douglass
3. Abraham Lincoln

DISCUSSION QUESTIONS

1. This chapter asserted that America is now a post-Christian nation in which the Bible is no longer a standard of right and wrong in social, political, and policy debates. Assume that is correct; why does it matter? Does it matter?
2. What is the significance of the *Somerset v. Stewart*, *Zong Massacre*, and *Dred Scott* cases to the issue of law and order and whether Blacks are equal under the law in relation to how Blacks are treated by the police today? Is there a relationship?
3. How did Lincoln view the Civil War? How did the war change over time in his mind? Why does that matter? Does it matter? How did the country view the purpose of the war over time? How did the Court reflect that change from the *Civil Rights Cases* to *Brown v. Board of Education*?
4. Why does it matter that White Christians used the Bible to justify slavery? How does the use of the Bible during slavery reflect current issues of social justice, criminal justice reform, and how the Black church advocates the meaning of the Bible in relation to stop and frisk, drug crime policy, and the incarceration of Black men?

5. Consider the Supreme Court opinion in *Dred Scott* (1857) ("they had no rights which the white man was bound to respect"), the *Civil Rights Cases* (1883), ("Mere discriminations on account of race or color were not regarded as badges of slavery"), *Plessy v. Ferguson* (1896) ("enforced separation of the two races stamps the colored race with a badge of inferiority. If this be so, it is ... but solely because the colored race chooses to put that construction upon it"), and Justice Harlan's dissent in *Plessy* ("The white race deems itself to be the dominant race in this country. And so it is in prestige, in achievements, in education, in wealth and in power. So, I doubt not, it will continue to be for all time ... "). Are these opinions still relevant to understanding criminal justice politics and policy today? Can these opinions be explained and found in current debates regarding Black crime and whether disproportionate minority confinement is the result of racism or by disproportionate criminality of Blacks? Can an argument be made that slavery and racism is over in America, and negative disproportionate involvement with the criminal justice system is a cultural problem that Blacks must solve.

Appendix

Jones v. Alfred H. Mayer Co
392 U.S. 409, 412, 417, 420–24, 437–39 (1968) (emphasis added)

In this case, we are called upon to determine the scope and the constitutionality of an Act of Congress, 42 U.S.C. § 1982 which provides that:

> All citizens of the United States shall have the same right, in every State and Territory, as is enjoyed by white citizens thereof to inherit, purchase lease, sell, hold, and convey real and personal property.

...

We begin with the language of the statute itself. In plain and unambiguous terms, § 1982 grants to all citizens, without regard to race or color, "the same right" to purchase and lease property "as is enjoyed by white citizens."

...

On its face, therefore, § 1982 appears to prohibit all discrimination against Negroes in the sale or rental of property—discrimination by private owners as well as discrimination by public authorities. Indeed, even the respondents seem to concede that, if § 1982 "means what it says"—to use the words of the respondents' brief—then it must encompass every racially motivated refusal to sell or rent, and cannot be confined to officially sanctioned segregation in housing. Stressing what they consider to be the revolutionary implications of so literal a reading of § 1982, the respondents argue that Congress cannot possibly have intended any such result. Our examination of the relevant history, however, persuades us that Congress meant exactly what it said.

...

In its original form, 42 U.S.C. § 1982 was part of § 1 of the Civil Rights Act of 1866. That section was cast in sweeping terms:

> *Be it enacted by the Senate and House of Representatives of the United States of America in Congress assembled*, That all persons born in the United States and not subject to any foreign power, ... are hereby declared to be citizens of the United States, and such citizens, of every race and color, without regard to any previous condition of slavery or involuntary servitude, ... shall have the same right, in every State and Territory in the United States, to make and enforce contracts, to sue, be parties, and give evidence, to inherit, purchase, lease, sell, hold, and convey real and personal property, and to full and equal benefit of all laws and proceedings for the security of person and property, as is enjoyed by white citizens, and shall be subject to like punishment, pains, and penalties, and to none other, any law, statute, ordinance, regulation, or custom, to the contrary notwithstanding. ...

To the Congress that passed the Civil Rights Act of 1866, it was clear that the right to do these things might be infringed not only by "State or local law", but also by "custom, or prejudice." Thus, when Congress provided in § 1 of the Civil Rights Act that the right to purchase and lease property was to be enjoyed equally throughout the United States by Negro and White citizens alike, it plainly meant to secure that right against interference from any source whatever, whether governmental or private.

...

The remaining question is whether Congress has power under the Constitution to do what § 1982 purports to do: to prohibit all racial discrimination, private and public, in the sale and rental of property. Our starting point is the Thirteenth Amendment ...

As its text reveals, the Thirteenth Amendment is not a mere prohibition of State laws establishing or upholding slavery, but an absolute declaration that slavery or involuntary servitude shall not exist in any part of the United States. ...

Thus, the fact that § 1982 operates upon the unofficial acts of private individuals, whether or not sanctioned by state law, presents no constitutional problem. If Congress has power under the Thirteenth Amendment to eradicate conditions that prevent Negroes from buying and renting property because of their race or color, then no federal statute calculated to achieve that objective can be thought to exceed the constitutional power of Congress simply because it reaches beyond state action to regulate the conduct of private individuals. The constitutional question in this case, therefore, comes to this: does the authority of Congress to enforce the Thirteenth Amendment "by appropriate legislation" include the power to eliminate all racial barriers to the acquisition of real and personal property? We think the answer to that question is plainly yes.

"By its own unaided force and effect," the Thirteenth Amendment "abolished slavery, and established universal freedom." *Civil Rights Cases*, 109 U.S. 3, 20. *Whether or not the Amendment itself did any more than that—a question not involved in this case—it is at least clear that the Enabling Clause of that Amendment empowered Congress to do much more. For that clause clothed "Congress with power to pass all laws necessary and proper for abolishing all badges and incidents of slavery in the United States"* Ibid.

CHAPTER SIX

Case Study in Police and Race

THE NYPD STOP AND FRISK CIVIL CASE

STUDENT LEARNING OBJECTIVES

1. Students will be able to explain what the New York City Police Department (NYPD) stop-and-frisk program was and why the U.S. District Court held that it violated the Fourth Amendment and the Equal Protection Clause of the Fourteenth Amendment.
2. Students will be able to differentiate between an investigatory tool and a crime suppression tool in policing. Students will be able to discuss and apply *Terry v. Ohio* to the distinction between the two tools of policing.
3. Students will be able to differentiate between the police officer's ability to stop as compared to frisk a person under the Reasonable Articulable Suspicion (RAS) burden of proof and explain how Fourth Amendment jurisprudence allows a stop and frisk on a lower level of proof than probable cause.
4. Students will be able to explain and differentiate between general population and reported crime statistics benchmarks versus suspect race–descriptive benchmarks to establish a disproportionate police activity based on race resulting in violation of the Fourth and Fourteenth Amendments.
5. Students will be able to explain how the NYPD stop-and-frisk program was defended both on the level of constitutional construction and political rhetoric by officials of the NYPD and the Office of the Mayor of New York. Students will be able to explain how criminal justice policy is subject to political dynamics and debates and how elections can change those dynamics and debates and thus change the political policy.

****

Parts of this chapter have been adapted from Arthur H. Garrison, "NYPD Stop and Frisk, Perceptions of Criminals, Race and the Meaning of Terry v Ohio: A Content Analysis of Floyd, et al. v City of New York," *Rutgers Race & the Law Review*, vol. 15. *Rutgers Race & the Law Review*, 2014.

In Chapter Two, the Fourth Amendment was discussed regarding the constitutionality of police use of force, both deadly and non-deadly. The Fourth Amendment allows the police to use reasonable force in situations that call for the use of force and that the police can be civilly and criminally culpable for the use of such force if it was unreasonable in either justification or application. In this chapter, we return to the Fourth Amendment with a focus on the authority and power of the police to stop and search an individual on suspicion that a person may, the key word is may, be involved in criminal activity and the how the police make a determination that a crime may be afoot.

While the authority of the police to make such a stop is not in dispute, what is in great dispute is how the police determine if a crime is afoot. As discussed in Chapter Three, that determination can be made through unconscious bias that Blacks are, on sight, dangerous and criminal. This bias can color innocent behavior to look like possible criminal behavior worthy of further investigation. This chapter will review the Federal District Court decision in *Floyd et al. v. City of New York* in which the NYPD was sued over its application of stop and frisk. It was alleged that the NYPD was unconstitutionally using stop and frisk and was disproportionately targeting Blacks based on race, rather than criminal behavior.

The district court issued a one hundred and ninety-five-page opinion on the NYPD use of stop and frisk and it would be unrealistic to review every aspect of the opinion in this chapter. After a summary review of the decision, this chapter will specifically analyze why the district court rejected the NYPD assertion that the use of criminal statistics—suspect descriptive data—provides a justification for focusing police attention on individuals of a racial group in specific neighborhoods. Review of the court decision will be put in context by a review of how each party focused on the use of crime statistics to support and oppose the agreed result of the NYPD use of stop and frisk, the disproportionate contact with Blacks. This focus will include a review of the politics of stop and frisk and how two city mayors defended and opposed the NYPD stop-and-frisk program. Before the legal and political review of the NYPD program in application of stop and frisk, a summary of the key legal precedent of stop and frisk is provided.

THE PURPOSE AND ORIGIN OF STOP AND FRISK

The NYPD has a long history with stop and frisk dating back to the 1964 state statute and the Supreme Court decision in *Sibron v. New York*, the companion case to *Terry v. Ohio*, which held that the statute was constitutional.[1] In 1968, the Supreme Court held in the landmark

1 *See* NY CLS CPL § 140.50; *see Sibron v. New York*, 392 U.S. 40 (1968); *see also* Complaint Demand for Jury Trial, *supra* note 3, at 9; *see also* John Q. Barrett, "Deciding the Stop and Frisk Cases: A Look Inside the Supreme Court Conference," St. John's Law Review 72 (1998): 749.

NYPD officers are governed by state law, which defines stop and frisk in terms of *Terry* under *People v. DeBour*, 40 N.Y. 2d 210 (1976). The city asserted to the Court Appeals that:

case, *Terry v. Ohio*, that the police are authorized to stop a person on the street and intrude upon his/her liberty without a warrant if the police have,

> specific and articulable facts which, taken together with rational inferences from those facts, reasonably warrant that intrusion [a]nd in making that assessment it is imperative that the facts be judged against an objective standard: would the facts available to the officer at the moment of the seizure or the search 'warrant a man of reasonable caution in the belief' that the action taken was appropriate? *Anything less would invite intrusions* upon constitutionally guaranteed rights *based on nothing more substantial than inarticulate hunches*, a result this Court has consistently refused to sanction.[2]

More importantly, the Court made clear what that the law enforcement purpose of stop and frisk.

> One general interest is of course that of effective crime prevention and detection; it is this interest which underlies the recognition that a police officer may in appropriate circumstances and in an appropriate manner approach a person for *purposes of investigating possibly criminal behavior* even though there is no probable cause to make an arrest. It was this legitimate *investigative function* Officer McFadden was discharging when he decided to approach petitioner and his companions.[3]

Stop and frisk is an investigatory tool based on specific behavior, "a series of acts, each of them perhaps innocent in itself, but which taken together warranted further investigation."[4] Stop and frisk, under the Fourth Amendment, is not a tool of police deterrence; it is an investigatory tool to determine if otherwise innocent behavior is criminal behavior. As discussed below, the NYPD was using stop and frisk as a crime suppression tool in general and, specifically, as a tool to reduce gun violence.

> [t]he Court was also misguided in its belief that New York's *DeBour* standards provide a lesser degree of protection than federal law (SPA68; *see* A7094-95). In *DeBour*, the New York Court of Appeals set forth a four-tiered framework for evaluating street encounters: (1) the "request for information," requiring some objective, credible reason not necessarily indicative of criminality; (2) the "common-law right of inquiry," requiring a "founded suspicion that criminal activity is afoot;" (3) the "forcible stop and detention," requiring RAS [reasonable articulable suspicion]; and (4) arrest, which demands probable cause. *DeBour*, 40 N.Y. 2d at 222–23.
> Notably, the third level of *DeBour* tracks *Terry* in all respects.

David Floyd, Lalit Clarkson, Deon Dennis, David Ourlicht v. City of New York et al., Defendant – Appellants Merits Brief, Appeal to the U.S. Court of Appeals Second Circuit, 13-3088-cv (L), 13-3461-cv(CON) and 13-1352-cv(CON) (December 10, 2013) at 78.

2 *Terry v. Ohio*, 392 U.S. 1, 21–22 (1968) (internal citation omitted) (emphasis added).

3 *Terry v. Ohio* at 22 (emphasis added).

4 *Terry v. Ohio* at 22.

The Court then proceeded to discuss the second aspect of the tool, frisk. Here the Court focused on the issue of police safety as primary to the right to be free from government having physical contact with one's person without consent.

> We are now concerned with more than the governmental interest in investigating crime; in addition, there is the more immediate interest of the police officer in taking steps to assure himself that the person with whom he is dealing is not armed with a weapon that could unexpectedly and fatally be used against him. Certainly it would be unreasonable to require that police officers take unnecessary risks in the performance of their duties.
>
> ...
>
> [W]e cannot blind ourselves to the need for law enforcement officers to protect themselves and other prospective victims of violence in situations where they may lack probable cause for an arrest. When an officer is justified in believing that the individual whose suspicious behavior he is investigating at close range is armed and presently dangerous to the officer or to others, it would appear to be clearly unreasonable to deny the officer the power to take necessary measures to determine whether the person is in fact carrying a weapon and to neutralize the threat of physical harm.[5]

But, the Court was clear to explain that, although it recognized that the police, in making a reasonable stop based on articulable facts that rise to reasonable suspicion, have a right to protect themselves from the possibility of the presence of a weapon, that right of protection does not authorize an unlimited right to conduct a search. Because "[e]ven a limited search of the outer clothing for weapons constitutes a severe, though brief, intrusion upon cherished personal security, and it must surely be an annoying, frightening, and perhaps humiliating experience."[6] The Court concluded that

> Our evaluation of the proper balance that has to be struck in this type of case leads us to conclude that there must be a narrowly drawn authority to permit a reasonable search for weapons for the protection of the police officer, where he has reason to believe that he is dealing with an armed and dangerous individual, regardless of whether he has probable cause to arrest the individual for a crime. The officer need not be absolutely certain that the individual is armed; *the issue is whether a reasonably prudent man in the circumstances would be warranted in the belief that his safety or that of others was in danger.*[7]

As with the standard to make the stop, the Court held that "in determining whether the officer acted reasonably in such circumstances, due weight must be given, not to his inchoate and

---

5 *Terry v. Ohio* at 24.

6 *Terry v. Ohio* at 24–25.

7 *Terry v. Ohio.* at 27 (emphasis added).

unparticularized suspicion or 'hunch,' but to the specific reasonable inferences which he is entitled to draw from the facts in light of his experience."[8]

In the *Terry* case, the officer watched Terry and his companions, and their actions were indicative of possible robbery.[9] The officer's suspicions did not rise to the level of probable cause, but their actions were such that "[i]t would have been poor police work indeed for an officer of thirty years' experience in the detection of thievery from stores in this same neighborhood to have failed to investigate this behavior further."[10] As to the frisk, the Court held

> We cannot say his decision at that point to seize Terry and pat his clothing for weapons was the product of a volatile or inventive imagination, or was undertaken simply as an act of harassment; the record evidences the tempered act of a policeman who in the course of an investigation had to make a quick decision as to how to protect himself and others from possible danger, and took limited steps to do so.[11]

Again, focus on the justification of the stop and the frisk—investigation of possible criminal activity. "Inventive imagination" or acts of "harassment" do not authorize individual stops, and neither do objective crime pattern statistics, as the district court made clear in *Floyd*.

To conclude, a stop and frisk is an investigatory tool of law enforcement, not a tool of crime deterrence. The tool is justified under the following dynamics, as summarized by the Court in *Terry*. The Court said,

> We merely hold today that [1]where a police officer observes unusual conduct which leads him reasonably to conclude in light of his experience that criminal activity may be afoot [2] and that the persons with whom he is dealing may be armed and presently dangerous, [3] where in the course of investigating this behavior he identifies himself as a policeman and makes reasonable inquiries, and where nothing in the initial stages of the encounter serves to dispel his reasonable fear for his own or others' safety, [4] he is entitled for the protection of himself and others in the area to conduct a carefully limited search of the outer clothing of such persons in an attempt to discover weapons which might be used to assault him.[12]

The Court also made clear that how the search is conducted is equally constitutionally important as the limited justification of the search.

---

8 *Terry v. Ohio*. at 27.

9 *Terry v. Ohio* at 28.

10 *Terry v. Ohio* at 23.

11 "The sole justification of the search in the present situation is the protection of the police officer and others nearby, and it must therefore be confined in scope to an intrusion reasonably designed to discover guns, knives, clubs, or other hidden instruments for the assault of the police officer." *Terry v. Ohio*. at 29.

12 *Terry v. Ohio* at 30.

> [A] search which is reasonable at its inception may violate the Fourth Amendment by virtue of its intolerable intensity and scope. The scope of the search must be strictly tied to and justified by the circumstances which rendered its initiation permissible.
>
> ...
>
> The scope of the search in this case presents no serious problem in light of these standards. Officer McFadden patted down the outer clothing of petitioner and his two companions. He did not place his hands in their pockets or under the outer surface of their garments until he had felt weapons, and then he merely reached for and removed the guns. He never did invade Katz' person beyond the outer surfaces of his clothes, since he discovered nothing in his patdown which might have been a weapon. Officer McFadden confined his search strictly to what was minimally necessary to learn whether the men were armed and to disarm them once he discovered the weapons. He did not conduct a general exploratory search for whatever evidence of criminal activity he might find.[13]

FLOYD ET AL. V. CITY OF NEW YORK

On January 31, 2008, David Floyd and Lalit Clarkson filed suit against the City of New York (NYC), NYPD Commissioner Ray Kelly, the Mayor of New York Michael Bloomberg, and two NYPD police officers for violation of Floyd and Clarkson's Fourth Amendment, Fourteenth Amendment Equal Protection Clause, and statutory civil rights. The plaintiffs claimed that the police policy of stop and frisk (1) subjected them to stops and frisks without specific reasonable articulated suspicion, and (2) that the two police officers, who conducted the stop and frisks, were engaged in "implement[ing] and are continuing to enforce, encourage and sanction a policy, practice and/or custom of unconstitutional stops and frisks of city residents by the New York City Police Department ("NYPD")."[14] The Complaint asserted that "NYPD officers, in violation of the Equal protection Clause of the Fourteenth Amendment, often have used, and continue to use, race and/or national origin—not reasonable suspicion—as the determinative factors in deciding to stop and frisk individuals."[15] The actions of the NYPD are the "result of, and are directly and proximately caused by, policies, practices and/or customs devised, implemented and enforced by the city, Kelly and Bloomberg."[16] The civil suit sought injunctive relief to end the asserted unconstitutional policies, as well as compensatory damages, punitive damages, and attorney's fees.[17] In subsequent filings in the litigation, the plaintiffs withdrew claims for

---

13 *Terry v. Ohio* at 18–19, 29–30 (internal citation omitted).

14 Complaint Demand for Jury Trial at 1–2, Floyd and Clarkson v. City of N.Y., 959 F. Supp. 540 (2013) (No. 08 Civ. 1034 (SAS)).

15 Complaint Demand for Jury Trial at 1–2, *Floyd and Clarkson v. City of N.Y.* at 2.

16 Complaint Demand for Jury Trial at 1–2, *Floyd and Clarkson v. City of N.Y.*

17 Complaint Demand for Jury Trial at 1–2, *Floyd and Clarkson v. City of N.Y.* at 10–11.

damages, dismissed their claims against the individual officers, dropped subsequent petitions for relief under state law, and certified the case as a class action asserting federal civil rights violations (Fourth and Fourteenth Amendments) seeking only injunctive relief.[18]

Five years later, and after a nine-week bench trial (March 18 through May 20, 2013), District Judge Shira A. Scheindlin of the U.S. District Court Southern District of New York ruled that "[b]ased on the preponderance of the credible evidence,"[19] the plaintiffs had established that

> (1) The NYPD carries out more stops where there are more blacks and Hispanic residents, even when other relevant variables are held constant ...
> (2) Blacks and Hispanics are more likely than whites to be stopped within precincts and census tracts, even after controlling for other relevant variables ...
> (3) For the period 2004 through 2009, when any law enforcement action was taken following a stop, blacks were 30% more likely to be arrested (as supposed to receiving a summons) than whites, for the same suspected crime.
> (4) For the period 2004 through 2009, after controlling for suspected crime and precinct characteristics, blacks who were stopped were about 14% more likely—and Hispanics 9% more likely—than whites to be subjected to the use of force.
> (5) For the period 2004 through 2009, all else being equal, the odds of a stop resulting in any further enforcement action were 8% *lower* if the person stopped was black than if the person stopped was white. In addition, the greater the black population in a precinct, the less likely that a stop would result in a sanction. ...
> (6) 78% of stops during the class period were self-initiated.[20]

The court concluded that "[t]ogether, these results show that blacks are likely targeted for stops based on a lesser degree of objectivity founded suspicion than whites."[21] As discussed below, the city asserted that police attention and deployment in Black and Hispanic neighborhoods were not done due to race but were done due to crime patterns within neighborhoods and that race concentration in stops and frisks is an unfortunate fact of crime patterns in those neighborhoods with high rates of crime. The court was not convinced: "I reject the testimony of the City's experts that the race of crime suspects is the appropriate benchmark for measuring racial bias in stops. The City and its highest officials believe that blacks and Hispanics should be stopped at the same rate as their proportion of the local criminal suspect population."[22]

The court held that the stop and frisk policy of the NYPD was unconstitutional because it did not make a distinction between the population and the subpart of the population that that was involved in crime. The policy, in implementation, was too broad in its application

---

18 Floyd et al. v. City of N.Y., 959 F. Supp. 2d 540, 557, 572 n.100 (S.D.N.Y. 2013), *appeal dismissed* (Sept. 25, 2013).

19 *Floyd et al. v. City of N.Y.* at 565, 572 n.101.

20 *Floyd et al. v. City of N.Y.* at 560; 574–75 n.121.

21 *Floyd et al. v. City of N.Y.* at 560.

22 *Floyd et al. v. City of N.Y.* at 560.

because innocent Blacks and Hispanics were stopped based on race not behavior. The court concluded that the policy was "flawed because the stopped population is overwhelmingly innocent—not criminal. There is no basis for assuming that an innocent population shares the same characteristics as the criminal suspect population in the same area."[23] Even more importantly, there is no basis at all for assuming that the innocent Blacks and Hispanics who share the same neighborhood as Black and Hispanic criminals share the same characteristics or behaviors. It's the criminal behavior that should be the defining factor, not race. As discussed below, it is that distinction—behavior—that defines the constitutional right of police to conduct a stop and frisk.

The court further held that, "the NYPD has an unwritten policy of targeting 'the right people' for stops. In practice, the policy encourages the targeting of young Black and Hispanic men based on their prevalence in local crime complaints."[24] The court concluded that one of the alleged nineteen incidents was not a *Terry* stop at all; of the remaining eighteen incidents, ten were unconstitutional stops, and eight were constitutional stops; and of the fifteen

---

23 *Floyd et al. v. City of N.Y.*; To the contrary, the RAND Corporation 2007 evaluation of the NYPD stop and frisk program asserted that:

> [R]esidential census data—that is, the racial distribution of the general population in New York—possibly provide an estimate of the racial distribution of those exposed to police but do not reflect rates of criminal participation. As a result, external benchmarks based on the census have been widely discredited. The racial distribution of arrestees has been proposed as a more reliable benchmark. A more promising external benchmark is the racial distribution of individuals identified in crime-suspect descriptions, though this benchmark also has serious pitfalls.

The RAND report concluded that:

> Evaluating racial disparities in pedestrian stops using external benchmarks is highly sensitive to the choice of benchmark. Therefore, analyses based on any of the external benchmarks developed to date are questionable.
>
> Benchmarks based on crime-suspect descriptions may provide a good measure of the rates of participation in certain types of crimes by race, but being a valid benchmark requires that suspects, regardless of race, are equally exposed to police officers.
>
> We found that black pedestrians were stopped at a rate that is 20 to 30 percent lower than their representation in crime-suspect descriptions. Hispanic pedestrians were stopped disproportionately more, by 5 to 10 percent, than their representation among crime-suspect descriptions would predict.

Greg Ridgeway, RAND, *Analysis of Racial Disparities in The New York Police Department's Stop, Question, and Frisk Practices*, xi-xii (2007) [hereafter RAND Report].

24 *Floyd et al. v. City of N.Y.* at 561.

involving frisks, nine were unconstitutional, and six were constitutional.[25] Thus, the court found seventy-two percent of the named plaintiffs suffered a constitutional violation (thirteen suffered an unconstitutional stop and/or frisk, and five suffered no constitutional violations out of the eighteen total incidents). The court concluded that the

> City acted with deliberate indifference toward the NYPD's practice of making unconstitutional stops and conducting unconstitutional frisks. Even if the City had not been deliberately indifferent, the NYPD's unconstitutional practices were sufficiently widespread as to have the force of law. In addition, the City adopted a policy of indirect racial profiling by targeting defined groups for stops based on local crime suspect data. This has resulted in the disproportionate and discriminatory stopping of blacks and Hispanics in violation of the Equal Protection Clause. Both statistical and anecdotal evidence showed that minorities are indeed treated differently than white. For example, once a stop is made, blacks and Hispanics are more likely to be subjected to the use of force than whites, despite the fact that whites are more likely to be found with weapons or contraband. I also conclude that the City's highest officials have turned a blind eye to the evidence that officers are conducting stops in a racially discriminatory manner. In their zeal to defend a policy that they believe to be effective, they have willfully ignored overwhelming proof that the policy of targeting "the right people" is racially discriminatory and therefore violates the United States Constitution. One NYPD official has even suggested that it is permissible to stop racially defined groups just to instill fear in them that they are subject to being stopped at any time for any reason—in the hope that this fear will deter them from carrying guns in the streets. The goal of deterring crime is laudable, but this method of doing so is unconstitutional.
>
> I recognize that the police will deploy their limited resources to high crime areas. This benefits the communities where the need for policing is greatest. But the police are not permitted to target people for stops based on their race ... [T]he Equal Protection Clause prohibits the practices described in *this* case. A police department may not target a racially defined group for stops *in general*—that is, for stops based on suspicions of general criminal wrongdoing—simply because members of that group appear frequently in the police department's suspect data. The Equal Protection Clause does not permit the police to target a racially defined group as a whole because of the misdeeds of some of its members.[26]

The court held that it would order various remedies, including (1) a change in the policies for stop and frisk, (2) a trial program for body-worn cameras in one precinct per borough, (3) a court-appointed facilitator to aid in a community-based remedial process, and (4) the appointment of an independent monitor to ensure the use of stop and frisks comply with

---

25 *Floyd et al. v. City of N.Y.* at 561–562.

26 *Floyd et al. v. City of N.Y.* at 562–63.

the Constitution and the "principles enunciated in this Opinion, and to monitor the NYPD's compliance with the ordered remedies."[27]

THE BATTLE OVER STATISTICS

Anytime a NYPD officer conducts a stop, he is required to complete a UF-250 form.[28] The UF-250 is a one-page, double-sided form on the front of which is gathered basic information including time, address of the stop, type of location, whether it occurred inside a structure or outside, the name of the officer, the duration of the stop, the name and address of the person stopped, identification provided by the person stopped, basic demographic information of the person stopped (age, race, sex, height, weight, etc.), level of force used, resolution of stop (whether the person was arrested or given a summons), whether the stopped person was frisked, and whether a reason for the stop was provided.[29] On the back of the form, if the person was frisked, the officer is given various choices (boxes) to check to justify the frisk.[30] The name of the person was searched. The officer is also provided with a set of choices under "Additional Circumstances/Factors" to justify the stop and/or frisk or search.[31] The officer is also required to record the incident in his activity log (memo books).[32] The data from the compliance of filling out the UF-250s created a database that the parties analyzed to establish the statistical occurrences of stop and frisks conducted by the NYPD.[33]

Both plaintiffs and the NYPD introduced evidence from liability experts[34] on the results of analysis of data available. The court held, regarding the data, that it was uncontested that

- Between January 2004 and June 2012, the NYPD conducted over 4.4 million *Terry* stops.
- The number of stops per year rose sharply from 314,000 in 2004 to a high of 686,000 in 2011.
- 52% of all stops were followed by a protective frisk for weapons. A weapon was found after 1.5% of these frisks. In other words, in 98.5% of the 2.3 million frisks, no weapon was found.

---

27 *Floyd et al. v. City of N.Y.* at 563.

28 *Floyd et al. v. City of N.Y.* at 572.

29 *Floyd et al. v. City of N.Y.* at 667.

30 See copy of the UF-250 form reproduced in Arthur H. Garrison, "NYPD Stop and Frisk, Perceptions Criminals, Race and the Meaning of *Terry v. Ohio*: A Content Analysis of *Floyd et al. v. City of New York*," *Rutgers Race and Law Review* 15 (2014): 65, Appendix A.

31 *Id.*

32 *Floyd et al. v. City of N.Y.* at 607.

33 *Floyd et al. v. City of N.Y.* at 572.

34 Dr. Jeffrey Fagan for the plaintiffs, Dr. Dennis C. Smith and Dr. Robert M. Purtell for the City and NYPD. *Floyd*, 959 F. Supp. 2d at 573 n.105.

- 8% of all stops led to a search into the stopped person's clothing, ostensibly based on the officer feeling an object during the frisk that he suspected to be a weapon, or immediately perceived to be contraband other than a weapon. In 9% of these searches, the felt object was in fact a weapon. 91% of the time, it was not. In 14% of these searches, the felt object was in fact contraband. 86% of the time it was not.
- 6% of all stops resulted in an arrest, and 6% resulted in a summons. The remaining 88% of the 4.4 million stops resulted in no further law enforcement action.
- In 52% of the 4.4 million stops, the person stopped was Black.
- In 31% of the stops, the person stopped was Hispanic.
- In 10% of the stops, the person stopped was White.
- In 2010, New York City's resident population was roughly 23% Black, 29% Hispanic, and 33% White.
- In 23% of the stops of Blacks, and 24% of the stops of Hispanics, the officer recorded using force. The number for Whites was 17%.
- Weapons were seized in 1.0% of the stops of Blacks, 1.1% of the stops of Hispanics, and 1.4% of the stops of Whites.
- Contraband other than weapons was seized in 1.8% of the stops of Blacks, 1.7% of the stops of Hispanics, and 2.3% of the stops of Whites.
- For the years 2004 to 2009, the two most commonly checked boxes indicating the reasons for a stop were "Furtive Movements" and "Area Has Incidence Of Reported Offense Of Type Under Investigation" ("High Crime Area"). Setting aside stops based on radio runs, officers marked "Furtive Movements" as a basis for the stop on 42% of the forms, and "High Crime Area" on 55% of the forms. In 2009, officers indicated "Furtive Movements" as a basis for the stop nearly 60% of the time.
- Both "Furtive Movements" and "High Crime Area" are weak indicators of criminal activity. For the years 2004 to 2009, stops were 22% more likely to result in arrest if "High Crime Area" was not checked, and 18% more likely to result in arrest if "Furtive Movements" was not checked.
- Between 2004 and 2009, as the number of stops per year soared from 314,000 to 576,000, the percentage of UF-250s on which the officer failed to state a specific suspected crime rose from 1% to 36%.[35]

Thus, the data showed that fifty-two percent of the stops were Black, while Blacks made up only 23 percent of the total NYC population. Hispanics accounted for 31 percent of the stops, but only 20 of the NYC population and Whites accounted for only 10 percent of the stops while making up 33 of the total population. As discussed later in this chapter, the main justification for the disproportionate stop and frisk results made by the Mayor and Police Commissioner was that the program reduced the number of gun homicides and other types of gun violence.

35 *Floyd et al. v. City of N.Y.* at 558–59.

But, the data showed that only 0.1 percent of stops resulted in gun seizures,[36] and more Whites (1.4 percent) were found with weapons during a stop than Blacks (1 percent) or Hispanics (1.1 percent). More interesting, more contraband was seized from Whites (2.3 percent) than Blacks (1.8 percent) or Hispanics (1.7 percent). Looking at what explanations were used to justify the *Terry* stops in the first place, not counting radio calls, "Furtive Movements" (sudden movements or suspicious movements) was the basis of 42 percent of the stops, and "High Crime Area" was the basis for 55 percent of the stops.

Placing this data together suggests that, while Whites are more likely to be armed and have some type of contraband, Blacks and Hispanics are more likely to be stopped and searched. Further, the single most used excuse (outside of furtive movements) is high crime area. But the NYPD, as the Mayor and Police Commission publicly assert, focused intensive law enforcement activity in high-crime Black and Hispanic communities and specifically targeted crime in those neighborhoods only. While the NYPD asserted that stops were the result of radio calls, it is significant that its own records showed that 78 percent of all stops between 2004 and 2009 were self-initiated;[37] in other words, stops were not because of service calls in which a victim give a description that includes race, which can justify a stop using race. As discussed in Chapter Three, self-initiated stops can be subject to implicit bias and suspicious behavior of Blacks stopped by the police can be explained by stereotype threat theory rather than furtive movements that imply criminal activity.

The fact that police stops were self-initiated and not the result of radio calls is important, because public statements by the Mayor and Police Commissioner would leave a person with the impression that because the stops were the result of radio calls or information provided by a victim regarding a specific incident racial bias could not be explanation of the data; but disproportionate criminality could be.[38] Because only 22 percent of the stops resulted from radio calls, race descriptions from victims don't explain the disproportionate contact with police.

The NYPD tried to justify the disproportionate stopping of Blacks and Hispanics, as well as justify the low rate of arrests (6 percent) and summonses (6 percent) resulting from stops, because as the former Chief of the Department Joseph Esposito testified, "many stops interrupt a crime from occurring."[39] The court was not convinced,[40] but more importantly, stop and frisk is not a preventive tool, it is an investigatory tool to determine if "criminal activity may be

36 *Floyd et al. v. City of N.Y.* at 574 n.118.

37 *Floyd et al. v. City of N.Y.* at 574 n.121.

38 *E.g.*, Mayor Michael Bloomberg, Press Release, Mayor Bloomberg Speaks to Parishioners of the First Baptist Church of Brownsville About How Crime Can be Driven Down even Further While Continuing to Improve Community Relations (June 10, 2012).

39 *Floyd et al. v. City of N.Y.* at 575.

40 *Floyd* at 575. "No evidence was offered at trial, however, of a single stop that was: (1) based on reasonable suspicion, and (2) prevented the commission of a crime, but (3) did not result in probable cause for an arrest. While I have no doubt that such a stop has taken place at some time, it is highly implausible that successful "preventive"

afoot."[41] Stop and frisk is not a crime suppression tool. The reason this is significant is that stop and frisk interferes with an individual's constitutional right to walk down the street without police obstruction, intimidation, or interference. The Constitution allows for interference when the police have a specific and justifiable reason for that interference. General crime suppression and prevention is not a specific and justifiable reason for that interference. This is all the more significant when "at least 88% of the NYPD's 4.4 million stops" did not result in any formal police action (arrest or summons).[42] Thus, 3.872 million people had their constitutional right to be left alone interfered with (if not unlawfully violated) on the say so of the police but afterwards were released with nothing to show for the interference.

The plaintiffs used two approaches to establish the NYPD had violated the Fourth Amendment by systematically conducting stops and frisks without specific individualized reasonable suspicion: statistically, by analyzing the NYPD UF-250 database, and through individual testimony of the named twelve plaintiffs and the corresponding nineteen stops.[43] Space would not allow for a complete review of seventy pages of analysis on these two pillars of the plaintiffs' case; such a review would be a chapter in itself. Rather, an overview of the courts' reasoning and conclusions regarding the use of race and crime statistics will be analyzed.

The court first conceded the limits to making conclusions on the NYPD stop-question-frisk program regarding violations of the Fourth Amendment based on the database, because "it is impossible to assess individually whether each of the 4.4 million stops at issue in this case was based on an officer's reasonable articulable suspicion."[44] The reason being the database information

> is highly flawed ... (1) Officers do not always prepare a UF-250 ... (2) A UF-250 is one-sided, in that the UF-250 only records the officer's version of the story[,] (3) ... UF-250s do not provide enough information to determine whether reasonable suspicion existed for a stop [and] (4) Many of the checkboxes on the UF-250 ... are problematic. "Furtive Movements" is vague and subjective. In fact, an officer's impression of whether a movement was "furtive" may be affected by unconscious racial biases. "Fits Description" is a troubling basis for a stop if the description is so general that it fits a large portion of the population in the area, such as black males between the ages of 18 and 24. "High Crime Area" is also of questionable value when it encompasses a large area or an entire borough, such as Queens or Staten Island.[45]

---

stops take place frequently enough to affect the conclusion that in at least 88% of the NYPD's 4.4 million stops between January 2004 and June 2012, the suspicion giving rise to the stop turned out to be misplaced."

41 *Terry v. Ohio*, 392 U.S. 1, 30 (1968).

42 *Floyd et al. v. City of N.Y.* at 575.

43 *Floyd et al. v. City of N.Y.* at 558–89, 624–58

44 *Floyd et al. v. City of N.Y.* at 578.

45 *Floyd et al. v. City of N.Y.* at 578.

In addition to these limitations, the court held that Dr. Fagan, plaintiff's expert, who the court found more credible than the experts for the NYPD,[46] used an "extremely conservative" method in analyzing the database in which he found only 6 percent of the stops in the database as "'apparently unjustified,' that is, lacking reasonable suspicion."[47] The court asserted that, although it had doubts as to whether the analysis of Dr. Fagan truly captured the actual percentage of unjustified stops, his 6 percent figure "represents 200,000 individuals who were stopped without reasonable suspicion. Even this number of wrongful stops produces a significant human toll."[48]

The court held that the two most-used justifications on the UF-250s, "Furtive Movements" and "High Crime Area" are highly suspect in establishing reasonable suspicion, because "stops were more likely to result in arrest when Furtive Movements and High Crime Areas were not checked than when they were."[49] Further, expert witness Dr. Fagan found "that the rate at which officers check High Crime Area in a precinct or census tract is roughly 55 percent, regardless of the amount of crime in the precinct or census tract as measured by crime complaints."[50] The point being police used these two descriptions regardless of the actual factors that led to the actual stop—police scripting.[51]

The court held that even assuming that the furtive movements truly reflect what the officer believes justifies the stop, "Courts have also recognized that furtive movements, standing alone, are a vague and unreliable indicator of criminality,"[52] because such movements standing alone do not establish reasonable suspicion.[53] The reason for the unreliability is that it is very subjective as to whether a behavior is furtive, and even if it is furtive, does it evidence criminality or fear of

46 *Floyd et al. v. City of N.Y.* at 580; *See also* Brief for Defendant-Appellants at 43, *Floyd et al. v. City of N.Y.*, No. 13-3088-cv (L) (2d Cir. Dec. 10, 2013) (detailing the attack on Dr. Fagan, the statistical analysis, and conclusions drawn from the UF-250 database). The city, in its appeal, made clear that "it was manifestly erroneous ... for the District Court to admit Fagan's Fourth Amendment analysis. First, while Fagan is a professor of criminology at Columbia Law School, he is not an attorney and has no formal legal training. Interpretation of legal precedent lies outside of his area of expertise." Brief for Defendant-Appellants at 43. (The city left aside that its own expert was also without formal legal training.); *See also Floyd*, 959 F. Supp. 2d at 557.

47 *Floyd et al. v. City of N.Y.* at 578. See also, 582–83

48 *Floyd et al. v. City of N.Y.* at 579.

49 *Floyd et al. v. City of N.Y.* at 580.

50 *Floyd et al. v. City of N.Y.* at 581.

51 *Floyd et al. v. City of N.Y.* at 581 n.162 (explaining "But, as Dr. Fagan noted at trial, *see id.* at 2360–2361, it is simply not plausible that 55% of all stops take place in an "area" whose particular crime characteristics objectively justified checking the High Crime Area box, *regardless* of the crime rate of the census tract or the precinct where the stop takes place. The unvarying rate of checking High Crime Area across locations and times is more likely a product of reflexive box-checking that is unrelated to any defined crime condition.").

52 *Floyd et al. v. City of N.Y.* at 580.

53 *See Illinois v. Wardlow*, 528 U.S. 119, 124 (2000).

being under police control *per se*, regardless of innocence. As discussed in Chapter Three furtive movements filtered and processed through implicit bias create RAS in the perceptions of the police; and police react with automatic mental processing due to pattern recognition/schema motor learning to furtive movements. Add to this the issue of police prior belief regarding the location and race of the stop further clouds the issue. As the court observed

> Recent psychological research has also provided evidence that officers may be more likely to perceive a movement as indicative of criminality if the officer has been primed to look for signs that 'crime is afoot.' As I stated in *Ligon*, '[g]iven the nature of their work on patrol, officers may have a systematic tendency to see and report furtive movements where none objectively exist.'
>
> Other recent psychological research has shown that unconscious racial bias continues to play an objectively measurable role in many people's decision processes. It would not be surprising if many police officers share the latent biases that pervade our society. If so, such biases could provide a further source of unreliability in officers' rapid, intuitive impressions of whether an individual's movements are furtive and indicate criminality. Unconscious bias could help explain the otherwise puzzling fact that NYPD officers check 'Furtive Movements' in 48% of the stops of blacks and 45% of the stops of Hispanics, but only 40% of the stops of whites. There is no evidence that black people's movements are objectively more furtive than the movements of white people.[54]

The court concluded that the use of the High Crime Area was suspect, because police were known to define entire precincts or boroughs as High Crime Areas.[55]

The real disagreement between the experts for the NYPD and the plaintiffs did not center on the truth of disproportionate stops, but rather was regarding whether they were the result of unlawful racial bias. To prevail on their Fourteenth Amendment Equal Protection Clause complaint, the plaintiffs must show, "that blacks and Hispanics are stopped more frequently than they would be if police officers did not discriminate based on race when deciding whom to stop."[56] In proving this, the dispute between the parties is what "standard, or point of reference" should the "statistics about rates of stops of blacks and Hispanics" be compared to—this is called setting a ***benchmark***.[57] The plaintiffs argued that the benchmark should be general

---

54 *Floyd et al. v. City of N.Y.* at 580–81 (internal citations omitted).

55 *Floyd et al. v. City of N.Y.* at 581 n.161.

56 *Floyd et al. v. City of N.Y.* at 583.

57 *Floyd et al. v. City of N.Y.* As Dr. Fagan explained:

> [A] valid benchmark requires estimates of the supply of individuals of each racial or ethnic group who are engaged in the targeted behaviors and who are available to the police as potential targets for the exercise of their stop authority. Since police often target resources to the places where crime rates and risks are highest, and where populations are highest, some measure of population that is conditioned on crime rates is an optimal candidate for inclusion as a benchmark.

population statistics,[58] and the NYPD advocated for the use of "a benchmark consisting of the rates at which various races appear in suspect descriptions from crime victims—in other words, 'suspect race descriptive data.'"[59] The former (***general population data***) approach will capture "who is available to be stopped in an area ... and ... local crime rates reflects the fact that stops are more likely to take place in areas with higher crime rates."[60] The latter approach (***suspect description data***) assumes that "if officers' stop decisions were racially unbiased, then the racial distribution of stopped pedestrians would be the same as the racial distribution of the criminal suspects in the area."[61] The NYPD advocated for a benchmark of suspects defined by race, not total population defined by race. Victim data describes criminal defendants regardless of ability of the police to close a case—which, as discussed in Chapter One, is what arrest data shows.

The NYPD benchmark focuses on the percentage of criminals described (***suspect description data***) *as Black or Hispanic* and then looks at who is being stopped. *The plaintiff benchmark focuses on the total population (the geographic community)* (***general population data***) *the police operate in* and looks at the percentage of people stopped compared to the population breakdown of those in the total population. Under the NYPD approach, disproportionate results should occur, because Blacks make up the majority of victim-identified suspects. Under the plaintiff approach, disproportionate results show racial bias.

As discussed above, 52 percent of the people stopped were Black, while Blacks only comprise 23 percent of the total NYC population. Hispanics account for 31 percent of the stops but only 20 percent of the population, and Whites account for only 10 percent of the stops while making up 33 percent of the total population. The NYPD asserted that this is to be expected if the correct benchmark is suspect race-descriptive data. As the Mayor and the Police Commissioner publicly stated in defense of the program, more than 90 percent of the victims and perpetrators of gun violence are young men of color. Thus, the stops disproportionately included Whites and underrepresented Blacks and Hispanics. As discussed below, the Mayor and the Police Commissioner made clear that to end the violence the police should have stopped more Blacks and Hispanics than Whites. The city asserted in court that there was no constitutional violation—race was not the operative factor in the stops; criminal activity was. The NYPD expert testified "that the disproportionate stopping of black people can be explained by the disproportionately black

---

58 *Floyd et al. v. City of N.Y.*

59 *Floyd et al. v. City of N.Y.* at 584–85 n.183 ("**Crime suspect description data** estimates the available **pool of *persons exhibiting suspicious behavior*** that could be observed by the police—**while population** merely **estimates the potential number of *persons* in a given area.**") (italics in the original, emphasis added).

60 *Floyd et al. v. City of N.Y.* at 585.

61 *Floyd et al. v. City of N.Y.* at 584; *see also* RAND Report discussion of benchmark *infra* note 73.

composition of the pool of criminals."[62] The NYPD experts, Drs. Smith and Purtell, were quite blunt on this point at trial.

> Obviously, if particular racial or ethnic groups in New York City participate in crime at a rate disproportionate to their share of the population, we would expect officers to conduct *Terry* stops for such groups at rates higher than each groups' respective share of the City's population. The benchmark of suspect race description allows us to measure if [the] NYPD's officers are stopping minorities at a rate *over and above* what could be explained by the racial composition of the criminally active population in New York.[63]

On appeal, the city asserted that, with the proper benchmark, the disproportionality found by Dr. Fagan disappears.

> Application of the suspect description benchmark reveals a far closer correlation to stops by race and ethnicity. In 2011 and 2012, 87% of stop subjects were black and Hispanic, as were approximately 83% of all known crime suspects and approximately 90% of all violent crime suspects. Defendants' experts ran several alternate regressions which included suspect race data, and evidence of disproportionate racial impact either disappeared, or the size of the disparity was greatly reduced. Other trial evidence strongly undermined plaintiffs' benchmark as producing an unwarranted inference of discrimination.[64]

---

62 *Floyd et al. v. City of N.Y.* at 585. But the court was not convinced and observed disproportionate criminal activity demonstrated in the database.

> *The suspect's race was unknown in 70% of crime complaints* in 2005 and 2006. Even after merging crime suspect data and arrestee data, the race of the perpetrator is only known for roughly 63% of crimes (using data from 2010 to 2011). In addition, based on this "merged" data, while the suspect's race is known for a high percentage of certain types of crime—such as felony violent crimes (86%), weapons crimes (98%), and drug offenses (99%)—race is known in only 22% of felony property crimes, which are the basis for 25% of all stops. Dr. Fagan persuasively showed that using data where almost 40% of the information is missing would introduce sample selection bias, and is not a reliable approach to drawing conclusions about the criminal suspect population. (Dr. Smith acknowledging that he had not found any scholarly support for estimating the demographics of crime suspects based on data that is nearly 40% incomplete).

Floyd et al. v. City of N.Y. at 588 n.193 (Dr. Smith acknowledging that he had not found any scholarly support for estimating the demographics of crime suspects based on data that is nearly 40% incomplete (internal citations omitted, emphasis added)); *see also infra* note 212, 218 (the logical conclusion of the proposition that blacks are criminogenic).

63 *Floyd et al. v. City of N.Y.*. at 585 n.184 (emphasis in original).

64 *See* Brief for Defendant-Appellants, *supra* note 46, at 15. In its post-trial memorandum of law, the city further minimized the statistical findings of Dr. Fagan.

The court was not so convinced.

> I conclude that Dr. Fagan's benchmark is the better choice. The reason is simple and reveals a serious flaw in the logic applied by the City's experts: there is no basis for assuming that the racial distribution of stopped pedestrians will resemble the racial distribution of the local criminal population if the people stopped are not criminals. The City defends the fact that blacks and Hispanics represent 87% of the persons stopped in 2011 and 2012 by noting that "approximately 83% of all known crime suspects and approximately 90% of all violent crime suspects were Black and Hispanic." *This might be a valid comparison if the people stopped were criminals ... To the contrary, nearly 90% of the people stopped are released without the officer finding any basis for a summons or arrest and only 13% of stops are based on fitting a specific suspect description.*[65]

The court concluded

> There is no reason to believe that the nearly 90% of people who are stopped and then subject to no further enforcement action are criminals. As a result, there is no reason to believe that their racial distribution should resemble that of the local criminal population, as opposed to that of the local population in general. If the police are stopping people in a race-neutral way, then the racial composition of innocent people stopped should more or less mirror the racial composition of the areas where they are stopped, all other things being equal.[66]

The NYPD expert countered in court,[67] as did the Mayor and Commissioner in public, with the proposition that stops do prevent crime, regardless of whether the person stopped in fact

---

> Assuming the accuracy of Fagan's statistics – which the City disputes – Fagan's analysis only purports to show that (1) blacks and Hispanics are more likely to be stopped than whites, and (2) the odds of an increase in stops given a 1% increase in the proportion of black or Hispanic population versus a 1% increase in the white population is a virtual coin toss

Defendant's Post-Trial Memorandum of Law (June 12, 2013) at 20 [hereinafter Defendant Memorandum].

65 *Floyd*, 959 F. Supp. 2d at 584 (emphasis added).

66 *Floyd et al. v. City of N.Y.* at 584–85.

67 *Floyd et al. v. City of N.Y.* at 586–87. "Dr. Smith's position, while surprising, is not illogical once his premises are accepted. Dr. Smith apparently does not find it plausible that an officers' decision to stop a person may be swayed by conscious or unconscious racial bias. If a researcher begins with this premise, he will attempt to find a credible, race-neutral explanation for the NYPD's stopping of blacks and Hispanics out of proportion to their share of the population. For example, the researcher may seek to explain the disproportionate stopping of minorities as the result of the characteristics of the criminal population. ... Next, the researcher may analyze the deployment of police to high crime areas or 'hot spots.' If these areas happen to be disproportionately minority,

committed a crime.[68] The cumulative effect of the stops prevents crime from occurring. As to those who are stopped and innocent, the expert asked rhetorically, "[H]ow do we know ... [i]f they were utterly innocent[?]"[69] His point being that a low arrest or hit rate only tells you that the police could not reach the required burden of proof, probable cause, to arrest the person stopped. It does not mean that they were innocent. Thus, the police could have a high hit rate on stopping the guilty and a low rate of proof regarding their guilt. Leaving aside the courts' correct retort that the NYPD expert's "theory that a significant number of these stops resulted in the prevention of the suspected crime is pure speculation and not reliable,"[70] the point is irrelevant.[71] A *Terry* stop is a tool to determine if a crime has or is about to be committed. Put simply, constitutional rules and limitations on police are just that, limitations. Crime investigation and prevention would, of course, be greatly improved if Fourth Amendment prohibition against unreasonable searches and seizures did not "handcuff" the police.

One last point on the distribution of race and crime statistics should be observed. The NYPD in court and the Mayor and Commissioner in public statements make clear that they don't believe all Blacks and Hispanics are criminal, but Blacks and Hispanics are

---

then heavy deployment to these areas will provide a race-neutral basis for the disproportionate stopping of minorities. ... In the end, if the researcher cannot think of any relevant race-neutral factors for which Dr. Fagan did not control, the only remaining race-neutral explanation for the NYPD's stop patterns may be that members of the over-stopped racial groups have a greater tendency to appear suspicious than members of other racial groups, even when they are not breaking the law."

68 *See generally Floyd et al. v. City of N.Y.* at 585.

69 *Floyd et al. v. City of N.Y.*; *see also*, Commissioner Kelly, comments, *infra* notes 115, 117.

70 *Floyd et al. v. City of N.Y.* at 586 (stating "[c]rime suspect data may serve as a reliable proxy for the pool of *criminals* exhibiting suspicious behavior. But there is no reason to believe that crime suspect data provides a reliable proxy for the pool of *non-criminals* exhibiting suspicious behavior. Because the overwhelming majority of people stopped fell into the latter category, there is no support for the City's position that crime suspect data provides a reliable proxy for the pool of people exhibiting suspicious behavior. Moreover, given my finding that a significant number of stops were *not* based on reasonable suspicion—and thus were stops drawn from the pool of *non*criminals *not* exhibiting suspicious behavior—the use of crime suspect data as a benchmark for the pool of people that would have been stopped in the absence of racial bias is even less appropriate.").

71 See *Floyd et al. v. City of N.Y.* at 586 n.186 (stating "[o]f course, if the real purpose of the stops is not to investigate suspected criminal activity based on individualized suspicion, but instead to deter criminals from carrying weapons or contraband by stopping people who fit a general profile of criminal suspects in an area, then criminal suspect data would *in a sense* be the appropriate benchmark for measuring racial disparities in stops. But the City does not make this argument, and if it did, the argument would fail for reasons related to plaintiffs' Fourth and Fourteenth Amendment claims. *First*, to the extent that such 'deterrence' stops were based solely on a person's resemblance to a general profile of the criminals in an area, the stop would not be based on *individualized* reasonable suspicion of criminal activity. *Second*, to the extent that 'the general profile of criminal suspects in an area' contains a racial description, the use of that description as a basis for stops would constitute racial profiling.").

overrepresented in the criminal population. Even if the latter part is true, it does not follow that the majority of those stopped should be people of color. The police should be expected to distill or differentiate the criminals within a race from the law-abiding members of the same race. The failure to do so raises racial bias. It does so because the police, rather than doing the difficult work of being able to tell the criminal from the law abiding, use a simpler tool of over-stopping all members of the race. When the police do this, as the court observed, they prove their detractors' case.

> Rather than being a defense against the charge of racial profiling, however, this reasoning is a defense of racial profiling. To say that black people in general are somehow more suspicious-looking, or criminal in appearance, than white people is not a race-neutral explanation for racial disparities in NYPD stops: it is itself a racially biased explanation. This explanation is especially troubling because it echoes the stereotype that black men are more likely to engage in criminal conduct than others.
>
> ...
>
> [R]ace alone is not an objective basis for suspicion by the police. Because there is no evidence that law-abiding blacks or Hispanics are more likely to behave objectively more suspiciously than law-abiding whites, Dr. Smith's—and the City's—refuge in this unsupported notion is no refuge at all. It is effectively an admission that there is no explanation for the NYPD's disproportionate stopping of blacks and Hispanics other than the NYPD's stop practices having become infected, somewhere along the chain of command, by racial bias.
>
> ...
>
> A simple explanation exists: the racial composition of the people stopped by the NYPD resembles what the NYPD perceives to be the racial composition of the criminal population because that is why they were stopped. Evidence discussed later in this Opinion shows that the NYPD has an unwritten policy of targeting racially defined groups for stops, based on the appearance of members of those groups in crime suspect data. A strong correlation between the races of people stopped and the known races of criminal suspects is the natural result.[72]

The city fundamentally rejected any negative association to the disproportionate stop and frisk of young men of color. To the NYPD, disproportionate impact is the natural result of effective and determined law enforcement applied to criminal concentrations. There was no

72 *Floyd et al. v. City of N.Y.* at 587–88 (also stating "In short, the correlation highlighted by the City and its experts in their attempt to refute the allegation of racial profiling in fact provides evidence of racial profiling. Rather than revealing a valid race-neutral variable that explains the NYPD's disproportionate stopping of blacks and Hispanics, the correlation highlighted by the City's experts suggests how the racial disparities identified by Dr. Fagan might have come about—namely, through a widespread practice of racial profiling based on local criminal suspect data.")

selective or indirect racial bias. The city, citing its RAND study, defended the use of suspect data over population data as a benchmark to establish that the stop-question-frisk program was free from racial bias. But, even the report by the RAND Corporation observed the following regarding the choice of benchmarks and what they prove:

> Regardless of the external benchmark selected—census, arrests, suspect descriptions, or any other—the *racial composition of the stops involves the interaction of the rates of criminal participation and the racial distribution of the population that the officer encounters.* To put some hypothetical numbers to this, **consider an unbiased officer who makes stops only when a pedestrian matches a suspect description. This officer works in a precinct with 40 blacks matching suspect descriptions and 40 whites matching suspect descriptions. If all 40 of the white suspects stay inside, travel only by car, or avoid the specific area in which the officer patrols, then this officer will stop only black pedestrians**, deviating substantially from the precinct's suspect description benchmark of 50 percent. Even the less extreme situation, in which 20 of the white suspects are exposed to the officer, results in the officer involving blacks in 67 percent of all of that officer's stops. The ***suspect benchmark is valid only if the suspects from the various racial groups are equally exposed to police officers.***[73]

Note the point that RAND makes. Regardless of the benchmark chosen, *if the distribution of the pool of suspects within the police field of vision is not equal—the use of suspect data for analysis of the stops is of no value.* If the police target a specific area for criminals, and they use race as a factor for police attention, they will intentionally avoid like criminals of a difference race in the same area. They will also avoid like criminals, regardless of race, in different areas. The use of suspect description data results in the police focusing and catching only those criminals it chooses to see acting as criminals. As discussed in Chapter One, police use of race to detect crime (1) puts a Black face on all crime and (2) makes White crime socially and politically invisible. Sociology and criminal justice implications aside, racial focus is unconstitutional. The constitutional violation is in the policy choice of picking a specific group, by race, to target police attention on and placing certain criminals within the line of sight of the local police officer on the street. This subtlety was lost on the defendants.

Consider this example. Whites and Blacks, by percentage, use marijuana equally, but Blacks tend to use it publicly, while Whites use it behind doors. When the police decide to make arrests for marijuana use they will focus on public use. The reason is simple, it's easier to arrest people who smoke in public. The police are aware that the result will be disproportionate arrests of Blacks. They also know that focusing on public use will remove from police attention marijuana use by Whites. The resulting police statistics (arrest statistics) will confirm the suspect race data that there is a disproportionate use of marijuana by Blacks, which in turn, justifies the police deployment and the resulting arrests of Blacks and not Whites.

73 RAND report, *supra* note 23 at 15 (emphasis added).

As discussed in Chapter One, this is how crime data is subject to manipulation regardless of actual crime commission. Leaving the manipulation aside, the decision to conduct a policy that will result in disproportionate arrests of Blacks creates the constitutional violation.

As discussed below regarding the legal and political defense of the stop and frisk initiative and advocating the use of suspect race data benchmarking, the NYPD rejected any assertion that racism was the result of the stops. As far as the Mayor and Commissioner were concerned, nothing short of the Commissioner ordering the police to "round up" men of color, because they are men of color living in a specific neighborhood, and the police saturation of a specific neighborhood for the purpose of enabling the officers to "round up" men of color will establish a constitutional violation. To the NYPD, there is no such thing as "indirect bias" or "unconscious bias" and only the KKK walking down Pennsylvania Avenue with torches and ropes and burning-crosses level "explicit bias" is unlawful and establishes civil liability. The problem, as discussed in Chapter Three, is that the definition and nature of racism is not that simple. But the NYPD approach allows the city to bypass what the plaintiffs alleged and simply assert that regardless of disproportionate impact, the statistics justify racially-based policing strategies. Concluding that since there was no unconstitutional purpose or intent based on race regarding the use of stop and frisk the city is not liable. Fortunately, the law is not that simple or myopic.

As the Plaintiffs answered, "The guarantee of equal protection goes beyond punishing racist men wearing white hoods; because of the harmful, stigmatizing and lingering effect of racial discrimination, the Fourteenth Amendment proscribes governmental policies or pronouncements that are even in part motivated by racial classification, identification or stereotype."[74] "Likewise, Plaintiffs need not prove that decision-makers exhibited overt racial hostility or antipathy, or that police officers candidly admitted their racial bias in order to prove intentional discrimination."[75] The use of racial stereotypes and the establishment of policy based on those stereotypes established a discriminatory, unconstitutional purpose. The fact that crime is disproportionately distributed in minority communities does not mean that people in minority communities are disproportionately criminal.

What is surprising in reviewing the NYPD use of *Terry* is the agency's fundamental failure to understand that stop and frisk is an investigatory tool, not a crime-suppression tool. The unconstitutional use of *Terry* along with the racial motivation in the deployment of the police (even taking the motivation of the NYPD on face value) together establish the "deliberate indifference" to the result of the policy in actual implementation. It is clearly foreseeable that the clear and direct public assertions by the Mayor and the Police Commissioner that minority youth commit crime disproportionately within the society, and as such, police are deployed in minority communities to reduce crime because that is where the perpetrators are, will result in greater stopping of minority youth by line police officers.

---

74 Post-Trial Memorandum of Law in Support of Plaintiffs' claims (June 12, 2013) at 12.

75 Post-Trial Memorandum of Law in Support of Plaintiffs' claims (June 12, 2013) at 12.

The city "purpose" and "intent" is further proven by the city's wholehearted defense of the "suspect race description" benchmark, which focuses the policy on race. The use of suspect race data makes the population of criminals within a larger racial population the only point of measurement that matters. Suspect race data defines a minority population into a criminal population. With such a policy, it is clearly foreseeable what street level police officers will do with the assumption. "Thus, the City's policy, at least in part, "expressly incorporate[s] racial bias" in a manner that violates the Fourteenth Amendment."[76]

> The City's crude presumption actually underscores the ongoing Equal Protection violation in this case. By justifying discriminatory stop and frisk rates on the theory that Blacks and Latinos in general commit more crime, the City affirmatively embraces a racial profile that incentivizes and generates more unlawful stops of Blacks and Latinos, including the innocent Plaintiffs and class members in this case. The City has wound itself into a vicious, discriminatory circle that discards the fundamental constitutional requirement that law enforcement sanction be based on individualized criteria.[77]

Put simply, "Reliance on overbroad generalizations about the propensities of classes of individuals to justify government policy is *per se* unconstitutional."[78] The city took offense to the conception that the stopping of innocent people established constitutional violation. As the city asserted on appeal,

> It is beyond question that officers may stop and frisk innocent people without offending the Fourth Amendment, because the compelling governmental interest in protecting citizens from crime balances the limited incursion. [*Illinois v.*] *Wardlow,* 528 U.S. at 126. Indeed, the innocent may be subject to the higher intrusion of arrest, provided probable cause is present. *E.g., Jocks v. Tavernier,* 316 F.3d 128, 135 (2d Cir. 2003). Likewise, innocence, known to police only with the benefit of hindsight, cannot establish a valid EPC claim. *See Brown,* [*v. City of Oneonta*] 221 F.3d at 339 (targeted stops of young black male subjects were constitutional although "understandably upsetting to the innocent plaintiffs who were stopped ... ").[79]

Such was the attitude of the city; the stopping of innocent people of color is of little constitutional matter, because the "compelling governmental interest in protecting citizens from crime balances the limited incursion" and embarrassment of the men of color stopped.

---

76 Post-Trial Memorandum of Law in Support of Plaintiffs' claims (June 12, 2013) at 14.

77 Post-Trial Memorandum of Law in Support of Plaintiffs' claims (June 12, 2013) at 15.

78 Post-Trial Memorandum of Law in Support of Plaintiffs' claims (June 12, 2013) at 16 (citing United States v. Virginia, 518 U.S. 515 (1996)).

79 Brief for Defendant-Appellant at 68, *Floyd et al. v. City of New York*, No. 13-3088 (2d Cir. Dec. 10, 2013), *available at* http://www.ccrjustice.org/files/City's%20Merits%20Brief%2012%2010%202013.pdf.

The district court disagreed. Having determined that that the NYPD has a "widespread practice of racial profiling based on local criminal suspect data," the court moved to the legal question of "NYPD's awareness of and response to those unconstitutional stops," or in other words, was the City "deliberately indifferent to the violations of the Plaintiff class's Fourth and Fourteenth Amendment rights?"[80]

THE POLITICAL RESPONSE BY THE MAYOR AND THE NYPD

Judge Scheindlin, at the beginning of her opinion, made clear that "this case is not about the effectiveness of stop and frisk in deterring or combating crime. This Court's mandate is solely to judge the *constitutionality* of police behavior, *not* its effectiveness as a law enforcement tool."[81] While the court made clear that ends don't justify the means, Mayor Bloomberg asserted that the end is the point. Mayor Bloomberg addressed the assertion that the NYPD racially targeted Black males directly at a community meeting in Brooklyn at the First Baptist Full Gospel Church of Brownsville.[82] At the meeting in June 2012, the Mayor defended the program by asserting that crime statistics don't follow the census tracks of NYC and that the police can't stop different groups according to relative population distribution based on census tracks.[83] The Mayor defended the program as a strategy that has reduced crime and, specifically, rates of murder and the reason for the reduction of murder has been the reduction of "guns ... being carried on our streets. That is our real goal—preventing violence before it occurs, not responding to victims after the fact."[84]

The Mayor addressed the disproportionate impact of stop and frisk by explaining a "harsh reality" that

> [t]he worst, most tragic disparity of all is that young black men are 36 times more likely to be murdered—and young Hispanic men are 12 times more likely to be murdered—than young white men, and sadly, they are also far more likely to commit murder.
>
> I mentioned earlier that 90 percent of all people murdered in our city are black or Hispanic. It's also true that 96 percent of shooting suspects are black and Hispanic. I don't

80 *Floyd et al. v. City of N.Y.* at 589–590.

81 *Floyd et al. v. City of N.Y.* at 556 (emphasis in original).

82 Kate Taylor, *Stop-and-Frisk Policy 'Saves Lives,' Mayor Tells Black Congregation,* N.Y. Times, June 10, 2012, *available at* http://www.nytimes.com/2012/06/11/nyregion/at-black-church-in-brooklyn-bloomberg-defends-stop-and-frisk-policy.html?_r=0.

83 Kate Taylor, "Stop-and-Frisk Policy 'Saves Lives,' Mayor Tells Black Congregation," *N.Y. Times.*

84 Kate Taylor, "Stop-and-Frisk Policy 'Saves Lives,' Mayor Tells Black Congregation," *N.Y. Times.*

> have to tell you about the tragedy of black-on-black crime. And I don't have to tell you that most of the shooters—and victims—are young men.[85]

Although the Mayor acknowledged that he understood why young Black men who had been stopped by police officers stated "that their interactions with police officers left them angry [e] ither because of disrespectful language or unnecessary force[,] there is no denying that stops take guns off the street and saves lives."[86]

> Last year, those frisks produced 780 guns, and 5,872 knives and 1,572 other dangerous weapons. Just as importantly, it unquestionably deterred many from carrying those weapons in the first place.
>
> By making it 'Too hot to carry,' the NYPD is preventing guns from being carried on our streets. That's our goal: preventing violence before it occurs, not responding to victims after the fact.[87]

The Mayor made clear that he understood the complaint that the stop-and-frisk program was "stopping too many black and Hispanic young men," but he analogized that the stops were due to disproportionate criminal activity by Blacks and Hispanics, not racial profiling by the police. He argued

> [s]omeone might say: It's unfair that men are stopped more often than women and that young people are stopped more often than old people. I hope we all live to see the day when men commit as few crimes as women and the young commit as few crimes as the old.
>
> But until that day arrives, we are not going to deny reality.
>
> In order to prevent crime, *police officers have to be able to make stops based on crime reports, not census reports.* If we stopped people based on census numbers, we would stop many fewer criminals, recover many fewer weapons and allow many more violent crimes to take place.
>
> We will not do that. We will not bury our heads in the sand. We can't ever forget who is being killed—and we can't deny what neighborhoods they are being killed in.
>
> *The reason police officers make stops in Brownsville and East New York is not because of race; it is because of crime.* Brownsville and East New York remain two of the

---

85 Mayor Michael Bloomberg, "Mayor Bloomberg Speaks to Parishioners of the First Baptist Church of Brownsville About How Crime Can be Driven Down even Further While Continuing to Improve Community Relations," Press release, (June 10, 2012).

86 Mayor Michael Bloomberg, "Mayor Bloomberg Speaks to Parishioners" ...

87 Mayor Michael Bloomberg, "Mayor Bloomberg Speaks to Parishioners" ...

> highest-crime areas in our city. We've cut crime here over the past 10 years, but not by enough. And we are not going to walk away from a strategy that we know saves lives.[88]

The Mayor concluded that the problem with stop and frisk was not that the police were making stops on rationalities less than reasonable suspicion, but that the police making the stops may not be doing so "in a respectful way," which results in the person being stopped left "hurt and angry."[89] Thus, he said the program would be "mended, not ended, to ensure that stops are conducted appropriately, with as much courtesy as possible."[90] To achieve this goal, he stated that "we will be putting a new emphasis on Courtesy, Respect, and Professionalism, so that when innocent people are stopped and questioned, the interaction does not leave them hurt and angry."[91] Leaving aside the patronizing tone of alleviating "hurt and angry" feelings, innocent people are not supposed to be unconstitutionally stopped in the first place, much less stopped because of their race.

A year later, the Mayor addressed the NYPD leadership at the main headquarters[92] and defended the stop-and-frisk program. He congratulated his command police officers that murder was down 32 percent compared to the year before and that "if you compare the first-third of this year to when we came into office, it's down 56 percent. And shootings also are down 22 percent compared to last year's record low."[93] In further congratulations of his officers, he proclaimed that "by cutting the murder rates to a new record low, we saved 96 lives compared to the year before, and since 2002, we've saved 7,364 lives compared to the decade before."[94] As the Mayor told the Brooklyn congregation the year before, the Mayor defined the NYPD as "First Preventers" not "First Responders" in regard to crime.[95] After recounting that the murder rate in NYC was down while in comparable cities the rate was significantly higher, he also informed his officers that rather than filling the prisons with young people, they were "keeping young people from going to jail and to prison. Unlike in the rest of the country ... here in New York City we've cut crime not by locking more people up, but in locking fewer people up."[96] This occurred, in part, due to the policy the Mayor had announced in Brooklyn.

> That's one reason why last year, Commissioner Kelly issued an order to clarify that when officers find someone carrying small amounts of marijuana, rather than making an arrest,

88 Mayor Michael Bloomberg, "Mayor Bloomberg Speaks to Parishioners" ... (emphasis added).

89 Mayor Michael Bloomberg, "Mayor Bloomberg Speaks to Parishioners" ...

90 Mayor Michael Bloomberg, "Mayor Bloomberg Speaks to Parishioners" ...

91 Mayor Michael Bloomberg, "Mayor Bloomberg Speaks to Parishioners" ...

92 Mayor Michael Bloomberg, "Mayor Bloomberg Delivers Address on Public Safety to NYPD Leadership," Press Release, (April 30, 2013).

93 Mayor Michael Bloomberg, "Mayor Bloomberg Delivers Address on Public Safety to NYPD Leadership" ...

94 Mayor Michael Bloomberg, "Mayor Bloomberg Delivers Address on Public Safety to NYPD Leadership" ...

95 Mayor Michael Bloomberg, "Mayor Bloomberg Delivers Address on Public Safety to NYPD Leadership" ...

96 Mayor Michael Bloomberg, "Mayor Bloomberg Delivers Address on Public Safety to NYPD Leadership" ...

> a summons should be issued—just as if the marijuana was found in the home. Since then, arrests have dropped by a quarter.
>
> Last week Commissioner Kelly and I joined Governor Cuomo in supporting an amendment to State law that would effectively codify the directive Commissioner Kelly has put in place. But no matter what happens in Albany, we are already reducing the number of arrests—and keeping more young people from having negative interactions with the criminal justice system.[97]

While the tone of the Mayor was conciliatory in Brooklyn, he was more hostile to critics of the stop-and-frisk program when he exhorted his police department.

Even with the excellent record of reducing crime, the Mayor complained that, "the NYPD is under attack."

> The attacks most often come from those who play no constructive role in keeping our city safe, but rather view their jobs as pointing fingers from the steps of City Hall. Some of them scream that they know better than you how to run the Department. Some have even sued the NYPD and demanded a Federal monitor over NYPD operations.
>
> ...
>
> As the ongoing Federal court case is now demonstrating for any objective observer to see, the NYPD conducts stops based on seeing something suspicious, or witnesses' descriptions of suspects, not on any preconceived notions, or on demographic data that would have you stopping old women as often as you stop young men.
>
> ...
>
> The second bill before the City Council is being sold as a law that bans racial profiling. Well the fact of the matter is racial profiling is already against the law. In fact, I signed that bill into law, because our Administration has absolutely zero tolerance for racial profiling.
>
> In addition, under Commissioner Kelly's leadership, we've made the NYPD the most diverse police force in the nation. Critics who claim that police stops are based on race never seem to mention the fact that the majority of the NYPD's patrolling officers are minorities, but that's true. And last year, Commissioner Kelly instituted more rigorous training and quality controls to ensure that officers conduct stops properly and respectfully.[98]

Leaving aside the ridiculous and absurd assertion that the fact that the police department is racially diversified proves that the stop-and-frisk program can't be racially biased because Black and Hispanic police officers are participating in the stops, the Mayor was blunt when

97 Mayor Michael Bloomberg, "Mayor Bloomberg Speaks to Parishioners" …

98 Mayor Michael Bloomberg, "Mayor Bloomberg Delivers Address on Public Safety to NYPD Leadership" …

he addressed why Blacks and Hispanic males were disproportionately being stopped and why proposed legislation in the city council to address it was wrong.

> The legislation is based on the false allegation that the NYPD disproportionately stops young men of color. But as you know, stops are made based on descriptions of suspects and suspicious activity only. And *the sad reality is on the streets of our city, 90 percent of murder suspects and murder victims are black and Latino. And black and Hispanics are the overwhelming majority of suspects in other violent crimes.* The truth of the matter is, comparing stops to the general population is just not rational. *Comparing stops to the witnesses' description of suspects and the identification of suspicious activity—which together reflect the racial and ethnic breakdown of criminal activity—is what matters.* And the numbers put the lie to the racist allegations. In fact, the percentage of stops of blacks is less than that of whites and Asians when adjusted for crime reports.[99]

The Mayor, both in this speech and in other statements, asserts that the stops are based on crime patterns within a geographic area and those who commit crimes within that area. If Blacks and Hispanics commit the most crimes in the area as a group, then the stops should reflect that reality. The Mayor neglected to mention 70 percent of the crime complaints were missing suspect race data. Only when merging suspect data with arrest data is race of suspects known in the majority of cases.[100]

The Mayor opposed proposed legislation to prevent racial profiling, because "[b]y their own admission, the supporters of these bills say they are designed to put pressure on the NYPD to make fewer stops,"[101] to which the Mayor responded, "Stop playing politics with public safety."[102] Further, the Mayor asserted that those who attack the stop-and-frisk program are hypocrites, because they rage at the injustice done to Black and Hispanic males when stopped by the police, but they are nowhere to be heard when a Black or Hispanic male is killed in a meaningless drive-by shooting. While "about 90 percent of all murder victims in our city are black and Latino ... there is no outrage from the Center for Constitutional Rights or the NYCLU [and there is] not even a mention ... in our paper of record, the New York Times, [but] when police stop and ask a 17-year-old a question based on reasonable suspicion of a crime, there is outrage. Yet when a 17-year-old is standing on the corner near his home at 8:15 in the evening and gets shot and killed, there is silence."[103]

---

99 Mayor Michael Bloomberg, "Mayor Bloomberg Delivers Address on Public Safety to NYPD Leadership" ... (Emphasis added)

100 See supra note 62.

101 Mayor Michael Bloomberg, "Mayor Bloomberg Delivers Address on Public Safety to NYPD Leadership" ...

102 Mayor Michael Bloomberg, "Mayor Bloomberg Delivers Address on Public Safety to NYPD Leadership" ...

103 Mayor Michael Bloomberg, "Mayor Bloomberg Delivers Address on Public Safety to NYPD Leadership" ...

As he explained to the community the year before, the Mayor said that the stop-and-frisk program was based on a deterrence model. The police are making stops to prevent people from carrying guns.

> Now, critics say that police stops have nothing to do with the reduction in crime we've achieved. But think about this: over the past eleven years, stops have taken 8,200 illegal guns off our streets—and murder-by-guns has dropped dramatically.

The fact that you can't use unconstitutional means to achieve a legitimate end was lost on the mayor. He continued,

> Critics say the fact that we're 'only' finding 800 guns a year through stops of people who fit a description or are engaged in suspicious activity means that we should end stop and frisk.
>
> Wrong. That's the reason we need it—to deter people from carrying guns. We are the First Preventers.
>
> Think about police department tactics, that they often announce they're setting up checks for DWI. The goal is deterrence. If you know you're likely to be stopped, you don't drink and drive.
>
> If you end DWI stops, more people will get killed in crashes. And if you end stops looking for guns, make no mistake there will be more guns in the hands of young people and more people will be getting killed. It's really that simple.[104]

While the district court held that the stops were occurring without specific reasonable suspicion, the Mayor assumes the stops are being carried out as such; thus, the attacks on the program result from people who want the NYPD to "run according to the standards of political correctness, not public safety,"[105]—a concept he, of course, rejected.

---

104 Mayor Michael Bloomberg, "Mayor Bloomberg Delivers Address on Public Safety to NYPD Leadership" .... *See also,* Mayor Bloomberg, Police Commissioner Kelly, Special Narcotics Prosecutor Brennan, District Attorneys Vance and Hynes and Criminal Justice Coordinator Feinblatt Announce Largest Seizure of Illegal Guns in City History, press conference (August 19, 2013).

At the press conference the Mayor announced that the police had seized 254 illegal guns and indictments of 19 people involved in illegal gun trafficking from North and South Carolina to New York City. The Mayor noted that wiretaps of the suspects revealed that the gun runners had changed their behavior because stop-question-frisk made selling illegal guns more difficult in the city. The Mayor played a taped conversation with one of the gun traffickers. On the tape, Defendant Earl Campbell said,

> yeah I'm in Charlotte now. I can't leave until you come, cause I can't take them [guns] to my house, to my side of town cause I'm in Brownsville. So we got like, whatchamacallit, stop and frisk.

105 Mayor Michael Bloomberg, "Mayor Bloomberg Speaks to Parishioners" ...

Commissioner Kelly, in an op-ed a month later,[106] stated that "[s]ince 2002, the New York Police Department has taken tens of thousands of weapons off the street through proactive policing strategies. The effect this has had on the murder rate is staggering. In the 11 years before Mayor Michael Bloomberg took office, there were 13,212 murders in New York City. During the 11 years of his administration, there have been 5,849. That's 7,383 lives saved—and if history is a guide, they are largely the lives of young men of color."[107] As did the Mayor, Commissioner Kelly rejects the assertion that individual men of color are being racially profiled, because "the race of those stopped highly correlates to descriptions provided by victims or witnesses of crimes."[108] Put simply, "96% of the individuals who were shot [in 2003] and 90% of those murdered were black and Hispanic [thus] we've [developed] a proactive policy of engagement. We stop and question individuals about whom we have reasonable suspicion."[109] Like the Mayor, Commissioner Kelly said, "[i]t's understandable that someone who has done nothing wrong will be angry if he is stopped [but] we have to face the reality that New York's minority communities experience a disproportionate share of violent crime. To ignore that fact, as our critics would have us do, would be a form of discrimination in itself."[110]

A month later, the district court issued its opinion of the stop-question-frisk policy, holding that it violated the Fourth Amendment, because the stops were not conducted on a basis of specific reasonable suspicion but upon "indirect racial profiling." The Mayor and the Police Commissioner held a press conference to voice their rejection of the decision.[111] After making similar statements on the utility of the program to prevent crime and, specifically, the murder rate, the Mayor complained that the "judge made it clear she was not at all interested in the crime reductions ... nowhere in her 195-page decision does she mention the historic cuts in crime or the number of lives that have been saved."[112] Aside from this major oversight, the Mayor complained

> She ignored the real-world realities of crime, the fact that stops match-up with crime statistics, and the fact that our police officers on patrol—the majority of whom are black, Hispanic, or members of other ethnic or racial minorities—make an average about less than one stop a week.

---

106 Ray Kelly, "Ray Kelly: The NYPD: Guilty of saving 7,383 Lives, Accusations of racial profiling ignore the fact that violent crime overwhelmingly occurs in minority neighborhoods," *THE WALL STREET JOURNAL*, Jul. 22, 2013 7:14 P.M. https://www.wsj.com/articles/SB10001424127887324448104578616333588719320

107 Ray Kelly, "The NYPD: Guilty of saving 7,383 Lives" ...

108 Ray Kelly, "The NYPD: Guilty of saving 7,383 Lives" ...

109 Ray Kelly, "The NYPD: Guilty of saving 7,383 Lives" ...

110 Ray Kelly, "The NYPD: Guilty of saving 7,383 Lives" ...

111 Press Release, Transcript of Statements of Mayor Bloomberg and Commissioner Kelly on Federal Court Ruling (Aug. 12, 2013) http://www1.nyc.gov/office-of-the-mayor/news/275-13/statements-mayor-bloomberg-commissioner-kelly-federal-court-ruling

112 Mayor Bloomberg and Kelly, press release.

His point being Blacks and Hispanics can't hold negative bias, stereotypes, racist views of other Blacks and Hispanics. The Mayor continued,

> And even though the plaintiff's own expert found that about 90 percent of stops have been conducted appropriately and lawfully, and another 5 percent may well have been conducted appropriately and lawfully, the judge still wants to put the NYPD into receivership based on the flimsiest of evidence in a handful of cases.

After claiming that the judge was biased from the beginning in favor of the plaintiffs[113] the Mayor made clear that stop-question-frisk is a key tool in law enforcement and "we have to give the members of our Police Department the tools they need to do their jobs without being micro-managed and second-guessed every day by a judge or a monitor."[114] Commissioner Kelly was just as incensed by the decision, taking particular umbrage to the assertion that the NYPD engages in racial profiling.[115] But more importantly, he continued to justify the program on a deterrence theory.

> Police stops are just one component of multiple efforts by the Department that have saved lives and driven the murder rate to record lows. In the first 11 years of Mayor Bloomberg's tenure there were 7,363 fewer murders in New York City compared to the 11 years prior

---

113 "Given the judge's public comments and media interviews throughout the case, this decision was certainly not a surprise. From even before the start of the case, when she offered some strategic advice to the plaintiffs that would allow her to hear the case, the judge clearly telegraphed her intentions. And she conveyed a disturbing disregard for the good intentions of our police officers, who form the most diverse Police Department in the country, and who put their lives on the line for us every single day. Throughout the case, we didn't believe that we were getting a fair trial. This decision confirms that suspicion, and we will be presenting evidence of that unfairness to the Appeals Court." *Id.*

The Second Circuit would find salience with this attack on the Judge and the Court removed Judge Scheindlin from case when it granted a stay of her ruling pending appeal by the City. See *Ligon et al. v. City of New York* (13-3123) and *David Floyd, et al. v. City of New York* (13-3088) U.S. Court of Appeals 2nd Cir (October 31, 2013), *David Floyd, et al. v. City of New York Plaintiffs Declaration in Support of Motion to Vacate the District Court Order* (13-2088(L)) (Nov. 9, 2013), *In re Motion of District Judge*, ____ F.3d____, Nos 13-3123, 13-3088 (2d Cir. Nov. 13, 2013) and *In re Reassignment of Cases*, ____ F3d.____, Nos. 13-3123, 13-3088 (2d Cir. Nov. 13, 2013), and *Ligon et al. v. City of New York* (13-3123) and *David Floyd et al. v. City of New York* (13-3088) U.S. Court of Appeals 2d Cir (Nov. 22, 2013).

114 Mayor Bloomberg and Kelly, press release, *supra* note 111.

115 Mayor Bloomberg and Kelly, press release. As previously asserted by the Commissioner, "To that point, last year 97 percent of all shooting victims were black or Hispanic and reside in low-income neighborhoods. Public housing where five percent of the city's population resides experiences 20 percent of the shootings. There were more stops with suspicious activity in neighborhoods with higher crime because that's where the crime is."

> to the Mayor taking office. And if history is any guide, those lives saved were overwhelmingly the lives of young men of color.
>
> Now, this didn't happen by accident, it was a result of proactive policing supported by this Mayor. There's little question that police stops in this case continue to be deeply misunderstood.
>
> The fact that they often do not lead to arrests or summonses misses the point. When a police officer stops and makes inquiry of an individual about to burglarize a location the officer has stopped a burglary. When officers stop and make inquiry of young men about to strong-arm a bodega owner as he leaves his store late at night they've stopped a robbery or perhaps worse.
>
> But obviously stops for suspicious behavior do lead to good arrests as well. We've taken about 8,000 guns from individuals over the last decade this way. Something our critics sneer because the number is 'too low' compared to the number of stops, despite the fact that stops average, as the Mayor said, less than one per week per officer on patrol.[116]

The Commissioner ended his rejection of the district court by quoting an article in the *Atlantic Magazine*, "But just as the cost of aggressive crime control are disproportionately borne by the disadvantaged, so too have been the benefits: the reduction in crime is one of the few public goods in New York that is truly progressive, benefiting disproportionately the poor and vulnerable, who need it most."[117]

In an op-ed a few days later[118] the Mayor asserted that statistics on crime should not be viewed from census tracks with a view of finding proportionate results of police interaction. Police activity should be viewed from the perspective of crime activity and those who, as a group, commit those crimes. Such an approach is not racism but active law enforcement applied to both location and crime perpetrators.

> That the proportion of stops generally reflects our crime numbers does not mean, as the judge wrongly concluded, that the police are engaged in racial profiling; it means they are stopping people in those communities who fit descriptions of suspects or are engaged in suspicious activity.[119]

---

116 Mayor Bloomberg and Kelly, press release.; *but see supra* notes 70–72.

117 Mayor Bloomberg and Kelly, press release

118 Michael R. Bloomberg, "Michael Bloomberg: 'Stop and frisk' keeps New York safe," WP OPINION, *Washington Post*, (Aug. 18, 2013), http://www.washingtonpost.com/opinions/michael-bloomberg-stop-and-frisk-keeps-new-york-safe/2013/08/18/8d4cd8c4-06cf-11e3-9259-e2aafe5a5f84_story.html.

119 Michael Bloomberg, "Stop and frisk' keeps New York safe,"

He also complained that the plaintiffs failed to prove their claim of racial profiling.

> Amazingly, out of several million stops that have happened over the past decade, the advocates who brought the case could identify only 19 stops that they believe were unjustified—and the judge disagreed with them on a majority of even those handpicked cases, finding that 10 of the 19 stops were in fact justified, even though they did not lead to an arrest. By doing so, the judge acknowledged that stops that do not end in arrest are often legitimate; those scoping out a robbery, or lying in wait of a potential victim, can be stopped and deterred even if they cannot be arrested. Nevertheless, the judge used a questionable analysis of police officers' paperwork, which found that only 6 percent of stops were unjustified, as a basis for imposing a court-appointed monitor to oversee the NYPD's practice of stop-question-frisk, as well as to mandate specific programmatic changes to policing, even though she has no experience in policing.[120]

It is clear that the Mayor and the NYPD viewed the issue of stop-question-frisk differently than the plaintiffs and the court. The program allowed the city to reduce crime, prevent crime, and remove guns from the street. They viewed the disproportionate impact as an inconvenience that is the natural result of Blacks and Hispanics committing crime disproportionately to their population. As the Mayor and Commissioner made clear in their public statements, it would make no sense to stop women over men and the old over the young, because the women and the old are not the drivers of crime, the young and the men are. Thus, it makes logical sense to stop them. By the analogy, it should be expected that the police will stop people of color more than Whites. To the claim that they are using a tool that has utility but is unconstitutional, they both made clear that they only stop people based on reasonable suspicion. But as the court observed, the police perceive anyone within the high-crime committing group as a possible criminal or, at the very least, a person to be considered for a stop-question-frisk encounter. As discussed in Chapter Three, the issue of race occurs in the mind of the police before the reasonable suspicion occurs. That is what the court held was "indirect racial profiling," and this is what the city rejects out of hand.

The perception that Blacks are a population to be controlled due to their threat to public peace and law and order is not a recent concept. As discussed in Chapter Seven, Blacks have been the focus of urban criminal justice and a perceived threat to be controlled for more that century. The point is the attitudes of the Mayor and Commissioner have a social political context outside of the debate between general population and criminal population benchmarking.

---

120 Michael Bloomberg, "Stop and frisk' keeps New York safe,"

When a group of Roman police officers[121] asked John the Baptist what they must do to be saved, John answered, "Do not intimidate anyone or accuse falsely."[122] It is nothing new in the history of mankind that the police must be warned not to use their authority to the detriment of those who are socially disadvantaged or incapable of defending themselves within society. Such protection, in the American context, is provided by the Constitution and the courts. In the case of *Floyd et al. v. City of New York*, the court held that the NYPD was, (1) as a matter of custom, practice, and policy, stopping young men of color based on their race and not—as required by *Terry* and *DeBour*—due to specific individual behavior that would invoke a reasonable person to believe a crime had been or was about to be committed warranting further investigation to determine if, in fact, a crime was in progress, and (2) deliberately indifferent to the widespread practice, and failed to adequately train and supervise officers to prevent the constitutional violations.[123] The court concluded

> [t]he NYPD has directed officers to target young black and Hispanic men because these groups are heavily represented in criminal suspect data—the reliability of which is questionable—in those areas where the NYPD carries out most of its stops. Under the NYPD's policy, targeting the "right people" means stopping people in part because of their race. Together with Commissioner Kelly's statement that the NYPD focuses stop and frisks on young blacks and Hispanics in order to instill in them a fear of being stopped, and other explicit references to race ... there is a sufficient basis for inferring discriminatory intent.
>
> The fact that the targeted racial groups were identified based on crime victim complaints does not eliminate the discriminatory intent. Just as it would be impermissible for a public housing agency to adopt a facially race-neutral policy of disfavoring applications from any group that is disproportionately subject to tenant complaints, and then apply

121 Although, the actual wording is "soldiers," John was most likely answering members of the Roman Urban Cohorts. The Urban Cohorts, in the days of ancient Rome, were a branch of the Army with the authority to arrest and enforce Roman law. *See* P. K. Baillie Reynolds, "The Police in Ancient Rome," *1The Police Journal: Theory, Practice and Principles* 1, no. 3 (1928): 432, *The Cambridge History of Greek and Roman Warfare: Volume II Rome from the Late Republic to the Late Empire*, eds. Philip Sabin, Hans Van Wees & Michael Whitby (Cambridge University Press, 2007), 217–18 and Kelly Martin, *The First Urban Policeman*, J. Police Sci. &Admin, 1, no. 1 (1973): 56.

122 Luke 3:14 (New King James Version); *see also*, Luke 3:14 (New Living Translation) ("Don't extort money or make false accusations"); Luke 3:14 (English Standard Version) ("Do not extort money from anyone by threats or by false accusation"); Luke 3:14 (Easy to Read Version) ("Don't use force or lies to make people give you money.")

123 *Terry v. Ohio*, 392 U.S. 1(1968). *See also, People v. DeBour*, 40 N.Y. 2d 210 (1976) and *Floyd,* 959 F. Supp. 2d at 658–667.

> this policy to disfavor applications from a racially defined group, so it is impermissible for a police department to target its general enforcement practices against racially defined groups based on crime suspect data.[124]

As the court observed, the constitutional error is that "[t]he policy assumes that *all* members of a racially defined group are 'the right people' to target for stops because *some* members of that group committed crimes."[125] Put simply,

> targeting young black and Hispanic men for stops based on the alleged criminal conduct of other young black and Hispanic men violates bedrock principles of equality. ... [T]he Equal Protection Clause does not sanction treating similarly situated members of a different racial groups differently based on racial disparities in crime data. Indeed, such treatment would eviscerate the core guarantees of the Equal Protection Clause. ... [I]ndividuals may not be punished or rewarded based on the government's views regarding their racial group, regardless of the source of those views.[126]

Additionally, the other constitutional error made by the NYPD and the mayor was viewing stop and frisk as a tool of crime deterrence, rather than a crime investigatory tool. Constitutionally, stop and frisk is a rule that governs the power of government to obstruct the liberty of a person to travel without government interference. The New York Court of Appeals in *People v. DeBour* (1976), and the Supreme Court in *Terry v. Ohio* (1968) and its companion case *Sibron v. New York*, held that stop and frisk is not a constitutional tool to create an environment of fear in the hearts of criminals or suppress criminal activity, but rather it was a constitutional rule to allow police to temporarily stop a person to determine if a crime is afoot or has been committed and that the police may frisk such a person if they have reasonable suspicion that the person is armed. Stop and frisk is not designed to prevent crime and reduce gun violence; it is a police investigatory tool to determine if a crime has been or is about to occur by a specific person at a specific time in a specific place. The NYPD changed stop and frisk into a tool that created an environment that criminals are afraid to operate within and justified the disproportionate impact as the natural result of crime statistic–driven policing and crime prevention.

---

124 *Floyd et al. v. City of N.Y.* at 662, (internal citation referring to the liability of criminal suspect data); "The NYPD's use of local crime suspect data to target racially defined groups for stops is not only a form of racial profiling, it is also a deeply flawed way of identifying the criminal population." *Id.* at 662 n. 764; *see also id.* at 666 n.776.

125 *Floyd et al. v. City of N.Y.* at 663 n767.

126 *Floyd et al. v. City of N.Y.* at 664.

The reason why it matters that the stop-and-frisk program by the NYPD needs to comply with *Terry* is because it is important that, under the American constitutional system, the government be bound and prevented from violating the rights and freedoms of individuals regardless and even though abridging those rights has utility in achieving a legitimate governmental goal—reduction of crime. The constitution established a limited government with limited powers. That is what makes the American republic a reality. In 1886, Supreme Court Justice Joseph Bradley wrote in that, "it is not the breaking of his doors, and the rummaging of his drawers, that constitutes the essence of the [Fourth Amendment] offense; but it is the invasion of his indefeasible right to personal security, personal liberty and private property."[127] Justice Bradley reminds us more than a century ago that obnoxious systematic and systemic violation of constitutional and individual rights begins with small procedural diversions from what the law requires.

> It may be that it is the obnoxious thing in its mildest and least repulsive form; but illegitimate and unconstitutional practices get their first footing in that way, namely, by silent approaches and slight deviations from legal modes of procedure. This can only be obviated by adhering to the rule that constitutional provisions for the security of person and property should be liberally construed. A close and literal construction deprives them of half their efficacy, and leads to gradual depreciation of the right, as if it consisted more in sound than in substance. It is the duty of the courts to be watchful for the constitutional rights of the citizen, and against any stealthy encroachments thereon. Their motto should be *obsta principiis*.[128]

The protection of the freedoms embedded in the Constitution and the enforcement of those freedoms and liberties is not handcuffing the police or allowing loopholes that criminals use to escape justice, because "freedoms are not loopholes in a system of limited government."[129] As Justice Douglas similarly observed

> The infringement on personal liberty of any 'seizure' of a person can only be 'reasonable' under the Fourth Amendment if we require the police to possess 'probable cause' before they seize him. Only that line draws a meaningful distinction between an officer's mere inkling and the presence of facts within the officer's personal knowledge which would convince a reasonable man that the person seized has committed, is committing, or is about to commit a particular crime. 'In dealing with probable cause ... as the very name implies, we deal with probabilities. These are not technical; they are the factual and practical considerations of everyday life on which reasonable and prudent men, not legal technicians, act.'

---

127 *Boyd v. United States*, 116 U.S. 616, 630 (1886).

128 *Boyd v. United States* at 635.

129 *A Conspiracy Against Obamacare: The Volokh Conspiracy and the Health Care Case*, The Heritage Foundation (Jan. 7, 2014)

> ***To give the police greater power than a magistrate is to take a long step down the totalitarian path.*** Perhaps such a step is desirable to cope with modern forms of lawlessness. But if it is taken, it should be the deliberate choice of the people through a constitutional amendment.
>
> Until the Fourth Amendment, which is closely allied with the Fifth, is rewritten, the person and the effects of the individual are beyond the reach of all government agencies until there are reasonable grounds to believe (probable cause) that a criminal venture has been launched or is about to be launched.[130]

Justice Douglass, in his dissent in *Terry* (he dissented on allowing a stop or a search on less than probable cause), defended both the text and the principal of the Fourth Amendment by concluding that the ends of crime suppression do not justify the means of violating the Constitution.

> There have been powerful hydraulic pressures throughout our history that bear heavily on the Court to water down constitutional guarantees and give the police the upper hand. That hydraulic pressure has probably never been greater than it is today.
>
> ***Yet if the individual is no longer to be sovereign, if the police can pick him up whenever*** they do not like the cut of his jib, ***if they can 'seize' and 'search' him in their discretion, we enter a new regime.*** The decision to enter it should be made only after a full debate by the people of this country.[131]

Protection of constitutional rights in the face of government assertion of crisis is no small matter. The only protection the individual has is the courts enforcing the law backed up by societal acceptance that the law must triumph regardless of who it triumphs for. As Justice Jackson wrote regarding the role of the judiciary,

> With all its defects, delays and inconveniences, men have discovered no technique for long preserving free government except that the Executive be under the law, and that the law be made by parliamentary deliberations.
>
> ***Such institutions may be destined to pass away. But it is the duty of the Court to be last, not first, to give them up.***[132]

Liberties are only safe in a society when the law protects the poor, the weak, and the despised. Although the law and the liberties they protect apply equally to protecting the powerful and respected, the protection of the law is more important for the poor because the powerful have less need for the protection of the law, they have other means to protect their rights and liberties.

---

130 *Terry v. Ohio*, 392 U.S. at 38–39 (internal citation omitted).

131 *Terry v. Ohio* at 39.

132 *Youngstown Sheet & Tube Co. v. Sawyer*, 343 U.S. 579, 655 (1952) (emphasis added)

EPILOGUE

The change to the NYPD stop-and-frisk program did not occur due to appellate review by federal courts but by the decision made by New Yorkers themselves in November 2013. Elections have consequences to policy. Bill de Blasio was elected Mayor of NYC in November 2013, and during the election, he had stated that he would withdraw the appeal and accept the district court's ruling if elected. On December 5, 2013, de Blasio announced that he was appointing Bill Bratton as the new Police Commissioner. During the press conference, de Blasio paraphrased his new police commissioner, who commented on the use of stop and frisk. Mayor de Blasio said that, "stop-and-frisk is like chemotherapy: Used in the right dose, it can save lives; used in the wrong dose, too heavy a dose, it can create its own dangers and problems, it can backfire."[133] At the press conference, Commissioner Bratton, while defending stop and frisk as a law enforcement tool, noted that "stop-and-frisk is essential to every police department in America. But it's also essential that it be done constitutionally and respectfully. And that is my commitment to this mayor and to the city—that it will be done that way."[134]

On December 29, 2013, while announcing the appointment of the new city corporate attorney, de Blasio stated that the city "will drop the appeal on the stop and frisk case because we think the judge was right about the reforms that we need to make."[135] On January 1, 2014, de Blasio stated in his inaugural address that, among the things his administration will seek to accomplish, "We will reform a broken stop-and-frisk policy, both to protect the dignity and rights of young men of color, and to give our brave police officers the partnership they need to continue their success in driving down crime."[136] On January 30, 2014, the de Blasio administration filed a motion to have the case returned to the district court in order to facilitate the settlement of the case.[137] In a press conference announcing the agreement between

---

133 Henry Goldman, "de Blasio Taking Office Citing Wealth Gap as Crime Falls," *Bloomberg Business Week* (Jan. 1, 2014), http://www.bloomberg.com/news/2013-12-31/de-blasio-taking-office-citing-wealth-gap-as-crime-falls.html.

134 Beth DeFalco and Bob Fredericks, "de Blasio names Bill Bratton next NYPD Commissioner," *New York Post* (Dec. 5, 2013), http://nypost.com/2013/12/05/de-blasio-to-tap-bill-bratton-to-run-nypd/.

135 Erin Durkin, "Bill de Blasio announces Zachary Carter as city's next top lawyer," *NY Daily News* (Dec. 29, 2013), http://www.nydailynews.com/news/politics/de-blasio-announces-zachary-carter-city-top-lawyer-article-1.1561084.

136 Bill de Blasio, "Text of Bill de Blasio's Inauguration speech," *New York Times* (Jan. 1, 2014), http://www.nytimes.com/2014/01/02/nyregion/complete-text-of-bill-de-blasios-inauguration-speech.html?_r=0.

137 Declaration in Support of Motion for Limited Remand to the District Court for the Purpose of Exploring a Resolution, *David Floyd, et al v. City of New York* and *Jaenean Ligon et al v. City of New York*, No. 13-3088 (2d Cir. Jan. 30, 2014), *available at* http://www.ccrjustice.org/files/City's%201%2030%202014%20Unopposed%20Motion%20for%20Remand..pdf.

the city and the plaintiffs, Mayor de Blasio made clear that, "the agreement we're announcing today accepts the facts and the roadmap laid out in last August's [sic] landmark Federal court ruling."[138] The Mayor stated that

> [n]either the police commissioner nor I believe it is acceptable when 90 percent of the people stopped and frisked are innocent of any crime. And so we are taking significant corrective action to fix what is broken. I am proud to announce today, that the City of New York is taking a major step to resolve the years-long legal battle over stop-and-frisk; and that we have reached accord with the plaintiffs in the landmark *Floyd vs. City of New York* case. We are doing it through a collective commitment to fix the fundamental problems that enabled stop-and-frisk to grow out of control and violate the rights of innocent New Yorkers. What we are doing here today will increase the quality of policing in New York City.[139]

Commissioner Bratton affirmed the views of the Mayor and was blunt regarding the need for the change. At the press conference, he said:

> The Mayor referenced that, in a democracy, the first obligation of government has to be—the first responsibility has to be public safety. Let's face it, stop, question, and frisk as it's been practiced in this city for the last several years, has not met that obligation or responsibility. Instead of securing confidence, instead of securing legitimacy and procedural justice in this city for the residents, it instead has raised doubts and concerns about the police force in this city. And to that end, we need to have resolution.

Noting that, "something that unites us all is we believe in the United States Constitution," and after citing Commissioner Bratton, that "you cannot break the law to enforce the law," the Mayor concluded that, "we have to bring our practices fully in line with the foundational document of the republic. I don't think there's anything more important you can do."[140] The Mayor announced a three-part settlement in the stop-and-frisk case. The three factors will include:

> [O]ne, a joint and ongoing reform process with direct police-community dialogue, ensuring that policies which are driving police and community apart are raised through a direct line of communication with the police leadership. Two, there will be for three years a court-appointed monitor to ensure the Police Department's compliance with the United States Constitution. And that limited period of oversight is contingent upon us meeting our obligations. Three, I want to emphasize as an explanation that this is a shorter window of monitoring than is customary, and that is in part because of our administration's

---

138 Mayor Bill de Blasio, Announcement of Agreement in Landmark Stop-And-Frisk Case (Jan.30, 2014) (transcript available at http://www1.nyc.gov/office-of-the-mayor/news/727-14/transcript-mayor-bill-de-blasio-agreement-landmark-stop-and-frisk-case/).

139 Mayor Bill de Blasio, Announcement of Agreement in Landmark Stop-And-Frisk Case (Jan.30, 2014)

140 Mayor Bill de Blasio, Announcement of Agreement in Landmark Stop-And-Frisk Case (Jan.30, 2014)

> explicit commitment to reform—including the installation of an independent NYPD Inspector General.[141]

At the same press conference, the City Corporate counsel affirmed that the city would comply with Judge Scheindlin's "order that the New York City Police Department comply with the Constitution, as she interpreted it, with respect to whether—or—the situations in which you can and cannot take race into account when you're making policing decisions." He also made clear that the city would support and comply with the consent order being agreed upon, which involved both internal and external compliance observation of the NYPD.

> One thing we have, the very positive change in circumstances that has been institutionalized in New York City—that creation of an independent Inspector General for the Police Department, and so what is envisioned is that what is temporary with respect with respect to the three-year monitorship, those responsibilities will naturally migrate over time to the Inspector General. And obviously that is permanent in reliable external oversight.

Subsequent to the district court affirming the agreement, Mayor de Blasio stated that, "the City of New York will officially drop its appeal in this case."[142] On February 21, 2014, the Court of Appeals for the Second Circuit granted the city's motion to have the case returned to the district court for purposes of settling the case and to vacate the court stay on the August 2013 decision.[143] Subsequently, the city filed a motion in the district court on April 3, 2014, that it had reached an agreement with the plaintiffs and that it accepts and will comply with the August 2013 Remedial Order enforcing the August 2013 Liability Opinion.[144]

KEY CONCEPTS AND CASES

1. *Sibron v. New York* (1968)
2. *Terry v. Ohio* (1968)
3. *People v. DeBour* (1976)
4. Stop and Frisk
5. *Floyd v. City of New York* (2013)
6. Suspect race descriptive crime data
7. General population and reported crime data

---

141 Mayor Bill de Blasio, Announcement of Agreement in Landmark Stop-And-Frisk Case (Jan.30, 2014)

142 Mayor Bill de Blasio, Announcement of Agreement in Landmark Stop-And-Frisk Case (Jan.30, 2014)

143 *Floyd v. City of New York and Ligon v. City of New York*, Docket Nos. 13—3123—cv, 13—3088—cv, 13—3461—cv (February 21, 2014).

144 *Floyd v. City of New York and Ligon v. City of New York*, Memorandum of Law in Support of Motion for Modification of Remedial Order 08 Civ.1034 (AT), 12 CIV. 2274 (AT) (April 3, 2014).

DISCUSSION QUESTIONS

1. The NYPD argued that, although a disproportionate percentage of Blacks and Hispanics were stopped by NYPD officers, the disproportionate percentage was proportionate to the suspect-descriptive data. The plaintiffs argued that the disproportionate percentage was not proportionate based on the population of Blacks and Hispanics in NYC. Explain and contrast the two competing benchmark measures? Why is the choice of benchmark significant? Which benchmark do you agree with? Why?
2. The RAND corporation asserted that it does not matter what benchmark is used if police exposure does not allow for the police to have access to all possible criminal perpetrators. Explain the RAND corporation discussion and compare to the two benchmarks advocated by the plaintiffs and the NYPD.
3. What is the politics of police crime suppression in minority communities? How did Mayor Bloomberg and Commissioner Kelly defend the actions and results of the NYPD stop and frisk policy? Were they correct? What is the significance of elections in policy disputes?
4. What is the difference between crime suppression strategies and crime investigation strategies? What is the difference from a constitutional law perspective, and what is the difference from a police operation perspective?
5. What issues are raised in the *Terry* case, and how were these issues balanced in the case? Do you agree or disagree with the logic and/or conclusions of *Terry*?

CHAPTER SEVEN

Black Incarceration and Social Control

AMERICAN POLITICAL CHOICES AND CRIMINAL JUSTICE POLICY

> Any society, any family, which cannot share or take seriously the pain of its children, and views that pain as something normal or to be expected, is a society "condemned" to remain a hostage to itself, prey to the very things which cause that pain.[1]

STUDENT LEARNING OBJECTIVES

1. Students will be able to explain the history of American criminal justice in the postbellum period and place that history in context with the criminal justice politics of the 1960s.
2. Students will be able to define peonage, convict leasing, criminal surety, and other forms of legal involuntary servitude laws that criminalized Blacks.
3. Students will be able to explain how the politics of World War II and the Cold War added to the social and political background that supported the civil rights movement of the 1960s.
4. Students will be able to explain and describe the link between the fall of Jim Crow and the rise of conservative political ideology and the crime-control policies of the 1970s to 1980s.

****

1 Pope Francis Remarks at the Curran-Fromhold Correctional Facility, Philadelphia, PA (September 27, 2015).

Timeline of Race, Law, and Criminal Justice in America

- 1619 First slaves are **brought to Jamestown, VA.**
- 1686 the rise of slave patrols and southern police
- 1776–1783 War of Independence
- 1789 U.S. Constitution
- Between 1777 (Vermont) and 1804 (N.J.) slavery is legally ended in the north
- 1861–1865 the Civil War and the end of slavery
- 1865-1870 13th, 14th and 15th Amendments

1863–1877 Reconstruction Era

- 1863 Emancipation Proclamation
- 1865–1872 Freeman's Bureau
- 1865 states pass the Black codes
- 1866 Congress passes the Civil Rights Act Southern states and the rise of convict leasing Alabama the first
- 1870 Congress passes the Reconstruction Acts
- 1870–1871 Congress passes three Ku Klux Klan Acts (§1983 civil liability passed in the 2nd Klan Act of 1871)
- 1872 Freeman's Bureau closed & 1874 the rise of vagrancy laws, convict leasing, Tenant farming, share cropping and peonage
- 1877 Tilden/Hayes election and the compromise of 1877 Reconstruction ends The rise of the "pig laws"

- 1886 modern southern police forces form to enforce pig laws and vagrancy statutes
- 1883 Supreme Court rules in the 1883 *Civil Rights Cases* that the 14th only applies to govt. discrimination
- 1896 Supreme Court rules in *Plessey v Ferguson*
- 1890–1908 Black disenfranchisement established across the nation
- 1908 the rise of chain gang and state convict labor
- 1928 Southern states the end of convict leasing Alabama the last to end the practice
- 1930s–1940s Modern Professionalization of policing

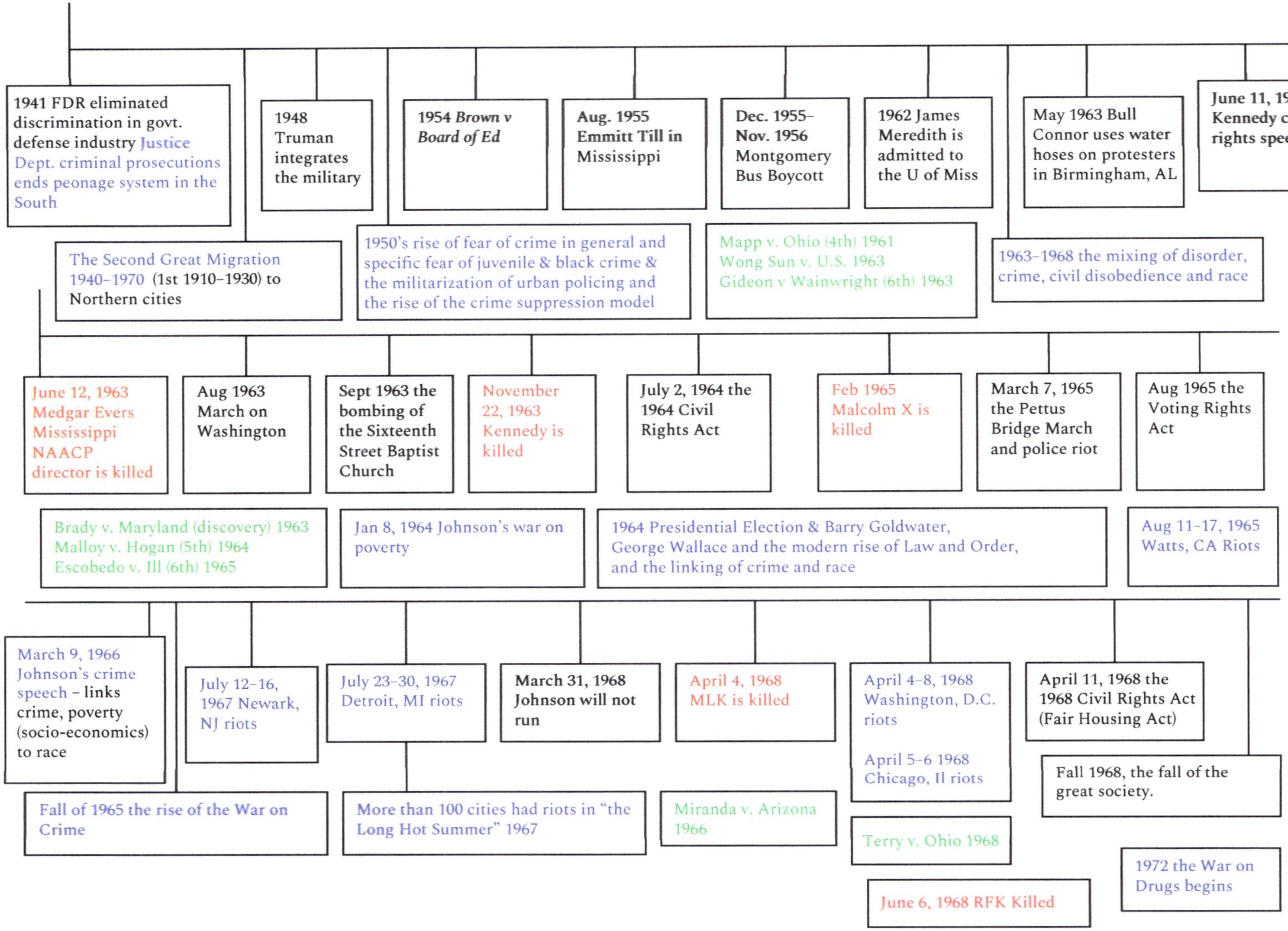
1941 FDR eliminated discrimination in govt. defense industry Justice Dept. criminal prosecutions ends peonage system in the South
1948 Truman integrates the military
1954 Brown v Board of Ed
Aug. 1955 Emmitt Till in Mississippi
Dec. 1955–Nov. 1956 Montgomery Bus Boycott
1962 James Meredith is admitted to the U of Miss
May 1963 Bull Connor uses water hoses on protesters in Birmingham, AL
June 11, 1963 Kennedy civil rights speech
The Second Great Migration 1940–1970 (1st 1910–1930) to Northern cities
1950's rise of fear of crime in general and specific fear of juvenile & black crime & the militarization of urban policing and the rise of the crime suppression model
Mapp v. Ohio (4th) 1961
Wong Sun v. U.S. 1963
Gideon v Wainwright (6th) 1963
1963–1968 the mixing of disorder, crime, civil disobedience and race
June 12, 1963 Medgar Evers Mississippi NAACP director is killed
Aug 1963 March on Washington
Sept 1963 the bombing of the Sixteenth Street Baptist Church
November 22, 1963 Kennedy is killed
July 2, 1964 the 1964 Civil Rights Act
Feb 1965 Malcolm X is killed
March 7, 1965 the Pettus Bridge March and police riot
Aug 1965 the Voting Rights Act
Brady v. Maryland (discovery) 1963
Malloy v. Hogan (5th) 1964
Escobedo v. Ill (6th) 1965
Jan 8, 1964 Johnson's war on poverty
1964 Presidential Election & Barry Goldwater, George Wallace and the modern rise of Law and Order, and the linking of crime and race
Aug 11–17, 1965 Watts, CA Riots
March 9, 1966 Johnson's crime speech – links crime, poverty (socio-economics) to race
July 12–16, 1967 Newark, NJ riots
July 23–30, 1967 Detroit, MI riots
March 31, 1968 Johnson will not run
April 4, 1968 MLK is killed
April 4–8, 1968 Washington, D.C. riots
April 5–6 1968 Chicago, Il riots
April 11, 1968 the 1968 Civil Rights Act (Fair Housing Act)
Fall 1968, the fall of the great society.
Fall of 1965 the rise of the War on Crime
More than 100 cities had riots in "the Long Hot Summer" 1967
Miranda v. Arizona 1966
Terry v. Ohio 1968
1972 the War on Drugs begins
June 6, 1968 RFK Killed

Beginning with Chapter One, this book proposed that understanding the criminal justice system in general, and criminal justice and race in particular, can only be understood through a multidisciplinary and multidirectional approach that includes American political, social, and policy history along with considering the social psychology of race and racism. In addition, race in America has a constitutional and legal history that adds additional support for the systematic and then systemic racism that influences the operation of policy making, criminal laws, and the daily operation of American criminal justice. The explanation for the disproportionate involvement of Blacks in the criminal justice system is not one-dimensional in that Blacks are more criminal or the criminal justice system is singularly racist by design and purpose. It's much more complicated than that.

The chronic incarceration of Blacks is the result of various factors. As discussed in Chapter One, Black disproportionate incarceration predates the arrival Lyndon Johnson to the House of Representatives in 1937.

Black incarceration after the civil war was the result of the passage of criminal and employment statutes that resulted in forced labor. How these statutes created both a chronic social dynamic of Black incarceration from 1865 through end of World War II is reviewed in this chapter. Chapter Eight will review the contemporary politics and policies of the middle and late twentieth century that continued the chronic incarceration of Blacks.

THE RISE OF JIM CROW CRIMINAL JUSTICE AND THE ORIGINAL INCARCERATION OF POST-ENSLAVED BLACKS

Blacks have been disproportionately involved in the criminal justice system since the Civil War. Black incarceration through the criminal justice system replaced slavery and Jim Crow as a social policy of controlling Blacks. That control began with the use of criminal peonage, convict leasing, criminal surety, and other systems of involuntary servitude.

The Black Codes and the Origins of Black Incarceration within American Criminal Justice

Blacks in chains were a social constant both before and after the Civil War. Slavery was replaced by the Southern development and Northern adoption of the "assumption that blacks would not work without compulsion. ... This assumption was also reflected in the so-called Black Codes that were adopted by the Southern states in 1865–1866 and that sought to perpetuate slavery in substance."[2] The significance of the Black Codes is that they replaced the control of Blacks through slavery with control through criminal justice statutes that made Blacks susceptible to slavery though conviction, which the Thirteenth Amendment authorized. These Black Codes,

---

2 Michael J. Klarman, *From Jim Crow to Civil Rights: The Supreme Court and the Struggle for Racial Equality* (2004) at 71.

which were followed by Jim Crow laws, supplemented the broader American policy determination to nullify as many of the rights Black citizens enjoyed, short of abolition of slavery, as possible.

As discussed in Chapter Five, the Supreme Court eliminated the ability of the Civil Rights Acts of 1871 and 1875 and the Civil War Amendments (the Thirteenth, Fourteenth, and Fifteenth) to outlaw and restrict individual and state discrimination of Blacks. The Black Codes involved criminal justice statutes and a system of "***mandatory contract laws*** supported by vagrancy provisions [that] required blacks to enter yearlong agricultural labor contracts ... or risk being convicted as vagrants and [be] compelled to work for planters under ***criminal-surety*** arrangements."[3] These criminal statutes supplemented other laws that put Blacks in a system of slavery by another name. These laws included ***criminal anti-enticement laws***, which forbade employers from hiring another's workers, which were backed up by ***contract enforcement laws***, which "criminalized entering into a contract without providing notice that the party was currently in breach of a similar contract."[4] Another system of controlling the right to contract and labor of Blacks were ***false-pretense laws***, which "criminalized a worker's breach of a labor contract after he had fraudulently accepted advanced wages."[5] These contract laws served two purposes: to protect landlords from sharecroppers abandoning the land before harvest (i.e., to protect the landlord's investment) and to maintain a stable labor force that could no longer be controlled by simple slavery.

The significance of these laws is that criminal law and the imposition of criminal sanctions were used to enforce contract law. While it was an abandonment of legal tradition in Western legal history, the criminalization of contract law occurred to solve a practical problem. Although landlords maintained the right to sue a sharecropper for leaving or otherwise not fulfilling the terms of the contract, as a practical matter this right had serious limits. Assuming the absconded sharecropper could be found, since he had no money or valuables, what purpose would a financial judgment be to the landlord? Thus, criminal penalty laws were instituted to enforce contracts. These laws were maintained for decades into the twentieth century.[6] These criminal laws that made it a crime to leave a plantation. The criminal antienticement laws, contract enforcement laws, and false-pretense laws forced Blacks to become permanently attached to the plantations with little difference to the antebellum period. These

---

3 Michael J. Klarman, *From Jim Crow to Civil Rights* ... (Emphasis added)

4 Michael J. Klarman, *From Jim Crow to Civil Rights* ... at 72.

5 Michael J. Klarman, *From Jim Crow to Civil Rights* ...

6 Harold D. Woodman, "Post-Civil War Southern Agriculture and the Law," *Agricultural History* 53, no. 1 (Jan., 1979): 319, 337, 335.

laws mirrored antebellum laws which prohibited slaves from running away, prohibited people from hiding slaves, and required people to return runaway slaves under the ***Fugitive Slave Laws*** of 1793 and 1850 and ***the Fugitive Slave Clause*** of the U.S. Constitution ("No person held to service or labour in one state, under the laws thereof, escaping into another, shall, in consequence of any law or regulation therein, be discharged from such service or labour, but shall be delivered up on claim of the party to whom such service or labour may be due").[7] Southern criminal justice used the pig laws, employment and apprentice laws (anti-vagrancy statutes), and antienticement laws, the criminalization of hiring workers (Blacks) under contract (the sharecropping system) to keep Blacks in a state of slavery by other means.[8] ***Pig laws*** were statutes that redefined formally misdemeanor or trivial offenses as felonies and imposed harsh sentences and fines. These laws were selectively enforced against Blacks to inject them into the criminal justice system and into forced labor through ***peonage, criminal surety***, and ***convict-leasing.***

As insidious as these laws were, the famous convict-lease system, criminal surety system, and criminal peonage firmly established the purpose of the Southern criminal justice as a system to keep Blacks not only in their place but to create a system that could produce the results of slavery in compliance with the Thirteenth Amendment, because involuntary service could be imposed, as the Thirteenth Amendment made clear, "as a punishment for crime whereof the party shall have been duly convicted." The system of peonage and criminal surety was not totally eradicated from the face of American criminal justice until the 1940s!

The systematic and systemic significance of the criminal anti-enticement laws, contract enforcement laws, the false-pretense laws, the convict-lease system, criminal surety system, and criminal peonage is that the state judiciaries and the U.S. Supreme Court found ways to either find these laws constitutional or failed to enforce their unconstitutionality. Although these laws were finally removed from the face of American criminal justice during the era of World War II, within only twenty years these laws were replaced with the rhetoric of "law and order" resulting in the "get tough on crime" policies of the late 1960s and 1970s, which were supplemented by the war on drugs in the 1980s and 1990s, all of which continued the chronic incarceration of Blacks in America.

---

7 U.S. Constitution Article IV, Section 2, Clause 3 (1789).

8 Douglas A. Blackmon, *Slavery by Another Name: The Re-Enslavement of Black Americans from the Civil War to World War II* (2008), See also, Christopher R Adamson, "Punishment after Slavery: Southern State Penal Systems, 1865–1890," *Social Problems* 30, no. 5 (June 1983): 555, Earl Smith and Angela J. Hattery, "African American Men and the Prison Industrial Complex," *Washington Journal of Black Studies* 34, no.4 (2010): 387, Eric Schlosser, "The Prison Industrial Complex," *Atlantic Monthly*, Dec. 1998, at 52, Philip L. Reichel, "Southern Slave Patrols as a Transitional Police," *American Journal of Police* 7(1988): 51, Bruce P. Smith, "The Fourth Amendment, 1789-1868: A Strange History," *Ohio State Journal of Criminal Law* 5(2008): 663, Michelle Alexander, *The New Jim Crow: Mass Incarceration in the Age of Colorblindness* (2010) and Carol A Archbold, *Policing: A Text Reader* (2013).

Peonage

Peonage was a tradition brought to the United States through its annexation of Texas in 1845 and the subsequent conquest of Mexico during the Mexican-American War (1846–1848). To prevent the spread of the practice, Congress passed the *Peonage Act of 1867*, which prohibited the practice of peonage in the New Mexico Territory specifically and in the United States generally. Specifically, the act made

> the holding of any person ... directly or indirectly, [for] the voluntary or involuntary service or labor [for the purpose of] liquidation of any debt or obligation and any person or persons who shall hold, arrest, or return, or cause to be held, arrested, or returned, or in any manner aid in the arrest or return of any person or persons to a condition of peonage, shall, upon conviction, be punished by fine not less than one thousand nor more than five thousand dollars, or by imprisonment not less than one nor more than five years, or both, at the discretion of the court. Sec. 2. And be it further enacted, That it shall be the duty of all persons in the military or civil service in the Territory of New Mexico to aid in the enforcement of the foregoing section of this act; and any person or persons who shall obstruct or attempt to obstruct, or in any way interfere with, or prevent the enforcement of this act, shall be liable to the pains and penalties hereby provided; and any officer or other person in the military service of the United States who shall so offend, directly or indirectly, shall, on conviction before a court-martial, be dishonorably dismissed the service of the United States, and shall thereafter be ineligible to reappointment to any office of trust, honor, or profit under the government.[9]

The federal law against peonage was passed (March 1867) sixteen months after the assassination of Lincoln (April 1865), fifteen months after the ratification of the Thirteenth Amendment (December 1865), which made clear "Neither slavery nor involuntary servitude ... shall exist within the United States." The Peonage Act was the first federal legislation to criminally outlaw involuntary servitude. Under the Peonage Act, involuntary service could not be compelled to liquidate any debt. The law specifically prohibited local law enforcement from enforcing peonage by making it illegal to "hold, arrest, or return, or cause to be held, arrested, or returned, or in any manner aid in the arrest or return of any person or persons to a condition of peonage." Enforcement of the Peonage Act was required by both local and federal civil and military authority. Thus, from earliest days of the postbellum period, it was the duty of the federal government to enforce laws preventing state-sponsored activities that put individuals in a state of involuntary servitude. The problem was not that involuntary servitude was not made illegal after the Civil War, the

---

9 United States Statutes at Large, 39th Cong., Sess. II., Chp. 187, p. 546 (March 2, 1867). *The Peonage Act* was amended in 1909 (60th Cong., Sess. II., Chp. 321, section 269 p. 1142, March 4, 1909) and amended into its modern form on June 25, 1948 (18 U.S.C. § 1581). See generally 18 U.S. C. Chapter 77 (18 U.S.C. §§1851–1897) for modern federal laws prohibiting various types of slavery, involuntary servitude, slave trafficking, and sex trafficking. The modern federal law prohibiting slavery is 18 U.S.C. 1589.

problem was that it was unenforced. Without federal enforcement of civil rights, Blacks were left to the mercy of state and local government officials, politics, and policy interests. A lesson not lost on Blacks; then or today.

Although peonage was illegal under federal law, it was not enforced after the fall of Reconstruction. The history of postbellum criminal justice and incarceration of Blacks begins with state policies to circumvent the federal law against criminal peonage. The origin of Southern policing begins with the slave patrols antebellum and the failure of the federal government to enforce the peonage law postbellum. The problem of non-enforcement of the law and Blacks being subjected to practices of peonage occurred when the North grew tired of controlling the South. When the North withdrew from the South, peonage was integrated with the Thirteenth Amendment in which the South passed laws that focused on criminalizing Black economic and social behavior so that Blacks could be forced to comply with employment contracts under the threat of criminal prosecution, or Blacks were required to liquidate criminal fines paid by others. The legal basis for this was that involuntary servitude was authorized by criminal convictions. Blacks went from slaves to criminals. The slave plantations changed to penal plantations.

After the North withdrew from the Confederate South, still an agricultural economy, the south needed labor to work the remaining plantation fields. The defeat of the South did not change the economic dynamics of the South. Blacks were free but still had to work, and the status of economic and intellectual ignorance that they were forced to endure before the war did not immediately change after the war. Blacks still worked the land as they struggled to educate themselves and become economically independent from White landowners. Southern criminal justice and the system of Jim Crow after Reconstruction would retard these efforts for a century.

Peonage occurred through the duel dynamics of the creation of criminal violations that required fines or high bail before trial. Blacks that did not have such funds were released under criminal surety bonds paid for by White property owners in need of labor. Blacks were then forced to work for those Whites to liquidate the debt. The Southern criminal justice system used conviction of minor crimes as a tool to force Blacks to work for White plantation owners to plant and maintain crops.

Peonage in the American South was built on two overall premises. First, peonage provided a means to maintain Black manual labor. The postbellum system which created the Black Codes and the system of peonage undergirded "the belief of most Southern whites that they had a 'proprietary interest in black labor and that Blacks would not work unless coerced to do so.'"[10] This was a belief that was shared by both former slave holders and Northern agents of the Freedman's Bureau. The demand for agricultural labor that had existed before the Civil War and supported the institution of slavery in the first place had not changed. Second, peonage was in congruence with the belief that Blacks were not able to care for themselves

10 Tamar R. Birckhead, "The New Peonage," *Washington and Lee Law Review* 72, no. 4 (2015): 1595, 1610.

after slavery and Blacks needed their former slave masters to provide for them. This belief that Blacks had to be cared for was also held by White Northerners from the Freedman's Bureau who believed they had to protect them from poverty. In either case, a paternal theory of Blacks resulted in forced work under peonage or the threat of it.

This system of laws, along with segregation laws, lasted for decades into the twentieth century. The systematic use of peonage was part of a larger system of social, economic, political, and legal oppression in the South after the Civil War. This oppression included the use of whitecapping, lynching, intimidation in voting, and simple murder of Blacks on sight. ***Whitecapping*** was a method of intimidation by poor Whites who had lost their land due to debt. These poor Whites would depose Blacks of their land by force or threat of force. This system of fear and oppression, both legal and illegal, lasted well into the twentieth century. As Pete Daniel explains in his book *The Shadow of Slavery*,

> By 1901 Southern society had reached the point where a debt-labor system characterized by violence and the corruption or acquiescence of local police officers was openly tolerated. In a section of the country characterized by illiteracy and poverty, vulnerable victims were in profusion, and most of the peons were black.
>
> Peonage infected the South like a cancer, eating away at the economic freedom of blacks, driving the poor whites to work harder in order to compete with virtual slave labor, and preserving the class structure inherited from slavery days.[11]

The significance of the rise of peonage and other systems of involuntary servitude developed by the states of the old Confederate South is that after the Civil War, the fall of Reconstruction, and the rise of the new South with peonage in operation, "southerners lost and then regained their power, and having vowed to continue slavery, they did not go back on their word. Replacing paternalism with violence which led back to paternalism, utilizing customs from the past and the freedmen's illiteracy, relying on contracts and Northern sympathy with the work ethic, and mouthing laws and threats, southern planters shaped a labor system that preserved the larva of slavery in the evolution of freedom."[12] As Douglas Blackmon writes in *Slavery By Another Name*,

> White southerners had clearly won the national debate over who would decide the future of the country's black population. As southerners had insisted for more than a decade, the nation's "Negro problem" would be dealt with using the southern, white man's solutions ...

---

11 Pete Daniel, *The Shadow of Slavery: Peonage in the South 1901–1969* at 10–11 (University of Illinois Press, 1972). See also, David M. Oshinsky, *Worse than Slavery: Parchman Farm and the Ordeal of Jim Crow Justice* (Prentice Hall, 1997) and Alex Lichtenstein, *Twice the Work of Free Labor: The Political Economy of Convict Labor in the New South* (Verso, 1996).

12 Pete Daniel, "The Metamorphosis of Slavery, 1865–1900," *The Journal of American History* 66, no. 1 (June 1979): 88–99, 92.

> From the perspective of most white Americans, the new racial order had been affirmed formally and informally at the highest levels of society. The U.S. Supreme Court ruling four years earlier in *Plessy v. Ferguson*, sanctioning "separate but equal" public facilities for blacks and whites, sanctified the wave of new legislation and business practices requiring disparate treatment of blacks and whites. The ruling's effects went far beyond the courts and legislative chambers. The open willingness of the highest court to base its seminal ruling on claims that were so clearly false—that train cars designated for blacks were no different from those of whites—sent a profound message to all Americans. ***So long as whites performed at least the bare rituals of due process and cloaked their actions behind claims of equality, the crudest abuses of blacks and violations of their protections under law would rarely ever be challenged.***
>
> The neo-slavery of the new century relied on a simple but extraordinary ruse that the Supreme Court's ruling implicitly endorsed. [Southern criminal justice] could safely force a black man into servitude for months or years as long as they pretended that the legal rights of those black men had not been violated. The implications were as deeply absorbed by black people as were the rhythms of farming in the era of old slavery. ***This long era of false trials and arrests would taint the African American view of legal processes and guarantees for generations to come.***[13]

Blacks and Whites tend to view the criminal justice system differently. Whites tend to see the criminal justice system contemporaneously, in that they view incidences in one moment in time without historical context. A police shooting is judged by the specific moment in time. Blacks view contemporaneous incidents of police actions within the context of historical abuse. Blacks evaluate the criminal justice system within the historical fact that the criminal justice system, from decades prior to and subsequently after the Civil War, was not designed to protect them. Those who suffered under peonage and the subsequent abuse that occurred under it suffered crimes of rape, lynching, assault, and false imprisonment. Blacks found neither relief or protection from these crimes from the criminal justice system. They found instead the protection of those who committed these crimes by those who operated the local system of justice.

> A victim of lawlessness usually turns to the nearest law-enforcement officer, but peonage victims found this avenue blocked. County sheriffs, constables, justices of the peace, and sometimes federal officials aided in preserving the nightmare world of peonage. ... Local law-enforcement officials, secure in their isolated domains, accepted the customs that encouraged peonage. ... Justices of the peace also contributed to peonage by cooperating

13 Douglas A. Blackmon, *Slavery By Another Name* (Doubleday, 2008) at 147–148 (emphasis added).

> closely with employers. Much of the local corruption throughout the rural South thrived on the apathy of white Southerners. ... Thus, from the lowest local official to the highest state and federal officials, peons customarily found no champion.[14]

It was not until the first decade of the twentieth century that a minority of federal prosecutors and local judges took an interest in ending peonage. But, they were the minority. The process of fully extracting peonage from America would not begin until 1940, and peonage would not be fully removed from the face and practice of American criminal justice until the post–World War II era.

As Pete Daniel explains, the system of peonage was defined by two elements: debt and coercion. And, both include of all levels and types of bondage of people who, due to race and economic status, are controlled by those with racial and/or economic power. Because the Thirteenth Amendment had created the social and political impression that slavery was a thing of the past, federal law enforcement that focused on Southern criminal justice only focused on the system of criminal peonage when the offense was servitude due to debt,[15] not conviction of crimes. Remember, the Thirteenth Amendment allows for servitude based on criminal conviction. Even though peonage was made illegal under federal law soon after the Civil War, the first challenge to the practice of forcing Blacks to work for Whites who asserted that Blacks owed them money by federal authorities under the Peonage Act did not occur until 1898.[16] The practice ran unchecked for more than thirty years[17] before initial enforcement by federal authorities. But peonage would last an additional forty years before its enforced prohibition.

The system of peonage was supportive of the broader system of indebting Blacks and the use of the local police force to maintain compliance of Blacks. The ***slave patrols*** before the Civil War were tasked with preventing slave revolts, slave escapes, returning runaway slaves, and keeping free Blacks under social control. After emancipation, slave patrols developed into local sheriff agencies. Sheriffs were used to support the new system of sharecropping that replaced slavery and peonage was used to enforce the system. ***Sharecropping*** was a system of debt against the value of the crop harvested in the spring. The system occurred, in part, due to the lack of cash on hand to pay base salaries. To address the lack of cash for both tenant

---

14 Pete Daniel, *The Shadow of Slavery: Peonage in the South 1901–1969* (1972) at 30–32.

15 Pete Daniel, *The Shadow of Slavery* ... at xi.

16 Pete Daniel, *The Shadow of Slavery* ... at 4.

17 William Cohen, "Negro Involuntary Servitude in the South, 1865–1940: A Preliminary Analysis," *The Journal of Southern History* 42, no. 1 at 34–35. See also, Risa L. Goluboff, "'Won't You Please Help Me Get My Son Home': Peonage, Patronage, and Protest in the World War II Urban South," *Law & Social Inquiry* 244, no. 4 (Autumn, 1999): 777–806, Richard B. Morris, "The Course of Peonage in a Slave State," *Political Science Quarterly* 65, no. 2 (Jun., 1950): 238–63, Ralph Shlomowitz, "The Origins of Southern Sharecropping," *Agricultural History* 53, no. 3 (Jul., 1979)557–75, and *Infra* note 25–30.

and landowner, two systems developed: the sharecropper and tenant-farmer. These systems were different in fact, practice, and in law.

Blacks were sharecroppers not tenant-farmers. ***Tenant-farmers*** paid rent for the land and owned the produce of their planting and harvest. ***Sharecroppers*** lived on the land, borrowed supplies from local store merchants for planting, and then split the produce of the land with the landowner. The loans Black sharecroppers secured were collateralized against their half of the harvest. The distinction also applied to how the famer was expected to be treated. The tenant-farmer owned his time and strategy for securing the harvest; the landowner received his payment through agreed-upon rent. The tenant-farmer "owned" his personhood regarding the labor required to secure the harvest. The sharecropper, as far as the landowner was concerned, was a wage worker and as such was under the supervision of the landowner. The landowner expected the sharecropper to work as they did under slavery. The sharecropper was under the control of the landowner overseer as he was under slavery. He could not remove his wife and children from enforced work nor from the intentions of rape by the overseer. This system was what southern legislation contemplated when the Black Codes were legislated.[18]

To make matters worse, if the crop had a lower yield than expected, the landowner still took his percentage, leaving the sharecropper in debt to the merchant under the supplier's lien. [19] The lien would carry over to the next year with new loans for supplies for the next year's planning and harvest. This system of economic bondage backed up by the fear of criminal justice enforcement of debt locked Blacks into systematic, systemic, and structural poverty though debt. Many families did not break this cycle of debt until they participated in the first great migration north during the first three decades of the twentieth century.

The problem of the harvest never alleviating the debt, was compounded by the fact that sharecroppers had a debt that was enforced by criminal sanctions. Under threat of criminal contract violation—a criminal offense that could result in arrest and incarceration for failure to pay debts when demanded, the 1867 peonage law prohibiting such incarceration notwithstanding. For example, Tennessee law[20] allowed land owners to control time and duration of work hours and conditions of labor under judicial enforcement if croppers' work failed to meet contractual obligations or fines imposed due to that failure. The system of peonage and criminal surety was also implemented through the enforcement of criminal activity and criminalizing immoral behavior. For example,

---

18 Harold Woodman, "Sequel to Slavery: The New History Views the Postbellum South," *The Journal of Southern History* 43, no. 4 (1977): 523, 551–53.

19 Devon Douglas-Bowers, "Debt Slavery: The Forgotten History of Sharecropping," *The Hampton Institute* (November 7, 2013) at http://www.hamptoninstitution.org/sharecropping.html#.WAfsWPT5iCk (internal citations omitted). See also Harold D. Woodman, "Post-Civil War Southern Agriculture and the Law," *Infra* notes 41–45.

20 Devon Douglas-Bowers, "Debt Slavery: The Forgotten History of Sharecropping," *The Hampton Institute*

> Florida's Black Code of 1865 stipulated that anyone who did not pay a fine should be hired out "at public outcry to any person who will take him or her for the shortest time and pay the fine, forfeiture and penalty imposed, and cost of prosecution." Such punishment resulted from convictions of assault, misdemeanors, malicious mischief, assault and battery, vagrancy and "all offenses against Religion, Chastity, Morality and Decency."[21]

"The Black Codes of 1865–1867, although short-lived and characterized by racially discriminatory terminology, presaged the system of peonage as the South's answer to the Thirteenth Amendment."[22] These Black Codes were predated by the southern slave codes which were passed after **Bacon's rebellion** (1676). Bacon's rebellion was an uprising of Virginia indentured servants and Black slaves resulting in the burning of Jamestown and the forced evacuation of the royal governor. After the rebellion was put down, laws were passed to strengthen slavery and socially separate poor Whites from Black slaves. These laws worked to separate the shared social and economic interests of the Virginia lower classes (African slaves from White indentured servants) for the benefit of the slave plantation aristocracy. The first laws were passed in 1705 in Virginia and then followed by Maryland, North Carolina, South Carolina, and Georgia. In Missouri, peonage was built upon the Slave Code of 1804. The system of the slave codes came with the Louisiana territory when it was seeded to the United States from Spain and France in the Louisiana Purchase in 1803.

> The customs established by France and Spain were quickly replaced with the customs and traditions of other Southern states such as Virginia and Kentucky with the creation of the Slave Code of 1804. Under the Slave Code of 1804, blacks were explicitly and implicitly denied rights which had previously existed under French and Spanish rule. The code denied blacks the right to testify against whites and forbade them from receiving medical care. The 1804 code not only restricted black rights, but it also failed to include protections such as requirements for slave owners to clothe, feed, or provide housing for slaves. Under the 1804 code, slaves could also be worked any day of the week and were no longer protected against physical abuse by their master. The extreme provisions of the new code stemmed from a fear of insurrection and in areas such as St. Louis, where black population was as high as twenty percent, additional ordinances were added to further restrict the black slave population. White Americans present in the new territory clearly restricted the black slave population out of a sense of fear.[23]

21 Gordon N. Carper, "Slavery revisited: peonage in the South," *Phylon* 37, no. 1 at 85.

22 Tamar R. Birckhead, "The New Peonage," Washington and Lee Law Review 72, no. 4 (2015): 1595, 1612–13.

23 Jonathan A. Klusmeyer, *Slavery Continued: Peonage in Missouri*, Master's Thesis, University of Central Missouri (November 2013) at 7–8.

These slave codes required free Blacks to carry their papers of manumission and, in 1835, Missouri passed legislation that required all free Blacks to be employed and under the supervision of a White employer, specifically "requiring any free black ages seven to twenty-one to be legally bound as an apprentice or servant"[24] under pain of criminal penalty.

These laws and contracts kept Blacks in a perpetual status of *subjugation* to White land owners. The system was based on economic domination and the idea that Blacks were supposed to be subjugated. This system of peonage pervaded the old Confederacy. It was found in the cotton belt from the Carolinas to Texas through the Mississippi Delta and in Florida, Georgia, Alabama, Missouri, Virginia, Kentucky, and Tennessee.[25]

Peonage was a system that naturally flowed from slavery.

> In order for peonage to occur, there was typically a combination of the following factors in existence. First, peonage generally occurred only in areas that had previously allowed for the holding of persons in involuntary servitude. Second, violence towards minorities and a general apathy towards individual rights was often the zeitgeist. Third, the political structure caused illiteracy, absence of political power, and an absence of participation of government officials in local, state, and often national positions. Lastly, the areas in which peons worked were generally isolated from main society, helping to maintain the general apathy of the population.
>
> Peonage is defined as a form of involuntary servitude based on alleged debt or indebtedness. It is a condition that plagued the American South from emancipation well into the second half of the twentieth century. Peonage was born in a transitional state from slave to wage labor and provided a way to control a predominately African American labor force and maintain a racial hierarchy. [26]

Slavery served a dual purpose. Slavery served the economic needs of large plantation owners who needed a perpetual labor force that did not need to be paid. As discussed in Chapter Three, Jefferson Davis asserted that slavery also served the need to create a homogenous relationship between poor Whites and rich land owners. They both shared one thing in common, socially they were equal in superiority to Blacks. That shared belief in racial superiority papered over the economic disparities between them. Although they were kept poor and illiterate, they were still White and superior to Blacks *per se*. And that status was enough. It was enough to live for, fight for, lynch for, and kill for, from the 1860s through the 1960s. The system of peonage

---

24 Jonathan A. Klusmeyer, *Slavery Continued: Peonage in Missouri*

25 Pete Daniel, *The Shadow of Slavery: Peonage in the South 1901–1969* (1972) at 21, Devon Douglas-Bowers, "Debt Slavery: The Forgotten History of Sharecropping," *The Hampton Institute* (November 7, 2013), Gordon N. Carper, "Slavery Revisited: Peonage in the South," *Phylon* 37, no. 1 (1976): 85–89, Jonathan A. Klusmeyer, *Slavery Continued: Peonage in Missouri*, Master's Thesis, University of Central Missouri (November 2013).

26 Jonathan A. Klusmeyer, *Slavery Continued: Peonage in Missouri* at 61, 54 respectively.

supported the desired result of White superiority and provided a legal way to achieve a state of near slavery in compliance with the Thirteenth Amendment.

The significance of the injustice of peonage was that it was illegal under federal law since 1867. Criminal Peonage in the south became systematic after the end of Reconstruction. The significance of southern criminal justice and peonage was that it was the result of the national government's abandonment of Blacks on the altar of national unification with the South.[27] The federal government did not engage in a serious effort to intervene and stop the states from operating under criminal peonage until the progressive era (1890–1920), resulting from U.S. Justice Department prosecutions[28] and by the Supreme Court ruling in *United States v. Clyatt* that criminal justice peonage was unconstitutional in 1905.[29] The Confederate states were recalcitrant in supporting their right to enforce these contracts. The defense of criminal penalties imposed on Blacks accused of committing criminal fraud by intentional abrogation of contract led to the Supreme Court rulings in *Bailey v. Alabama* (1911) and *United States v. Reynolds* (1914) that state laws that allowed private contracts to be enforced by criminal sanctions were unconstitutional.[30] But what the Court says is unconstitutional and what the national government enforces is not always the same thing. Not until the federal prosecutions got serious in the 1940s did the practice disappear from southern criminal justice.

With the reemergence of the agricultural industry in the rural South, the chronic agricultural needs for labor to maintain cotton and tobacco plantations, and the fact that the old system of slavery to provide that labor was gone, a new system developed that trapped Blacks. Blacks were forced to sharecrop to avoid criminal vagrancy. The sharecropping system forced them to take on debt. The inability to pay off the debt resulted in criminal conviction, which allowed involuntary servitude under the Thirteenth Amendment. Such servitude made them subject to being placed in the system of convict leasing, a state worse than slavery. With peonage came convict leasing and criminal surety.

---

27 Jonathan A. Klusmeyer, *Slavery Continued: Peonage in Missouri* at 54 (Internal citations omitted). See also, Tamar R. Birckhead, "The New Peonage," *Washington and Lee Law Review* 72, no. 4 (2015): 1595, 1610.

28 See Pete Daniel (ed.) *The Peonage Files of the Department of Justice, 1901–1945* (1989). "This microfilm publication contains fresh material on the first federal prosecution under the peonage statute, *U.S. v. Eberhart*, in 1898. The first Supreme Court case dealing with peonage, *Clyatt v. United States*, began in 1901 in Florida." Id at v.

29 *United States v. Clyatt*, 197 U.S. 201 (1905).

30 *United States v. Reynolds*, 235 U.S. 133 (1914). For further discussion see, William Wirt Howe, "The Peonage Cases," *Columbia Law Review* 4, no. 4 (April 1904): 279–86, Pete Daniel, "Up from Slavery and Down to Peonage: The Alonzo Bailey Case," *The Journal of American History* 57, no. 3 (December, 1970): 654–70, Aziz H. Huq "Peonage and Contractual Liberty," *Columbia Law Review* 101, no. 2 (March 2001): 351–91, Aviam Soifer, "Federal Protection, Paternalism, and the Virtually Forgotten Prohibition of Voluntary Peonage," *Columbia Law Review* 112, no. 7 (November 2012): 1607–39, and Benno C. Schmidt Jr., "Principle and Prejudice: The Supreme Court and Race in the Progressive Era. Part 2: The 'Peonage Cases,'" *Columbia Law Review* 82, no. 4 (May 1982): 646–718.

Convict Leasing

With the death of Reconstruction due to the disputed election of 1876 and the corrupt bargain of 1877, any pretense of freedom for Blacks and their equality to Whites disappeared. The need for labor to rebuild the South, both in agriculture and the newly developing industrial capacity due to the building of railroads and coal mining, a systematic need for continuous labor at low cost in the life-threatening work of private industry produced a secondary system of Black servitude almost equal to slavery—the convict leasing system. During slavery, Blacks had economic value to both the slave owner and the Southern society as a whole; as convicts, Blacks again had economic value to both the plantation owner and/or the coal mine owner in need of cheap labor and to Southern society as a whole—their labor was a source of governmental revenue. Although convict leasing was a major factor in meeting employment needs postbellum, its roots dates to the antebellum period of the 1840s–1850s in which slaves were imprisoned and sentenced to periods of hard labor as an alternative to hanging them for crimes.[31] Prisoners who were slaves were worked and sold as non-convicted slaves were.

The overarching concept of convict leasing, regardless of operation, is that the convict has financial value to the criminal justice system. Convict leasing removed from the purpose of criminal justice the principles of rehabilitation of the offender or retribution on the offender and replaced it with the purpose of securing financial profit. Southern policing had enough of an original sin in that it was birthed from the sole purpose of oppressing free Blacks, and law and order was solely defined by controlling the slave population and preventing slave escapes and rebellions. But after the Civil War, slave patrols become Southern police forces, and the purpose of the Southern police was to arrest Blacks for financial gain, regardless of actual guilt.

After the Civil War, sheriffs and constables maintained the classical Southern way of life, which included keeping the former slaves subservient and maintaining White supremacy. In this post–Civil War system of social control southern police and local judges were paid through fines and bonds[32] which through peonage were paid by White plantation owners. The system of police having a financial incentive to make arrests did not end with convict-leasing and peonage in the 1940s. Since the 1980s police financial incentive to make arrests exists through the federal and state system of asset forfeiture and arrest requirements under Justice Department state-local police drug units, a policy that we will return to in Chapter Eight. In many localities, government operational budgets are supplemented by police issuing parking tickets and other fines for minor violations that carry fines for failure to pay. The violence resulting from the shooting of Michael Brown by Darren Wilson in Ferguson, Missouri, in

---

31 For example, see Jeff Forret "Before Angola: Enslaved Prisoners in the Louisiana State Penitentiary," *Louisiana History* 54, no. 2 (2013): 133–71.

32 Jonathan A. Klusmeyer, *Slavery Continued: Peonage in Missouri* at 63 (internal citation omitted) and Douglas A. Blackmon, *Slavery By Another Name* (2008) at 100–102.

August 2014, was partially explained by community outrage at the systematic use of the Ferguson police and courts using fees imposed on the majority poor Black residents to cover the operational budget of the city.[33]

Under the convict-lease system, the charges made against Blacks included serious felonies, but mostly, they were petty crimes, like vagrancy, gambling, and loitering or violations of civil contracts resulting in an unpaid debt or a charge of breach of contract (intentional financial fraud). These petty crimes or civil contract claims, when convicted, would require fines, which the accused could not pay. "If the black man was unable to pay the fine, a local White man would 'graciously' pay the fine allowing the black man, and occasionally a black woman, to work off the debt over time. Once in this system, time could be added to the original contract simply by accusing the peon of another crime. The key to the entire process was the swift arrest, trial, and sentencing of the black person and the absence of witnesses and lawyers for defense."[34] This system of criminal peonage was supplemented by the state or county renting convicts to industry for a fee—convict leasing. The convict was trapped, first he worked to pay off the fines of the conviction which were paid by the land owner—peonage—then when he left he was arrested, served time for violating the contract, and rented out to the same land owner under convict-lease.[35]

Criminal peonage and convict leasing worked together within Southern criminal justice. Under the convict-lease system the convict, now subject to "involuntary servitude" under the Thirteenth Amendment could be rented or leased out to a private company for a fee. The landowner or company got free labor and the county got a fee for the labor. A system of slavery by another name. The significance of this system is that it was state sanctioned, and both judges and police officers had to be in the corrupt system for it to function. In addition, apathy by those outside of the system—both local and national—supported the outcomes of the system with their silence. This dynamic of silence in the face of abuse of Blacks is even more significant than the actual injustice of the system, because the only reason the system existed at all was because lives of Blacks caught in the system were of so little moral value that their suffering did not matter. On the other hand the forced Black labor did have significant economic labor value. This value was not superseded until the international politics of World War II and the Cold War that followed, along with Black protest and the rise of the civil rights

33 See, NPR, "In Ferguson, Court Fines And Fees Fuel Anger" (August 25, 2014) at https://www.npr.org/2014/08/25/343143937/in-ferguson-court-fines-and-fees-fuel-anger, "Ferguson's Conspiracy Against Black Citizens: How the city's leadership harassed and brutalized their way to multiple civil-rights violations," (March 5, 2015) at https://www.theatlantic.com/national/archive/2015/03/ferguson-as-a-criminal-conspiracy-against-its-black-residents-michael-brown-department-of-justice-report/386887/ and United States Department of Justice Civil Rights Division, *Investigation of the Ferguson Police Department* (March 4, 2015).

34 Jonathan A. Klusmeyer, *Slavery Continued: Peonage in Missouri* at 67 (Internal citation omitted).

35 Gordon N. Carper, "Slavery Revisited: Peonage in the South," *Phylon* 37, no. 1 at 86, 93–94.

movement, changed the dynamics of postbellum Jim Crow America and made the system peonage and southern criminal justice untenable.

Criminal peonage and convict leasing worked together by charging Blacks with crimes, regardless of actual guilt, that carried felony sentences of years in duration. This system of criminalizing Black behavior and focusing law enforcement to capture Blacks was based on the Black Codes that outlawed offenses that were considered prominent with Black behavior.[36]

> Of all the Black Codes, that section dealing with vagrancy was applied most often to freed Negroes. And few convicted of vagrancy were able to pay their fines and court costs. As a result they took the second alternative, one to six months as a county convict. At this point they were usually leased to the highest bidder and privileged to participate in another peculiarly Southern institution, the convict-lease system. Frequently, the convicts were detained beyond the term of sentence. When this happened a condition of peonage existed. Throughout the South the convict-lease system directly led to and brought about peonage [and] there was a positive relationship between peonage and convict leasing [in which] convicts were leased and subleased and not allowed to depart upon the expiration of their sentences[37]

The infamous 1922 case of Captain Alston Brown's turpentine camp in Dixie County, Florida is an example of how the peonage and convict-leasing system were intertwined to permanently make Blacks subject to the criminal system.[38] "If a peon tried to leave he was placed back into the system as a convict. If a convict served out his sentence, he found himself in debt to Brown via the commissary system and forced back into the system as a peon ... In essence there was no way out of the system."[39]

What is important in understanding this system is that it did not occur in a vacuum, the system served to maintain a social order that was centuries old in the new realities of a post-slavery social dynamic.[40] This system of peonage and convict leasing had long-term effects on the South that can be seen today. The South, in general, and the Deep South, specifically, are poorer than the North, and both Southern economic and industrial backwardness,[41]

36 Douglas A. Blackmon, *Slavery By Another Name* (2008) at 99.

37 Gordon N. Carper, "Slavery revisited: peonage in the South," *Phylon* 37, no. 1 at 86.

38 See Pete Daniel, *The Shadow of Slavery: Peonage in the South 1901–1969* (1972) and Douglas A. Blacmon, *Slavery By Another Name* (2008) for descriptions and individual stories of peonage, convict leasing and prisoner treatment in private and government prisoner work camps.

39 Gordon N. Carper, "Slavery Revisited: Peonage in the South," *Phylon* 37, no. 1 at 97.

40 Harold D. Woodman, "Sequel to Slavery: The New History Views the Postbellum South," *The Journal of Southern History* 43, no. 4 (1977): 523–54, 535.

41 Harold D. Woodman, "Sequel to Slavery: The New History Views the Postbellum South," at 549, 550, 553.

as well as Black poverty, has been traced back to the Southern policies of sharecropping[42] and the cultural incalcitrant defense of racial oppression and discrimination.[43]

As previously discussed, local sheriffs and courts were paid by fines collected due to arrests for minor crimes. Blacks were arrested on sight for vagrancy, petty theft, offensive language, or any other "Negro Crimes," which included failure to prove employment, loitering, gambling, staring at a White woman, not stepping aside for a White man in the street, or being accused of being in debt to a White landowner or merchant. A vagrancy charge could be established by nothing more than walking on the road. Two or more Blacks standing at a location could establish loitering. The Southern criminal justice system was such that it was in the financial interests of the local judge and sheriff to find guilt, because the conviction resulted in bids for the labor of the convict, and the highest bidder would pay the fine and costs in exchange for judicial orders to have the convict work off the fines. The bid could be more than the statutory fine. Blacks with financial means would pay more than the lawful fines and costs to escape conviction or being "sold" into the system of convict leasing. This system lasted for decades despite the Supreme Court decision in 1914 that held that the practice of incarceration for financial crimes or inability to pay fines were unconstitutional under the Thirteenth

---

42 Harold D. Woodman, "Post–Civil War Southern Agriculture and the Law," *Agricultural History* 53, no. 1 (Jan., 1979): 319–37, 324–25.

The law in every southern state, usually as early as the 1870s, sharply distinguished between the landlord-tenant relationship (which included payment of rent in the form of a share of the crop) and the landlord-cropper relationship. A South Carolina Court of Appeals succinctly summarized the difference:

> The fundamental distinction between the relationships of landlord and cropper and landlord and tenant is in the fact that the status of a cropper is that of a laborer who has agreed to work for and under the landlord for a certain proportion of the crop as wages, but who does not thereby acquire any dominion or control over the premises upon which such labor is to be performed, the cropper having the right merely to enter and remain thereupon for the purpose of performing his engagement; whereas a tenant does not occupy the status of a laborer, but under such a contract acquires possession, dominion, and control over the premises for the term covered by the agreement, usually paying therefore a fixed amount either in money or specifics, and in making the crop performs the labor for himself and not for the landlord.
>
> The cropper, then, was a wage laborer, his wages being a portion of what he produced paid *to* him *by* the landlord. The tenant was a renter who paid rent *to* the landlord for use of the land; it did not alter that relationship if the rent was a portion of the crop produced.

See also Devon Douglas-Bowers, "Debt Slavery: The Forgotten History of Sharecropping." *Supra* note 19.

43 William Cohen, "Negro Involuntary Servitude in the South, 1865–1940: A Preliminary Analysis," *The Journal of Southern History* 42, no. 1 (Feb., 1976): 31–60, 31.

Amendment and illegal under the Peonage Act of 1867.[44] Its actual end did not occur until federal prosecutions for the practice occurred in the 1940s.

By the late nineteenth century, the states of the Deep South were renting out state prisoners for labor when not using them for state labor projects. Such was the birth of chain gangs, work gangs, and the sentence of twenty years at hard labor. And in the Southern prisons, a man could be beaten and worked to death in a convict lease work camp, if not killed by disease first[45] and race was at the heart of the harshness of the Southern system.[46] The convict-lease system began in 1844 in Louisiana and did not formally end until 1928 when abandoned by Alabama. The convict-lease system, like the criminal-peonage system, did not functionally begin to end until the 1940s when Attorney General Biddle issued orders for federal prosecutions under circular 3591 on December 12, 1941. The point being these systems did not end, like slavery before them, until federal government power was imposed. A lesson not lost on either states' rights social conservatives or those who advocate for civil rights.

Criminal Surety, Enticement Laws, and Other Systems of Involuntary Servitude

Criminal surety, along with convict leasing,[47] occurred shortly after the end of the Civil War. The system involved using convict labor to meet state, local, and private labor needs. ***Criminal surety***, established by state statute or by custom dating back to the antebellum period of the Confederate South, authorized county governments and local police officers to allow to private agricultural, construction, coal mining companies, and/or private plantation owners to pay the bail of accused people in exchange for promises of labor from these misdemeanants, and sometimes felons.[48] Charges would be stayed in exchange for labor for set period of time which could be weeks to months.

The insidiousness of the criminal surety system was that it supplemented the system of pig laws and the purpose of those laws. This system, on its face, was non-racial, but in fact the application was designed to place Blacks in as close a position of slavery they held in the antebellum period as possible.[49] Another way to keep the former slaves in a status close to slavery was to control employment because that minimized economic independence. Between

44 *United States v. Reynolds*, 235 U.S. 133 (1914)

45 Douglas A. Blackmon, *Slavery by Another Name* (2008) at 95–96, 109–110.

46 William Cohen, "Negro Involuntary Servitude in the South, 1865-1940: A Preliminary Analysis," *The Journal of Southern History* 42, no. 1 (Feb., 1976): 31–60, 56–57.

47 William Cohen, "Negro Involuntary Servitude in the South ... " at 55.

48 Michael J. Klarman, *From Jim Crow to Civil Rights: The Supreme Court and the Struggle for Racial Equality* (Oxford University Press, 2004) at 74. See also, Douglas A. Blackmon, *Slavery by another Name* (2008) at 53–57.

49 William Cohen, "Negro Involuntary Servitude in the South, 1865–1940: A Preliminary Analysis," *The Journal of Southern History* 42, no. 1 (Feb., 1976): 31–60, 34.

1865 and 1867, ten Southern states passed ***antienticement laws.***[50] These laws made it a crime to try and hire away a laborer already under contract to another person. The result of these laws was the control of the Black labor force, specifically its mobility. The statutes were passed in Alabama, Georgia, Florida, North Carolina, Arkansas, South Carolina, Louisiana, and Mississippi just before and after the fall of Reconstruction.[51] These laws not only outlawed the hiring of Blacks under contract, many authorized the employer to send the police or private "man catchers" to secure runaway contracted Blacks and return them to the employer.[52] Tennessee (1917), Virginia (1924), and Texas (1929) also passed ***anti-emigrant-agent laws*** during the first great migration (1916–1920s) of Blacks from the South to the North.[53]

While anti-emigrant-agent laws were designed to control Whites and to prevent them from "stealing" Blacks from their White landlords who needed Black labor, ***contract-labor statutes*** were specifically designed to keep Blacks in their place. For example, various southern states required Blacks to carry papers proving that they left their employers legitimately and that they were gainfully employed.[54] These laws were little different than the ***manumission statutes*** that required freed Blacks to carry their freedom papers on demand of any White man or police officer to prove they were free during the days of slavery. Although these statutes fell out of favor during Reconstruction, they reemerged in the 1880s and 1890s, after the North abandoned Blacks to the mercy of Southern Democrats in 1877, in which it was made unlawful for a Black to look for better employment while under contract.[55] These ***false-pretense laws*** were clearly an attempt to criminalize breach of contract under the guise of asserting that the failure to comply with a contractual obligation was an act of fraud with the intent to injure the employer. The use of civil contract breach as a strategy to criminalize Black labor disputes in order to bring Blacks to heel was too much even for the separate but equal Supreme Court and in 1911 the Court held,[56] the false-pretenses laws unconstitutional.[57] But many former Confederate states (North and South Carolina, Florida, and Georgia) remained *incalcitrant regarding maintaining false-pretense statutes until the 1940s.*

It was one thing to have methods to enforce a contract already made; it was something else to force Blacks to enter into those labor contracts. That is where the criminal justice system came in with laws outlawing vagrancy and loitering, requiring apprenticeship and

---

50 William Cohen, "Negro Involuntary Servitude in the South … "at 35.

51 William Cohen, "Negro Involuntary Servitude in the South … " at 36.

52 Pete Daniel, *The Shadow of Slavery: Peonage in the South 1901–1969* (1972) at 3.

53 William Cohen, "Negro Involuntary Servitude in the South, 1865–1940: A Preliminary Analysis," *The Journal of Southern History* 42, no. 1 at 39.

54 William Cohen, "Negro Involuntary Servitude in the South … " at 42.

55 William Cohen, "Negro Involuntary Servitude in the South … "

56 *Bailey v. Alabama,* 219 U.S. 219 (1911).

57 William Cohen, "Negro Involuntary Servitude in the South, 1865-1940: A Preliminary Analysis," *The Journal of Southern History* 42, no. 1 at 43.

proof of employment. These Black Codes, passed in 1865–1866, in North Carolina, Florida, Louisiana, Georgia, South Carolina, Alabama, Virginia, Texas and Mississippi defined the crime of vagrancy in sweeping terms which included anyone without a labor contract.[58] The ***vagrancy laws*** made being out of work or unable to prove employment a crime punishable by fines and it provided a source of forced labor of Blacks when the need for labor increased due to economic conditions.[59] The ***apprentice laws*** focused on Black children and forced them to work Whites under the theory that they needed to be prevented from idleness and crime. The courts would receive a fee from Whites taking the responsibility to "train" Black youth in a trade. The fact that Blacks, through various ***commercial and trade restrictive laws***, were banned from various trades and ownership of property almost guaranteed unemployment, which lead to vagrancy violations, which subjected them to criminal surety, peonage, and convict leasing. The criminal surety laws gave a convict a choice: sign the labor contract and work for a person for six months or a year or in the alternative serve months in a jail or prison work camp at hard labor.[60]

The system of involuntary servitude was made of more than the sum of its parts: peonage, vagrancy statutes, forced labor contracts, the sharecropper system, convict-leasing, and criminal surety; all of which had their high-water mark between the late nineteenth and early twentieth centuries. But, as the nation moved from the Great Depression to the war of the Greatest Generation and its fight against Nazism and, after the war, its fight against communism, the legality and political and social support for the system of involuntary servitude of Blacks began to come to an end. Jim Crow would be dead two decades after the guns were silenced in 1945. But, the lasting and enduring damage of the system was the systemic disproportionate confinement of Blacks in the criminal justice system. The history of the involuntary servitude makes clear that, from 1865 through World War II, Blacks were sought by the criminal justice system to benefit former slave holders, business interests, and government labor needs. Actual criminal behavior of Blacks was secondary, if not tertiary, in explaining Black incarceration. But with the systematic policy of the social control of Blacks (slavery, followed by the Black Codes, and Jim Crow) dispensed with, the systemic political and social assumption that Blacks are criminal and need to be controlled has remained. This assumption has resulted in social policy outputs and outcomes that support a belief that Blacks are supposed to be disproportionately represented within the criminal justice system. The modern systemic policies that support disproportionate representation will be discussed in Chapter Eight.

---

58 William Cohen, "Negro Involuntary Servitude in the South ... " at 47.

59 William Cohen, "Negro Involuntary Servitude in the South ... " at 50, 51.

60 William Cohen, "Negro Involuntary Servitude in the South ... " at 55.

THE FALL OF JIM CROW, THE RISE OF ITS SUCCESSOR CRIME CONTROL THEORY, AND THE POLITICAL RHETORIC OF NON-RACIAL STATES' RIGHTS

World War II and the Fall of Jim Crow

There are multiple reasons for the fall of the postbellum Black Code/Jim Crow era, one of them being World War II. The United States, during the war, expended much "blood and treasure" and rhetorical energy asserting that it was fighting totalitarian governments that asserted racial superiority over the rest of the world. Germany had taken the theory of White racial superiority to its logical conclusion, and twelve million people, including six million Jews, were wiped off the face of the earth, because the Germans said they were racially inferior. In opposing Hitler and the Axis Powers, the United States had to come to terms with its own White racial superiority practices. Although America was not in the same class as Germany regarding racial prejudice and policies to enforce those ideals, America practiced segregation, and its criminal justice system was geared to imprison Blacks, because they were Black. The United States asserted to the world that America and the democracies of the world were better than Germany. Practices to the contrary like peonage and criminal surety, had to be terminated. In the early 1940s the federal government finally acted to enforce the Peonage statute and ended the practice of peonage in the South. The practices of sharecropping would also come to an end during this period. The practice of convict leasing was replaced by convict labor during the 1920s.

All this being true, Blacks still had to prove that they were not only worthy of equality and freedom, but they had to fight for the right to fight for America in World War II. Integration of the American armed forces occurred after World War II as a direct result of the demonstrated loyalty and fighting ability of Blacks, under racism, during the war. One of the famous stories of Blacks fighting while suffering overt racism is the story of the Tuskegee Airmen. The experiences of the airmen during training were fictionalized in the 1995 movie *The Tuskegee Airmen*. Sometimes fictional movies about actual events serve as the best way to make a point. The 1995 HBO movie begins with the new Black recruits being introduced to their commanding officers. The White training base commander told them that they were an experiment to see if Blacks had the academic, intellectual, physical, and psychological ability to fly planes and fight as pilots. He said that, in the experiment, no corners would be cut, but as to the results, if he had anything to do with it, the experiment would succeed. Fair enough. But, his second in command was not so convinced. He asked one cadet, played by Laurence Fishburne, why he had joined the Air Corp. The cadet answered that he had joined to fight for his country. The officer responded, "Boy, are you stupid? Don't you know how bad we treat you people? Serving your country. This ain't your country. Your country's full of apes and gorillas, malaria, missionaries." The cadet responded that America had enemies, and Blacks were not being spared by the German army. The officer responded, "to my knowledge, the colored aren't up to fightin' the Germans, let alone, beatin' 'em." The officer lost the engagement when the cadet responded, "Max Schmeling found out differently, sir." Defeated, the officer disengaged from the cadet saying, "Well you know what, my job is to see if you Joe Louises can fly. In case the Colonel gave you the wrong impression, let me clear it up. You are nothing special."

Well, they were! The Tuskegee Airmen of the 99th Pursuit (Fighter) Squadron, 332nd Fighter Group and 477th Bombardment Group, along with Blacks who served in the Army "Red Ball Express," the 327th Quartermaster Service Company, the 320th Anti-Aircraft Barrage Balloon Battalion, the U.S. Army 369th Infantry "Harlem Hell Fighters," among countless others who fought in World War II and World War I, as did the men of Massachusetts 54th Regiment half a century before, proved the bravery and heroism of Black men who fought for the United States while considered second-class citizens at home. Lt. Colonel Benjamin O. Davis Jr., the commanding officer of the 99th Pursuit (Fighter) Squadron and 332nd Fighter Group, was portrayed in the HBO movie as attending a U.S. Senate hearing in which the airmen were accused of poor military performance, incompetence, and poor leadership in order to disband the unit. In the movie, Lt. Colonel Benjamin O. Davis Jr. gave the following defense of the unit and responded to the racism underlying the false charges against his men.

> All we asked for was a chance to prove ourselves. A fair and impartial opportunity. We thought we had that chance. But you invite us to a poker game, hand us a fixed deck and then wonder why we can't win? Every colored pilot in the 99th went through his own private hell to wear those wings. Every one of those men carry not only the burden of their dreams of becoming American Military Aviators but the hopes of an entire people, as well. Am I the only one in this room who understands what that means? I was brought up to believe that, beneath it all, Americans are a decent people with an abiding sense of integrity and fair play. The cheers I heard across this country when Joe Louis and Jesse Owens humiliated Hitler's "Master Race" didn't just come from proud colored folks. They came from everyone. How are we to interpret that? As a United States Army Officer who gladly puts his life on the line every day, there's no greater conflict within me. How do I feel about my country? And how does my country feel about me? Are we only to be Americans when the mood suits you? A fair and impartial opportunity is all we ask. Nothing that you yourselves wouldn't demand.

As Sergeant Waters, introduced in Chapter One, said, "The First War didn't change nothing for the Negro. But this one's gonna change everything." It did. In World War II Blacks fought and died for freedom from totalitarian racial tyranny and injustice, and they proved that they were, indeed, equal to Whites in war. In the 2012 movie, *Red Tails*, about the airmen in Italy, the movie portrayed their historic air cover of U.S. Army Bomber Squads that cemented their reputation as fighters and proved that Blacks could fight as pilots. In the movie, they were shown to have a prayer of both humility and courage in battle. Before battle, they would pray,

> Heavenly Father, we thank you for this glorious day. We ask that you send your angels down to surround us as we fly through the sky. We know that it's part of your master plan that we've made it all the way from Tuskegee here to Ramitelli. We are very confident in our abilities, but we ask that you give us the vision, the sight, and the speed and power to

> make it through this mission. All the airmen say, "In Jesus' name we pray." Amen. Amen. Nothing's difficult! Everything's a challenge! Through adversity to the stars! From the last plane, to the last bullet, to the last minute, to the last man, we fight! We fight! We fight! We fight!

"We are men, soldiers," Waters proudly proclaimed, asserting Blacks had earned "its place of honor and respect in this war." As Black soldiers returned, they were not going to lose that place in the post-war peace. Blacks within the Greatest Generation would demand political, social, and legal equality in American life back home.

After World War II, the United States found itself in an ideological war with the Soviet Union. It was a war of international ideological suppositions between two opposing systems of governance—communism versus capitalism, slavery versus freedom. The Soviet Union took pleasure in telling the world and newly freed colonial nations in Africa and Asia that the West was racist and continues to seek to take advantage of them. They proposed America and its treatment of its own Black citizens as proof. The United States could no longer enjoy having Blacks as second-class citizens by law and in practice. These geopolitical dynamics aided in creating a historical and political background for the civil rights movement to achieve the end of Jim Crow.

Although this demand for legal and political equality would be fulfilled during the civil rights movement between 1954 and 1968, there was a backlash to the movement, which was operationalized within criminal justice and the politics of race and crime. Beginning in 1968 and developing through the 1980s and 1990s, the modern process of Black disproportionate conviction and incarceration in the criminal justice system developed. The nationalization of criminal justice politics under the Nixon Administration and the rise of the War on Drugs, the abandonment of rehabilitation in the early 1980s, the rise of "get tough on crime" policies of the mid-1980s, the rise of broken windows theory and racial profiling in the 1990s, and the misapplication of stop and frisk and the abandonment of community policing in the first decade of the twenty-first century all support the continued incarceration of Blacks that began with Black Codes after the Civil War.

The system of peonage, convict leasing, criminal surety, vagrancy, loitering, and involuntary servitude that were designed to incarcerate Blacks between 1865 and 1941 was replaced by the War on Drugs, the war on crack, and the system of mandatory and minimum sentencing for drug violations that were concentrated in Black communities in the 1980s through the first decade of the twenty-first century. The result of both systems was the same.

The Rise of Modern States' Rights Political Rhetoric as Criminal Justice Policy

Understanding the complexity of the criminal justice system begins with understanding that it is a multidimensional institution and a political machine that has multiple, and sometimes contradictory, purposes. Think of the criminal justice system as a machine with three dominant wheels; the police, the courts, and corrections. Within these wheels, there are various interlocking smaller wheels, gears, and belts that move people from arrest to incarceration. Politics governs which wheels are perceived as more significant and worthy of support. Thus, the wheels and subparts have their own political constituency that is both coveted and utilized for the benefit of the machine as a whole and/or for the benefit of a particular part of the machine. Politics also governs how laws are used to define the purpose of the machine—a point we will return to.

Understanding criminal justice also requires the acknowledgment of its power within American society. That acknowledgment aids in understanding the differential in White and Black fear of the various parts of the criminal justice system. The criminal justice system is the singular most powerful institution within American governmental structures. The criminal justice system is the only governmental system in the United States that has a range of power that can, at its beginning stage (the police), seize an American citizen and deny him/her the right to walk away (deny the right to liberty) and, as discussed in Chapter Two, can take the life of the person leaving him dead in the street. This power over life, both the denying of liberty and the taking the life of an individual, held by the criminal justice system can be exercised both at its beginning at the hands of the police on the street or at its end in prison in which a warden can order the imposition of drugs to cause death during an execution after decades of legal proceedings.

The criminal justice system stands as more than an institution with power over life and death; it reflects the greater politics and philosophy of America. The criminal justice system has no powers that the political and historical forces of America over past two centuries have not given it. The criminal justice system reflects what America is and requires for it to feel safe within its borders. This fear and desire for safety and safety from what and from whom is the background for race and criminal justice.

The criminal justice system is a creation of government for a specific purpose. The ability of government to act in the personal life of the individual and the limits upon that power is what defines the politics of conservatives and liberals. As professor Harold Dwight Lasswell famously wrote, politics is about who gets what, when, how, and why.[61] Politics is about gaining the power to decide. Politics is about the power to define problems, the power to make solutions, the power to decide when a problem is to be solved, the power to decide if a problem is a problem and should be solved, the power to decide who solves a problem, and the power to decide to whom a problem belongs.

Barry Goldwater defined conservative philosophy of government by stating that

> politics [is] the art of achieving the maximum amount of freedom for individuals that is consistent with the maintenance of social order. The Conservative is the first to understand that the practice of freedom requires the establishment of order: it is impossible

61 Harold Dwight Lasswell, *Politics: Who Gets What, When, How* (1936). For discussion on how politics affects criminal justice policy making see, Arthur Garrison, "The Influence of Research on Criminal Justice Policy Making," *Professional Issues in Criminal Justice* 4, no. 1 (2009): 9–21.

> for one man to be free if another is able to deny him the exercise of his freedom. But the Conservative also recognizes that the political power on which order is based is a self-aggrandizing force; that its appetite grows with eating. He knows that the utmost vigilance and care are required to keep political power within its proper bounds.[62]

Thus, the purpose of government is to maintain order, but no more. This explains why conservatives can bristle and oppose laws that overturn and ameliorate the evil of Jim Crow discrimination in America and claim, as Thurmond, Faubus, Wallace, and Goldwater did, that such laws are an affront to liberty and are the harbingers of tyranny while supporting the growth of federal and state criminal justice systems. To conservatives, the role of government is to maintain order, so people can enjoy liberty. The role of government is not to address the evil and injustice of men that is short of physical interference with the individual liberties of others to do all that they desire. This is how Goldwater, as discussed in Chapter Four, could conclude that Jim Crow discrimination and segregation was not the business of the federal government and that time and persuasion were the only tools available to end the private and social discrimination and segregation of Blacks in a free nation.

It is important to understand modern American conservative theory is not concerned with social freedom or rights; it is concerned only with individual liberty. It is not concerned with broader definitions of justice; it is only concerned with order. Conservative theory, as defined and established by Goldwater, fears governmental power and its growth and seeks to limit such growth as a singular primary goal. Conservatives can tolerate, as a political and social and even as a moral matter, the evil of discrimination or social injustice. What they cannot tolerate is federal government ending of injustice. The former is bad, but only bad, while the latter is tyranny.

In 1960 and 1964 Goldwater established the model for the moral philosophical underpinnings of the political advocacy conservative candidates in presidential election campaigns for the remainder of the century and into the first decade of the next. He wrote,

> Our tendency to concentrate power in the hands of a few men deeply concerns me. We can be conquered by bombs or by subversion; but we can also be conquered by neglect—by ignoring the Constitution and disregarding the principles of limited government. Our defenses against the accumulation of unlimited power in Washington are in poorer shape, I fear, than our defenses against the aggressive designs of Moscow. Like so many other nations before us, we may succumb through internal weakness rather than fall before a foreign foe.
>
> I am convinced that most Americans now want to reverse the trend. I think that concern for our vanishing freedoms is genuine. I think that the people's uneasiness in the

62 Barry Goldwater, *The Conscience of a Conservative* (1960), 13.

> stifling omnipresence of government has turned into something approaching alarm. But bemoaning the evil will not drive it back, and accusing fingers will not shrink government.
>
> *The turn will come when we entrust the conduct of our affairs to men who understand that their first duty as public officials is to divest themselves of the power they have been given.* It will come when Americans, in hundreds of communities throughout the nation, decide to put the man in office who is pledged to enforce the Constitution and restore the Republic. Who will proclaim in a campaign speech: "I have little interest in streamlining government or in making it more efficient, for *I mean to reduce its size.* I do not undertake to promote welfare, for *I propose to extend freedom.*[63]

From 1964 through the election of Donald Trump in 2016, no Republican has run for president without giving at least lip service in some manner to the principles that Goldwater said in 1964.

> My aim is *not to pass laws, but to repeal them.* It is *not to inaugurate new programs, but to cancel old ones* that do violence to the Constitution, or that have failed in their purpose, or that impose on the people an unwarranted financial burden. I will *not attempt to discover whether legislation is 'needed' before I have first determined whether it is constitutionally permissible.* And if I should later be attacked for neglecting my constituents' 'interests,' I shall reply that I was informed their main interest is liberty and that in that cause I am doing the very best I can."[64]

The good that the federal government did to kill Jim Crow was irrelevant. The injustice and racism that the federal government removed from the shores of America, first in 1865 and then in 1964–1968 is irrelevant to the fact that it had the power to act in the first place. Ronald Reagan before his election in 1980, in two speeches, supplemented the orthodoxy of Goldwater and, later, would supersede him as the modern embodiment of conservative ideology within the Republican Party. Ronald Reagan asserted in his speech, ***A Time for Choosing*** (October 27, 1964), that social programs on the national level would destroy liberty and freedom in America and under the guise of providing for the poor, the Federal government sought to take liberty and freedom from an otherwise free people. In line with the rhetoric of Thurmond, Wallace, and Goldwater, Reagan claimed that America was faced with a time to choose between liberty and tyranny.

Although the Time for Choosing is known in conservative circles as "The speech," which elevated Reagan to national prominence, the speech he gave in 1961 was much clearer in giving voice to the orthodoxy that would take over the Republican Party within the decade. Entitled ***Encroaching Control,*** his speech before the Phoenix Chamber of Commerce on March 30, 1961, proclaimed that international communism had laid plans for the conquering

---

63 Barry Goldwater, *The Conscience of a Conservative* (1960 at 22–23.

64 Barry Goldwater, *The Conscience of a Conservative* (1960) at 23–24 (Emphasis added).

of America. The conquering would not be by military force but through a gradual incrementalism of American acceptance of socialism—then communism—through social programs designed to aid the poor, the sick, the elderly, and the young. Through this incrementalism, America would lose social and societal strength to resist government control of all aspects of life. Reagan crystalized the orthodoxy that social programs in the hands of the federal government, which brings social control, is the definition of tyranny upon the many by the few. Reagan argued federal control of local issues of poverty lodged in the hands of Washington, D.C., bureaucrats only brings government waste, government-created corporations (private or publicly operationalized), progressive over-proportional taxes, higher federal tax rates, socialized medicine (birthed in the Medicare and social security programs), artificially created prices through manipulated supply and demand (the antipathy of free market capitalism), and the regulation of the individual lives of citizens—totalitarianism in the guise social justice.

Reagan made clear in his *Encroaching Control* speech that the purpose of government is not to establish freedom from want. The purpose of government is to protect individual liberty and economic independence which allows individuals to care for themselves and have the liberty to make decisions without government oversight. From this logic, Reagan said the goal should be to reduce the size of the federal government and to do that, reduction in taxes must be the primary objective—a proposition that is Republican orthodoxy to this day. The good that the federal government does is minimal in comparison to the tyranny that comes with the power of the government to do good in the first place. Reagan explained that the key to reducing the size of government is to reduce its ability to intake taxes. The cure for government is not reduced spending, its reduced taxes.

> And if your Congressman is one who writes back and says he, too, is for economy, but we must reduce government spending before we reduce taxes, you write back and tell him this is a dishonest theory. Because no government in history has ever voluntarily reduced itself in size. Government doesn't tax to get the money it needs. Government will always find a need for the money it gets. ... Our Founding Fathers, here in this country, brought about the only true revolution that has ever taken place in man's history. Every other revolution simply exchanged one set of rulers for another set of rulers. But only here did that little band of men so advanced beyond their time that the world has never seen their like since. Evolve the idea that you and I have within ourselves the God-given right and the ability to determine our own destiny.

Reagan then concluded his *Encroaching Control* speech with the most famous and regularly repeated idea in conservative circles.

> *But freedom is never more than one generation away from extinction. We didn't pass it on to our children in the bloodstream. The only way they can inherit the freedom we have known is if we fight for it, protect it, defend it and then hand it to them with the well thought lessons of how they in their lifetime must do the same. And if you and I don't do this, then*

> *you and I may well spend our sunset years telling our children and our children's children what it once was like in America when men were free.*

Note the historical context of Reagan's defense of states' rights. He stated that the federal government was getting too big and was engaged in tyranny when the federal government imposed its will to end Jim Crow and American apartheid. The states' rights rhetoric of the 1940s and 1950s was being was replaced by the states' rights rhetoric of protecting of individual liberty from a tyrannical federal government. The former rhetoric of Thurmond and Wallace was changing to the race-neutral rhetoric of Goldwater and Reagan. The end result for civil rights was the same, but the rhetoric was changing with the abandonment of explicit racism. The point is that either version of the theory of states' rights would strip the federal government of power to end the second-class status for Blacks. States' rights remained orthodoxy in the mouth of Calhoun and in Reagan; the difference between the two was in the tone of the delivery.

In his *Time for Choosing* speech three years later in support for Goldwater in 1964, Reagan said "a government can't control the economy without controlling people [and] that outside of its legitimate functions, government does nothing as well or as economically as the private sector of the economy." Government seeks taxes and power for its own sake under the guise of providing aid but only delivers debt and then slavery through debt, while in fact it does not meet the needs of poor. Reagan famously said of government officials and bureaucrats, "[t]he more the plans fail, the more the planners plan." Reagan, as Goldwater did, modernized the arguments of Thurmond and Wallace, and Calhoun before them, by focusing on the oppression of an increasingly powerful federal government. In his *Time for Choosing* speech, he asserted in 1964 that

> No government ever voluntarily reduces itself in size. So governments' programs, once launched, never disappear. Actually, a government bureau is the nearest thing to eternal life we'll ever see on this earth. Federal employees—federal employees number two and a half million; and federal, state, and local, one out of six of the nation's work force employed by government. These proliferating bureaus with their thousands of regulations have cost us many of our constitutional safeguards. How many of us realize that ***today federal agents can invade a man's property without a warrant***? They can impose a fine without a formal hearing, let alone a trial by jury? And they can seize and sell his property at auction to enforce the payment of that fine. In Chico County, Arkansas, James Wier over-planted his rice allotment. The government obtained a 17,000 dollar judgment. And a U.S. marshal sold his 960-acre farm at auction. The government said it was necessary as a warning to others to make the system work.

Reagan complained of federal agents entering the home of a man without a warrant. That was false. He knew it was false, for he was an educated man and he had access to basic Supreme Court rulings. But, the truth has little currency in political rhetoric. The fear of federal government tyranny and its use of the courts to create a political utopia (as Strom Thurmond warned) on the backs of White American citizens had taken hold in the Republican Party dating back to the days of Supreme Court enforced integration and its abandonment of Jim Crow in 1954.

Reagan's 1964 statement "that today federal agents can invade a man's property without a warrant" was false, because the Supreme Court had ruled that in *Weeks v. United States (1914) and in Silverthorne Lumber Co. v. United States (1920)* that the federal government needed a warrant to enter private property, and failure to do so would prohibit the use of any evidence secured by the unlawful entry inadmissible in court. By the time Reagan gave his "Time for Choosing" speech (1964) in which he decried the overreach abuse of federal power to issue fines the criminal justice system, the most powerful arm of the government, criminal court judges, both state and federal, were relatively free from constitutional control. The only significant limits on government power was that the Supreme Court ruled that the state judges could not convict a person in secret trials *(In re Oliver,* 1948*)* and *that* the police could not break into the home of man without a warrant and, by force, beat and extract evidence of a crime from his stomach and use the evidence at trial (*Rochin v. California*, 1952). The implementation of states' rights principles had required the Supreme Court to rule in 1936 that the police, under the Fourteenth Amendment Due Process Clause, could not tie three "defendants, all ignorant negroes" to a tree and a chair and whip confessions out of them and then use the confessions against them in court (*Brown v. Mississippi*) and to rule in 1931 that the state judges must appoint indigent defendants competent counsel in death penalty cases (*Powell v. Alabama*).

In defending the Fourteenth Amendment Due Process Clause, prohibition of beating physical evidence out of a suspect's stomach the Supreme Court held in *Rochin v. California* that such methods

> do more than offend some fastidious squeamishness or private sentimentalism about combating crime too energetically. This is conduct that shocks the conscience. Illegally breaking into the privacy of the petitioner, the struggle to open his mouth and remove what was there, the forcible extraction of his stomach's contents — this course of proceeding by agents of government to obtain evidence is bound to offend even hardened sensibilities. They are methods too close to the rack and the screw to permit of constitutional differentiation ... the conviction of the petitioner has been obtained by methods that offend the Due Process Clause. [65]

In the famous ***Brown v. Mississippi*** case of the police being free to whip confessions out of three Black defendants, prior to Reagan's speech decrying the tyranny of federal encroachment on the freedom of the states to handle its social issues as it deemed appropriate, a police officer in open court could be

> put on the stand by the state in rebuttal, and admitted the whippings. It is interesting to note that, in his testimony with reference to the whipping of the defendant Ellington, and ***in response to the inquiry as to how severely he was whipped, the deputy stated,***

65 *Rochin v. California* 342 U.S. 165, 172, 174 (1952).

> ***'Not too much for a negro; not as much as I would have done if it were left to me.'*** Two others who had participated in these whippings were introduced and admitted it—not a single witness was introduced who denied it. The facts are not only undisputed, they are admitted, and admitted to have been done by officers of the state, in conjunction with other participants, and all this was definitely well known to everybody connected with the trial, and during the trial, including the state's prosecuting attorney and the trial judge presiding.

To the assertion of states' rights prevailing over Fourteenth Amendment due process requirements and the prohibition of evidence secured by torture being introduced and used in open court, the Supreme Court responded

> The State is free to regulate the procedure of its courts in accordance with its own conceptions of policy. ... But the freedom of the State ... is limited by the requirement of due process of law. ***Because a State may dispense with a jury trial, it does not follow that it may substitute trial by ordeal. The rack and torture chamber may not be substituted for the witness stand.*** ... [A trial] is a mere pretense where the state authorities have contrived a conviction resting solely upon confessions obtained by violence. ... It would be difficult to conceive of methods more revolting to the sense of justice than those taken to procure the confessions of these petitioners, and the use of the confessions thus obtained as the basis for conviction and sentence was a clear denial of due process.[66]

---

66 *Brown v. Mississippi*, 297 U.S. 278, 284–86 (1936) (Internal citations omitted). The Court concluded, "We are not concerned with a mere question of state practice, or whether counsel assigned to petitioners were competent or mistakenly assumed that their first objections were sufficient. In an earlier case, the Supreme Court of the State had recognized the duty of the court to supply corrective process where due process of law had been denied. In *Fisher v. State,* 145 Miss. 116, 134, 110 So. 361, 365, [1926] the court said:

> Coercing the supposed state's criminals into confessions and using such confessions so coerced from them against them in trials has been the curse of all countries. It was the chief inequity, the crowning infamy, of the Star Chamber and the Inquisition, and other similar institutions. The constitution recognized the evils that lay behind these practices, and prohibited them in this country. ... The duty of maintaining constitutional rights of a person on trial for his life rises above mere rules of procedure, and wherever the court is clearly satisfied that such violations exist, it will refuse to sanction such violations and will apply the corrective.

In the instant case, the trial court was fully advised by the undisputed evidence of the way in which the confessions had been procured. The trial court knew that there was no other evidence upon which conviction and sentence could be based. Yet it proceeded to permit conviction, and to pronounce sentence. The conviction and sentence were void for want of the essential elements of due process, and the proceeding thus vitiated could be challenged in any appropriate manner. It was challenged before the Supreme Court of the State by the express invocation of the Fourteenth Amendment. That court entertained the challenge, considered the federal question

Secret trials were prohibited, state courts were prohibited from using evidence and confessions physically beaten out of Black defendants, the police could not prevent an attorney from seeing his client during police interrogation, and indigent defendants had a right to an attorney in felony cases. These were the only limits imposed upon the states under the U.S. Constitution when Reagan complained of the power of the federal government over the lives of citizens. Clearly, federal government tyranny was truly at the gates in 1964!

While Reagan decried the tyranny of the federal government in his *Encroaching Control* speech, the states argued before the Supreme Court that the Fourth Amendment did not prohibit the states from searching the homes of citizens without warrants and using warrantless seized evidence in criminal trials.

Reagan's *Encroaching Control* speech (1961) was three months before the Court overruled *Wolf v. Colorado* (1949), which held that the Fourth Amendment prohibition against unreasonable search and seizure could not be applied to the states through the Fourteenth Amendment, in ***Mapp v. Ohio*** (1961). His speech was

- One year before the Court ruled that the right against cruel and unusual punishment applied to the states (***Robinson v. California***, 1962),
- Two years before the Court ruled that the states must appoint counsel to indigent defendants in all felony cases (***Gideon v. Wainwright***, 1963),
- Three before the Court ruled that the states could not interrogate a confession out of an accused while he was in custody and asking for an attorney before he was arrested (***Escobedo v. Illinois***, 1964),
- Three years before the Court held that the Fifth Amendment right against forced confessions applies to the states (***Malloy v. Hogan***, 1964),
- Four years before the Court held that the right to cross-examine witnesses applies to the states (***Pointer v. Texas***, 1965),
- Five years before the Court held that the right to an impartial jury applied to the states (***Parker v. Gladded***, 1966),
- Five years before the Court ruled that the states were required to inform the defendant that he had a right to an attorney and to remain silent (***Miranda v. Arizona***, 1966),
- Six years before the Court ruled that juveniles could not be imprisoned in juvenile prisons without the protections of due process under the theory of *in loco parentis* (***In Re Gault***, 1967),
- Six years before the Court ruled that the police needed a warrant to conduct a wiretap on a private phone (***Berger v. New York***, 1967),

---

thus presented, but declined to enforce petitioners' constitutional right. The court thus denied a federal right fully established and specially set up and claimed, and the judgment must be *Reversed.*"
Brown v. Mississippi, 297 U.S. at 286–87.

- Six years before the Court ruled that the federal government could not arrange a lineup without defense counsel being present to assure the lineup was not manipulated by law enforcement to the detriment of the accused (***United States v. Wade***, 1967),
- Six years before the Court held that the right to a speedy trial applied to the states (***Klopfer v. North Carolina***, 1967),
- Seven years before the Court held that the right against double jeopardy applies to the states (***Benton v. Maryland***, 1968), and
- Seven years before the Court held that the Sixth Amendment right to a jury trial for felonies applies to the states (***Duncan v. Louisiana***, 1968).

States' rights criminal justice practices had produced the need for the ***criminal justice due process revolution*** (1961–1968) in which the Supreme Court would rule that the Fourth, Fifth, Sixth, and Eighth Amendments were incorporated into the Fourteenth Amendment and applicable to the states. This revolution, despised by social conservatives and later Republicans, was barely at its dawn when Reagan decried government tyranny—defined exclusively as federal government action.

When Reagan delivered his *Encroaching Control* (1961) and, later, in his *Time for Choosing* speech (1964), the established policy and the practice of the states allowed the police to conduct searches without warrants and interrogations without attorneys, convict the indigent without counsel, and imprison juveniles with no concern for procedural due process. Such judicial processes were apparently of no consequence to Reagan in the face of the tyranny of the federal government being able to "impose a fine without a formal hearing, let alone a trial by jury [and being able to] seize and sell his property at auction to enforce the payment of that fine."

Leaving that aside, Reagan's *Time for Choosing* speech was also a full endorsement of Goldwater and what he represented. Reagan stated that "last February 19th at the University of Minnesota, Norman Thomas, six-time candidate for president on the Socialist Party ticket, said, 'If Barry Goldwater became president, he would stop the advance of socialism in the United States.' I think that's exactly what he will do." Reagan concluded,

> Those who would trade our freedom for the soup kitchen of the welfare state have told us they have a utopian solution of peace without victory. ... Alexander Hamilton said, "A nation which can prefer disgrace to danger is prepared for a master, and deserves one." ... If we continue to accommodate, continue to back and retreat, eventually we have to face the final demand—the ultimatum [and] someday when the time comes to deliver the final ultimatum, our surrender will be voluntary, because by that time we will have been weakened from within spiritually, morally, and economically. ... You and I know and do not believe that life is so dear and peace so sweet as to be purchased at the price of chains and slavery. ... You and I have the courage to say to our enemies, "There is a price we will not pay." "There is a point beyond which they must not advance." And this—this is the meaning in the phrase of Barry Goldwater's "peace through strength." Winston Churchill

> said, "The destiny of man is not measured by material computations. When great forces are on the move in the world, we learn we're spirits—not animals." And he said, "There's something going on in time and space, and beyond time and space, which, whether we like it or not, spells duty." You and I have a rendezvous with destiny. We'll preserve for our children this, the last best hope of man on earth, or we'll sentence them to take the last step into a thousand years of darkness. We will keep in mind and remember that Barry Goldwater has faith in us. He has faith that you and I have the ability and the dignity and the right to make our own decisions and determine our own destiny.

Goldwater and Reagan laid the foundation for Republican politics regarding social policy. The purpose of the federal government is to preserve liberty. Individual dignity, they asserted, flows from the ability to enjoy liberty, not enjoy freedom from injustice and inequality. The individual liberty advocated by Goldwater and Reagan included preventing the federal government from ending the social policy of telling Black individuals your right to liberty includes your mandatory status to sit in the back of the bus. Goldwater and Reagan made clear that Black civil rights is not for the federal government to protect.

As discussed in Chapter Four, Goldwater, in his 1964 *Civil Rights and the Common Good* speech and in his 1960 book *The Conscience of a Conservative*, said let the states and local government address the social evil of Jim Crow, but if they don't—it's no business of the federal government, and the people who suffer under Jim Crow had no right to appeal to the federal government for aid. The reason being civil rights, like other social programs of the Great Society, was the foot in the door opening to tyranny. As a social commentator complained,

> The civil-rights movement set in motion what has been undoubtedly the most extensive and pervasive expansion of government power over society. It was to American culture what the New Deal was to the economy.
>
> Responding to entrenched and systemic racial discrimination, the Civil Rights Act of 1964 did not just dismantle Jim Crow as a legal regime in the South. It prohibited racial discrimination in nearly all aspects of American economic and social life. Along with the Voting Rights Act of 1965 and subsequent Supreme Court decisions, this seminal legislation created an energetic bureaucracy and expansive body of law that sought to stamp out racial discrimination.
>
> ...
>
> [Goldwater] ... insisted that trying to prohibit discrimination in employment and public accommodations empowered the government to interpose itself into the everyday lives of citizens to an unprecedented degree. With his characteristic bluntness, he warned that a government mandate to prevent and correct discrimination at all levels of society would require a "police state."[67]

---

67 R.R. Reno, "The Selma Analogy," *First Things* at 4 (May 2012) reprinted at http://www.firstthings.com/article/2012/05/the-selma-analogy

The point can be summarized by the observation that conservatives, as a rule, do not seek nor favor the use of the coercive power of government to achieve social ends, but liberals have no hesitation in doing so.

The same commentator begrudgingly admitted racism and ending it produced positive results, but the positive should be considered alongside the equally unsatisfactory result of increasing the power of the national government by allowing it to enforce and protect civil rights from state laws and private actions.[68] Today's conservatives assert that they are pleased that the days of Jim Crow are over, but they fail to admit that their theory of states' rights would not have ended Jim Crow. Furthermore, what conservatives resent is that the federal government was used in the first place to achieve this victory over Jim Crow, and that the resulting growth of government has remained after its victory over Jim Crow. To compound this growth, the federal government, and the states to a lesser degree, have continued to claim the power to impact the individual lives of Americans—the definition of tyranny.

States' rights theory was operationalized through opposition to attacks on the system of Jim Crow segregation and discrimination. As discussed in Chapter Four, the rise of Thurmond, Faubus, Wallace, and Goldwater fostered and supported the abandonment of Southern Democrats to the Republicans as the Democrats began to support civil rights legislation and desegregation beginning with President Truman in 1948. Wallace, in his 1958 run for Governor of Alabama, learned that support of racists and segregationist was essential for Southern politics. As a recent book on the period observed, "Before that January day, Wallace had not been a rabid segregationist; indeed, by Southern standards, Wallace had been a racial moderate. ... When Wallace initially ran for governor in 1958, the NAACP endorsed him; his opponent had the blessing of the Ku Klux Klan." His opponent was John Malcolm Patterson, and he later explained that his victory over Wallace could be distilled to Wallace being "out-niggered."[69] Wallace determined that he was not going to lose another election because he was perceived as soft on the segregation question again. In 1962 he ran and won as a ravenous segregationist. During the election he promised to stand in the door of the University of Alabama to prevent the integration of the university and in June 1963 he did just that.

The significance of Wallace standing in the doorway of the admissions office of the University of Alabama in 1963 is multidimensional, because it involved the conflating of states' rights, with opposition to the federal government, with White fear of Black integration, with conservative theory of government, and foreshadowed the politics that would result in the rise Republican Party control of national and state politics and policy in 1966 and 1968.

> Many observers have cited a white backlash to civil rights. Surely this played an important role, but conservatism seemed to benefit from a complex convergence of forces, only

---

68 R.R. Reno, "The Selma Analogy" at 3–5.

69 Ian Haney López. *Dog Whistle Politics: How Coded Racial Appeals Have Reinvented Racism and Wrecked the Middle Class* (2013), 14–15, reprinted at http://www.salon.com/2013/12/22/how_the_gop_became_the_white_mans_party/

> some of which had to do with race. Unprecedented prosperity, for example, gave rise to a new middle class that was hostile to high taxes and to many of the social programs they financed. Social unrest—most notably urban riots, violent crime, and student protests—also pushed many Americans toward conservative candidates who promised to restore law and order. But perhaps most important was a growing disillusionment with the federal government. Vietnam, deteriorating conditions in the cities, and forced busing affected the lives of working-and middle-class Americans in profound and often unsettling ways, and led them to believe that government no longer served their interests.[70]

Wallace, in 1963, learned three things about America, race, and civil rights politics. The first lesson was also impressed upon Martin Luther King Jr. when he tried to integrate Chicago in 1966:

> First, Wallace realized with a shock that hostility toward blacks was not confined to the South. He had looked out upon those white Americans north of Alabama and suddenly been awakened by a blinding vision: "They all hate black people, all of them. They're all afraid, all of them. Great god! That's it! They're all Southern. The whole United States is Southern." Wallace suddenly knew that overtures to racial resentment would resonate across the country.
>
> His second startling realization, [he] had figured out how to exploit that pervasive animosity. The key lay in seemingly non-racial language. At his inauguration, Wallace had defended segregation and extolled the proud Anglo-Saxon Southland, thereby earning national ridicule as an unrepentant redneck. Six months later, talking not about stopping integration but about states' rights and arrogant federal authority—and visually aided by footage showing him facing down a powerful Department of Justice official rather than vulnerable black students attired in their Sunday best—Wallace was a countrywide hero.[71]

This realization birthed **Dog Whistle** racial code speech into American political rhetoric. Wallace helped pioneer states' rights as a code in which "fear and hate could be mobilized without mentioning race itself except to deny that one is a racist." Wallace established that states' rights must be used "in the language of state-federal relations rather than white supremacy." He also established that states' rights "was enough of a fig leaf to allow persons queasy about black equality to oppose integration without having to admit, to others and perhaps even to themselves, their racial attitudes."[72]

---

70 Matthew Dalleck, "The Conservative 1960s," *The Atlantic Monthly* 276, no. 6 (December 1995): 130–35 at http://www.theatlantic.com/magazine/archive/1995/12/the-conservative-1960s/376506

71 Ian Haney López. *Dog Whistle Politics: How Coded Racial Appeals Have Reinvented Racism and Wrecked the Middle Class* (2013), 16, reprinted at http://www.salon.com/2013/12/22/how_the_gop_became_the_white_mans_party/

72 Ian Haney López. *Dog Whistle Politics ...*

As discussed in Chapter Four, the politics and policies of states' rights has changed over time. States' rights under Calhoun was a tool to defend slavery and assert Black inferiority. States' rights under Thurmond and Wallace was a tool to defend segregation and Black second-class citizenship. States' rights under Goldwater was a tool to prevent the tyranny of a strong federal government and its enforcement of federal civil rights law. States' rights under Nixon and Reagan was a tool to support law and order policies. All of these iterations of states' rights had one shared focus—the social control of Blacks and fear of Blacks by middle-class Whites. The focus remained the same, what changed was the language of the rhetoric.

The third lesson Wallace drew from 1963 was that he could ride this conceptualization of racism to the presidency, which he attempted in 1964, 1968, 1972, and 1976. As discussed in Chapters One and Four, the combination of the rise of Goldwater and the popularity of his book *The Conscience of a Conservative* in 1960,[73] the midterm elections of 1966, and the Wallace campaigns in the presidential elections of 1964 and 1968 all transformed the modern Republican Party into a formal proponent of states' rights, and Goldwater and Wallace laid the foundation for Republican politics for the next three decades. By the dawn of the 1972 elections, Nixon had learned from Wallace and Thurmond the science and art of **race coding**.[74] Nixon used middle-class fear of urban crime, race riots, and social disorder as a foundation for his law and order campaign and established two political truths. *First, **elections can be won by harnessing White working class and middle-class voters*** by focusing on their fear and resentment with non-racial code words. *Second, **elections can be won by focusing White working class and middle-class resentment*** against the policies of the national government. These two truths, along with Nixon's ***Southern Strategy***, became the dominant theory of Republican election politics for the remainder of the twentieth century. The lessons taught by Goldwater, Wallace, and Nixon were not lost on Ronald Reagan in 1980.

Reagan, in his election, redefined and continued papering over the original meaning and purpose of states' rights. Calhoun said states' rights meant that the national government had no power to contain or oppose slavery in the South or in the West. Faubus and Wallace said states' rights meant that the national government had no power to end or mitigate Southern segregation and Jim Crow. Reagan said states' rights meant that the national government was too large, and it interfered with individual liberty. Under Reagan, states' rights papered over the racial purpose of states' rights by asserting it was about protection of individual liberty, which is threatened, by definition, by a strong national government.

Reagan adopted the Goldwater conception of states' rights. In his acceptance speech for the Republican nomination on July 17, 1980, he said,

---

73 Matthew Dalleck, "The Conservative 1960s," *The Atlantic Monthly* 276, no. 6 (December 1995): 130–35 at http://www.theatlantic.com/magazine/archive/1995/12/the-conservative-1960s/376506/

74 Ian Haney López. *Dog Whistle Politics: How Coded Racial Appeals Have Reinvented Racism and Wrecked the Middle Class* (2013), 27, reprinted at http://www.salon.com/2013/12/22/how_the_gop_became_the_white_mans_party/

> As your nominee, I pledge to restore to the federal government the capacity to do the people's work without dominating their lives. I pledge to you a government that will not only work well, but wisely; its ability to act tempered by prudence and its willingness to do good balanced by the knowledge that government is never more dangerous than when our desire to have it help us blinds us to its great power to harm us.
>
> ...
>
> Beyond these essentials, I believe it is clear our federal government is overgrown and overweight. Indeed, it is time for our government to go on a diet. Therefore, my first act as chief executive will be to impose an immediate and thorough freeze on federal hiring. Then, we are going to enlist the very best minds from business, labor and whatever quarter to conduct a detailed review of every department, bureau and agency that lives by federal appropriations. We are also going to enlist the help and ideas of many dedicated and hard working government employees at all levels who want a more efficient government as much as the rest of us do. I know that many are demoralized by the confusion and waste they confront in their work as a result of failed and failing policies.
>
> Our instructions to the groups we enlist will be simple and direct. We will remind them that government programs exist at the sufferance of the American taxpayer and are paid for with money earned by working men and women. Any program that represents a waste of their money—a theft from their pocketbooks—must have that waste eliminated or the program must go—by executive order where possible; by congressional action where necessary. Everything that can be run more effectively by state and local government we shall turn over to state and local government, along with the funding sources to pay for it. We are going to put an end to the money merry-go-round where our money becomes Washington's money, to be spent by the states and cities exactly the way the federal bureaucrats tell them to.

States' rights theory was now about reducing the cost, incompetence, and general influence of the federal government. This villainization of the national government was the seed that would lead to the rise of Tea Party political rhetoric, the rejection of establishment republican politics, and the election Trump forty years later.

Reagan proclaimed this new definition of states' rights on August 3, 1980, in his first campaign speech after accepting the nomination. The significance of the declaration was in its location. Reagan went to Neshoba County, in Philadelphia, Mississippi, to give his speech at a local fair. The significance was not that a Republican went down South to build up support—it was the post–1964 Republican Party, after all. But the significance of Reagan's visit in 1980 was that he went to the location of the famous murder of the three civil rights workers, James Earl Chaney, Andrew Goodman, and Michael "Mickey" Schwerner, at the hands of the Ku Klux Klan with the support and assistance of the Neshoba County sheriff's office in 1964. Politics is about symbolism, as well as rhetoric. Reagan went to the location of the famous killing (which was only solved, because President Johnson ordered the national government and the Federal Bureau of Investigation to do so, over the objections of the local authorities) and said,

> I believe in state's rights; I believe in people doing as much as they can for themselves at the community level and at the private level. And I believe that we've distorted the balance of our government today by giving powers that were never intended in the constitution to that federal establishment. And if I do get the job I'm looking for, I'm going to devote myself to trying to reorder those priorities and to restore to the states and local communities those functions which properly belong there.[75]

True, his statement regarding states' rights was within the context of the Great Society welfare programs and how they only trap people in poverty, and it was not about federal enforcement of civil rights laws, but that's not the point. The point is not even that he defended states' rights in the first place. The point is he used the phrase and defended the concept to an audience that sixteen years ago advocated states' rights standing over the dead bodies of three civil rights workers murdered by the KKK for trying to get Blacks registered to vote! He made no mention of the events of 1964 or even an attempt to say the days of 1964 were over in Neshoba County. He said the federal government is too big, too intrusive, and "I'm going to devote myself to trying to reorder those priorities and to restore to the states and local communities those functions which properly belong there." Giving Reagan the benefit of the doubt that he did intend to blow a dog whistle, it was nonetheless both seen and heard.

Five months later, on the steps of the National Capitol, after being sworn in as the fortieth president of the United States he said,

> The economic ills we suffer have come upon us over several decades. They will not go away in days, weeks, or months, but they will go away. They will go away because we as Americans have the capacity now, as we've had in the past, to do whatever needs to be done to preserve this last and greatest bastion of freedom. ***In this present crisis, government is not the solution to our problem; government is the problem.*** From time to time we've been tempted to believe that society has become too complex to be managed by self-rule, that government by an elite group is superior to government for, by, and of the people. Well, if no one among us is capable of governing himself, then who among us has the capacity to govern someone else? All of us together, in and out of government, must bear the burden. The solutions we seek must be equitable, with no one group singled out to pay a higher price.
>
> ...
>
> So, as we begin, let us take inventory. We are a nation that has a government—not the other way around. And this makes us special among the nations of the Earth. Our government has no power except that granted it by the people. It is time to check and reverse

75 Ronald Reagan, speech at Neshoba County, Philadelphia Mississippi August 3, 1980, *The Neshoba Democrat* online at http://neshobademocrat.com/Content/NEWS/News/Article/Transcript-of-Ronald-Reagan-s-1980-Neshoba-County-Fair-speech/2/297/15599

the growth of government, which shows signs of having grown beyond the consent of the governed.

It is my intention to curb the size and influence of the Federal establishment and to demand recognition of the distinction between the powers granted to the Federal Government and those reserved to the States or to the people. ***All of us need to be reminded that the Federal Government did not create the States; the States created the Federal Government.***

Now, so there will be no misunderstanding, it's not my intention to do away with government. It is rather to make it work—work with us, not over us; to stand by our side, not ride on our back. Government can and must provide opportunity, not smother it; foster productivity, not stifle it.

If we look to the answer as to why for so many years we achieved so much, prospered as no other people on Earth, it was because here in this land we unleashed the energy and individual genius of man to a greater extent than has ever been done before. Freedom and the dignity of the individual have been more available and assured here than in any other place on Earth. The price for this freedom at times has been high, but we have never been unwilling to pay that price.

It is no coincidence that our present troubles parallel and are proportionate to the intervention and intrusion in our lives that result from unnecessary and excessive growth of government. It is time for us to realize that we're too great a nation to limit ourselves to small dreams. We're not, as some would have us believe, doomed to an inevitable decline. I do not believe in a fate that will fall on us no matter what we do. I do believe in a fate that will fall on us if we do nothing. So, with all the creative energy at our command, let us begin an era of national renewal. Let us renew our determination, our courage, and our strength. And let us renew our faith and our hope.

...

In the days ahead I will propose removing the roadblocks that have slowed our economy and reduced productivity. Steps will be taken aimed at restoring the balance between the various levels of government. Progress may be slow, measured in inches and feet, not miles, but we will progress. It is time to reawaken this industrial giant, to get government back within its means, and to lighten our punitive tax burden. And these will be our first priorities, and on these principles there will be no compromise.

President Reagan said that, "in this present crisis, government is not the solution to our problem; government is the problem." Not only was it "time to check and reverse the growth of government," it was time "to curb the size and influence of the Federal establishment and to demand recognition of the distinction between the powers granted to the Federal Government and those reserved to the States or to the people. All of us need to be reminded that the Federal Government did not create the States; the States created the Federal Government."

Excerpt from Ronald Reagan, "Inaugural Address." 1981.

President Reagan knew this last statement, that the states created the national government, was a blatant falsehood. Reagan was an educated man, so he knew the text of the Constitution says, "We the people of the United States, in Order to form a more perfect Union ... do ordain and establish this Constitution for the United States of America." The people not the states created the Constitution. The federalists won that debate in 1789, the North won that debate in 1865, and the segregationists lost that debate during the civil rights movement (1954–1968).

More importantly, Reagan's rewriting to make the preamble "we the states" was in line with classical Calhoun, Thurmond, Faubus, Wallace, and Goldwater. Both his supporters and detractors heard the whistle. In 1980, the ideas of the confederacy and Jim Crow defenders, both advocated through states' rights, found utterance in the mouth of a president, and Reagan established the permanency of these ideas within the Republican Party orthodoxy to this day. As Conservative Republicans say to this day, regarding the principles of free trade, low taxes, reduction of government regulation, protection of private property rights, limited national government, strong national defense, individual responsibility, rule of law, law and order in the streets, unquestioned support for local urban police and their tactics to suppress urban crime, and support for the second amendment right of individual private citizens to keep and bear arms, "on these principles there will be no compromise."

This political and historical background of American politics provides the canvas on which American criminal justice policy has been drawn for more than fifty years. The racial social turmoil of the decade of the 1960s, followed by the rise of Blacks as equals to Whites and the fall of systematic White superiority and the uncertainty that it brought in 1970s, resulted in the fall of rehabilitation as a theory of crime and punishment. As discussed in Chapter Eight, the fall of rehabilitation was followed by the rise of the retribution, incapacitation, and incarceration criminal justice policy in the 1980s and 1990s. The rise of conservative politics and White backlash in the 1980s combined with the rise of urban crime and crack in the 1980s and 1990s, exacerbated the historical disproportionate minority confinement of Blacks in the late 1980s through the 1990s.

KEY CONCEPTS AND CASES

1. Black Codes
2. Civil Rights Acts of 1871 and 1875
3. Mandatory contract laws
4. Criminal anti-enticement laws
5. Contract enforcement laws
6. False-pretense laws
7. Manumission statutes
8. Apprentice laws
9. Commercial and trade restrictive laws
10. Criminalization of contract law

11. Fugitive Slave Laws of 1793 and 1850
12. Fugitive Slave Clause of the U.S. Constitution
13. Slave patrols
14. Vagrancy laws
15. Peonage Act of 1867
16. Freedman's Bureau
17. Whitecapping
18. System of involuntary servitude
19. Sharecropper
20. Supplier's lien
21. Tenant-farmer
22. *United States v. Clyatt* (1905)
23. *Bailey v. Alabama* (1914)
24. Convict-leasing
25. Criminal peonage
26. Negro crime
27. Anti-emigrant-agent laws
28. The Tuskegee Airmen
29. Nationalization of criminal justice
30. Ronald Reagan's "Encroaching Control" (1961) and "A Time for Choosing" (1964) speeches
31. *Powell v. Alabama* (1931)
32. *Brown v. Mississippi* (1936)
33. *Rochin v. California* (1952)
34. Due process revolution (1961–1968)

DISCUSSION QUESTIONS

1. Describe, define, and explain the Black Codes and the involuntary servitude laws that were passed after the Civil War.
2. Describe and explain the system of sharecropping and tenant farming. How did these systems support the system of involuntary servitude, and how did the system of involuntary servitude support the economic system of sharecropping?
3. What is the relationship between the Black Codes and the status of slavery? How did the criminal justice system return a person to a state of slavery, both legally and functionally?
4. Why does the system of Black Codes and involuntary servitude matter in relation to the modern criminal justice operations that began in the 1960s? Compare and contrast the purpose of the criminal justice system in the 1860s with the system in

the 1960s. How did the system change regarding the purpose of the criminal justice system in the 1960s?

5. In line with the history of Jim Crow, what is legacy of these laws on how Blacks view the purpose and legitimacy of the criminal justice system? How does this legacy impact and explain the views Blacks of how the criminal justice system functions today?
6. What is the significance of World War II and the Cold War on how the American criminal justice system functions today? Why and how did the international politics of the Cold War impact local criminal justice laws and role of the federal government in local criminal justice operations?
7. Compare and contrast the views of Calhoun and Reagan? Are their thoughts in conflict or congruence? Is it fair to conflate their ideas when explaining and examining criminal justice history and current operations?

CHAPTER EIGHT

The Modern Incarceration of Blacks within the Criminal Justice System

STUDENT LEARNING OBJECTIVES

1. Students will be able to explain the politics and policy dynamics of the 1980s and 1990s to explain modern criminal justice policy and its relation to disproportionate Black incarceration.
2. Students will be able to explain how the crack epidemic started and how federal laws under Ronald Reagan and Bill Clinton formed the modern American criminal justice system. Students will be able discuss and describe how the political rhetoric of both Democrats and Republicans merged to negatively impact Blacks in urban neighborhoods and in public housing by both supporting a crime control model of criminal justice.
3. Students will be able to define the due process and crime control models and how each was adopted by various presidents in the second half of the twentieth century into the first decade of the twenty-first.
4. Students will be able to discuss how the modern narratives of crime and criminality have been used to shape and create criminal justice policy post-1960s, as well as differentiate the policies and politics of the 1970s, 1980s, 1990s, and 2000s.
5. Students will be able to compare and contrast the criminal justice policies of presidents Reagan, Bush 41, Clinton, Bush 43, Obama, and Trump and the policy determinations each president made and the impact of those policies.

****

In a republic like the United States, ideas and the values that support them create political attitudes, which create political narratives and those advocating winning narratives gain political power, which they use to create and implement policy. These policies define societal and social realities that govern and describe political disputes and subsequent elections, which redefine, reverse, and/or reinforce political narratives and subsequent policies. Although truth has its utility, truth pales in significance to the omnipresent (all encompassing), omniscient (all defining), and omnipotent (all controlling) need to secure a victorious political narrative.

In the United States, ideas and political narratives about Blacks are historically, politically, and socially derived. The history of racism provides America with a negative narrative of Blacks, which has been reflected in criminal justice policy for centuries; from slave ships to the slave patrols, to the pre-Reconstruction period of the Black Codes, to the post-Reconstruction policies of peonage, and convict-leasing resulting in disproportionate incarceration under Jim Crow, to the post–Jim Crow policies of the War on Drugs and war on crime, the militarization of the police and the use of militarized equipment on Black communities, to the strategy of police saturation and the tactics of stop and frisk to suppress violence in Black communities. All of which, together and separately, resulted in and has continued the disproportionate incarceration of Blacks. The manifestations of blacks in chains in America dates back to more than a century before the birth of the generation of the founding fathers.

****

CONTEMPORARY RACE NARRATIVES OF BLACKS AND CRIME

> *So long as whites performed at least the bare rituals of due process and cloaked their actions behind claims of equality, the crudest abuses of blacks and violations of their protections under law would rarely ever be challenged.* The neo-slavery of the new century relied on a simple but extraordinary ruse that the Supreme Court's ruling[s] implicitly endorsed. [Southern criminal justice] could safely force a black man into servitude for months or years as long as they pretended that the legal rights of those black men had not been violated. The implications were as deeply absorbed by black people as were the rhythms of farming in the era of old slavery. *This long era of false trials and arrests would taint the African American view of legal processes and guarantees for generations to come.*[1]

As discussed in Chapter Three, there is a psychological social link between being Black and being criminal. This link is socially, culturally, and historically derived and maintained. The link, in post 1960s America, is systemic not systematic. This link has a long intellectual history. It begins with the link between blackness and sin and the devil. As discussed in Chapter Five, European and American Christian theology asserted that slavery of Africans was the natural result stemming from the events of Genesis when Noah cursed Canaan—people of color—the

1 Douglas A. Blackmon, *Slavery by Another Name* (Anchor, 2008) at 147–148 (emphasis added).

sons of his son Ham, to serve his other sons, Japheth and Shem.[2] By the sixteenth century people of color were considered not equal to Europeans, and Christian Europe believed people of color were supposed to be their servants because they, Europeans, were the descendants of Japheth. These racist ideas were later translated into defining Black slaves as criminals when they resisted their enslavement. To resist slavery was to break both the law of man and God. Remember, slaves who ran away were, by definition, fugitives from the law. When a slave ran away he stole his master's property. The belief that fugitives were to be hunted down by law enforcement and returned to their slave masters was enshrined into the Constitution itself and subsequent federal law. One of the two main complaints the South had against Lincoln and the North was that the latter refused to obey the fugitive slave laws and chase down Blacks and return them to slavery; the other complaint, of course, was the North's opposition to slavery in the first place. The point is this: as a factual and cultural historical matter in America, in both North and South before and after the Civil War, the purpose of American law enforcement was to control and/or hunt down Blacks. When police use unlawful force on Blacks today, Blacks view it through this contextual historical fact. Black people evaluate police action in a historical context that begins in 1619 while White social conservatives, and Blacks who see the world through White conservative eyes, evaluate police action in the specific moment in time with no historical context.

After the Civil War, the rise of crime statistics began to replace biblical theories justifying control of Blacks and as an explanation of their behavior. Crime statistics were used as a justification and explanation for Black disproportionate incarceration; they were disproportionately incarcerated, because they are disproportionately criminal. As Ibram X. Kendi, author of *Stamped from the Beginning: The Definitive History of Racist Ideas in America*, explained during a panel discussion on race and criminal justice,

> Roughly by sort of the 1890s you had more and more reports of crime data specifically from census data and that census data started showing that black people were more likely to be arrested. Black people were more likely to be in prison. And of course, those racial disparities have continued to this day. Of course scholars in 1890 took that data and stated this means black people are by nature criminals.
>
> Now, of course, most scholars took this crime data as actual fact. Meaning they took it as actual crime rates meaning they stated that since black people are more likely to be arrested and imprisoned, they are more likely to commit crimes; so in being more likely to commit crimes they are more criminal-like. And that criminality emerges from either their nature or their culture.
>
> These are the theories that scholars put forth over the course of the 20th century. And those are the theories that are put forth by police officers, by prosecutors, by politicians and by many other people today to justify why 40% of the incarcerated population in this country is Black even though Black people represent 13% of the [total population. The

2 Genesis 9:22–27 (NKJV).

> reason why this disproportionate representation exists is internal to Blacks. The simple reason is that] Black people are recklessly violent and criminals. That is the reason why.
>
> These racist ideas, blaming Black people to justify racial disparities. Which is essentially the history of racist ideas. ... Typically there are three responses ... people have utilized to explain racial disparity over the course of American history. There was something wrong with Black people, something wrong with discrimination or racial profiling or both and we see that constantly playing out. ... We know there is a direct link for instance between unemployment and violence. Meaning there is no such thing a violent Black neighborhood. But there is such a thing as a violent unemployed neighborhood. But of course, we're not going to think of it that way because that would call for a war against unemployment as opposed to a war against drugs and criminals.[3]

As discussed in Chapter One, crime is explained by a complicated and nuanced group of social and structural factors, including the physical dynamics of concentrated poverty, which concentrate in separate geographic areas (1) low employment; (2) no home ownership; (3) political, economic, and social isolation; (4) predatory financial practices by banks and other types financial institutions; (5) poor supermarket and nutrition options; and (6) increased stress and deviant social behavior, all of which combine to result in violence and crime.

Concentrated poverty creates emotional and psychological dysfunction, including depression, hopelessness, fear, anger, resentment, illicit economic systems, purposeless aggression, and crime. This physical and psychological concentration became problematic in some urban centers during the 1970s when ***Black flight*** from ghettos to middle-class communities followed ***White flight*** from middle-class communities to the suburbs. Both flights followed the flight of low-skill working class and middle class industrial jobs from the cities into the suburbs in the 1960s. With the rise of affirmative action, educated Blacks like Clarence Thomas, Henry Lewis Gates Jr., Sheila Jackson Lee, and Ben Carson were able to enter Yale and Harvard in the late 1960s and early 1970s and enter the upper American middle class and professional ranks. With that entering the Black community lost its cohesion. The dark side of integration resulted in Black communities losing the middle-class moral underpinning that was imposed by segregation. Under segregation Blacks, regardless of success, were forced to live together. The counterintuitive result of forced racial segregation was the sustainment of the middle class base within poor and urban working class communities. The doctors, lawyers, and other professionals, who could not leave the inner city, maintained a presence within the community which provided the moral counterbalance to negative behavior of other residents. With the rise of integration, successful educated Black middle class residents left the inner cities for middle class White neighborhoods.

The consequences of the splitting off the Black middle class positive role models from the poor and less educated class was the creation of a concentrated poor, both economically

3 Ibram X. Kendi, *Panel Discussion on Race in America* (April 16, 2016) at https://www.c-span.org/video/?408008-104/discussion-focuses-race-relations

and socially, in concentrated geographic areas. Although crime, drugs, and gangs became a problem in parts of inner city communities in the early 1960s, these problems became exacerbated by Black flight in the 1970s. Concentrated lack of jobs in a community produces chronic structural poverty. Chronic structural poverty creates intractable social problems of crime, gangs, family disruption, educational failure, and a hopelessness that becomes intergenerational. In the inner cities, chronic structural poverty replaced simple low-wage poverty in the middle- and late-1970s. As Cornel West observed, "in the 1950s Black communities were the most civilized communities in America. There were ties of empathy and bonds of sympathy. Unbelievable embrace of others who came in. Out of the seventies, we don't have neighborhoods as much as we got hoods."[4]

But integration in the 1970s exposed a latent racism that was not eradicated by the end of Jim Crow. The social policies of the 1970s exposed racism in Northern working class White neighborhoods that were thought to only exist in the South of the 1950s. In 1966, Martin Luther King Jr. learned and stated that the poor and working-class Whites in Chicago were more racist and violent to the idea of integration than the Whites in Mississippi and Alabama that he had encountered in the 1950s when they rioted in Chicago upon his arrival to end housing discrimination and segregation. In 1966, Dr. King began to shift his strategy for the civil rights movement from opposing structural Jim Crow to opposing economic injustice. In 1968, he died in a struggle for economic justice for garbage workers.

In 1974, working class Whites in South Boston rioted in front of the South Boston High School upon the integration of the school through bussing. The parents and students rioted in reaction to the fact that they would lose their right to the privilege of being able to attend a segregated, fully funded and supported, all-White high school. The rejection and avoidance of accepting enforced school integration by Whites resulted in the rise of private schools in the North, as did the closing of all public schools in many Southern states in the 1950s–1960s. This latent racism and resentment of Black advancement, believed to be at the expense of low skilled and educated working-class Whites, manifested in White middle- and working-class opposition to affirmative action, the rise of the politics of reverse discrimination (1974–1990s), and the rise and fall of bussing (1974–1980) in Northern cities like Boston.

Between 1966 and 1976 a White backlash to Black integration provided the fertile ground for Nixon and Reagan to run campaigns to secure both Northern and Southern White votes and create a permanent voter base for the Republican Party. During this period, the modern social and political link of crime and Blacks in the American mind was formed by White fear of crime in general in the late 1970s, with the rise of crack cocaine (1981–1983), and the violence that accompanied the drug epidemic (1983 through 1995). Further, the politics of the 1980s under Reagan linked Blacks with welfare fraud and laziness at the expense of working-class Whites. In the 1980s, Blacks were portrayed as out of control, criminal, and the reason for the loss of social and economic power and status of poor White and working-class

---

4 *Black America Since MLK: And I Still Rise* Documentary Series (2016).

America. Republican Party tactics ginned up these voters and their fears and resentments, creating an unfailing voting block that supported every Republican presidential candidate from Nixon to Trump.

The politics of Black crime is supported by a historical perception of Blacks. The historical constant is Blacks, at worst, are inferior or, at least, are criminal and need to be placed under social control. This historical constant has manifested in various iterations in America, beginning with the idea that Blacks were born to be slaves which was replaced in late nineteenth century with the science of eugenics, the philosophy of Social Darwinism and positivist (biological) criminology. These new iterations provided a non-religious explanation for Black inferiority. These iterations used crime statistics to support the assertion that Blacks are violent and criminal. These nineteenth and twentieth century ideas support the modern assertions of today that Black culture is criminogenic. The historical perception and beliefs about Blacks, from being cursed by God because of the sin they committed on Noah, to their natural criminal behavior, to their deviant culture which celebrates and indulges laziness, to their aversion to hard work, as discussed in Chapter Three, create racist results and policies without overt racist intent.

Modern criminal justice policies that result in negative disproportionate impact on Blacks in poor neighborhoods or Blacks driving down the street are built on the proposition that Blacks are to blame for their condition. For example, consider the opinions of the formerly national syndicated television political commentator Bill O'Reilly. Before O'Reilly was fired from FOX in Spring 2017 for sexual harassment and paying off his victims with million-dollar settlements, O'Reilly was the top social commentator on FOX with a show that had a viewership of millions of people every night. His influence on popular and Republican/social conservative political opinion was without dispute. As discussed in Chapter One, O'Reilly, along with other social conservative commentators, assert that crime and violence within the Black community are self-inflicted, because their culture is criminogenic.

O'Reilly started all of his shows with an opinion monologue he called the memo. In a 2016 episode of his show,[5] O'Reilly opined on the Black Lives Matters movement and its threat to America:

> How Black Lives Matter is killing Americans. That is the subject of tonight's talking points memo. First, the stats, and they are stunning. Since the Ferguson chaos, murders in the USA's fifteen largest cities are up close to 17 percent. And much higher in cities with large black populations. In Chicago, for example, this year alone, shootings up around 80 percent. Why? Because Chicago police have stopped stopping suspicious people.

Note his point, crime is birthed by two factors: (1) large Black populations and (2) police withdrawal of aggressive policing in Black populations due to political pressure. The latter

---

5 Bill O'Reilly, "How Black Lives Matter is killing Americans" O'Reilly Factor Talking Points (May 25, 2016) at https://www.youtube.com/watch?v=t4D6f13ctJE&app=desktop (Emphasis added).

creates crime, because the former is not under the control of the police. Further, Black protest of police violence or general criminal justice unfairness is "chaos," which results in nationwide increases in violent crime. O'Reilly continued,

> So-called pedestrian stops are down 90 percent in the windy city. *When you fail to police people proactively, people commit more crimes. The media will not spotlight that much of the violent crime in America is being committed right now by young black men.* In fact, Black males between the ages of fourteen and seventeen commit homicide at a rate ten times higher than White and Hispanic male teenagers combined. And Blacks of all ages commit homicide at a rate of eight times higher than Whites and Hispanics combined.

Again, these Black people, especially Black youth, are naturally criminal, and crime will increase if these people are not properly socially controlled. Socially controlled—not controlled by excellent education, not by employment opportunities, not by public transportation attached to suburban job opportunities, not by all the social dynamics that keep communities together—but socially controlled exclusively by aggressive policing. Why control only and exclusively by aggressive policing? Because Blacks are criminogenic by their nature, as evidenced by their culture. The political choice of this narrative over the narrative that crime is multifaceted and not caused by the single factor of Blacks being criminogenic is how disproportionate incarceration has remained a criminal justice constant for centuries.

What should America do regarding Black crime? More importantly, what should Blacks do about it? O'Reilly continued his monologue by providing the following answer.

> Conclusion? *There is a violent subculture in the African-American community that should be exposed and confronted.* Enter the Black Lives Matter crew which roams around the country promoting a false narrative that American police officers are actively hunting down and killing blacks. Here's the truth. Police shot Whites at a rate of 50 percent in 2015. Police shot blacks at a rate of 26 percent. In addition, Black Lives Matter is now infringing on freedom of assembly and freedom of expression. In Chicago, at DePauw University, this happened Tuesday night.

There you have it. America must confront Black criminogenic culture in the face of Black failure to do so. America must accept the fact that, rather than admit their culture is criminogenic, Blacks always blame the police and accuse them of violence and racism. As O'Reilly makes clear, White America must oppose the politically correct answer of police racism with the truth that police use of force doesn't involve racism, because police shoot more Whites than Blacks. Rather than cleaning up their own culture, Blacks prefer to blame the White society by focusing on the police and racism. Also note his use of statistics of police shootings. O'Reilly does not consider Blacks being less than 13% of the population but making up 26%

of the people being shot by the police as a problem. O'Reilly was most likely citing 2015 data from the *Washington Post* National Police Shooting Database.[6]

Research on the 2015 database showed that 990 people were shot and killed by police in 2015 and

> Roughly 18% of the deadly shootings involved officers employed in jurisdictions with *high crime*, whereas about 33% and 17% involved officers employed in jurisdictions with *moderate* and *low crime*, respectively.
>
> ...
>
> Fifteen percent of Black civilians shot and killed by police last year were unarmed at the time of their death compared with 6% of White civilians and 11% of other civilians. In fact, although roughly twice as many White civilians died by police gunfire as Black civilians (495 vs. 258), *more unarmed Black civilians (38) were shot and killed than unarmed White civilians (32).* Similar findings emerged with respect to threat level: 24% of Black civilians and 31% of civilians from other racial/ethnic groups were *not* attacking the officer(s) or other civilians, whereas the same was true of approximately 17% of White civilians. These simplistic findings provided preliminary evidence of an implicit bias effect, but they did not permit us to rule out the potential confounding influence of other relevant variables.
>
> ...
>
> Black civilians were no more or less likely than White civilians to have been attacking the officer(s) or other civilians when they were fatally shot by police. These results provide support for an implicit bias effect with respect to non-Black minority groups. That is, civilians of other races/ethnicities were significantly more likely than Whites to have been fatally shot because of an apparent threat perception failure.
>
> ... Black civilians were significantly *more* likely than White civilians to have been unarmed when they were shot and killed by police, net of other factors. Indeed, the odds ratio indicates that Black civilians who died by police gunfire were more than twice as likely as Whites to have been unarmed, holding all else constant. This is further evidence of implicit bias as race was again significantly associated with one of our indicators of threat perception failure.[7]

This research is in line with the literature on police use of force that shows that race bias is significant in the decision of police to use force, exclusive of other factors, including threat to police officers and possession of a weapon. Police officers, as discussed in Chapter Three, are

---

6 See Justin Nix, Bradley A. Campbell, Edward H. Byers and Geoffrey P. Alpert, "A Bird's Eye View of Civilians Killed by Police in 2015 Further Evidence of Implicit Bias," *Criminology & Public Policy* 16, no. 1 (2017): 309–40, 322.

7 Justin Nix et al., "A Bird's Eye View of Civilians Killed by Police in 2015 Further Evidence of Implicit Bias"at 324, 324, 325–326 respectively (emphasis in original).

more likely to perceive Blacks as armed, regardless of the fact that they are not armed. The same attribution error explains police decisions that observed behavior establishes reasonable suspicion to justify a stop and search of Blacks. Whites tend to see Blacks as dangerous and criminal, and this attribution error is reflected within law enforcement.

O'Reilly, representing White middle-class social conservative perceptions of Blacks, makes the explanation of crime quite simple. Black opposition to how police treat Blacks is a threat to society as a whole—the threat being the lack of law and order and control of criminals, i.e., Blacks. This belief is not held by just Whites, because, as discussed in Chapter One, Black social conservatives like David Clarke and Larry Elder believe the same thing. Police and the criminal justice system operationalize the desire for safety and the practical maintenance of law and order. The criminal justice system is the only way for society to socially control Blacks in general, and young Black males specifically, after the demise of slavery and the social and legal system of Jim Crow. O'Reilly reinforces this need when he makes clear that the police must be defended at all costs regardless of abuses they may inflict upon the modern threat to society—the Black culture and the crime it produces. After noting that more Whites than Blacks are shot and killed by police and complaining about an incident in which Black Lives Matter disrupted a college forum, O'Reilly concluded,

> [s]o, there is no question Black Lives Matter is affecting what we do here in the USA. A new book by Heather McDonald entitled "The war on cops: How the new attack on law and order makes everyone less safe" starkly lays out the threat from the radical group which openly attacks COMPSTAT, a policy placing police officers where violent crime is taking place. Here is a quote from Miss McDonald.
>
> > "In terms of economic stimulus alone no other government program has come close to the success of COMPSTAT. In New York City, businesses that had previously shunned drug infested areas now set-up shops there. Offering residents a choice in shopping and creating a demand for workers. Children could ride their bikes on city sidewalks without their mothers worrying they could be shot. But the crime victories of the last two decades and the moral support on which law and order depends are now in jeopardy, thanks to the falsehoods of the Black Lives Matter movement."
>
> So, summing up, *thousands more Americans are being murdered because police are being more passive.* Since the Ferguson situation and the Black Lives Matter protests. Talking Points believes every American should know that, should know the truth. Sympathetic media and many race hustlers are backing Black Lives Matter and the final indignity—members of the group have even been invited to the White House. And that's "The Memo".

So to be clear, public safety is reduced, *per se*, when Blacks are not subjected to aggressive militarized policing, because they are criminogenic as a factual issue. Aggressive policing in Black communities by the police is a direct result and consequence of Black criminogenic behavior. To believe otherwise is to be sympathetic to the race hustlers among honest people.

After his opine, he had the following debate on the issue of Black crime and the nature of Black criminality.

> **O'Reilly:** Now for the top story reaction with us here in New York City Eric Guster an attorney and political commentator. So the unintended consequences for the Black Lives Matter movement is a rise in murder. Do you buy that?
> **Guster:** I don't buy that at all Bill.
> **O'Reilly:** The stats are no, there're just an accident, coincidence what?

To start with, as discussed in Chapter One, criminal justice arrest statistics are used as a proxy of crime commission. But they do not explain crime commission. Explaining crime patterns is complicated, and the fact that two events are present together does not establish causation. Human social behavior can be explained by coincidence, correlation, or causation. The occurrence of a political event (police ordered to stop aggressive use of stop and frisk) followed by a rise in the number of shootings does not mean the political event caused the increase in shootings. The debate continued,

> **Guster:** No. The police officers need to do their jobs. And if they did their jobs effectively that would calm down the murder rate. Because the police officers after Ferguson, they say we're just not going to police because we're being held accountable for what we have done, then they are not doing their job.
> **O'Reilly:** Then you see that policing is less aggressive then?
> **Guster:** Oh that's true.
> **O'Reilly:** And you say they are being less aggressive because what it was being abusive, uh, and they have stopped being abusive. Is that the point you are trying to make?
> **Guster:** Some of the abuse has been brought to light. For example, many police departments have gone to body cameras in order to hold police accountable for the things that they do
> **O'Reilly:** or vice versa
> **Guster:** Right. Or people pull out their camera phones. But if police officers are doing the right thing then they are going to be OK and that was the problem.
> **O'Reilly:** Do you believe that Black Lives Matter has a right to interrupt that speech at DePauw University and turn it into a circus?
> **Guster:** I don't necessarily agree with what they did at DePauw.
> **O'Reilly:** Wait. Necessarily, what does that mean?
> **Guster:** I don't agree on what they did at DePauw.
> **O'Reilly:** Alright, you think that's wrong.
> **Guster:** I do think that's wrong.

Police stopping Black males, young Black males specifically, because they are walking down the street and police presuming they could be guilty and stopping them is a clear violation of their Fourth Amendment rights. The violation invokes no sympathy from O'Reilly. But, he demands a definitive statement of condemnation regarding the disruption of a college student panel, which he views as a violation of law and order. The debate continued,

> **O'Reilly:** OK. *Do you believe that Black Lives Matter has put out a propaganda about American police, generally, hunting down young black men* when the stats show twice as many white men are killed by police than black men?
> **Guster:** *Oh, that's not propaganda. Let me tell you why. In many communities when you're being over policed, when you're being harassed by police, when you're being stopped unnecessarily by police. That's what these young people are experiencing. So they're talking about their truths and what they experience on a daily basis.*
> **O'Reilly:** *And they don't understand the big picture on why they're being stopped.*[8]

Wait! Don't read over that discourse.

O'Reilly did not dispute that young Black men were being harassed. He said there is a greater good, and they simply "don't understand the big picture on why they're being stopped," which is to reduce crime. If they must suffer the inconvenience and humiliation of being stopped because they are Black and look guilty, which results in achieving that greater good—reduction in crime, then that's the burden they will have to endure for being Black. This is an example of infrahumanization, a lack of sympathy and empathy for abuse and unjust treatment of an out group—Blacks—as discussed in Chapter Three.

As O'Reilly makes clear, if the loss of constitutional rights suffered by young Black men in poor Black communities produces a public safety gain by society as a whole, the loss of rights by young Black males is an acceptable loss. And to prove his point, he asserts that the result of the number of unlawful stops being reduced by 90% is shootings being up by 80%. The debate continued,

> **O'Reilly:** *And they don't understand the big picture on why they're being stopped.* In Chicago the stat is, that stops that you're talking about, and you don't like, are down 90 percent, OK. Ninety percent. Shootings are up 80 percent. Counselor, do you see any correspondence between not stopping and the rise in shooting?
> **Guster:** There may be.
> **O'Reilly:** Yes or no.
> **Guster:** I'm not sure because it depends on the rest of the statistics.
> **O'Reilly:** A shooting is a shooting is a shooting.
> **Guster:** You are talking about stopping vs. shooting. If the police officers had their presence and they were doing their jobs instead of pulling off and not doing their jobs then they would possibly reduce the crime.
> **O'Reilly:** I don't understand. If you are a linear thinker and police in Chicago 90 percent they don't stop suspicious people anymore and then correspondingly the shootings have

8 Bill O'Reilly, "How Black Lives Matter is killing Americans" O'Reilly Factor Talking Points (May 25, 2016) at https://www.youtube.com/watch?v=t4D6f13ctJE&app=desktop (Emphasis added).

> risen 80 percent it seems to me that the policy of not stopping suspicious people is leading to the rise in shootings. Are you disputing that?
> **O'Reilly:** I don't understand. If you are a linear thinker and police in Chicago ... 90 percent they don't stop suspicious people anymore and then correspondingly the shootings have risen 80 percent it seems to me that the policy of not stopping suspicious people is leading to the rise in shootings. Are you disputing that?
> **Guster:** I am saying it depends on the rest of the data Bill.
> **O'Reilly:** That data stands alone. It stands alone.
> **Guster:** No it does not.
> **O'Reilly:** Sure it does.

No it doesn't. Just because two events occur, that does not mean there is a causal relationship. A causal relationship means that there is no other variable or explanation to explain the result. Shootings are explained by countless factors besides the factor of reduced police stops. Mr. Guster was correct when he noted that police behavior to stop crime is not limited to stop and frisk. The positive physical presence of the police can stop shootings without the use of indiscriminate stopping of young Black males. The failure of police to maintain a physical presence is not exclusively explained by preventing them from conducting stops without reasonable suspicion.

But, here is the problem; the law does not mean anything to O'Reilly. The narrative of Black crime justifies police behavior. If the police conduct stops in violation of the Fourth Amendment, as discussed in Chapters Two and Six, but happen to find guns or drugs nonetheless, who cares about Fourth Amendment niceties! O'Reilly's attitude is simple, that's one less criminal off the street, and if aggressive police saturation will deter other criminals from walking the streets armed and with drugs, what's the problem.

White conservatives like O'Reilly can have this attitude because after all, it's not O'Reilly or his sons that are stopped and frisked on the hood of the police car or against the wall, nor are the police aggressively saturating his neighborhood. Conservatives like O'Reilly explain that the inconvenience to innocent Blacks stopped and searched by the police is just that, an inconvenience. This is the crime control perspective and policy, discussed below, that has dominated American politics for more than three decades.

The debate concluded,

> **Guster:** With any type of data, with any statistics, there are other factors that go into it.
> **O'Reilly:** I don't know why. I mean, I am giving you the shootings. The shooting is a shooting. And the lack of police stops are the lack of police stops.
> **Guster:** Are thefts up as well?
> **O'Reilly:** In Chicago violent crime is up almost in every category. Theft I am not sure. Alright counselor, good debate. We appreciate you taking the fire. Thank you very much.

Again, Mr. Guster was correct to ask if other types of crime are up, because an increase in theft could explain an increase in shooting completely independent of police stops. But, the most important point is O'Reilly's base narrative. When police use aggressive tactics in Black communities, they keep crime down, because the aggressive tactics keeps the criminals down—Blacks and criminals being the same thing. Any innocent Blacks harassed is an unfortunate collateral sacrifice to the societal need to reduce criminal behavior. Crime in Black neighborhoods does not result from unemployment or the various factors discussed in Chapter One and Seven; crime according to social conservatives in Black communities is solely explained by the Black culture of violence and the failure of Blacks to take ownership of that culture and change it. I quote O'Reilly here and in Chapter One, because he best reflects the ideas and narratives that have governed American criminal justice philosophy and racialized thinking regarding the cause of crime that has governed since the mid-1960s.

This line of political thinking gave rise to the crime control politics of the late 1960s, which flourished in the 1980s and 1990s. The politics of race and crime between 1964 and 1968, followed by the demise of the due process model replaced by the crime control model in the late 1970s, did not grow out of a vacuum. It grew out of the backlash to the Great Society and fears of urban crime and social resentment of the changes forced into society by the rise of the civil rights movement. Look at the late 1960s from the perspective of social conservative, Southern Democrat, non–college educated, semi-skilled or low-skilled, non-professional White working class and/or White suburban middle-class voters. Such voters could look at 1954–1968 and conclude,

> we up rooted and up ended almost a century of social order (Jim Crow), we unleashed the army to integrate our schools, we enlarged the power of the federal government, we increased social spending for Black neighborhoods, we increased welfare payments for the poor, we made Blacks equal to Whites under the law; and what did we get—increased government debt, the Vietnam war, weakened state governments, increased urban crime and the summer riots of 1964–1968. Something needs to change to get order back into our country.

The Republican Party provided voice to these concerns and conclusions. These voices found actual political operationalization in the backlash election of 1966 in which the Democrats lost forty-seven seats to the Republicans in the House of Representatives, three seats in the Senate, and seven governorships. Although the Democrats held both houses of Congress, there was an increase in conservative members of Congress that would oppose any further expansion of the Great Society.[9]

> That November, 27 of the 48 Democratic House freshmen elected as part of Johnson's 1964 landslide lost office. Of the 10 new governors elected that fall, nine were Republicans, and the GOP now controlled 12 of 13 Western state legislatures. The number of Americans identifying themselves as Republicans increased. The conservative coalition in

9 Doug McAdam and Karina Kloos, *Deeply Divided: Racial Politics and Social Movements in Post-War America* (2014), 109.

> Congress—made up of segregationist Southern Democrats and Northern Republicans—doubled after the 1966 elections.[10]

The policies that came with the backlash of 1966 and 1968 elections was the rise of law and order politics, the development of the Southern strategy and the modern Republican Party politics of states' rights, limited government, reduced taxes, opposition to busing, and affirmative action. The change in criminal justice policy that followed was the abandonment of the due process model which was replaced by the crime control model. This change corresponded with the change in philosophy on the purpose of prisons and the treatment of offenders from rehabilitation to incarceration (social banishment), incapacitation, and retribution. All these changes culminated in the rise of the modern disproportionate incarceration of Blacks.

AMERICAN THEORIES OF CRIME AND PUNISHMENT

Purpose of Criminal Justice: The Due Process and Crime Control Models

In 1968, Herbert L. Packer published his famous book, *The Limits of the Criminal Sanction*, which provided a theoretical framework for understanding how the American criminal justice system operated and what the purpose and goal of the system was. He proposed that the system can be defined by two opposing models: due process and crime control. These models were originally used to explain how the criminal justice system functions and how the various parts interacted on the level of purpose and social expectation. By the 1980s and 1990s, these two models expanded to provide a foundation for moral explanations of crime and why crime occurs, as supposed to sociological explanations, which had dominated academic and public discourse during the 1950s and 1970s. As discussed below, these differing models can explain how criminal justice policy is justified politically and morally.

Advocates of the ***Crime Control Model*** assert that the explanation of crime is in the fact that crime is an individual moral issue. Crime results from a lack of behavioral moral clarity. The focus of analysis is the individual. Crime is explained as the result of sub-group cultural failures. Crime is about the values an individual chooses to adopt. The crime control model places primacy on maintaining society/social order and protecting civilization from anarchy and lawlessness. The social assumptions of the crime control model regarding the purpose of the criminal justice system as a system are as follows:

1. Protect society from crime and disorder
    - Justification of punishment is retribution, incapacitation, and incarceration (social banishment)

---

10 Michael Phillips, January 17, 2011 blog post "White Backlash in the 1966 Off-Year Elections" at http://jmichaelphillips.blogspot.com/2011/01/white-backlash-in-1966-off-year.html

- Acceptance of collateral sanctions (informal sanctions) in addition to formal statutory prison incarceration

2. Secure and punish the guilty
3. The criminal justice system is efficient—specifically it does not arrest the innocent because that would be a waste of time.
4. The system, specifically the police, should enjoy the benefit of any doubt when a conflict occurs between the police and an individual
5. Assumption of factual guilt
    - Only the guilty are arrested and they are arrested because they are guilty. Trials are legal formalities whose purpose is to affirm factual guilt.
6. Justice is outcome based—was the guilty convicted
    - Justice is defined by a criminal trial resulting in the guilty getting punished.
    - Rejects the assertion it's better for nine guilty to go free than to convict one innocent person.

Advocates of the ***Due Process Model*** assert that the explanation of crime is in the fact that crime is a social issue and relates to how society treats the individual. Crime results from unfair and unequal societal structures imposed on the individual. The focus of analysis is society. Crime is explained as the result of poverty and social and economic injustice. Due process places primacy on controlling societal power and protecting the individual from tyranny and oppression by government. The social assumptions of the due process model regarding the purpose of the criminal justice system as a system are as follows:

1. Protect individual freedom and liberty from the power of government to take away that freedom and liberty under the guise of punishing the guilty
    - Justification of punishment is rehabilitation along with restitution
    - Rejection of collateral sanctions (informal sanctions) in addition to formal statutory prison incarceration
2. Prove the guilt of the accused
3. The criminal justice system is not efficient in determining guilt—specifically it does arrest the innocent
4. The system, specifically the police, should not enjoy the benefit of the doubt but rather the individual should enjoy the benefit of the doubt when a conflict occurs between the police and an individual
5. Assumption of legal innocence
    - The assumption creates a legal duty of the government to prove guilt. The assumption protects the right of people to be free from government tyranny and interference with individual freedom and liberty.
6. Justice is process based—was the accused given a fair trial
    - Justice is defined by a criminal trial resulting from a fair process in which the law was properly, correctly, and objectively applied.

- Defends assertion that it's better for nine guilty to go free than to convict one innocent person.

Another way of understanding the difference between the two models would be to consider the following dynamics of power within the criminal justice system. There are only two governmental institutions in America that can physically take hold of a person and control their lives and take away their ability to act as they please (freedom and liberty), to force them to act and behave in a certain manner, to change their name, to redefine their status in society, to control their associations, to move them to locations at will, to force them to fight or surrender their right to protect themselves from physical threat, and can take their lives from them. These two institutions are the military, in times of the draft and war, and the criminal justice system. The military in time of war can get you killed. It can put you in situations of serious life-threatening danger with no social consequences. Since the draft is no longer implemented, the criminal justice system remains the only agency in America that, under the law, can define and control an individual on its own determination with no appeal outside of the system. With a voluntary military, to be subject to danger, you must voluntarily place yourself in the military. The criminal justice system can come and get you and inject you into its world on its own determinations by its own rules.

As Justice Sotomayor, discussed in Chapter Nine, observed, the criminal justice system with nothing more than probable cause can seize people, strip them of their clothes, search them in their nakedness, confine them in dangerous environments, detain them for hours or years before trial, and if convicted, can confine them and separate them from society for months, for years, or for the rest of their lives and even take their lives strapped down on a gurney for all to see. The criminal justice system can stamp upon a person the label of felon and subsequently prevent a person from holding professions, skilled employment, business licenses, prevent them from living in certain places, prevent them from residing with certain family members, prevent them from being free to move and build a family, and/or enjoy the most basic of civil rights in America—the ability to vote. In addition, the criminal justice stamp of felon puts a social stigma on a person that is impossible to fully remove. As discussed in Chapter Two, the gatekeepers of the criminal justice system, the police, can shoot a person dead in the street with nothing more than asserting it was objectively, under the totality of circumstances, reasonable. This burden of proof is one step lower than probable cause and one step higher than hunch or no reason at all.

Because of the significant power of the criminal justice system, the due process model asserts that the purpose of criminal justice is to control this power in the interest of the individual who is injected into it by police actions. The crime control model discounts and minimizes the power of the system and prioritizes the need to protect society from criminals. It assumes that the criminal justice system, its individual parts and the system as a whole, has no interest in the innocent, because its purpose is to protect society from criminals. The assumption is that it functions with desire to seize the guilty with limited resources. To focus on the innocent would be a waste of resources.

Thus, returning to O'Reilly and social conservatives' discussion of police deployment—it would be a waste of police resources to saturate poor White rural or middle class suburban neighborhoods with militarized police tactics, because drug, gang, and violent crime doesn't exist there. These types of crime, they imply, if not actually assert, are not committed by Whites, they are committed by Blacks as a cultural fact. After all, Whites don't steal, use drugs, nor commit violence worthy of police attention, but Blacks do. Because crime is committed in urban Black neighborhoods, society should saturate those neighborhoods with police attention. That's why prisons are disproportionally Black. It's not about racism; it's about disproportionate criminality, social conservatives conclude.

Regarding the power of the criminal justice system to change lives and impose formal and informal (collateral) sanctions, crime control model advocates assert it is of no consequence to society as a whole, because only the guilty suffer the sanctions and they deserve to suffer. Crime control focuses not on the suffering of the criminal but the suffering of the victim of the criminal. The life of the criminal being immeasurably altered is of no or little account compared to the life of the victim being altered by the offender. The focus of sympathy belongs to the victim, not the offender. To the crime control model advocate, justice is done when the factually guilty (assumed by the arrest, because it would be inefficient to arrest the innocent) are found legally guilty by the court (which is its only purpose). Thus, innocent until proven guilty really means the court has not sanctioned and affirmed what is the truth—the accused is guilty.

The due process model rejects the initial assumption that the criminal justice system only secures the guilty. Due process assumes that the system can and does make errors and is not efficient in separating the innocent from the guilty. Thus, the purpose of a trial is not to affirm a police arrest but to require the government to prove guilt as a matter of fact and law, and until that is done, the individual is legally and factually innocent.

Of course, the two models by Packer were drafted in the extremes in order to expose the differences in how criminal justice can be defined as to purpose and whether it is just. Of course, American justice is not exclusively one or the other but a combination of both. But the models help explain why certain criminal justice policies are supported when others are rejected. Due process model holders pay more attention to rehabilitation and control of police than crime control model holders. Crime-control-model holders reject criminal procedures that seem to control police actions and how evidence can be secured and used in court than due-process-model holders. Due process holders focus on how the wheels and belts of the criminal justice system function and if the wheels and belts are fair to the accused. Crime control model holders focus on whether the result—the outcome—protects society as a whole. They focus on societal and victim protection more than whether the system was fair to the accused.

The due process model rejects retribution over rehabilitation, while crime control rejects rehabilitation as a purpose of the criminal justice system in the first place. To crime control model holders, the purpose of the criminal justice system is retribution (revenge—social payback), incapacitation (making sure the offender can't commit additional crime), and incarceration (banishment for society). Crime control rejects the proposition that the system can rehabilitate or fix the offender. Only the offender can fix or change his behavior. Crime control has little concern for the nature of prisons, while due process places more attention on how prisoners are treated. Due process places significant value on appeals after conviction and seeks to expand that ability as a policy matter to control the power of the government through the criminal justice system. Crime control model advocates seek finality in convictions and seek to limit appeals of convictions as much as possible to secure the goals of retribution, incapacitation, and incarceration. Due process model holders tend to support judicial oversight of prisons and expanded ability for prisoners to enjoy constitutional protections from the decisions and policies of prison officials' determinations of prison conditions. Crime control model holders seek to limit judicial application of constitutional rights to prisoners and those convicted of crimes on the premise that such people have lost the constitutional rights that law abiding citizens enjoy as a matter of principle. Felons and convicts, both in prison and on probation/parole, are property of the state, not free citizens, and they should be treated as such for the safety of those who obey the law and have a right to protection from criminals.

Packer's models provide a way to understand the history of American punishment and the abandonment of rehabilitation as an underlying theory of American justice since the 1980s.

A Brief History of American Criminal Justice Systems

When the first American settlements were established in May 1607 (Jamestown, Virginia), and in November 1620 (Cape Cod, Massachusetts), they brought with them the ideals and principles of justice practiced in Great Britain. The Puritans in Massachusetts brought the concept that crime and sin were synonymous, and that public power was required to punish sin. Crimes were defined by sin, as defined in the scriptures of the Bible, specifically crimes defined in the books of Exodus and Deuteronomy.[11] As defined by Moses, punishments were corporal in nature, and in the colonies, they included whipping, the use of the stocks, branding, banishment, and public humiliation. The punishments did have a rehabilitative premise. The use of corporal punishment was to break the pride and will of the sinner in order for him or her to soften his or her heart and repent. Repentance was significant in the colonists' thinking of crime and sin, because "all have sinned and come short of the glory of God." The colonists applied a Christian proposition to rehabilitation, repentance. The Christian proposition was that, through repentance, a person can be reconciled with God and society. Once a sinner became repentant, he or she was accepted back into the community as a full member because the goal of corporal punishment, as Paul told the Corinthians, was restoration through repentance. After the colonies freed themselves from Great Britain, the question arose as to how criminals should be treated.

---

11 Arthur H. Garrison, "Defining the Meaning and Purpose of Justice, Law, and Criminal Justice: A Hermeneutical Judeo-Christian Biblical Perspective," *Journal of Catholic Legal Studies* 55, no. 1 (2016): 1.

Timeline of Criminal Justice Theory in American Criminal Justice

The Penance Era (1790–1876)	The Reform Era (1876–1935)	The First Punitive Era (1935–1945)	The Rehabilitative Era (1945–1980)	The Second Punitive Era (1980–2000)	The Post-Second Punitive Era (2000-present)

The Penance Era (1790–1876) involved the beginning of the use of prisons as a place to incur repentance and rehabilitation of a criminal in the United States. Corporal punishment as a response to criminal behavior was abandoned for the proposition that forced solitary confinement would soften that heart of the offender through isolation and prayer. The offender would be isolated from the criminal associations that he or she may have been exposed to and, with pure isolation and the presence of a Bible and time, the evil of their ways would come to the offender and, upon repentance, they would no longer commit crime. The theory of the penance model is rehabilitative. Incarceration was not to protect society or to inflict pain and suffering on the offender as punishment, but penance was built on the premise that the individual was responsible for his or her actions, and through imposed discipline and enforced silence, rehabilitation would occur. During this time America used prisons for mass incarceration.

The penance era can be divided into two periods. The first is ***the penitentiary period*** (1790–1825) in which the Quakers developed the theory of penance through isolation, which was operationalized in ***the Pennsylvania system*** at the Walnut Street Jail and Eastern State Penitentiary. This is where the word penitentiaries came from. During ***the mass prison period*** (1825–1876) an alternative theory, known as ***the Auburn system***, of penance was implemented at the Auburn State and Sing Sing prisons, in which isolation was abandoned for rehabilitation through forced silence, corporal punishment, hard labor, and prisoner regimentation. It was during this period that prisoner industry, in which prisoners were required to work at trades in order to develop skills that they could utilize when released, was first attempted as a mode of rehabilitation. Over time *the Auburn system* replaced *the Pennsylvania system* as the primary theory of prison construction and operation. Of course, as the North developed the penance theory, the South utilized slavery and forced labor as the operational strategy for criminals in its criminal justice system.

The Reform Era (1876–1935) marked the abandonment of the religious Christian explanation of crime (crime is sin) and the adoption of ***the medical model*** for explaining crime. During this period, the professions of criminal justice (probation and parole officers, judges, youth workers, social workers, police officers, criminal defense attorneys, juvenile court officers and judges, full-time prosecutors, prison wardens, and court administrators) formalized the operation of formal societal criminal justice. During this period, plea bargaining began to become a method of resolving criminal charges, and criminal trials became longer, more complex, professional, and systemized with the rise of rules of evidence and formal court procedures and operations. During this period, the concepts of indeterminate sentencing, probation and parole boards, prison reform, prisoner good time towards early release, separate prisons for women, gender-specific theories of crime and rehabilitation, separate courts for juveniles, and separate detention of juveniles from adults were implemented under the concept that dealing with criminal offenders, like dealing with the sick, was for professionals.

The Auburn system was replaced with rehabilitation through education, diversion from prison, release from prison due to good behavior, and the theory that crime is like being sick with pneumonia. If isolation due to the pneumonia is required, it should last no longer than is required to make the person better, after which the patient should be released with additional medicine and sent home to loved ones who will continue his or her care. Likewise, criminal behavior is a sickness of behavior, and if prison (a hospital by analogy) is required, the person should be held only as long as the professionals (prison wardens) determine is required to fix the behavior illness. When the offender is no longer a danger to society, the person should be released under the care of a criminal justice professional (parole officer) who will supervise the release and make sure relapse of criminal behavior does not occur.

If a person has a bad cold you don't expose him or her to people with pneumonia so they get infected with a more serious disease. You control their cold with medicine but let them go home. In line with the medical analogy, in the criminal justice context, the offender that is not a direct threat to society has a professional (probation officer) who will work to control the behavior of the offender so that they will become a productive member of society. The overall assumption during *the Reform Era* is that the criminal can be fixed. The purpose of the criminal justice system was to fix the offender, not to punish them for its own sake, because you don't punish a person with pneumonia; you heal them. The moral condemnation theory of *the penance era* was replaced by the illness theory of reform. While, in the North the principles of the reform era took hold with the retention of mass incarceration and industrial prisons, the South utilized convict-leasing, chain gangs, and prison labor camps. Reform did not take place in the South, but rather, it retained and maintained a system that put Blacks, as discussed in Chapter Seven, in a state of neo-slavery.

The First Punitive Era (1935–1945) marked America's first abandonment of rehabilitation and reform for retribution as the governing theory for the criminal justice system and use of prisons. During this period, America suffered crime waves across state lines and birthed the need for the federal government to become a key agent of criminal justice and crime control. The dark side of the Roaring Twenties brought increases in bank robberies, prostitution, kidnappings, auto theft, racketeering, gambling, and drug trafficking, all committed by criminals who crossed state lines with faster cars and the use of guns more powerful than those carried by local police. The 1920s had birthed organized crime, which had a nationalized criminal reach during prohibition (1920–1933), with famous criminal names like Al "Scarface" Capone, George "Bugs" Moran, Bonnie and Clyde, "Machine Gun" Kelly, Lucky Luciano, John Dillinger, and other organized crime families in Chicago and New York, along with corruption in government (Teapot Dome Scandal of 1923).

In addition to the rise in violent interstate crime, the lack of middle class and working-class American compliance with Prohibition, and the resulting rise of bootleggers, rumrunners, and speakeasies produced in America the normalization of open defiance of the law (scofflaws) and a reduced belief that certain laws had legitimacy. This belief reduced societal law and order.

The growth in violent and organized crime, along with the uncertainty and disorder of the Great Depression moved American sensibilities on crime from rehabilitation to incapacitation, incarceration, and retribution. During this period, the Federal Bureau of Investigation (FBI) was created (1935) out of the Department of Justice Bureau of Investigation (1908). The Bureau of Investigation, in 1924, was placed under the command of J. Edger Hoover, who governed it through its renaming as the FBI in 1935 and continued to govern it until he died in 1972.

With rise of fear of crime, the purpose of prison was not to rehabilitate, but instead it focused on the incapacitation and incarceration of criminals with the political rhetoric of just deserts and the policy of warehousing offenders. The purpose of the criminal justice system was protection of society, and that birthed ***the rise of maximum security prisons*** on the state and federal level, the most famous being the opening of ***Alcatraz*** (August 1934). Alcatraz was the model for the theory that the purpose of prison was to make the offender "pay his debt to society" with the return of regimentation and prisoner control. Alcatraz also operationalized the ***Concentration Model*** of prisoner control. Alcatraz was designed to hold the most dangerous and incorrigible prisoners within the federal prison system in one place—the theory being to confine the most dangerous in one place and that will increase the safety of all other prisoners in the system. Although this model would be abandoned during *the rehabilitation era*, it would return in the *second punitive era* and form the basis for supermax prisons in the 1990s.

The first punitive era involved the rise of striped uniforms and long prison terms at hard labor and replaced the idea of fixing the offender as one would heal a patient with pneumonia. The significance of this period was the rise of the role of national government in criminal justice and crime control, which up until this period, was always a local matter. The rise of the FBI helped foster ***the rise of professionalism of law enforcement*** in general under Hoover and, later, the abandonment of the community support–based crime prevention and police presence model of Robert Peel (the Guardian model). ***The guardian model*** of policing was replaced by ***the Warrior Model*** of community control and crime investigation and suppression. *The warrior model* adopted a militaristic organizational approach to achieve professionalism in policing and this model was first pioneered and operationalized in the Los Angeles Police Department under Chief William Parker which was adopted by police agencies across the United States from the 1950s through the 1990s.

The Rehabilitation Era (1945–1980) was birthed, in part, due to the lessons of World War II. In Germany, Italy, Spain, and France, dictators rose to power in functioning democracies. The military and police forces were unleashed on civilian populations to maintain order, and individual liberty was to be sacrificed for the good of society as a whole. The Axis Powers took this principle to its most logical conclusion, and gas chambers and political prisons spread across Europe. The lessons gained in the United States and Western Europe were that government power must be controlled at all levels and that the rights of the individual under the law and through the courts must be valued above governmental claims of needing to prevent crime and disorder. The crimes of Nazi Germany proved that totalitarian tyranny can function in a Republic under procedural rule of law. This lesson reintroduced the ideals of *the* *due process model* in criminal justice policy and the return of rehabilitation as the governing of theory of American prisons. The lessons of the war provided a reminder that positive law (written law) is not the definition or the purpose of justice. The purpose of the law is to uphold the higher concepts of justice as well as equality. Justice is accomplished through the application of the higher principles of the *Law* and the supremacy of the *Law* over governmental power to act. Unjust laws that are efficient and legally passed are still unjust are not laws that should be obeyed. These lessons were not lost on the generation of Thurgood Marshal, Martin Luther King, and the Black leaders of civil rights after World War II.

The Rehabilitative Era regarding criminal justice occurred in concurrence with the rise of the civil rights movement, the second wave of the women's movement, and then the homosexual rights movement in the early 1970s. The rise of the 1960s and the values of Martian Luther King Jr., John F. Kennedy, Robert Kennedy, Lyndon Johnson, and the due process revolution (applying the Fourth, Fifth, Sixth, and Eighth Amendments to the states, specifically to local police and criminal justice systems, through the Fourteenth Amendment) at the hands of the U.S. Supreme Court all provided the background for the idea that American prisons and criminal justice policy should focus on the offender.

During this period, the rise of ***the treatment model***, akin to the reform medical model, reached its golden age. Crime was not only perceived as a social sickness that should be treated like an illness, crime resulted from social, structural, racial, and economic injustice imposed upon people who had no choice but to commit crime. During this period, every possible concept of rehabilitation and that crime is the result of social and societal structure found advocacy and policy justification. This period saw the rise of prisoner rights advocacy groups and prison reform, including religious rights for inmates and prisoner advisory boards and the right to have access to law libraries in prisons for appeals. This period also involved the rise of diversion programs and community correction initiatives, alternative sentencing, community-based programs, drug treatment programs, various types of alternatives to incarceration, the deinstitutionalization of the mentally ill from state mental hospitals, the rise of re-entry programming, the constitutionalization of the juvenile justice system, and work-release and furlough programs. In the golden age of rehabilitation, it was believed that crime was socially imposed, and criminals had rights in prisons that mirrored the rights they had before conviction.

Beginning with the politics of Goldwater in 1964, the urban riots of 1964–1968, the election of Richard Nixon, and the rise of "law and order" politics in the early 1970s, politics began to change. The golden age of the rehabilitation era was slowly replaced with public skepticism over whether rehabilitation programs worked, a general resentment of the social changes that the 1960s had inflicted upon American middle class social and Christian values, and the rise of the militarization of policing. During the middle to late 1970s the narrative that crime occurs due to the lack of law enforcement and the coddling of criminals was replacing the theory that crime was the result of social and structural injustices. The rise of law and order politics, the resentment of the policies of the 1960s, and the belief crime results from weak law enforcement culminated in the election of Ronald Reagan in 1980, which marked the beginning of a new era in American social politics in general and, specifically, in criminal justice policy.

The Second Punitive Era (1980–2000) ushered the end of *the rehabilitative period* as the *first punitive era* ended *the reform era*. With the rise of crime, urban crime (Black crime), and the general change in political sentiment that abandoned the idea that prisoners could be fixed. America returned to the ideal that the purpose of the criminal justice system and prisons was the incapacitation and incarceration of prisoners and justice required retribution not rehabilitation.

The fall of *the rehabilitation era* occurred for various reasons:

1. The fear of crime and rising crime (supplemented by societal unrest in the face of the prison riots in the early 1970s),
2. The actual failure to rehabilitate offenders (high recidivism rates),
3. Poor planning and implementation of rehabilitative programs and initiatives,
4. Theory error on what causes people to commit crime and the belief that all offenders could be rehabilitated with similar programs (i.e., not all offenders are the same),
5. Failure to address the social need for retribution and incapacitation, and
6. The failure to politically fight off the "nothing works" movement of the late 1970s.

These failures were compounded by the rise of the "soft on crime" political rhetoric of the late 1970s and early 1980s and the failure of rehabilitation advocates to defend, as a political matter, why offenders should be rehabilitated in the first place.

The rise in violent crime, violent juvenile crime, gun violence, sensational cases of child abductions, and the crack epidemic of the 1980s ushered in a return of the ideals of incapacitation, incarceration, the protection of society, and make the offender "pay his debt to society." These political sentiments gave rise to the policies of ***determinant sentencing*** for violent crime and drug offenses; ***the policy of juvenile transfer***, the transferring serious juvenile offenders and juvenile "super predators" to adult court, so they could be tried and punished like adults; the total ***abandonment of parole*** and good time policies; and the rise of ***supermax prisons***. During this period, the federal government provided states with trillions of dollars to build prisons, and supermax prisons (23-hour lockdowns). Federal funds were provided to states that implemented various crime-control policies including the ***establishment of sex offender databases***, passage of legislation giving victims of crime the right to be heard at sentencing hearings, and passage of ***truth-in-sentencing statutes***. The result of these policies was significant increases in prison populations for longer periods of time.

This period also introduced the policy of ***sentencing guidelines*** that imposed ***mandatory sentencing*** of offenders for crimes. The guidelines were designed to remove discretion from judges in sentencing offenders, which was hailed by both liberals and conservatives. Liberals or due process model holders supported sentencing guidelines because the guidelines ended vast variances between sentencing for individuals of different races who had committed the same offense (racial bias by judges). Conservatives or crime control model holders supported sentencing guidelines to prevent the imposition of "soft" sentences by liberal anti-police judges. The impact of increased incarceration rates due to the mandatory sentence guidelines were supplemented by the ***policy of three strikes***. Under this policy offenders who were convicted of a third, and sometimes a second, serious offense would be sentenced to life without the possibility of parole.

The Post-Second Punitive Era (2000–present) did not return to the rehabilitation era as a theory of criminal justice and prison operation, but the post-second punitive era allowed for the softening of retribution politics while maintaining the idea of incapacitation and incarceration. As the lowering of the national and local crime rates occurred, policies that allowed for the reduction in mandatory minimum sentences for drugs occurred under the ***Fair Sentencing Act (2010)***, and during this period, the Supreme Court ruled in ***U.S. v. Booker*** (2005) and ***Kimbrough v. U.S.*** (2007) that the federal and state sentencing guidelines were presumptive but not mandatory. The treatment of the guidelines as discretionary allowed for judges to have discretion in sentencing and allowed them to develop programs designed to divert offenders from incarceration through specialty courts. ***Specialty courts*** were initiatives in which court personnel received training to deal with certain type of offenders and these offenders were exclusively handled by these courts. The idea was for the courts to craft rehabilitative and when necessary retributive outcomes to deal with the specific issues the offenders had. These courts included DUI courts, mental health courts, truancy courts, first offender courts, and domestic violence courts.

The withdrawal from the policies of *the second punitive era* resulted, in part, from the reality of the high cost of mass incarceration, and with state and federal budgets no longer supplemented by deficit spending to build and maintain prisons, the utilization of rehabilitation as a less expensive way to deal with offenders forced political change. While the idea that offenders can be fixed or rehabilitated has been abandoned and has not returned as the primary theory of criminal justice, the idea of retribution at all costs has also been abandoned.

During the heyday of *the second punitive era*, the disproportionate incarceration of Blacks was defended by the assertion that it was the sole and natural consequence of deviant Black behavior and culture. In other words, it was not a problem to be fixed by reforming the criminal justice system but a reality to be accepted, so long as the Black community did not change the behavior of young Black men. The problem was cultural and not due to the operation of the criminal justice system. During the *post-secondary punitive era*, the disproportionate incarceration was recognized as a problem to be fixed, not accepted as normal.

With this background, we will turn to the specific policy determinations during *the rehabilitative era* through *the second-punitive era* that has formed the modern criminal justice system and defined the contemporary disproportionate incarceration of Blacks from the last half of the twentieth century to the present.

CRIME SUPPRESSION AND POLITICS 1966–1990S

By the late 1940s, the practice of peonage which was made a federal crime in 1867 was finally enforced and the practice was ended in the former Confederate South. Convict leasing was abandoned, as well as criminal surety and criminalization of unemployment. The late 1940s left America as the sole superpower defending the West from communism. Blacks, after the war, were at the dawn of demanding their social and political rights that they were promised almost a century before but were denied. The days of overt racism would come to an end within two decades. By the late 1960s the rhetoric of Thurmond and Wallace were no longer acceptable, and their politics of the 1940s and 1950s had lost to those of Kennedy and King.

But the civil rights movement, which began with the victory in *Brown v. Board of Education*, would also hold the seeds for the rise of the modern foundation for Black incarceration. With the rise of civil rights and the fall of Jim Crow, two political and psychological events occurred simultaneously. Great enthusiasm and pleasure that Jim Crow was dead and promises of freedom made to Blacks would be granted, along with an undercurrent of great fear and resentment to the upending of a social structure that conservatives believed was forced upon them without their consent. This resentment was followed by fear of social change, social disorder, crime, and Black crime. During the civil rights movement, all four fears became synonymous in the politics of the 1960s, which gave rise to the modern criminal justice system to this day. It all began with the rise of urban crime in the 1950s through 1968.

The beginning of the modern link of crime and Blacks began in the 1960s with a significant increase in the fear of crime. The total U.S. population between 1960 and 1970 increased by 13.3%, but the rate of violent crime increased 156%. During this period, the murder rate increased 75.6%, the incidents of rape increased 121%, the incidents of robbery increased 224%, and incidents of aggravated assault increased 117%. The total property crime rate increased by 137.7%, with incidents of burglary increased by 141.7%, theft increased by 127.7%, and motor vehicle theft increased by 128.8%. While the Johnson Administration (1963–1968) was advocating for civil rights for Blacks and asserting the social policy that the Great Society would address social and racial inequity, social conservatives were pointing out incidents of crime—both violent and property—had increased. Violent crime increased 87.7% between 1963 and 1968. During the same period, incidents of murder showed an increase of 59.7%, incidents of rape increased 79.4%, the rate of assault increased 64.5%, and the biggest crime increase involved incidents of robbery at 125.6%. This increase in crime coincided with the upending of Jim Crow and the civil rights movement's strategy of civil disobedience, which included the breaking of segregation laws. The point is this: social unrest, crime, Black civil rights, and Blacks intentionally breaking segregation laws all occurred at the same time, and middle-class fears regarding the lack of law and order and social stability resulted in the modern conflation of Blacks and crime. Black resistance became Black criminality.

The significance of the increase in the crime rate between 1960 and 1970 is not why it increased, but how the increase was defined and used politically. The increase occurred at a time when the Democrats were supporting civil rights and anti-poverty programs and

CRIME IN UNITED STATES 1960–1970										
YEAR	POPULATION	TOTAL VIOLENT CRIME	MURDER AND NON-NEGLIGENT MANSLAUGHTER	FORCIBLE RAPE	ROBBERY	AGGRAVATED ASSAULT	TOTAL PROPERTY CRIME	BURGLARY	LARCENY-THEFT	MOTOR VEHICLE THEFT
1960	179,323,175	288,460	9,110	17,190	107,840	154,320	3,095700	912,100	1,855,400	328,200
1961	182,992,000	289,390	8,740	17,220	106,670	156,760	3,198600	949,600	1,913,000	336,000
1962	185,771,000	301,510	8,530	17,550	110,860	164,570	3,450700	994,300	2,089,600	366,000
1963	188,483,000	316,970	8,640	17,650	116,470	174,210	3,792500	1,086,400	2,297,800	408,300
1964	191,141,000	364,220	9,360	21,420	130,390	203,050	4,200400	1,213,200	2,514,400	472,800
1965	193,526, 000	387,390	9,960	23,410	138,690	215,330	4,352000	1,282,500	2,572,600	496,900
1966	195,576,000	430,180	11,040	25,820	157,990	235,330	4,793300	1,410,100	2,822,000	561,200
1967	197,457, 000	499,930	12,240	27,620	202,910	257,160	5,403500	1,632,100	3,111,600	659,800
1968	199,399,000	595,010	13,800	31,670	262,840	286,700	6,125200	1,858,900	3,482,700	783,600
1969	201,385,000	661,870	14,760	37,170	298,850	311,090	6,749000	1,981,900	3,888,600	878,500
1970	203,235,298	738,820	16,000	37,990	349,860	334,970	7,359200	2,205,000	4,225,800	928,400

Source: FBI Uniform Crime Reports as prepared by the National Archive of Criminal Justice Data Web page https:/ /www.ucrdatatool.gov/Search/Crime/State/RunCrimeStatebyState.cfm

embracing the theory that crime was the result of poverty and social structure inequities; the Supreme Court was issuing decisions that expanded due process rights for the accused at each stage of the criminal justice system, and later in the decade (1968–1970) when the Vietnam War became a quagmire that the United States seemed unable to win or retreat from, the second wave of the women's movement began, and the overall social fabric of White middle class America values were perceived to be under assault from various quarters of society. Into this time of social distress, the politics of Thurmond, Wallace, Goldwater, Reagan, and Nixon provided an answer to working and middle-class Whites who thought they were losing their country. The verbiage of "nigger" and "segregation today, segregation tomorrow and segregation forever" was abandoned and replaced by the language of "law and order" and "war on crime." The Ku Klux Klan and White citizens leagues were replaced by the "silent majority" and the Southern Strategy which was followed by a "War on Drugs" and the politics and policy of retribution.

The politics of the late 1960s through 1980s was such that law and order became code to the voters who rejected and opposed civil rights, affirmative action, bussing, and integration—those who opposed the latter were spoken to in the language of the former. *Newsweek Magazine* in its special issue in October 1969, reported that 85% of Whites thought Blacks were getting too much, and more than 60% thought the police needed more power and Whites were getting shortchanged in getting government aid in comparison to Blacks.[12] In the politics of the middle and late 1960s, the *ascriptive authority* (the ability and power to ascribe negative values and perceptions onto other people or another race) of White America defined Black demands for civil rights as lawless and criminal and used its v*olitional authority* (the ability and power to ascribe positive values and perceptions onto oneself or ones group) to define itself as the moral majority that had lost its place and its country to those who sought to destroy it or turn it into a socialistic utopia.

As explained by Thurmond, Wallace, Goldwater, Reagan, and Nixon, the people who sought to do this were those who rejected states' rights for forced integration, supported rehabilitation over retribution and the protection of law-abiding citizens. These people were the social engineers who sought to change the political and moral dynamics of the America of the 1940s and 1950s. When social conservatives complain of progressivism or "the left" they are complaining about the social engineers of the 1960s who upended a century of social policy of Jim Crow, with the result being increased crime and the power of the national government to interfere with individual citizens and dictate policy to the states. The politics of crime control and law and order served as a vehicle to reject these social changes and a unifying political rhetoric to achieve political obstruction of the social change of the 1960s, the flashpoint being crime and integration post 1964–1968 civil rights laws.

---

12 Newsweek, "The troubled American: A Special Report on the White Majority" (October 6, 1969).

President Johnson and Crime Policy

In 1964, President Johnson spearheaded the war on poverty. His goal was to end hunger, increase educational opportunities for the poor, provide social programs to rural and urban neighborhoods, provide medical care for the elderly and those who could not afford it, provide financial assistance to single-parent mothers, provide medical coverage to children, and provide financial aid for young people trying to secure an education. His policies had broad support within the Congress that was controlled by his party. He had defeated Goldwater in a decisive victory.

Between 1964 and 1968 President Johnson passed civil rights legislation and Great Society programs including Medicare and Medicaid. But, behind these achievements and political victories was the growing backlash to these very same programs. Recognizing that crime was a major political issue within the country President Johnson sought to get ahead of demand for law and order. Johnson sought to broaden the acceptance of his social programs by linking them to the other social problem at the time—the rising crime rate. Crime, according to the Democrats and liberals, is the reaction to poverty. That was the link Johnson used to make his programs palatable to a growing skepticism in the country. The war on poverty would be an answer to crime. Johnson linked crime and poverty together and then linked both to race. Under Johnson, the policy assertion was that war on crime will be won by victories in the war on poverty. This logic has served as liberal orthodoxy to this day.

The Republicans and social conservatives adopted this logic with one distinction. They agreed that Black crime was the source of the overall crime rate but rejected the proposition that poverty had anything to do with it, and even if it did, it was not the role of the federal government to end poverty. From 1964 to the present both Republicans and Democrats agree that crime and race were linked, their dispute was on how. Although the Great Society programs were designed to aid rural Whites as much as urban Blacks, as a political and rhetorical matter, the face of the recipients of the Great Society (and those in need of it) were Black. This is how urban inner cities became code for Blacks and Blacks became code for poverty, and how the demarcation line was drawn between the politics of the two parties regarding the type of social engineering that was required to control Black crime. Democrats proposed the Great Society while Republicans would propose crime control model statutes and increased construction of prisons.

By 1966 the Johnson Administration began to abandon the Great Society as the policy to reduce crime with adoption of law and order policies. Johnson's law and order policy began with providing direct support to local law enforcement to deal with crime, and on this policy the Republicans were in agreement. While the Johnson Administration sought to include law and order policies with the Great Society to address urban crime, the Republicans proposed that law and order policies should be the exclusive policy, since crime is caused by individual behavior not social structural iniquities. But both were in policy agreement that the federal government should provide funding to the local police to deal with crime—i.e., Blacks.

The Johnson Administration began the federalization of the politics and policy of law and order when, on August 20, 1964, President Johnson signed the ***Federal Criminal Justice Act of 1964***. That act provided funding for indigent defense counsel. This act was followed by the President signing the ***Law Enforcement Assistance Act of 1965*** on September 22, 1965, which provided block grant funding for the education and support of local police officers.[13] But a year later, the politics of crime had shifted, and the need for law and order—control of the streets from criminals, i.e., Blacks—had to be addressed. Johnson met the challenge when he gave his special message to Congress on crime on March 9, 1966.

After President Truman created the President's Committee on Civil Rights in December 1946, the commission asserted a year later that safety from violence was the first civil right of all citizens. The context of of the report and Truman's approval of it in his 1948 special message to Congress was that Blacks have a right to be free from lynch mobs, police brutality, and racial violence. But Johnson misappropriated his statement, in his March 1966 speech, to mean all people should be able to live free from urban crime.

Johnson delivered a special message to Congress on Crime and Law Enforcement on March 9, 1966 (see appendix at the end of this chapter), and established the foundation of the modern Democratic Party approach to criminal justice policy. Johnson asserted seven major principles: (1) crime is a problem; (2) the federal government has a role in maintaining safety on the streets of America; (3) crime is a holistic problem which requires a holistic response; (4) all aspects of the criminal justice system are required to address crime, not the police exclusively; (5) rehabilitation is key to reducing crime; (6) federal regulation and prohibition of gun sales across state lines; and (7) crime has root causes. Johnson asserted that by addressing the root causes (poverty and racial injustice) the rate of crime could be significantly and permanently reduced. This message supplemented his special message to Congress on Law Enforcement and the Administration of Justice (see appendix at the end of this chapter) a day before. In that massage, Johnson declared that "crime is a national problem" which requires "a national effort to resolve the problems of law enforcement and the administration of justice."

To deal with the threat and fear of crime, President Johnson stated that the main parts of the system—the police, courts, and corrections—need to be modernized. The treatment of the accused and the convicted must be such that rehabilitation and deterrence can be operationalized. The system of bail should avoid preventive detention or detention because of inability to pay the bail set by the court. While the police officer is the frontline soldier in the war on crime, courts must be made to support their efforts in making society safe, and the root cause of crime is injustice. Here is where Johnson linked crime to poverty and both to race. The president said, "*The programs now underway to eliminate the degradation of poverty, the decay of our cities, the disgrace of racial discrimination, the despair of illiteracy—are all vitally important to crime prevention.*" More importantly, "*where legitimate opportunities are*

---

13 Statement by the President Following the Signing of Law Enforcement Assistance Bills September 22, 1965, at http://www.presidency.ucsb.edu/ws/?pid=27270

closed, illegitimate opportunities are seized. Whatever opens opportunity and hope will help to prevent crime and foster responsibility. Effective law enforcement and social justice must be pursued together, as the foundation of our efforts against crime."

Congress complied with the president. On June 22, 1966, President Johnson signed the ***Bail Reform Act of 1966***, which was to "assure that all persons, regardless of their financial status, shall not needlessly be detained pending their appearance to answer charges, to testify, or pending appeal, when detention serves neither the ends of justice nor the public interest." The law required that

> Any person charged with an offense, other than an offense punishable by death, shall, at his appearance before a judicial officer, be ordered released pending trial on his personal recognizance or upon the execution of an unsecured appearance bond in an amount specified by the judicial officer, unless the officer determines, in the exercise of his discretion, that such a release will not reasonably assure the appearance of the person as required.

The concept that bail only involved the issue of guaranteeing the appearance of the defendant, and preventive detention would be prohibited in the federal courts was American policy until the Reagan era and the passage the *Bail Reform Act of 1984*.

Two years later, at President Johnson's urging, Congress passed the ***Omnibus Crime Control and Safe Streets Act of 1968***.[14] The new law provided more than $400 million dollars for a block grant and training for police agencies, authorized the president to order wiretapping for national security and homeland defense purposes, prohibited private employers from wiretapping employees, overruled the *Miranda* decision by allowing the admission of confessions at trials when those confessions were voluntarily secured from a defendant regardless of whether the actual warnings required by the Supreme Court were given, and outlawed interstate sales of handguns, along with raising the minimum age to buy a handgun in interstate commerce to be 21 years old.

The *Miranda* provision was not used by federal law enforcement and when it was, the Supreme Court held it unconstitutional in *Dickerson v. United States* in 2000.[15]

By June 1968, the Democrats developed the political orthodoxy that crime control included gun control. The president made clear in his signing of the of the Omnibus Act,

> [t]he measure also ends three decades of inaction on the problem of gun controls. Interstate traffic in handguns and their sales to minors will now be prohibited by law. The majority of all the murders by firearms in this Nation are committed by these small but deadly weapons.

---

14 Statement by the President Upon Signing the Omnibus Crime Control and Safe Streets Act of 1968 June 19, 1968 at http://www.presidency.ucsb.edu/ws/index.php?pid=28939&st=&st1=

15 See, United States v. Dickerson, 530 U.S. 428, 120 S.Ct. 2326, 147 L.Ed. 2d 405 (2000) and Arthur H. Garrison, "Rehnquist v. Scalia – The Dickerson and Miranda Cases: A Debate on What Makes a Decision Constitutional" *American Journal of Trial Advocacy* 25 no.1 (2001): 91

> But as I have told the Nation and the Congress repeatedly, this is only a halfway step toward the protection of our families and homes. We must go further and stop mail order murder by rifle and shotgun. We must close a glaring loophole in the law by controlling the sale of these lethal weapons, as well as the sale of ammunition for all guns.

Under the national radar of the politics of the war on poverty and the Great Society, crime policies slowly shifted law enforcement toward a more militant and militarized approach to crime. In the 1950s, ***the Los Angeles Police Department (LAPD)***, under ***Chief William Parker***, established the professionalization model for his officers. They were no longer the political pawns of politicians. Their honesty was to be without reproach. But more importantly, Chief Parker believed that crime was the sole result of disrespect for the police. He believed that crime resulted from the disregard and disrespect of the law. The problem of crime was easily resolved. The police officer was a warrior who enforced the law with brute force upon the criminal. Communities were safe because they were under control. Communities that were not under control were to be made so by force. Chief Parker believed that Blacks were not under control. Civil disobedience resulted in criminal behavior. The law is the law—whether those are laws enforcing segregation and Jim Crow or laws prohibiting burglary and theft. The law was to be obeyed. Parker's view found a similar perspective in the Director of the FBI, ***John Edgar Hoover***. Between these two men, a new generation of police officer ethos was being created in the public eye. ***The warrior model*** was the template of the modern police officer and purpose of the policing. Crime was about social disorder, and the warrior police officer was the sole agent to solve and prevent disorder. Where Parker and Hoover parted company with President Johnson was on whether the police were the sole agents responsible for solving social disorder. Johnson believed the entire criminal justice system was the wall that prevented crime and disorder. The *warrior model* under Parker and Hoover believed the thin blue line, the warrior cop, is the sole separation between society and an ever-encroaching jungle. A concept that would find support in mouth of a president in 1980.

Another public official would introduce and support another key tool of law enforcement and maintenance of law and order by brute force—***Governor Nelson Rockefeller*** and his policies of no-knock warrants and use of stop and frisk of pedestrians on the street.[16] The ***no knock warrants statute*** allows the police to secure a special warrant that allowed them to enter a house without knocking and allowing the owner or occupant to answer the door. The ***stop-and-frisk statute*** allows the police to stop a person on the street and detain them upon suspicion of crime. Both pieces of legislation became effective on July 1, 1964. Over the next decade, both policies underlying the statutes were adopted by the states, the federal

---

16 New York Consolidated Laws, Criminal Procedure Law—CPL § 690.35(4)(b) (No-Knock warrants) and New York Consolidated Laws, Criminal Procedure Law—CPL § 140.50 (stop-and-frisk). See also, discussion of stop-and-frisk law in Chapter six and Note, "The 'No-Knock' and 'Stop and Frisk' Provisions of the New York Code of Criminal Procedure" 38(2) *St. John's Law Review* 38 no. 2 (1964); 392.

government, and the U.S. Supreme Court as legitimate law enforcement tools to suppress crime. The problem with both laws is not their existence but how they were implemented. Over the proceeding decades, reports and cases would arise showing how the police entered and destroyed the homes of people under the authority of no-knock warrants and Blacks being stopped with little more reason than that they were Black, and Blacks tend to be criminal.

The middle- and late-1960s also birthed another aspect of the militarization of the police—the need for the police to deal with armed, organized, radicalized political criminal gangs; mass shooters; and radical racial groups, like the Black Panthers. There was a need for special police units. This need resulted in the formation of the LAPD ***Special Weapons and Tactics team*** (SWAT), the brainchild of then LAPD Inspector ***Daryl Gates***. The idea of SWAT was birthed after ***the Charles Whitman massacre at the University of Texas at Austin clock tower*** on August 11, 1966.[17] The lack of preparedness of law enforcement to deal with Whitman and the urban riots of '64 and '65 instilled in Gates the need for police departments to have officers trained in military tactics to deal with disturbances that regular officers were not trained or equipped to handle. Aside from the epiphany of SWAT in the mind of Gates, the "riots in Watts and other urban areas" left an impression on middle class suburban voters who feared the "rising black criminal class" but who had felt immune from criminal violence were dissuaded of that immunity by "Whitman's rampage on a college campus. ... And all of this came as the country was still reeling from Richard Speck's trial for torturing, raping, and murdering eight nurses from South Chicago Community Hospital a month earlier. The criminal threat no longer seemed to be limited to the inner cities."[18] Middle-class America wanted to feel safe, and the rise and support of militarized police would provide a source of comfort. Although Gates found it hard to convince his superiors that SWAT should be supported, the urban riots of 1967 and 1968 and the police riot at the 1968 Democratic Convention in Chicago had provided fertile ground for law enforcement acceptance of the SWAT idea. In December 1969, Gates and the LAPD SWAT team entered the national limelight with its raid on the Los Angeles headquarters of the Black Panthers.[19]

Gates and his SWAT team raided the headquarters of the Black Panthers to execute a warrant for possession of illegal firearms. The Panthers were ready for a fight due to the killing of Fred Hampton, the deputy chairman of the Illinois chapter, by the Chicago police.[20] The raid resulted in three hours of exchanged gunfire and after Gates secured permission from the Department of Defense to use a Marine grenade launcher on the house the Panthers surrendered, all in front of the national media.[21] This raid, along with the LAPD SWAT raid on

17 Radley Balko, *Rise of the Warrior Cop: The Militarization of America's Police Forces* (PublicAffairs, 2013) at 56–57.

18 Radley Balko, *Rise of the Warrior Cop* at 58–59.

19 Radley Balko, *Rise of the Warrior Cop* at 76–80.

20 Radley Balko, *Rise of the Warrior Cop* at 77.

21 Radley Balko, *Rise of the Warrior Cop* 78–80.

the Symbionese Liberation Army (SLA), famously known for the kidnapping of Patty Hearst, in November 1973 made both Gates and SWAT sensations in the national consciousness and within law enforcement.[22] By the early 1980s, every police department in America had some type of SWAT-trained officer corp.

With the 1968 assassinations of Dr. King and Robert Kennedy, American politics was changing. Both parties in Congress defined law and order as the need to control and suppress crime. The Supreme Court was abandoning the due process revolution as exemplified by its decision in ***Terry v. Ohio*** in which the Court held ***reasonable articulable suspicion*** (RAS) was all that was required for police to stop a person the police believed could be involved in criminal activity. The Court in *Terry* affirmed the New York stop and frisk statute. The American public was becoming convinced that crime should be defined as social disorder and disobedience, not the result of social injustice or economic inequalities.

In the wake of a decade of civil rights marches and civil disobedience, 1968 witnessed the abandonment of non-violent civil protest for civil rights and the advocacy for a militant civil rights movement. The Great Society had not ended social disorder and the 1968 riots became a major political issue in the 1968 elections. In the politics of crime, race became the euphemism for disorder and a threat to law and order with the war on poverty being blamed by both the left and the right on having failed to reduce poverty, which was supposed to reduce crime and increase public safety. With the failure of the war on poverty and Great Society programs becoming clear, but race being irrevocably linked to crime, the crime control model as an answer to crime was ready to make its appearance with the election of Richard Nixon. If social programs won't reduce Black crime, law enforcement will.

The 1970s and the Incremental Fall of the Due Process Model

By the 1968 presidential election, crime was a defining election topic. During the campaign, Nixon was famously quoted as saying the "solution to the crime problem is not the quadrupling of funds for any governmental war on poverty but more convictions."[23] After receiving the Republican Party the nomination for president, Nixon asserted that crime was the main question for America to answer. Nixon announced the "silent majority" saw what the problem in America was.[24] As Johnson established the orthodoxy of liberal theory of crime reduction in his 1966 address to Congress, Nixon established the orthodoxy of social conservatives in his acceptance speech at the 1968 Republican convention.

> And tonight, it is time for some honest talk about the problem of order in the United States.

---

22 Radley Balko, *Rise of the Warrior Cop* at 126–37.

23 Katherine Beckett and Theodore Sasson, *The Politics of Injustice: Crime and Punishment in America* (SAGE Publications, 2004) at 52.

24 Richard Nixon, Address Accepting the Presidential Nomination at the Republican National Convention in Miami Beach, Florida August 8, 1968 at http://www.presidency.ucsb.edu/ws/?pid=25968

> Let us always respect, as I do, our courts and those who serve on them. But ***let us also recognize that some of our courts in their decisions have gone too far in weakening the peace forces as against the criminal forces in this country and we must act to restore that balance.***
>
> Let those who have the responsibility to enforce our laws and our judges who have the responsibility to interpret them be dedicated to the great principles of civil rights.
>
> But let them also recognize that ***the first civil right of every American is to be free from domestic violence, and that right must be guaranteed*** in this country.

Nixon, misappropriating what Truman said in 1948, begins with the right to be free from domestic violence and crime. Nixon said, "Let's never forget that despite her faults, America is a great nation ... When the nation with the greatest tradition of the rule of law is plagued by unprecedented lawlessness [and] [w]hen a nation that has been known for a century for equality of opportunity is torn by unprecedented racial violence. [It is clear that] America is in trouble today not because her people have failed but because her leaders have failed." That failure he laid at the feet of the federal government failure to end crime and the courts for limiting the police in their ability to stop crime. Nixon continued,

> And if we are to restore order and respect for law in this country there is one place we are going to begin. We are going to have a new Attorney General of the United States of America.
>
> I pledge to you that our new Attorney General will be directed by the President of the United States to ***launch a war against organized crime*** in this country.
>
> I pledge to you that the new Attorney General of the United States will be an active belligerent ***against the loan sharks and the numbers racketeers*** that rob the urban poor in our cities.
>
> I pledge to you that the new Attorney General will open ***a new front against the filth peddlers and the narcotics peddlers who are corrupting the lives of the children*** of this country.
>
> Because, my friends, let this message come through clear from what I say tonight. ***Time is running out for the merchants of crime and corruption in American society.***
>
> The wave of crime is not going to be the wave of the future in the United States of America.
>
> ...
>
> ***For the past five years we have been deluged by government programs for the unemployed; programs for the cities; programs for the poor. And we have reaped from these programs an ugly harvest of frustration, violence and failure across the land.***
>
> And now our opponents will be offering more of the same—more billions for government jobs, government housing, government welfare.
>
> I say it is time to quit pouring billions of dollars into programs that have failed in the United States of America.

The Great Society had failed; it was time "to restore order and respect for law in this country" and it was time to open new fronts on crime and corruption and "the merchants of crime and corruption in American society." It was that simple.

After winning the election, Nixon opened the first salvo in the war on crime by backing proposals to allow no-knock warrants and stop and frisk in the District of Columbia. On July 29, 1970, he signed the ***D.C. Crime Bill***, which authorized the D.C. police to conduct no-knock warrants, conduct field urine testing during drug raids, and conduct preventive detentions. The law also expanded police wiretapping authority and allowed the police to seize evidence that was not listed in warrants.[25] Nixon then turned to illegal drug use. He famously declared a War on Drugs and signed the ***Comprehensive Drug Abuse Prevention and Control Act of 1970*** on October 27, 1970. The legislation revolutionized federal power to deal with illegal drug use. The legislation abandoned all previous national illegal possession legislation and placed enforcement of illegal drug use within the Justice Department on a constitutional theory that Congress could outlaw illicit drug use under the commerce clause, rather than the tax power of Congress. Title II of the Act, the ***Controlled Substances Act***, created a system of making drugs illegal to use and established a schedule system for all drugs in which schedule one drugs were illegal to use or possess.

Nixon then reorganized federal law enforcement to wage this newly declared War on Drugs. The lead federal agency in illegal drug interdiction in 1973 was the Bureau of Narcotics and Dangerous Drugs (BNDD), a creation of the merging of the Bureau of Internal Revenue, the Bureau of Drug Abuse Control (BDAC), and the Federal Bureau of Narcotics (FBN) in the 1960s. Three years after the passage of the *Comprehensive Drug Abuse Prevention and Control Act*, Nixon, under the ***Reorganization Plan No. 2 of 1973***, created the ***Drug Enforcement Agency*** (DEA) and made it the primary agency to enforce federal illegal drug use laws.[26] The DEA was comprised of the merging of the BNDD and the Office of Drug Abuse Law Enforcement (ODALE), an agency Nixon created within the White House in January, 1972, in addition to securing agents from the U.S. Customs Service and the Office of National Narcotics Intelligence. The *Controlled Substances Act* was amended to allow the DEA, jointly in consultation with the Department of Health and Human Services (HHS) and the Food and Drug Administration (FDA), to define which drugs would be classified as schedule one drugs and, thus, be illegal to use or possess.[27] For drugs to be classified as schedule one, the HHS must certify that medical and scientific data evaluation of the drug establishes that it has the potential for abuse, and as such, it should be controlled—"If a drug does not have a potential for abuse, it cannot be controlled."[28] "Once the DEA has received the scientific and medical

25 Radley Balko, *Rise of the Warrior Cop* (2013) at 84.

26 See Drug Enforcement Agency history 1970–1975 at https://www.dea.gov/about/history/1970-1975.pdf

27 DEA, *Drugs of Abuse 2011 Edition: A DEA Resource Guide* (2011) at https://www.dea.gov/docs/drugs_of_abuse_2011.pdf

28 DEA, *Drugs of Abuse 2011 Edition: A DEA Resource Guide* (2011) at 8

evaluation from HHS, the [DEA] will evaluate all available data and make a final decision whether to propose that a drug or other substance should be removed or controlled and into which schedule it should be placed."[29]

Nixon supplemented his actions in the War on Drugs with political rhetoric against judges who were "soft on crime" and his opposition to parole. By the elections of 1972 Nixon was taking credit for reductions in urban crime and asserted that the sole cause of the reduction was effective federal law enforcement and prosecution of criminals. Nixon said,

> A key to our successes against the drug menace has been the all-out attack on drug pushers. The pusher's crime is one of the most reprehensible known to man-the enslavement of other human beings to a life of degradation, dependence, and suffering. The punishment for this crime must be strict, and it must be certain.
>
> We can be encouraged that Federal narcotics law enforcement officials are arresting pushers at twice the rate of the previous Administration, that illicit drug seizures have quadrupled in the past 4 years, and that more narcotics traffickers are being brought to justice than ever before.

After giving credit to law enforcement, Nixon made clear he would "expand our present massive funding for local law enforcement assistance and will again ask the Congress … for law enforcement special revenue sharing [,] appoint judges who will help to strengthen the peace forces as against the criminal forces in our country, and who will oppose without equivocation the permissive trend toward light or suspended sentences for convicted drug pushers [, and] amend the Federal drug statutes so as to require tough, mandatory sentences for heroin traffickers." Nixon concluded that

> My goal for the next 4 years is for every American city to begin realizing the kind of victories in the war on crime which we have already achieved in the Nation's Capital—where the crime rate has been cut in half since my Administration took office, and where heroin overdose deaths have almost disappeared.
>
> This kind of progress can and must be made all across America. By winning the war on crime and drugs, we can restore the social climate of order and justice which will assure our society of the freedom it must have to build and grow.[30]

Nixon was not alone in his attack on crime through a War on Drugs. The crime control model found support with ***Governor Nelson Rockefeller*** with the passage of his no-knock and stop-and-frisk policy legislation in 1964 and, in 1971 New York, passed the first modern mandatory sentencing statutes for drug possession, the ***Rockefeller Drug Laws of 1973***.

---

29 DEA, *Drugs of Abuse 2011 Edition: A DEA Resource Guide* (2011)

30 Richard Nixon, Campaign Statement About Crime and Drug Abuse October 28, 1972, at http://www.presidency.ucsb.edu/ws/?pid=3665

> The statutory design, like the reasoning upon which it rests, is simple and straightforward. The legislature chose to impose lengthy and frequently mandatory sentences for possession and distribution of controlled substances, on the assumption that harsh and certain punishment would deter and reduce drug abuse and related crime. Under this system, drug offenses are graded according to the dangerousness and the quantity of the drug involved. Dangerousness of a drug is determined by consulting detailed schedules of controlled substances, with the drugs considered most harmful listed in schedule I, and those classified as the least harmful in schedule V. Dangerousness is also evaluated by criteria described as objectively verifiable: potential for abuse, existence of approved medical uses, and safety. Grading is according to the quantity of the drug involved: the greater the quantity, the greater the sentence. Possession of half an ounce of methamphetamine, for example, is a class C felony, punishable by a term of imprisonment up to fifteen years. Possession of two or more ounces of methamphetamine, on the other hand, is a class A-II felony carrying a term of up to life imprisonment.
>
> ...
>
> Governor Rockefeller believed that drug pushers were responsible for increases in addiction and in nondrug crime, and declared that the threat of harsh sentences would "establish an effective deterrent to illegal drug use and drug-related crime." His favored sentencing structure, in its magnitude and its rigidity, reflected the opinion of many respondents to contemporaneous polls that the harm caused by drugs was the most serious problem facing the nation. Punishment of drug possession and distribution in New York is still severe. Possession of half an ounce of methamphetamine, a class C felony, is treated as the equivalent of third degree arson, or second degree burglary. Sale of two ounces of heroin, a class A-I felony, is treated as the equivalent of murder in the first degree.[31]

The *Rockefeller Drug Laws of 1973*, for the first time, elevated drug possession and distribution crimes as equivalent to violent crimes like murder, rape, and arson. The drug war created a system of equating the drug dealer with the violent criminal. This strategy greatly increased the number of criminals sentenced to long prison terms for non-violent offenses. This approach to drug crimes would drive the increases in the U.S. prison population for decades. On the political ground laid by Nixon and Rockefeller that drug crimes deserved the full dropping of the criminal justice system on the heads of those who use and sell drugs, under Presidents Reagan through Clinton, anti-drug legislation would decimate the Black community and support the modern disproportionate incarceration of Blacks for three decades.

---

31 Susan Herman, "Measuring Culpability by Measuring Drugs? Three Reasons to Re-evaluate the Rockefeller Drug Laws," *Albany Law Review* 63 (2000): 777, 777–78, 781–82. See also, The Joint Committee on New York Drug Law Evaluation, *The Nation's Toughest Drug law: Evaluating the New York Experience: Final Report* (1977) at 33–40 at https://www.ncjrs.gov/pdffiles1/Digitization/47795NCJRS.pdf

Four years after winning the presidency, Nixon continued to focus on crime as the domestic issue of the election. The criminalization of drug use and the incarceration of drug users and dealers as the backbone to crime reduction was again emphasized in political rhetoric and policy. In his 1972 acceptance speech at the Republican convention he said,

> Four years ago crime was rising all over America at an unprecedented rate. Even our Nation's Capital was called the crime capital of the world. I pledged to stop the rise in crime. In order to keep that pledge, ***I promised in the election campaign that I would appoint judges to the Federal courts, and particularly to the Supreme Court, who would recognize that the first civil right of every American is to be free from domestic violence.***
>
> I have kept that promise. I am proud of the appointments I have made to the courts, and particularly proud of those I have made to the Supreme Court of the United States. And I pledge again tonight, as I did 4 years ago, that ***whenever I have the opportunity to make more appointments to the courts, I shall continue to appoint judges who share my philosophy that we must strengthen the peace forces as against the criminal forces in the United States.***
>
> We have launched an all-out offensive against crime, against narcotics, against permissiveness in our country.
>
> I want the peace officers across America to know that they have the total backing of their President in their fight against crime.[32]

From the presidency of Nixon, no Republican presidential candidate has not made judicial appointment a major domestic policy issue. From Nixon through Reagan they promised to appoint judges that will support crime control policies. From Bush to Trump they promised judges who would be strict constructionists. In Republican orthodoxy, the constant in rhetoric for fifty years has been law and order, tough on crime, and the appointing judges that support law and order over concern for expanding due process rights for offenders.

The 1972 election made clear that the Great Society approach to explaining crime was completely abandoned. Crime resulted from failure to support the police. Under Nixon and the rise of the crime control model the police were to be honored, supported, and funded as the warriors against crime.

The ethos that the police were warriors against what Reagan called "the jungle" ever encroaching upon civilization was exemplified by the image of the LAPD officer. During the 1970s, the LAPD formed in the national popular consciousness the example of what the warrior cop should be. Popular police dramas of the 1960s and 1970s, such as *Adam 12*, *Dragnet*, *The Rookies*, and *SWAT*, all used the LAPD as the model for fictional police departments or dramatized the LAPD directly. These television series, as well as the series of the 1970s, *The FBI*, which dramatized actual FBI investigations, and shows like *Hawaii Five-O*,

32 Richard Nixon, Remarks on Accepting the Presidential Nomination of the Republican National Convention August 23, 1972, at http://www.presidency.ucsb.edu/ws/?pid=3537

CHIPS, *Starsky and Hutch*, and *Barretta*, all supported the crime control model of the police. Police officers were brave, overworked, and despite working within a system that favored criminal defendant rights—letting them go on "technicalities"—they were, above all, honest, incorruptible, and did not use force unless it was required. Suburban middle class White and Black voters who were exposed to the police and the criminal justice system only through television were prone to support Nixon and, later, Reagan's view that law and order was exclusively maintained by the men in blue, as shown on the T.V. The police warrior model was defined in terms of the strong and tough but fair arbiter of justice on the street who guarded the gates from the barbaric hoards. Police abuses of Blacks was neither seen nor believed by these voters. This dynamic allowed for the policies of the 1980s in which the police in general, and militarized SWAT unites in particular, were unleashed to deal with the scourge of the 1980s—crack cocaine and the crime and violence that came with it.

The 1980s-1990s and the Rise of Crime Control Model

The fear of crime in America was a potent political tool that had held the Republican Party voting base together for twenty years. It was also a political reality that changed the politics of the Democratic Party to require them to catch up on the "get tough on crime" rhetoric and politics of the post-1960s America. This dynamic forced the party to abandon the defense of the politics and policies of the Great Society of President Johnson. In the 1980s, the new focal point of law-and-order politics was the politics of crime and race in the era of crack cocaine in Black urban neighborhoods. Because of the nature of crack drug trafficking and the gang and gun violence that came with it, the constant of disproportionate arrest and incarceration of Blacks was taken to a new level. To the detriment of Blacks, the plague of crack concentrated in urban neighborhoods, and the criminalization of crack was the funnel in which millions of young men of color were poured into the criminal justice system. With groundwork laid by Nixon and Rockefeller, those young men of color would be incarcerated for decades, if not life, under the new drug policies and laws under Reagan, Bush, and Clinton.

President Reagan: Crime Control Takes Center Stage—the Great Society is Dead

Ronald Reagan ushered in policies that, to this day, have supported critical race theorists' assertions that the 1980s were the modern demarcation line and evidence that the purpose of the criminal justice system is to incarcerate Blacks. Reagan was always crime control oriented and was not new to the crime rhetoric game before his ascension to the presidency. In 1967 while governor of California, he gave a speech to the National Sheriffs' Association and made clear he was not supportive of any theory of crime reduction other than the exclusive use of the police. Any concepts of controlling the police were, to him, equal to trying to take their guns away. In his 1967 speech to the National Sheriffs Association,[33] as he did in his

33 Ronald Reagan, Speech by the Governor to the National Sheriffs' Association – Riviera Hotel – Los Vegas, Nevada June 19, 1967.

1961 *Encroaching Control* speech,[34] he asserted that significant federal involvement in local responsibilities, like crime control, would usher in tyranny and loss of freedom and that

> there are those who've done everything but tie your hands and take your guns. It is time for society to give to those on the firing line the weapons needed in this fight against crime.
>
> ...
>
> Law-abiding citizens are genially concerned. And so are those of us who are ultimately charged with providing protection, maintaining law and order, solving and preventing crime and finding the causes of crime, and juvenile delinquency.
>
> ...
>
> [W]e must never forget that the basic tasks of crime prevention and control belongs at the local level ...
>
> ...
>
> It is important to recognize that unless both local and state law enforcement agencies meet their responsibilities, we may find them usurped by the federal government or ceded to it by default.
>
> When this happens we will have, in effect, a national police force. And we will have taken steps to abolish crime only at the risk of our freedom.

After parroting Wallace and Thurmond on the fear of a federal police force and tyranny being the price for solving local problems with federal action; Reagan parroted Nixon regarding the cause of crime. He said,

> I do not hold with the theory that says society is to blame when a man commits a robbery or a murder and therefore we must be understanding and a sympathetic for the criminal as we are for the victim.
>
> Nor do I hold with the spirit of permissiveness around the land that has undoubtedly added to the juvenile delinquency problem.
>
> ... [W]e should question perhaps that part of the President's crime report that lays such emphasis on curing crime by eliminating poverty. ... [W]e should not delude ourselves that simply by improving social conditions we can automatically eliminate crime.
>
> ...
>
> I believe in the carrot and the stick philosophy ...
>
> There is talk these days that punishment is not a deterrent, and I believe that talk is partially responsible for our increase in crime.
>
> As punishment becomes more difficult to mete out those who would be deterred by its threat feel free-er to resort to crime and acts of violence.
>
> Some court decisions have narrowed the difference between liberty and license and in some areas have overbalanced the scales of justice so that the right of society are outweighed by decisions granting new rights to individuals accused of crimes.

34 See Chapter Seven.

Since 1954 conservatives have laid the blame of social disorder on the courts. First, the courts let Blacks run wild in opposing Jim Crow by allowing civil disobedience and the breaking segregation laws daring the state to arrest them in the 1950s. This abomination, in social conservative eyes, is made all the worse when the Supreme Court held that the states could not require school children to salute the flag and recite the pledge of allegiance, nor could religious readings of the Bible be required in the public schools, and that separate but equal was unconstitutional on golf courses, public beaches and bathhouses, public transportation, public parks and school athletic competitions.[35] To make things worse, the Court was seen as letting criminals run wild in the 1960s by applying the Bill of Rights to the states and issuing decisions that "handcuffed" the police.[36] As Nixon said, Reagan agreed, that the federal courts, and specifically the Supreme Court, had to be brought to heel. This is why every Republican president since Nixon has made the selection of federal judges and justices a central part of domestic policy election rhetoric.

Reagan continued to assert republican orthodoxy that poverty does not explain crime and the Great Society explanation of crime is to be rejected.

> [L]et us have an end to this idea that society is responsible for each and every wrong doer. We must return to a belief in every individual being responsible for his conduct and his misdeeds with punishment immediate and certain.
>
> ... [T]he jungle still is waiting to take over. The man with the badge holds it back.
>
> ... [M]ass criminal violations and mob violence are increasingly endangering our communities. Some euphemistically call this "civil disobedience." It is nothing more or less than deliberate and premeditated violations of the law by groups of people. Protest that takes the form of criminal violations, leads to violence, mob rule, and ultimately to anarchy, where no man has either freedom or rights.

---

35 See, *West Virginia State Board of Education v. Barnette*, 319 U.S. 624 (1943)(salute the flag and pledge of allegiance), *Engle v. Vitale*, 370 U.S. 421 (1962)(prayer in school), *Abington School District v. Schempp*, 374 U.S. 203 (1963)(required Bible recitation), *State of Illinois ex rel McCollum v. Board of Education*, 333 U.S. 203 (1948) (mandatory religious instruction), *Holmes v. City of Atlanta*, 350 U.S. 877 (1955)(desegregation of golf courses), *Mayor of Baltimore v. Dawson*, 350 U.S. 877 (1955) (desegregation of beaches and bathhouses), *Gayle v. Bowder*, 352 U.S. 903 (1956) (the Montgomery boycott case), *New Orleans City Park Improvement Association v. Detiege*, 358 U.S. 54 (1958) (desegregation of public parks), and *State Athletic Commission v. Dorsey*, 359 U.S. 533 (1959) (desegregation of school athletic competitions). To matters all the worse, the Court also held at the height of the second red scare and the during the cold war that membership in the communist party, standing alone, was not enough to allow the firing of government employees and that the government could not use secrete evidence of communist activity in a criminal trial by not allowing the defendant to see the evidence. See, Arthur H. Garrison, *Supreme Court Jurisprudence in Times of National Crisis, Terrorism, and War* (2011) at 159–87.

36 See list of cases and discussion in Chapter Seven.

> Those who go about the country forecasting "a long hot summer" and predicting where the next riot will take place contribute to disturbances and disorders because some of the more irresponsible elements seem to feel an obligation to justify these predictions.
>
> I am also a little tired of those who proclaim that we must pour so much money into community programs ... or else we face a wave of riots and unrest. Government ... must not bow to threats of violence which amounts to political extortion.

Six years later, he echoed his remarks speaking to the Citizens Committee for Law Enforcement Needs[37] and made clear that increased crime was the result of court decisions that, in seeking to make the system fair for the accused, endangered public safety. In very subtle code, he stated that the reason for the increase in crime, aside from liberal judges handcuffing the police, has been "major social upheavals. ... Great migrations of people, the growth of vast metropolitan areas," along with declines in religion, ethics, and the rise of the drug culture. In his 1973 speech to Citizen Committee, when he spoke about crime increasing due to "great migrations" of people and growth in "metropolitan areas," who do you think he was referring to? He echoed his 1967 speech that America has become too permissive of law breakers, and the criminal justice system is too slow in applying punishment. As to the criminal justice system, Reagan listed the causes of crime and signaled what would become his policies as president to fix those problems.

> **Court rulings stacked almost entirely on the side of the law breaker**, a **lack of uniform sentencing** patters for identical crimes, an **over reliance on probation** and perhaps, a **too optimistic view that hardened criminals can be easily rehabilitated**; all those things add up to a seemingly inability, a failure of the criminal justice system to fulfill its basic purpose. To most of our people, the purpose of the law and the criminal justice system is clear and simple: it is to protect the innocent and bring the guilty to justice.
>
> ...
>
> [I]n our zeal to be progressive and compassionate, the rights of society have been eroded.
>
> . ...
>
> When a **law breaker can kill without facing the prospect of the ultimate penalty**, when most **convicted criminals know that they probably will not wind up in prison**, we cannot say we have effective deterrents. ...
>
> ...
>
> **[A]bolish the so-called "exclusionary rule"** and instead adopt a substitute that would allow the victims of illegal search and seizure to recover damages but would not result in suppressing evidence that might otherwise convict a guilty offender. More than any other single court decision, the "exclusionary rule" had had the most devastating impact on effective law enforcement.

37 Ronald Reagan speech to the Citizens Committee for Law Enforcement Needs Los Angeles August 1, 1973

. ...

> Our committee proposed that the public entity employing the policeman be made liable for ordinary damages plus attorney's fees for any unlawful searches and seizures by law enforcement officers. In this way, the law would provide an effective means of redress for the victim of unlawful searches. But it would not be at the cost of suppressing evidence necessary to bring the guilty to justice.
>
> In the final analysis, the primary purpose of the trial, the whole reason for a court and a legal system, is to determine the truth.
>
> When valid evidence is suppressed, the truth is mocked. And injustice is the result.
>
> We must find ways of re-establishing the court as a citadel of truth [and] our system of criminal justice must always be prepared to vigorously act to protect society.

As the crime control model found pure enunciation in the mouth and policies of President Nixon, it found support in the mouth of the future President Reagan. In 1981, Reagan addressed the International Association of Chiefs of Police,[38] and he stated that crime is not complicated to understand, for it is, in the end, a moral issue. He said,

> Controlling crime in American society is not simply a question of more money, more police, more courts, more prosecutors; it's ultimately a moral dilemma, one that calls for a moral or, if you will, a spiritual solution. In dealing with crime, new programs may help; more law-and-order rhetoric may be justified; the studies and surveys may still be needed; the blue ribbon panels may keep investigating. But in the end, the war on crime will only be won when an attitude of mind and a change of heart takes place in America, when certain truths take hold again and plant their roots deep in our national consciousness, truths like: Right and wrong matters; Individuals are responsible for their actions; **Retribution should be swift and sure for those who prey on the innocent.**
>
> We must understand that basic moral principles lie at the heart of our criminal justice system, that our system of law acts as the collective moral voice of society. There's nothing wrong with these values ... **Theft is not a form of political or cultural expression;** it is theft, and it is wrong. Murder is not forbidden as a matter of subjective opinion; it is objectively evil, and we must prohibit it. And no one but the thief and murderer benefits when we think and act otherwise.
>
> ...
>
> A tendency to downplay the permanent moral values has helped make crime the enormous problem that it is today, one that this administration has, as I've told you, made one of its top domestic priorities. But it has occurred to me that the root causes of our other major domestic problem, the growth of government and the decay of the economy, can be traced to many of the same sources of the crime problem. This is because the same

38 Ronald Reagan, Remarks in New Orleans, Louisiana, at the Annual Meeting of the International Association of Chiefs of Police September 28, 1981, at http://www.presidency.ucsb.edu/ws/?pid=44300

> utopian presumptions about human nature that hinder the swift administration of justice have also helped fuel the expansion of government.

His point, Great Society thinking results in big government and the erroneous idea that human behavior is about economics not moral clarity. Reagan continued,

> Many of the social thinkers of the 1950's and 60's who discussed crime only in the context of disadvantaged childhoods and poverty-stricken neighborhoods were the same people who thought that massive government spending could wipe away our social ills. The underlying premise in both cases was a belief that there was nothing permanent or absolute about any man's nature, that he was a product of his material environment, and that by changing that environment—with government as the chief vehicle of change through educational, health, housing, and other programs—we could permanently change man and usher in a great new era.
>
> Well, we've learned the price of too much government: runaway inflation, soaring unemployment, impossible interest rates. We've learned that Federal subsidies and government bureaucrats not only fail to solve social problems but frequently make them worse.
>
> It's time, too, that we acknowledge the solution to the crime problem will not be found in the social worker's files, the psychiatrist's notes, or the bureaucrats budgets. It's a problem of the human heart, and it's there we must look for the answer. We can begin by acknowledging some of those permanent things, those absolute truths I mentioned before. Two of those truths are that men are basically good but prone to evil, and society has a right to be protected from them.
>
> ...
>
> [F]or all our science and sophistication, for all of our justified pride in intellectual accomplishment, **we must never forget the jungle is always there waiting to take us over.** Only our deep moral values and our strong social institutions can hold back that jungle and restrain the darker impulses of human nature.

President Reagan put these principles into operation and set the terms of his criminal justice policy in 1982 when he addressed the employees of the Department of Justice.[39] He began his speech with his traditional decry that the criminal justice system was broken, it was not punishing criminals, and described modern crime as the result of what, in the 1990s, would be termed "super predators." He said,

> As all of you know, crime today is an American epidemic. It takes the lives of over 20,000 Americans a year, touches nearly a third of America's homes, and results in about $8.8 billion a year in financial losses. I've resisted figuring out and doing what is sometimes

39 Ronald Reagan, Remarks Announcing Federal Initiatives Against Drug Trafficking and Organized Crime October 14, 1982, at http://www.presidency.ucsb.edu/ws/?pid=43127

> typical in remarks of this kind, and that is to tell you how many people are going to be murdered while I'm talking to you.
>
> But these statistics suggest that our criminal justice system has broken down, that it just isn't working, and many Americans are losing faith in it. Nine out of ten Americans believe that the courts in their home areas aren't tough enough on criminals, and the **cold statistics do demonstrate the failure of our criminal justice system to adequately pursue, prosecute, and punish criminals**. In New York City, for example, less than 1 percent of reported felonies end in a prison term for the offender.
>
> The perception is growing that the crime problem stems from the emergence of a new privileged class in America, a class of **repeat offenders and career criminals**. ... They **don't believe they'll be caught, and if they are caught, they're confident that once their cases enter our legal system, the charges will be dropped, postponed, plea-bargained away, or lost in a maze of legal technicalities** that make a mockery of our legitimate and honorable concern with civil liberties.

Reagan also made clear that he rejected the proposition that crime is explained by sociological and environmental factors. He stated that crime is an evil that is decided by the individual. Crime is personal, not societal. But punishment of crime—that is societal. President Reagan continued,

> Once again the research shows that this common perception has a strong basis in fact. Just take one limited part of the crime picture. Transit police in New York estimate that **only 500 habitual offenders were responsible for nearly half of the crimes** committed in their subways last year. This rise in **crime**, this growth of a hardened criminal class, **has partly been the result of misplaced government priorities and a misguided social philosophy.**
>
> At the root of this philosophy lies **utopian presumptions** about human nature that see **man** as primarily a **creature of his material environment**. By changing this environment through expensive social programs, this philosophy holds thatgovernment can permanently change man and usher in an era of prosperity and virtue. In much the same way, **individual wrongdoing is seen as the result of poor socioeconomic conditions or an underprivileged background**. This philosophy suggests in short that there is crime or wrongdoing, and **that society, not the individual, is to blame.**
>
> But what has also become abundantly clear in the last few years is that **a new political consensus among the American people utterly rejects this point of view.** The increase in citizen involvement of the crime problem and the tough new State statutes directed at repeat offenders make it clear that the American people are reasserting certain enduring truths—the belief that right and wrong do matter, that **individuals are responsible for their actions**, that **evil is frequently a conscious choice**, and that **retribution must be swift and sure** for those who decide to make a career of preying on the innocent.
>
> This administration, even as we're struggling with our economic and international problems, has also been attempting to deal with the threat of crime and to speak for this new consensus.

> ...
>
> When I spoke in New Orleans last year to the International Association of Chiefs of Police, I made the point then, as Bill has told you—and I don't think that I should repeat it now—but we do draw distinctions between violent crime, sophisticated crime, or between crimes like drug pushing and crimes like bribery. The truth is, crime doesn't come in categories. It's part of a pattern. If one sector prospers in the community of crime, so ultimately do all the others.
>
> As I said then, the street criminal, the drug pusher, the mobster, the corrupt policeman, public official, they form their own criminal subculture. They contribute to and they prosper in a climate of lawlessness. They need each other. They use each other. They protect each other. And that brings us to the major and sweeping effort that I'm announcing this morning.
>
> ...
>
> **[T]his administration will open a new legislative offensive** that is aimed to win approval of reforms in criminal statutes **dealing with bail, sentencing, criminal forfeiture, the exclusionary rule, and labor racketeering,** that are essential in the fight against organized crime.
>
> ...
>
> **[M]illions of dollars will be allocated for prison and jail facilities** so that the mistake of releasing dangerous criminals because of overcrowded prisons will not be repeated.
>
> ...
>
> "Justice," James Madison wrote in "The Federalist Papers," "is the end of government. It is the end of civil society. It ever has [been] and ever will be [pursued until it be] obtained, or until liberty be lost in the pursuit." For the sake of our children, for the sake of all the magnificent accomplishments of the American past, today I ask for your support and the support of our people in this effort to fight the drug menace, to eradicate the cancers of organized crime and public corruption, to make our streets and houses safe again, and to return America to the days of respect for the law and the rights of the innocent.

Reagan made clear that rising crime is simply explained by a criminal justice system that is more interested in coddling criminals than deterring them or punishing them. The answer is simple. Change the law to require the courts to sentence criminals and not release them—thus he announced his support for the policy of establishing sentencing guidelines and ending probation/parole through the creation of minimum and mandatory sentences. Reagan's policy desires were implemented two years later in the ***Comprehensive Crime Control Act of 1984***.

The Comprehensive Crime Control Act was signed by President Reagan on October 12, 1984, and the bill revolutionized federal criminal justice. The act touched on almost every major law enforcement aspect of criminal justice.[40] Some of the key provisions of the act included the following changes.

---

40 See summary of the twelve titles in the Senate Bill that was signed by President Reagan at https://www.congress.gov/bill/98th-congress/senate-bill/1762

Significant Criminal Justice Policy Initiatives: Johnson to Clinton

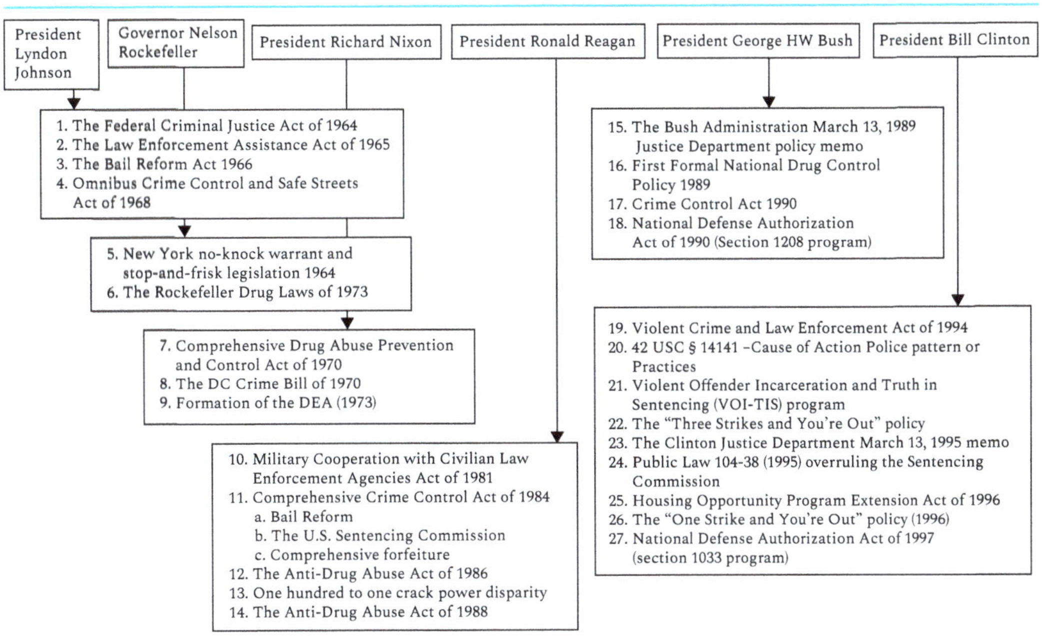

Title One, the ***Bail Reform Act of 1984***, repealed the *Bail Reform Act of 1966* and authorized preventive detention if the court found that a defendant posed a danger to the community outside and independent of the defendant likelihood of appearing in court for future hearings. Title One allowed the government to appeal an order granting bail and established addition penalties for the commission of a crime while on bail.

Title Two, the ***Sentencing Reform Act of 1984*** established the Sentencing Guidelines Commission with a mandate to create a set of federal sentencing guidelines that would be mandatory for the judiciary. Title Two also established maximum terms of imprisonment for certain types of felonies and misdemeanors. One of the key policy initiatives that Reagan supported from 1973 was achieved in Title Two, which eliminated parole in the federal correctional system and provided for special sentencing for violent juvenile offenders. By statute, criminal sanctions were

> to reflect the seriousness of the offense, to promote respect for the law, and to provide just punishment for the offense; to afford adequate deterrence to criminal conduct; to protect the public from further crimes of the defendant; and to provide the defendant with needed educational or vocational training, medical care, or other correctional treatment in the most effective manner [and sentences] need to avoid unwarranted sentence disparities among defendants with similar records who have been found guilty of similar conduct [as well as meet] the need to provide restitution to any victims of the offense.[41]

41 See 18 U.S. Code § 3553 (a)(2)(A-D)(6)(7) Factors To Be Considered in Imposing a Sentence.

America had officially changed the purpose of American correctional theory by abandoning rehabilitation for incapacitation, incarceration, and retribution in addition to victim restoration.

Title Three, **the *Comprehensive Forfeiture Act of 1984***, authorized federal law enforcement to secure property gained through criminal activity—both personal and real property. It also authorized the government to seize property believed to be the fruit of criminal activity *before* conviction. It authorized drug crimes to be subject to asset forfeiture by federal law enforcement. The burden of proof to secure property was placed on the same level as securing a search warrant and authorized judges to issue asset forfeiture warrants for property involved or gained through criminal activity. Title Three also authorized the Attorney General to transfer drug-related forfeited property to other federal, state, or local agencies. It also authorized law enforcement to use forfeited property for official law enforcement purposes. Put simply, law enforcement was given a financial incentive to make arrests, the modern return of the policy outcome of convict leasing, criminal surety, and peonage.

Title Seven authorized the Attorney General to authorize the Administrator of the General Services Administration to transfer to any state or local government federal government surplus property for correctional use. Title Ten established minimum mandatory sentences for the use of firearms during a federal crime of violence, made it a federal crime to attack or threaten a federal employee during the commission of his/her duties, or to kidnap such federal employee or his/her family. Title Eleven made it a crime to warn a person of an impending federal warrant issuance. Title Twelve allowed the government to appeal any district court order for a new trial.

The Comprehensive Crime Control Act of 1984 was followed by the ***Anti-Drug Abuse Act of 1986***, which President Reagan signed on October 27, 1986. The key aspect of the Act was to change the criminal penalty for crack cocaine compared to powder cocaine. The bill famously created a one hundred to one crack–powder disparity in which five grams of crack and five hundred grams of powder cocaine were punished with at least a five-year sentence, regardless of any mitigating factors. A conviction of possession of fifty grams of crack and five thousand grams of powder cocaine were punished by a sentence of at least ten years. These statutory minimum mandatory sentences were adopted by the U.S. Sentencing Guidelines. This 1986 act was followed by the ***Anti-Drug Abuse Act of 1988***, which President Reagan signed on November 18, 1986, which created a five-year mandatory minimum and a twenty-year maximum sentence for simple possession of five grams and fifty grams of crack cocaine respectively for first-time offenders.

As discussed in Chapter One, these laws, together, resulted in the increase in the disproportionate incarceration rate of Blacks from 41% in state and federal prisons in 1980 to 49% in 1989. Half of the total number of people in prison were Black, while Blacks only accounted for 13% of the total U.S. population. The explanation for this increase was the social and political landscape that crack created along with the general "get tough on crime" policies that had preceded the arrive of crack by a decade.

The modern foundation for the incarceration of Blacks is the plague of crack and its arrival in the Black community. In 1981, a new version of cocaine was introduced in Los Angeles, California. Powder cocaine had maxed out its demand by the late 1970s, and a new market was required. To increase the demand and reduce the cost of powder cocaine, the drug was mixed with baking soda or any other powder product and then cooked. This resulted in a crystalized version of cocaine that could be smoked and inhaled directly into the lungs and brain, resulting for some users, in a faster and more intense high from the drug. Further, this form could be sold at a very low cost. A pound of powder cocaine could be increased to three pounds of pre-crack product that, when cooked down to crystal crack "rocks," could be sold as low as a dollar and as high as five dollars for a single use. The crack user found a cheap quick high that required additional hits and drug sellers created a customer base that would return for additional product sometimes three to five times per day. The economic laws of capitalism worked, and a permanent and loyal customer base was created. With demand high and cost for manufacturing low, millions of dollars were generated on the sale of crack. By 1983, crack had spread to every major city in the United States.

Because crack was the way to get the non-affluent to use cocaine in large numbers, crack was a product tailor-made for the Black and Hispanic inner-city drug user, while the affluent drug user still used powder cocaine. Crack cocaine also had a different physiological reaction for some users. It proved to be more addictive and established addiction faster than powder cocaine in some users. A single hit could produce dependency. Drug users shifted from heroin to crack and new drug users were created by experimentation with crack by first-time drug users.

Crack was a plague that aggravated the criminal problems that had already weakened the Black community. As discussed in Chapter Seven, the negative results of desegregation had reduced working class employment and the middle class moral underpinning of the Black community. Federal law enforcement in the late 1960s through the 1970s had decimated large organized crime organizations and gangs that controlled the nature of criminal activity in the community. The leaders of these criminal enterprises were arrested and sentenced to decades in prison. The unintended consequence of this law enforcement activity was that there was no longer a unified control of lower level and younger gang members. Within larger gangs, the older members disciplined and controlled the violent tendencies of the younger gang members. When law enforcement broke the leadership of the larger gangs, control of the younger gang members was lost. Smaller gangs resulted from the breakup of the larger gangs and violence among the smaller gangs by younger members increased. At this time, crack appeared. The sale of crack did not require the significant criminal organization to profitably sell it, as heroin did. To sell crack, all that was required was some powder, some other material to mix it with, and a corner to sell it from. The smaller gangs had a product that sold for thousands of dollars at the street level. The laws of economics were applied, and positive law-abiding employment lost in the competition for employees. But because crack was a cash business, sellers were prone to robbery. Thus, entered the plague that accompanied crack, the significant increase in guns, and the resulting gun violence. Smaller gangs and individual drug dealers used semi-automatic weapons to protect themselves from robbery and maintain control of drug sale territory.

The result was a drastic increase in murder and shooting injuries in the Black community, which—and this is the important part—was public for all of America to see. Young Black males getting shot and shooting each other, which seemed purposeless, was sensationalized on the local news. The news was full of showing Black men either dead on the street or in handcuffs on the hood of police cars. To make matters worse, stories on the local news showed drug addicted babies and mothers selling themselves to get the drug and innocent people getting shot when two young Black males started shooting at each other with no ability to shoot straight—thus hitting everyone but the person they were shooting at. Crime news stories in the 1980s showed Blacks in cars driven by rival Black and Hispanic gang members and shooting indiscriminately, resulting in retaliation shootings of the same type. The political reaction was that this level of violence by unconstrained young Black males was getting out of hand, and laws had to be passed to deal with it. Local police departments said that they were overwhelmed by the violence and needed both equipment and training, as well as support from the national government.

President Reagan, who decried that the failure of local law enforcement to deal with crime would require federal intervention (the very definition of tyranny), found no hesitation in providing federal help to the states to unleash the hammer of law enforcement on the Black community. That help came from unleashing federal law enforcement in the form of federal prosecution for drug use—in this case, simple possession. Federal prosecutions that resulted in conviction of federal drug laws had more draconian sentencing possibilities. More important, federal prosecutions could result in making an offender disappear. Conviction in federal court resulted in being sent to a federal facility anywhere in the country. State prosecutions only resulted in incarceration within the state allowing the offender to maintain contact with his neighborhood and criminal associates. More significantly, federal assistance brought law enforcement support from the DEA and the FBI. Under Reagan, federal support also gave local police agencies access to military bases in which they received military training (SWAT training), equipment, and criminal intelligence training and technical support under the ***Military Cooperation with Civilian Law Enforcement Agencies Act of 1981.***

The result of the federal assistance, the Black community suffered increases in prosecution of Blacks for low-level possession of crack cocaine with minimum mandatory sentences in federal prisons. Urban communities were besieged with militarized police units, special drug units, joint federal state and local drug forces, and militarized drug warrant units comprised of federal and local officers, as well as special probation/parole police units, which had the authority to enter the homes of people on probation and parole without the need for warrants *en masse* from the late 1980s through the 1990s under President Reagan, followed by Presidents Bush and Clinton. The Black community was under siege either by crack violence on one side or federal and local law enforcement on the other. The target of attention, from either side, was the young Black male. Drug gangs sought Black males as either participants or clients, and law enforcement sought them as targets for arrest, imprisonment, and their property as sources of revenue through asset forfeiture.

To make this dynamic all the worse, the Democrats had surrendered to the Republicans the argument on the causes of crime and they were in active competition with the Republicans on who could be tougher on crime. The political ground of "tough on crime" that was owned by the Republicans in the late 1970s and early 1980s was now open to dispute by the Democratic Party by the late 1980s and 1990s. Neither party talked about the root causes of crime, and neither party advocated Great Society solutions to the crack epidemic in the Black community. Under both parties, the answer was to let the prison building begin, both full well knowing who was ending up in them.

The plague of crack cocaine also provided evidence of the general perception of Blacks as criminals, that they were out of control, and that they had to be put under control. According to Dan Baum of *Harper's Magazine*, this view of Blacks was the true reason for Nixon's War on Drugs. Baum wrote in an April 2016 article[42] that, in a 1994 interview with **John Ehrlichman**, the Nixon Administration used the **War on Drugs** as a cover to deal with what they perceived as social threats to his silent majority. Baum directly quotes Ehrlichman as saying,

> The Nixon campaign in 1968, and the Nixon White House after that, had two enemies: the antiwar left and black people. You understand what I'm saying? We knew we couldn't make it illegal to be either against the war or black, but **by getting the public to associate** the hippies with marijuana and **blacks with heroin,** and then criminalizing both heavily, we could disrupt those communities. **We could** arrest their leaders, raid their homes, break up their meetings, and **vilify them night after night on the evening news**. Did we know we were lying about the drugs? Of course we did.

The point is less about whether Ehrlichman actually said this, but the fact that what he said actually occurred in the 1980s and 1990s. Black homes were raided, Black communities were disrupted, and Blacks were vilified night after night on the evening news. The belief by many within the Black community that the government allowed heroin and later crack cocaine to settle in Black communities in order to give the government the justification to unleash law enforcement and the criminal justice system with the goal to incarcerate Blacks disproportionately is a deep-seated belief, and it colors how Blacks view crime control advocates. Putting Ehrlichman's statement in historical context with peonage, criminal surety, and convict leasing, the belief is not unreasonable.

---

42 Dan Baum, "Legalize It All: How to win the war on drugs," *Harper's Magazine* (April 2016) at https://harpers.org/archive/2016/04/legalize-it-all/. For commentary on why the statement can be believed, see Erik Sherman, "Nixon's Drug War, An Excuse To Lock Up Blacks And Protesters, Continues," *Forbes Magazine* (March 23, 2016) at https://www.forbes.com/sites/eriksherman/2016/03/23/nixons-drug-war-an-excuse-to-lock-up-blacks-and-protesters-continues/#5333aaec42c8

But regardless of its origin, crack was a plague in the Black community, and my point is not that crack was not a problem that needed attention, but the only attention it got was cops, courts, and corrections. Only the hammer of government and the unleased warrior cop philosophy was applied to the problem. Politically, that could be done, because crack was viewed as a Black drug and a Black crime. The fact that Whites used crack by the late 1980s and 1990s equally to Blacks was lost in the politics of crime control. News stories of crack babies[43] born addicted to crack and mothers abandoning them *en masse* for the need to get the next crack high were a nightly event. The entertainment industry in movies and rap music that romanticized the use of crack in the 1990s just made the problem all the worse with rap artists and movies glorifying those who sold crack as being authentically Black.

Between 1991 and 1995 under the George H.W. Bush and Clinton Administrations, Blacks accounted 51% of the total U.S. prison population. In 1994, America broke the one million mark of people incarcerated in federal and state prisons. The 1990s was the high-water mark in the get tough on crime rhetoric and policies of the *second punitive era*. No politician could get elected if they were perceived as soft on crime. Justice Department grants required state criminal justice policies and programs be geared to deal with serious violent crime. During this period, catch phrases like "super predators" and "adult time for adult crime" supported policies for treating juveniles as adults for certain types of crimes and the general political attack on the operating principle of juvenile court (rehabilitation). This period also saw the overall nationwide abandonment of parole through "truth in sentencing" statutes that required both mandatory and minimum sentences for certain crimes, which removed judicial discretion in setting prison terms and fostered overcrowding.

The Bush Administration: The Reagan Years Continue—"We Will Build More Prisons"

President George H.W. Bush continued the trend established by President Reagan. Soon after assuming the presidency, on September 5, 1989, President Bush announced from the White House a new strategy[44] focusing on crack cocaine:

> Good evening. This is the first time since taking the oath of office that I felt an issue was so important, so threatening, that it warranted talking directly with you, the American people. All of us agree that the gravest domestic threat facing our nation today is drugs. ... Our most serious problem today is cocaine, and in particular, crack.
>
> ...
>
> This is crack cocaine seized a few days ago by Drug Enforcement agents in a park just across the street from the White House.

43 See Jason E. Glenn, "The Birth of the Crack Baby and the History that "Myths" Make" (2006) at https://biblio.csusm.edu/sites/default/files/reserves/birth_of_the_crack_baby_and_the_history_that_myths_make.pdf

44 George H.W. Bush Address to the Nation on the National Drug Control Strategy September 5, 1989, at http://www.presidency.ucsb.edu/ws/?pid=17472

Bush released the **1989 National Drug Control Strategy**. "Earlier today, I sent this document, our first such national strategy, to the Congress."[45] This speech was made famous when Bush held up a DEA evidence bag of crack cocaine and said this crack was bought a block away from the White House as evidence that crack was openly available everywhere in America. The speech then became embroiled in scandal when it was reported that the DEA, under White House orders, arraigned for a drug dealer to go to the park by the White House to sell the crack. The DEA had to give the drug dealer directions because he had never been the park before. The scandal notwithstanding, Bush had made his point—crack was a national law enforcement problem and it would receive national law enforcement response.

Theatrics aside, President Bush continued the policy of President Reagan that drugs, and crack specifically, was to be controlled by crime control policies. Bush made clear

> [b]ecause we changed our national attitude toward drugs, casual drug use has declined. We have many to thank: our brave law enforcement officers, religious leaders, teachers, community activists, and leaders of business and labor. We should also thank the media for their exhaustive news and editorial coverage and for their air time and space for antidrug messages. And finally, I want to thank President and Mrs. Reagan for their leadership. All of these good people told the truth: that drug use is wrong and dangerous.
>
> ...
>
> Tonight, I'm announcing a strategy that reflects the coordinated, cooperative commitment of all our Federal agencies. ...
>
> **First, we are determined to enforce the law, to make our streets and neighborhoods safe. So, to start, I'm proposing that we more than double Federal assistance to State and local law enforcement**. Americans have a right to safety in and around their homes. And we won't have safe neighborhoods unless we're tough on drug criminals—much tougher than we are now. Sometimes that means **tougher penalties**, but more often it just means **punishment that is swift and certain**. We've all heard stories about drug dealers who are caught and arrested again and again but never punished. Well, here **the rules have changed**: If you sell drugs, **you will be caught**. And when you're caught, **you will be prosecuted**. And once you're convicted, **you will do time**. Caught—prosecuted—punished.
>
> I'm also proposing that we enlarge our criminal justice system across the board—at the local, State, and Federal levels alike. **We need more prisons, more jails, more courts, more prosecutors.** So, tonight **I'm requesting**—all together—an almost **$1.5 billion increase in drug-related Federal spending on law enforcement.**

President Bush was clear in who would be on the receiving end of this enhanced law enforcement, crime control, and use of prisons approach to deal with crack cocaine. ***Bush stated quite simply***, "while ***illegal drug use*** is found in every community, ***nowhere*** is it ***worse than in our public housing projects***." Public housing, for various reasons, concentrated ***poor Blacks***

45 See National Drug Policy 1989 at https://www.ncjrs.gov/pdffiles1/ondcp/119466.pdf

in geographically ***poor neighborhoods. More prosecutors, more jails, more courts were unleashed on them.*** The president made clear that "Congress needs not only to act on this national drug strategy but also to act on our crime package announced last May, a package to ***toughen sentences, beef up law enforcement***, and ***build new prison space*** for 24,000 inmates." Additionally, the President explained, "You and I both know the Federal Government can't do it alone. ***The States need*** to match tougher Federal laws with ***tougher laws of their own***: stiffer bail, probation, parole, and sentencing."

After requesting a $1.5 billion increase in law enforcement and $65 million in emergency funding to support international drug interdiction and crop eradication in Columbia, Bush asked for $321 million in Federal spending on drug treatment. Although Bush advocated for treatment, it was with a crime control perspective. In addition to funding treatment, he advocated for zero tolerance treatment of people addicted to drugs:

> The third part of our strategy concerns drug treatment. Experts believe that there are 2 million American drug users who may be able to get off drugs with proper treatment, but right now only 40 percent of them are actually getting help. This is simply not good enough. Many people who need treatment won't seek it on their own, and some who do seek it are put on a waiting list. Most programs were set up to deal with heroin addicts, but today the major problem is cocaine users. It's time we expand our treatment systems and do a better job of providing services to those who need them.
>
> Fourth, we must stop illegal drug use before it starts. Unfortunately, it begins early—for many kids, before their teens. But it doesn't start the way you might think, from a dealer or an addict hanging around a school playground. More often, our kids first get their drugs free, from friends or even from older brothers or sisters. Peer pressure spreads drug use; peer pressure can help stop it. I am proposing a quarter-of-a-billion-dollar increase in Federal funds for school and community prevention programs that help young people and adults reject enticements to try drugs. And I'm proposing something else. Every school, college, and university, and every workplace must adopt tough but fair policies about drug use by students and employees. And those that will not adopt such policies will not get Federal funds—period!

The president, in total, asked Congress for $8 billion in additional spending to deal with drugs and crack cocaine. He asked Congress for stronger law enforcement support and tougher laws. He was not rebuffed.

On November 29, 1990, President Bush signed the ***Crime Control Act of 1990***, which focused on victims' rights (*Criminal Victims Protection Act of 1990*) and provided federal grants and funding for anti-drug task forces. But most significantly, Title Nine of the act (*Mandatory Detention for Offenders Convicted of Serious Crimes Act of 1990*) required mandatory detention for convicted drug offenders facing ten years or more who had filed for appeal of convictions, and Title Thirty provided support for placement of offenders facing twelve to thirty months' incarceration to accept in the alternative incarceration in a military type boot camp (shock incarceration) for six months followed by release. Bush also signed the ***National Defense Authorization Act of 1990***, which authorized the Pentagon to provide local police departments with surplus military equipment. The ***section 1208 program*** provided such equipment for anti-drug operations. The 1208 program, which expanded military partnerships with local police authorized by President Reagan in 1981, was expanded from anti-drug operations to any and all bona fide police uses by President Clinton in 1997.

President Bush continued to fertilize the ground for establishing the national policy of punitive drug sanctions to address illegal drug use. President Bush continued the Reagan Administration strategy of focusing on demand and on Nancy Reagan's focus on adolescent and teen demand for drugs. In a national televised Nancy Reagan–type speech geared towards teens, President Bush focused on the moral issues of drugs and asserted that drugs were evil, they bring death and destruction, they bring crime, and they are the cause of babies being born with physical defects that affect them for the rest of their lives. President Bush made the case that drugs were evil and that alone should deter youth from using it or tolerating those who do. The carrot of morality was followed by the stick of criminal justice punishment as a supplemental reason to avoid drugs. The president told his adolescent audience things had changed regarding how the criminal justice system would deal with drug dealers and users.

> But if that's not enough reason, there's another side: Using illegal drugs is against the law. And if you break the law, you pay the price. Because **the rules have changed. If you do drugs you will be caught, and when you're caught you will be punished.** You might lose your driver's license—some States have started revoking users' driving privileges. Or you might lose the college loan you wanted—because we're not helping those who break the law. These are privileges, not rights. And if you risk doing drugs, you risk everything, even your freedom. Because you will be punished.

What also had changed was the government policy towards drug sellers:

> Now, I can imagine a few whispers out there: Maybe you think we'll never get drugs under control, that it's too easy for the dealers to get back on the street. Well, those days are over, too. The revolving door just jammed. **Some think there won't be room for them in jail. We'll make room. We're almost doubling prison space.** Some think there aren't enough prosecutors. We'll hire them, with the largest increase in Federal prosecutors in history. The day of the dealer is drawing to a close.[46]

Under the crime control model, the drug user and the drug dealer ("pusher") were dealt with in the same way, both were criminals, and both were a plague on society that must be addressed with punishment. As the president made clear in his State of the Union Address to Congress in January 1989,

46 George H.W. Bush, Address to Students on Drug Abuse September 12, 1989, at http://www.presidency.ucsb.edu/ws/index.php?pid=17509&st=students&st1

> [t]here are few clear areas in which we as a society must rise up united and express our intolerance. The most obvious now is drugs. And when that first cocaine was smuggled in on a ship, it may as well have been a deadly bacteria, so much has it hurt the body, the soul of our country. And there is much to be done and to be said, but take my word for it: **This scourge will stop!**

President Bush backed up this rhetoric with the issuance of the ***March 13, 1989 Plea Policy for Federal Prosecutors memo*** which ordered U.S. Attorneys to use the process of plea bargaining to extract the most serious sanctions from defendants. According to the memo, "The basic policy is that charges are not to be bargained away or dropped, unless the prosecutor has a good faith doubt as to the government's ability readily to prove a charge for legal or evidentiary reasons. … The policy is to bring cases that the government should win if there were a trial."[47] The policy instructed U.S. Attorneys that "the Department will expect plea bargains to support, not undermine, the guidelines. Once prosecutors have indicted, they should find themselves bargaining about charges which they have determined are readily provable and reflect the seriousness of the defendant's conduct."[48] "In sum, plea bargaining, both charge bargaining and sentence bargaining, is legitimate. But, such bargaining must honestly reflect the totality and seriousness of the defendant's conduct and any departure to which the prosecutor is agreeing, and must be accomplished through appropriate guideline provisions."[49]

On May 19, 1989, the president issued a fact sheet that announced the Justice Department policy.

> If our criminal justice system is to achieve its objective of ensuring that those who commit violent firearms offenses are held fully accountable for their actions, plea bargaining practices nationwide must be reformed. Too often, serious felons walk away from court after pleading guilty to minor offenses and misdemeanors because overburdened prosecutors have accepted plea agreements rather than going to trial. The lesser charges result in lesser sentences or probation, and repeat offenders continue to beat the system. To speed an end to such plea bargaining:
>
> 1. The President directed the Attorney General to issue and fully implement guidelines for Federal prosecutors regarding plea bargaining under the Sentencing Reform Act to ensure that Federal charges always reflect both the seriousness of the defendant's conduct and the Department's commitment to statutory sentencing goals and procedures. This

---

47 United States Department of Justice, "March 13, 1989 Memorandum from Dick Thornburgh, Attorney General, to Federal Prosecutors, Plea Bargaining Under the Sentencing Reform Act" at, https://www.fd.org/sites/default/files/criminal_defense_topics/essential_topics/sentencing_resources/useful_reports/thornburgh_memos_3.13.89_and_6.16.89.pdf. *Federal Sentencing Reporter* 1, no. 9 (Apr., 1989): 421–23, 421.

48 United States Department of Justice, "March 13, 1989 Plea Policy for Federal Prosecutors"

49 United States Department of Justice, "March 13, 1989 Plea Policy for Federal Prosecutors "

> will ensure that Federal prosecutors seek minimum mandatory penalties for all violent firearms offenses.
> 2. The President urged State and local governments to reform their plea bargaining and sentencing practices along similar lines and to devote increased resources to prosecutions.[50]

The White House announcement of the policy was more emphatic than the actual Justice Department policy on rejecting plea bargaining to reduce workload, because the Justice Department policy made clear that

> Second, federal prosecutors may drop readily provable charges. ... This exception recognizes that the aims of the Sentencing Reform Act must be sought without ignoring other, critical aspects of the federal criminal justice system. For example, approval to drop charges in a particular case might be given because the United States Attorney's office is particularly overburdened, the case would be time-consuming to try, and proceeding to trial would significantly reduce the total number of cases disposed of by the office.[51]

But nonetheless, the policy was designed to support the purpose and outcome of the sentencing guidelines. Because federal sanctions under the guidelines can be draconian and result in decades, if not life, for non-homicide or violent criminal acts, defendants are inclined to take pleas, rather than risk the full weight of mandatory sanctions after convictions. The Bush Administration policy goal of securing from the defendant an acceptance of the most seriously charged felony count resulted in significantly increased length of time federal prisoners remaining in prison.

President Bush's impact on the "get tough" policies of the late 1980s was limited, because he only had one term. But, the president gave significant support to laying the foundation of the get-tough policies that would govern the 1990s. President Bush's support for a crime control approach to drugs and violence and the support for police strike forces and increased prosecutions of drug users, along with significant building of prisons, all made palatable the result of disproportionate incarceration of Blacks. The drug war was a war on crack dealers and gangs—which, in the public consciousness, meant young Black males. Thus, dropping the full power of the criminal justice and law enforcement machine on the heads of Blacks garnered little sympathy. Bush's successor, a Democrat, took hold of the well-plowed land made clear by his predecessor. President Clinton signed legislation and advocated for policies in congruence with those of President Reagan that resulted in the incarceration of Blacks and that lasted for more than a decade after he left office.

---

50 White House Fact Sheet on Combating Violent Crime May 15, 1989, at http://www.presidency.ucsb.edu/ws/?pid=17030

51 United States Department of Justice, "March 13, 1989 Plea Policy for Federal Prosecutors" at 422.

The Clinton Administration: Democrats Take Command of the Get Tough on Crime Landscape

Since the late 1960s, the Democratic Party was stigmatized by the label that it was soft on crime. It was the party of President Johnson, the Great Society, welfare, and protection of the due process rights of murderers and rapists. It was the party of opposition to the rights of victims and the strengthening the power of police to be the thin blue line of civilization against the advancement of the jungle. President Clinton successfully changed that narrative. After winning the presidency, Clinton's contribution to the "get tough" policies of the 1990s was the passage of a comprehensive crime bill that rivaled the one signed by President Reagan in 1984.

In his first formal State of the Union Address on January 25, 1994, Clinton took control of the "get tough on crime" politics from the exclusive ownership by Republicans:

> But while Americans are more secure from threats abroad, I think we all know that in many ways we are less secure from threats here at home. Every day the national peace is shattered by crime. In Petaluma, California, an innocent slumber party gives way to agonizing tragedy for the family of Polly Klaas. An ordinary train ride on Long Island ends in a hail of 9-millimeter rounds. A tourist in Florida is nearly burned alive by bigots simply because he is black. Right here in our Nation's Capital, a brave young man named Jason White, a policeman, the son and grandson of policemen, is ruthlessly gunned down. Violent crime and the fear it provokes are crippling our society, limiting personal freedom, and fraying the ties that bind us.
>
> The crime bill before Congress gives you a chance to do something about it, a chance to be tough and smart. What does that mean? Let me begin by saying I care a lot about this issue. Many years ago, when I started out in public life, I was the attorney general of my State. I served as a Governor for a dozen years. I know what it's like to sign laws increasing penalties, to build more prison cells, to carry out the death penalty. I understand this issue. And it is not a simple thing.
>
> **First, we must recognize that most violent crimes are committed by a small percentage of criminals who too often break the laws even when they are on parole.** Now those who commit crimes should be punished. **And those who commit repeated violent crimes should be told**, "When you commit a third violent crime, you will be put away, and put away for good; **three strikes and you are out.**"
>
> **Second,** we must take serious steps to reduce violence and prevent crime, beginning with **more police officers** and more community policing. We know right now that police who work the streets, know the folks, have the respect of the neighborhood kids, focus on high crime areas, we know that they are more likely to prevent crime as well as catch criminals. Look at the experience of Houston, where the crime rate dropped 17 percent in one year when that approach was taken.
>
> ...
>
> You have before you crime legislation which also establishes a police corps to encourage young people to get an education and pay it off by serving as police officers; which

> encourages retiring military personnel to move into police forces, an inordinate resource for our country; one which has a safe schools provision which will give our young people the chance to walk to school in safety and to be in school in safety instead of dodging bullets. These are important things.
>
> **The third thing** we have to do is to build on **the Brady bill**. ... There is no sporting purpose on Earth that should stop the United States Congress from banishing assault weapons that out-gun police and cut down children.
>
> **Fourth,** we must remember that drugs are a factor in an enormous percentage of crimes. Recent studies indicate, sadly, that drug use is on the rise again among our young people. The crime bill contains—all the crime bills contain—more money for **drug treatment** for criminal addicts and **boot camps** for youthful offenders that include incentives to get off drugs and to stay off drugs. Our administration's budget, with all its cuts, contains a large increase in funding for drug treatment and drug education. You must pass them both. We need them desperately.
>
> My fellow Americans, the problem of violence is an American problem. It has no partisan or philosophical element. Therefore, I urge you to find ways as quickly as possible to set aside partisan differences and pass a strong, smart, tough crime bill. But further, I urge you to consider this: As you demand tougher penalties for those who choose violence, let us also remember how we came to this sad point. In our toughest neighborhoods, on our meanest streets, in our poorest rural areas, we have seen a stunning and simultaneous breakdown of community, family, and work, the heart and soul of civilized society. This has created a vast vacuum which has been filled by violence and drugs and gangs. So I ask you to remember that even as we say no to crime, we must give people, especially our young people, something to say yes to.

President Clinton got his crime bill eight months later. His rhetoric on the social factors that contributed to and created crime found much less support, both from Congress and in time from his administration.

The Violent Crime and Law Enforcement Act of 1994, which President Clinton signed on September 13, 1994, was a comprehensive crime control theory inspired piece of legislation. The Act ***eliminated Pell Grants for prisoners***, thus ending the ability for prisoners to gain a college education while in prison. The Pell grant elimination would remain until restored under ***the Second Chance Pell Experiment*** under the Obama Administration in 2015. Title Four of the Act, the ***Violence Against Women Act of 1994***, established federal funding to prevent domestic violence, and it granted women who suffered violence with the ability to sue for civil damages in federal court. The act also increased the number of crimes that could receive the federal death penalty, ***required states to track sex offenders*** (*Jacob Wetterling Crimes Against Children and Sexually Violent Offender Registration Act of 1994*), and put a ***ban on the sale of semi-automatic and assault weapons*** (*The Public Safety and Recreational Firearms Act of 1994*). The Act, through Community Oriented Policing Services Grants, sought to ***put***

100,000 police officers on the street. The program provided funding for police agencies to increase the number officers dedicated to community policing.

In his 1994 State of the Union speech Clinton, as did presidents Bush, Reagan, and Nixon, before him, complained that convicted offenders were not being punished. Clinton sought to change this by linking federal funds to state laws that increased the percentage of time offenders were incarcerated. President Reagan's abandonment of federal parole in 1984 was now supplemented by state government abandonment of parole under Clinton's crime control law in 1994. The Act established the ***Violent Offender Incarceration and Truth in Sentencing (VOI-TIS) program***, which provided special federal grants to states that provide

> assurances that the State has implemented, or will implement, correctional policies and programs, including ***truth-in-sentencing laws that ensure that violent offenders serve a substantial portion of the sentences imposed***, that are designed to provide sufficiently severe punishment for violent offenders, including violent juvenile offenders, and that the prison time served is appropriately related to the determination that the inmate is a violent offender and for a period of time deemed necessary to protect the public.[52]

States complied by passing laws that required prisoners to serve at least 85% of their sentence before being eligible for parole.[53] In Fiscal Year (FY) 1996 the VOI-TIS grant awarded $65,252,476 to states that passed truth-in-sentencing laws, in FY2001 $435,273,543 was awarded, and between FY1996 and 2001, a total of $2,707,534,780 was awarded to the states.[54] The *VOI-TIS grant* effectively ended parole from American criminal justice.

But the crowning jewel of the ***Violent Crime and Law Enforcement Act of 1994*** was the ***three strikes*** provision. Codified under 18 USC § 3559(c) Imprisonment of Certain Violent Felons the statute imposed a life sentence for a violent felony if the convict had two prior serious felony convictions or two drug convictions.

> (1) Notwithstanding any other provision of law, a person who is convicted in a court of the United States of a serious violent felony shall be sentenced to life imprisonment if—
> (A) the person has been convicted (and those convictions have become final) on separate prior occasions in a court of the United States or of a State of—
> (i) 2 or more serious violent felonies; or
> (ii) one or more serious violent felonies and one or more serious drug offenses; and
> (B) each serious violent felony or serious drug offense used as a basis for sentencing under this subsection, other than the first, was committed after the defendant's conviction of the preceding serious violent felony or serious drug offense

52 42 U.S. Code § 13703(a)—Violent offender incarceration grants

53 BJA, *Report to Congress: Violent Offender Incarceration and Truth-In-Sentencing Incentive Formula Grant Program* (February 2012) at 3

54 BJA, *Report to Congress: Violent Offender Incarceration and Truth-In-Sentencing Incentive Formula Grant Program* (February 2012) at 2.

The Clinton Administration viewed the three-strikes statute as a key tool in dealing with violent crime. In like manner of the Bush Justice Department memo on plea bargaining on March 13, 1989, On March 13, 1995, the Clinton Justice Department issued a memo[55] instructing U.S. Attorneys that the three-strikes law "should play a key role in every district's anti-violent crime strategy" in order to "to take violent criminals off the streets" through coordination with state and local prosecutors. The memo summarized that the administration's ***Anti-Violent Crime Initiative***, which had "long used the Armed Career Criminal Act, 18 U.S.C. § 924(e), to achieve the prolonged incarceration of armed, violent offenders" was now supplemented by "a powerful new federal tool, the so-called "Three Strikes, You're Out" provision, to help us deal with violent repeat offenders." The three-strikes statute, the memo asserted "provides a vehicle to take the most dangerous offenders out of the community and keep them out. This is particularly important in states where prison overcrowding results in early release even for violent criminals."

Clinton Administration policy authorized U.S. Attorneys to use three strikes on non-federal violators by transferring offenders to the federal system and reducing state overcrowding legal problems. The memo instructed U.S. Attorneys that any serious violent crime, defined as "murder, manslaughter, sex offenses, kidnapping, robbery, and any offense punishable by 10 years or more which includes as an element the use of force or that, by its nature, involves a significant risk of force," as well as unarmed robbery and the "distribution, manufacture, or possession with intent to distribute significant quantities of controlled substances, or equivalent state offenses" were covered under the three-strikes statute. The memo concluded that

> [f]urthermore, you should aggressively use all available federal violent felony provisions, including the Hobbs Act, to achieve prolonged incarceration for "Three Strikes"-eligible defendants. Under 18 U.S.C. § 1951, the Hobbs Act covers a robbery that in any way affects interstate commerce, including the robbery of a convenience store or other commercial establishment. While the Department has promoted use of the Hobbs Act robbery provision primarily in cases involving criminal organizations or gangs, you also should consider using it where a defendant's criminal history would support a life sentence under "Three Strikes." These decisions, of course, should be carefully coordinated with state and local prosecutors, taking into account the availability in each case of a state statute that will result in prolonged incarceration of the defendant. The Hobbs Act also prohibits an attempt or conspiracy to commit such a robbery.

Under these instructions, it was Clinton Administration policy for the three-strikes law to be utilized to apply to almost any state offense with the specific objective of increasing incarceration.

---

55 Jo Ann Harris Assistant Attorney General, *Memorandum for all Unites States Attorneys Subject: Three Strikes* March 13, 1995, at https://www.justice.gov/usam/criminal-resource-manual-1032-sentencing-enhancement-three-strikes-law

The VOI-TIS truth-in-sentencing grants, along with the three-strikes law and the Clinton Administration policy of applying it, ushered in the nationwide passage of state statutes and prosecutorial policies that increased prison populations. These new statutes and prosecution policies contributed to longer sentences for inmates through plea bargain-based convictions in which defendants pled guilty to avoid more stringent sanctions after trial because they were declared three-strike eligible. As to its impact, in states like California with stringent three-strike laws, "African-Americans comprise[d] 31% of inmates in the state's prisons, but 37% of offenders convicted under two strikes and 44% of three strikes offenders."[56]

Although the *Violent Crime and Law Enforcement Act of 1994* was a crime-control oriented piece of legislation, it did include legislation that authorized the U.S. Justice Department to file civil cases against police agencies that demonstrated a pattern and practice of violation of civil rights. Codified under ***42 USC §14141*** Cause of Action Police Pattern or Practice:

> (a) Unlawful conduct
>
> It shall be unlawful for any governmental authority, or any agent thereof, or any person acting on behalf of a governmental authority, to engage in a pattern or practice of conduct by law enforcement officers or by officials or employees of any governmental agency with responsibility for the administration of juvenile justice or the incarceration of juveniles that deprives persons of rights, privileges, or immunities secured or protected by the Constitution or laws of the United States.
>
> (b) Civil action by Attorney General
>
> Whenever the Attorney General has reasonable cause to believe that a violation of paragraph (1) has occurred, the Attorney General, for or in the name of the United States, may in a civil action obtain appropriate equitable and declaratory relief to eliminate the pattern or practice.

Section 14141 was passed in the wake of the Rodney King beating on March 3, 1991 and the subsequent riots in Los Angles on April 29 through May 4, 1992, when the officers were acquitted by an almost all-White jury.

Section 14141 provides the Justice Department with civil enforcement authority to enforce the three predominant federal laws prohibiting discrimination: ***Title VI of the 1964 Civil Rights Act*** ("No person in the United States shall, on the ground of race, color, or national origin, be excluded from participation in, be denied the benefits of, or be subjected to discrimination under any program or activity receiving Federal financial assistance"), the ***Omnibus Crime Control and Safe Streets Act of 1968*** ("No person in any State shall on the ground of race, color, religion, national origin, or sex be excluded from participation in, be denied the benefits of, or be subjected to discrimination under or denied employment in connection

56 Walter J. Dickey and Pam Hollenhorst, "Three-Strikes Laws: Five Years Later," *Corrections Management* 3, no. 3 (1999): 1, 3.

with any programs or activity funded in whole or in part with funds made available under this chapter."), and ***Title II of the Americans with Disabilities Act of 1990*** ("no qualified individual with a disability shall, by reason of such disability, be excluded from participation in or be denied the benefits of the services, programs, or activities of a public entity, or be subjected to discrimination by any such entity.")[57]

The Omnibus Crime Control and Safe Streets Act of 1968 authorized the Justice Department to file civil lawsuits when police violated rights based on a racial or religious basis. Originally codified as § 3789d(c)(E) and now codified in 41 USC §10228(c)(2)(E) Civil Action by Attorney General, the 1968 legislation established that

> Whenever the Attorney General files a civil action alleging a pattern or practice of discriminatory conduct … the Office of Justice Programs shall cause to have suspended further payment of any funds under this chapter to that specific program or activity alleged by the Attorney General to be in violation of the provisions of this subsection until such time as the court orders resumption of payment.

Both sections 14141 and 10228 provide the Attorney General with the authority to seek consent decrees between the Justice Department and a police agency to change its practices when they are found to be discriminatory. The role of the court is to make sure that any mutually agreed upon consent decree addresses the asserted discriminatory practice and the resolutions provide an "appropriate equitable and declaratory relief to eliminate the pattern or practice"[58] and that "the agreement is fair, adequate, and reasonable and is not illegal, a product of collusion, or against the public interest."[59] In the event consent decrees cannot be mutually secured, the Justice Department can seek court orders mandating changes in an agency's discriminatory practice or policy. Conservative complaints notwithstanding, these laws do not authorize and seek to allow the Justice Department to take over the operations of local police agency. As section 10228(a) makes clear

> (a) General rule
> Nothing in this chapter or any other Act shall be construed to authorize any department, agency, officer, or employee of the United States to exercise any direction, supervision,

57 The 1964 Civil Rights Act, 42 U.S.C. § 2000d, Omnibus Crime Control and Safe Streets Act of 1968, 42 U.S.C. § 3789d(c)(1) and Title II of the Americans with Disabilities Act of 1990, 42 U.S.C. § 12132. For an example of a 14141 complaint see, Justice Department complaint against the Baltimore Police Department on January 12, 2017 at http://www.mdd.uscourts.gov./sites/mdd/files/Complaint-JKB-17-99.pdf. The city of Baltimore and the Baltimore Police Department entered a mutual agreed upon consent decree with the Justice Department on April 7, 2017. See, *United States v. Baltimore Police Department, Memorandum and Order* (April 7, 2017) http://www.mdd.uscourts.gov./sites/mdd/files/OrderEnteringConsentDecree.pdf

58 Violent Crime Control and Law Enforcement Act of 1994,42 USC §14141(b)

59 *United States v. Baltimore Police Department, Memorandum and Order* (April 7, 2017) at 2 (internal citation omitted).

> or control over any police force or any other criminal justice agency of any State or any political subdivision thereof.

Under section 14141 the Justice Department can secure a court order requiring the local agency to change its policies of discrimination, if a voluntary consent decree is not agreed upon, and failure of the agency to comply with the court order can result in the court exercising its equitable powers to enforce its orders which can include placing the police agency in receivership.[60] Under ***receivership*** an agency can be placed under direct control of a receiver appointed by the court to enforce the court order and make changes to the agency pursuant to that order.[61] To determine whether a police agency should be placed under receivership the court must determine,

> (1) Whether there is a grave and immediate threat or actuality of harm to plaintiffs;
> (2) Whether the use of less extreme measures of remediation have been exhausted or prove futile;
> (3) Whether continued insistence that compliance with the Court's orders would lead only to confrontation and delay;
> (4) Whether there is a lack of leadership to turn the tide within a reasonable period of time;
> (5) Whether there is bad faith;
> (6) Whether resources are being wasted; and
> (7) Whether a receiver is likely to provide a relatively quick and efficient remedy.

The first two factors holding the predominant weight.[62] Receivership is an extraordinary remedy to a police agency failure to comply with a court order and in fashioning an appropriate remedy for failure to comply with a court order, "the Court must exercise restraint, using the least possible power adequate to the remediation of constitutional violations. However, the Court is not required to restrict its powers to those means that have proven inadequate, or that show no promise of being fruitful. Rather, as the Supreme Court has held, federal courts are not reduced to issuing injunctions against state officers and hoping for compliance. Once issued, an injunction may be enforced."[63]

---

60 For example, see Case note, "Receivership as a Remedy in Civil Rights Cases," *Rutgers Law Review* 24, no. 1 (1969): 115, and Robert F. Nagel "Separation of Powers and the Scope of Federal Equitable Remedies," *Stanford Law Review* 30, no. 4 (1978): 661.

61 Liat Weingart, "Receiverships in the Prison Litigation Context: Factors Necessary for An Effective Judicial Remedy of last resort," *Cardozo Public Law Policy and Ethics Journal* 9 (2010): 193, and Schlanger, Margo, "Plata v. Brown and Realignment: Jails, Prisons, Courts, and Politics," *Harvard Civil Rights-Civil Liberties Law* Review 48, no. 1 (2013): 165.

62 *Plata v. Schwarzenegger* 2005 U.S. Dist. LEXIS 43796, at * 66–67, 2005 WL 2932253, at *23.

63 *Plata v. Schwarzenegger* at LEXIS 43796, at * 70, WL 2932253, at 24. Citing *Hutto v. Finney*, 437 U.S. 678, 690, 98 S. Ct. 2565, 57 L. Ed. 2d 522 (1979).

The power of the judiciary to enforce of its powers flows from its equity jurisdiction. To an argument that a district court acted outside its authority when it placed a state agency under receivership and that the state agency did not have the authority to act under a receiver's orders, the Supreme Court held that the "federal court unquestionably has the power to enter the various orders that state officials and private parties have chosen to ignore, and even to displace local enforcement ... if necessary to remedy the violation of federal law found by the Court. Even if those orders may have been erroneous in some respects, all parties have an unequivocal obligation to obey them while they remain in effect. ... [T]he District Court has the power to undertake the necessary remedial steps and to enlist the aid of the appropriate federal law enforcement agents in carrying out those steps. Moreover, the comments by the Court of Appeals strongly imply that it is prepared to uphold the use of stern measures to require respect for federal court orders."[64]

Regarding the enforcement and available ***readies for police violation of civil rights***, the remedies are ***three-fold. One, the civil authority of the Attorney General to sue*** local law enforcement agencies for practices and patterns of discrimination and abuse[65] (police use of force) under 42 USC §14141. This includes judicial authority to enforce a consent decree or court order. ***Two, private civil liability lawsuits***[66] through 42 USC §1983. ***Third, federal government pursuit of criminal culpability*** cases under 18 USC § 242. These three avenues form the sum total of legal remedies to police abuse of power.

Notwithstanding support for federal legislation to allow the Justice Department to take police agencies that violated civil rights of those most likely to be abused by the police, Blacks living in urban communities, to court, the Clinton Administration was clearly crime control oriented and it proved its credentials in 1995.

---

64 *Washington v. Washington State Commercial Passenger Fishing Vessel Assoc.*, 443 U.S. 658, 695–96 (1979)

65 For discussion on the impact of Justice Department civil litigation to change police operations and practices of discrimination and the utility of such litigation see story on the civil litigation brought against the Oakland Police Department. Kelly Kimbriell, Sarah Childress and Steven Rich, "Justice Department forces police reforms. But have they worked?" *The Washington Post* at http://www.washingtonpost.com/sf/investigative/2015/11/13/forced-reforms-mixed-results/?utm_term=.5188a0e6bcfa

66 For examples of private civil litigation to enforce court orders and address violations of civil rights by law enforcement agencies including the request for placing an agency under receivership see, *Jones and United States vs. Gusman*, Memorandum in Support of Plaintiffs' Motion for an Order to Show cause and Appointment of a Receiver to Implement Consent Judgment, Civil Action No. 2:12-cv-00859 4/25/2016 at http://neworleans.macarthurjusticecenter.org/uploads/rsmjc-neworleans/documents/2016-04-25_1007-2_memo_in_support.pdf. See also *United States v. Territory of the Virgin Islands*, Memorandum of Points and Authorities in Support of United States' Motion for Appointment of a Receiver pursuant to Fed. R. Civ. P. 66 and This Court's Equity Jurisdiction, Civil No. 86/265 6/9/2011 at https://www.justice.gov/sites/default/files/crt/legacy/2011/06/13/GoldenGrove_MemoinSupportMtnforReceiver.pdf

The support and passage of the *Violent Crime and Law Enforcement Act of 1994* and its impact on Black incarceration paled in comparison to Clinton directly overruling the U.S. Sentencing Commission recommendation that the one hundred to one ratio of crack to powder cocaine passed in 1986 should be changed. In 1995, the U.S. Sentencing Commission issued a report, ***Special Report to the Congress: Cocaine and Federal Sentencing Policy***, on cocaine and crack use and reviewed the various reasons justifying the one hundred to one ratio created in the *Anti-Drug Abuse Act of 1986* and found that cocaine was no more addictive than crack—that use of cocaine, whether smoked, snorted, injected or ingested produces the same psychological effect; and

> Blacks accounted for 88.3 percent of federal crack cocaine distribution convictions in 1993, Hispanics 7.1 percent, Whites 4.1 percent, and others 0.5 percent. The racial breakdown for powder cocaine distribution offenses sentenced in 1993 shows 32.0 percent White, 27.4 percent Black, 39.3 percent Hispanic, and 1.3 percent other. On the other hand, the 1991 Household Survey shows that 52 percent of those reporting crack use in the past year, as opposed to distribution, were White, 38 percent were Black, and 10 percent Hispanic; 75 percent of those reporting powder use in the past year were White, 15 percent were Black, and 10 percent Hispanic.[67]

The Commission concluded that

> Federal sentencing data leads to the inescapable conclusion that Blacks comprise the largest percentage of those affected by the penalties associated with crack cocaine. This does not mean, however, that the penalties are racially motivated. Clearly the penalties (both statutory and guideline-based) apply equally to similar defendants regardless of race. Many individual criminal statutes, when enforced, produce a pool of defendants who are not representative of the racial make-up of criminal law violators generally or of society. However, as all appellate courts have found, there is no evidence that Congress or the Sentencing Commission acted with any discriminatory intent in setting different statutory and guideline penalties for different forms of cocaine.
>
> Nevertheless, the high percentage of Blacks convicted of crack cocaine offenses is a matter of great concern to the Sentencing Commission. Penalties clearly must be racially neutral on their face and by design. The Sentencing Commission is committed to these goals. When one form of a drug can be rather easily converted to another form of the same drug and when that second form is punished at a quantity ratio 100 times greater than the original form, it would appear reasonable to require the existence of sufficient policy bases to support such a sentencing scheme regardless of racial impact. Moreover, when such an enhanced ratio for a particular form of a drug has a disproportionate effect

67 U.S. Sentencing Commission, *Special Report to the Congress: Cocaine and Federal Sentencing Policy* (Feb 1995) at vi–xi.

> on one segment of the population, it is particularly important that sufficient policy bases exist in support of the enhanced ratio.[68]

To address the disparity of crack to powder cocaine, the Commission proposed to establish guidelines that would use the impact of powder and crack cocaine on the community rather than focus exclusively on the one hundred to one ratio for sentencing decisions by the court.[69] "[T]he Sentencing Commission concludes that Congress's objectives with regard to punishing crack cocaine trafficking can be achieved more effectively without relying on the current federal sentencing scheme for crack cocaine offenses that includes the 100-to-1 quantity ratio." As to sentencing, the Commission proposed

> [a]s a priority matter upon completion of this report, the Sentencing Commission will further develop appropriately weighted guideline enhancements (i.e., specific offense characteristics, general adjustments, offender characteristics) corresponding to important offense and offender characteristics present in crack cases that justify higher sentences. The guidelines currently provide enhancements for a number of societal harms associated with crack; to the extent Congress factored in these same harms in establishing the 100-to-1 quantity ratio, double punishment occurs. If guideline enhancements cannot sufficiently account for harms associated with crack, the guidelines can provide an increased ratio through the base offense level. Workable guideline provisions can be developed to account fully for harms related to crack and powder cocaine without the difficulties associated with an automatic 100-to-1 ratio.
>
> In setting these guidelines, the Commission will consider, to the extent relevant to congressional concern and the purposes of sentencing as set forth at 18 U.S.C. § 3553(a)(2), the following: 1) the form of cocaine involved; 2) whether a firearm or other dangerous weapon was involved; 3) whether the offense resulted in serious bodily injury or death to another person; 4) the quantity of cocaine involved; 5) the extent to which the powder cocaine defendant knew the drug would be converted into crack; 6) the extent to which the offense involved systemic crime, that is, crime related to the drug's marketing, distribution, and control; 7) the extent to which the offense involved social harms, that is, harms associated with increased addictiveness, parental neglect, child and domestic abuse, and high risk sexual behaviors; 8) whether the offense involved the use or employment of any person under the age of 18; 9) whether the defendant performed a managerial or leadership role in the offense; 10) the defendant's prior criminal record; and 11) any

68 U.S. Sentencing Commission, *Special Report to the Congress: Cocaine and Federal Sentencing Policy* (Feb 1995) at xii

69 U.S. Sentencing Commission, *Special Report to the Congress: Cocaine and Federal Sentencing Policy* (Feb 1995) at xiv–xv

> other aggravating or mitigating factors necessary to ensure adequate and appropriate punishment for defendants convicted of cocaine offenses.[70]

President Clinton and Congress were having none of this. For the first time in the history of the Commission, Congress passed legislation rejecting a finding of the Commission.

On October 30, 1995, Clinton signed ***Public Law 104–38*** entitled ***To disapprove of amendments to the Federal Sentencing Guidelines relating to lowering of crack sentences and sentences for money laundering and transactions in property derived from unlawful activity.*** The act required the Commission to make the following recommendation to Congress,

> (A) the sentence imposed for trafficking in a quantity of crack cocaine should generally exceed the sentence imposed for trafficking in a like quantity of powder cocaine [and] The recommendations described in the preceding subsection [regarding the] ratio of crack cocaine to powder cocaine under the relevant statutes and guidelines [shall be] consistent with ... section 3553(a) of title 28 United States Code [Factors To Be Considered in Imposing a Sentence].

Clinton and Congress rejected the Commission's assertion that the application of the one hundred to one ratio and the factors to be used for sentencing is a "double punishment."

Upon signing the legislative rejection of the Commission and its findings, Clinton defended and asserted his "tough on crime" credentials:[71]

> Today I reject United States Sentencing Commission proposals that would equalize penalties for crack and powder cocaine distribution by dramatically reducing the penalties for crack. The Sentencing Commission would also reduce the penalties for money laundering by combining the guidelines on money laundering with those on transactions in unlawfully acquired property. I am opposed to both of these changes.
>
> Since I took office, my Administration has fought to stop drug abuse and to stamp out the crime and violence that are its constant companions. We are battling drug traffickers at every level of their networks—from the very top to the very bottom.
>
> The Cali Cartel, which pumped drugs into America with seeming impunity, is now on the run. We have intensified our efforts to work with drug producing countries to stop drugs from coming into the United States and to capture major drug traffickers. We told criminals convicted time and again for serious violent crimes or drug trafficking that from now on, its three strikes and you're out. And we established the death penalty for drug kingpins, because they should reap what they sow.

---

70 U.S. Sentencing Commission, *Special Report to the Congress: Cocaine and Federal Sentencing Policy* (Feb 1995)

71 William J. Clinton, Statement on Signing Legislation Rejecting U.S. Sentencing Commission Recommendations October 30, 1995, at http://www.presidency.ucsb.edu/ws/?pid=50716

> We are putting 100,000 police officers on America's streets. We banned assault weapons because America doesn't want drug dealers to be better armed than police officers. We are helping schools to rid themselves of guns, and we are also helping schools to prevent teenage drug use by teaching children about the dangers of drugs and gangs. And we support schools who test student athletes for drugs.
>
> All of this is beginning to work. For the first time in a very long time, crime has decreased around the country. But we cannot stop now.
>
> We have to send a constant message to our children that drugs are illegal, drugs are dangerous, drugs may cost you your life—and the penalties for dealing drugs are severe. I am not going to let anyone who peddles drugs get the idea that the cost of doing business is going down.

President Reagan said the exact same thing when he signed the *Anti-Drug Act of 1986*:

> Well, today it gives me great pleasure to sign legislation that reflects the total commitment of the American people and their government to fight the evil of drugs. Drug use extracts a high cost on America: the cost of suffering and unhappiness, particularly among the young; the cost of lost productivity at the workplace; and the cost of drug-related crime. Drug use is too costly for us not to do everything in our power, not just to fight it but to subdue it and conquer it. The magnitude of today's drug problem can be traced to past unwillingness to recognize and confront this problem. And the vaccine that's going to end the epidemic is a combination of tough laws—like the one we sign today—and a dramatic change in public attitude. We must be intolerant of drug use and drug sellers. We must be intolerant of drug use on the campus and at the workplace. We must be intolerant of drugs not because we want to punish drug users, but because we care about them and want to help them. This legislation is not intended as a means of filling our jails with drug users. What we must do as a society is identify those who use drugs, reach out to them, help them quit, and give them the support they need to live right.
>
> ...
>
> ... Nevertheless, today marks a major victory in our crusade against drugs—a victory for safer neighborhoods, a victory for the protection of the American family. The American people want their government to get tough and to go on the offensive. And that's exactly what we intend, with more ferocity than ever before.[72]

In the face of proved disproportionate incarceration of Blacks under the one hundred-to-one ratio, Clinton offered the following,

---

72 Ronald Reagan, Remarks on Signing the Anti-Drug Abuse Act of 1986, October 27, 1986 at http://www.presidency.ucsb.edu/ws/?pid=36654

> Trafficking in crack, and the violence it fosters, has a devastating impact on communities across America, especially inner-city communities. Tough penalties for crack trafficking are required because of the effect on individuals and families, related gang activity, turf battles, and other violence.
>
> Current law does require a substantial disparity between sentences for crack as compared to equal amounts of powder cocaine. Some adjustment is warranted, and the bill I am signing today, S. 1254, directs the Sentencing Commission to undertake additional review of these issues and to report back with new recommendations.
>
> Furthermore, the sentencing structure should reflect the fact that all crack starts as powder. When large-scale cocaine traffickers sell powder with the knowledge that it will be converted into crack, they should be punished as severely as those who distribute the crack itself. I have asked the Attorney General to immediately develop enforcement strategies to bring about this result. As I said before, we are going after drug traffickers at every level of their networks.

The two parties had found congruence. It would be a decade into the following century, fifteen years, before the one hundred to one ratio was addressed and changed by President Obama in 2010.

When Clinton ran for the presidency, he ran a political campaign that went out of its way to establish that he was not the pawn of liberal Black politicians to secure the vote of middle class and rural Whites. Yet, he was able to hold the traditional coalition of Democrats, which included Black urban voters. Clinton's political ability to hold Black votes and support while supporting "get tough" policies that he knew would have a disparate impact on Blacks is legendary within the annals of politics and political science. Clinton, as did Reagan, asserted that the primary goal of these policies was not to incarcerate Blacks disproportionately, but that was the exact result. Fifteen years after he left office, in an act of political chutzpah that only he could get away with, Clinton went to the National Association for the Advancement of Colored People (NAACP) convention in July 2015 and responded to the initiatives of President Obama on reducing Black incarceration through criminal justice reform. He said,

> And the president spoke a long time yesterday and very well about this criminal justice reform and appreciate what he has done, but I want to say a few words about it because *I signed a bill that made the problem worse and I want to admit it.*
>
> But here's what happened. When I took office we had had a roaring decade of rising crime. We had gang warfare on the streets. We had little children being shot dead on the streets who were just innocent bystanders in the wrong place. We had kids in Los Angeles doing drills in their schools to learn how to drop down because of people just doing random drive-by shootings. And violent crime in America had tripled in the previous thirty years and police force had only increased by ten percent.
>
> So we put a hundred thousand more police on the street so they could be tighter tied to the community and we passed the Brady bill and the assault weapons ban which had

> an ammunition limit on the clips as I remember of about ten bullets and we passed funds to give people something to say yes to in the after-school area hours not just to say no to.
>
> But *in that bill there were longer sentences* and most of these people are in prison under state law but the federal law sets a trend *and that was overdone, we were wrong about that.* That percentage of it we were wrong about. So the good news is we had the biggest drop in crime in history in the first eight years decline in crime in history. The bad news is *we had a lot of people who are essentially locked up who were minor actors for way too long.*[73]

He "apologized" for supporting the three-strikes legislation, saying he "signed a bill that made the problem" of incarceration "worse"; "it was overdone" and "I want to admit it." He received applause for his honesty and integrity and the press reported his speech as asserting that he apologized and was wrong in supporting the crime bill. Now let's be serious. First, he did not say the bill was wrong. He said the bill was overdone. That aside, the chutzpah of his "apology" is not in the statement that the three strikes and the minimum mandatory were too harsh, the chutzpah was in the fact that he signed legislation, a year after the 1994 crime bill, which overruled the Sentencing Commission initiative to address the one hundred to one crack to powder cocaine rules that the Commission asserted was driving the disproportionate incarceration of Blacks.

Almost a year later, in April 2016, he gave a full-throated defense of the crime bill when his wife ran for president in 2016. While at an event supporting her election, Bill Clinton was heckled by a Black Lives Matter supporter, and she heckled that Blacks suffered mass incarceration due to his 1994 crime bill. Bill Clinton, first amused, answered the protester saying,

> I heard it, can I answer. No you see here's the thing. I like protesters but the ones that won't let you answer are afraid of the truth. That's a simple rule. At every campaign rally I welcome the protesters. ... Now look, what she is referring to are the increased sentencing provisions of the 1994 crime bill. Ninety percent of the people in prison too long are in state prison and local jails, more than ninety percent. But it's also true that there are too many people in the state prisons, I mean the federal prisons. President Obama is trying to let them out.
>
> Here's what happened, let's just tell the whole story. ... Here's what happened. Vice President Biden ... he was the chairmen of the committee that had to jurisdiction over this crime bill. I had an assault weapons ban in it, I had money for inner city kids for out of school activities, we had a hundred and ten thousand police officers so we could be people on the street not in these military vehicles and the police would look like the people they were policing, we did all that. And Biden said we can't pass this bill the Republicans will kill it if you don't put more sentencing in.

---

73 Former President Bill Clinton Speech at the 2015 NAACP meeting at https://www.youtube.com/watch?v=8RXZSFtbwU8 (26:46-28:57) (emphasis added)

But his defense of the bill became more hostile upon pushback from the Black Lives Matter supporter, and he forcefully defended his crime bill, utilizing crime-control model rhetoric. He said,

> I talked to a lot of African-American groups. They thought black lives matter. They said take this bill, because our kids are being shot in the street by gangs. We have 13-year-old kids planning their own funerals. She don't want to hear any of that!
>
> You know what else you don't want to hear, because of that bill we had a twenty five year low in crime, a thirty three low in the murder rate and listen to this. Because of that and the background check law we had a forty six year low in the deaths of people by gun violence. And who do you think those lives were? That mattered! Whose lives were saved, that mattered!

After his defense, Clinton tried to move on to defending his wife's record on health care and her current record on criminal justice reform, but the heckler and her supporters would not back down. Clinton attacked back, saying,

> I don't know how you would characterize the gang leaders who got 13-year-old kids hopped up on crack and sent them out onto the street to murder other African-American children. Maybe you thought they were good citizens. You are defending the people who kill the lives you say matter. Tell the truth. You are defending the people who cause young people to go out and take guns. There was a thirteen–year-old girl in Washington D.C. who was planning her own funeral.[74]

He said this less than a year after saying that he had gone too far with the crime bill he signed, and after signing a bill overruling the Sentencing Commission attempt to reduce the impact of the one hundred-to-one ratio which he knew at the time was driving Black disproportionate incarceration. Classic Bill Clinton.

While an argument could be made that gives Reagan the benefit of the doubt as to him not knowing what the full impact of his policies would be on Blacks. The same cannot be said of Clinton. Clinton overruled the U.S. Sentencing Commission, which asserted outright that the one hundred to one ratio was discriminatory in fact. He knew signing the bill overruling the Sentencing Commission would *continue* the one hundred-to-one ratio that was having a direct discriminatory impact on Blacks and would *continue* to increase their incarceration, and he did it anyway in order to maintain and command the "get tough on crime" political high ground.

President Clinton supported all types of "get tough on crime" legislation, including signing *Megan's Law* in 1995, the *Pam Lychner Sexual Offender Tracking and Identification Act of 1996*, the *Prison Litigation Reform Act of 1996, the Jacob Wetterling Amendment Act of 1998*,

---

74 Black Lives Matter protesters and Bill Clinton repeatedly clash in Philadelphia at https://www.youtube.com/watch?v=xRrVI5gHVyo

and his signature social legislation—the ***Personal Responsibility and Work Opportunity Reconciliation Act of 1996*** (the welfare to work law, which allowed drug testing for people on Temporary Assistance for Needy Families - TANF). Three months after seeking and signing legislation reversing the Sentencing Commission, Clinton, in his 1996 annual address to Congress, continued to bask in his ownership of the "get tough on crime" politics of the 1990s by making clear,

> [o]ur fourth great challenge is to take our streets back from crime and gangs and drugs. At last we have begun to find a way to reduce crime, forming community partnerships with local police forces to catch criminals and prevent crime. This strategy, called community policing, is clearly working. Violent crime is coming down all across America. In New York City, murders are down 25 percent; in St. Louis, 18 percent; in Seattle, 32 percent. But we still have a long way to go before our streets are safe and our people are free from fear.
>
> The crime bill of 1994 is critical to the success of community policing. It provides funds for 100,000 new police in communities of all sizes. We're already a third of the way there. And I challenge the Congress to finish the job. Let us stick with a strategy that's working and keep the crime rate coming down.
>
> Community policing also requires bonds of trust between citizens and police. I ask all Americans to respect and support our law enforcement officers. And to our police, I say, our children need you as role models and heroes. Don't let them down.
>
> The Brady bill has already stopped 44,000 people with criminal records from buying guns. The assault weapons ban is keeping 19 kinds of assault weapons out of the hands of violent gangs. I challenge the Congress to keep those laws on the books.
>
> Our next step in the fight against crime is to take on gangs the way we once took on the mob. I'm directing the FBI and other investigative agencies to target gangs that involve juveniles in violent crime, and to seek authority to prosecute as adults teenagers who maim and kill like adults.
>
> And I challenge local housing authorities and tenant associations: Criminal gang members and drug dealers are destroying the lives of decent tenants. From now on, the rule for residents who commit crime and peddle drugs should be "one strike and you're out."

Congress complied and passed the *Housing Opportunity Program Extension Act of 1996* (Extension Act) and the *Quality Housing and Work Responsibility Act of 1998*. Under the ***Quality Housing and Work Responsibility Act of 1988***, which was passed as ***part of the Anti-drug Abuse Act of 1988***, owners of federally subsidized housing and public housing agencies were authorized to place in leases a notice of authority to evict residents for illegal drug use or alcohol abuse and that prior illegal drug use or alcohol abuse can be terms for permanent ineligibility for public or subsidized housing.[75]

75 42 U.S.C. § § 13661 *Screening of applicants for federally assisted housing (a) Ineligibility because of eviction for drug crimes (b) Ineligibility of illegal drug users and alcohol abusers* and § 13662 *Termination of tenancy and assistance for illegal drug users and alcohol abusers in federally assisted housing.*

The ***Housing Opportunity Program Extension Act of 1996*** gave local Public Housing Authorities (PHAs) "new authority and obligations to deny occupancy on the basis of illegal drug-related activity and alcohol abuse."[76] In the *Anti–Drug Abuse Act of 1988*, Congress authorized Housing and Urban Development (HUD) and PHAs to put in all leases the following language,

> that any criminal activity that threatens the health, safety, or right to peaceful enjoyment of the premises by other tenants or any drug-related criminal activity on or off such premises, engaged in by a public housing tenant, any member of the tenant's household, or any guest or other person under the tenant's control, shall be cause for termination of tenancy[77]

The Clinton Administration asserted that the 1988 Quality housing law had not been properly enforced and that would end with his ***"One Strike and You're Out"*** policy. The Clinton Administration issued guidelines that required local PHAs to require criminal background checks for all people applying for public housing and to have procedures to evict any current residents for drug or alcohol use. The guidelines made clear

> Current law requires all PHAs to use leases that expressly state that (1) any criminal activity is grounds for eviction if it threatens the health, safety, or right to peaceful enjoyment of the premises by other tenants, and (2) all drug-related criminal activity occurring on or off the premises is cause for eviction. Under the required lease terms, a tenancy can be terminated and the household evicted when the tenant, any member of the tenant's household, or a guest engages in the prohibited criminal activity. In addition, the Extension Act requires PHAs to establish standards for occupancy that allow PHAs to evict any person who the PHA determines is illegally using a controlled substance, or whose illegal use of a controlled substance is determined by the PHA to interfere with the rights of other tenants.
>
> ...
>
> 1. Put the policy in the lease.
>
> PHAs must make their eviction policies clear in every lease. At a minimum, this means including the HUD-required language obligating tenants to assure that neither they nor any household member or guest, or other person under their control, will engage in the prohibited drug-related or other criminal activities, and providing that failure to abide by this lease term is grounds for eviction. It is highly recommended that the lease also contain language expressly stating that any drug-related or criminal activity in violation of this term will be treated as "a serious violation of the material terms of the lease." Finally, PHAs should consider additional language specifying that the PHA has a One Strike or

76 U.S. Department of Housing and Urban Development Officer of Public and Indian Housing, "Subject: 'One Strike and You're Out' Screening and Eviction Guidelines for Public Housing Authorities (HAs)" March 1996 at 1 .

77 42 U. S. C. § 1437d (l)(6) *Leases; terms and conditions; maintenance; termination.*

> "zero tolerance" policy with respect to violations of lease terms regarding criminal activity. To ensure that their leases are sufficiently explicit, PHAs should have them reviewed by experienced attorneys in their jurisdictions.
>
> Under the Extension Act, alcohol abuse is grounds for termination of tenancy if a PHA determines that such abuse interferes with the health, safety, or right to peaceful enjoyment of the premises by other tenants. To make this policy clear, PHAs should include a lease term allowing for eviction under these circumstances.
>
> ...
>
> 5. Make tenants responsible for the conduct of everyone in their households.
>
> The lease language mandated by federal law imposes on tenants an affirmative obligation to assure that neither they nor any member of their household or guest or other person under their control will engage in prohibited drug-related or other criminal activities. PHAs can generally enforce this obligation by terminating leases and evicting entire households when a household member or guest commits a crime in violation of lease provisions. A promise is a promise. Where the tenant has promised in a lease to ensure a crime-free household, the tenant is responsible for the household, regardless of whether he or she was personally engaged in the prohibited drug or other criminal activity.[78]

In justifying this policy and the new HUD guidelines implementing the policy, Clinton spoke in clear crime control terms:

> In my State of the Union Address I challenged local housing authorities and tenant associations to adopt this "one strike and you're out" policy to restore the rule of law to public housing, to simply say, "If you mess up your community, you have to turn in your key. If you insist on abusing or intimidating or hurting other people, you'll have to live somewhere else."
>
> It seems so simple, it's hard to imagine how we ever went so wrong. Public housing was created with a simple purpose in mind, to provide good, inexpensive homes for good, hard-working people, so they could care for their children, hold down their jobs, and eventually save enough, if they chose, to move into homes of their own. ***Public housing has never been a right; it has always been a privilege.*** And it is amazing how far some people in some places have strayed from that original mission.
>
> ...
>
> ***The only people who deserve to live in public housing are those who live responsibly there and those who honor the rule of law.*** We've worked hard to protect public housing residents with Operation Safe Home and public housing drug elimination programs. We've made 6,800 arrests, seized hundreds of weapons, [and] confiscated $3 million

78 U.S. Department of Housing and Urban Development Officer of Public and Indian Housing, "Subject: 'One Strike and You're Out' Screening and Eviction Guidelines for Public Housing Authorities (HAs)," March, 1996 at 7–8.

worth of illegal drugs. And coupled with our other anticrime initiatives, we're helping to restore order in our cities, to our one stoplight towns, and in our public housing. But we know we have to do more.

This policy today is a clear signal to drug dealers and to gangs: If you break the law, you no longer have a home in public housing, "one strike and you're out." That should be the law everywhere in America.

...

Believe it or not, the Federal law has actually authorized "one strike" eviction since 1988. ... For whatever reason, the sad fact is that in most places in this country, "one strike" has not been carried out. ...

Now there will be no more excuses, for these national guidelines tell public housing authorities the steps they must take to evict drug dealers and other criminals. They explain how housing authorities must work with tenants, with the police, with the courts, with our Government to get the job done. They also tell housing authorities how to screen tenants for criminal records. With effective screening, many of the bad people we're trying hard to remove today won't get into public housing in the first place.

The second thing we're going to do is to make sure these guidelines don't sit around and gather dust. ***Under the new rules HUD will propose, for the first time there will actually be penalties for housing projects that do not fight crime and enforce "one strike and you're out."*** Superior housing authorities that live up to their responsibilities will improve their chances for increased funding and for greater flexibility in how the housing authority is run by the local people. Those that don't will face increased supervision and might lose out on extra financial help.

I know that for some, "one strike and you're out" sounds like hardball. Well, it is. It is because ***it's morally wrong for criminals to use up homes that could make a big difference in the lives of decent families.*** And as Leora said better than I could have, if people aren't going to do anything wrong in public housing, they have nothing to fear from "one strike and you're out."

After all, it's not as if nobody wants to live there. There are three people in line for every one person who has a slot in public housing. In many places, the waiting list today is up to 4 years. This is a privilege, not a right. ***The people who are living there deserve to be protected***, and the good people who want to live in public housing deserve to have a chance. The people who are in the middle, doing the wrong thing, must be removed.

...

For too many years, the chaos in some of our public housing units has been a national blind spot and a national disgrace. Most Americans probably think it has to be that way. Many of them who have had no personal experience with tenants may even believe most people who live in public housing are lawless, are not working, are not concerned parents. All of that is wrong.

> Now we are going to give the good, decent, law-abiding citizens in public housing the life they deserve, and we're going to give the kids the future they deserve by doing what we should have been doing all along, and doing it together.
>
> I want every American to believe that if he or she works hard and plays by the rules, they can share in the American dream. I want every parent to believe that if he or she works hard, they can do a better job raising their kids in a country that's supporting them, not undermining them. I want this country to come together across the lines of income and race, not be divided. Surely, our dreams of opportunity and decent childhoods and strong families and unity in this country can be furthered by what we're doing here today. And surely, others will see this and say that they have to do the same.
>
> I want to now sign this Executive order ... [79]

On the same day, President Clinton issued a memorandum to the Secretary of HUD confirming the policy justification and the new HUD policy of linking local PHA compliance with the new policy and subsequent federal funding:

> Today, the majority of the Nation's approximately 3,400 public housing authorities provide safe, attractive, quality homes. But there remains too much public housing in this country that is ravaged by drugs, crime, and violence.
>
> It is imperative that we protect the ability of all individuals to live in safety and free from fear, intimidation, and abuse. It is also imperative that our precious public housing resources be made available only to responsible, law-abiding individuals. We must have zero tolerance for those who threaten the safety and well-being of decent families and innocent children who live in public housing.
>
> That is why, in my State of the Union Address, I expressed my strong support for a clear and straightforward rule for those who endanger public housing communities by dealing drugs or engaging in other criminal activity: One Strike and You're Out of public housing.
>
> At my request, HUD has now developed, in consultation with the Department of Justice, new national Guidelines on One Strike and You're Out. These new Guidelines set forth how each public housing authority should use applicant screening and tenant eviction procedures to keep out drug dealers and other criminals who threaten the safety and the well-being of residents. These Guidelines are meant to ensure that One Strike and You're Out is effective and that it is fair.
>
> You have advised me that HUD intends to amend its public housing performance evaluation regulations so that the overall "grade" HUD gives annually to each local housing authority will be based, in part, on how effectively it has implemented the type of

---

79 William J. Clinton, Remarks Announcing the "One Strike and You're Out" Initiative in Public Housing, March 28, 1996 at http://www.presidency.ucsb.edu/ws/?pid=52598 (emphasis added)

> applicant screening and tenant eviction policies set forth in the new Guidelines. I understand that this "grade" can affect both the amount of Federal funding a public housing authority receives and the degree of Federal oversight to which a public housing authority will be subject.
>
> I hereby direct you to disseminate these important new Guidelines on One Strike and You're Out to each of this Nation's public housing authorities …
>
> One Strike and You're Out is one component of comprehensive initiatives already underway to improve safety and quality of life in public housing. We will continue to work with the Congress, and with public housing authorities, residents, local officials, and law enforcement agencies, to rid our public housing of drugs, violence, and crime.[80]

Under a Democratic president, the policy of removing poor rural and urban Black and White people from public housing on conviction or suspected drug use found national support and presidential advocacy. The policy, according to President Clinton, was supported by the fact that public housing residency is a privilege not a right. So much for the progressive theory that housing is a human right.

The One Strike and You're Out policy applied by vicarious liability to all residents in public housing. The policy applied to all members of the household regardless of their knowledge of any criminal activity of any individual member residing in the house. This "no fault" clause that applied eviction to an entire household for the sins of one member was affirmed by the Supreme Court in *Department of Housing and Urban Development v. Rucker* (2002). The Court held

> The HUD regulations closely track the statutory language, and provide that in deciding to evict for criminal activity, the public housing authority shall have discretion to consider all of the circumstances of the case. … " 24 CFR § 966.4(l)(5)(i) (2001). The agency made clear that local public housing authorities' discretion to evict for drug-related activity includes those situations in which "the tenant did not know, could not foresee, or could not control behavior by other occupants of the unit." 56 Fed. Reg. 51560, 51567 (1991).[81]

Rucker argued that the *Anti–Drug Abuse Act of 1988* did not authorize eviction when the tenant did not know of the criminal activity of a member of the household. The Court rejected that assertion. The Court also rejected the assertion that the eviction policy violated the Due Process clause because it applied the application of government sanction without any culpability. The Court held unanimously

80 William J. Clinton, Memorandum on the "One Strike and You're Out" Guidelines, March 28, 1996, at http://www.presidency.ucsb.edu/ws/?pid=52599

81 Department of Housing and Urban Development v. Rucker 535 U. S. 125, 129 (2002) (internal citation brackets omitted)

> that 42 U. S. C. § 1437d(l)(6) unambiguously requires lease terms that vest local public housing authorities with the discretion to evict tenants for the drug-related activity of household members and guests whether or not the tenant knew, or should have known, about the activity.
>
> ...
>
> The government is not attempting to criminally punish or civilly regulate respondents as members of the general populace. It is instead acting as a landlord of property that it owns, invoking a clause in a lease to which respondents have agreed and which Congress has expressly required.[82]

The Court held that Congress clearly wanted to allow for eviction for criminal activity either on or off public housing when it passed the *Housing Opportunity Program Extension Act of 1996.*

> A 1996 amendment to § 1437d(l)(6), enacted five years after HUD issued its interpretation of the statute, supports our holding. The 1996 amendment expanded the reach of § 1437d(l)(6), changing the language of the lease provision from applying to activity taking place "on or near" the public housing premises, to activity occurring "on or off" the public housing premises. See Housing Opportunity Program Extension Act of 1996, § 9(a)(2), 110 Stat. 836. But Congress, "presumed to be aware" of HUD's interpretation rejecting a knowledge requirement, made no other change to the statute.[83]

The Supreme Court also affirmed the link between "no fault" eviction and crime control as reasonable.

> And, of course, there is an obvious reason why Congress would have permitted local public housing authorities to conduct no-fault evictions: Regardless of knowledge, a tenant who "cannot control drug crime, or other criminal activities by a household member which threaten health or safety of other residents, is a threat to other residents and the project." 56 Fed. Reg., at 51567. With drugs leading to "murders, muggings, and other forms of violence against tenants," and to the "deterioration of the physical environment that requires substantial government expenditures," 42 U. S. C. § 11901(4) (1994 ed., Supp. V), it was reasonable for Congress to permit no-fault evictions in order to "provide public and other federally assisted low-income housing that is decent, safe, and free from illegal drugs," § 11901(1) (1994 ed.).[84]

Leaving aside the ability to make an entire family homeless for the sins of one member, the real impact of the policy was that it was issued during the crime-control period of the 1990s in

---

82 *Department of Housing and Urban Development v. Rucker* at 130, 135 respectively.

83 *Department of Housing and Urban Development v. Rucker* at 133 fn 3.

84 *Department of Housing and Urban Development v. Rucker* at 134.

which police had a financial incentive (asset forfeiture) to make and secure more convictions of minor drug dealers and users. During this period, local police agencies secured federal anti-drug funding by establishing high arrest and conviction rates. During this period, poor Black communities were suffering from intense anti-crime police activities, including the use of SWAT teams to execute drug warrants, the formation of local–federal drug task forces, which specifically targeted open-air drug trafficking in Black communities, and the use of "jump-out squads" that would conduct random sweeps of residents to find and arrest residents with drugs. Prosecutors were engaged in using plea bargaining to secure convictions through overcharging and by pretrial incarceration. Prosecutors could secure pleas from suspects who feared incarceration or needed to be released to take care of family members. When prosecutors opposed bail or requested bail that would result in incarceration due to the inability to pay the court ordered bond, offenders where more amenable to taking a plea – regardless of guilt – to be released. The "one strike and you're out" policy would make people who pled guilty to minor or reduced charges to get out of jail due to the lack of ability to secure bail ineligible to maintain residency in public housing and could result in entire families being evicted. Thus, from this policy, countless stories of family dislocation occurred over the past decades.

In the ***National Defense Authorization Act of 1997*** under ***section 1033***, Clinton authorized the Pentagon to provide surplus military equipment to local law enforcement agencies. Under the 1033 program, the Pentagon provided local agencies with military weapons, including armored vehicles, helicopters, ordinance, gas and grenade launchers, and high caliber rifles to local police without charge. The 1033 program expanded the 1208 program under President Bush. The program was curtailed under President Obama by executive order in 2014, which was withdrawn by President Trump in 2017.

Clinton continued to advocate for crime control policies in 1997. In Clinton's 1997 annual speech to Congress, he said "And I ask you to mount a full-scale assault on juvenile crime with legislation that declares war on gangs with new prosecutors and tougher penalties." In 1998, he asked for the same legislation. In his 1999 annual speech to Congress,

> Tonight I propose a 21st century crime bill to deploy the latest technologies and tactics to make our communities even safer. Our balanced budget will help put up to 50,000 more police on the street in the areas hardest hit by crime and then to equip them with new tools, from crime-mapping computers to digital mug shots.
>
> We must break the deadly cycle of drugs and crime. Our budget expands support for drug testing and treatment, saying to prisoners: If you stay on drugs, you have to stay behind bars; and to those on parole: If you want to keep your freedom, you must stay free of drugs.[85]

85 William J. Clinton, Address Before a Joint Session of the Congress on the State of the Union January 19, 1999, at http://www.presidency.ucsb.edu/ws/index.php?pid=57577&st=&st1=

In 2000, in his last speech before Congress, Clinton took credit and a final bow for reducing crime through his crime control model policies:

> And our economic revolution has been matched by a revival of the American spirit: crime down by 20 percent, to its lowest level in 25 years; teen births down 7 years in a row; adoptions up by 30 percent; welfare rolls cut in half, to their lowest levels in 30 years.
>
> ...
>
> With the smallest Federal work force in 40 years, we turned record deficits into record surpluses and doubled our investment in education. We cut crime with 100,000 community police and the Brady law, which has kept guns out of the hands of half a million criminals.[86]

Clinton stole the "tough on crime" mantle from the Republican Party, and under his presidency, more people were incarcerated than under Reagan and Bush. In "President Clinton's first-term (1992–1996), 148,000 more state and federal prisoners were added than under President Reagan's first term (1980–1984), and 34,000 more than were added under President Bush's four-year term (1988–1992)."[87] Under President Reagan, during his first term, the number of people incarcerated increased by 129,000, while under Bush, the number increased by 243,000, and under Clinton, during his first term, it increased by 277,000.[88] Comparing Clinton's and Reagan's eight years in office each, under Reagan, there was an increase of 448,000, but under Clinton, there was an increase of 673,000 people. Thus under Clinton, 225,000 more people were incarcerated than under Reagan.[89] Under Reagan, the incarceration rate per 100,000 was 247; under Bush, it was 332; and under Clinton, it was 476.[90] The Clinton Justice Department policy of using the three-strikes law to increase both prosecutions and long-term incarceration bore fruit. Under Clinton, the federal incarceration rate outstripped the rate of the Reagan and Bush Administrations combined.

> Under President Reagan's eight year term, the number of prisoners under federal jurisdiction rose from 24,363 (1980) to 49,928 (1988), and under President George Bush's four-year term, the federal system grew to 80,259 (1992). However, under President Bill Clinton, the number of prisoners under federal jurisdiction doubled, and grew more than it did under the previous 12-years of Republican rule, combined (to 147,126 by February, 2001). As of December 31, 1999, a year prior to the completion of his term in office, the Clinton Administration already well outstripped the Reagan and Bush Administrations with a federal incarceration rate of rate of 42 per 100,000. This was more than double

---

86 William J. Clinton, Address Before a Joint Session of the Congress on the State of the Union January 27, 2000, at http://www.presidency.ucsb.edu/ws/index.php?pid=58708&st=&st1=

87 Justice Policy Institute, *Too Little Too Late: President Clinton's Prison Legacy* (2001) at 3.

88 Justice Policy Institute, *Too Little Too Late: President Clinton's Prison Legacy* (2001)

89 Justice Policy Institute, *Too Little Too Late: President Clinton's Prison Legacy* (2001) at 4.

90 Justice Policy Institute, *Too Little Too Late: President Clinton's Prison Legacy* (2001) at 8.

> the federal incarceration rate at the end of President Reagan's term (17 per 100,000), and 61% higher than at the end of President George Bush's term (25 per 100,000). Fifty-eight percent of these inmates (63,448) are serving time for drug offenses—a 62% increase since 1990.[91]

As discussed in Chapter One, the net result during the 1980s and 1990s under Reagan, Bush, and Clinton Black incarceration rose from 41% under Reagan to a high of 51% under Clinton in 1994. The Black incarceration dropped during Clinton's final years in office from 49% in 1997 to 46% in 2001. The reduction occurred simultaneously with the beginning of the end of the crack epidemic in 1993, culminating in 1996.[92]

Needless to say that one of the results of the second punitive era between 1980 and 2000 was a significant increase in prison and corrections spending, as well as increased prison population. In 1982, states spent $15 billion on corrections, and by 2002, states had spent $53.4 billion on corrections.[93] Each and every year for two decades, the amount spent increased.

****

In summary, various policy initiatives led directly to disproportionate Black incarcerations. These included the *Comprehensive Crime Control Act of 1984*, which established mandatory sentencing guidelines system and ended federal parole; the *Anti–Drug Abuse Act of 1986*, which established the one hundred-to-one crack-powder disparity in which five grams of crack and five hundred grams of powder cocaine were punished with at least five years; *the Anti–Drug Abuse Act of 1988*, which created the five-year mandatory minimum sentence for simple possession of five grams of crack cocaine for first-time offenders; the *Bush Administration March 13, 1989, Justice Department Policy* that plea bargains should support the objective of sentencing guideline sanctions and prosecutors were prohibited from dropping charges in an effort to arrive at a bargain that fails to reflect the seriousness of the defendant's conduct; the *Violent Crime and Law Enforcement Act of 1994*, which established three strikes and truth in sentencing; the *Clinton Justice Department March 13, 1995, Memo*, which established the prosecution policy that the three-strikes legislation was to be used to achieve the specific purpose of increased incarceration; and *Public Law 104–38* the 1995 legislation that overruled the U.S. Sentencing Commission.

---

91 Justice Policy Institute, *Too Little Too Late: President Clinton's Prison Legacy* (2001) at 6.

92 Andrew Lang Golub and Bruce D. Johnson, *Crack's Decline: Some Surprises Across U.S. Cities*, National Institute of Justice (July 1997) at https://www.ncjrs.gov/pdffiles/165707.pdf

93 Bureau of Justice Statistics, *State Corrections Expenditures, 1982–2010* (December 2012) at 10. https://www.bjs.gov/content/pub/pdf/scefy8210.pdf

CRIME SUPPRESSION AND POLITICS 2000–PRESENT

President Bush and a New Century

Under the presidency of George W. Bush, Attorney General John Ashcroft defended the Bush Administration's approach to criminal justice. As did Nixon and Reagan, Ashcroft defined criminal justice as a civil right.[94]

> I believe a citizen's paramount civil right is safety. Americans have a right to be secure in their persons, homes and communities. Gun violence, violence against women, drug crime, and sexual predators all threaten to deny this most fundamental right. It is a core responsibility of government, led by the Attorney General and the Department of Justice, cooperating with local law enforcement officials, to secure this right. Our FY 2002 budget provides $650 million in additional funding to advance this effort. Children do not learn in schools overrun by neighborhood violence. Jobs will not be found in communities where criminals own the streets, and no American who now feels threatened should have to move to live in a safer neighborhood.

To back up this view, the Attorney General asserted that funding for the Department of Justice would "shift in spending from state and local law enforcement in order to support our core federal law enforcement mission, and better target assistance to areas of greatest need, such as crime in our schools, crimes committed with firearms, and violence against women." To meet these responsibilities, the Justice Department would focus on building and maintaining prisons:

> The number of inmates in the Federal Prison System has more than doubled since 1990 as a result of tougher sentencing guidelines, mandatory minimum sentences, the abolition of parole, and increased federal law enforcement efforts. This surge in the prison population continually tests the limits of our detention and incarceration capacity. The FY 2002 budget for the Department of Justice includes a $949.5 million increase in funding to support the federal responsibility of detaining individuals awaiting trial or sentencing in federal court, and incarcerating inmates who have been sentenced to prison for federal crimes.
>
> The rapid growth in the federal inmate population is expected to continue. Despite the investment of nearly $5 billion for prison construction over the past decade, the prison system is currently operating at 32 percent over its rated capacity—up from 22 percent at the end of 1997. These conditions could jeopardize public safety and cannot be ignored. The FY 2002 budget seeks an additional $809.27 million for the Bureau of Prisons to reduce overcrowding and accommodate future growth. Specifically, $669.97 million is requested to fund the construction of three Federal Corrections Institutions and four

94 Department of Justice Press Release, Attorney General Testimony Before the Senate Committee on Appropriations April 26, 2001, at https://www.justice.gov/archive/opa/pr/2001/April/189ag.htm

> United States Penitentiaries; partial site and planning funds for two female facilities and two male facilities; and $139.3 million is requested for the activation of the Federal Corrections Institute in Petersburg, Virginia, and the United States Penitentiary and work camp in Lee County, Virginia; and, the contract confinement costs to meet the anticipated increase in the federal prison population.
>
> To increase the detention capacity and staffing necessary to keep pace with the growth in INS enforcement activities, the Department's request includes an increase of $74.2 million. …

The Administration requested "$77.2 million in additional resources for law enforcement agencies to combat illegal drug use," all of which was to support law enforcement capacities for the DEA. After requesting more than $1.6 billion for prisons and law enforcement, the Administration requested

> $5 million for the development of a faith-based, pre-release pilot program at four federal prisons. The pilot [is a] faith-based initiative which ... aims to combat crime and curb recidivism so that ex-offenders can remain ex-offenders. Religion and crime are age-old enemies, and a growing body of empirical evidence shows the potency of the "faith factor" to change behavior. This model initiative, with a strong focus on one-on-one, post-prison aftercare, will offer moral guidance and a caring community to help ex-offenders re-enter society with hope and responsibility.

An additional $240.14 million was requested for border and immigration enforcement (INS).

The first president of the twenty-first century followed the policies of his predecessors with a general "get tough" approach to criminals in which the focus would be on increased federal funding for prisons and law enforcement. This would have been President Bush's response to what was perceived as the greatest threat of domestic violence—crime. September 11th would moderate the Bush Administration domestic law enforcement policy. After September 11, domestic security policy shifted from crime or counterterrorism. Federal law enforcement and domestic safety agencies were reorganized to focus on protecting America from terrorism and from this new priority came the founding of the Department of Homeland Security on November 25, 2002. Political focus changed from inner city crime suppression to the war on terror. Federal funds shifted accordingly. Now, local police focused grant writing on securing federal funding to support domestic terrorism monitoring and suppression. This would drive American domestic policy for more than a decade into the new century.

But even under the shift in policy to deal with the war on terror, the crime-control model of the 1990s found support. After the officers in the Rodney King beating were acquitted in 1992, two of the officers, Stacy Koon and Lawrence Powell, were convicted in federal court under section 242 for violating King's civil rights. The District Judge reduced the sentence of both officers from the presumptive sentence of 70 to 87 months to a sentence of 30 to

37 months, a downgrade of eight levels in the sentencing guidelines.[95] The District Court reasoned that the beating resulted in part due to Rodney King's wrongful conduct which the court held resulted in a five level reduction and an additional three level reduction was justified because (1) the officers would be subject to abuse in prison, (2) neither men would ever be law enforcement officers again and had suffered public humiliation due to the publicity of the case, (3) the officers had been "significantly burdened by being subjected to successive state and federal prosecutions," and (4) since the officers were not "violent, dangerous, or likely to engage in future criminal conduct" they were not a threat to society. "The court concluded these factors justified a departure when taken together, although none would have been sufficient standing alone."[96]

The government appealed the reduction and the Court of Appeals "reviewed '*de novo* whether the district court had authority to depart' [from the guidelines and it] reversed the five-level departure for victim misconduct, reasoning that misbehavior by suspects is typical in cases involving excessive use of force by police and is thus comprehended by the applicable Guideline. As for the three-level departure, the court rejected each factor cited."[97] The Supreme Court on appeal held that the Court of Appeals used the wrong standard for review. Rather than using *de novo* which allows the court to review the issue on its own determinations, the Supreme Court held that a reviewing court should only determine if the district court abused its discretion. Under this burden the legal question is whether the original court applied the law incorrectly. Abuse of discretion does not allow the reviewing court to substitute its opinion on how the case should have been resolved with the decision by the original court. Abuse of discretion is a much more deferential approach.

The Supreme Court in *Koon v. United States* (1996) held that the sentencing guidelines allowed district court judges to deviate from the presumptive guidelines when the court finds certain aggravating or mitigating circumstances should be considered that were not considered by the sentencing guidelines. The Court held that trial courts had not lost all discretion when issuing a sentence under the Sentencing Guidelines. The Court wrote that the District Court did not get the law wrong in the five-level downward departure due to King's conduct but it did get the law wrong regarding the three-level reduction. The Court held that the career loss and threat to society factors cited by the District Court did not authorize departure but the remaining two factors, their susceptibility to abuse in prison and the successive prosecutions in state and federal courts did authorize departure. The case was remanded for a new sentencing hearing.

In 2003 President Bush approved Congressional reversal of the proposition that judges could depart from presumptive guidelines. The ***USA PROTECT Act***, signed by President Bush on April 30, 2003, reaffirmed the crime control model policies of the 1980s and 1990s which

---

95 Koon v. United States, 518 U.S. (1996), 81, 89.

96 *Koon v. United States*, 518 U.S. at 89–90.

97 *Koon v. United States*, 518 U.S. at 90.

Significant Criminal Justice Policy Initiatives: Bush to Trump

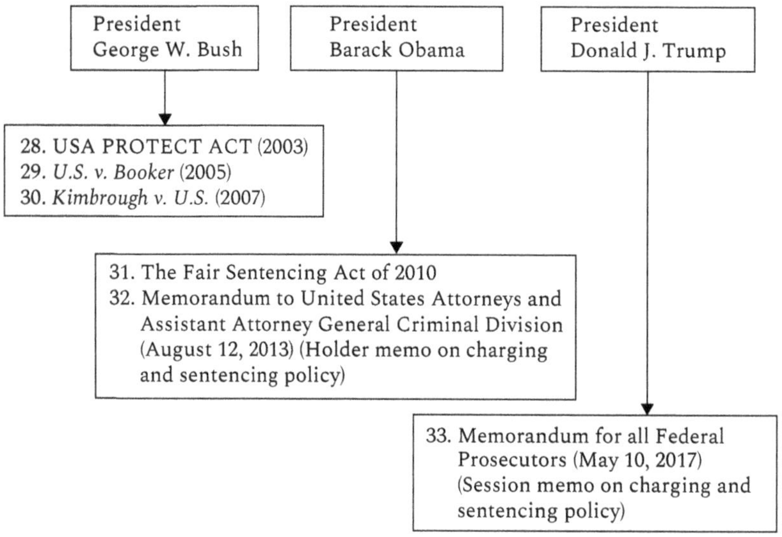

rejected judicial discretion in sentencing convicted criminals. The act reaffirmed the policy of "truth in sentencing" and rejected the idea that a check was needed to be placed on prosecutors and legislators regarding the harsh sentences of criminals. Specifically, the policies of the 1980s and 1990s made clear that the courts were not to be a check on either prosecutors or legislatures that increased sentences of offenders.

The USA PROTECT Act made five changes to the Sentencing Guidelines under the *Sentencing Reform Act of 1984*. The last three overruling *Koon v. United States.*

> First, the PROTECT Act amended 18 U.S.C. § 3553(c) (Imposition of a sentence) to require the court to include specific *written* reasons for departures in the judgment and commitment order (unless the court relied on *in camera* evidence under Fed. R. Crim. P. 32).
>
> Second, the PROTECT Act amended 28 U.S.C. § 994(w) to require the Chief Judge of each district court to ensure that, within 30 days following entry of judgment, the sentencing court submits to the Commission certain sentencing documents, including the Statement of Reasons for the sentence imposed, which must include, in the case of a departure, the reason for departure. The potential effect of these documentation requirements on the Commission's data collection and reporting is discussed in Chapter 2 of this report.
>
> Third, by amending 18 U.S.C. § 3742 (Review of a sentence), the PROTECT Act specifically requires sentencing courts to base departures on a factor that advances the statutory purposes of sentencing set forth in 18 U.S.C. § 3553(a)(2).
>
> Fourth, the PROTECT Act modifies appellate review for departure decisions. The PROTECT Act now generally requires *de novo* review of a district court's departure decision.

> Fifth, the PROTECT Act adds restrictions to limit the district courts' discretion when sentencing upon remand. Newly enacted 18 U.S.C. § 3742(g) prohibits the district court, upon remand, from sentencing outside the applicable guideline range, except upon a ground that was (i) "specifically and affirmatively" included in the written statement of reasons given by the district court pursuant to section 3553(c) in connection with sentencing of the defendant prior to the appeal *and* (ii) was held by the court of appeals, in remanding the case, to be a permissible ground for departure.[98]

The act authorized the Courts of Appeals to review sentencing departures *de novo* and required departures to be governed only by the factors dictated by the Sentencing Commission or by factors that supported the purpose of the guidelines.

The guidelines were mandatory and would remain so until the Court held that under the Sixth Amendment they were advisory only in *U.S. v. Booker* (2005) and *Kimbrough v. United States* (2007). In *Booker* the Court held that the Sixth Amendment right to jury trial required that factors that could increase a sanction must be proved before a jury and since the guidelines allow such to be proved only before a judge, that part of the guidelines violates the Sixth Amendment. The Court held that guidelines were to be read by the courts as advisory.[99] In *Kimbrough* the Court held the one hundred-to-one crack-to-powder cocaine sentence is advisory and that the courts, although they must take into account the presumptive sentence, can consider the purpose of the guidelines regarding fairness and "[i]n making that determination, the judge may consider the disparity between the Guidelines' treatment of crack and powder

---

98 U.S. Sentencing Commission, Report to the Congress: Downward Departures from the Federal Sentencing Guidelines (2003) at ii-iii at https://www.ussc.gov/sites/default/files/pdf/news/congressional-testimony-and-reports/departures/200310-rtc-downward-departures/departrpt03.pdf

99 *U.S. v. Booker*, 543 U.S. ___, Slip opinion by Justice Stevens speaking for the Court at 2 (2005). The Court concluded,

> Any fact (other than a prior conviction) which is necessary to support a sentence exceeding the maximum authorized by the facts established by a plea of guilty or a jury verdict must be admitted by the defendant or proved to a jury beyond a reasonable doubt.

U.S. Sentencing Commission, Report to the Congress: Downward Departures from the Federal Sentencing Guidelines (2003) at 20.

> As to the status of the Sentencing Guidelines, the Court held the provision of the federal sentencing statute that makes the Guidelines mandatory [is] incompatible with today's constitutional holding. We conclude that this provision must be severed and excised ... So modified, the Federal Sentencing Act makes the Guidelines effectively advisory. It requires a sentencing court to consider Guidelines ranges, but it permits the court to tailor the sentence in light of other statutory concerns as well.

Slip opinion by Justice Breyer speaking for the Court at 2 (2005) (internal citations omitted) cocaine offenses."[100] The Court redeemed the sentencing Commission's position rejected by Clinton twelve years earlier.

After signing the USA PROTECT Act the Bush Justice Department issued a memo[101] to prosecutors regarding plea agreements and charge bargaining affirming the memos issued by the Bush 41 and Clinton Administrations. On September 22, 2003 Attorney General Ashcroft issued the ***Department Policy Concerning Charging Criminal Offenses, Disposition of Charges, and Sentencing*** memo which instructed the U.S. Attorneys that, "It is the policy of the Department of Justice that, in all federal criminal cases, federal prosecutors must charge and pursue the most serious, readily provable offense or offenses that are supported by the facts of the case. ... The most serious offense or offenses are those that generate the most substantial sentence under the Sentencing Guidelines, unless a mandatory minimum sentence or count requiring a consecutive sentence would generate a longer sentence."

It has been Justice Department policy since the early 1980s that the purpose of plea negotiations is to secure the most stringent sanction possible and the most serious charge that can be proven was not to be dismissed through plea agreements. This approach would not find challenge until the Obama Administration in 2013.[102]

By the middle of the first decade of the new century, the politics of "get tough on crime" and policy of prison construction during the *second punitive era* were coming to an end. Starting in 2003, state spending on corrections began to decrease from $51.7 billion to $48.5

---

100 *Kimbrough v. United States*, 552 U.S. ____, Slip opinion at 2 (2007).

> Under the statute criminalizing the manufacture and distribution of crack cocaine and the relevant Guidelines prescription a drug trafficker dealing in crack cocaine is subject to the same sentence as one dealing in 100 times more powder cocaine. The question here presented is whether, as the Court of Appeals held in this case, "a sentence ... outside the guidelines range is *per se* unreasonable when it is based on a disagreement with the sentencing disparity for crack and powder cocaine offenses." We hold that, under *Booker*, the cocaine Guidelines, like all other Guidelines, are advisory only, and that the Court of Appeals erred in holding the crack/powder disparity effectively mandatory. A district judge must include the Guidelines range in the array of factors warranting consideration. The judge may determine, however, that, in the particular case, a within-Guidelines sentence is "greater than necessary" to serve the objectives of sentencing. In making that determination, the judge may consider the disparity between the Guidelines' treatment of crack and powder cocaine offenses.

U.S. v. Booker at 1–2 (internal citations omitted).

101 John Ashcroft, "Department Policy Concerning Charging Criminal Offenses, Disposition of Charges, and Sentencing" (September 22, 2003) at https://www.justice.gov/archive/opa/pr/2003/September/03_ag_516.htm

102 For additional discussion on the history of Justice Department policy of plea bargaining see, Alan Vinegrad, "The Sessions Memo: Back to the Past?" (May 25, 2017) *The Vera Institute of Justice* at https://www.vera.org/blog/the-sessions-memo-back-to-the-past

billion in 2010.[103] In the year 2000, the total number of people incarcerated in America was 1,945,400; by 2005, it was 2,200,400, increasing every consecutive year until 2008 with 2,310,300 incarcerated. Beginning in 2009 through 2015, each consecutive year, the number of people incarcerated decreased, resulting in 2,173,800 in 2015.[104] From 2008 through 2015, those under probation and parole also consecutively decreased from 5,093,400 to 4,650,900. "At yearend 2015, an estimated 6,741,400 persons were under the supervision of U.S. adult correctional systems, about 115,600 fewer persons than yearend 2014. This was the first time since 2002 (6,730,900) that the correctional population fell below 6.8 million."[105]

The political necessity for members of Congress to prove they were strong on drugs and violent crime was beginning to shift to other concerns. Congressional attention shifted to other criminal justice issues, including dealing with child and victim protection statutes to deal with sexual predators. These laws included the *Campus Sex Crimes Prevention Act of 2000, the Prosecutorial Remedies and Other Tools to end the Exploitation of Children Today Act of 2003, the Justice For All Act of 2004* (Scott Campbell, Stephanie Roper, Wendy Preston, Louarna Gillis, and Nila Lynn Crime Victims' Rights Act of 2003–2004), and *the Walsh Child Protection and Safety Act of 2006* (Sex Offender Registration and Notification Act).

By the end of the first decade of the new century, politics had changed, and President Barack Obama was able to secure passage of ***the Fair Sentencing Act 2010***, which changed the one hundred-to-one ratio under the *Anti–Drug Abuse Act of 1986* to a ratio of eighteen to one and changed the five-year minimum mandatory sentence for five grams of cocaine under the *Anti–Drug Abuse Act of 1988* to 28 grams. These changes, along with the Supreme Court ruling in *U.S. v. Booker* (2005) that, for the federal guidelines to be constitutional, they had to be treated as advisory not mandatory, and the one hundred-to-one ratio guidelines were also to be treated as advisory not mandatory in *Kimbrough v. U.S.* (2007), resulted in a reduction of Black incarceration from 41% in 2009 to 33% in 2016.

President Obama and Trump and Criminal Justice: Three Strikes, and Minimum Mandatory Sentencing in Prosecutorial Charging

In the election politics of 2016, Trump proposed returning blue-collar employment to Black communities, rather than increased militarized police and stop and frisk. Trump was not a dog whistle Republican running the classical law-and-order rhetoric that held the Republican electoral base together in the 1970s through the 1990s. Although Trump did not engage in classical dog whistle politics, that didn't mean that his choice for Attorney General wouldn't engage in blowing the dog whistle.

---

103 Bureau of Justice Statistics, *State Corrections Expenditures, 1982–2010* (December 2012) at 10.

104 Bureau of Justice Statistics, *Correctional Populations in the United States, 2015* (December 2016) at 2. https://www.bjs.gov/content/pub/pdf/cpus15.pdf

105 Bureau of Justice Statistics, *Correctional Populations in the United States, 2015* at 1.

On February 9, 2017, Jefferson Beauregard Sessions III assumed the office of the U.S. Attorney General. Sessions was the U.S. Senator from Alabama before being nominated by President Trump. Sessions was a social conservative senator that believed in the traditional Republican use of law and order. On May 10, 2017, he acted on his belief and reversed Justice Department policy on the use of the three strikes and minimum mandatory sentencing in prosecutorial charging decisions that reverted to the Clinton Administration policy and revoked the policy of the Obama Administration.

On August 12, 2013, Attorney General Holder, reversed the Clinton Administration policy on charging offenders under the three-strikes legislation. In the ***Memorandum to United States Attorneys and Assistant Attorney General Criminal Division***[106] General Holder announced the change was based on the assertion that "mandatory minimum and recidivist enhancement statutes have resulted in unduly harsh sentences and perceived or actual disparities that do not reflect our Principles of Federal Prosecution. Long sentences for low-level, non-violent drug offenses do not promote public safety, deterrence, and rehabilitation." He ordered his U.S. Attorneys

> to ***conduct an individualized assessment*** of the extent to which charges fit the specific circumstances of the case, are consistent with the purpose of the federal criminal code, and maximize the impact of federal resources on crime. When making these individualized assessments, ***prosecutors must take into account*** numerous factors, such as ***the defendant's conduct and criminal history*** and the circumstances relating to the commission of the offense, the needs of the communities we serve, and federal resources and priorities. Now that our charging decisions also affect when a defendant is subject to a mandatory minimum sentence, prosecutors must evaluate these factors in an equally thoughtful and reasoned manner.
>
> It is with full consideration of these factors that we now refine our charging policy regarding mandatory minimums for certain nonviolent, low-level drug offenders. We must ensure that our most ***severe mandatory minimum penalties are reserved for serious, high-level, or violent drug traffickers.***

The policy change required prosecutors to charge and/or make recommendations for sentencing utilizing the full impact of three strikes only for certain types of offenders. The new policy sought to focus federal prosecution and sanctions on the more serious and violent offenders and relieve low level non-violent first-time offenders the impact and severity of federal law:

> **Certain Mandatory Minimum Sentencing Statutes Based on Drug Quantity:** Prosecutors should continue to ascertain whether a defendant is eligible for any statutory mandatory minimum statute or enhancement. However, in cases involving the

---

106 *Memorandum to United States Attorneys and Assistant Attorney General Criminal Division* (August 12, 2013) at https://www.justice.gov/sites/default/files/oip/legacy/2014/07/23/ag-memo-department-policy-pon-charging-mandatory-minimum-sentences-recidivist-enhancements-in-certain-drugcases.pdf

applicability of Title 21 mandatory minimum sentences based on drug type and quantity, ***prosecutors should decline to charge the quantity necessary to trigger a mandatory minimum sentence if the defendant meets each of the following criteria***:

- The defendant's relevant ***conduct does not involve the use of violence***, the credible threat of violence, the possession of a weapon, the trafficking of drugs to or with minors, or the death or serious bodily injury of any person;
- The ***defendant is not an organizer, leader, manager*** or supervisor of others within a criminal organization;
- The defendant ***does not have significant ties to large-scale drug trafficking*** organizations, gangs, or cartels; and
- The defendant ***does not have a significant criminal history***. A significant criminal history will normally be evidenced by three or more criminal history points but may involve fewer or greater depending on the nature of any prior convictions.

Timing and Plea Agreements: If information sufficient to determine that ***a defendant meets the above criteria*** is available at the time initial charges are filed, ***prosecutors should decline to pursue charges triggering a mandatory minimum sentence*** ... If the defendant ultimately meets the criteria, prosecutors should pursue a disposition that does not require a Title 21 mandatory minimum sentence. For example, a prosecutor could ask the grand jury to supersede the indictment with charges that do not trigger the mandatory minimum, or a defendant could plead guilty to a lesser included offense, or waive indictment and plead guilty to a superseding information that does not charge the quantity necessary to trigger the mandatory minimum.

Advocacy at Sentencing: ... In cases where the properly calculated guideline range meets or exceeds the mandatory minimum, prosecutors should consider whether a below-guidelines sentence is sufficient to satisfy the purposes of sentencing as set forth in 18 U.S.C. § 3553(a). In determining the appropriate sentence to recommend to the Court, prosecutors should consider whether the defendant truthfully and in a timely way provided to the Government all information the defendant has concerning the offense or offenses that were part of the same course of conduct, common scheme, or plan.

Recidivist Enhancements: Prosecutors should decline to file an information pursuant to 21 U.S.C. § 851 unless the defendant is involved in conduct that makes the case appropriate for severe sanctions. When determining whether an enhancement is appropriate, prosecutors should consider the following factors:

- Whether the defendant was an organizer, leader, manager or supervisor of others within a criminal organization;
- Whether the defendant was involved in the use or threat of violence in connection with the offense;
- The nature of the defendant's criminal history, including any prior history of violent conduct or recent prior convictions for serious offenses;
- Whether the defendant has significant ties to large-scale drug trafficking organizations, gangs, or cartels;

> - Whether the filing would create a gross sentencing disparity with equally or more culpable co-defendants; and
> - Other case-specific aggravating or mitigating factors.
>
> In keeping with current policy, prosecutors are reminded that all charging decisions must be reviewed by a supervisory attorney to ensure adherence to the Principles of Federal Prosecution, the guidance provided by my May 19, 2010 memorandum, and the policy outlined in this memorandum.

The goal of the new policy was to limit the impact of sentencing that increased the federal prison population and the length of time people spent incarcerated. General Holder sought to revoke the Clinton Administration policy of utilizing mandatory sentencing and three strikes for the sole purpose of increasing the prison population and the length of stay in prison.

General Sessions was not in support of this approach. On May 10th, General Sessions issued ***Memorandum for all Federal Prosecutors***[107] which announced a new policy of charging and sentencing:

> This memorandum establishes charging and sentencing policy for the Department of Justice. Our responsibility is to fulfill our role in a way that accords with the law, advances public safety, and promotes respect for our legal system....
>
> First, it is ***a core principle that prosecutors should charge and pursue the most serious, readily provable offense.*** This policy affirms our responsibility to enforce the law, is moral and just, and produces consistency. This policy fully utilizes the tools Congress has given us. ***By definition, the most serious offenses are those that carry the most substantial guidelines sentence, including mandatory minimum sentences.***

This policy change was a return to the policies of the *second punitive era*. is significant. It is now Justice Department policy that the most serious charge that can be proved, and the sanction attached to that charge, is to be pursued. The factor of individual dangerousness and criminal culpability is no longer definitive or dispositive. The policy specifically reversed the Obama Administration policy that facts that invoke the three strikes and you're out legislation could be withheld in charging.

> There will be circumstances in which good judgment would lead a prosecutor to conclude that a strict application of the above charging policy is not warranted. In that case, prosecutors should carefully consider whether an exception may be justified. ...
>
> Second, ***prosecutors must disclose to the sentencing court all facts that impact the sentencing guidelines or mandatory minimum sentences***, and should in all cases seek a

107 *Memorandum for all Federal Prosecutors* (May 10, 2017) at https://www.justice.gov/sites/default/files/oip/legacy/2014/07/23/ag-memo-department-policypon-charging-mandatory-minimum-sentences-recidivist-enhancements-in-certain-drugcases.pdf

> reasonable sentence under the factors in 18 U.S.C. § 3553. In most cases, recommending a sentence within the advisory guideline range will be appropriate.

The policy makes clear that it is now an exception to charge outside of the facts and to make recommendations for sentencing below the presumptive sentence under the guidelines. Any exception required U.S. Attorney or Assistant Attorney General level approval. "Any inconsistent previous policy of the Department of Justice relating to these matters is rescinded, effective today." The policy specifically stated that the previous policy rescinded included General Holder's "Department Policy on Charging Mandatory Minimum Sentences and Recidivist Enhancements in Certain Drug Cases (August 12, 2013); and Guidance Regarding § 851 Enhancements in Plea Negotiations (September 24, 2014)."

General Sessions, in an op-ed in the *Washington Post*,[108] defended the policy change. He first rejected the proposition that a criminal engaged in the drug trade should be classified as non-violent and that the federal prisons are filled with non-violent drug offenders:

> Drug trafficking is an inherently violent business. If you want to collect a drug debt, you can't, and don't, file a lawsuit in court. You collect it by the barrel of a gun. For the approximately 52,000 Americans who died of a drug overdose in 2015, drug trafficking was a deadly business.

Reflecting and affirming the policies of Governor Rockefeller and Presidents Nixon and then Reagan, Sessions asserted that the War on Drugs in the 1970s and 1980s was correct and these policies should be the policy of the second decade of the new century. Session continued,

> Defenders of the status quo perpetuate the false story that federal prisons are filled with low-level, nonviolent drug offenders. The truth is less than 3 percent of federal offenders sentenced to imprisonment in 2016 were convicted of simple possession, and in most of those cases the defendants were drug dealers who accepted plea bargains in return for reduced sentences.

General Sessions was correct that 3.4% of all federal and state prisoner are in prison for simple possession (15.2% for all drug offenses)[109] but he neglected to note that almost half (47.5%) of all federal prisoners were incarcerated for drug offenses (99% of drug offenses were for drug trafficking).[110] Furthermore, more than a third (37.8%) of all federal prisoners for drug offenses were Black and another third were Hispanic (38.5%) while Whites only accounted for 21.6% of

---

108 Jeff Sessions, "Being soft on sentencing means more violent crime. It's time to get tough again" *Washington Post* (June 19, 2017) at https://www.washingtonpost.com/opinions/jeff-sessions-being-soft-on-sentencing-means-more-violent-crime-its-time-to-get-tough-again/2017/06/16/618ef1fe-4a19-11e7-9669-250d0b15f83b_story.html?utm_term=.c16553a2540b

109 E. Ann Carson, *Prisoners in 2016*, Bureau of Justice Statistics (January 2018) at 18

110 E. Ann Carson, *Prisoners in 2016*, Bureau of Justice Statistics (January 2018) at 20.

those incarcerated for drug offenses.[111] There is no research that shows Blacks and Hispanics are responsible for 76% of all drug crime in America worthy of Federal incarceration. Looking at these disparities another way, in 2016, 56.5% of all Hispanics in federal incarceration and 48.5% of all Blacks were there for drugs while only 37.5% of Whites were incarcerated for federal drug crimes.[112] Thus Blacks and Hispanics are disproportionately incarcerated in federal prisons and they are disproportionately incarcerated for drug offenses which carry more serious mandatory sentencing.

The disproportionate incarceration of Blacks and Hispanic is also reflected in State incarceration rates. In 2015, Hispanics accounted for 19.6% of all drug offenders, Blacks accounted for 31.2% and Whites accounted for 30.9%.[113] The disproportionality is amplified when incarceration for violent crimes is considered. In 2016, Hispanics accounted for 9.7% of violent offenders, Blacks 50%, and Whites 24.6% in federal prisons[114] and in 2015, Hispanics accounted 23.6%, Blacks 35.6%, and Whites 30.9%.[115]

Ignoring these disparities, Sessions implied in his op-ed that federal prisoners are not simple drug users but major drug traffickers.

> Federal drug offenders include major drug traffickers, gang members, importers, manufacturers and international drug cartel members. To be subject to a five-year mandatory sentence, a criminal would have to be arrested with 100 grams or more of heroin with the intent to distribute it—that is 1,000 doses of heroin.

But an offender does not need to be a trafficker to be subject to the five-year mandatory sentence. The five-year mandatory statute, 21 U.S.C. § 841, only requires possession of one hundred grams of heroin and five hundred grams of powder cocaine but only twenty-eight grams of crack to secure the same five-year sentence. And to secure the ten-year mandatory sentence, it requires one kilo of heroin and five kilos of powder cocaine but only two hundred and eighty grams of crack.

But drug weight disparities aside, it's the disparity of sentence that General Holder sought to address. A disparity created under the *Ant-Drug Abuse Act of 1986* (one hundred to one ratio punishment crack to powder cocaine) and the *Ant-Drug Abuse Act of 1988* (five-year mandatory for five grams of crack cocaine) that was in effect for more than two decades before it was changed by the *Fair Sentencing Act of 2010.* The result of the Holder policy was a reduction of Black incarceration. Between 2013 and 2016 the number of Blacks incarcerated

---

111 E. Ann Carson, *Prisoners in 2016*, Bureau of Justice Statistics (January 2018) at 20.

112 E. Ann Carson, *Prisoners in 2016*, Bureau of Justice Statistics (January 2018)

113 E. Ann Carson, *Prisoners in 2016*, Bureau of Justice Statistics (January 2018) at 19

114 E. Ann Carson, *Prisoners in 2016*, Bureau of Justice Statistics (January 2018) at 20

115 E. Ann Carson, *Prisoners in 2016*, Bureau of Justice Statistics (January 2018) at 19

dropped 8%.[116] Overall, under the Obama Presidency Black (2009 and 2016) incarceration decreased by 16.7%[117] which was more than three times the decrease under the Bush Administration (4.8%).[118] In 2009 when President Obama took office the percentage of Black federal and state incarceration was 41% and at the end of the Obama presidency in 2016, the percentage of Black federal and state incarceration had dropped to 33%, which was the lowest since 1964 (33%).[119]

Although this accomplishment is significant, the systemic incarceration of Blacks remains. In 2016 there are 1,608 Blacks for every 100,000 resident adults (18 and over) in the United States, while only 274 Whites and 856 Hispanics for every 100,000 adult residents in the United States.[120] The total number of people incarcerated in 2016 per 100,000 adults was only 582. Between 2015 and 2016, the rate of Black imprisonment decreased 4% (from 1,670 per 100,000 in 2015 to 1,608 per 100,000 in 2016) while the rate of White imprisonment decreased 2% (from 281 per 100,000 in 2015 to 274 per 100,000 in 2016) and the rate of Hispanic incarceration decreased only 1% (862 per 100,000 in 2015 to 856 per 100,000 in 2016). Since 2006, the imprisonment rate for Hispanics declined 20% (1,073 per 100,000 in 2006) and the imprisonment rate for Blacks declined 29% since 2006 (2,261 per 100,000).[121] Although the rates of Black incarceration are decreasing, "Black males ages 18 to 19 were 11.8 times more likely to be imprisoned than White males of the same age. This age group had the highest Black-to-White racial disparity in 2016."[122]

The impact of this disparity on Black communities and its justification for the Holder policy attempt to mitigate the disproportionate impact of the 1986 and 1988 drug laws was irrelevant to General Sessions. Session wrote in his op-ed that under the Holder policy, "federal drug prosecutions went down dramatically—from 2011 to 2016, federal prosecutions fell by 23 percent. Meanwhile, the average sentence length for a convicted federal drug offender decreased 18 percent from 2009 to 2016." The result being, "[w]ithin one year after the Justice Department softened its approach to drug offenders, the trend of decreasing violent crime reversed. In 2015, the United States suffered the largest single-year increase in the overall violent crime rate since 1991." He asserted that the lack of absolute federal prosecution of crime resulted in an increase in crime:

---

116 E. Ann Carson, *Prisoners in 2016*, Bureau of Justice Statistics (January 2018) at 5.

117 E. Ann Carson, *Prisoners in 2016*, Bureau of Justice Statistics (January 2018)

118 Under President Bush 2002 (622,700) and 2008 (592,800) and Under President Obama 2009 (584,800) and 2016 (486,900). E. Ann Carson, *Prisoners in 2002*, Bureau of Justice Statistics (July 2003—revised August 2003) at 9 and E. Ann Carson, *Prisoners in 2016*, Bureau of Justice Statistics (January 2018) at 5.

119 See Chapter One and E. Ann Carson, *Prisoners in 2016*, Bureau of Justice Statistics (January 2018) at 5.

120 E. Ann Carson, *Prisoners in 2016*, Bureau of Justice Statistics (January 2018) at 8

121 E. Ann Carson, *Prisoners in 2016*, Bureau of Justice Statistics (January 2018) at 10

122 E. Ann Carson, *Prisoners in 2016*, Bureau of Justice Statistics (January 2018) at 13

> The truth is that while the federal government softened its approach to drug enforcement, drug abuse and violent crime surged. The availability of dangerous drugs is up, the price has dropped and the purity is at dangerously high levels. Overdose deaths from opioids have nearly tripled since 2002. Overdose deaths involving synthetic opioids rose an astonishing 73 percent in 2015. My fear is that this surge in violent crime is not a "blip," but the start of a dangerous new trend—one that puts at risk the hard-won gains that have made our country a safer place.[123]

Note the conflating of violent crime with the rise of opioid addiction with the failure of the federal government to prosecute drug cases. The fact that violent crime—even drug related violent crime—is a different dynamic than the opioid crisis (which is driven by abuse of prescription drugs) is lost on Sessions. To Sessions, in line with the crime control policies of Nixon, Reagan, Bush, and Clinton, crime is solely the result of lax and weak application of **formal social control**—the application of **police** and **prosecutions in court** and the utilization of **prison incarceration** after conviction.

Sessions concluded his op-ed by evoking the rhetoric of President Nixon that the first civil right is to be free from violence and the political rhetoric of President Clinton that the first community that deserves that protection are the less affluent who suffer the brunt of crime.

> Some skeptics prefer to sit on the sidelines and criticize federal efforts to combat crime. But it's not our privileged communities that suffer the most from crime and violence. Minority communities are disproportionately impacted by violent drug trafficking. Poor neighborhoods are too often ignored in these conversations. Regardless of wealth or race, every American has the right to demand a safe neighborhood. Those of us who are responsible for promoting public safety cannot sit back while any American communities are ravaged by crime and violence.
>
> There are those who are concerned about the fate of drug traffickers, but the law demands I protect the lives of victims that are ruined by drug trafficking and violent

---

123 Jeff Sessions, "Being soft on sentencing means more violent crime. It's time to get tough again" Washington Post (June 19, 2017) at https://www.washingtonpost.com/opinions/jeff-sessions-being-soft-on-sentencing-means-more-violent-crime-its-time-to-get-tough-again/2017/06/16/618ef1fe-4a19-11e7-9669-250d0b15f83b_story.html?utm_term=.c16553a2540b

For rebuttal to General Sessions op-ed see David Cole and Marc Mauer, "Jeff Sessions wants a new war on drugs. It won't work" Op-ed *Washington Post* (June 22, 2017) at https://www.washingtonpost.com/opinions/the-new-war-on-drugs-wont-be-any-more-effective-than-the-old-one/2017/06/22/669260ee-56c3-11e7-a204-ad706461fa4f_story.html?utm_term=.3ccfb75cb818 and op-ed by former Acting Attorney General Jessica Yates, "Making America scared again won't make us safer" Op-ed *Washington Post* (June 23, 2017) at https://www.washingtonpost.com/opinions/making-america-scared-again-wont-make-us-safer/2017/06/23/f53d238e-578a-11e7-ba90-f5875b7d1876_story.html?utm_term=.aea9b6a119ab

> crime infecting their communities. Our new, time-tested policy empowers police and prosecutors to save lives.

On December 15, 2017 General Sessions announced a new Justice Department initiative to add an additional 40 Assistant U.S. Attorneys (AUSAs) specializing in violent crime and drug prosecutions.[124] He asserted that violent crime had increased over the past two years. "The overall violent crime rate is up by nearly 7% … rape is up by nearly 11% and murder up by more than 20%" and that 25% of the increase in the murder rate is caused by increases in drug related homicides. To address the increase in crime and to return neighborhoods to law and order, Sessions announced new funding for Project Safe Neighborhoods streets task forces. These task forces coordinate federal, state, and local law enforcement under the leadership of AUSAs that focus on prosecutions of violent crimes. Sessions asserted that the new AUSAs, funded through "shifting department resources and priorities," will "repurpose existing funds [by] reducing wasteful spending" to support the appointment of AUSAs in communities that are suffering from higher crime than the national average. He announced that over the next few months he plans on appointing an additional 260 AUSAs. He concluded, "To the communities that are suffering, hear this. Help is on the way. We are marshalling our resources and will be relentless in our pursuit of violent criminals that are victimizing your neighborhoods."

After his prepared remakes, he answered a question as to whether more AUSAs and partnerships will reduce crime by asserting that the project safe neighborhood strategy "if sustained, is somewhat akin to the New York City–proven COMSTAT model where you use good intelligence, you identify what the commissioner told me the *alpha criminal*, and you make those top priority in your investigations and prosecutions. And you can see, hopefully for America, what they have seen in New York is a steady decline in homicides and violent crime. So, I believe it's a proven technique." The reduction of crime is not complicated to General Sessions, simply focus on *the alpha criminal* (*the super predator of the 1990s*). Clinton could not have said it better himself.

On January 4, 2018 General Sessions continued to assert the need for a reinvigorated law and order policy to replace the policies of the Obama Administration. Sessions announced that the policy of the Obama Administration regarding federal prosecutions for marijuana prosecutions was reversed. Under the Obama Administration, ***Justice Department policy announcement: Justice Department Announces Update to Marijuana Enforcement Policy August 29, 2013***, "federal marijuana enforcement policy in light of recent state ballot initiatives that legalize, under state law, the possession of small amounts of marijuana and provide for the regulation of marijuana production, processing, and sale … the Department identifie[d]

124 See, General Jeff Session Press Conference December 15, 2017 at https://www.c-span.org/video/?438603-1/attorney-general-jeff-sessions-holds-news-conference

eight (8) enforcement areas that federal prosecutors should prioritize."[125] These enforcement areas included (1) selling marijuana to minors, (2) preventing sales of marijuana to drug gangs and other criminal organizations, (3) preventing sales of marijuana from states that allow such sales to states that do not, (4) preventing state-authorized marijuana activities from being co-opted by criminal organizations for illegal drug activity or money laundering, (5) preventing gun violence in the cultivation and distribution of marijuana, (6) preventing marijuana cultivation on federal lands, (7) preventing marijuana use on federal land, and (8) preventing driving while intoxicated on marijuana. The policy left prosecution of minor marijuana possession and sale to state and local prosecution priorities and policies.[126]

Sessions reversed this policy and in the ***Memorandum to all U.S. Attorneys issued by Attorney General Jeffery Sessions January 4, 2018*** he instructed his U.S. Attorneys to use "well-established principles that govern all federal prosecutions" which include "federal law enforcement priorities set by the Attorney General, the seriousness of the crime, the deterrent effect of criminal prosecution, and the cumulative impact of particular crime on the community" to determine whether to prosecute marijuana cases under federal law.[127] Sessions explained in his announcement of the new policy announced that he was "direct[ing] all U.S. Attorneys to enforce the laws enacted by Congress and to follow well-established principles when pursuing prosecutions related to marijuana activities. This return to the rule of law is also a return of trust and local control to federal prosecutors who know where and how to deploy Justice Department resources most effectively to reduce violent crime, stem the tide of the drug crisis, and dismantle criminal gangs."[128]

The policies implemented by Sessions open the possibility that the fifteen-year (2001–2016, 46% to 33%) decline in disproportionate incarceration of Blacks in general and Black males specifically, and the overall six-year (2009–2015, 2.3 million to 2.1 million) reduction in the U.S. prison population, will be reversed.

Although General Sessions and his policy changes to federal prosecutions are in alignment with the Clinton policies instituted at the height of the crime control *second punitive era*, the golden age of these crime control politics is past. In terms of both politics and governmental budgeting restraints on both the federal and state levels, the glory days of unrestrained

---

125 Justice Department policy announcement: Justice Department Announces Update to Marijuana Enforcement Policy August 29, 2013 at https://www.justice.gov/opa/pr/justice-department-announces-update-marijuana-enforcement-policy

126 Memorandum to all U.S. Attorneys issued by Deputy Attorney General James M. Cole August 29, 2013 at https://www.justice.gov/iso/opa/resources/3052013829132756857467.pdf

127 Memorandum to all U.S. Attorneys issued by Attorney General Jeffery Sessions January 4, 2018 at https://www.justice.gov/opa/press-release/file/1022196/download

128 Justice Department policy announcement: Justice Department Issues Memo on Marijuana Enforcement January 4, 2018 at https://www.justice.gov/opa/pr/justice-department-issues-memo-marijuana-enforcement

funding and building of prisons and the political acceptance of the disproportionate filling of prisons with Blacks, Hispanics, and poor Whites will not return. Sessions never had the opportunity to make a good faith effort to bring back the Clinton years because he was forced to resign on November 7, 2018, due to Trump's disfavor with Sessions' recusal from overseeing the Russia election interference investigation by the special counsel.

***

During the second decade of the twenty-first century, Black incarceration as a major political issue was supplanted by the issue of police use of force and killing of Black males during police encounters. These two issues, together, are the modern issues that are used to assert the criminal justice system is the new Jim Crow for Blacks in general and specifically for young Black males. In his documentary on Blacks in America and criminal justice policy, social historian Henry Louis Gates observed that,

> from 1983 and 1997 the number of African Americans incarcerated for drug offense grew by over 2000 percent. That's more than six times the rate of increase for white Americans. The rise of crack cocaine birthed the new war on crime and drugs and created the avenue that criminalized Black men and Black behavior. Crack gave birth to significant increases in funding for police, special drug task forces, asset forfeiture, militarization of police to deal with drug gangs, and the rise of increased prison construction.[129]

Other social commentators in his documentary came to the similar conclusions on the impact of the policies of the 1980s and 1990s on the Black community. Historian Lawrence D. Bobo reflected that during the 1980s and 1990s, "we have a circumstance of this persistent and rising joblessness in urban Black communities and rather than major investment in education or training or jobs, we get a major investment in policing and prison building and incarceration." Sherrilyn Ifill, President, NAACP Legal Defense Fund, observed that rather than providing support to those needing jobs and education, "We have used the prisons essentially as a warehouse for our race problem. We used that as the place where we could warehouse particularly young African American men." Attorney General Eric Holder concluded that "We looked for simple solutions to complex problems as opposed to asking ourselves what are the sociological reasons? What are the social dysfunctions, the deficits that we see in the people who are committing these crimes? What are we going to do to deal with those? The thought was never to deal with those. The thought was always simply to get them locked up, get them away from us, and hopefully they will stay there for an extended period of time."

When the issue of race and crime shifted from concern of disproportionate incarceration to police use of force and the lack of securing prosecutions and convictions of police killing Black males, Cornel West observed, regarding the rise of the Black Lives Matter movement, "We know Black lives matter the way all lives matter. But unfortunately, in America you got

---

129 Henry Louis Gates, *Black America Since MLK and Still We Rise,* PBS documentary 2016.

to say Black lives matter because when you say all lives matter often times you don't get to the Black lives." With the failure to indict the police officers in the death of Black men like John Crawford and Freddie Gray by police officers, Brittney Cooper observed, "So we know now, really clearly, whether we begin at hurricane Katrina or we begin at Travon Martin or we begin at Michael Brown that this country's having a problem affirming at the level of policy and treatment that Black lives matter."

KEY CONCEPTS AND LAWS

1. Eugenics
2. Social Darwinism
3. Bill O'Reilly Debate
4. Due Process Model
5. Crime Control Model
6. The Penance Era (1790–1876)
7. The Reform Era (1876–1936)
8. The Punitive Era (1935–1945)
9. The Rehabilitative Era (1945–1980)
10. The Second Punitive Era (1980–2000)
11. The Post-Second Punitive Era (2000–present)
12. The Federal Criminal Justice Act of 1964
13. The Law Enforcement Assistance Act of 1965
14. The Bail Reform Act 1966
15. Omnibus Crime Control and Safe Streets Act of 1968
16. New York no-knock warrant stop-and-frisk legislation
17. Militarization of the police
18. Special Weapons and Tactics (SWAT) teams
19. The silent majority
20. The DC Crime Bill of 1970
21. Comprehensive Drug Abuse Prevention and Control Act of 1970
22. Formation of the DEA (1973)
23. The Rockefeller Drug Laws of 1973
24. The criminalization of drug use
25. Military Cooperation with Civilian Law Enforcement Agencies Act of 1981
26. Comprehensive Crime Control Act of 1984
27. The U.S. Sentencing Commission
28. The Anti–Drug Abuse Act of 1986
29. One hundred to one crack power disparity
30. The Anti-Drug Abuse Act of 1988
31. The Bush Administration March 13, 1989 Justice Department policy memo

32. Five-year mandatory minimum sentence for five grams of crack cocaine
33. Crime Control Act of 1990
34. The National Defense Authorization Act of 1990 section 1208 program
35. Violent Crime and Law Enforcement Act of 1994
36. 42 USC § 14141 – Cause of Action Police pattern or Practices
37. Violent Offender Incarceration and Truth in Sentencing (VOI-TIS) program
38. The "Three Strikes and You're Out" policy
39. The Clinton Justice Department March 13, 1995 memo
40. Housing Opportunity Program Extension Act of 1996
41. Quality Housing and Work Responsibilities Act of 1998
42. The "One Strike and You're Out" policy
43. National Defense Authorization Act of 1997 section 1033 program
44. The Fair Sentencing Act of 2010
45. *U.S. v. Booker* (2005)
46. *Kimbrough v. U.S.* (2007)
47. *Koon v. United States* (1996)
48. USA PROTECT ACT (2003)
49. *Department Policy Concerning Charging Criminal Offenses, Disposition of Charges, and Sentencing* (September 22, 2003) (Attorney General Ashcroft sentencing policy memo)
50. Memorandum to United States Attorneys and Assistant Attorney General Criminal Division (August 12, 2013) (Holder memo on charging and sentencing policy)
51. *Justice Department policy announcement: Justice Department Announces Update to Marijuana Enforcement Policy* August 29, 2013
52. *Memorandum for all Federal Prosecutors* (May 10, 2017) (Session memo on charging and sentencing policy)
53. *Memorandum to all U.S. Attorneys issued by Attorney General Jeffery Sessions* January 4, 2018
54. Federal consent decrees through the Violent Crime and Law Enforcement Act of 1994, 42 U.S.C. § 14141 enforcing the 1964 Civil Rights Act, 42 U.S.C. § 2000d, the Omnibus Crime Control and Safe Streets Act of 1968, 42 U.S.C. § 3789d(c)(1) and Title II of the Americans with Disabilities Act of 1990, 42 U.S.C. § 12132.

KEY PEOPLE

1. Bill O'Reilly
2. Chief William Parker
3. Director John Edger Hoover
4. Governor Nelson Rockefeller
5. Chief Daryl Gates
6. Attorney General Jeff Sessions
7. Attorney General Eric Holder

DISCUSSION QUESTIONS

1. Describe the O'Reilly debate. What was the point each participant was making? Do you agree or disagree?
2. What are the various aspects and principles in the Due Process and Crime Control models? Which do you agree with? Which do you not agree with? How would you describe a fair, just, and functional criminal justice system?
3. Summarize and explain the various criminal justice eras and the purpose for each? Which do you think was the best answer to why people commit crime and the best solution for the crime problem in society?
4. Explain and contrast the criminal justice policies of various time periods in American modern criminal justice history. What made the 1960s so different than the 1970s? What made the 1980s and 1990s so similar, considering they were dominated by presidents of two different parties?
5. Explain and contrast the rhetoric of Presidents Reagan and Clinton? How did they agree on criminal justice policy? Why do you think their rhetoric and policies agreed?
6. Explain the history of criminal justice drug policy from President Nixon through Clinton? How did each president deal with the criminalization of drug use?
7. This chapter asserted that the modern explanation of disproportionate incarceration of Blacks occurred under the plague of crack cocaine. What was the history of the crack epidemic, and why did it have such a disproportionate impact of the Black and Hispanic communities? How did modern criminal justice policies address the crack epidemic?
8. The militarization of policing has a long history. Explain the historical and policy development of SWAT and federal support for the militarization of policing in America and why it matters? Should police have access to weapons designed for the military?
9. What is the significance of the end of the second punitive era in American criminal justice? What policies resulted? Do you think those policies have been beneficial or detrimental to American criminal justice and public safety?
10. *The Violent Crime and Law Enforcement Act of 1994* (42 USC § 14141 – Cause of Action Police pattern or Practices) authorized the Justice Department to sue local law enforcement agencies that were found to have a pattern and practice of violating the civil rights of citizens. This law, supplementing *the Omnibus Crime Control Act of 1968*, allows for the Justice Department to investigate and either (1) establish consent decrees with police agencies to make changes to end discrimination or (2) secure judicial court orders and monitoring to enforce policy changes in police agencies. Should the federal government have the power to interfere with a state and local function – the operation of police agencies? How and does American history, politics, policy, and rhetoric justify federal intervention in a traditionally locally governmental function? Is a consent decree or judicial monitoring of a police agency equal federal taking over

of local policing as social conservatives claim? Should a local police agency be taken over by the federal government if it is discriminatory in practice?

11. In looking at *Koon v. United States* (1996), the *USA PROTECT ACT* (2003), *U.S. v. Booker* (2005), *Kimbrough v. U.S.* (2007) and *The Fair Sentencing Act of 2010* together, what are the issues they raise and settle regarding sentencing guidelines?
12. Compare and contrast the Holder and Sessions memos regarding charging and sentencing policy. What was the policy goal of each memo, what policies did each memo change, and what was the impact of each policy?
13. Compare and contrast the Bush Administration March 13, 1989 Justice Department policy memo and the Clinton Justice Department March 13, 1995 regarding the use of three-strikes charging. What was the policy goal of each memo, what policies did each memo change, and what was the impact of each policy?

Appendix
President Johnson Special Message to the Congress on Crime and Law Enforcement (March 9, 1966)

Crime—the fact of crime and the fear of crime—marks the life of every American. .... We know the cost it inflicts on thousands—in death, injury, suffering and anguish. We know the still more widespread cost it exacts from millions in fear:

—Fear that can turn us into a nation of captives imprisoned nightly behind chained doors, double locks, barred windows.

—Fear that can make us afraid to walk city streets by night or public parks by day. These are costs a truly free people cannot tolerate. ...

The entire nation is united in concern over crime. The entire nation shares in the resolution to deal effectively with crime. But national concern is not enough. National resolution is not enough. ...

Today, therefore, I call on the Congress and the nation to join in a three-stage national strategy against crime, welding together the efforts of local, state, and federal governments.

WHAT WE HAVE DONE

This Administration—with the support of this Congress—is committed to assist local authorities. For the first time in our history, an Administration has pledged to the American people that the growth of crime—local, state, and national—will be checked.

We are working in a creative federal partnership to fulfill that pledge.

1. The Law Enforcement Assistance Act, passed last fall, provides a sound foundation upon which we can now build. Under its imaginative scope, we have already launched

Lyndon B. Johnson, "Selection from 'Special Message to the Congress on Crime and Law Enforcement'," 1966.

local and federal action—generations overdue-to modernize not only police work but all aspects of the system of criminal justice.

2. The Prisoner Rehabilitation Act, passed last fall, is the most significant legislative reform in modern American penology. Hundreds of prisoners already are working in daytime jobs as they finish their sentences at night. They are learning job skills that will bring dignity to themselves and support to their families.
3. The National Crime Commission and the District of Columbia Crime Commission, established last year, have launched searching studies into the causes of crime and our present shortcomings in dealing with it.
4. The Federal Bureau of Investigation is expanding its National Academy six-fold. It will soon be able to train 1,200 rather than 200 law enforcement officials each year. It will provide special training for an additional 1,000 officers.
5. Federal efforts against organized crime have continued to increase. Racketeering indictments last year rose to a record 674, compared with 535 in 1964 and only 19 in 1960.

A UNIFIED ATTACK

. . . .

Despite the devotion of our law enforcement officials, our law enforcement system does not deter enough of those who can be deterred. It does not detect and convict enough of those who cannot be deterred. It does not restore enough rehabilitated offenders into the law-abiding community.

Despite the dedication of our law enforcement officials, reforms too often defeat themselves because they do not go far enough.

There is a fundamental lesson we have too often ignored. The problems of crime and law enforcement are closely interrelated. One interlocking tie is within the very system of law enforcement.

Making police more effective is fruitless-if we continue to permit the overburdening of judges and the clogging of courts.

Increasing the number of judges is futile-if the number of competent prosecutors and defense attorneys remains inadequate.

An expanded judiciary cannot take advantage of modern thinking in sentencing-if new correctional facilities are not provided.

The best correctional programs will fail-if legitimate avenues of employment are forever closed to reformed offenders.

. . . .

We must mobilize all of the resources of our creative federal system if we are to repel the threat of crime to our common well-being. The problems of crime bring us together. We must make a common response. There is no other way.

OUR NATIONAL STRATEGY

. . .

I propose a three-stage national strategy.

. . . .

FIRST: THE IMMEDIATE ATTACK

Each of the four aspects of law enforcement calls for reform. There are steps we can now take.

A. To Improve Crime Prevention and Detection

We must improve the quality of local law enforcement throughout the country.

The front-line soldier in the war on crime is the local law enforcement officer. Federal aid to law enforcement at the state and local level was made possible by the Law Enforcement Assistance Act of 1965. Police, court, correctional, and university authorities have responded to the newly created Office of Law Enforcement Assistance with hundreds of imaginative ideas and proposals ...

. . . .

If crime is to be controlled, we must control the weapons with which so many crimes are committed.

We must end the easy availability of deadly weapons to professional criminals, to delinquent youth, and to the disturbed and deranged.

We must stop the flow of firearms into dangerous hands.

It is not enough to say that gun control is a state responsibility. States with gun control laws now stand helplessly by while those laws are flouted daily by the unchecked sales of guns by mail.

Our Federal responsibility is clear. It is promptly to enact legislation, such as S. 1592, to regulate and control interstate traffic in dangerous firearms.

The front pages of our newspapers make us acutely aware of the human tragedies that flow daily from the unchecked purchase of firearms. Recent Congressional hearings added abundant evidence of the gravity of this problem.

There is no need to curtail the right of citizens to keep arms for such traditional pastimes as hunting and marksmanship. But there is a pressing need to halt blind, unquestioned mail-order sales of guns, and over-the-counter sales to buyers from out of state whose credentials cannot be known.

Only the federal government can give the several states and cities their first real chance to enforce their own gun laws. We must do so without further delay.

. . . .

I recommend a pistol registration act prohibiting the sale of deadly weapons to those who have been convicted of violent crimes, to those with a history of mental instability, and to habitual alcoholics.

B. To Facilitate the Prosecution of Criminals

We must intensify our campaign against organized crime.

...

I propose the appointment of a Commission to conduct a comprehensive review of all the Federal criminal laws and to recommend total revision by 1968.

A number of our criminal laws are obsolete. Many are inconsistent in their efforts to make the penalty fit the crime. Many-which treat essentially the same crimes—are scattered in a crazy-quilt patchwork throughout our criminal code.

...

C. To Enhance Justice in Our Courts

We must reform our bail system. The administration of criminal justice must be fair as well as effective. Whether a person, released after arrest, is likely to flee before trial or endanger society is not determined by the wealth he commands. Yet all too often we imprison men for weeks, months, and even years—before we give them their day in court—solely because they cannot afford bail.

Effective law enforcement does not require such imprisonment.

To correct this injustice, I urge the Congress to complete action on the pending Federal Bail Reform Act and to give favorable consideration to the District of Columbia Bail Agency bill.

These measures will insure fairness. They will provide an enlightened model for those states and communities which have not already undertaken bail reform.

D. To Reclaim and Rehabilitate Lives in Our Prisons

We must establish a rational, coordinated correctional system.

No national strategy against crime can succeed if we do not restore more of our first offenders to productive society. The best law enforcement has little value if prison sentences are only temporary and embittering way stations for men whose release means a return to crime.

.....

At present, we administer the prison, parole, and probation functions partly in the executive branch and partly in the judicial branch. I believe the effectiveness of our corrections programs depends on a rational, coordinated and unified approach.

Consolidating federal correctional efforts can reduce the number of repeaters. ... I recommend that the Federal prison, parole, and probation Junctions be unified within the Department of Justice to consolidate our presently fragmented correctional system.

We must capitalize on the beginning already made in rehabilitating prisoners.

The importance of up-to-date vocational training for inmates is clear. Chronic underemployment often goes hand-in-hand with crime. In our federal prisons, one of every three prisoners worked less than 6 months of the two years before confinement.

...

> We must deal realistically with drug addiction …
> Drug addiction is a double curse. It saps life from the afflicted.

…

SECOND: A COMPREHENSIVE AGENDA

…

We must press forward for greater knowledge, better tools, and deeper insights. This is the task on which the National Crime Commission has already embarked. … .

…

I am asking the Attorney General to work with the governors of the 50 states to establish statewide committees on law enforcement and criminal justice.

Such state committees can assist—and be assisted by—the National Commission. They can stimulate the growth of public involvement and the development of a comprehensive anti-crime agenda in every part of the country.

THIRD: ATTACKING CRIME AT THE ROOTS

A century ago, Thoreau wrote that "There are a thousand hacking at the branches of evil to one who is striking at the root." So it remains today.

The efforts I have described—more effective police action, more efficient courts, improved corrections, comprehensive planning for major reform—all are urgently needed.

And yet all of them together can permit us only to strike more quickly and surely at the branches. The roots of crime will remain.

An effective strategy against crime must also rest on a base of prevention. And that base can come only from action against the wellsprings of crime in our society.

Our commitment to insuring social justice and personal dignity for all Americans does not flow from a desire to fight crime. We are committed to those goals because they are right.

But social conditions which foster a sense of injustice or exploitation also breed crime. But social conditions which foster a sense of injustice or exploitation also breed crime. More than thirty years ago, Clarence Darrow observed:

> "It is very seldom that any one is in prison for an ordinary crime unless early in life he entered a path that almost invariably led to the prison gate. Most of the inmates are the children of the poor. In many instances they are either orphans or half-orphans; their homes were the streets and byways of big cities, and their paths naturally and inevitably took them to their final fate."

The programs now underway to eliminate the degradation of poverty, the decay of our cities, the disgrace of racial discrimination, the despair of illiteracy—are all vitally important to crime prevention.

At the same time, even as we seek to fight crime by fighting injustice, the ways we deal with crime should not foster further injustice:

—Bail requirements need not add families to the welfare rolls.
—Court procedures need not increase a sense of unfair and differential treatment.
—Sentencing practices need not require that the poor go to jail while others pay fines.
—Imprisonment need not result in loss of job skills. Social injustice is not the sole reason for crime. Social justice is not the sole cure.

Even the broadest social programs cannot be panaceas. The lives and attitudes of persons long neglected do not change upon command. The effects of even the most energetic programs may be long in coming. The vast majority of our citizens who suffer poverty and discrimination do not turn to crime.

But where legitimate opportunities are closed, illegitimate opportunities are seized. Whatever opens opportunity and hope will help to prevent crime and foster responsibility.

Effective law enforcement and social justice must be pursued together, as the foundation of our efforts against crime.

The proposals I am making today will not solve the problem of crime in this country. The war on crime will be waged by our children and our children's children. But the difficulty and complexity of the problem cannot be permitted to lead us to despair. They must lead us rather to bring greater efforts, greater ingenuity and greater determination to do battle.

Appendix
Special Message to the Congress on Law Enforcement and the Administration of Justice (March 8, 1966)

To the Congress of the United States:

Crime has become a malignant enemy in America's midst.

Since 1940 the crime rate in this country has doubled. It has increased five times as fast as our population since 1958.

In dollars the cost of crime runs to tens of billions annually. The human costs are simply not measurable.

The problems run deep and will not yield to quick and easy answers. We must identify and eliminate the causes of criminal activity whether they lie in the environment around us or deep in the nature of individual men. This is a major purpose of all we are doing in combatting poverty and improving education, health, welfare, housing, and recreation.

All these are vital, but they are not enough. Crime will not wait while we pull it up by the roots. We must arrest and reverse the trend toward lawlessness.

This active combat against crime calls for...

... improved training of policemen...

....

—to our correctional agencies. We cannot tolerate an endless, self-defeating cycle of imprisonment, release, and reimprisonment which fails to alter undesirable attitudes and behavior. We must find ways to help the first offender avoid a continuing career of crime.

No right is more elemental to our society than the right to personal security and no right needs more urgent protection.

Our streets must be safe. Our homes and places of business must be secure. Experience and wisdom dictate that one of the most legitimate functions of government is the preservation of law and order.

Our system rejects the concept of a national police force. The protection responsibilities lie primarily with state and local governments.

That is right and proper.

Yet, crime is no longer merely a local problem. Every city, every state is troubled by the same hard statistical—and human-facts. The extent and seriousness of the problem have made it of great national concern.

....

I believe the way to do so is to give new recognition to the fact that crime is a national problem—and to intensify our crime prevention and crime-fighting at all levels of government.

....

It has been said, for example, that the fault lies with courts which "coddle criminals," or, on the other hand, that police officers do not observe the rights of the individual.

.... Yet there is the undoubted necessity that society be protected from the criminal and that the rights of society be recognized along with the rights of the individual.

As Mr. Justice Frankfurter once said, "A democratic society, in which respect for the dignity of all men is central, naturally guards against the misuse of the law enforcement process."

It has been said that the fault lies in poor living conditions, limited education, and the denial of opportunity.

Plainly, laws are less likely to command the respect of those forced to live at the margins of our society. Stability and order have little meaning and small advantage to those who exist in poverty, hopelessness, and despair.

The long-run solution to the view of crime is jobs, education and hope. This is a goal to which this country is now committed. But we should remember that not all crime is committed by those who are impoverished or those denied equal opportunity. ....

....

Thus, while recognizing that the basic responsibility rests on local authorities, we must also recognize the burdens they now bear. To assist them in bearing these burdens successfully, I propose:

—increased federal law enforcement efforts;

—assistance to local law enforcement efforts;

—a comprehensive, penetrating analysis of the origins and nature of crime in modern America.

FEDERAL LAW ENFORCEMENT EFFORTS The average citizen is most directly concerned with what is called "crime in the streets". Crime of this kind—robberies, muggings, housebreakings—are the primary law enforcement responsibility of state and local governments. When criminals cross state lines, however, federal enforcement is also available. Thus, federal, state and local investigators may all join to pursue the bank robber, the kidnapper or the auto thief. Federal assistance in these activities has been and can continue to be helpful.

In some areas, however, the Federal Government has a special responsibility…, narcotic and drug control, regulation of gun sales….

2. Drug Control.

The return of narcotic and marihuana users to useful, productive lives is of obvious benefit to them and to society at large. But at the same time, it is essential to assure adequate protection of the general public.

…

… provide an alternative means of dealing with those narcotic and marihuana users likely to respond to treatment and achieve rehabilitation. … [P]enalty provisions of the federal narcotics and marihuana laws requiring mandatory minimum sentences and precluding probation or parole be applied restrictively in order to provide a greater incentive for rehabilitation.

The Justice Department will shortly submit proposals for a federal civil commitment statute to the Congress and for limiting the coverage of the mandatory minimum penalty sentences. The proposals will seek to the fullest extent consistent with the public safety to give offenders a maximum opportunity for return to a normal life.

…

3. Firearms Control.

Drugs are, of course, only one cause of the rise in violent crime in the United States. Another significant factor is the ease with which any person can acquire firearms. Lee Oswald sent for and received a rifle through the United States mail. I believe that the people of the United States have learned, through the recent tragic loss of President Kennedy the need for strengthened control.

Here the Federal Government's jurisdiction is limited. State and local action will be necessary. But at minimum, we must make effective local regulation of firearms possible by increasing Federal control over interstate shipment of firearms. In addition, limits must be imposed on the importation into this country of surplus military weapons and other used firearms.

I am proposing [to] amend the Federal Firearms Act to prohibit firearms shipments in interstate commerce except among importers, manufacturers and dealers licensed by the Treasury Department.

Mail-order sales to individuals would thus stop. … I urge the Governors of our states and mayors and other local public officials to review their existing legislation in this critical field with a view to keeping lethal weapons out of the wrong hands.

I recommend this legislation to the Congress as a sensible use of Federal authority to assist local authorities in coping with an undeniable menace to law and order and to the lives of innocent people.

....

ASSISTANCE TO LOCAL AUTHORITIES Whatever we may do to strengthen federal law enforcement, the principal enforcement responsibility still rests on state and local governments—and that has become a very large burden indeed.

....

...I believe a major opportunity lies in the development and testing of experimental methods of crime control. To this end, I am proposing the Law Enforcement Assistance Act of 1965. This legislation would authorize the Attorney General to assist state, local and private groups to improve and strengthen crime control programs and make generally available information as to their effectiveness.

This Act would bolster present training programs for local law enforcement personnel and would support the development of new training methods. Fighting crime effectively under modern conditions requires professional police who are expertly trained in a variety of skills....

...

PRESIDENTIAL COMMISSION The proposals which I have discussed are promising immediate approaches to a number of the specific problems of controlling crime. In the longer run we must also deepen our understanding of the causes of crime and of how our society should respond to the challenge of our present levels of crime. Only with such understanding can we undertake more fundamental, far-reaching and imaginative programs.

As the first step, l am establishing the President's Commission on Law Enforcement and Administration of Justice. The Commission will be composed of men and women of distinction who share my belief that we need to know far more about the prevention and control of crime. I will ask the Commission to make a comprehensive report to me by the summer of 1966 and to make interim reports when early action on the basis of its recommendations may be possible.

...

CONCLUSION This message recognizes that crime is a national problem.

That recognition does not carry with it any threat to the basic prerogatives of state and local governments. It means, rather, that the Federal Government will henceforth take a more meaningful role in meeting the whole spectrum of problems posed by crime.

It means that the Federal Government will seek to exercise leadership and to assist local authorities in meeting their responsibilities.

It means that we will make a national effort to resolve the problems of law enforcement and the administration of justice—and to direct the attention of the Nation to the problems of crime and the steps that must be taken to meet them.

CHAPTER NINE

Epilogue

STUDENT LEARNING OBJECTIVES

1. Students will be able to summarize the historical, social, political and societal factors that influence and define disproportionate involvement of Blacks in the criminal justice system.
2. Students will be able to explain and discuss the views of Frederick Douglass regarding the proposition that the U.S. Constitution is a pro-slave document and how Douglass rejected that proposition.
3. Students will be able to define social conservative political theory and understand its relationship to police use of force and the politics of police use of force as well as be able to distinguish the politics of police use of force from the law that governs police use of force.
4. Students will be able to explain and discuss recent research on police use of force and will be familiar with data from the Washington Post database on police use of force.

In 1776 when the founding fathers of the American Revolution debated and decided to assert independence from Great Britain, they decided that they should assert the reasons why the colonies had decided to reject further rule by the king and demanded their freedom and independence. In the draft of the great document penned by Thomas Jefferson, with minor additions from John Adams and Benjamin Franklin, an interesting *crime* was asserted to have been committed by the king worthy of disownment by the colonies that would become the United States. The crime was

> He has waged cruel war against human nature itself, violating its most sacred rights of life and liberty in the persons of distant people, who never offended

Parts of this chapter have been adapted from Arthur H. Garrison, "Arthur H. Garrison: Viewing Ferguson And Staten Island In Historical Context Of Race," *The Morning Call*, 2014.

> him, captivating and carrying them into slavery in another hemisphere, or to incur miserable death in their transportation thither. This piratical warfare, the opprobrium of infidel powers, is the warfare of the Christian king of Great Britain. Determined to keep open a market where Men should be bought and sold, he has prostituted his negative for suppressing every legislative attempt to prohibit or to restrain this execrable commerce: and that this assemblage of horrors might want no fact of distinguished dye, he is now exciting those very people to rise in arms among us, and to purchase that liberty of which he has deprived them by murdering the people upon whom he also obtruded them; thus paying off former crime committed against the liberties of one people, with crimes which he urges them to commit against the lives of another.

Note the three aspects of the crime. First, the king invaded a nation of people that had not "offended him" and carried them away as slaves. Second, the king imposed the institution of slavery on the colonies in 1619. Most significantly, third, the king was actively fermenting, agitating, and inciting rebellion among those African slaves against their colonial masters by 1776. Black Africans were imposed on the Christian White colonies, and then, they were made a physical threat to those same colonies. Consider Jefferson's description of the third aspect of the king's crime and then the negative psychological and sociological perceptions of Blacks held today as discussed in Chapter Three. As it is written, there is nothing new under the sun.

Upon receiving Jefferson's draft, the Southern colonies led by Georgia and South Carolina threatened not to sign the **Declaration of Independence** if Jefferson's **slave clause** was listed among the crimes of King Charles to justified independence. The Southern rebellion was supplemented by Northern slave merchant interests that profited from a system of slavery and the industry of the international slave trade. The result of the rebellion was the removal of the slave clause of Jefferson's draft of the Declaration of Independence. In 1787, when some of the same men gathered to draft the U.S. Constitution, the Southern states again demanded that slavery be protected at most and not be prohibited at least, the result being that the slavery was not only not prohibited, but Congress was prohibited from outlawing the importation of slaves until 1808! Again, under threat of not agreeing to the constitution, slavery was tolerated, not abolished.

Social conservatives, both Black and White, look at this history and admit, with little shame, that, indeed, it was expedient to the writing of the Declaration of Independence and the U.S. Constitution and to the signing and ratification of both to allow African slavery in a nation premised on individual liberty and freedom. Social conservatives argue that neither document would have seen the light of day if the high-minded ideals of "all men are created equal" and "We the people" required opposition to the institution of slavery and extended freedom, much less equality, to Blacks in the new nation they were creating. Social conservatives make clear that the founding generation was trying to create a nation (1776) and form a lasting government (1787), and sacrifices had to be made for the greater good. Slavery and the racism that undergirded it had to be left to later generations—all true as a raw historical and political matter. The point is, however, not that sacrifices had to be made, but who was sacrificed to create this "land of the free and home of the brave."

****

When consider the following interaction between race, criminal justice, and perceptions of Blacks in American history: between 1619 and 1865 is two hundred and forty six years; between 1789 and 2018 is two hundred and twenty nine years; between 1865 and 1968 is one hundred and three years; and between 1968 and 2018 is fifty years.

Summary Timeline Chart of American Race and Criminal Justice History

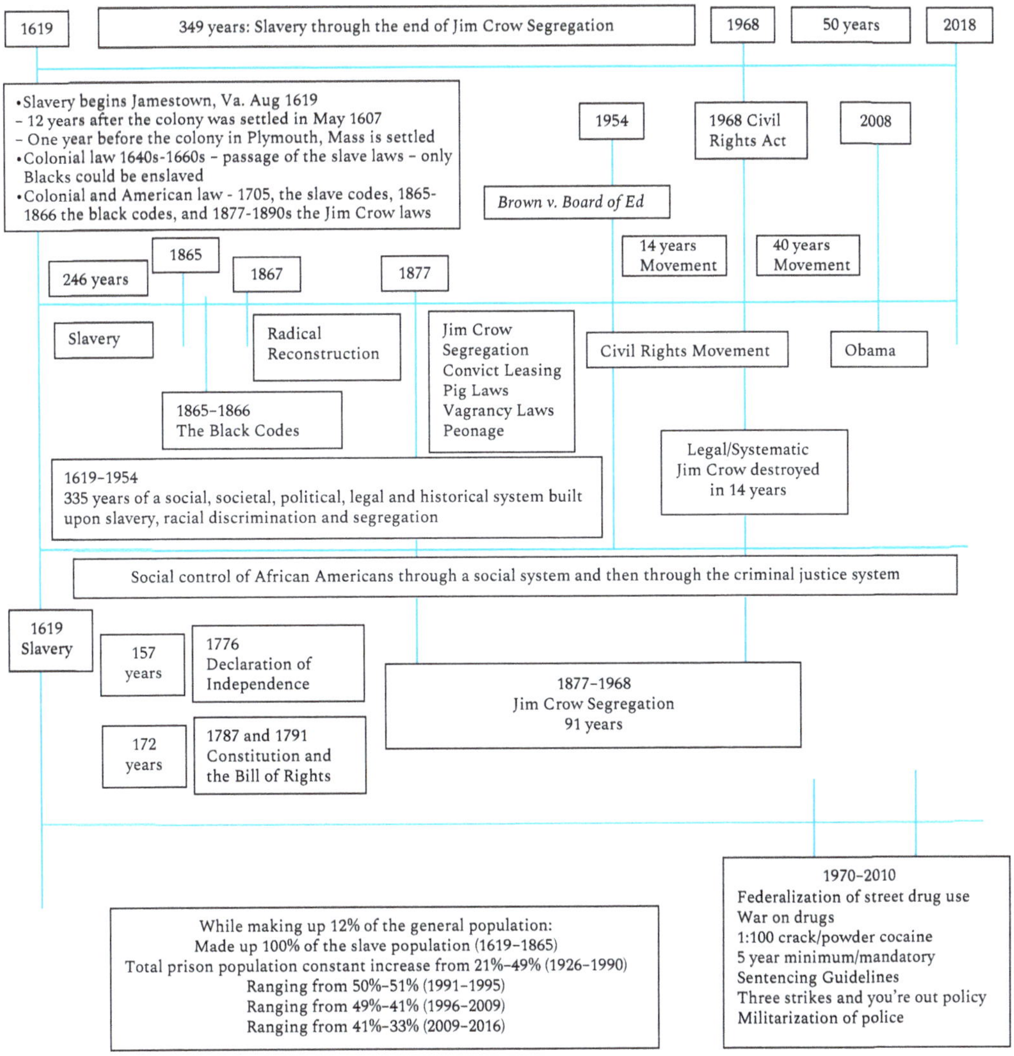

Slavery of Blacks in the colonies and then in the United States lasted two hundred and forty-six years, which means slavery and the racism that undergirded it in North America is seventeen years older than the entire history of the constitutional United States!

The history of the Black Codes, Jim Crow, and Blacks being second class citizens by statute (one hundred and three years) is slightly less than half as old as the entire constitutional history of the United States.

Blacks being free from Jim Crow (statutory second-class citizenship) is only fifty years old in a country that is two hundred and twenty-nine years old.

Now consider the historical, political, economic, sociological, and psychological development and the operation of the government institutions built upon them and their relation to Blacks when Blacks have only been equal under the law for fifty years of a nation that is two hundred and twenty-nine years old.

CRIMINAL JUSTICE AND RACE VS EDUCATION INVOLVEMENT: RHETORIC AND POLICY OUTCOMES

The significance of the constitutional and legal history of slavery and race in America is that there is a socio-legal historical context for how Blacks are perceived. The perception that Blacks are supposed to be watched and controlled dates back to slavery and the assertion of inferiority of Blacks remained and developed within the social and legal culture of American for more than a century after the Civil War. After the modern civil rights movement (1968), the social control of Blacks—under intentional and specific law—was replaced by unconscious racial bias, in general, and the fear of Black crime, specifically. This resulted in increased use of federal and state criminal justice laws, which resulted in the use of prisons and the criminal justice system as the modern replacement of slavery and Jim Crow as a method of the social and physical control of Blacks. As the great Thirteenth Amendment makes clear, "Neither slavery nor involuntary servitude, *except as a punishment for crime whereof the party shall have been duly convicted*, shall exist within the United States, or any place subject to their jurisdiction." From 1865 to the present, the Constitution has made clear that slavery is abolished for all except those convicted of crime. For those convicted, the vestiges of slavery can be inflicted. Under the Constitution, a person convicted can be discriminated against in employment, housing, education, receiving governmental assistance, eligibility for military service, financial opportunities, and political rights, including the right to vote and hold elective office. A criminal conviction can bar a person from all of these privileges of citizenship. In other words, the vestiges of slavery can be lawfully inflicted after the Civil War and after the Second Reconstruction (1950s–1960s) With the fall of slavery as an institution of social control, criminal justice rose as the new system of social control. From the late 1870s to the present, these vestiges of slavery have been inflicted disproportionately on Blacks in America, all under the auspices the criminal justice system.

The criminal justice system is not the cause of the need to socially control Blacks, but it is the reflection of that need. As President Obama observed,

> And I don't think that the criminal justice system is obviously the sole source of racial tension in this country, or the key institution to resolving the opportunity gap. But I think it is a part of the broader set of challenges that we face in creating a more perfect union ... the most important goal is keeping folks from getting in the criminal justice system in the first place, which means early childhood education and good jobs, and making sure that we're not segregating folks in impoverished communities that have no contact with opportunity.
>
> ...
>
> ... part of our question should be, how about somebody reaching out to these guys when they're 10, or 11, or 12, or eight, as opposed to waiting until they've already gone through a criminal justice program.[1]

The history of Jim Crow provides the context for understanding Black disproportionate incarceration and how Blacks perceive their treatment by the criminal justice system and, particularly, their treatment by police officers in the street. As Attorney General Lynch explained, the racial history of America

> is really a deeper issue than just the individual discrimination many of us have seen in whether or not we didn't get the job or the opportunity, or if someone didn't speak to us. We are talking about the pain that comes up when these deeply rooted injustices get shrugged off and they get ignored.[2]

Attorney General Loretta Lynch related a story about criminal justice in the 1930s and how her grandfather would hide boys that were being pursued by the local police. She said,

> Sometimes the sheriff would come by the house and ask my grandfather, "Have you seen so-and-so?" My grandfather would say, "Well not lately." So-and-so is hiding in a closet or hiding under the floorboards. Because in those days, 1930's North Carolina, there was no justice in the dark of night on a rural road. No Miranda warnings. No procedural protections. None of the things we take for granted today. And so despite what happened with these individuals, my grandfather knew that sometimes in order to preserve the fight for justice into the future we had to take action in the moment—you had to take action in the moment.
>
> Now of course things are much better now.[3]

---

1 President Obama Press Conference July 15, 2015, at https://www.whitehouse.gov/the-press-office/2015/07/15/press-conference-president

2 Attorney General Loretta Lynch, Remarks at the Congressional Black Caucus 45th Annual Legislative Conference Judiciary Brain Trust Panel (September 18, 2015).

3 Attorney General Loretta Lynch

Racial bias in policing is not a trivial thing. It is about the personal "frustration that comes up when we are treated unfairly because of race. But this is really about more than just that. This is really about being treated unfairly because of race by those who are sworn to protect you, by those who wear the uniform of protection."[4] There is a difference between being harassed or killed by a criminal and being harassed or killed by an arm of the government.

While America has moved on from legal and systematic segregation, the history of racial, social, economic, and political segregation has caused structural distortions in the Black community. ***Just as those who assert that what the founding generation believed and wrote regarding the Constitution matters in interpreting and applying that document two hundred years later, the legal and social history of racial discrimination and its results in policy over two centuries has present day consequences.*** It has been observed that American contemporary society, when looking at a video of Blacks being beaten by police, needs to

> acknowledge the anger and the despair that develops when these things that we now see on tape are still pushed aside by so many people as if they don't exist. You have to acknowledge the kind of pain that develops. You have to acknowledge that feeling—and you know people say "I don't think it was that bad," "Well I don't think they meant it that way," or even "That just didn't even happen." And so when that happens to people—to a people, to our people—time and time again, you have within our community a sense of disconnection and despair that is a dangerous as any bullet or any billy club.[5]

The point General Lynch was making is simple: the racism of police beating a Black man in the street is only surpassed by American political indifference or policy-making apathy to it. This racism is all the more distressing when police abuse is seen as an aberration, thus not a problem to be addressed. This indifference has a history that Black parents have had to contend with for generations. As General Lynch explained,

> 52 years ago my father, like all parents, looked at me and my two brothers and wondered, "How do I protect my children? How do I keep them safe?" Not just from the enemy next door but the world that wants to tell them they are less than. A world that wants to tell them that they are different. A world that tells them they don't matter and that they are simply cannon fire.[6]

The point is not that the parents of the generation of General Lynch "couldn't see who would be sitting in the White House today and sitting in a meeting with the Attorney General who was that little girl whose father looked at her 52 years ago and said I have to protect."[7] The

---

4 Attorney General Loretta Lynch

5 Attorney General Loretta Lynch

6 Attorney General Loretta Lynch

7 Attorney General Loretta Lynch

point she was making was that her father's generation had to worry in the first place, and the worry was not shared by White parents of the same generation about their children's future.

This fear was not new in the time of General Lynch's father, for in 1883, **Frederick Douglass**, the great orator of Black thought, both before and after the Civil War, observed the following regarding the state of race in America in his ***Address to the People of the United States***:[8]

> It is our lot to live among a people whose laws, traditions, and prejudices have been against us for centuries, and from these they are not yet free. To assume that they are free from these evils simply because they have changed their laws is to assume what is utterly unreasonable and contrary to facts ... Though the colored man is no longer subject to be bought and sold, he is still surrounded by an adverse sentiment which fetters all his movements. In his downward course he meets with no resistance, but his course upward is resented and resisted at every step of his progress. If he comes in ignorance, rags, and wretchedness, he conforms to the popular belief of his character, and in that character he is welcome. But if he shall come as a gentleman, a scholar, and a statesman, he is hailed as a contradiction to the national faith concerning his race, and his coming is resented as impudence. In the one case he may provoke contempt and derision, but in the other he is an affront to pride, and provokes malice. Let him do what he will, there is at present, therefore, no escape for him. The color line meets him everywhere, and in a measure shuts him out from all respectable and profitable trades and callings. In spite of all your religion and laws he is a rejected man.

As discussed in Chapter Three, racism is not simply defined as hatred, it's manifested in the dehumanization of low expectations and either refusal to accept Blacks as equal and, through study and hard work, superior to Whites or the belief that there is a default subservient place for Blacks. In the times of Frederick Douglass, the expected place of Blacks was "ignorance, rags, and wretchedness;" today, it's prison. In his time, there was no surprise to find Blacks poor, as today there is no surprise to find a disproportionate number of people under the control of the criminal justice system are Black. The assumption is that they are supposed to be there. It's the Black man without a criminal record that is a surprise, as the educated Black man was in times of Douglass.

Frederick Douglass continued his assessment of the social environment the freed slave found himself in by noting that the racism he faced was found not only in the perceptions Whites had for him but in how those perceptions defined his relation to both church and law. He observed that

> He is rejected by trade unions, of every trade, and refused work while he lives, and burial when he dies, and yet he is asked to forget his color, and forget that which everybody

8 Frederick Douglass, "Address to the People of the United States," delivered at a Convention of Colored Men, Louisville, Kentucky, Sept. 25, 1883 at http://coloredconventions.org/items/show/554

> else remembers. If he offers himself to a builder as a mechanic, to a client as a lawyer, to a patient as a physician, to a college as a professor, to a 'firm as a clerk, to a Government Department as an agent, or an officer, he is sternly met on the color line, and his claim to consideration in some way is disputed on the ground of color.
>
> Not even our churches ... have yet conquered this feeling of color madness, and what is true of our churches is also true of our courts of law. Neither is free from this all-pervading atmosphere of color hate. The one describes the Deity as impartial, no respecter of persons, and the other the Goddess of Justice as blindfolded, with sword by her side and scales in her hand held evenly between high and low, rich and poor, white and black, but both are the images of American imagination, rather than American practices.
>
> Taking advantage of the general disposition in this country to impute crime to color, white men color their faces to commit crime and wash off the hated color to escape punishment. In many places where the commission of crime is alleged against one of our color, the ordinary processes of the law are set aside as too slow for the impetuous justice of the infuriated populace. They take the law into their own bloody hands and proceed to whip, stab, shoot, hang, or burn the alleged culprit, without the intervention of courts, counsel, judges, juries, or witnesses. In such cases it is not the business of the accusers to prove guilt, but it is for the accused to prove his innocence, a thing hard for any man to do, even in a court of law, and utterly impossible for him to do in these infernal Lynch courts. A man accused, surprised, frightened and captured by a motley crowd, dragged with a rope about his neck in midnight-darkness to the nearest tree, and told in the coarsest terms of profanity to prepare for death, would be more than human if he did not, in his terror-stricken appearance, must confirm suspicion of guilt than the contrary. Worse still, in the presence of such hell-black outrages, the pulpit is usually dumb, and the press in the neighborhood is silent or openly takes side with the mob. There are occasional cases in which white men are lynched, but one sparrow does not make a summer. Everyone knows that what is called Lynch law is peculiarly the law for colored people and for nobody else. If there were no other grievance than this horrible and barbarous Lynch law custom, we should be justified in assembling, as we have now done, to expose and denounce it. But this is not all. Even now, after twenty years of so-called emancipation, we are subject to lawless raids of midnight riders, who, with blackened faces, invade our homes and perpetrate the foulest of crimes upon us and our families. This condition of things is too flagrant and notorious to require specifications or proof. Thus in all the relations of life and death we are met by the color line. We cannot ignore it if we would, and ought not if we could. It hunts us at midnight, it denies us accommodation in hotels and justice in the courts; excludes our children from schools, refuses our sons the chance to learn trades, and compels us to pursue only such labor as will bring the least reward.

As General Lynch explained, the distrust of the criminal justice system because the system had no relation to fair and just outcomes when it came to Blacks has existed for centuries, both before and a century after the Civil War. A Black man accused was a Black man convicted by the rope of the mob. The point is not that today criminal justice functions as a modern day lynch mob or with the mentality of a lynch mob. The point is that, culturally and historically, the criminal justice system has not been an institution with a history of protection and valuation of Black lives. Its history has been quite the opposite. It's that history that breeds general Black distrust of the system. For Whites, it's the lack of a negative history regarding their rights that explains their support for the system. There is a profound point in the simple truth that the pursuit of federal anti-lynching laws were necessary in the first place in America, that they were requested for the sole purpose of preventing Blacks from being lynched by White mobs, and it took more than a century to pass an anti-lynching bill in the Senate.

Like Martin Luther King Jr. after him, Frederick Douglass expressed in his *Address to the People of the United States*, that he also had a dream:

> While we recognize the color line as a hurtful force, a mountain barrier to our progress, wounding our bleeding feet with its flinty rocks at every step, we do not despair. We are a hopeful people. This convention is a proof of our faith in you, in reason, in truth and justice our belief that prejudice, with all its malign accompaniments, may yet be removed by peaceful means; that, assisted by time and events and the growing enlightenment of both races, the color line will ultimately become harmless. When this shall come it will then only be used, as it should be, to distinguish one variety of the human family from another. It will cease to have any civil, political, or moral significance, and colored conventions will then be dispensed with as anachronisms, wholly out of place, but not till then. Do not marvel that we are not discouraged. The faith within us has a rational basis, and is confirmed by facts. When we consider how deep-seated this feeling against us is the long centuries it has been forming; the forces of avarice which have been marshaled to sustain it; how the language and literature of the country have been pervaded with it; how the church, the press, the play-house, and other influences of the country have been arrayed in its support, the progress toward its extinction must be considered vast and wonderful.

Just as Dr. King said we must fight to make sure justice rolls down like a mighty stream, Douglass said that until justice is found in America Blacks must not accept injustice:

> If liberty, with us, is yet but a name, our citizenship is but a sham, and our suffrage thus far only a cruel mockery, we may yet congratulate ourselves upon the fact that the laws and institutions of the country are sound, just and liberal. There is hope for a people when their laws are righteous whether for the moment they conform to their requirements or not. But until this nation shall make its practice accord with its Constitution and its righteous laws, it will not do to reproach the colored people of this country with keeping up the color line for that people would prove themselves scarcely worthy of even theoretical freedom, to say nothing of practical freedom, if they settled down in silent, servile and cowardly submission to their wrongs, from fear of making their color visible. They are bound by every element of manhood to hold conventions in their own name and on their

> own behalf, to keep their grievances before the people and make every organized protest against the wrongs inflicted upon them within their power.

It was this battle to "keep their grievances before the people and make every organized protest against the wrongs inflicted upon them within their power" that ended Jim Crow fifty years ago and seeks to end the political expectation and acceptation of disproportionate incarceration of Blacks today as normal.

The fall of Jim Crow resulted from the ratification of the Twenty-Fourth Amendment (outlawing the poll tax—January 1964), the passage of the Civil Rights Acts of 1964 and 1968, and the enforcement of the Fifteenth Amendment (1870) through the passage of the Voting Rights Act of 1965. The death of Jim Crow allowed the Black middle class to flourish like at no other time in American history and allowed it to take its place among the White middle class as the social and political backbone of society. The result of the fall of Jim Crow resulted in the election of the first Black president only fifty-four years after *Brown*, and the achievements of the Black middle class include Barack Obama, Michael Steele, Eric Holder, and Loretta E. Lynch and, before them, General Colin Powell and Condoleezza Rice.[9] Although the fall of Jim Crow resulted from the social and societal successes built upon the victories of Lincoln over Stephens; Kennedy over Wallace; Warren over Taney; they did not change the fact that more Blacks are disproportionately represented in the population of prison, as compared to college.

In 2012, the Department of Education[10] released a report asserting that in 2010 Blacks accounted for 15% of undergraduate enrollment of U.S. residents in degree-granting post-secondary institutions[11] and 14% of post-baccalaureate enrollment of U.S. residents in degree-granting post-baccalaureate institutions.[12] While it is true that the percentage of participation in undergraduate enrollment has increased from 10% in 1980 and 1990 to 12% in 2000 to 15% in 2010 with corresponding increases in post-baccalaureate enrollment (6% in 1980 and 1990, 9% in 2000, and 14% in 2010)[13] the percentage of Black "enrollment" in prison has not been below 20% since official data has been collected dating back to the

9 The first Black elected president of the United States, the first Black elected Chairman of the National Republican Party, the first Black appointed to the position of U.S. Attorney General, the first Black female appointed to the position of U.S. Attorney General, the first Black appointed to the position of Secretary of State (and Chairman of the Joint Chief of Staff), and the first Black female appointed to the position of National Security Advisor (later Secretary of State) respectively.

10 Susan Aud, William Hussar, Frank Johnson, Grace Kena, Erin Roth, Eileen Manning, Xiaolei Wang, Jijun Zhang, and Liz Notter, *The Condition of Education 2012* Department of Education, National Center for Education Statistics (September 2012)

11 Susan Aud et al., *The Condition of Education 2012*, Department of Education, National Center for Education Statistics (September 2012) at 35.

12 Susan Aud et al., *The Condition of Education 2012*, Department of Education, National Center for Education Statistics (September 2012) at 37.

13 *Supra* notes 10–12.

early 1920s.[14] Blacks account for 13% of the total population, yet they account for 35% of the prison population 15% of undergraduate population and 14% of the post-baccalaureate population.

In 2013, the Department of Education[15] reported that Blacks accounted for 14% of undergraduate enrollment of U.S. residents in degree-granting postsecondary institutions[16] and 12.6% of post-baccalaureate enrollment of U.S. residents in degree-granting post-baccalaureate institutions.[17] While Blacks, in 2013, accounted for 14% of undergraduate enrollment, they also accounted for 36% of those "enrolled" in prison.[18] As the Department of Justice reported,

---

14 See discussion in Chapter One

15 Grace Kena, Lauren Musu-Gillette, Jennifer Robinson, Xiaolei Wang, Amy Rathbun, Jijun Zhang, Sidney Wilkinson-Flicker, Amy Barmer, Erin Dunlop Velez, *The Condition of Education 2015* Department of Education, National Center for Education Statistics (May 2015).

16 Grace Kena et al., *The Condition of Education 2015*, Department of Education, National Center for Education Statistics (May 2015) at 93. In regard to the percentage decrease, the report noted that "[b]etween 1990 and 2013, Hispanic enrollment nearly quadrupled (from 0.7 million to 2.9 million students) and Black enrollment more than doubled (from 1.1 million to 2.5 million students), while White enrollment increased 7 percent (from 9.3 million to 9.9 million students). However, the number of undergraduate students was lower in 2013 than in 2010 for most groups; the exception was Hispanic students, whose enrollment increased by 13 percent during this period." Id.

17 Grace Kena et al., *The Condition of Education 2015*, Department of Education, National Center for Education Statistics (May 2015) at 99. Although the percentage of Blacks in post-baccalaureate programs decreased, "[b] etween 1990 and 2013, both Black and Hispanic enrollments nearly quadrupled, with Black enrollment increasing from 100,000 to 367,000 students [and] the number of post-baccalaureate students was higher in 2013 than in 2010 for most groups; the exceptions were White and American Indian/Alaska Native students, whose enrollment decreased during this period.".

18 See discussion in Chapter One. See also, E. Ann Carson, *Prisoners in 2013*, Bureau of Justice Statistics, Department of Justice (September 2014) at 8. Although Blacks make up 13.3% percent of the U.S. population in 2016,

> During the early days of the Republic the population of blacks was much higher:
>
> - Between 1790 and 1810 the population ranged between 19.3 and 19.0%
> - Between 1820 and 1830 the population ranged between 18.4 and 18.1%
> - Between 1840 and 1860 the population ranged between 16.8 and 14.1%
> - Between 1870 and 1890 the population ranged between 12.7 and 11.9%
> - Between 1890 and 2000 the population ranged between 11.9 and 12.3%
> - Between 2000 and 2010 the population ranged between 12.3 and 12.3%

Arthur H. Garrison, "Disproportionate Incarceration of African Americans: What History and the First Decade of the Twenty-First Century Have Brought," *Journal of the Institute of Justice & International Studies* 11 (2011):

> [a]lmost 3% of black male U.S. residents of all ages were imprisoned on December 31, 2013 (2,805 inmates per 100,000 black male U.S. residents), compared to 1% of Hispanic males (1,134 per 100,000) and 0.5% of white males (466 per 100,000). While there were fewer black females in state or federal prison at yearend 2013 than in 2012, black females were imprisoned at more than twice the rate of white females.
>
> Black males had higher imprisonment rates across all age groups than all other races and Hispanic males. In the age range with the highest imprisonment rates for males (ages 25 to 39), black males were imprisoned at rates at least 2.5 times greater than Hispanic males and 6 times greater than white males. For males ages 18 to 19—the age range with the greatest difference in imprisonment rates between whites and blacks—black males (1,092 inmates per 100,000 black males) were more than 9 times more likely to be imprisoned than white males (115 inmates per 100,000 white males). The difference between black and white female inmates of the same age was smaller, but still substantial. Black females ages 18 to 19 (33 inmates per 100,000) were almost 5 times more likely to be imprisoned than white females (7 inmates per 100,000).[19]

Although Blacks are imprisoned at higher rates than all other groups, the comparison of prison to college for young Black males is more positive. In 2013, college age (eighteen to twenty-four) Black males accounted for 14% of college age inmates in prison compared to 31% of all Black males age eighteen to twenty-four in the United States were in college.[20] Thus by percentage more college age Black males are in college than in prison. In 2013, the total percentage of males eighteen to twenty-four in the United States that were in college was 37%.[21]

In its 2016 report the Department of Education[22] reported that in 2014 Blacks accounted for 13% of post-baccalaureate enrollment of U.S. Residents in degree-granting post-graduate institutions[23] and 14% of undergraduate enrollment of U.S.

87, 92. For additional information on Black population statistics see, African American Population 1790–2000 at https://www.infoplease.com/us/race-population/african-american-population

19 E. Ann Carson, *Prisoners in 2013* at 8.

20 E. Ann Carson, *Prisoners in 2013* and *Supra* note 15 at 18. In 2013, 31% of Black males 18–24 in the United States were in college, compared to 29% of Hispanic, 38% of White, 64% of Asian males in the same group. "From 2000 to 2013, the percentage of male young adults who were enrolled in college increased for Blacks (25 vs. 31 percent) and Hispanics (18 vs. 29 percent)." *Supra* note 14 at 19.

21 *Supra* note 15 at 18.

22 Grace Kena, William Hussar, Joel McFarland, Cristobal de Brey, Lauren Musu-Gillette, Xiaolei Wang, Amy Rathbun, Jijun Zhang, Sidney Wilkinson-Flicker, Amy Barmer, Erin Dunlop Velez,Melissa Diliberti, Farrah Bullock Mann, Thomas Machazel, Wyatt Smith and Mark Ossolinski, *The Condition of Education 2016* Department of Education, National Center for Education Statistics (May 2016).

23 Grace Kena et al., *The Condition of Education 2016*, Department of Education, National Center for Education Statistics (May 2016) at 107 "Of the 2.9 million postbaccalaureate students enrolled in fall 2014, some …

residents in degree-granting postsecondary institutions.[24] In 2014 Black males eighteen to twenty-four years old accounted for 28% of college-age students[25] a 3% decrease from 2013. In 2014 Black males eighteen to twenty-four years old accounted for14% of the prison population and White males of the same age account for 9% of the prison population.[26] In 2014 White males of college age accounted for 68% of the U.S. college age population and Black males of the same age accounted 15% of the total U.S. college-age population.[27]

In the most recent report by the Department of Education [28] in 2015 Blacks accounted for 12% of post-baccalaureate enrollment of U.S. Residents in degree-granting post-graduate institutions[29] and 13% of undergraduate enrollment of U.S. residents in degree-granting postsecondary institutions.[30] From 2000 to 2015, college enrollment rates increased for Whites between eighteen and twenty-four years old from 39 to 42%, Blacks from 31 to 35%, and Hispanics from 22 to 37%.[31] "In 2015, the college enrollment rate was higher for Asian young adults (63 percent) than for young adults who were White (42 percent), Black (35 percent), and Hispanic (37 percent); and the rate for White young adults was higher than the rates for

---

366,000 were Black . ... Between 2000 and 2014, both Black and Hispanic enrollment more than doubled, with Black enrollment increasing from 181,000 to 366,000 students ... "

24 Grace Kena et al., *The Condition of Education 2016*, Department of Education, National Center for Education Statistics (May 2016) at 101. "Of the 17.3 million undergraduate students in fall 2014, some ... 2.4 million were Black ... Between 2000 and 2014 ... Black enrollment increased by 57 percent (from 1.5 million to 2.4 million students)."

25 Grace Kena et al., *The Condition of Education 2016*, Department of Education, National Center for Education Statistics (May 2016) at 208. "From 1990 to 2014, the college enrollment rate increased for young adults who were White (from 35 to 42 percent), Black (from 25 to 33 percent). ... In 2014, the college enrollment rate was higher for Asian young adults (65 percent) than for young adults who were White (42 percent), Black (33 percent), and Hispanic (35 percent)—a pattern that has held for the past two decades." Id at 207.

26 E. Ann Carson, *Prisoners in 2014* Bureau of Justice Statistics, Department of Justice (September 2015) at 29.

27 U.S. Census Bureau America Fact Finder Database Search sex by age 2014 at https://factfinder.census.gov/faces/nav/jsf/pages/searchresults.xhtml?refresh=t#none

28 Joel McFarland, Bill Hussar, Cristobal de Brey, Tom Snyder, Xiaolei Wang, Sidney Wilkinson-Flicker, Semhar Gebrekristos, Jijun Zhang, Amy Rathbun, Amy Barmer, Farrah Bullock Mann, Serena Hinz, Thomas Nachazel, Wyatt Smith, and Mark Ossolinski, *The Condition of Education 2016 Department of Education*, National Center for Education Statistics (May 2017).

29 Joel McFarland et al., *The Condition of Education 2016 Department of Education*, National Center for Education Statistics (May 2017) at 123.

30 Joel McFarland et al., *The Condition of Education 2016 Department of Education*, National Center for Education Statistics (May 2017) at 117.

31 Joel McFarland et al., *The Condition of Education 2016 Department of Education*, National Center for Education Statistics (May 2017) at 237

young adults who were Black and Hispanic."[32] The total enrolment rate for youth 18-24 in undergraduate college was 40 percent in 2015.

For young adult males (eighteen to twenty-four years old) enrollment rates were higher in 2015 than in 2000 in which White males accounted for 39 vs. 36%, Black males accounted for 34 vs. 25%, and Hispanic males accounted for 33 vs. 18%.[33] In 2015 young males (eighteen to twenty-four years old) comprised 38% of the total undergraduate college population.[34] In 2015 the young adult male (eighteen to twenty-four years old) "enrollment" rate in prison was 11% and the enrollment rate for young Black and Hispanic males was 13% and Whites was 8%.[35] In comparing percentages of attendance in college to percentages of attendance to prison; more Black and Hispanic young males are "enrolled" in prison (13%) than young White males (8%) and more young White males are in college (39%) than young Black and Hispanic males (34% and 33%).

RACE, POLICE, AND THE CRIMINAL JUSTICE SYSTEM—FINAL SUMMARY

> Conservatives had always held the somewhat contradictory position that government can't be trusted in any area of society except when it comes to the power to arrest, detain, imprison, and execute people. But Reagan didn't dance around the contradiction, he embraced it.[36]

Part of the ease of conservatives in holding this contradiction lies in two simple truths. First, conservatives don't think that the machine of the criminal justice system will land on their heads. Historically, the sword of the criminal justice system has been unleashed on Blacks, other minorities, and poor rural Whites. As discussed in Chapter Eight, middle-class America embraces the crime control model assuming that if the criminal justice system lays its hands on you, you must have done something wrong. The result being it has insensitivity to the harm the system can do—after all you deserved the harm because you did something wrong. Secondly, because the contradiction lays in focusing in on who is arrested, detained, imprisoned, and executed and not the power government is given, conservative don't have the same

32 Joel McFarland et al., *The Condition of Education 2016 Department of Education*, National Center for Education Statistics (May 2017)

33 Joel McFarland et al., *The Condition of Education 2016 Department of Education*, National Center for Education Statistics (May 2017) at 238

34 Joel McFarland et al., *The Condition of Education 2016 Department of Education*, National Center for Education Statistics (May 2017).

35 E. Ann Carson, *Prisoners in 2015* Bureau of Justice Statistics, Department of Justice (December 2016) at 13.

36 Radley Balko, *Rise of the Warrior Cop: The Militarization of America's Police Forces* (2013) at 144.

rejection of empowering the government over the lives of the individual when the police are empowered. Put simply, when police were given the power to break down doors in the night with Special Weapons and Tactics (SWAT) teams and to use force to subdue poor Blacks in crime-infested communities, middle-America in the 1980s and 1990s had little sympathy. It wasn't their doors that were broken down, and their children put face down on the hood of police cars, and their neighborhoods over policed but under protected.

This apathy and indifference to the power of government, the police, began to change when a new category of people suffered the impact of the criminal justice system—innocent Whites mistaken for being in one of the three categories of described above. They, like the former three, received the same treatment. Only when mistaken SWAT raids resulting in property damage, police killing of pets, and police shooting of people defending their property began to occur in suburban and rural White America did the blind support for the police began to change. Only when police focus was expanded to include drug crimes in rural and suburban America in the first two decades of twenty-first century did society begin to question the militarization of the police. Only when the police response in Ferguson got out of hand did the general public of America question the use of armored cars, automatic weapons, and tear gas by police in military uniforms. Only when asset forfeiture found White America has its morality been challenged by social conservatives and legality been challenged in the Supreme Court.

Another explanation for the contradiction is the nature of American conservative theory as applied to race. Conservative theory is based on liberty, not freedom. Liberty is the lack of government control over the individual; it is what the government can't do. To conservatives liberty is about being *left alone from government* to live as one chooses. Freedom is what the individual has a right to do or not do and freedom includes the right to enjoy social and political rights of society. Freedom is a broader concept than liberty. Freedom includes social outcomes. Social conservatism rejects this broader idea. Freedom to social conservatives is only liberty.

Conservative Americanism is about lack of government in social outcomes, not the justice in social outcomes. Justice is not defined by the fairness of social outcome. Thus, an evil can be recognized under conservative theory, but that does not mean the evil must be eradicated and, in fact, can be lived with if the cure contradicts liberty. That is why racism can be tolerated by conservatives if the cure is government action to prevent it. Slavery may have been bad, but the federal government swooping down on the individual Southern slaveholders and commanding them to stop was worse. Jim Crow discrimination may have been bad, but the federal government swooping down on the individual White individuals, regardless of whether they are barefoot and ignorant or rich and sophisticated, and commanding them to see Blacks as equals and to allow their children to sit next to them in school was worse. Such government action, by definition, violated liberty which by definition means tyranny; and government tyranny was worse than the evil of slavery and Jim Crow. States rights' advocates honor liberty, the lack of government action over individual behavior, more than the justice of ending slavery and Jim Crow by the hand of the federal government; so said Calhoun in

1838, Stephens in 1861, and the fathers of the modern Republican Party/social conservative thought: Thurmond in 1948, Goldwater in 1960, and Wallace in 1963.

Lastly, because of this dynamic of liberty over justice and liberty before freedom, racists ideas and attitudes can hide in and unjust social policy results can be served by conservative theory without check. The problem with the Republican Party, as discussed in Chapters Four and Eight, is that it adopted American conservatism as defined by John Calhoun, Alexander Stephens, Jefferson Davis, Strom Thurmond, George Wallace, Orval Faubus, Barry Goldwater, Richard Nixon, and Ronald Reagan. Goldwater, Nixon, and Reagan asserted that they were not racists, but the results of their states' rights advocacy and adoption of Southern Democrats into the Republican Party resulted in achieving the racist ideals of Calhoun, Davis, and Stephens. Jim Crow/states' rights advocates Thurmond, Wallace, and Faubus were the bridge between antebellum Calhoun, Davis, and Stephens on one side and Goldwater, Nixon, and Reagan on the other. The adoption of the racism of Southern Democrats dressed up as noble assertions of individual liberty has hounded conservatives and Republicans ever since—a hounding we will return to when we discuss the post-election of Donald Trump.

****

The positive social results of the fall of Jim Crow have not blunted the perception by the police that young Black males, at the very least, are prone to criminal activity that requires inquiry and control—which can lead to confrontations that can lead to young Black men being shot in the street, because the officer fears for his life in the face of a non-subservient Black man. The racial bias is in what causes the officer to engage in the first place and, even more important, how the officer engages the confrontation (either by imposing physical domination or engaging with respect) and how that young Black man perceives that engagement.

Policing of Blacks in America reflects a larger American historical context. That American context is more than a century older than the writing of America's founding documents and its writers. The context dates back to how and why Blacks were brought to America.

In May 1607, the Virginia Company of London established the first colony on the North American continent in Jamestown, Virginia, thirteen years before the arrival of the Puritans in Cape Cod, Massachusetts, in November 1620. The Jamestown settlement was a financial venture to establish an English foothold on the continent, establish a system of trade for North American raw materials, and find a trade route to the Orient and a way to Christianize the Indians living in Virginia. After a period of starvation and unprofitable ventures, in 1613, John Rolfe introduced tobacco as a cash crop in Jamestown.[37] Tobacco proved to be the most profitable export and industry of the colony, and by 1617–1618, more than forty thousand pounds of tobacco was shipped to England. Tobacco was profitable but required large tracks of land and labor to plant and cultivate. The need for large tracks of land and labor birthed

37 History of Jamestown Web page—http://www.historyisfun.org/jamestown-settlement/history-jamestown/

the Southern system of plantations, the plantation aristocracy in the South, and Southern wealth fueled and defined by slavery.

In August 1619, only thirteen years after the colony was established, twenty African slaves arrived in Jamestown, Virginia, from Angola. They were captured and brought by a Dutch warship looking for supplies.[38] They were subsequently used as laborers in raising tobacco. The arrival of the slaves proved to be very beneficial to the developing the tobacco-growing agricultural aristocracy of Virginia. Farming tobacco proved to be profitable, but it was very labor intensive and "white Virginians, who increasingly shunned field work" needed laborers, and they used African slaves to work "long hard hours in the fields" to solve the problem of a lack of availability of White labor.[39] Within twelve years of the importation of slaves, more than half a million pounds of tobacco were exported. "The first great American enterprise had been established."[40] Tobacco was the first of many colonial products farmed to meet European demands for luxury and commercial goods.

The European demand for tobacco and sugar and the rise of the need for large agricultural lands resulted in the importation of more than ten million Africans by the European nations to farm these agricultural estates in the Americas. The Portuguese between 1441–1836 imported 5.8 million Africans, the French between 1549–1818 imported 1.4 million, Great Britain between 1562–1807 imported 3.3 million, the Netherlands (Dutch) between 1619–1814 imported 555,300, and Denmark between 1649–1802 imported 85,000.[41]As professor Andrew Isenberg summarized,

> [b]ecause of the rapid depopulation of the Americas owing to disease, Europeans faced a shortage of labor in their effort to exploit the resources in the new world particularly to exploit the soil. So the Europeans, first the Portuguese and then the Dutch and then eventually the English imported slaves from West Africa to cultivate sugar in the Caribbean and Brazil, tobacco and Virginia rice in South Carolina and by the 19th century in mainland North America cotton. It's no exaggeration to say that these cash commodities produced by slave labor were essential to the export economies of the Americas.[42]

Although these export economies used indentured servants, as well as slaves, for labor in the early North American colonial period, and indentured servants could be Black or White, "by the mid-seventeenth century it was becoming clear that Africans and white servants received different treatment."[43] The American context of race, from the date of early slavery, was that

38 James Oliver Horton and Lois E. Horton, *Slave and the Making of America* at 27 (2005).

39 James Oliver Horton and Lois E. Horton, *Slave and the Making of America* (2005) at 29.

40 John Rolfe, National Park Service Web page—https://www.nps.gov/jame/learn/historyculture/john-rolfe.htm

41 Smithsonian National Museum of African History and Culture.

42 National Geographic Channel, *America Before Columbus,* Documentary (2009).

43 James Oliver Horton and Lois E. Horton, *Slave and the Making of America* at 29.

Blacks were no more than a means to an end and were not equal to those who came to the colonies, whether rich or poor.

By the 1640s, Whites in Virginia who escaped from service were punished by having time added to their service, but Blacks were sentenced to life service. By the 1660s, slave laws were being passed in the colonies, including changing the common law of rights of inheritance for Blacks by linking their legal and social status to the mother, rather than to the father. Thus children produced when White slave owners raped their slaves did not have the legal status of White men. These laws were followed by laws against interracial marriage and laws that made children of White women who married their Black slaves, property of the owner of the Black slaves.[44]

By the 1670s, Virginia was fearful of the growing Black population and feared poor Whites and Black slave alliances that could result in rebellion against the growing Southern aristocracy. Thus laws were made to discourage poor White and Black associations, and these laws, as discussed in Chapter Three, formed the foundation of the social dynamic of poor Whites being placed on a higher social status that Blacks. By the mid- to late-seventeenth century, Black slaves replaced White indentured servants as the main source of imported labor in the colonies. By middle 1770s, the colonies had passed laws that only allowed Africans to be enslaved and classified them as aliens, having no legal rights, and that Black slavery was attached to the land and was perpetual through maternal generations. Race (Black skin) was used as the physical, visual, and legal designation for slavery; Black skin was the demarcation line regarding the inapplicability of the law and its protections. By the middle 1770s, enforcement of these laws were given to local law enforcement, which were composed of poor Whites and White slave overseers hired by the slave aristocracy.

In 1787 at the Constitutional Convention, slavery was an institution that was one hundred and sixty-eight years old and was entrenched in the social, political, and legal framework of the Southern states. At the convention when voting and counting population for representation in the Congress was an issue that nearly destroyed the formation of the meeting, the writers of the Constitution agreed that Black slaves would be counted as three-fifths of other persons (Article 1, Section 2) for representation in Congress. They also determined that the international slave trade could not be limited by Congress (Article 1, Section 9) until 1808. They also determined that the Constitution would require Northern authorities to secure escaped slaves and return them (Article 4, Section 2, Clause 3), which was backed up by the Fugitive Slave Act of 1793. Between 1774 through 1850, an economic and political schism developed between the North and South, which cemented slavery in the South and free labor in the North.

This does not mean, of course, that the Constitution should be understood as a slave constitution. In 1860 at the Scottish Anti-Slavery Society in Glasgow, Scotland on March 26, 1860, Frederick Douglass debated the assertion made by both abolitionists like William Lloyd

---

44 James Oliver Horton and Lois E. Horton, *Slave and the Making of America* (2005) at 30.

Garrison and slave-owners that the Constitution itself authorized slavery. Both asserted that it was a pro-slavery document. Douglass asserted both were *wrong*.[45] Douglass addressed the following arguments of Garrison and the slave owners that are still asserted for the proposition that the Constitution favored slavery.

1. *Article 1, section 9, provides for the continuance of the African slave trade for the 20 years.* Douglass responded:

> It so happens that no such words as "African slave trade," no such words as "slave insurrections," are anywhere used in that instrument. These are the words of that orator, and not the words of the Constitution of the United States. …
>
> …
>
> I come to the next, that which it is said guaranteed the continuance of the African slave trade for twenty years. I will also take that for just what my opponent alleges it to have been, although the Constitution does not warrant any such conclusion. But, to be liberal, let us suppose it did, and what follows? Why, this—that this part of the Constitution, so far as the slave trade is concerned, became a dead letter more than 50 years ago, and now binds no man's conscience for the continuance of any slave trade whatsoever. … Men, at that time, both in England and in America, looked upon the slave trade as the life of slavery. The abolition of the slave trade was supposed to be the certain death of slavery. Cut off the stream, and the pond will dry up, was the common notion at the time.
>
> Wilberforce and Clarkson, clear-sighted as they were, took this view; and the American statesmen, in providing for the abolition of the slave trade, thought they were providing for the abolition of the slavery. This view is quite consistent with the history of the times. All regarded slavery as an expiring and doomed system, destined to speedily disappear from the country. But, again, it should be remembered that this very provision, if made to refer to the African slave trade at all, makes the Constitution anti-slavery rather than for slavery; for it says to the slave States, the price you will have to pay for coming into the American Union is, that the slave trade, which you would carry on indefinitely out of the Union, shall be put an end to in twenty years if you come into the Union. Secondly, if it does apply, it expired by its own limitation more than fifty years ago. Thirdly, it is anti-slavery, because it looked to the abolition of slavery rather than to its perpetuity. Fourthly, it showed that the intentions of the framers of the Constitution were good, not bad. I think this is quite enough for this point.

2. *Article 4, section 9, provides for the recovery from the other States of fugitive slaves.* Douglass responded to the debater who made the argument:

> This is called the "Fugitive Slave Provision." It is called so by those who wish to make it subserve the interest of slavery in America. … It is quite true [at the Constitutional

45 Frederick Douglass, "The Constitution of the United States: Is It Pro-Slavery or Anti-slavery?" at http://www.blackpast.org/1860-frederick-douglass-constitution-united-states-it-pro-slavery-or-anti-slavery

> Convention] that Mr. Butler and Mr. Pinckney introduced a provision expressly with a view to the recapture of fugitive slaves: it is quite true also that there was some discussion on the subject—and just here the truth shall come out. These illustrious kidnappers were told promptly in that discussion that no such idea as property in man should be admitted into the Constitution. The speaker in question might have told you, and he would have told you but the simple truth, if he had told you that the proposition of Mr. Butler and Mr. Pinckney—which he leads you to infer was adopted by the convention that from the Constitution—was, in fact, promptly and indignantly rejected by that convention. He might have told you, had it suited his purpose to do so, that the words employed in the first draft of the fugitive slave clause were such as applied to the condition of slaves, and expressly declared that persons held to "servitude" should be given up; but that the word "servitude" was struck from the provision, for the very reason that it applied to slaves. He might have told you that the same Mr. Madison declared that the word was struck out because the convention would not consent that the idea of property in men should be admitted into the Constitution. The fact that Mr. Madison can be cited on both sides of this question is another evidence of the folly and absurdity of making the secret intentions of the framers the criterion by which the Constitution is to be construed. But it may be asked—if this clause does not apply to slaves, to whom does it apply?
>
> I answer, that when adopted, it applies to a very large class of persons—namely, redemptioners—persons who had come to America from Holland, from Ireland, and other quarters of the globe—like the Coolies to the West Indies—and had, for a consideration duly paid, become bound to "serve and labour" for the parties two whom their service and labour was due. It applies to indentured apprentices and others who have become bound for a consideration, under contract duly made, to serve and labour, to such persons this provision applies, and only to such persons. The plain reading of this provision shows that it applies, and that it can only properly and legally apply, to persons "bound to service." Its object plainly is, to secure the fulfillment of contracts for "service and labour." It applies to indentured apprentices, and any other persons from whom service and labour may be due. The legal condition of the slave puts him beyond the operation of this provision. He is not described in it. He is a simple article of property. He does not owe and cannot owe service. He cannot even make a contract. It is impossible for him to do so. He can no more make such a contract than a horse or an ox can make one. This provision, then, only respects persons who owe service, and they only can owe service who can receive an equivalent and make a bargain. The slave cannot do that, and is therefore exempted from the operation of this fugitive provision.

3. *Art. 1, section 2, gives the slave States a representation of the three-fifths of all the slave population.* Douglass responded:

> I answer—It is a downright disability laid upon the slaveholding States; one which deprives those States of two-fifths of their natural basis of representation. A black man

> in a free State is worth just two-fifths more than a black man in a slave State, as a basis of political power under the Constitution. Therefore, instead of encouraging slavery, the Constitution encourages freedom by giving an increase of "two-fifths" of political power to free over slave States. So much for the three-fifths clause; taking it at is worst, it still leans to freedom, not slavery; for, be it remembered that the Constitution nowhere forbids a coloured man to vote.

4. *Article 1, section 8, requires the President to use the military, naval, ordnance, and militia resources of the entire country for the suppression of slave insurrection, in the same manner as he would employ them to repel invasion.* Douglass responded:

> I go to the "slave insurrection" clause, though, in truth, there is no such clause. The one which is called so has nothing whatever to do with slaves or slaveholders any more than your laws for suppression of popular outbreaks has to do with making slaves of you and your children. It is only a law for suppression of riots or insurrections. But I will be generous here, as well as elsewhere, and grant that it applies to slave insurrections. Let us suppose that an anti-slavery man is President of the United States (and the day that shall see this the case is not distant) and this very power of suppressing slave insurrections would put an end to slavery. The right to put down an insurrection carries with it the right to determine the means by which it shall be put down. If it should turn out that slavery is a source of insurrection, that there is no security from insurrection while slavery lasts, why, the Constitution would be best obeyed by putting an end to slavery, and an anti-slavery Congress would do the very same thing. Thus, you see, the so-called slave-holding provisions of the American Constitution, which a little while ago looked so formidable, are, after all, no defense or guarantee for slavery whatever.

While a full debate on Douglass's answers are not within the focus of this book, they are reprinted for discussion and contemplation by the reader. But his views on interpretation of the Constitution and the value of law regarding its application to Blacks is worth some additional discussion.

When Douglass addressed the argument regarding the fugitive slave clause and the assertion that the writers of the Constitution intended for the clause to apply to Black slaves he concluded that the history of the debate could go either way—"The fact that Mr. Madison can be cited on both sides of this question is another evidence of the folly and absurdity of making the secret intentions of the framers the criterion by which the Constitution is to be construed."

Douglass in his speech rejected the theory of original intent as a mode of interpreting the Constitution. He argued that the Constitution should be interpreted by its text with attention to the purpose of the document. He was a strict construction/textualist. But he also asserted that the Constitution should be read with the purpose of establishing justice. Douglass said,

> In all matters where laws are taught to be made the means of oppression, cruelty, and wickedness, I am for strict construction. I will concede nothing. It must be shown that

> it is so nominated in the bond. The pound of flesh, but not one drop of blood. The very nature of law is opposed to all such wickedness, and makes it difficult to accomplish such objects under the forms of law. Law is not merely an arbitrary enactment with regard to justice, reason, or humanity. Blackstone defines it to be a rule prescribed by the supreme power of the State commanding what is right and forbidding what is wrong. The speaker at the City Hall laid down some rules of legal interpretation. These rules send us to the history of the law for its meaning. I have no objection to such a course in ordinary cases of doubt. But where human liberty and justice are at stake, the case falls under an entirely different class of rules. There must be something more than history—something more than tradition. The Supreme Court of the United States lays down this rule, and it meets the case exactly—"Where rights are infringed—where the fundamental principles of the law are overthrown—where the general system of the law is departed from, the legislative intention must be expressed with irresistible clearness."[46] The same court says that the language of the law must be construed strictly in favour of justice and liberty. Again, there is another rule of law. It is — where a law is susceptible of two meanings, the one making it accomplish an innocent purpose, and the other making it accomplish a wicked purpose, we must in all cases adopt that which makes it accomplish an innocent purpose. Again, the details of a law are to be interpreted in the light of the declared objects sought by the law.

46 *United States v. Fisher*, 6 U.S. 2 Cranch 358, 390 (1805). This case involved an appeal by the United States regarding its rights as creditor. The full quote from the decision is as follows:

> That the consequences are to be considered in expounding laws where the intent is doubtful is a principle not to be controverted, but it is also true that it is a principle which must be applied with caution, and which has a degree of influence dependent on the nature of the case to which it is applied. Where rights are infringed, where fundamental principles are overthrown, where the general system of the laws is departed from, the legislative intention must be expressed with irresistible clearness to induce a court of justice to suppose a design to effect such objects. But where only a political regulation is made, which is inconvenient, if the intention of the legislature be expressed in terms which are sufficiently intelligible to leave no doubt in the mind when the words are taken in their ordinary sense, it would be going a great way to say that a constrained interpretation must be put upon them to avoid an inconvenience which ought to have been contemplated in the legislature when the act was passed and which, in their opinion, was probably overbalanced by the particular advantages it was calculated to produce.
>
> Of the latter description of inconveniences are those occasioned by the act in question. It is for the legislature to appreciate them. They are not of such magnitude as to induce an opinion that the legislature could not intend to expose the citizens of the United States to them when words are used which manifest that intent.

Fisher, 6 U.S. at 389–390.

Douglass then argued that not only does the Constitution not use the word slavery and Black slaves as something to be protected by its text, Douglass argued that the text of the Constitution uses words that reject slavery. He said,

> I set these rules down against those employed at the City Hall. To me they seem just and rational. I only ask you to look at the American Constitution in the light of them, and you will see with me that no man is guaranteed a right of property in man, under the provisions of that instrument. If there are two ideas more distinct in their character and essence than another, those ideas are "persons" and "property," "men" and "things." Now, when it is proposed to transform persons into "property" and men into beasts of burden, I demand that the law that completes such a purpose shall be expressed with irresistible clearness. The thing must not be left to inference, but must be done in plain English.
>
> I know how this view of the subject is treated by the class represented at the City Hall. They are in the habit of treating the Negro as an exception to general rules. When their own liberty is in question they will avail themselves of all rules of law which protect and defend their freedom; but when the black man's rights are in question they concede everything, admit everything for slavery, and put liberty to the proof. They reserve the common law usage, and presume the Negro a slave unless he can prove himself free. I, on the other hand, presume him free unless he is proved to be otherwise.

Regarding the preamble of the Constitution, Douglass argued, "The objects here set forth are six in number: union, defence, welfare, tranquility, justice, and liberty. These are all good objects, and slavery, so far from being among them, is a foe of them all. But it has been said that Negroes are not included within the benefits sought under this declaration. This is said by the slaveholders in America—it is said by the City Hall orator—but it is not said by the Constitution itself." In a rebuke of the abolitionists assertion that the Constitution was not intended to apply to the Negro, he answered,

> But how dare any man who pretends to be a friend to the Negro thus gratuitously concede away what the Negro has a right to claim under the Constitution? Why should such friends invent new arguments to increase the hopelessness of his bondage? This, I undertake to say, as the conclusion of the whole matter, that the constitutionality of slavery can be made out only by disregarding the plain and common-sense reading of the Constitution itself; by discrediting and casting away as worthless the most beneficent rules of legal interpretation; by ruling the Negro outside of these beneficent rules; by claiming that the Constitution does not mean what it says, and that it says what it does not mean; by disregarding the written Constitution, and interpreting it in the light of a secret understanding.

In summarizing the text of the Constitution, he said, "the Constitution declares that no person shall be deprived of life, liberty, or property without due process of law; it secures to every man the right of trial by jury, the privilege of the writ of habeas corpus—the great writ that put an end to slavery and slave-hunting in England—and it secures to every State a republican form of government. Anyone of these provisions in the hands of abolition statesmen, and backed up by a right moral sentiment, would put an end to slavery in America. The Constitution forbids the passing of a bill of attainder: that is, a law entailing upon the child the disabilities and hardships imposed upon the parent. Every slave law in America might be repealed on this very ground."

"But to all this it is said that the practice of the American people is against my view" Douglass admitted, "They have given the Constitution a slaveholding interpretation. I admit it. They have committed innumerable wrongs against the Negro in the name of the Constitution. Yes, I admit it all; and I go with him who goes farthest in denouncing these wrongs. But it does not follow that the Constitution is in favour of these wrongs because the slaveholders have given it that interpretation." Douglass separated the Constitution from politics. His distinction was correct. "Thus, for instance, the American Government and the American Constitution are spoken of in a manner which would naturally lead the hearer to believe that one is identical with the other; when the truth is, they are distinct in character as is a ship and a compass. The one may point right and the other steer wrong. A chart is one thing; the course of the vessel is another. The Constitution may be right, the Government is wrong. ***If the Government has been governed by mean, sordid, and wicked passions, it does not follow that the Constitution is mean, sordid, and wicked.*** " As discussed throughout this book, in regard to Blacks—"the Government has been governed by mean, sordid, and wicked passions." And those passions lead to laws that attempted to hold a nation built on freedom together with a practice of slavery based on race.

Congress passed the Missouri Compromise in 1820, then the Compromise of 1850 (Fugitive Slave Act), and in 1854, it passed the Kansas–Nebraska Act, all of which were compromises to ease tensions over slavery, which together, allowed for the spread of slavery to the new Western territories of the United States through popular sovereignty, required local law enforcement in the North to secure Blacks and return them to slavery, and maintained the balance of power in the Senate between slave and free states. In 1857, the Supreme Court held in *Dred Scott v. Sanford* that Blacks, *per se*, were not and never were citizens of the United States, and there were no laws regarding their protection that a White man had to respect. By the election of Lincoln in 1860, the dance with the devil had run its course, and payment came due. The Civil War and the carnage it brought humbled Lincoln to admit the true cause of the war. In 1864, he said "in the providence of God, ... He gives to both North and South this terrible war ... Yet, if God wills that it continue until all the wealth piled by the bondsman's two hundred and fifty years of unrequited toil shall be sunk, and until every drop of blood drawn with the lash shall be paid by another drawn with the sword ... the judgments of the Lord are true and righteous altogether." Jefferson, a slave owner himself, in a moment of honesty and reflection was in agreement with Lincoln regarding the institution of slavery and the judgment that was due to the enslavement of Blacks.

> ... There must doubtless be an unhappy influence on the manners of our people produced by the existence of slavery among us. ... Indeed I tremble for my country when I reflect that God is just: that his justice cannot sleep for ever: ...[47]

Jefferson's prayers that emancipation would occur under heaven through the consent of the masters and the values of natural law and liberty at the heart the American Revolution ("We hold these truths to be self-evident, that all men are created equal, that they are endowed by their Creator with certain unalienable Rights, that among these are Life, Liberty and the pursuit of Happiness. That to secure these rights, Governments are instituted among Men, deriving their just powers from the consent of the governed") rather than extirpation were not answered. It took the deaths of more than 300,000 union soldiers and the decimation of much of the South and its wealth to end slavery. But the defeat of slavery did not mean the defeat of racism. The latter existed before and after the Civil War both in policy and the development of policing Blacks, both free and slave.

In the antebellum period, Southern policing was born out of the need to control the African slave population. The governments of the Deep South created slave patrols (the origin of Southern policing) with the sole purpose of enforcing slavery, which included controlling free Blacks, preventing slave revolts, and capturing escaped slaves. Northern police justice, to Blacks both slave and free, was defined by the Fugitive Slave Acts of 1793 and 1850. The Fugitive Slave Acts defined Northern police action as the pursuit of Blacks as far as the Canadian border and returning them to slavery or the capture of free Blacks and selling them into slavery. After the Civil War, law enforcement in the South changed from slave patrols to local police enforcing the sharecropper system. Laws in the South were passed to entrap former slaves to the land, and the police were authorized to make sure that happened. Some of the local police officers during the day were members of the night riders (Ku Klux Klan) at night. Both had the purpose of controlling former slaves and keeping them in their place. After the North abandoned Reconstruction in 1877, the North adopted, and in some cases improved upon the system of segregation. With Jim Crow firmly in place by the early 1880s, the criminal justice system, nationally, enforced laws that imprisoned Blacks disproportionately to their population or criminal activity. A system of laws (pig laws, anti-vagrancy statutes, peonage, convict leasing, the criminalization of hiring Blacks under contract and other types of unemployment laws) were instituted to place Blacks in a position of servitude as close to slavery as possible. The Supreme Court added its imprimatur to Jim Crow, when in 1883, it held in the *Civil Rights Cases* that Blacks were relieved from slavery, they needed to stop seeking to be the special favorite of the law and its protection, and mere discrimination on the basis of race was not a badge of slavery. In 1896, the Supreme Court held in *Plessy v. Ferguson* that Jim Crow and the doctrine of separate but equal was constitutional and that the separation of the

47 Thomas Jefferson, Notes on the State of Virginia, Query XVIII: Manners, The particular customs and manners that may happen to be received in that state? (1781).

races based on race, if such a system holds negative connotations, was negative only by choice in the minds of Blacks. The legal statutory system of Jim Crow would not suffer significant challenge or change until World War II and would not be fully repealed until twenty-three years after the war.

After World War II, Black male soldiers were excluded from many of the aspects of the G.I. Bill and the rise of suburban housing. This segregation resulted in excluding Blacks from participation in the formation of the modern middle class in America. This discrimination, in conjunction with White and employment flight in the 1940s–1950s, concentrated Blacks in urban neighborhoods, which resulted in social and political isolation and containment. This isolation fostered long-term intergenerational desperation, poverty, anger, and crime. While the civil rights movement (1953–1968) rendered more than three centuries of structural and legal racism and second-class citizenship to the dustbin of history, the racism that undergirded the system remained. Large police departments in Los Angeles and other urban cities recruited officers from the Deep South to control Black neighborhoods in the 1940s and 1950s.

By the late 1970s, Black middle-class flight followed White flight. This flight further exacerbated the loss of positive structures within urban neighborhoods. Between 1983 and 1985, the plague of crack cocaine arrived, and it wreaked havoc for more than a decade over urban neighborhoods already damaged by the scourge of heroin and street gang violence dating back to the early 1960s. In the late 1980s, America responded to open air violent urban crime by creating militarized police drug units, increasing sentences for drug use and possession, increasing the number of Blacks in prison, and building prisons (and supermax prisons) to house them in. Insensitive and power-oriented policing was the norm, and it was not until the 1990s, after the Los Angeles riots and major police scandals in Los Angeles, New York City, and other large urban cities that some departments changed from community control to the philosophy of Sir Robert Peel and community policing. Non–criminal justice system answers to Black crime would not be politically viable until the middle of the new century.

During slavery, the Black male was viewed as physically powerful, intellectually limited, and when properly controlled, trustworthy. During the early postbellum period, former slave owners changed the method of control by changing how the Black male was perceived. He was now viewed as lazy, violent, criminal, and powerful. This negative image has remained a social constant, although it evolved over time. In the 1920s, it was the fear of the violent cocaine-crazed Negro. In the 1920s–1930s, it was the fear of Black men, sober or not, who, if given the opportunity, would hunt down White women to rape on sight. It was up to White men, in organizations like the Ku Klux Klan, to protect White womanhood. At the peak of its power in 1925, the Klan walked 25,000 of its members in full regalia down Pennsylvania Avenue in Washington, D.C. Before the famous march, the film *The Birth of a Nation* was released in 1915, which portrayed and romanticized the concept of the Southern lost cause and the utility of the Klan as a bulwark against Black rapists of White women. The movie, originally entitled *The Clansmen*, ignited riots of White gangs upon Blacks and was honored by President Woodrow Wilson with a screening in the White House in which he is reported to have said after seeing the movie that "It is like writing history with lightning, and my only regret is that it is all so terribly true." This perception of Blacks as dangerous entities to be controlled was backed by racial violence and White riots against Blacks in the first two decades of the twentieth century. The National Association for the Advancement of Colored People was born in 1909, not out of the need for affirmative action—it was born after the 1908 White race riots in Springfield, Illinois, and the need to end lynching.

In the 1860s, Blacks were described as lazy *per se* and would only work under slavery; in the 1920s, Blacks were described as cocaine-crazed Negroes looking for White women; in the 1960s, Blacks were the source of violent crime and social unrest (urban riots), as well as the beneficiaries of government handouts; in the 1970s, through affirmative action, Blacks received social promotion, educational rewards, and career advancement without work or merit at the expense of Whites; and in the 1980s, Black communities were described as crack cocaine saturated areas producing crack babies, which required law and order to control homicidal gangs that killed for no reason. In today's language, Blacks are described in terms of being disproportionately criminal, and the result of disproportionate incarceration is to be expected. Today's explanation for Black male criminality is failure of the Black family structure (fatherless homes) and criminogenic aggression. The belief that Black males are dangerous operates within the subconscious of law enforcement and manifests itself in suspicion, fear, and the determination to physically control young Black men when interacting with them. The assumed dangerousness of the young Black male creates the environment for aggressive policing. Aggressive policing leads to police use of force, which leads to police shooting those upon whom aggressive policing is applied.

Consider the recent shooting of **John Crawford** who was in a Wal-Mart, looking at a BB gun for sale in the store, and was reported to the police as a Black man with a gun. The police shot and killed him on August 5, 2014. Consider **Tamir Rice**, a twelve-year-old who was playing with a toy gun but was reported to the police as menacing and was shot to death by two police officers immediately after they stopped their car in front of him on November 22, 2014. Consider **Akai Gurley** and **Timothy Stansbury** who were both shot by New York Police Department (NYPD) officers on November 20, 2014, when they were entering a darkened stairwell in their own building. The NYPD publicly stated that neither of the men were doing anything illegal or threatening to the officers. The officers were in the building with their guns drawn, because they were afraid of the building they were in and accidently shot the two men upon seeing them. One of those officers, Peter Liang, was found guilty of manslaughter for the killing of Akai Gurley in February 2016 and after the Brooklyn DA recommended no jail time for the officer in March, Officer Liang was sentenced to five years of probation after the judge reduced the conviction to criminally negligent homicide in April 2016. The conviction was the first conviction of an on duty police officer for the shooting of a civilian in a decade.[48]

---

48 See generally, Thomas Tracy, Christina Carrega-Woodby, John Marzulli, Denis Slattery, Stephen Rex Brown "NYPD Officer Peter Liang found guilty of manslaughter in fatal shooting of Akai Gurley in Brooklyn housing development," *New York Times* (February 12, 2016) at http://www.nydailynews.com/new-york/nyc-crime/nypd-peter-liang-guilty-fatal-shooting-akai-gurley-article-1.2528827. See also

According to the *Washington Post Database* on police shootings, in 2015, police killed nine hundred and ninety-five people (995), in 2016, police killed nine hundred and sixty-three people (963), in 2017, police had shot and killed nine hundred and eighty-seven people (987), and in 2018 the police had killed nine hundred and ninety-five (995); including the case of **Stephon Clark** who was shot at twenty times and hit eight times mostly in the back by the Sacramento, California police on March 18, 2018. Some of the more famous killings in 2017 included the shooting of fifteen-year-old **Jordan Edwards** who was killed in Balch Springs, Texas, on April 29, 2017 and **Justine Ruszczyk**, an Australian who was killed in Minneapolis, Minnesota, on July 15, 2017.

Edwards was in a car driving away from the police when he was shot. Edwards was shot by Officer Roy Oliver of the Balch Springs, Texas police department when he fired his rifle into a car of four Black teenagers. Oliver claimed that the car was aggressively approaching him, but body camera recordings established that the car was not. Oliver was indicted on July 17, 2017 for murder and four counts of aggravated assault with a deadly weapon by a public servant in addition to two charges of aggravated assault relating to a use of force in an unrelated prior incident.[49] On August 28, 2018 Oliver was convicted for murder and on August 29, 2018 he was sentenced to fifteen years imprisonment.

Ruszczyk, a White woman, had called the police to report a possible assault near her home and was shot by police while speaking with them next to their car. Officer Mohamed Noor shot Ruszczyk from inside his police vehicle while sitting in the passenger seat as Ruszczyk was standing outside of the car and speaking to his partner who was seated in the drivers' seat. Noor was indicted on March 20, 2018 with third degree murder (depraved heart indifference) and second degree manslaughter (culpable negligence reckless behavior). Officer Noor was fired the same day.

Emily Saul, "DA recommends ex-NYPD cop Peter Liang not serve jail time in fatal shooting," *New York Post* (March 23, 2016) at http://nypost.com/2016/03/23/brooklyn-da-to-recommend-liang-not-serve-jail-time-for-stairwell-shooting/. See also Emily Saul, Kevin Fasick and Kate Sheehy "NYPD cop Peter Liang dodges prison for killing Akai Gurley," *New York Post* (April 19, 2016) at http://nypost.com/2016/04/19/nypd-cop-peter-liang-gets-community-service-for-killing-akai-gurley/.

49 Jennifer Emily Tasha Tsiaperas, "Fired cop who killed 15-year-old Jordan Edwards indicted on murder charge," *Dallas Morning News* July 17, 2017 at https://www.dallasnews.com/news/crime/2017/07/17/fired-cop-killed-15-year-old-jordan-edwards-indicted-murder; Sara Hoye, "Fired Officer gives detailed account of shooting teen Jordan Edwards," July 19, 2017 *WFAA* at http://www.wfaa.com/news/local/fired-officer-gives-detailed-account-of-shooting-teen-jordan-edwards/457774294; and Eva Ruth Moravec, "Former Texas police officer sentenced to 15 years in prison for fatally shooting teen," *The Washington Post* (August 30, 2018) at https://www.washingtonpost.com/news/post-nation/wp/2018/08/29/former-texas-police-officer-sentenced-to-15-years-in-prison-for-fatally-shooting-teen/?noredirect=on&utm_term=.13d46fbde25f

The moral significance of all these shootings was summarized by the father of Ruszczyk at her funeral. "Justine, my daughter, was killed by a bullet fired by an agent of the state."[50] There is a difference between being shot and killed by a criminal and being shot by an agent of the state. The difference tends to be lost on social conservatives. It is true, as they say with great enthusiasm, that more Black males are killed by other Black males than by police officers. But the distinction is in the fact that when a Black male is killed by criminal, there is moral and social and political value placed on the victim. The point being it matters who killed the Black male because the killing by the criminal does not represent society, the killing by a police officer directly represents society. Society and the law says that the killing by the criminal was wrong and the life taken has legal value. But when the agent of the state kills a Black male the killing automatically carries moral and legal justification. Politically, police shootings assume the Black life was worth being taken. The moral support is for the agent of the state. As discussed in Chapter Two, it is the agent that is supported by the law and given the benefit of the doubt. Thus that Black males' life is not of legal value or worthy of social and political support. In other words, that Black life does not matter.

These shootings in 2017 followed two previous years, 2015 and 2016, which resulted in almost two thousand people killed by the police. Many of the cases involved police killings of Blacks during traffic stops or Blacks dying in police custody. Some of the more famous incidents included the cases of **Keith Lamont Scott** (September 20, 2016, Charlotte, North Carolina), **Terence Crutcher** (September 16, 2016, Tulsa, Oklahoma), **Sylville Smith** (August 13, 2016, Milwaukee, Wisconsin), **Philando Castile** (July 6, 2016, Falcon Heights, Minnesota), **Alton Sterling** (July 5, 2016, Baton Rouge, Louisiana), **Daniel Shaver** (January 18, 2016, Mesa, Arizona), **Jeremy McDole** (September 23, 2015, Wilmington, Delaware), **Samuel DuBose** (July 19, 2015, Cincinnati, Ohio), **Sandra Bland** (July 13, 2015, Hempstead, Texas), **Freddie Gray** (April 12, 2015, Baltimore, Maryland) and **Walter Scott** (April 4, 2015, North Charleston, South Carolina). These shootings followed the infamous police killings of **Laquan McDonald** (October 20, 2014, Chicago, Illinois), **Ezell Ford** (August 11, 2014, Los Angeles, California), **Michael Brown** (August 1, 2014, Ferguson, Maryland), **Eric Garner** (July 17, 2014, Staten Island, New York) and the killing of **Trayvon Martin** (February 26, 2012, Sanford, Florida) by a White Hispanic community watch leader in a gated community.

The 2015, the killing of **Walter Scott** in North Charleston, South Carolina, was especially compelling regarding Black experience with police, in that it involved a shooting resulting from a traffic stop. The officer shot at Scott eight times, hitting him five times in the back, while Scott ran away and then attempted to plant his Taser on the dead body in order to claim self-defense. His assertion of self-defense failed when a video was posted showing him shooting Scott and planting the Taser. After a mistrial in which one White woman refused to

50 Melissa Gray, "Memorial held for Minneapolis police shooting victim Justine Ruszczyk," CNN (August 11, 2017) at http://www.cnn.com/2017/08/11/us/justine-ruszczyk-memorial-minneapolis-police-shooting/index.html

convict the officer for murder, Officer Michael T. Slager pleaded guilty to federal civil rights charges. On May 2, 2017, he plead guilty to violating 18 U.S.C. § 242 Deprivation of Rights under the Color of Law in that he, as a police officer, acted under the color of law and

> deprived Walter Lamar Scott, Jr., of the right to be free from the unreasonable and excessive use of force ... a right secured by the Fourth Amendment to the United States Constitution [in] That the defendant acted willfully; and that bodily injury or death resulted ... [which] involved the use of a dangerous weapon ... The defendant used deadly force even though it was objectively unreasonable under the circumstances. The defendant acknowledges that his actions were done willfully, that he acted voluntarily and intentionally and with specific intent to do something that the law forbids.[51]

In the 2014 **Laquan McDonald** killing in Chicago, Illinois, police video showed him walking away from the police when he was killed. Officer Jason Van Dyke was indicted on December 15, 2015, and charged with first degree murder for shooting McDonald sixteen times after McDonald was shot and on the ground helpless and not moving.[52] On October 5, 2018, Van Dyke was convicted of second-degree murder of McDonald as well as sixteen charges of aggravated battery (one for each gun discharge at McDonald). In addition, three officers were charged on June 27, 2017, with conspiracy, official misconduct, and obstruction of justice, because they entered into

> [a] conspiracy to conceal the true facts of the events surrounding the killing [of McDonald by Van Dyke] in order to shield their fellow officer from criminal investigation and prosecution. In order to accomplish this goal, the co-conspirators lied about what occurred and mischaracterized the video recordings [in order to prevent the public from seeing the video]. The co-conspirators understood that public airing of the events ... including the video recordings, would inexorably lead to a thorough criminal investigation ... and criminal charges.[53]

The criminal convictions in the Scott and McDonald cases are exceptions to the general outcome of police killings of Blacks, which usually results in no charges being filed. Criminologist Philip Stinson, who created a database on police deviance and secured a National Institute

---

51 *United States of America v. Michael Slager* United States District Court for the District of South Carolina Criminal No: 2:16-378 Global Plea Agreement (May 2, 2017) at 1–3. In agreement to the plea, the two remaining federal charges and state murder charges were dropped.

52 Monica Davey and Mitch Smith, "3 Chicago Officers Charged With Conspiracy in Laquan McDonald Case." *New York Times* (June 27, 2017)at https://www.nytimes.com/2017/06/27/us/chicago-officers-indicted-laquan-mcdonald-shooting.html

53 Grand Jury, Cook County, Ill. Indictment of David Marsh, Joseph Walsh, and Thomas Gaffney 2 (June 27, 2017) at https://assets.documentcloud.org/documents/3878758/Indictment-of-3-Chicago-cops-in-Laquan-McDonald.pdf

of Justice grant to study police criminal activity reported "that on-duty police officers across the country shoot and kill someone about 1,000 times each year. Almost all of the cases end with a determination by a prosecutor that a police shooting was legally justified."[54]

> Since 2005, there have been 82 police officers across the country charged with murder or manslaughter resulting from an on-duty shooting. That includes 18 officers charged in 2015, 13 in 2016, and three charged with murder or manslaughter resulting from an on-duty shooting so far in 2017. It is a rare event for a police officer to be charged with a crime resulting from a fatal on-duty shooting, and even rarer for an officer to be convicted in one of these cases. In the past 13 years, only 29 officers have been convicted and most of those convictions were for lesser manslaughter offenses. Only one officer has been convicted of intentional murder during that time period ... There have been 15 officers convicted at a jury trial (the other 14 convictions were by guilty pleas). The criminal cases for 31 officers ended in a non-conviction.[55]

According to the *Washington Post*, since 2005 "54 officers nationwide have been criminally charged after they shot and killed someone in the line of duty. When prosecutors filed charges, there were often additional factors. In 80% of the cases, at least one of the following occurred: the victim was shot in the back, there was a video recording of the incident, other officers testified against the shooter or a cover up was alleged."[56] When police shootings are not cleared as "justified," accountability for the death has not resulted in incarceration, but rather in the police officers being acquitted, as they were in the Freddie Gray, Terence Crutcher, Philando Castile, Sylville Smith, Anthony Smith[57] and Daniel Shaver[58] cases; criminal trials resulting in

---

54 Philip M. Stinson, "Op-Ed: Cops shoot and kill someone about 1,000 times a year: Few are prosecuted: What can be done?" *Los Angeles Times*, December 15, 2016, at http://scholarworks.bgsu.edu/cgi/viewcontent.cgi?article=1072&context=crim_just_pub

55 Philip M. Stinson, "Charging a Police Officer in Fatal Shooting Case is Rare, and a Conviction is Even Rarer," *New York Daily News* (Wednesday, May 31, 2017) at http://scholarworks.bgsu.edu/cgi/viewcontent.cgi?article=1079&context=crim_just_pub

56 See Kimberly Kindy and Elliot Kennedy data page, "Police officers prosecuted for use of deadly force" at https://www.wsj.com/articles/police-rarely-criminally-charged-for-on-duty-shootings-1416874955 linked to *Washington Post* article by Kimberly Kindy and Elliot Kennedy "Thousands Dead, Few Prosecuted," *The Washington Post* (April 11, 2015) at http://www.washingtonpost.com/sf/investigative/2015/04/11/thousands-dead-few-prosecuted/?utm_term=.a0b55c6c0293

57 On December 20, 2011 Anthony Smith was shot and killed Officer Jason Stockley of the St. Louis Missouri police department after a high-speed chase. Stockley was charged with first degree murder in August 2016 and on September 15, 2017 was acquitted after a bench trial conducted by Judge Timothy Wilson.

58 On January 16, 2016 Daniel Shaver was shot while crawling on his knees by Officer Philip "Mitch" Brailsford of the Mesa Police Department after the officer told Shaver not to move his hands but to crawl to him. When Shaver moved his hands to pull up his pants as he crawled, begging not to be shot, he was

a mistrial due to a hung jury, as in the first trial in the Freddie Gray case and the twice hung jury trials in the Samuel DuBose case; the officers suffering administrative sanctions (being fired or suspended), as Officer Timothy Loehmann (fired) and Frank Garmback (suspended for ten days) were in the Tamir Rice case and Officers Blane Salamoni (fired) and Howie Lake (suspend for three days) were in the Alton Sterling cases; or officers accepting non-criminal sanction plea agreements, as in the Sandra Bland case.

In the **Sandra Bland** case, the Texas State Trooper accepted a plea of surrendering his state law enforcement license and agreeing never to seek a law enforcement position in exchange for the dropping of a misdemeanor charge of perjury regarding his justification for removing Bland from her car, which resulted in her arrest and later suicide in the Waller County Jail. According to the indictment, the trooper asserted that he "had Sandra Bland exit the vehicle to further conduct a safe traffic investigation [and] such sworn statement [was] false in that Defendant Brian T. Encinia removed Sandra Bland from her vehicle because he was angry she would not put out her cigarette."[59] Bland ended up hanging from a jail cell, because the officer was angered by her behavior. She was not contrite and submissive enough for him.

These cases provide support for the negative perception Blacks have for the criminal justice system due to the lack of criminal culpability being imposed on police officers for the killing of Blacks. Additionally, there is a consequence for police shooting without sanction—it creates a fear of police in general and encourages police officers to believe that they can act without accountability. On July 26, 2017, Salt Lake City, Utah, police Detective Jeff Payne forcibly grabbed, pushed against a wall, handcuffed, and arrested head trauma room nurse **Alex Wubbels** who failed to obey his request for a blood withdrawal from an unconscious patient when such withdrawal was against a written policy agreed to between the hospital and the Salt Lake City police department. She explained to the detective that, unless the patient was under arrest, the detective had a warrant, or the patient consented (the patient was unconscious at the time), she could not draw blood. Payne knew she was correct, because the Supreme Court in *Birchfield v. North Dakota* (2016) wrote clearly that "we conclude that a breath test, but not a blood test, may be administered as a search incident to a lawful arrest for drunk driving. As in all cases involving reasonable searches incident to arrest, a warrant is not needed in this situation ... the search incident to arrest doctrine does not justify the warrantless taking of a

---

shot by Brailsford. The incident involved a suspected active shooter and the police had ordered Shaver to crawl over to them under threat of being shot. The encounter was filed by body cameras (see at https://www.youtube.com/watch?v=VBUUx0jUKxc). The jury found the officer not guilty of second degree murder. Uriel J. Garcia, "Ex-Mesa Officer Philip Brailsford found not guilty of murder in shooting of unarmed man" December 8, 2017 at https://www.azcentral.com/story/news/local/mesa-breaking/2017/12/07/philip-brailsford-verdict-daniel-shaver-killing/927052001/

59 Brian T. Encinia Criminal Indictment at https://assets.documentcloud.org/documents/2678589/Trooper-Brian-Encinia.pdf

blood sample."[60] Even more significant was the fact that the patient was not a suspect in car accident. Payne wanted the blood sample simply because he wanted it.

When the nurse, Wubbels, showed Payne the written policy between the hospital and the police department in compliance (in part anyway) with the Supreme Court ruling defending her refusal and after her supervisor informed Payne that nurse Wubbels was correct and that the officer was making a mistake and chided him for threatening her, Payne lost his temper with her presumption to tell him what she would not do under his direction and arrested her and pushed her into his police car. It was her attitude and lack of contriteness and submissiveness that resulted in her arrest.[61] Twenty minutes after the arrest, while sitting in his car, she was released, and she later received apologies from the police department chief and the mayor. Both the mayor and the chief admitted that the arrest was not lawful and the amount of forced used to make the arrest was not appropriate. Payne was removed from the blood draw unit, placed on administrative leave pending a department investigation, which occurred simultaneously with a criminal investigation.[62] When it was revealed that Payne said after the encounter that, "I'll bring them all the transients and take good patients elsewhere" in order to retaliate against the nurse and the hospital, he was fired from his part-time job as a paramedic. After an administrative investigation Payne was fired and his supervisor, who authorized Payne's arresting Nurse Wubbels, was demoted from lieutenant to officer.[63]

Nurse Wubbels, a White female, and Sandra Bland, were arrested and manhandled not for violation of the law but for not having an attitude sufficiently subservient to the liking of the police officer. It's the abuse of power and the sense of entitlement to abuse their power that is the point. That sense of entitlement has consequences, in the case of Bland—her death—and in the case of nurse Wubbels—a physical assault, being publicly dragged out of her emergency room in terror, and being thrown into the back of a police car.

This sense of entitlement by the police to use force due to an insufficiently subservient attitude of a citizen creates a logical fear of the police, because criminality is not the focal point of police use of force. Consider the following case of a White woman who refused to move her hands, because she did not want to be shot by the officer during a Driving Under the Influence (DUI) traffic stop. On July 10, 2016, four days after the Philando Castile shooting, the following conversation occurred when Cobb County, Georgia, police lieutenant Greg Abbott conducted a traffic DUI stop.

---

60 Birchfield v. North Dakota 579 U. S. ____, Slip op at (35–36) (2016).

61 See Nurse Alex Wubbels Arrested for Doing Her Job at https://www.youtube.com/watch?v=JFxe86QQKF8 and Mayor, Police Chief Respond to Cop Arresting *Nurse* at https://www.youtube.com/watch?v=cITA9HcX77I

62 Id. See also, Melissa Gray, "'I've done nothing wrong': Utah nurse's arrest prompts police apology," CNN (September 2, 2017) at http://www.cnn.com/2017/09/01/health/utah-nurse-arrest-police-video/

63 Derek Hawkins "Utah police officer fired after manhandling, arresting nurse who was doing her job," *Washington Post* (October 11, 2017) at https://www.washingtonpost.com/news/morning-mix/wp/2017/10/10/utah-police-officer-fired-after-manhandling-arresting-nurse-who-was-doing-her-job/?utm_term=.0e9a00242d33

Abbott: Now Listen to me. Call the person who is coming to get you. Tell them they don't need to come. All right? Yes. OK. Go ahead and call them. I am going to take you to jail and then I am going to impound the car.
Passenger: Before that [inaudible]
Abbott: No
Passenger: I can't call them if you don't open the car door.
Abbott: Why can't you?
Passenger: I just want to put myself in that
Abbott: Use your phone. It's in your lap right there
Passenger: Okay, I will, I just don't want to put my hands down. I'm really sorry
Abbott: Is something wrong
Passenger: No, **I've just seen way too many videos of cops shooting people**
Abbott: But **you're not black. Remember, we only kill black people**. Yeah, we only kill black people, right? All the videos you've seen, have you seen any white people get killed?
Passenger: Yes
Abbot: You have.
Passenger: An eighteen-year-old white boy killed in twenty three seconds [inaudible]
Abbot: Yeah
Passenger: [inaudible] I'm not saying you're a bad cop [inaudible]
Abbott: Right[64]

During a DUI traffic stop, a White police lieutenant with twenty-eight years of experience, with a purpose of comforting a White woman who was drunk, told her that she did not need to worry and could lower her hands, because police only shoot Black people.

Consider the dynamics of this encounter and what it means both socially and politically. Since she was not Black, she had nothing to fear from the police. There is a reason why Blacks fear police in general and specifically when alone during a police stop. Blacks define both police action and the criminal justice system through the lens of history. That history is defined by abuse and discrimination at the hands of government power based on skin color. And, that abuse has been specifically unleased by the police dating back to 1619.

While police shootings are perceived by many Whites in America as the result of Blacks being unwilling to respond appropriately to lawful police officer commands that must be enforced, Blacks view use of force by the police that results in the shootings of young Black men as nothing out of the ordinary. Blacks being abused by law enforcement dates back to the beginning of American policing—the beginning of that abuse being the slave patrols of the antebellum period, followed by police enforcement of the black codes and Jim Crow in the postbellum period (1865 to 1918), the militarization of policing in the late 1960s, the

64 The officer was subsequently fired from the police department on August 31, 2017. See "We only shoot black people"—Georgia police officer at https://www.youtube.com/watch?v=YBRIHNn78dc

federalization of illicit drug policy in the 1970s, the rise of police drug task forces in the 1980s, and the imposition of police drug suppression "jump out squads" on Black communities in the 1990s.

Consider policing from a philosophical inquiry, *Quis Custodiet Ipso Custodies*, "Who will guard the guards themselves?" The police have a power that the president of the United States does not have. They have power, on the street, to take the life and liberty of any person they choose. They can take life with less legal justification (objective reasonableness) than is required to secure a warrant (probable cause to believe). When police take action, the question is how this power is controlled and is it controlled when it's applied to Black males. As discussed in Chapter Two, the Fourth Amendment provides a very limited check on police power. The true control on police power is political. The enforcement of control of police power is dictated by the level of societal fear of crime and who commits that crime. While Blacks tend to ask, "Who will watch our watchers—who will protect us from our protectors when it comes to police," Whites tend to support the police, because they are perceived as protectors of them.

Policing is a system of control and the use of force. Police work is about the officers going home alive after an altercation. Police encounters are about police control and domination, which to the police officer equals officer safety. The loss of physical control leads to a fear of personal safety in the police officer. The lack of dominance equals lack of safety. This fear for safety leads to police aggression. The subconscious fear of young Black males leads the police to perceive a threat and then act aggressively to maintain control. The result can lead to a Black man face down on the hood of a car or dead in the street.

An example of this dynamic is the Crutcher killing. Officer Betty Shelby shot and killed **Terence Crutcher** on September 16, 2016, in Tulsa, Oklahoma, while being backed up by three other officers and a police helicopter. In a *60 minutes* interview regarding the killing, Selby said, regarding why she chose to use deadly force when in an ambiguous confrontation with a Black male bigger than she was and whom she feared had a gun, "If I wait to find out if he had a gun or not I could very well be dead. There is something that we always say: I would rather be tried by twelve than carried by six."[65] Consider the dehumanization of Crutcher and the privilege enjoyed by Shelby that she felt free to be so honest regarding the taking of Crutcher's life with nothing more than the explanation that he could have had a gun, not that he did.

Race, she said, had nothing to do with the shooting. The social psychology research of implicit bias, involuntary psychological upload of negative racial stereotypes of Blacks, and physiological fear of Blacks, as discussed in Chapter Three, says otherwise. In her interview she, in tears, said that if he had only obeyed her, she would not have had to shoot him. The confrontation began when she saw him standing next to his car, and she thought his standing still was "zombielike behavior" and that standing still next to her car led her to fear that Crutcher was on PCP. The helicopter pilot hovering over the scene when Crutcher was facing four armed police officers with their guns drawn, said Crutcher, "looks like a bad dude too."

---

65 *60 Minutes*, CBS (April 4, 2017).

When Crutcher walked towards Shelby with his hands in his pocket and then removed them at her command, his behavior left her with the fear that he had a gun. She drew her weapon, even though he was not being belligerent, because he did not follow her command not to approach his car. She explained in the interview that as he walked toward his car, she thought he was looking for a gun that he did not have in his pocket. When he walked to his car and, to her, he looked like he was putting his hands into the window, she shot him dead. The police watched him bleed in the street for two minutes before attempting to give aid. The police found no gun. They did find a small amount of PCP in his car and in his system.

When asked about how she felt about killing Crutcher and why it happened, she stated that his disobedience and walking away from her and looking at his car meant he was looking to do her harm. Shelby said that his movements alone justified his killing. Officer Shelby said Crutcher is dead because of his own actions. He caused his own death, and "If he would have complied. If he would have communicated with me. If he would have just done what as I asked him to do." The jury agreed and acquitted her of manslaughter charges in May 2017. It's this dynamic that causes Black parents in Black communities to have "The Talk" with their children and, especially, their young Black males.

One of the dynamics of the need for "The Talk" is because of crime concentration in Black communities and aggressive police responses to Black crime. Crime is never evenly distributed in a city; it is concentrated in specific geographical areas. The concentration produces certain structural social dynamics. These dynamics can be grouped into three overarching problems; first, chronic violent crime; second, chronic intractable poverty and the psychological problems that come with poverty; and third, police saturation policies, which involve aggressive police attention and abusive treatment of all of the people in those sections as if they were the cause of the first problem.

Police operations in neighborhoods with these three problems include the abandonment of community-policing/problem-solving philosophy for the politically more popular law-and-order policy of the illegal operational use of stop and frisk. The illegality of stop and frisk is in its use, as done in New York City, as a crime suppression tool rather than a crime investigatory tool. The NYPD used it as the latter to reduce gun violence. The illegal operationalized use of stop and frisk was publicly defended by then Mayor Bloomberg and Police Commissioner Kelly with the assertion that the police were stopping Blacks, because criminals in high-crime neighborhoods were Black, and that the Blacks stopped were more likely to be armed. The rage of innocent Black males being stopped and treated as if they were the cause of first factor adds to the desperation and feelings isolation caused by the second factor.

How the Supreme Court and the judiciary has fashioned the law to provide the police, specifically, and the criminal justice system, generally, with life-altering power is another factor behind Black distrust of the criminal justice system. There are only two institutions in America that have the power to physically take away your liberty and change your life. The first is the military in times of a draft—which no longer exists in America. The second is the criminal justice system. With nothing more than reasonable suspicion, the police can seize you and prevent you from going about your business on one end of the continuum and can shoot you dead in the street on the other end. With nothing more than probable cause, the police can arrest you, put you in jail, and leave you to your own devices with hardened criminals in the same cell—all that before a judge lays eyes upon you.

Consider the eloquent description of criminal justice written by Supreme Court Justice Sonia Sotomayor in her dissent in the 2016 case *Utah v. Strieff* on the power of the criminal justice system. After reading her opinion, consider her conclusion, "unlawful police stops corrode all our civil liberties and threaten all our lives. Until their voices matter too, our justice system will continue to be anything but."

> Writing only for myself, and drawing on my professional experiences, I would add that unlawful "stops" have severe consequences much greater than the inconvenience suggested by the name. This Court has given officers an array of instruments to probe and examine you. When we condone officers' use of these devices without adequate cause, we give them reason to target pedestrians in an arbitrary manner. We also risk treating members of our communities as second-class citizens.
>
> Although many Americans have been stopped for speeding or jaywalking, few may realize how degrading a stop can be when the officer is looking for more. This Court has allowed an officer to stop you for whatever reason he wants—so long as he can point to a pretextual justification after the fact. *Whren* v. *United States*. That justification must provide specific reasons why the officer suspected you were breaking the law, *Terry v. Ohio*, but it may factor in your ethnicity, *United States* v. *Brignoni-Ponce*, where you live, *Adams* v. *Williams*, what you were wearing, *United States* v. *Sokolow*, and how you behaved, *Illinois* v. *Wardlow*. The officer does not even need to know which law you might have broken so long as he can later point to any possible infraction—even one that is minor, unrelated, or ambiguous. *Devenpeck* v. *Alford* and *Heien* v. *North Carolina*.
>
> The indignity of the stop is not limited to an officer telling you that you look like a criminal. The officer may next ask for your "consent" to inspect your bag or purse without telling you that you can decline, *Florida* v. *Bostick*. Regardless of your answer, he may order you to stand "helpless, perhaps facing a wall with [your] hands raised." *Terry v. Ohio*. If the officer thinks you might be dangerous, he may then "frisk" you for weapons. This involves more than just a pat down. As onlookers pass by, the officer may "'feel with sensitive fingers every portion of [your] body. A thorough search [may] be made of [your] arms and armpits, waistline and back, the groin and area about the testicles, and entire surface of the legs down to the feet.'" *Terry v. Ohio*.
>
> The officer's control over you does not end with the stop. If the officer chooses, he may handcuff you and take you to jail for doing nothing more than speeding, jaywalking, or "driving [your] pickup truck ... with [your] 3-year-old son and 5-year-old daughter ... without [your] seatbelt fastened." *Atwater* v. *Lago Vista*. At the jail, he can fingerprint you, swab DNA from the inside of your mouth, and force you to "shower with a delousing agent" while you "lift [your] tongue, hold out [your] arms, turn around, and lift [your] genitals." *Florence* v. *Board of Chosen Freeholders of County of Burlington* and *Maryland*

> v. *King*. Even if you are innocent, you will now join the 65 million Americans with an arrest record and experience the "civil death" of discrimination by employers, landlords, and whoever else conducts a background check. And, of course, if you fail to pay bail or appear for court, a judge will issue a warrant to render you "arrestable on sight" in the future.
>
> This case involves a *suspicionless* stop, one in which the officer initiated this chain of events without justification. As the Justice Department notes many innocent people are subjected to the humiliations of these unconstitutional searches. The white defendant in this case shows that anyone's dignity can be violated in this manner. But it is no secret that people of color are disproportionate victims of this type of scrutiny. For generations, Black and brown parents have given their children "the talk"—instructing them never to run down the street; always keep your hands where they can be seen; do not even think of talking back to a stranger—all out of fear of how an officer with a gun will react to them.[66]

These "humiliations of these unconstitutional searches" are compounded by the fact that the Fourth Amendment provides very limited civil liability protection. Police officers carry qualified immunity for their actions, even when they are factually wrong.

> "The doctrine of qualified immunity shields officials from civil liability so long as their conduct 'does not violate clearly established ... constitutional rights of which a reasonable person would have known.'" *Mullenix v. Luna*, 577 U. S. ___, ___ (2015) (per curiam) (slip op., at 4–5) (quoting *Pearson v. Callahan*, 555 U. S. 223, 231 (2009)). The "dispositive inquiry in determining whether a right is clearly established is whether it would be clear to a reasonable officer that his conduct was unlawful in the situation he confronted." *Saucier v. Katz*, 533 U. S. 194, 202 (2001). The qualified immunity analysis thus is limited to "the facts that were knowable to the defendant officers" at the time they engaged in the conduct in question. *White v. Pauly*, 580 U. S. ___, ___ (2017) (per curiam) (slip op., at3). Facts an officer learns after the incident ends–whether those facts would support granting immunity or denying it—are not relevant.[67]
>
> The Fourth Amendmen ... forbids unreasonable searches and seizures, yet it may be difficult for an officer to know whether a search or seizure will be deemed reasonable given the precise situation encountered. See *Saucier v. Katz*, 533 U. S. 194, 205 (2001) ("It is sometimes difficult for an officer to determine how the relevant legal doctrine, here excessive force, will apply to the factual situation the officer confronts"). For this reason, "[t]he dispositive question is 'whether the violative nature of particular conduct is clearly established.'" *Mullenix v. Luna*, 577 U. S. ___, ___ (2015) (per curiam) (slip op., at 5) (quoting *Ashcroft* [*v. al-Kidd, 563 U. S.*], supra, at 742).

---

66 *Utah v. Strieff*, 579 U.S. ____(2016) Slip Op., 9–12 Sotomayor, dissenting opinion.

67 *Hernandez v. Mesa*, 582 U.S. ____(2017) Slip Op. at 6

> It is not necessary, of course, that "the very action in question has previously been held unlawful." Anderson, supra, at 640. That is, an officer might lose qualified immunity even if there is no reported case "directly on point." Ashcroft, supra, at 741. But "in the light of preexisting law," the unlawfulness of the officer's conduct "must be apparent." Anderson, supra, at 640. To subject officers to any broader liability would be to "disrupt the balance that our cases strike between the interests in vindication of citizens' constitutional rights and in public officials' effective performance of their duties." *Davis v. Scherer*, 468 U. S. 183, 195 (1984). For then, both as a practical and legal matter, it would be difficult for officials "reasonably [to] anticipate when their conduct may give rise to liability for damages." Ibid.
>
> In light of these concerns, the Court has held that qualified immunity protects "all but the plainly incompetent or those who knowingly violate the law." *Malley v. Briggs*, 475 U. S. 335, 341 (1986). To determine whether a given officer falls into either of those two categories, a court must ask whether it would have been clear to a reasonable officer that the alleged conduct "was unlawful in the situation he confronted." Saucier, supra, at 202. If so, then the defendant officer must have been either incompetent or else a knowing violator of the law, and thus not entitled to qualified immunity. If not, however—i.e., if a reasonable officer might not have known for certain that the conduct was unlawful—then the officer is immune from liability.[68]

The result being that it doesn't matter if the police make a decision in error that results in police use of force or deadly force. The Fourth Amendment begins with the presumption that the police have the right to seize at their discretion, limited only by the objective question of reasonableness, not correctness. That reasonableness, as discussed in Chapter Two, is governed by what the individual does when confronted by the police. This fact led Justice Sotomayor to lament that under the law

> your body is subject to invasion while courts excuse the violation of your rights. It implies that you are not a citizen of a democracy but the subject of a carceral [a prison] state, just waiting to be cataloged. We must not pretend that the countless people who are routinely targeted by police are "isolated." They are the canaries in the coal mine whose deaths, civil and literal, warn us that no one can breathe in this atmosphere. They are the ones who recognize that unlawful police stops corrode all our civil liberties and threaten all our lives. Until their voices matter too, our justice system will continue to be anything but.[69]

The value placed on Black bodies under police control raises another issue—moral equivalency. On December 20, 2014, two New York City Police Department officers, Rafael Ramos and Wenjian Liu, were sitting in their car and were ambushed and killed by Ismaaiyl Abdullah

---

68 *Ziglar v. Abbasi*, 582 U.S. ____ (2017) Slip Op., 28–29

69 *Utah v. Strieff*, 579 U.S. ____(2016) Slip Op., 12 Sotomayor, dissenting opinion.

Brinsley, who later shot and killed himself. Brinsley had posted on social media that he hated cops and that he was going to shoot some police officers in retaliation for the killings of Eric Garner and Michael Brown by the New York and Ferguson Police Departments. In both killings, the officers were not charged with a crime.

If Brinsley would have lived, what would have happened? He would have been arrested, indicted, tried, and convicted. The police would not have called for justice for the officers, because they would have gotten it without a word. This uncontroverted fact raises a question: why would Brinsley's arrest and conviction been assured? There would have been no question, because the value of the lives of the officers was not open to dispute as to whether criminal accountability for their deaths was required. No one would have tried to justify the murderer and his actions. No one would have asked "what were the officers doing that caused Brinsley to shoot them?"

The deaths of Garner and Brown did not receive the same absolute reaction as the murder of Officers Ramos and Liu, because Garner and Brown were labeled as criminals and a threat to the police. Those who spoke out against the killing of Garner and Brown had to first elevate the lives of these men to a level deserving of accountability. Such is the sin of moral equivalency.

The Bible tells the story that God created male and female, that He created human life, and it was precious in His eyes. When the son of the generation that ate the fruit of the forbidden tree spilled blood in murder, the answer from Heaven was not, "Abel what did you do to Cain to make him kill you," but rather Heaven said to Cain, "[Abel's] blood cries out to Me from the ground." From then until now, human life has not been measured by its inherent value from creation, but rather by comparing the value of one person to another. In the American context, that comparison is based on wealth, race, gender, and personal behavior. Justice is defined by a moral equivalency defined subjectively and politically.

Moral equivalency is used to make distinctions between evil (one evil is not as bad as another) or to make distinctions between events in which one requires a certain result, while another does not. Historically, the lives of Black males have not held the same moral equivalency as White lives and certainly not equivalent to police lives. While the days of Jim Crow's lack of equivalency are a thing of the past, subtle expressions of the lack of equivalency are still voiced. In cases of a Black man killed by the police, an assumption is made at the outset that the Black man must have been doing something that resulted in his own death. Questions are raised about his criminal history or behavior before the police shooting.

It's the lack of equivalency at the beginning of the inquiry that sparks protesters to claim "Black lives matter" and to demand the same result that would have occurred if the murderer of Officers Ramos and Liu had lived—that result being, at the very least, an arrest, an indictment, and a trial.

Arrests, indictments, and trials are social actions that publically vindicate the value of a life under the law. They also vindicate the moral value and purpose of the law. It should be remembered that the enforcement of law is the only thing that ensures that the value of a man's life is equal to all other lives in society. The law is the beginning of justice, and justice is what is sought when a Black man is shot by the agents of government—the police. As Lord

Chief Justice Hewart said in 1924, "it is not merely of some importance but is of fundamental importance that justice should not only be done, but should manifestly and undoubtedly be seen to be done."[70] As Justice Frankfurter wrote in 1954, "justice must satisfy the appearance of justice."[71] Public trials establish a social minimum equality under law.

The sin of moral equivalency is manifested by the justification for the police. The role of the police is to protect society. The subtly of the sin of moral equivalency is in the answer to the question, "who are the police to protect and from whom?" Those who stand protected behind the shield of the police will oppose those who are subjected to the sword of the police, and they will defend them for that protection.

When protesters and politicians demand accountability in the use of the sword, they are seen as opposing the saviors of society; they are "soft on crime." When the police commit an injustice, that injustice is not perceived as morally equivalent to the harm caused by those who the police seek to control. In the American context, those who are to be socially controlled by the police are young Black males who are the source of crime and, thus, a threat to the greater society. The result of this is that the life of the young Black male is not assumed, much less treated, to be morally equivalent to the protection of society and the value of the police. With that assumption, it's less likely that the criminal justice system will vindicate the value of a Black man killed by the police. The sin of moral equivalency manifests itself in the protests and complaints by Blacks and how those complaints are minimized and met with contempt by the defenders of the police.

As discussed throughout this book, there are various and complicated reasons why Blacks and Whites perceive the legitimacy of the criminal justice system differently, both in purpose and in operation. These distinctions have historical, political, economic, and legal origins. While true that America has become a great nation and has put its racist Jim Crow laws into the dust bin of history, it is nonetheless true that negative perceptions of Blacks and support for aggressive policing and control of Blacks have been linked together since before the founding of the Constitution. The purpose of policing can only be understood within the broader context of a complicated American history. Policing has a purpose, to protect (to be a shield) some and to be a sword upon (to control) others. In relation to Blacks, policing can be summarized as follows: Policing has always been about protecting Whites, it was certainly about controlling Blacks in the past, and it is open to debate if it's only about controlling Blacks now. If it's only about controlling Blacks now, the resentment, distrust, and riots resulting from police shootings of Blacks should not be a surprise.

A social context exists to explain how Blacks and Whites perceive the criminal justice system. This context is based on historical memory and lasting impact. Blacks and Whites don't share the same historical perspective. In regards to the discussion of policing in American political discourse, when American society as whole is the focus, the police are discussed

70 *R v. Sussex Justices, Ex parte McCarthy* ([1924] 1 KB 256, [1923]

71 *Offutt v. United States*, 348 U.S. 11, 14 (1954)

in terms of "to serve and protect," but when the focus is on Blacks, the language changes to the terms of "law and order." While all people in all communities deserve policing in both terms (serve and protect, as well as law and order), the truth is Black communities are only discussed in terms of the latter. The former involves respect from the police, the latter requires obedience to the police and control by the police.

KEY CONCEPTS AND LAWS

1. Declaration of Independence slave clause
2. Lost Cause Theory
3. Thirteenth Amendment
4. European Slave Trade
5. America—antebellum period
6. America—Jim Crow period
7. Washington Post Police Use of Force Database

KEY PEOPLE

1. Thomas Jefferson
2. President Obama
3. Attorney General Lynch
4. Frederick Douglass
5. Justice Sotomayor

DISCUSSION QUESTIONS

1. What is the significance of the slave clause of the Declaration of Independence that was rejected by the Continental Congress? How does the clause relate to what Jefferson thought was illegal and immoral about slavery? Compare on contrast Jefferson's view on the legality of slavery and his perception on Black intelligence and social and biological equality to Whites discussed at the end of chapter three. Why and how does the difference matter in modern criminal justice rhetoric and policy making regarding explanations of Black and White criminality?
2. What were the politics of slavery during the drafting of the Declaration of Independence and the U.S. Constitution and how does that relate to how Blacks were perceived under the law after the Civil War? Further how does this history relate to police use of force today?

3. Compare and contrast the ideas of President Obama, Attorney General Lynch, and Frederick Douglass on race, crime, justice, and American politics.
4. In recent years there have been more than 2000 people killed by the police. There have been few trials of police officers and even fewer convictions of those officers. Discuss and explain the shootings discussed in this chapter and the reasons and politics for the lack of prosecution and conviction.
5. What is the Lost Cause theory and why does it matter?
6. Discuss the opinion by Justice Sotomayor and whether she is correct in her opinion.
7. Discuss the assertion that moral equivalency is part of the problem of the lack of police accountability in police use of force.
8. Frederick Douglass asserted that the U.S. Constitution was not only not a pro-slavery document but in fact it was clear in opposing slavery. Was Douglass correct? What is the distinction between what the text of the Constitution says and the policies that were passed by the government under the Constitution? Assuming Douglass is correct in his arguments regarding the various clauses used to define the Constitution as a pro-slavery document, does it matter historically, politically, or socially today?
9. Frederick Douglass rejected original intent for strict scrutiny/textualism regarding how the Constitution should be interpreted. Define both approaches and discuss which theory is best in applying the Constitution and its protections to minority groups in today's politics. Review the discussion of the *Dred Scott* and *Brown v. Board of Education* cases in light of Douglass's approach to constitutional interpretation.

CHAPTER TEN

Post-Script: The Rise of President Trump and Republican Rhetoric, Narratives, Politics, and Policy on Race

Political *rhetoric* leads to the development of political *narratives* which in turn define *politics* (elections) which result in the development and implementation of *policy*. This book is premised on the assertion that to understand the American criminal justice system when it comes to law enforcement policy and its intersectionality with race, the narratives and politics of race in America must be understood from a historical perspective. The fear and animosity Blacks have towards the criminal justice system and the policies of the system that have led to disproportionate incarceration is not spontaneous. The criminal justice system is the creation of politics, policy, and the rhetoric of politicians. While many of the injustices of slavery and Jim Crow have been relegated to the dustbin of history, the effects of those policies remain and the modern demarcation line in debate on the manifestation of those effects is seen and debated within the operation and policies of American criminal justice.

Blacks since the end of the Civil War and the fall of Reconstruction have been controlled by the power of criminal justice. But that control is not endemic to criminal justice. The control has been the result of American politics. This chapter concludes this book with a discussion on the modern politics of the Republican Party considering the election of Donald Trump. From politics comes policy, not the reverse. With the rise of President Trump the Republican Party's racial and social control rhetoric is changing from fear of crime and focusing that fear on Blacks to resentment of party elites who have abandoned the party faithful for economic globalization. The party has also embraced a politics in which the "Lost Cause" of the southern rebellion has been reborn and modernized to defend confederate statues and the confederate flag. The "Lost Cause" asserts there was no moral difference between the South and North and the South was fighting for freedom and for states' rights. Although this defense is hardly new, what is new is the assertion that today's judgement that slavery was evil cannot be applied to the practice of slavery in the South then. Thus, the men who

This section has been adapted from Arthur H. Garrison, "Trump: Fifty Years In The Making," *The Keystone Newspaper*, 2016.

fought to destroy the Union then cannot be judged as evil now. More, they can be judged as men who fought honorably. The implication is that slavery was something worthy to defend because slavery was not an abomination. That being true, where does that leave Blacks who suffered under slavery? If slavery was not wrong, then the racism that undergirded slavery was not wrong. If so, as a matter of policy what does that mean for criminal justice policy outcomes of disproportionate incarceration and police use of force in the street? It is because of these questions—and the answers that follow—that it matters how presidents in general, and how President Trump now, think. It matters if the "Lost Cause" is the new theory of Republican Party rhetoric and policy.

As discussed in Chapter Eight, Attorney General Sessions was not sympathetic to the underlying theory behind Attorney General Holder's policy on mandatory sentencing. Elections have consequences—winners make and implement policy and losers go home and write memoirs. To the victor go the spoils.

TRUMP AND 2016 ELECTION: VICTORY OF A COUNTER-INSURGENCY

Throughout this book it has been asserted that the modern Republican Party traces its ideological and political philosophical underpinnings of states' rights and opposition to a strong national government to John Calhoun, Strom Thurmond, George Wallace, Barry Goldwater, Richard Nixon, and Ronald Reagan. The Republican Party, for more than fifty years, has cultivated a narrative to attract and hold working class, high-school educated, anti-intellectual White voters who felt politically and economically emasculated in their own country. The party sought to attract and hold the voter who resented and feared the disappearance of the 1950s *Father Knows Best*, *Make Room for Daddy*, *Adventures of Ozzie and Harriet* America. The party began recruitment of this type of voter when it welcomed defecting Southern Democratic voters into the party after the passage of the 1964 Civil Rights Act. From 1966 through the 1970s, the party built a political voting base by taking advantage of White fear of the rise of Blacks, women, homosexuals, the poor, Hispanics, people of color, immigrants, and liberals of all stripes who were changing the American social and political culture. In the 1980s, beginning with Reagan, the Republican Party added to this fear by focusing blame on the federal government and asserted that the federal government (run by Democrats who favored minorities at White expense with government-run social welfare programs) was incompetent, untrustworthy, violent to middle-class Christian values, and an impediment to individual success.

In the 1990s, the party encouraged voters to believe that the blame for the lack of social, economic, and political success of middle-class White males was affirmative action (Blacks, Hispanics, and women) and liberals masquerading as Republicans. The party promoted a narrative that made clear whom was at fault and to blame for the cultural and economic changes in America. In the 1990s, the assertion that only conservative ideological purity would restore

America began to take root within the party. The culmination of these narratives and perspectives was the formation within the Republican Party of the Tea Party after the election of the first Black President, Barak Obama, in 2008. The Tea Party insurgency was fostered and encouraged by the Republican establishment to be used as a weapon against President Obama.

The Tea Party was comprised of middle and working class non-college educated voters whose wages had remained stagnant under the Republican domination of Congress beginning in the last two decades of the twentieth century through the first decade of the twenty-first century. Under Republican control of Congress and the presidencies held by both Presidents Bush, the loss of high-wage, blue collar jobs continued. The size of the federal government and the budget deficit increased under the Republican Congress without any serious resistance. The Tea Party, a conservative insurgency within the party, first focused its ire on the Democrats, energized the Republicans, and bore fruit when the party took control of the House (2010) and Senate (2014). The Tea Party base expected that decades-old promises made by the party would be fulfilled and the policies of Obama would be turned back. The base of the Tea Party, in victory, gained no tangible policy success in 2010 through 2016. President Obama's chief policy achievement, the Affordable Care Act ("Obamacare"), was not repealed even with Republican control of the House and Senate; in fact, it was fully funded. Full funding for Planned Parenthood continued. Homosexual marriage became the law of the land by a Supreme Court decree written by Justice Kennedy, a Reagan appointee! The Republican base voter felt it had been lied to, and they resented it. To make things worse, the political influence of Tea Party activists was actively resented by the party establishment. The Tea Party base resentment of the party establishment selection of Mitt Romney in 2012 was further compounded by the fact that he lost to Obama.

Into this decades-old resentment stepped Donald Trump. When he declared his candidacy for the presidency on June 16, 2015, he instantly took primary control of the long-standing issue of immigration (code for people coming from Mexico) from the party establishment by asserting that Mexico was sending rapists, murderers, and other criminals into America, and that is why a great wall must be built separating Mexico from the United States. While in politics, some level of civility is required, Trump rejected political correctness asserting, "political correctness is killing us" and we don't have time for it, because America is going down the tubes. On December 7, 2015 Trump called for a complete ban on all Muslims entering America until the incompetent federal government "figures out what the hell is going on."

Trump also gave voice to White social conservatives who held resentment of political correctness. Political correctness is a social concept that has long been opposed by Republican social conservative ideology because political correctness is interpreted as a means of muzzling White Christian conservatives who advocate for traditional American family values. Republicans view political correctness as an enforced proposition that White guilt should be accepted by White America for its centuries-old discrimination of minorities and women. Political correctness, in the eyes of political and social conservatives, has weakened American politics from asserting unpopular truths—for example, Black deviant culture, not racism, explains Black failure when compared to White and Asian groups that maintain non-deviant social and family dynamics in their homes and communities. The desire of many to be able to speak the truth, without fear of being called a racist or worrying about the "hurt feelings" of other social groups is what Donald Trump capitalized on.

Trump established his anti-political correctness *bona fides* when he said John McCain was not a real war hero, because all he did was get captured. Trump said, "I like people who were not captured." Trump ran a campaign that made clear to the press (another despised social institution in the Tea Party ideological worldview of politics) that they "can't toy with me like they toy with everyone else." Trump capitalized on his *bona fides* as the leading birther, (those who asserted President Obama was not born in the United States but in Africa—thus, he was an illegitimate president) during the 2008 election. Upon entering the 2016 race and he broke the presidential hopes of long time social conservatives like Rick Perry, Bobby Jindal, Lindsey Graham, and Scott Walker with little more than his physical presence. He made the Christian conservative *bona fides of* Rick Santorum and Mike Huckabee irrelevant. With nothing more than his bluster and presence, he commandeered the exclusive command of the Tea Party credentials of Ted Cruz.

Trump was the beneficiary of the creation of the confrontational, anti-establishment politics created by the Republican Party in 1968, 1980, and 2008. Trump was popular not only because he tapped into the politics of anti-government resentment that the Party had nurtured since 1980 under Reagan, he also tapped into the base Republican voter who resented the Republican Party itself. Trump took advantage of the Party establishment disdain for the Tea Party. Trump commandeered and expanded upon Tea Party resentment and broadened it to be a general insurgency of a grassroots rejection of the economic internationalists, Wall Street bailout, deficit spending, neo-con foreign policy, free trade Washington leadership of the Party. Trump was elected by harnessing an insurgency of rural, Rust Belt state, working class, non-college educated, low-skill workers who believed that the policies of both parties over the past fifty years have taken away from them their country and their opportunities in a free nation. The Trump insurgency was a reincarnation and combination of the Nixon hard hats of 1972, the Reagan Democrats of 1980, the Buchanan voters of 1992; the voters who opposed civil rights in the 1950s and 1960s and opposed affirmative action programs of the 1970s; and the voters who supported the war on drugs and crime policies of the 1980s through the 1990s.

The Trump insurgency also included a coalition of states' rights, balanced budget, anti-entitlement spending, limited government, social conservative, evangelical Christian, anti-neo-con foreign policy, isolationist voters who rejected the post 9/11 wars in the Middle East, opposed the idea of spreading democracy through international nation building, and wanted America to focus on itself. Trump campaigned with a simple slogan, "Make America Great Again." Trump laid claim to the insurgency by attacking the record of George W. Bush and the Iraq War, blaming the turmoil in the Middle East on the Iraq invasion and claiming he was the only Republican running that opposed it. He advocated for the exclusion of Muslims from the United States, called for the building of a wall on the Mexican border, and bragged that he would make Mexico pay for it.

Trump, unlike Reagan and Goldwater, was not an ideological candidate. He was a nationalist populist candidate with a campaign of flamboyant narratives—"Make America Great Again"—not a candidate with hard ideological philosophy. He ran his campaign as a pragmatist who asserted that, as a businessman, he would get things done and would not be owned by any political ideology. In addition to asserting independence, he was portrayed a masculine persona that was not present with the other Republican candidates running for president. He had his own plane, which arrived at locations like it was Air Force One. Trump was brash and not obedient to conventional rules for running for president. When attacked by opponents or by the media, he demanded public apologies and got them. He did not need funding from Wall Street or the Republican political donor class. He commanded the attention of the media by the force of his personality. He was not beholden to conservative media (Fox News and conservative talk radio) to connect with voters. He ran for office with a persona of being politically incorrect, as well as confrontational. After fifty years of party weakness, to his supporters, Trump was someone who would not only fight both the political left (Democrats) and the ineffective Republican establishment; he, like Reagan and Goldwater, would change the party.

Starting with his book in 1960 and during the election of 1964, Goldwater redefined the ideological principles of Republican Party. This ideological definition was made permanent with the election of 1980. The elections in 1988 and the 1990s were the elections of the culture wars, which pitted Blacks against Whites, Goldwater/Reagan conservatives against liberal Republicans, Great Society Democrats against Republicans, law-and-order voters against Democrats, free traders against protectionists, labor against right-to-work advocates, isolationists against interventionists, those advocating pro-family traditional values against those supporting rights for people with alternative life styles, and pro-life against pro-choice.

In the elections of 2008 and 2012, America elected and re-elected the first Black President. But these elections also gave birth to the rise of the Tea Party and a civil war within the ideological heart of the Republican Party. The Tea Party was a grass roots rejection of establishment politicians who failed to stop the policies of President Obama and reduce the size of the federal government after having control of both houses of Congress. The primary election of 2016 was an election over the internal control of the Party, the Reagan/Goldwater philosophy championed by Ted Cruz vs. the Trump coalition of insurgencies. The Reagan coalition of 1980, in which Reagan papered over the differences between the various wings of conservatism within the Republican Party, was ended. Cruz and Trump fought for the support of the populist, libertarian, Tea Party, anti-government, social and Christian conservative wings of the party. Marco Rubio, Jeb Bush, and John Kasich fought for the Republican establishment, mainstream conservative, neo-con foreign policy, limited-government wings. Cruz and Trump defeated the establishment candidates, and then, Trump defeated Cruz for the party nomination. Trump, in the general election, defeated Hillary Clinton and became the forty-fifth president of the United States.

Trump is a reflection of the disdain held by Republican voters. He has created a constituency of voters that cuts across various ideological lines. He merged non-ideological, social conservative, libertarian, economic nationalist and protectionist, free market, non-interventionist foreign policy, limited government, and anti-government voters together under the broad concept that America is no longer great, but it can be again under his business leadership style in which the goal will be getting things done. Trump combined various voters under American nativism and nationalism, not the ideology of the past four decades.

Like Goldwater in 1964, Trump has changed the definition of the Republican Party. Politically Trump is a combination of Andrew Jackson in 1828, Barry Goldwater in 1964, and George Wallace in 1968. Like Jackson, he exhibits an authoritarian persona in which things will get done his way, because he says so. Like Jackson, Trump claimed his election was the vote of the majority against the Washington elites of both parties and financial interests that sought to profit at the expense of the working man. Like Jackson, Trump claimed that he was part of the people who had been forgotten and whom political leaders are to serve, not to be served by. Like Goldwater, he represents a rejection of the prevailing ideological definition for the Republican Party. Like Wallace, he is a populist who has a disdain for the political media and the establishment elites of both parties that he says do not care about the average American. Trump was able to merge pragmatism and economic nationalism with "dog whistle" politics that united both Southern, Midwestern, and Rust Belt voters. Trump not only commandeered the party social conservative narrative without being a social conservative, Trump commandeered the entire conservative movement of the past fifty years without being beholden to any of those who created it or to all of its canons.

Because the election of Trump was based on a general insurgency against both the Republican intellectual political establishment and structure in Washington, D.C., as well as an election against Hillary Clinton, his election politics were more narrative than specific policy focused. In his effort to secure the Republican nomination and the general election, he did not build his campaign on the tradition of the Republican Party politics of the 1980s and 1990s. Trump changed the meaning of the rhetoric of law and order. He did not advocate the need to restore law and order in its classical Republican Party meaning—code for White fear of Black criminality. Rather, he asserted that restore law and order meant enforcement of immigration law—the arrest of illegal aliens on sight and their swift deportation regardless of whether the aliens have a criminal record.

Nor did he advocate that social programs like affirmative action (code for incompetent Blacks taking jobs from competent Whites) were the exclusive reason why middle class and working-class Whites were not successful in America. Rather than parroting the traditional view of social conservatives like O'Reilly, who assert Whites were held back by unjust social programs of redistribution of wealth to the poor and those on welfare (code for Blacks), Trump attended a Black church and asserted that the problems in the Black community were caused by lack of employment. He abandoned the narrative O'Reilly and the Republicans have asserted for decades that the singular problem of the Black community is the deviant Black culture and the lack of control in the schools along with single motherhood.

But upon entering the presidency Trump showed little policy or rhetorical understanding of American racial history or how the symbols of that history matter as demonstrated by the Charlottesville incident.

PRESIDENT TRUMP, THE KLAN, NAZIS, AND THE CHARLOTTESVILLE INCIDENT

On August 11, 2017, hundreds of Nazis, Ku Klux Klan members, and White Nationalists held a torch fire protest on the campus of the University of Virginia, Charlottesville campus. The mob marched and chanted racist slogans, including "Jews will not replace us" and stated that they would fight to protect the blood and soil of America. The protest was due to the decision of Charlottesville to remove two Civil War statues of Civil War generals. The next day, the Nazis marched in downtown Charlottesville and were met by anti-Nazi marchers, and fights broke out between the two groups.

The various skirmishes between the Nazi and anti-Nazi groups resulted in a media spectacle in which Trump tweeted (1:19 p.m.), "We ALL must be united & condemn all that hate stands for. There is no place for this kind of violence in America. Let's come together as one!" Soon after (1:31 p.m.) David Duke, a former Ku Klux Klan Grand Wizard, former Republican Louisiana State Representative, and multiple failed Republican candidate for the U.S. Senate, stated in an interview regarding the march and the confrontation with anti-Nazi protestors, "We're going to fulfill the promises of Donald Trump. That's what we believed in. That's why we voted for Donald Trump, because he said we're going to take our country back. And that's what we gotta do." To make matters worse, Duke tweeted again (2:01–2:03p.m.) in response to Trump's 1:19 tweet, "So, after decades of White Americans being targeted for discriminated & anti-White hatred, we come together as a people, and you attack us? I would recommend you take a good look in the mirror & remember it was White Americans who put you in the presidency, not radical leftists." At 1:40 p.m., a twenty-one-year-old Nazi, James Alex Fields Jr., drives his car into a crowd of anti-Nazi protesters and killed a twenty-year-old woman, Heather Heyer, and injured nineteen other people. At 3:33 p.m., Trump makes a formal statement about the violence while at an event to showcase an executive order regarding the treatment of veterans.[1]

By the time Trump made his formal statement, it was all over national and international news that the violence was the result of Nazi, Klan, and White Nationalists protesting the taking down of Confederate statues and that a woman had been killed as a result of the violence. The reason this event matters in regard to race and the Republican Party is that the Party, since George Wallace, Barry Goldwater, Richard Nixon, and Ronald Reagan, has been accused of accepting the support of racists as a key voting bloc. Trump had the same reputation, built from his days of supporting the "birther movement," both before and after President Obama was elected and during his own campaign in 2016. This, in addition to his often quick and decisive responses to terrorism when committed by Muslims and his campaign announcement that Mexico was sending rapists and murderers and other criminals to

1 Eugene Kiely and Robert Farley, "Trump Press Conference, in Context," (August 16, 2017) http://www.factcheck.org/2017/08/trump-press-conference-context/

America, all combined to label Trump as an outright racist at worst or an apologist for racists at best. So when an incident of White terrorists occurred, Trump's less-than-forthright condemnation was deafening.

Under political pressure to make a statement, Trump did not condemn the White Nazi protestors as terrorists and in his statement he failed to condemn them by name. Throughout the Obama years, Trump and Republicans condemned Obama for not using the label "Islamic Terrorism" when discussing terrorist attacks committed by Muslims. But when it came to White racists and terrorists, Trump's condemnation was generic and implied moral equivalence regarding the fight between the Nazi and anti-Nazi protestors. Trump said,

> But we're closely following the terrible events unfolding in Charlottesville, Va. *We condemn in the strongest possible terms this egregious display of hatred, bigotry and violence on many sides, on many sides.* It's been going on for a long time in our country. Not Donald Trump, not Barack Obama. This has been going on for a long, long time. It has no place in America. What is vital now is a swift restoration of law and order and the protection of innocent lives. No citizen should ever fear for their safety and security in our society. And no child should ever be afraid to go outside and play or be with their parents and have a good time.
>
> ...
>
> Above all else, we must remember this truth: no matter our color, creed, religion or political party, we are all Americans first. We love our country. We love our God. We love our flag. We're proud of our country. We're proud of who we are. So, we want to get the situation straightened out in Charlottesville, and we want to study it. And we want to see what we're doing wrong as a country where things like this can happen. My administration is restoring the sacred bonds of loyalty between this nation and its citizens, but our citizens must also restore the bonds of trust and loyalty between one another. We must love each other, respect each other and cherish our history and our future together. So important. We have to respect each other. Ideally we have to love each other.

The response to his statement, "*we condemn in the strongest possible terms this egregious display of hatred, bigotry and violence on many sides, on many sides,*" received universal disdain. A group of Nazis, Ku Klux Klan members, and White Nationalists are forcefully confronted (both groups were armed with bats and sticks, and some of the White Nationalists had guns) by anti-Nazi protestors, and Trump condemns, "hatred, bigotry, and violence on many sides, on many sides."

Trump sustained political condemnation across the board all weekend, so on Monday, August 14th, he was "forced" to give another statement on the weekend. In this speech, he was more condemning of the White Nazi groups. He said,

> And as I have said many times before, no matter the color of our skin, we all live under the same laws. We all salute the same great flag, and we are all made by the same almighty God.
>
> We must love each other, show affection for each other and unite together in condemnation of hatred, bigotry and violence. We must rediscover the bonds of love and loyalty that bring us together as Americans.
>
> *Racism is evil. And those who cause violence in its name are criminals and thugs, including the K.K.K., neo-Nazis, white supremacists and other hate groups that are repugnant to everything we hold dear as Americans.*
>
> We are a nation founded on the truth that all of us are created equal. We are equal in the eyes of our creator. We are equal under the law. And we are equal under our Constitution.
>
> Those who spread violence in the name of bigotry strike at the very core of America.

Trump had specifically focused on the Nazi groups, but the problem was two-fold. First, he "abandoned" the moral equivalency statement only after a weekend of political beating, and second, he did not demonstrate the passion of condemnation that he had for Muslim terrorist and Mexican criminals that he had demonstrated in the past. Both the press, left and right, and both the Democrats and Republicans attacked Trump for saying too little and too late. This was the background for the August 15th press conference, which was supposed to be about his support for a new infrastructure initiative.

From the start, the press asked him about the reactions to his statements about Charlottesville.

> **TRUMP:** ... And honestly, if the press were not fake and if it was honest, the press would have said what I said was very nice. But unlike you … [cross talk] ... and unlike the media, before I make a statement, I like to know the facts.

In regard to the Nazi who intentionally drove his car into a group of anti-Nazi protestors, Trump said,

> **TRUMP: I think the driver of the car is a disgrace** to himself, his family and this country. And that is—you can call it terrorism, you can call it murder. **You can call it whatever you want**. I would just call it as the fastest one to come up with a good verdict. That's what I'd call it. And there is a question. **Is it murder? Is it terrorism? Then you get into legal semantics.** The driver of the car is a murderer, and what he did was a horrible, horrible, inexcusable thing.

If the driver had been Muslim or even worse had acted in the name of Islam, would Trump have said he did not know if the driver was a terrorist or not? Would Trump have said the driver was much more than a disgrace? If the driver was Muslim would Trump have implied the difference between terrorism and murder was nothing more than legal semantics?

When the press asked him about the link between the Nazi groups and the rise of the alt-right—the alt-right being an ultra-conservative political wing of conservative Republican politics—Trump attacked the questioner and the implication that the alt-right supports conservative racist beliefs. Trump's temper and disdain for the press was on full display and the press conference degraded into a direct confrontation between Trump and the reporters who challenged his description of the incident. In part, the press conference commenced as follows:

> **REPORTER:** Senator McCain said that the alt-right is behind these and he linked that same group to those that perpetrated the attack in Charlottesville.
> **TRUMP:** Well, I don't know. I can't tell you. I'm sure Senator McCain must know what he is talking about. **When you say the alt-right. Define alt-right to me. You define it! Go ahead! No, define it for me! Come on. Let's go!**
> **REPORTER:** Senator McCain defined them as the same group—
> [cross talk]
> **TRUMP: What about the alt-left** that came charging at—Excuse me—What about the alt-left that came charging at the, as you say, the alt-right? **Do they have any semblance of guilt?**
> [cross talk]
> **Let me ask you this: What about the fact that they came charging, that they came charging with clubs in their hands swinging clubs?** Do they have any problem? I think they do. So, you know, as far as I'm concerned, that was a horrible, horrible day.
> [cross talk]
> Wait a minute. I'm not finished. **I'm not finished, fake news.** That was a horrible day.
> [cross talk]
> **TRUMP:** I will tell you something. **I watched those very closely, much more closely than you people watched it.** And you had a group on one side that was bad and you had a group on the other side that was also very violent. And nobody wants to say that. But I'll say it right now.
> [cross talk]
> You had a group on the other side that came charging in without a permit and they were very, very violent.
> **REPORTER:** Do you think that what you call the alt-left is the same as neo-Nazis?
> **TRUMP:** All of those people—Excuse me—I've condemned neo-Nazis. I've condemned many different groups. **But not all of those people were neo-Nazis**, believe me. Not all of those people were white supremacists by any stretch. **Those people were also there because they wanted to protest the taking down of a statue, Robert E. Lee.**
> So—excuse me—and you take a look at some of the groups and you see and **you would know it if you were honest reporters, which in many cases, you are not**. But, many of those people were there to protest the taking down of the statue of Robert E. Lee. So **this week, it is Robert E. Lee. I noticed that Stonewall Jackson is coming down. I wonder, is it George Washington next week? And is it Thomas Jefferson the week after?** You know, you really do have to ask yourself, where does it stop?

But they were there to protest—excuse me—you take a look, the night before, they were there to protest the taking down of the statue of Robert E. Lee. Infrastructure question. Go ahead.

At this point the fight shifted from the protesters to what the protest was about, the confederate statues and the social meaning various sides place on removing and protecting the confederate monuments. Here is where Trump begins his defense of the "Lost Cause."

REPORTER: Does the statue of Robert E. Lee stay up?
TRUMP: I would say that is up to a local town, community or the federal government, depending on where it is located.
REPORTER: Are you against the Confederacy?
REPORTER: How concerned are you about race relations in America and do you think things have gotten worse or better since you took office?
TRUMP: I think they've gotten better or the same. Look they have been frayed for a long time. And you can ask President Obama about that because he would make speeches about it.
But I believe that the fact that I brought in, it will be soon, millions of jobs, you see where companies are moving back into our country. I think that's going to have a tremendous positive impact on race relations.
We have companies coming back into our country. We have two car companies that just announced. We have Foxconn in Wisconsin, just announced. We have many companies, I say, pouring back into the country. I think that's going to have a huge, positive impact on race relations.
You know why? It is jobs. What people want now, they want jobs. They want great jobs with good pay. And when they have that, you watch how race relations will be. And I'll tell you we are spending a lot of money on the inner cities. We are gonna fix, we are fixing the inner cities. We are doing far more than anybody has done with respect to the inner cities. It is a priority for me. And it's very important.
REPORTER: Mr. President, are you putting what you are calling the alt-left and white supremacists on the same moral plane?
TRUMP: I am not putting anybody on a moral plane. What I'm saying is this: You had a group on one side and you had a group on the other and they came at each other with clubs and it was vicious and horrible. And it was a horrible thing to watch. But there is another side. There was a group on this side—you can call them the left. You have just called them the left—that came violently attacking the other group. So you can say what you want, but that's the way it is.
REPORTER: You said there was hatred; there was violence on both sides?
TRUMP: Well I do think there's blame. Yes, **I think there is blame on both sides.** You look at both sides. **I think there is blame on both sides**. And **I have no doubt about**

> **it! And you don't have doubt about it either!** And if you reported it accurately, you would say.
> **REPORTER: The neo-Nazis started this thing**. They showed up in Charlottesville to protest —
> **TRUMP:** Excuse me. They didn't put themselves down as neo-Nazis. And **you had some very bad people in that group. But you also had people that were very fine people on both sides.**
> **You had people in that group**—excuse me, excuse me—I saw the same pictures as you did. You had people in that **group that were there to protest the taking down, of to them, a very, very important statue** and the renaming of a park from Robert E. Lee to another name.
>
> [cross talk]

In this colloquy, Trump has asserted that on the side of the Nazis you had very fine people and those very find people were defending the statue of Robert E. Lee, the General that fought to destroy the Union over the issue of slavery. The press challenged the moral equivalency that Trump was proposing.

> **REPORTER: George Washington and Robert E. Lee are not the same, Mr. President.**
> **TRUMP: George Washington was a slave owner.** Was George Washington a slave owner? **So will George Washington now lose his status?** Are we going to take down—excuse me—are we going to take down statues to George Washington? **How about Thomas Jefferson?** What do you think of Thomas Jefferson? You like him. Good.
> Are we going to take down the statue? **Cause he was a major slave owner.** Are we going to take down his statue? So you know what? It's fine. **You are changing history, you're changing culture.** You had people and I'm not talking about the neo-Nazis and the white nationalists, because they should be condemned totally. You had many people in that group other than neo-Nazis and white nationalists. O.K.? And the press has treated them absolutely unfairly.
> Now, in the other group also, you had some fine people but you also had troublemakers and you see them come with the black outfits and with the helmets and with the baseball bats. You had a lot of bad people in the other group too.

Perplexed, the Press asked for clarification.

> **REPORTER:** Who has the press treated unfairly? Sir, I'm sorry, I just didn't understand what you were saying. You were saying the press has treated white nationalists unfairly? I just didn't understand what you were saying.
>
> **TRUMP:** No, no. There were people in that rally. I looked the night before. If you look, they were people protesting very quietly the taking down the statue of Robert E. Lee. I am sure in that group there were some bad ones. **The following day, it looked like they had** some rough, bad people, **neo-Nazis, white nationalists**, whatever you want to call

> them. **But you had a lot of people in that group that were there to innocently protest** and very legally protest. Because I don't know if you know, they had a permit. The other group didn't have a permit. So I only tell you this. **There are two sides to a story.** I thought what took place was a horrible moment for our country, a horrible moment. But **there are two sides to the country.** Does anybody have a final question? Do you have an infrastructure question?[2]

The political outrage and response was without equal for weeks. It took the news of two major hurricanes over Texas and Florida to remove the topic from the national news and public debate. It was bad enough that Trump did not instinctually condemn uniformed Ku Klux Klan and Neo-Nazis marching in the street, but that he provided support for what they were protesting against—the taking down of confederate monuments.

The Civil War, like World War II, is viewed in a moral context and not simply as a war the United States fought. The Civil War was a war to "make men free"; it was a war to end slavery! As Lincoln learned, it was not simply a war to maintain the Union. In World War II, Americans fought Nazis to purge the world from the idea of racial nationalism in which twelve million people were gassed to death for not being White and Arian!

To make matters worse, Trump put George Washington and Robert E. Lee on the same moral plane. At the press conference, Trump said, "So this week, it's Robert E. Lee; I noticed that Stonewall Jackson's coming down. I wonder, is it George Washington next week? And is it Thomas Jefferson the week after? You know, you really do have to ask yourself, where does it stop?" To the assertion by a reporter that "George Washington and Robert E. Lee are not the same," Trump answered, "George Washington was a slave owner ... How about Thomas Jefferson? ... He was a major slave owner. Are we going to take down his statue?" After Trump said that there was blame on both sides and Washington and Jefferson were slave owners too, David Duke, who rebuked Trump after his initial response to the Charlottesville incident and told him to remember who elected him and why, tweeted, "Thank you President Trump for your honesty & courage to tell the truth about #Charlottesville & condemn the leftist terrorists in BLM/Antifa."

The praises of David Duke notwithstanding, history and moral argument has settled that the Civil War and World War II were wars against evil—and the Nazis and the Confederate slave owners were evil! The condemnation of Trump was for his failure to condemn the Nazi marchers with political decisiveness without equivocation. His moral equivalence between the Nazis and those who marched in opposition to them provides a backdrop to his implicit support for the "Lost Cause" narrative which took hold in the late nineteenth century.

---

2 See Donald Trump, Press conference August 15, 2017 at https://www.youtube.com/watch?v=alc_x49hLuw and Full Transcript: Trump's News Conference in New York August 15, 2017, at http://www.bellinghamherald.com/news/politics-government/article167364607.html (Emphasis added)

Between 1860 and the middle 1880s the meaning, purpose, and cause of the Civil War was not disputed. But subsequently with the Northern abandonment of Blacks to the racism of Southern Democrats and the fall of Reconstruction, the South created a new narrative of the war. The South was not at war to protect slavery but to oppose "Northern aggression" and defend individual freedom under states' rights. This narrative was adopted by the North, in part, to "bind up the nation's wounds" and make peace with racial discrimination. It was during the late 1890s through the first two decades of the twentieth century that the South erected the monuments to Southern generals, including Robert E. Lee. The monuments were statements that what the South fought to protect was respectable. They were representative of Southern honor in the defense of slavery in the face of Northern arrogance—Northern arrogance that asserted that slavery was wrong and should not spread across the entire nation. The "Lost Cause" narrative and the monuments were developed to erect physical symbols of support of the system of Jim Crow laws that were strengthened and made uniform across the South and into the North in the 1920s and 1930s and that were defended in the 1950s and 1960s under the arguments of states' rights and interposition.

Trump's defense and legitimizing of the "Lost Cause" narrative of the moral equivalency of George Washington and Robert E. Lee or the "bravery" of those who fought for the Confederacy and the Union, is not new in popular culture. In the popular 1950s–1960s television series *The Riflemen,* the sympathy for the "Lost Cause" was the basis for the episode "The Prisoner."[3] In that episode two former confederate soldiers kidnapped the hero of the series, Lucas McCain, blaming him for the abuse they suffered at a Union prison camp that the two soldiers said was worse than the infamous Confederate prison camp Andersonville. The subtle point being there were Union atrocities that were worse than if not equal to confederate atrocities—again the point is moral equivalency. The episode ends with McCain explaining to his son what the Confederate flag symbolizes. He said, "This flag stands for the bravery of all the men who fought and died under it—the men who fought against it. Only to prove in the end that victor and loser were one and the same—free men in a free country."

The defense of the "Lost Cause" has found a rebirth and political legitimacy in the wake of the Trump victory. Social conservatives have drawn the line at political correctness and assert that regarding slavery, mistakes were made, but the generals of the Confederacy were honorable in what they were fighting for. In an interview on October 30, 2017, Chief of Staff and retired four-star general John Kelly was interviewed by social conservative Laura Ingraham on her Fox News TV show *The Ingraham Angle.* In her debut episode she asked Kelly, "A prominent church in Alexandra Virginia where George Washington worshiped, it's historic of course, and Robert E. Lee… They decided to pull the plaques memorializing both George Washington and Robert E. Lee because they want the church to be inclusive and be considered more tolerant. What is your reaction to that type of attempt to pull down little markers of history?" Kelly answered,

---

3 *The Rifleman*, Season 3 Episode 25, "The Prisoner," (March 14, 1961)

> Well, history's history. And there are certain things in history that were not so good and other things that were very, very good.
>
> **I think we make a mistake**, though, and as a society, and certainly as individuals, **when we take what is today accepted as right and wrong and go back 100, 200, 300 years or more and say, 'What Christopher Columbus did was wrong.'** Ah, you know 500 years later, **it's inconceivable to me that you would take what we think now and apply it back then.** I think it's just very, very dangerous. It shows you just how much of a lack of appreciation of history and what history is. I would tell you that **Robert E. Lee was an honorable man**. He was a man that **gave up his country to fight for his state**, which in 150 years ago was more important than country. It was always loyalty to state first back in those days. Now it's different today. But **the lack of an ability to compromise led to the Civil War**, and men and women of good faith on both sides made their stand where their conscience had them make their stand.

To which Ingraham responded, "I think pulling down the Washington monuments, what are we going to rename it? We're running out of names." To which Kelly responded, "No, No. We can find some cult hero we can put up there, and say he ... well, he was the real one—Andy Warhol or someone like that. Yea."[4] As discussed in Chapter Four, President Garfield said in 1881 at his inauguration,

> My countrymen, we do not now differ in our judgment concerning the controversies of past generations, and fifty years hence our children will not be divided in their opinions concerning our controversies. ***They will surely bless their fathers and their fathers' God that the Union was preserved, that slavery was overthrown, and that both races were made equal before the law.***

With the rise of the ideas advocated by Kelly, Trump, and other social conservatives of today, it is clear we do "differ in our judgment concerning the controversies of past generations" and "fifty years hence our children" are "divided in their opinions concerning our controversies."

The purpose of the modern incantation of the "Lost Cause" as annunciated by Trump, Kelly, Ingraham, and other social conservatives is that slavery was not evil then and we can't judge slavery by today's standards. As Kelly said, slavery is evil today, but we can't make it evil then because of our standards now. Regarding whether slavery was morally evil then by the moral standards that existed then, I submit Frederick Douglass, then; Abraham Lincoln, then; Harriet Tubman, then; William Lloyd Garrison, then; and President James Garfield, then; just to name a few asserted slavery was morally wrong, then. To again quote President James Garfield, who at the Republican convention in 1880 said of the Civil War and its purpose as well as the nature of reunifying the nation,

---

4 Kelly on Wilson dispute, monuments uproar, never Trumpers (5:29-7:30) (10/30/2017) at https://www.youtube.com/watch?v=RrRe4BAjffk

> ***The Republican party offers to our brethren of the South the olive branch*** of Peace, and invites them to renewed brotherhood, ***on this supreme condition: That it shall be admitted, forever, that in the War for the Union we were right and they were wrong.***

More than 300,000 Union troops fought to prove the South was wrong and slavery was wrong. Even Thomas Jefferson, with his racists views regarding the humanity of Blacks—see Chapter Three—said slavery was wrong, then. But who are they to say it was wrong then, when people like Kelly and Ingram say it was not.

Kelly said, "Robert E. Lee was an honorable man [who] gave up his country to fight for his state." Here is my disagreement. An honorable man does not destroy his country and betray his position to defend slavery. Remember *Colonel* Robert E. Lee resigned his commission in the Union Army to take command of the confederate army to fight the army he once served. The confederacy, not the Union, fired the first shot at Fort Sumter in 1861.

Kelly said, it was "the lack of an ability to compromise led to the Civil War," Really! A brief list of the compromises over slavery include, the compromise over Jefferson's slave clause to the Declaration of Independence, the three-fifths compromise at the constitutional convention, the compromise to prevent the federal government from regulating the international slave trade until 1808, the passage of the Fugitive Slave Act of 1793, the compromise of 1820[5], the compromise of 1850[6], and the Kansas-Nebraska Act of 1854.[7] American history is full of nuances and debatable issues, but the inability to compromise over slavery to hold the Union together is not one of them. American history is littered with lasting compromises, both moral and political, over slavery to maintain the Union. In 1860 the dance with the devil ended and payment came due. For that matter, what does it say about conservatives like Kelly that assert that compromise with the devil was acceptable.

Kelly is retired four star general and White House Chief of Staff and he gets on a national conservative opinion show and says the Civil War was due to the lack of the ability to compromise. Either Kelly was able to rise through his career without the need for a minimal college level grasp of American history or he knew what he was saying was not historically correct. If the latter, the question is why?

The subtler assertion of modern "Lost Cause" advocacy is what it tells Blacks now. The implication of the modern "Lost Cause" and protection of confederate monuments is to tell

---

5 Admitting Missouri as a slave state and Maine as a free state to maintain the equal balance in the U.S. Senate and prohibited the spread of slavery north of 36°30′paralell.

6 Admitted California as a free state, ended the slave trade in Washington D.C., strengthened the Fugitive Slave Act of 1793, and established that in the New Mexico and Utah territories popular sovereignty would determine if slavery would be instituted.

7 Repealed the ban on slavery north of the 36 parallel and allowed popular sovereignty in the Kansas and Nebraska territories. The Kansas-Nebraska Act of 1854 led to the breakup of the Whig Party and formation of the Republican Party and the rise of Abraham Lincoln.

Blacks, "let it go, it's over; you're not slaves or niggers now. Stop trying to remind White America about your suffering at our hands. It's over. And stop trying to take away our heroes by tainting them with slavery. They owned slaves then, like we own cars now." Besides as social conservative radio host Dennis Prager explains, American slavery in the context of world history is nothing special or unique, although America is a unique and special country in world history. Prager defended America and Americanism by saying,

> I love this country. I think having been to 130 countries has made me aware, from, but it did from a very early age, I knew it was special. **You have to compare America to other places. You can't, you can't, do what the left does and compare America to some utopian dream**. "You know America allowed slavery." Yes, America did allow slavery. But America abolished slavery too. And since every country on earth allowed slavery, the question is not who allowed slavery it's who abolished slavery. **And had America abolished slavery at the outset there wouldn't have been a United States of America** to do all the good that it has done. Because America would not have incorporated the southern colonies if it had abolished slavery from the beginning.[8]

Really! The only question regarding slavery is who abolished slavery and you can't compare America to an ideal but only to other places. Fine. First, America was founded on a social and political ideal—all men are created by God with certain rights that can't be taken away by government. Not living up to that ideal means something—unless we are only talking about not living up to the ideal when Blacks are concerned. Second, consider what Prager and other White social conservatives don't say regarding the end of slavery. America was the only country that had to have a civil war to end slavery! All the other slave nations of Europe ended slavery by statute, judicial decision, or decision by royal decree. Furthermore, America was the last among the industrialized western countries to end domestic slavery!

In any event, Prager then explained why the Bible allowed slavery, and he asserted that biblical slavery was not the same as American slavery. Biblical slavery was not the kidnapping and enslavement of Africans. Correct. He correctly asserted that biblical slavery did not include the kidnapping of people to make them slaves because such an act, as discussed in Chapter Five, was man-stealing, which under Deuteronomy was punishable by death. Prager asserted that slavery under the Bible was a system of indentured servants paying off debts or people trying to get out of poverty. From this point, he returns to America and concluded

> Half the people who settled the U.S., I don't know if it's half it might have been more might have been less. But it's an immense number of people who came over to America came over as bonded indentured slaves if you will, servants. That's how they got out of poverty. But if you want to feel good about yourself you say no slaves, same with America.

8 Dennis Prager, Radio show Archive 12/01/17—Dennis Prager Show—Full Show (1:22:51—1:25:34) at https://www.youtube.com/watch?v=3NKPVvOlvpY&app=desktop

> Had America said no slavery there wouldn't have been an America. The world would not have been a better place had there not been an America! Okay![9]

Notice how he conflates the asserted positive nature of indentured service with American slavery of Blacks to imply there was little difference between the two and then asserts people who condemn slavery are people who don't understand that the greatness of America had to endure slavery so America could become great.

The idea that America is great, as advocated by social conservatives like Prager, is also reflected by conservatives who lament that America is in social decline. For example, Roy Moore, the Republican Party senatorial candidate for the December 2017 Alabama special election, was endorsed by President Trump in last few days of the campaign. Roy Moore was a controversial candidate because he had been accused of sexual assault and having intercourse with girls fourteen through eighteen years old when he was in his early thirties and while he was a district attorney. In September 2017 Moore was asked by an elderly Black man, "What does Trump mean, what does he mean, 'make it great again'?" Moore gave the following answer.

> Well, I think (inaudible). I think we've been striving for that greatness all the way through. I think you are right about that. And I think it was great in the minds of those who formed the Declaration, though they were not perfect people. They had problems. Those problems have been corrected by—unfortunately by war, by constitutional amendment. We've had to—corrected a lot of our problems. I think it was great at time when families were united, even though we had slavery, they cared for one another. People were strong in the families. Our families were strong, our country had a direction, and we corrected many of the problems. Today, I see our families divided, I see people in prison, young men, and women, that have a life ahead of them that have not been fed and nurtured in the families like they used to be. And I know I'm talking to you because you, like me, you're an age when you remember when your families used to care, when fathers used to care, when mothers used to care and children used to care and weren't disrespectful. The greatness I see was in our culture, not in our policies. There were problems—we had slavery. We've overcome slavery. We had prejudice. We still have prejudice. But we've turned the tide on civil rights, we've done a lot of things to bring this country around and I think we can still make it better.[10]

In December 2017 part of his answer was re-reported and it caused a public outcry. His answer was reported as follows.

---

9 Id.

10 Listen to Roy Moore comments on family, slavery and when America was great—*LA Times* at http://www.latimes.com/politics/95396983-132.html

> In response to a question from one of the only African Americans in the audience—who asked when Moore thought America was last "great"—Moore acknowledged the nation's history of racial divisions, but said: "I think it was great at the time when families were united—even though we had slavery—they cared for one another.... Our families were strong, our country had a direction."[11]

The report made it seem that Moore asserted that the last time America was great was during slavery. The problem with Moore's statement when he spoke of the greatness of America and the American nuclear family is that he failed to note that Black nuclear families were intentionally destroyed under slavery.

Nonetheless, the abomination is in the subtlety of the placing of American greatness and slavery in the same context. It's the placing of nostalgic views of America in same time context as when slavery existed and the describing slavery in America as a policy problem to be discussed on the same level of discussion as tax policy. It's the subtle placing of Jim Crow in America's better days that is the modern incarnation of the Lost Cause.

O'Reilly, Prager, and social conservatives consistently assert regarding slavery, true America had slavery, but slavery was a universal system on the face of the earth and throughout history. Nothing in American slavery was different they assert. But more importantly, they assert, Blacks need to let go of slavery and deal with their own house. As Rev. Jamie Johnson, Director of the Department of Homeland Security's Center for Faith-Based & Neighborhood Partnerships, said in 2008 in a radio interview, "It's an indictment of America's Black community that has turned America's major cities into slums because of laziness, drug use, and sexual promiscuity."[12] Although his statement received negative commentary when published by CNN in 2017, the commentary did not examine the full context of Johnson's beliefs about Blacks.

In 2008, the same year of the election of the first Black president, who was forced to justify his beliefs about race and prove to White America that he was not an "angry Black man" like his pastor Jeramiah Wright, Johnson was a guest on the conservative radio show *The Right Balance* which was aired on the Accent Radio Network. The host asserted that Blacks were anti-Semitic and asked why. Johnson gave the following explanation.

---

11 Lisa Mascaro, "In Alabama, the heart of Trump country, many think he's backing the wrong candidate in Senate race," *Los Angeles Times*, September 21, 2017 at http://beta.latimes.com/politics/la-na-pol-alabama-senate-runoff-20170921-story.html. See also, John Haltiwanger, "Roy Moore: Last Time America Was 'Great' Was During 'Slavery'," *Newsweek*, December 7, 2017 at http://www.newsweek.com/roy-moore-last-time-america-great-during-slavery-741845

12 Eli Rosenberg, "Homeland Security official resigns after comments linking blacks to 'laziness' and 'promiscuity' come to light," *Washington Post* (11/17/2017) at https://www.washingtonpost.com/news/powerpost/wp/2017/11/16/republican-appointee-resigns-from-the-dhs-after-past-comments-about-blacks-muslims-come-to-light/?utm_term=.2e2d39a74478

> I think one of the reasons why is because **Jewish people** from their coming to America in great waves in the early part of the 1800s immediately **rolled up their sleeves and began to work** so hard and **applied themselves** to education and other means of improvement and other means of climbing the, I hate this phrase, but the social ladder if you will, and they have done exceptionally well for themselves. For only representing about 1.4 percent of America's population, they make up 12% of America's millionaires. Why? Because **they work**!
>
> And **it's an indictment of America's Black community that has turned America's major cities into slums because of laziness, drug use, and sexual promiscuity.**[13]

After making this pronouncement, Johnson agreed with his co-guest who asserted that Jews have taken away the right of Blacks to assert that their failures are due to slavery because Jews were slaves, too. Since Jews succeeded, that means Blacks should be expected to succeed and blame for not doing so belongs to them, not White America and the history of slavery. The guest asserted that Blacks were anti-Semitic because they were jealous of Jews and resented them proving a slave background was no excuse to not succeed in America. Johnson then agreed with the radio host who asserted that Blacks were lazy and that was the explanation for their lack of performance. The proof, the radio host asserted, of Black laziness and immorality was the experience of Jamaicans and other Blacks from former Caribbean slave nations who came to America poor and almost illiterate and within one generation their children were at the top of American education and they were darker skinned Blacks than native Blacks. His point is that it's not skin color and racism that explains native urban poverty, but urban Black laziness. After agreeing with a full-throated attack on affirmative action and how Blacks—urban Blacks—were lazy and anti-sematic, the radio host finally conditioned his remarks to apply to those Blacks who lived with an entitlement and welfare mentality for four or five generations.[14] The conversation then moved on to Islam and Johnson asserted violence in Islam is not the result of extremism but rather the natural result of the dictates of Islam itself.[15]

Although Johnson made these comments before his appointment to the DHS, these statements must have—or should have—come to light in the extensive security background check that all executive level political appointees must submit to. The Trump Administration should not have been surprised by these statements, both because of the background check and because Johnson was well known in socially conservative, White evangelical, and Republican

13 Jamie Johnson, "Blacks made cities into slums with "laziness, drug use, and sexual promiscuity," The Right Balance, Accent Radio Network, Rhode Island, 2008. at https://soundcloud.com/user-429524614/jamie-johnson-in-2008-on-african-americans

14 Jamie Johnson, "Blacks made cities into slums" …

15 For links to audio of Johnson's comments see CNN Politics, "Homeland Security's head of community outreach once said blacks turned cities to 'slums' with 'laziness, drug use, and sexual promiscuity'" at http://www.cnn.com/2017/11/16/politics/kfile-jamie-johnson-dhs/index.html.

circles that support and assert these views. In any event, the publication of Johnson's blunt annunciation of his socially conservative opinion of Blacks was too much for the Trump Administration and Johnson resigned a day after the news of his statements were published by CNN.

As discussed throughout this book, there is a continuity in racism in America regarding the need to socially control Blacks and why. In the days of slavery, the justification was that Blacks were inferior by design and were intended to be slaves. After slavery the justification shifted to the laziness and later to the criminality of Blacks and the need to control them.

Racism is a constant; it's the justifications that are variant in American politics. The rise of the modern "Lost Cause" narrative under Trump is part of that variation. Trump, Kelly, O'Reilly, Prager, and Johnson, backing up the ideas of David Duke and those of Wallace and Thurmond before him, assert that the South was fighting for principles worth fighting for. They were fighting for states' rights or they were fighting for their home state because that was more important than country or they were fighting against northern aggression. What they were not fighting for, according to social conservatives, was the right to enslave Blacks. But as discussed in Chapter Four the secession ordinances made clear that the Civil War was fought to defend the fact that Blacks were inferior and were designated to be slaves by God, and for the right of White slave owners to take their slaves anywhere in the America, and that included spreading slavery in America from the South into the West. The goal of the modern "Lost Cause" argument is not only to whitewash the evil of slavery inflicted on Blacks from American social history, but to whitewash the racism that undergirded slavery from American history, and to whitewash racism from the system of Jim Crow that for a century governed race after slavery.

According to Trump, and those who support him, General Lee was a great man who fought bravely. What Trump wants to whitewash is that General Lee fought to destroy the United States over Congressional actions to limit the spread of slavery and Northern assertions that slavery was morally wrong. When Trump said, "George Washington was a slave owner … How about Thomas Jefferson? … He was a major slave owner. Are we going to take down his statue?" he was lending credence to the "Lost Cause" theory that the Union and the Confederacy were on the same moral plane with no moral distinction between the soldiers of the Union and the Confederacy and what they were fighting for. According to Trump, Generals Lee and Grant both fought bravely and that's all that matters and that is what makes them equivalent. The distinction between what each was fighting to preserve is of no moral, political, or historical consequence.

America, despite some of her historical sins, slavery backed by racism for one, is a great country. I am totally supportive with America being said to be the greatest country on earth. That is why support for the "Lost Cause" as articulated by social conservatives and people like Trump is such an abomination. The Civil War was not a military end to an intractable political debate or the result of, as Kelly said, a "lack of an ability to compromise"—as if the devil demands no price after dancing with him. The Civil War ended a great evil and those who fought the Confederacy died for something worth dying over. The men of the Union found support and affirmation from the famous social conservative libertarian John Stuart Mill, who said in 1862 during the Civil War,

> War is an ugly thing, but not the ugliest of things: the decayed and degraded state of moral and patriotic feeling which thinks that nothing is worth a war, is much worse. When a people are used as mere human instruments for firing cannon or thrusting bayonets, in the service and for the selfish purposes of a master, such war degrades a people. ***A war to protect other human beings against tyrannical injustice; a war to give victory to their own ideas of right and good, and which is their own war, carried on for an honest purpose by their free choice, — is often the means of their regeneration.*** A man who has nothing which he is willing to fight for, nothing which he cares more about than he does about his personal safety, is a miserable creature who has no chance of being free, unless made and kept so by the exertions of better men than himself. ***As long as justice and injustice have not terminated their ever-renewing fight for ascendancy in the affairs of mankind, human beings must be willing, when need is, to do battle for the one against the other.***[16]

To equate Northern soldiers dying, as the song says, "to make men free" with confederates fighting to prevent the end of slavery and to maintain the states' rights of slavery based on race in the "land of the free and the home of the brave" which was built on the ideal and proposition that all mankind have inalienable rights of "life, liberty and the pursuit of property" is an abomination. To those who assert moral equivalency between those who fought to end slavery and those who fought to protect it, I would remind them of the quote of Samuel Adams. When Adams was faced with men who would rather live with slavery rather than fight against it, he said

> [To] the men who have let loose on us the dogs of war to riot in our blood and hunt us from the face of the earth? If ye love wealth better than liberty, the tranquillity of servitude than the animating contest of freedom—go from us in peace. We ask not your counsels or arms. Crouch down and lick the hands which feed you. May your chains sit lightly upon you, and may posterity forget that ye were our countrymen![17]

The same should be said of those who during the Civil War fought to preserve slavery and destroy the Union, "may posterity forget that ye were our countrymen." Let the same be said of those today who morally equate the defenders of liberty in the days of the Civil War with the defenders of racial slavery and the confederacy—which were the same.

---

16 John Stuart Mill, "The Contest in America," *Dissertations and Discussions*, Vol. I at 26 (1668). Originally in "The Contest in America," *Fraser's Magazine* (February 1862) (emphasis added).

17 Samuel Adams, "On American Independence," (Speech delivered at the State House in Philadelphia, August 1, 1776) at http://www.bartleby.com/268/8/18.html

Returning to the Charlottesville incident and why Trump's statements at the press conference are significant; the problem with the "Lost cause" ideal is not that the justification and legitimization of the defenders of the slave owning Confederacy found support in the 1880s or the 1920s or in a 1950s television show. The problem is that these narratives found support in the mouth of the president of the United States in 2017! It should be clear that these were the same arguments of those who instituted the Jim Crow laws and advocated the "Lost Cause" view of the Civil War after the fall of Reconstruction. These were the same arguments of those who defended Jim Crow in the 1950s and 1960s. These are the same arguments of those who supported states' rights in the face of Dr. King and the civil rights marchers demanding the ability to eat at breakfast counters. These are the same arguments of David Duke! Trump said, "You know what? It's fine, you're changing history; you're changing culture." Within this context, he said, "Some of the people who were marching alongside the Nazi mob, I'm not talking about the neo-Nazis and the white nationalists, because they should be condemned totally—but you had many people in that group other than neo-Nazis and white nationalists." Good people can walk alongside Nazis! Really!

Of those who opposed the Nazis, Trump said, "Now, in the other group also, you had some fine people, but you also had troublemakers and you see them come with the black outfits and with the helmets and with the baseball bats—you had a lot of bad people in the other group too." Trump asserted the people who faced down armed Nazis with bats of their own were equal for condemnation. When commenting on the French resistance during the German occupation, according to the logic of Trump, it could be said, "Yes, but look at the French and Jewish resistance; they used violence, too." As Winston Churchill once said, "I decline utterly to be impartial between the fire brigade and the fire."[18] Both the Allied and the Axis powers used the tools of war, but that fact does not make them morally equivalent. Ask the German Jews after the Nuremberg Laws in September 1935, Kristallnacht in November 1938, and the Wannsee Conference in January 1942, which authorized the "final solution"; if they had it to do again, what would they have done when the Nazi party was formed in 1919, when Hitler took control of the party in July 1921, when the Sturmabteilung (SA) was formed in November 1921, or when the Munich Putsch headed by Hitler occurred in November 1923? There is a difference between the righteous use of force against evil and the force used to perpetuate evil. As President Bush said after 9/11, "Freedom and fear, justice and cruelty, have always been at war, and we know that God is not neutral between them."[19]

In American politics, racism, insensitivity, and ignorance can sit and function alongside conservativism. But what could not sit alongside American conservativism was Nazis. What was thought not to be open to debate was whether American conservativism could sit

---

18 For the background to this quote, See Christopher C. Harmon, *Anarchism and Fire: What We Can Learn from Sidney Street* (Spring, 2011) at https://www.winstonchurchill.org/publications/finest-hour/finest-hour-150/anarchism-and-fire-what-we-can-learn-from-sidney-street

19 George W. Bush, Address to a Joint Session of Congress and the American People, September 20, 2001.

alongside any moral equivalence between Nazi marchers with bats and torches in America in 2017 and those who resisted them with bats of their own. Trump brought that assumption into dispute. The Civil War was about ending slavery, the single most unjust treatment of Blacks in American History. The North fought to remove the evil of slavery from the face of American politics and social structure, and the Confederacy defended the morality of slavery and fighting for the right to own slaves under the law. The Civil War was good versus evil. Except for White nationalists and Nazis in 2017 and states' rights advocates of the 1950s and 1960s, this conclusion of history was also thought to be settled in 2017. Trump and social conservatives now put these assumptions into question.

The August 2017 event was not the last Charlottesville would suffer regarding the Nazi protestors. In September 2017, Trump entered a public rhetoric and twitter war with some NFL football players who did not stand when the national anthem was played in protest to police brutality and social injustice regarding Blacks. Trump tweeted that these players, mostly Black, should be fired. When the players and some team owners in subsequent games "took a knee" in protest to Trump, Trump called the owners cowards and said the players were destroying the game and that the NFL were losing fans who wanted to be entertained and not be exposed to left-wing politics. With this background of Trump taking on the NFL players for not standing, on October 7, 2017, a group of Nazis returned to Charlottesville and again marched and chanted "Jews will not replace us" and "blood and soil" we will protect. The same chants of the German Nazis as they rose to power. The point is this: Trump did not tweet a sound! Nazis on American soil chanting ideas that the *Greatest Generation* fought to wipe off the face of the earth received no condemnation from Trump. But a bunch of NFL players silently "taking a knee" at the playing of the national anthem sparked weeks of Trump commentary without restraint. As discussed in Chapter Three, infrahumanization is in what is not said in the face of racism as well as what is affirmatively done to implement racism. Trump's silence on Nazis speech and clear condemnation on the silent protest of the NFL players makes his sympathies clear as to what is worth condemning and what is not. The choice is the point.

One of the propositions of this book is that political rhetoric is a reflection of the normative values of a nation and those normative values through political rhetoric leads to politics which creates policy. This is why it matters what a president says. Trump entered American politics arguing that Mexico was sending illegal aliens and they were sending rapists and other criminals not people simply trying to find work. Then during the 2016 election he said that there should be a stop on all immigration of Muslims. Throughout the election he said he would bring back law and order to America. Trump was elected, and he instituted a ban on immigration from seven Muslim countries. Trump was elected, and he demanded a wall along the southern boarder as a price for any immigration reform. Trump was elected, and he appointed Jeff Sessions as Attorney General, who instituted crime control model policies reminiscent of the Clinton Administration in the 1990s. Rhetoric matters. Again, to the victor goes the spoils.

On January 11, 2018, it was reported that Trump, in a meeting with leaders of both parties on the issue of immigration reform, asked, "Why do we want all these people from shithole countries coming here? We need more people from Norway." The report started a firestorm.

What was interesting is that after his statements were made public, the White House did not deny the statements. The White House issued a written statement that said, "Certain Washington politicians choose to fight for foreign countries, but President Trump will always fight for the American people [and] [l]ike other nations that have merit-based immigration, President Trump is fighting for permanent solutions that make our country stronger by welcoming those who can contribute to our society, grow our economy and assimilate into our great nation."[20]

But more significantly it was reported that inside the White House, Trump's statements regarding immigration—and stopping immigration—from Haiti, Africa, and South America were not being resisted as intensely as his comments regarding Charlottesville were. It was reported that a staffer explained that, "The President's 'shithole' remark is being received much differently inside of the White House than it is outside of it. Though this might enrage Washington, staffers predict the comment will resonate with his base, much like his attacks on NFL players who kneel during the National Anthem did not alienate it."[21] This view was affirmed by social conservatives on Fox News and conservative talk radio. As the lead Trump supporter on *The Five*, a Fox News public policy debate show, made clear,

> **This is how the forgotten men and women in America talk in the bar. This is how Trump relates to people if you're in a bar** and you're in Wisconsin and you're thinking they're bringing in a bunch of Haiti people or el Salvadorians or people from Niger, this is how some people talk. Is it graceful, no! Is it polite or delicate, absolutely not! **Is it a little offensive, of course it is!** But you know what, this doesn't move the needle at all. **This is who Trump is. He doesn't care.** He shoots from the hip and **if he offends some people, fine.** There are so many more offensive things that are happening in this world. We just talked about ISIS beheading people, there is crime in the inner city, people are getting—you know—kicked off welfare. I am trying to put it in perspective here, and an off the cuff comment by President Trump is not a big deal. I think he was talking about third world countries and you are bringing in people that have very low skills and low education. It was in the context of the immigration debate.[22]

---

20 Josh Dawsey, "Trump derides protections for immigrants from 'shithole' countries," *Washington Post*, January 12, 2018 at https://www.washingtonpost.com/politics/trump-attacks-protections-for-immigrants-from-shithole-countries-in-oval-office-meeting/2018/01/11/bfc0725c-f711-11e7-91af-31ac729add94_story.html?utm_term=.857a3016cfad

21 Chris Cillizza, "Trump's 'shithole' comment is his new rock bottom," CNN, January 12, 2018 at http://www.cnn.com/2018/01/11/politics/trump-rock-bottom/index.html

22 Jesse Watters, The Five, Fox News, (32:08-33:08) at https://www.youtube.com/watch?v=kOumX9o3tQ8&app=desktop

In case one would dismiss the Fox commentator as young and intemperate regarding his characterization of Trump and the voters who support him, consider the following story that is recounted regarding how Trump thinks of himself.

> Once, coming back on his plane with a billionaire friend who had brought along a foreign model, Trump, trying to move in on his friend's date, urged a stop in Atlantic City. He would provide a tour of his casino. His friend assured the model that there was nothing to recommend Atlantic City. It was a place overrun by white trash. "What is this 'white trash'?" asked the model. "They're people just like me," said Trump, "only they're poor."[23]

On March 29, 2018 Trump held a political rally in Cleveland, Ohio and during his remarks he congratulated Roseanne Barr on the ratings of her new T.V. show which reprised her show by the same name in the 1990s. The show *Roseanne* was a comedy about a poor, uneducated, blue collar White family in rural America. Roseanne Barr and her character in the show are both Trump supporters. The show enjoyed major success during spring 2018 until it was abruptly cancelled on May 29, 2018 when Roseanne Barr tweeted, "muslim brotherhood & planet of the apes had a baby=vj" vj referring to former Obama senior advisor Valarie Jarrett. During the rally Trump said, "Look at Roseanne, look at her ratings. Over 18 million people. And it was about us." As Trump said on his plane, White trash, "they're people just like me."

The truth behind what both Trump said about himself and what the Fox commentator said about the Trump voter is that Trump was elected, in no small part, because he represented the white non-college educated, bar drinking, politically incorrect forgotten man and woman. Trump tapped into a vein of voters who felt abandoned by the elites of America—abandoned to the interests of Blacks, gays, women, and social liberals who rejected the traditional America of the 1940s and 1950s. These voters resented both parties due to their support of economic globalists who supported international free trade agreements. Free trade agreements that resulted in the loss of blue collar jobs that employed voters who worked with their hands and provided pensions in their old age. As one Democratic political operative explained regarding the Democratic Party, "You know how off message we are? A guy that shits in gold-plated toilets is talking to blue collar workers and we're not. … He is talking to those voters and they are relating to a billionaire."[24] Trump was perceived as being respectful of these voters while Clinton was not.[25] "That is why the great blue wall became the great blue paper wall."[26]

23 Michael Wolff, *Fire and Fury: Inside the Trump White House* at 23 (2018).

24 David Betras, Chairman, Mahoning County, Ohio Democratic Party in CNN Special Reports, "Special Report: Why Trump Won," November 26, 2017 at http://transcripts.cnn.com/TRANSCRIPTS/1711/26/csr.01.html

25 David Betras, Chairman, Mahoning County, Ohio Democratic Party memo to David Pepper Ohio Democratic Party Chair (May 12, 2016) at http://businessjournaldaily.com/wp-content/uploads/2016/11/Blue-collar-famil-MEMORANDUM.pdf. See also, *Supra* notes 91 and 92.

26 David Betras quoted by James Hohmann, "The Daily 202: Rust Belt Dems broke for Trump because they thought Clinton cared more about bathrooms than jobs," *Washington Post*, November 22, 2016 at https://www.

These voters also welcomed Trump because he was not cowed by political correctness. To these voters, stopping political correctness means being able to say incendiary—if not racist—things without having the social cost of having it be labeled racists. As Derbyshire said,[27] rejecting political correctness is not being sensitive to the feelings of Blacks and being able to say that Blacks and other people of color are a threat to White people and America as a whole.

Tea Party/anti-republican establishment radio host Mark Levin defended Trump's statement regarding immigration from Haiti and other countries by saying Haiti and the other countries are hellholes and those nations are hellholes because they don't operate under American social and political values.[28] Social conservatives like Levin assert that it's political correctness that translates the truth that Haiti is run by corrupt leaders and incompetents and that immigration laws should be obeyed into racism. Social conservatives and Trump supporters assert it's not racist to say these countries are run by Black criminals and that's why they are "shitholes" as Trump said. Social conservatives and Trump voters welcome Trump because he normalized the assertion that political correctness translates people who assert these truths into racists and being labeled racist is a tool to quiet White people. But the election of Trump changed that. At the 2018 convention of the Conservative Political Action Committee (CPAC) the spokesman of the American Conservative Union (ACU) announced on stage at the meeting, "In 2009 … we made a little bit of history, we were somewhat lost as a group. We had just elected the first African-American president and that was a big deal and that was a hill that we got over and it was something that we were all proud of and weren't sure what to do. And in a little bit of cynicism what did we do, it's a terrible thing, we elected Mike Steele to be the RNC chair because he's a black guy and that was the wrong thing to do."[29]

As discussed in Chapter One, political correctness is defined by the oversensitivity to Black assertions of racism and Whites must admit that Black belief in White discrimination makes Blacks a threat to society—a threat that must be recognized and dealt with. This normalizing of racist rhetoric to the point where it's no longer recognized as racist has political implications for criminal justice policy. By the end of the first decade of the new century it was settled in American political discourse that the disproportionate incarceration of Blacks was a problem to be fixed. The 1980s and 1990s narrative that disproportionate incarceration was to be expected was abandoned by 2010. The rhetoric of Trump makes the return of the

---

washingtonpost.com/news/powerpost/paloma/daily-202/2016/11/22/daily-202-rust-belt-dems-broke-for-trump-because-they-thought-clinton-cared-more-about-bathrooms-than-jobs/58339cf3e9b69b7e58e45f1b/?utm_term=.1dc70093ec19

27 See Chapter One

28 Mark Levin, Mark Levin Show, Westwood One, January 11, 2018. Full Podcast at https://www.youtube.com/watch?v=94vfWn_IFEA&app=desktop and Mark Levin on Pres. Trump's "shithole" comment... Audio Only—1/11/18 (5:30–6:18) at https://www.youtube.com/watch?v=RVGjpvXdypw&app=desktop

29 Ian Walters, ACU Spokesman Walters at CPAC says RNC hired Steele 'because he's a black guy' (2/24/2018) at https://www.youtube.com/watch?v=llf_gpg129g

1980s and 1990s rhetoric and the politics and policies that followed more likely. This is why it matters what a president says.

As discussed throughout this book, political sympathies and rhetoric are the beginning of politics and the resulting policy priorities implemented by government.

****

Criminal justice policy flows from the politics of the nation as a whole and from the moral and intellectual beliefs of elected officials that turn political narratives into policy. What presidents believe becomes policy that impacts the lives of all. When Blacks are seen as the other or a people to be controlled, the policies that flow from that narrative explain, in part, the historical incarceration of Blacks—from slavery to prison.

Index

C

D

I

J

K

L

M

Q

R

S

Z

Printed in the USA
CPSIA information can be obtained
at www.ICGtesting.com
LVHW070138230224
772611LV00006B/10